D1629613

PRINCIPLES OF SCOTTISH
PRIVATE LAW

PRINCIPLES OF
SCOTTISH
PRIVATE LAW

by

DAVID M. WALKER

M.A., Ph.D., LL.D., Hon. LL.D., F.B.A., F.R.S.E., F.S.A. Scot.,
One of Her Majesty's Counsel in Scotland,
Of the Middle Temple, Barrister,
Regius Professor of Law in the
University of Glasgow

Volume III
Book V: Law of Property

THIRD EDITION

CLARENDON PRESS · OXFORD
1983

Oxford University Press, Walton Street, Oxford OX2 6DP

London Glasgow New York Toronto
Delhi Bombay Calcutta Madras Karachi
Kuala Lumpur Singapore Hong Kong Tokyo
Nairobi Dar es Salaam Cape Town
Melbourne Wellington
and associates in
Beirut Berlin Ibadan Mexico City Nicosia

Oxford is a trade mark of Oxford University Press

Published in the United States by
Oxford University Press, New York

© David M. Walker 1983

All rights reserved. No part of this publication may be reproduced,
stored in a retrieval system, or transmitted, in any form or by any means,
electronic, mechanical, photocopying, recording, or otherwise, without
the prior permission of Oxford University Press

First published 1970
Second edition 1975
Third Edition 1983

British Library Cataloguing in Publication Data

Walker, David M.
    Principles of Scottish private law.–3rd ed.
    Vol. 3
    Bk. 5: Law of property
    1. Civil law–Scotland
    I. Title
    344.1106   KDC330
ISBN 0-19-876134-1

Library of Congress Cataloging in Publication Data

Walker, David M.
    Principles of Scottish private law.

    Includes bibliographies and indexes.
    1. Civil law—Scotland.   I. Title.
KDC330.W35   1983   346.411   82-6387
ISBN 0-19-876134-1 (v.3)   344.1106   AACR2

Typeset by Oxford Verbatim Limited
Printed in Great Britain
at Thomson Litho Ltd. (East Kilbride).

PREFACE

In this edition the text has been further revised to try to take account of developments down to 1 January 1982.

Glasgow   D.M.W.
1 October 1982

CONTENTS

BOOK V
LAW OF PROPERTY

PART 1
PROPERTY IN GENERAL

PART 2
RIGHTS IN CORPOREAL HERITABLE OBJECTS OF PROPERTY

TABLE OF CASES

TABLE OF STATUTES

AUTHORITIES AND ABBREVIATIONS

A.A.   Act of Adjournal.

A.Ass.   Act of the General Assembly of the Church of Scotland.

A.P.S.   Acts of the Parliaments of Scotland, 1124–1707, ed. Cosmo Innes and Thomas Thomson, 11 vols. in 12, 1814–1875.

A.S.   Act of Sederunt.

Anton.   Professor A. E. Anton, *Private International Law,* 1967.

Balf.   Sir James Balfour of Pittendreich, *Practicks: or a System of the more Ancient Law of Scotland,* 1754 and (Stair Socy.) 1962–3.

Bankt.   Andrew McDouall, Lord Bankton, *Institute of the Laws of Scotland in Civil Rights,* 3 vols., 1751–3.

Begg.   J. Henderson Begg, *Law of Scotland relating to Law Agents,* 2nd ed., 1883.

Bell, *Arb.*   J. M. Bell, *Law of Arbitration in Scotland,* 2nd ed., 1877.

Bell, *Comm.*   Professor G. J. Bell, *Commentaries on the Law of Scotland and the Principles of Mercantile Jurisprudence,* 7th ed., 1870.

Bell, *Conv.*   Professor A. Montgomery Bell, *Lectures on Conveyancing,* 3rd ed., 2 vols., 1882.

Bell, *Dict.*   William Bell, *Dictionary and Digest of the Law of Scotland,* 7th ed., 1890.

Bell, *Prin.*   Professor G. J. Bell, *Principles of the Law of Scotland,* 10th ed., 1899.

Borthwick.   J. Borthwick, *Law of Libel and Slander in Scotland,* 1826.

Broun.   J. C. C. Broun, *Law of Nuisance in Scotland,* 1891.

M. P. Brown.   M. P. Brown, *Law of Sale,* 1821.

Brown.   Richard Brown, *Sale of Goods Act, 1893,* 2nd ed., 1911.

Burn-Murdoch.   H. Burn-Murdoch, *Interdict in the Law of Scotland,* 1933.

Burns.   John Burns, *Conveyancing Practice,* 4th ed., 1957.

C.   Code (Corpus Juris Civilis).

C.L.J.   Cambridge Law Journal.

Cheshire and North.   G. C. Cheshire and P. M. North, *Private International Law,* 10th ed., 1979.

Clark. F. W. Clark, *Law of Partnership and Joint Stock Companies*, 2 vols., 1866.

Clive and Wilson. E. Clive and J. G. Wilson, *Law of Husband and Wife*, 1974.

Cooper. F. T. Cooper, *Law of Defamation and Verbal Injury*, 2nd ed., 1906.

Craig. Sir Thomas Craig, *Jus Feudale*, 3rd ed., 1732, and trs. Lord President Clyde, 2 vols., 1934.

D. Digest (Corpus Juris Civilis).

Dallas. George Dallas of St. Martin's, *Styles of Writs*, 2nd ed., 1774.

Dicey and Morris. A. V. Dicey and J. H. C. Morris, *Conflict of Laws*, 10th ed., 1980.

Dickson. W. G. Dickson, *Law of Evidence in Scotland*, 3rd ed., 2 vols., 1887.

Dirleton. Sir George Nisbet, Lord Dirleton, *Doubts and Questions in the Law, especially of Scotland*, 1698.

Dobie. W. J. Dobie, *Manual of the Law of Liferent and Fee in Scotland*, 1941.

Dobie, *Prac.* W. J. Dobie, *Law and Practice in the Sheriff Court*, 1948.

Duff, *Deeds.* A. Duff, *Treatise on Deeds, chiefly affecting moveables*, 1840.

Duff, *Feudal.* A. Duff, *Treatise on Deeds and Forms used in the Constitution Transmission and Extinction of Feudal Rights*, 1838.

Duncan and Dykes. G. Duncan and D. Oswald Dykes, *Principles of Civil Jurisdiction as applied in the Law of Scotland*, 1911.

Encyc. *Encyclopaedia of the Laws of Scotland*, 18 vols., 1926–52.

Ersk. Professor John Erskine of Carnock, *An Institute of the Law of Scotland*, 8th ed., 2 vols., 1871.

Ersk., *Prin.* Professor John Erskine of Carnock, *Principles of the Law of Scotland*, 21st ed., 1911.

Ferguson, *Roads.* J. Ferguson, *Law of Roads, Streets, Rights of Way, Bridges and Ferries*, 1904.

Ferguson, *Water.* J. Ferguson, *Law of Water and Water Rights in Scotland*, 1907.

Forbes. Professor William Forbes, *Institutes of the Law of Scotland*, 2 vols., 1722–30.

Fraser, *H. & W.* Patrick, Lord Fraser, *Husband and Wife according to the Law of Scotland*, 2nd ed., 2 vols., 1876–8.

Fraser, *M. & S.* Patrick, Lord Fraser, *Master and Servant, Employer and Workman, Master and Apprentice*, 3rd ed., 1882.

Fraser, *P. & Ch.* Patrick, Lord Fraser, *Law of Scotland relative to Parent and Child and Guardian and Ward*, 3rd ed., 1906.

Gibb.   Professor A. Dewar Gibb, *International Law of Jurisdiction in England and Scotland*, 1926.

Gibb and Dalrymple.   *Scottish Judicial Dictionary*, 1946.

Gloag.   Professor W. M. Gloag, *Law of Contract*, 2nd ed., 1929.

Gloag and Henderson.   Professor W. M. Gloag and Professor R. C. Henderson, *Introduction to the Law of Scotland*, 8th ed., 1981.

Gloag and Irvine.   Professor W. M. Gloag and J. M. Irvine, *Law of Rights in Security, Heritable and Moveable, and Cautionary Obligations*, 1897.

Goudy.   Henry Goudy, *Law of Bankruptcy in Scotland*, 4th ed., 1914.

Gow.   J. J. Gow, *Mercantile and Industrial Law of Scotland*, 1964.

Graham Stewart.   J. Graham Stewart, *Law of Diligence*, 1898.

Halsbury.   Laws of England, 4th ed., in progress.

Henderson.   Professor R. C. Henderson, *Principles of Vesting in the Law of Succession*, 2nd ed., 1938.

Hope, *Major Prac.*   Sir Thomas Hope, *Major Practicks*, 1608–33, 2 vols. (Stair Socy.), 1937–8.

Hope, *Minor Prac.*   Sir Thomas Hope, *Minor Practicks*, 1726.

Hume.   Baron David Hume, *Decisions*, 1781–1822, 1839.

Hume, *Comm.*   Baron David Hume, *Commentaries on the Law of Scotland respecting Crimes*, 4th ed., 2 vols., 1844.

Hume, *Lect.*   Baron David Hume, *Lectures on the Law of Scotland*, 6 vols. (Stair Socy.), 1939–58.

Hunter.   R. Hunter, *Law of Landlord and Tenant*, 4th ed., 2 vols., 1876.

I.C.L.Q.   International and Comparative Law Quarterly, 1952–.

Inst.   Institutes (Corpus Juris Civilis).

Irons.   J. Campbell Irons, *Judicial Factors*, 1908.

J.R.   Juridical Review, 1889–.

Kames, *Eluc.*   Henry Home, Lord Kames, *Elucidations respecting the Law of Scotland*, 1777.

Kames, *H.L.T.*   Henry Home, Lord Kames, *Historical Law Tracts*, 4th ed., 1817.

Kames, *Equity.*   Henry Home, Lord Kames, *Principles of Equity*, 5th ed., 1825.

L.Q.R.   Law Quarterly Review, 1886–.

Mor.   W. M. Morison's *Dictionary of Decisions*, 22 vols.

M.L.R.   Modern Law Review, 1937–.

Mackay, *Manual.*   Aeneas J. G. Mackay, *Manual of Practice in the Court of Session*, 1893.

Mackay, *Prac.*   Aeneas J. G. Mackay, *Practice of the Court of Session*, 2 vols., 1877–9.

Mack.   Sir George Mackenzie of Rosehaugh, *Institutions of the Law of Scotland*, 1684.

Mack., *Crim.*   Sir George Mackenzie of Rosehaugh, *Laws and Customs of Scotland in Matters Criminal,* 2nd ed., 1699.

Mackenzie Stuart.   Professor A. Mackenzie Stuart, *Law of Trusts,* 1932.

Maclaren.   J. A. Maclaren, *Court of Session Practice,* 1916.

McLaren.   John, Lord McLaren, *Law of Wills and Succession,* 3rd ed., 1894; Supplement by Dykes, 1934.

Menzies.   Professor Allan Menzies, *Lectures on Conveyancing according to the Law of Scotland,* revised ed., 1900.

Menzies, *Trs.*   A. J. P. Menzies, *Law of Scotland affecting Trustees,* 2nd ed., 1913.

Millar.   J. H. Millar, *Handbook of Prescription according to the Law of Scotland,* 1893.

Miller, *Partnership.*   Professor J. Bennett Miller, *Law of Partnership in Scotland,* 1973.

More, *Lect.*   Professor J. S. More, *Lectures on the Law of Scotland,* ed. McLaren, 2 vols., 1864.

More, *Notes.*   Professor J. S. More, *Notes to Stair's Institutions,* in fifth edition thereof, 1832.

Morris.   J. H. C. Morris, *The Conflict of Laws,* 2nd ed., 1981.

Napier.   Mark Napier, *Law of Prescription in Scotland,* 2nd ed., 1854.

N.I.L.Q.   Northern Ireland Legal Quarterly.

Nov.   Novels (Corpus Juris Civilis).

Paton and Cameron.   G. C. H. Paton and J. G. S. Cameron, *Law of Landlord and Tenant,* 1967.

Q.A.   *Quoniam Attachiamenta.*

R.C.   Rules of the Court of Session, 1965.

R.M.   *Regiam Majestatem,* ed. Skene, 1609, and ed. Cooper (Stair Socy.), 1947.

Rankine, *Bar.*   Professor Sir John Rankine, *Law of Personal Bar in Scotland,* 1921.

Rankine, *L.O.*   Professor Sir John Rankine, *Law of Land Ownership in Scotland,* 4th ed., 1909.

Rankine, *Leases.*   Professor Sir John Rankine, *Law of Leases in Scotland,* 3rd ed., 1916.

Ross, *Lect.*   Walter Ross, *Lectures on the History and Practice of the Law of Scotland relative to Conveyancing and Legal Diligence,* 2nd ed., 2 vols., 1822.

S.L.R.   Scottish Law Review, 1886–1963.

S.L.T. (News).   Scots Law Times, News portion.

Skene, *D.V.S.*   Sir John Skene, *De Verborum Significatione,* 1597.

Smith, *British Justice.*   Professor T. B. Smith, *British Justice—The Scottish Contribution,* 1961.

Smith, *Precedent.*   Professor T. B. Smith, *Doctrines of Judicial Precedent in Scots Law,* 1952.

Smith, *Studies.*   Professor T. B. Smith, *Studies Critical and Comparative,* 1963.

Smith, *Sh. Comm.*   Professor T. B. Smith, *A Short Commentary on the Law of Scotland,* 1963.

Spotiswoode.   Sir Robert Spotiswoode, *Practicks of the Laws of Scotland,* 1706.

Stair.   Sir James Dalrymple, Viscount Stair, *Institutions of the Law of Scotland,* 6th ed., 1981.

Thoms.   G. H. Thoms, *Judicial Factors,* 2nd ed., 1881.

Steuart.   Sir James Steuart, *Answers to Dirleton's Doubts in the Laws of Scotland,* 1715.

Umpherston.   F. Umpherston, *Master and Servant,* 1904.

Walker, *Civil Remedies.*   Professor D. M. Walker, *Law of Civil Remedies in Scotland,* 1974.

Walker, *Contracts.*   Professor D. M. Walker, *Law of Contracts and Related Obligations in Scotland,* 1980.

Walker, *Damages.*   Professor D. M. Walker, *Law of Damages in Scotland,* 1955.

Walker, *Delict.*   Professor D. M. Walker, *Law of Delict in Scotland,* 2nd ed., 1981.

Walker, *Judicial Factors.*   Sheriff N. M. L. Walker, *Judicial Factors,* 1974.

Walker, *Prescription.*   Professor D. M. Walker, *Law of Prescription and Limitation of Actions in Scotland,* 3rd ed., 1981.

Walker, *S.L.S.*   Professor D. M. Walker, *The Scottish Legal System,* 5th ed., 1981.

Walkers.   Sheriffs A. G. Walker and N. M. L. Walker, *Law of Evidence in Scotland,* 1964.

Wallace.   G. Wallace, *System of the Principles of the Law of Scotland,* 1760.

Walton.   F. P. Walton, *Handbook of the Law of Husband and Wife in Scotland,* 3rd ed., 1951.

Wilson.   Professor W. A. Wilson, *Law of Trusts and Trustees in Scotland,* 1974.

Wood.   Professor J. P. Wood, *Lectures on Conveyancing,* 1903.

BOOK V

LAW OF PROPERTY

PART 1
PROPERTY IN GENERAL

CHAPTER 5.1

NATURE AND CLASSIFICATION OF PROPERTY

The law of property is concerned with proprietary rights, with the legal rights which persons have over and in respect of certain objects of property, both material things, and those bodies of rights which are held collectively to amount to immaterial things, and with the relations between persons in respect of such things, material and immaterial. It is concerned with real rights or *jura in re*, rights to and in things enforceable against persons generally, as contrasted with rights of obligation, which are *jura in personam* and enforceable only by legal claims against the other party to the obligation.[1] A real right, such as ownership of a vehicle, sometimes gives rise to a personal right, such as to claim damages from one who has damaged the vehicle.

Proprietary rights include a number of distinguishable rights, such as to own, to possess, to use, to transfer temporarily, to transfer to another in security, to transfer outright, as by gift, sale or bequest, and to use up or consume, though the exercise of some of these rights is qualified and restricted in certain cases by law.[2]

The objects of property rights, or things, material and immaterial, in respect of which persons may have proprietary rights are all elements of that person's assets or patrimony. Some are material and have a physical existence, such as land, buildings, vehicles, and animals. Some are immaterial, groups of rights which collectively amount to a legal thing, such as patent rights and copyrights. Some things, both material and immaterial, are represented and evidenced by documents showing a person's title to them, some are not, but any such document, itself also an object of property, should not be confused with the object of right of property which it evidences.[3]

---

[1] cf. Bell, *Comm.* I, 298.

[2] cf. Stair II, 1, 28; Ersk. II, 1, 1, 'property, which is the right of using and disposing of a subject as our own, except in so far as we are restrained by law or paction.'

[3] e.g. the title-deeds of land and the rights in land evidenced thereby are separate objects of property. Loss of the title deeds does not infer loss of rights in the land.

In respect of one object of property the various rights which exist, such as ownership, possession, security-holding and so on, may be separated so that several persons may simultaneously have rights of different kinds in one object of property, and each right may be dealt with and transferred separately from the others. Thus A may own a house, B be the tenant of it, and C have a right in security over it.

Some things are not deemed objects of property and cannot be appropriated; a person does not have a proprietary right in his own person, nor in that of another,[4] nor can anyone acquire a proprietary right in *res communes* such as the sea or the air,[5] nor in *res universitatis*, things belonging to corporations.[6] But a person can acquire property in some *res communes*, such as fish, by catching them. *Res publicae* such as navigable rivers and public roads are vested in the Crown for the benefit of the public generally.[7]

The word 'property' is also sometimes used for the right of ownership of the property, or the right to that property;[8] and sometimes merely as a synonym for the material object of the right of property itself.[9] So too 'possession' is used both of a kind of right in certain property and as a synonym for the objects themselves which are possessed.

Title

The relationship between a person and some object of property is constituted by title. There are various kinds of title, each defining the particular rights which a title-holder, of such a class as owner, borrower or custodier or security holder, has in relation to such a kind of object of property, and a considerable part of property law is concerned with the grounds on which and ways in which various kinds of title may be acquired, transferred and extinguished, while the rules of conveyancing are concerned with the methods and deeds necessary to effect transfers of title, according to the kind of property and the ground of creation, transfer or extinction of the title.

CLASSIFICATIONS OF OBJECTS OF PROPERTY

The objects in respect of which persons may have proprietary rights are divided, firstly, into those things deemed heritable, of kinds which formerly descended on the owner's death to his heir-at-law, and those

---

[4] *Reavis* v. *Clan Line Steamers*, 1925 S.C. 725; cf. *Williams* v. *W.* (1882) 20 Ch. D. 659.
[5] Stair II, 1, 5; Ersk. II, 1, 5–8; Bell, *Prin.* §639.
[6] Ersk. II, 1, 7.
[7] Bell, *Prin.* §638.
[8] e.g. Sale of Goods Act 1979, S. 17—passing of property in goods.
[9] e.g. 'This desirable property' in an advertisement of a house.

deemed moveable, of kinds which alone formerly descended on his death to his executors.[10] This division corresponds closely but not exactly to that between immoveable and moveable property,[11] and to that of English law between real and personal property.

Secondly, objects of property are cross-divided into those kinds of objects which are corporeal, being physical, material, tangible, and visible, such as buildings and vehicles, and those which are incorporeal, being metaphysical, immaterial, intangible, and invisible, such as claims to money or rights of copyright.[12] A further distinction sometimes drawn is between fungibles, articles which can be valued by weight, measure or number, and replaced by equal amount of the like thing, and non-fungibles, which are unique, have individual qualities and are not exactly replaceable.

The law of property accordingly falls into four divisions: (1) property in corporeal heritable objects, such as land or buildings; (2) property in incorporeal heritable objects, such as titles of honour; (3) property in corporeal moveable objects, such as vehicles and animals; and (4) property in incorporeal moveable objects, such as copyrights and claims of debt.[13] Different rules apply to each of these branches, partly for historical reasons and partly by reason of the natural differences between the kinds of things.

In relation to each division consideration must be given to the kinds of objects of property which fall under that heading, the relations in which persons may stand to those objects, the titles by which they hold their rights, and how their titles are created, evidenced, transferred, and extinguished.

Rights heritable and moveable

Rights in themselves are always incorporeal as being purely claims which the courts may recognize and enforce; they consist *in jure* and cannot be seen or handled, but they may exist in respect of either of corporeal or of incorporeal objects of property, e.g. of rights to land or vehicles, or rights to an annuity or a claim of debt or a copyright. A right to or in objects of property deemed heritable such as land is deemed a heritable right, and a right to or in objects of property deemed moveable such as vehicles and money is deemed a moveable right.[14] Such would be properly called incorporeal rights to or in corporeal

---

[10] Stair II, 1, 2; Ersk. II, 2, 3; Bell, *Prin.* §636, 1283, 1470.

[11] The distinction between immoveables and moveables was drawn in the Roman law, and is still relevant in problems of conflict of laws.

[12] Ersk. II, 2, 1–2; Bell, *Prin.* §1471–1505. cf. *Burghead Harbour Co. v. George* (1906) 8 F. 982, 996.

[13] Ersk. II, 2, 1–2; Bell, *Prin.* §1471–1505. cf. *Burghead Harbour Co. v. George* (1906) 8 F. 982, 996.

[14] Stair II, 1, 3; More's Note R; Ersk. II, 2, 5; see also *Burghead Harbour Co., supra.*

heritable or moveable objects. What is called an 'incorporeal heritable right' is properly an incorporeal right to an incorporeal heritable object of property, such as a right of servitude, and an 'incorporeal moveable right' is properly an incorporeal right to an incorporeal moveable object of property, such as a claim of copyright.

Rights in relation to objects of property

A major distinction of rights is between *jura in re propria*, rights which an individual may exercise over or in relation to objects of his own property, whether material or immaterial; these are ownership, with the consequential rights of enjoyment, use, lending, selling, giving or bequeathing, and possession;[15] and, on the other hand, *jura in re aliena*, rights which an individual may exercise over or in relation to objects of another person's property, whether material or immaterial; these include possession and use of another's property under a hiring or lease, holding the other's thing in security for debt, and the exercise of a servitude right over the other's land. All these are derogations from and limitations on the other person's more general rights, particularly ownership, in the same subject matter, and co-exist with it. Several persons may accordingly have different kinds of rights simultaneously in one object of property. These kinds of rights must be considered separately in relation to each of the divisions of property.

The classes of objects of property

The main classification of objects of property is important in relation to the proprietary rights which may exist in the particular object, to the modes of acquisition and transfer, to completion of title, to succession on death and to diligence.[16] The date relevant for classification is the date of the event, death, marriage, sale or diligence which raises the question, and later events do not in general alter the character of a thing or right.[17]

The character of a subject may be determines as heritable or moveable by its physical nature, as physically immoveable or moveable, by connection or accession to another subject which is actually immoveable or moveable, or by destination indicated by the owner.[18]

Heritable property

Heritable property includes all objects naturally immoveable, such as land and minerals, or united to the ground, such as buildings.[19]

---

[15] cf. Bell, *Prin.* §1284.
[16] Stair II, 1, 2; Ersk. II, 2, 3; Bell, *Comm.* II, 1; *Prin.* §1470–1, 1746.
[17] Ersk. II, 2, 20.
[18] Bell, *Prin.* §1470–1.
[19] Stair II, 1, 40; Ersk. II, 2, 4; Bell, *Prin.* §636, 1471.

Trees and annual fruits of the soil are demed heritable until cut and separated from the soil, when they become moveable;[20] cultivated crops are similarly heritable until harvested, when they become moveable.[21]

Rights connected with heritage

Rights connected with or affecting any heritable subject are also heritable, such as rights of superiority, of fee, of leases,[22] or of servitude,[23] and the former bonds of annual rent.[23] Similarly rights to feu-duties and rents are heritable, though each payment when made is moveable, and unpaid arrears are moveable, being deemed as paid;[24] liability for unpaid arrears falls on the executor and not on the heir of the vassal or tenant. A *jus crediti* in respect of heritable property is heritable,[25] as is a right to demand reconveyance of heritage given subject to condition, on failure of that condition.[26]

Business goodwill is heritable if and so far as the business connection of the undertaking depends on the premises and their situation rather than on any personal qualities;[27] it may be partly heritable and partly moveable.[28]

Rights having a tract of future time

Rights having a tract of future time are heritable, even though unconnected with land; these continue for a period of time, carry a yearly profit to the creditor, but are not related to any particular capital sum, e.g. a yearly premium or annuity.[29] Such debts are burdens on the debtor's heritable succession,[29] though termly payments, when they become due, are moveable.[30] But a legacy of the annual interest

---

[20] *Paul* v. *Cuthbertson* (1840) 2 D. 1286; *Nisbet* v. *Mitchell-Innes* (1880) 7 R. 575; *Burns* v. *Fleming* (1880) 8 R. 226; cf. *Breadalbane's Trs.* v. *Pringle* (1854) 16 D. 359; *Allan* v. *Millar*, 1932 S.C. 620; *Munro* v. *Balnagown Estates Co.*, 1949 S.C. 49.

[21] *Chalmer's Tr.* v. *Dick's Tr.*, 1909 S.C. 761, correcting Ersk. II, 2, 4; Bell, *Prin.* §1473; see also *Nisbet*, *supra*; *Morrison* v. *Lockhart*, 1912 S.C. 1017; *McKinlay* v. *Hutchison's Tr.*, 1935 S.L.T. 62.

[22] Ersk. II, 2, 6; Bell, *Prin.* §1478.

[23] Ersk. II, 2, 5.

[24] Bell, *Prin.* §1505; *Martin* v. *Agnew* (1755) Mor. 5457; 5 B.S. 830; *Logan's Trs.* v. *L.* (1896) 23 R. 848; *Watson's Trs.* v. *Brown*, 1923 S.C. 228.

[25] *Thain* v. *T.* (1891) 18 R. 1196.

[26] *Connell's J.F.* v. *MacWatt*, 1961 S.L.T. 203.

[27] *Bell's Trs.* v. *B.* (1884) 12 R. 85; *Graham* v. *G.* (1898) 5 S.L.T. 319; *Ross* v. *Ross's Trs.* (1901) 9 S.L.T. 340; *Town and County Bank* v. *McBain* (1902) 9 S.L.T. 485; *Graham* v. *G's Trs.* (1904) 6 F. 1015; *Muirhead Trs.* v. *M.* (1905) 7 F. 496; *Edinburgh Assessor* v. *Caira and Crolla*, 1928 S.C. 398.

[28] *Murray's Tr.* v. *McIntyre* (1904) 6 F. 588.

[29] Stair II, 1, 4; Ersk. II, 2, 6; Bell, *Prin.* §1480; *Crawford's Trs.* v. *C.* (1867) 5 M. 275.

[30] *Hill* v. *H.* (1872) 11 M. 247; *Breadalbane's Trs.* v. *Jamieson* (1873) 11 M. 912; *Reid* v. *McWalter* (1878) 5 R. 630; *de Serra Largo* v. *L's Trs.*, 1933 S.L.T. 391.

for a series of years of a capital sum bequeathed to another has been held moveable.[31]

Titles and honours

Also heritable are titles, coats of arms and honours and dignities if transmissible on the holder's death and not purely personal.[32]

Jura crediti

If the *jus crediti* under a trust entitles the beneficiary to demand delivery or conveyance of heritable subjects, it is heritable, descending to the heirs of the beneficiaries.[33] If, however, it be merely to demand money, or a share of the trust fund, it is moveable.[34] If the nature of the right is uncertain, it is deemed moveable.[35] The *jura crediti* of rents, and of principal and annual payments of interest on heritable bonds, are heritable, but accruing payments are moveable as soon as they vest in the creditor.[36] An assignee's right to a *spes successionis* to heritable property is a heritable *jus crediti*.[37]

At common law annuities, rents, and payments connected with land did not vest till the term of payment arrived, so that a creditor's executor could claim nothing if the creditor did not survive a term of payment, whereas the interest of money and the profits of daily work vested *de die in diem*. The Apportionment Act, 1870, provides that, unless it is stipulated that no apportionment is to take place,[38] all rents, annuities, dividends, and other periodical payments in the nature of income accrue from day to day and are apportionable accordingly, both as regards liability to make, and the right to receive, the payments.[39]

Moveable property

Things physically moveable are deemed legally moveable, such as money, animals, clothing, books, furniture, machinery, vessels, vehicles, and aircraft,[40] and also the fruits or income of such moveables, such as the young of animals and the income of money.[41] Debts and

---

[31] *Hill, supra;* cf. *Shaw's Trs.* v. *S.* (1870) 8 M. 419.

[32] Ersk. II, 2, 6; Bell, *Comm.* I, 120; *Prin.* §1481; cf. Succession (Sc.) Act, 1964, S. 37 (1)(a).

[33] Bell, *Prin.* §1482; *Durie* v. *Coutts* (1791) Mor. 4264; *Thain* v. *T.* (1891) 18 R. 1196.

[34] *Wardlaw's Trs.* v. *W.* (1880) 7 R. 1070; see also *Gilligan, infra; Borland's Trs., infra.*

[35] Bell, *supra; Somerville's Trs.* v. *Gillespie* (1859) 21 D. 1148; *Learmonts* v. *Shearer* (1866) 4 M. 540; *Auld* v. *Anderson* (1876) 4 R. 211; *Kippen's Trs.* v. *K's Exors.* (1889) 16 R. 668; *Gilligan* v. *G.* (1891) 18 R. 387; *Borland's Trs.* v. *B.,* 1917 S.C. 704.

[36] Bell, *Prin.* §1496.

[37] *Thain* v. *T.* (1891) 18 R. 1196.

[38] *Macpherson's Trs.* v. *M.,* 1907 S.C. 1067.

[39] *Learmonth* v. *Sinclair's Trs.* (1878) 5 R. 548.

[40] Stair, II, 1, 2; Ersk. II, 2, 7; Bell, *Prin.* §1472.

[41] *Adv. Gen.* v. *Oswald* (1848) 10 D. 969; *Hill* v. *H.* (1872) 11 M. 247.

undertakings to pay are moveable,[42] as are government stock, shares in companies, claims of damages, though arising in respect of heritable property,[43] a right to a share of the proceeds of heritage,[44] patent rights,[45] and copyrights.[46]

Also moveable are arrears of money due on an annuity, of feu-duty or rent, of interest on a bond,[47] and claims to money, such as money sunk in a partnership, or represented by shares in a company,[48] even though the assets of the firm or company consist of or comprise heritable property, and money presently due. A *jus crediti* under a marriage contract to estate which might be heritable or moveable has been held moveable.[49]

Business goodwill is moveable is dependent more on the reputation and connection of the firm than on the situation where it does business;[50] it may be partly heritable and partly moveable.[51]

Things in their nature heritable may be deemed moveable is part of a *universitas* or mixed unity which is regarded as moveable.[52]

The price of land voluntarily sold is moveable, unless payment is heritably secured rather than paid,[53] and even a compulsory sale makes the price moveable in the owner's succession, if he should die before granting a conveyance.[54]

But where land is judicially sold the interest of the heritable creditors therein remains heritable and the shares of the price to which they are entitled continue heritable till their debts are discharged, and fall to their heirs.[55] And sale of a pupils' heritage by his tutor or factor *loco tutoris* leaves the proceeds heritable until the pupil attains minority, when he may dispose of the proceeds as moveable estate.[56]

Obligations bearing interest *ex lege*, independently of stipulation of parties, are moveable for all purposes.[57]

---

[42] Even where lent on the security of a long lease: *Stroyan v. Murray* (1890) 17 R. 1170.

[43] Ersk. II, 2, 7; Bell, *Prin.* §1479; *Gray v. Walker* (1859) 21 D. 709; *Muirhead v. M's Factor* (1867) 6 M. 95; *Caledonian Ry. v. Watt* (1875) 2 R. 917; *Kelvinside Estate Co. v. Donaldson's Trs.* (1879) 6 R. 995; *Fairlie's Trs. v. F's C.B.*, 1932 S.C. 216.

[44] *Gilligan v. G.* (1891) 18 R. 387.

[45] *Adv. Gen. v. Oswald, supra.*

[46] Copyright Act, 1956, S. 36(1).

[47] Ersk. II, 2, 8; Bell, *Prin.* §1479, 1505; *Martin v. Agnew* (1755) Mor. 5457; 5 B.S. 830; *Logan's Trs. v. L.* (1896) 23 R. 848; *Watson's Trs. v. Brown*, 1923 S.C. 228.

[48] *Minto v. Kilpatrick* (1832) 11 S. 632; *L.A. v. Macfarlane's Trs.* (1893) 31 S.L.R. 357; Partnership Act, 1890, S. 22; Companies Act, 1948, S. 73; cf. *Shaw's Trs. v. S.* (1870) 8 M. 419.

[49] *Wardlaw's Trs. v. W.* (1880) 7 R. 1070; cf. *Gilligan v. G.* (1891) 18 R. 387; *Borland's Trs. v. B.*, 1917 S.C. 704.

[50] *Muirhead's Trs. v. M.* (1905) 7 F. 496.

[51] *Murray's Tr. v. McIntyre* (1904) 6 F. 588.

[52] Bell, *Prin.* §1474; *Allan v. Millar*, 1932 S.C. 620.

[53] Ersk. II, 2, 17; *McLellan v. McL.*, 1960 S.C. 348.

[54] *Heron v. Espie* (1856) 18 D. 917.

[55] Ersk. II, 2, 17.

[56] *Brown's Tr. v. B.* (1897) 24 R. 962.   [57] Ersk. II, 2, 13.

Heritable securities

Bonds to pay money secured by a disposition of heritage in security or by real burden on land were at common law, by reason of their inherent connection with land, deemed heritable in the succession of both debtor and creditor.[58] By statute,[59] however, such securities have been made moveable in the creditor's succession,[60] except *quoad fiscum*, i.e. as to the Crown's right of escheat,[61] and as to the legal rights of children.[62] The change might formerly be defeated by the creditor taking the bond expressly in favour of himself and his heirs, excluding executors, or by executing a minute excluding executors.[63] Such debts remain burdens on the debtor's heirs rather than his executors.[64] The change does not affect the mode of completing title to the bond,[65] Nor does it affect the succession to the debtor, in whose succession such a bond is always heritable.[66] The change has been held, where wills destined heritable and moveable portions of the estate differently, to put heritable securities into the moveable portion of the estate.[67]

The common law rule does not hold in respect of the constructive security of a ranking and sale, or in sequestration, nor as to securities taken by a tutor, factor *loco tutoris, curator bonis* or father as administrator in law, and such acts of administration do not alter the succession to the pupil.[68]

Personal bonds

Personal bonds, containing a merely personal promise to pay money and not secured over land, were at common law deemed moveable

[58] Ersk. II, 2, 5; Bell, *Prin.* §1485.
[59] Titles to Land Consolidation (Sc.) Act, 1868, S. 117; heritable securities affected are defined in S. 3. See also *Stroyan* v. *Murray* (1890) 17 R. 1170 (recorded long lease: moveable); *Peterkin* v. *Harvey* (1902) 9 S.L.T. 434 (decree of Dean of Guild Court declaring holder real creditor: moveable).
[60] *Hughes's Trs.* v. *Corsane* (1890) 18 R. 299.
[61] 1868 Act, S. 117.
[62] *Wingate's Trs.* v. *W.*, 1917, 1 S.L.T. 75; Succession (Sc.) Act, 1964, S. 34 and Sch. 3, amending 1868 Act, S. 117. Until 1964 such bonds were heritable as regards legal rights of surviving spouses (courtesy and terce) also. See e.g. *Heath* v. *Grant's Trs.*, 1913 S.C. 78.
[63] Succession (Sc.) Act, 1964, S. 34 and Sch. 3, amending 1868 act, S. 117.
[64] *Bell's Trs.* v. *B.* (1884) 12 R. 85; *Ferrier* v. *Cowan* (1896) 23 R. 703; see also *Brand* v. *Scott's Trs.* (1892) 19 R. 768; *Muir's Trs.* v. *M.*, 1916, 1 S.L.T. 372; *Ballantyne's Trs.* v. *B's Trs.*, 1941 S.C. 35.
[65] *Hare* (1889) 17 R. 105.
[66] *Bell's Trs., supra.*
[67] *Guthrie* (1880) 8 R. 34; *Hughes' Trs.* v. *Corsane* (1890) 18 R. 299; but see opinions in *Hare, supra,* and *Cunningham* v. *C.* (1889) 17 R. 218, that the section applied only in cases of intestate succession.
[68] Bell, *Prin.* §1486; *Lady Graham* v. *E. Hopetoun* (1798) Mor. 5599; *Kennedy* v. *K.* (1843) 6 D. 40; *Heron* v. *Espie* (1853) 18 D. 917.

initially, but, by reason of their resemblance to the annual profits of heritage, deemed heritable in the creditor's succession after the due date for repayment of the capital, when interest started to run, and heritable from the start if interest ran at once, or if the term of payment was a distant or uncertain day which evidenced an intention to leave the capital for a period at interest.[69]

By the Bonds Act, 1661 (c. 244) all sums contained in contracts and obligations carrying a clause of interest were declared moveable in the creditor's succession,[70] but to remain heritable if containing an express obligation to infeft, *quoad fiscum*, i.e. as respects liablility to escheat to the Crown, and in respect of the legal rights of husband and wife, so that neither spouse had a claim, under legal rights to moveables arising on death, to any bond due to the other.[71] Though to remain heritable *quoad* a spouse's legal rights, such bonds are made moveable *quoad* children's legal rights,[72] and statute,[73] by providing that what estate is subject to legitim shall be subject to *jus relictae* or *jus relicti*, has impliedly repealed the exception dealing with spouses' legal rights. This Act does not affect bonds taken expressly in favour of the creditor and his heirs in heritage, or a specified series of such heirs, or otherwise excluding the creditor's executors.[74] The Act also excepts bonds containing a clause of infeftment and providing for heritable security for the debt, and bonds expressly excluding executors.[75] Such bonds are, however, always moveable in the debtor's succession, unless the heir in heritage is expressly bound.

The statutes regulating the issue of certain securities sometimes also provide expressly that, notwithstanding the running of interest thereon, the bonds shall be moveable in succession.[76]

Heritable things becoming moveable

Things heritable such as minerals, trees[77] or crops become moveable when severed from the soil; for the purposes of sale 'goods' includes industrial growing crops and things attached to or forming part of the

---

[69] Stair II, 1, 3; Ersk. II, 2, 9; Bell, *Prin.* §1495; *Gray* v. *Walker* (1859) 21 D. 709; *Dawson's Trs.* v. *D.* (1896) 23 R. 1006; *Bennett's Exrx.* v. *B's Exors.*, 1907 S.C. 598; *Stark* v. *S.*, 1910 S.C. 397; *Heath* v. *Grant's Trs.*, 1913 S.C. 78.

[70] *Muirhead* v. *M's Factor* (1867) 6 M. 95.

[71] Ersk. II, 2, 10; *Downie* v. *D's Trs.* (1866) 4 M. 1067; *Dawson's Trs., supra; Stark, supra; Heath, supra.*

[72] *Dawson's Trs., supra.*

[73] Conveyancing (Sc.) Act, 1924, S. 22.

[74] *Duffs* v. *D.* (1754) Mor. 5429.

[75] *Mackay* v. *Robertson* (1725) Mor. 3224; *Kennedy* v. *K.* (1747) Mor. 5499.

[76] *Robertson's Trs.* v. *Maxwell*, 1922 S.C. 267; *McWiggan's Trs.* v. *McW.*, 1922 S.C. 276; cf. *Stewart's Trs.* v. *Battcock*, 1914 S.C. 179.

[77] *Munro* v. *Balnagown Estates Liqdrs.*, 1949 S.C. 49.

land which are agreed to be severed before sale or under the contract of sale.[78]

Moveable things become heritable by accession — fixtures

Where a thing by itself moveable is connected with heritage a question may arise whether it remains moveable or has become so annexed to the heritage as to become heritable by accession, to pass with it, and not to be again removeable.[79] While the principle is *accessorium sequitur principale*,[80] it is a question whether accession has taken place or is to be presumed.

The cases usually raise two questions, whether the thing has become a fixture, and, if so, whether some person is entitled to sever and remove it.

In accordance with the maxims *inaedificatum solo, solo cedit*, and *quicquid plantatur solo, solo cedit* anything built on or into or affixed to the ground is deemed annexed thereto.[81] Conversely a thing merely resting on the ground is not necessarily annexed thereto, though articles annexed only by their own weight may be so adapted to a building or its surroundings as to be deemed fixtures,[82] and moveable things so annexed or adapted that they cannot be removed without destruction of or damage to principal or accessory may be deemed heritable by accession.[83]

Also moveable articles accessory to a principal thing which is heritable may be deemed constructive fixtures, such as a factory bell,[84] or moveable accessories of fixed machinery,[85] though not themselves attached to the heritage.

Degree of fixation

One major point for consideration is the degree or permanence of the affixing, whether the article has been so permanently fixed as to have become part of the heritage, so that it cannot be disjoined without injury to itself or to the heritage, or on the other hand is so lightly attached as to be removeable without damage to itself or to the

[78] Sale of Goods Act, 1979, S. 61.
[79] On what are 'fixtures' and 'fittings' see *Jamieson* v. *Welsh* (1900) 3 F. 176.
[80] *Brand's Trs.* v. *B's Trs.* (1876) 3 R. (H.L.) 16, 20.
[81] Stair II, 1, 40; *Dowall* v. *Miln* (1874) 1 R. 1180; *Brand's Trs.* v. *B's Trs.* (1876) 3 R. (H.L.) 16, 23; *Nisbet* v. *Mitchell-Innes* (1880) 7 R. 575; *Burns* v. *Fleming* (1880) 8 R. 256; *Miller* v. *Muirhead* (1894) 21 R. 658; *Howie's Trs.* v. *McLay* (1902) 5 F. 214; *S.C.W.S.* v. *Glasgow Assessor*, 1938 S.C. 323.
[82] *Howie's Trs., supra; Christie* v. *Smith*, 1949 S.C. 572.
[83] Bell, *Prin.* §1473; *Dowall, supra*.
[84] *Barr* v. *McIlwham* (1821) 1 S. 124.
[85] *Fisher* v. *Dixon* (1845) 4 Bell 286; *Brand's Trs., supra*.

heritage.[86] Things attached to the ground or a building are fixtures.[87] A thing fixed for a substantial period and substantial in itself may be held heritable though in fact it could be, or even had been, removed without damage.[88] A mobile home in a caravan park may be heritable.[89] Machinery may be a fixture though attached only by its own weight.[90] A lesser degree of fixation renders the article heritable if the article is also essential or material to the use of the heritage,[91] or have special adaptation to the use or improvement of the heritage which it would not have if placed elsewhere,[92] or there be express declaration by the owner that the article should be annexed to the heritage.[93] Growing plants are fixtures passing on sale with the land.[94] A slag heap may be a heritable subject though removeable over a period.[95] For purposes of valuation for rating there have been held heritable: cable carrying power up a television mast;[96] car wash unit;[97] and chains running from land out to sea, to which mooring buoys were attached;[98] but not an old ship moored to a quay and used as a club.[99]

The duration of attachment is material and the permanency or quasi-permanency of the fixture is of great significance.[1]

Purpose of attachment

A further question of importance is the object and purpose of the annexation, whether the article was attached for the improvement of the heritage or the better use and enjoyment of the thing annexed. Ornamental shrubs and turf and gravel walks in a garden have been held improvements and not removeable.[2] Tile-hearths have been held

---

[86] *Fisher* v. *Dixon* (1845) 4 Bell 286; *Dowall, supra; Nisbet* v. *Mitchell-Innes* (1880) 7 R. 575; *Marshall* v. *Tannoch Chemical Co.* (1886) 13 R. 1042; *Cochrane* v. *Stevenson* (1891) 18 R. 1208; *Luke* v. *Smith* (1894) 1 S.L.T. 545; *Jamieson* v. *Welsh* (1900) 3 F. 176; *Dundee Assessor* v. *Carmicheal* (1902) 4 F. 525.

[87] *Tod's Trs.* v. *Finlay* (1872) 10 M. 422; *Graham* v. *Lamont* (1875) 2 R. 438; *Reid's Exors.* v. *R.* (1890) 17 R. 519; *Hobson* v. *Gorringe* [1897] 1 Ch. 182; *Edinburgh Gas Commissioners* v. *Smart*, 1918, 1 S.L.T. 80; *Glasgow Assessor* v. *Watson*, 1920 S.C. 517.

[88] *Glasgow Assessor* v. *Gilmartin*, 1920 S.C. 488; *Christie* v. *Smith's Exrx.*, 1949 S.C. 572.

[89] *Renfrewshire Assessor* v. *Mitchell*, 1965 S.C. 271; *Redgates Caravan Parks* v. *Ayrshire Assessor*, 1973 S.L.T. 52.

[90] *Brand's Trs.* v. *B's Trs.* (1878) 5 R. 607; *Howie's Trs.* v. *McLay* (1902) 5 F. 214; contrast *Dowall, supra.*

[91] *Fisher, supra; Dowall, supra.*

[92] *D'Eyncourt* v. *Gregory* (1866) L.R. 3 Eq. 382; *Dowall, supra.*

[93] *Dowall, supra.*

[94] *Nisbet* v. *Mitchell-Innes* (1880) 7 R. 575.

[95] *Collective Securities Co.* v. *Ayrshire Assessor*, 1946 S.C. 244; *Wemyss Coal Co.* v. *Fifeshire Assessor*, 1949 S.C. 207.

[96] *I.T.A.* v. *Lanarkshire Assessor*, 1968 S.C. 249.

[97] *Shell and B.P. Ltd.* v. *Renfrewshire Assessor*, 1973 S.C. 303.

[98] *Forth Yacht Marina Ltd.* v. *Fife Assessor*, 1976 S.C. 201.

[99] *Glasgow Assessor* v. *R.N.V.R. Club (Scotland)*, 1974 S.L.T. 291.

[1] *Christie* v. *Smith's Exrx.*, 1949 S.C. 572, 579.

[2] *Burns* v. *Fleming* (1880) 8 R. 226.

heritable, but grates, gas brackets, picture rods, a mirror, ornamental stone lions and fireclay vases to be moveable.[3] Particularly in the case of a tenant fixtures made by him for the better use of heritage for the purposes of his trade are readily held removeable.[4] Such trade fixtures, until removed, are *partes soli* and the property of the landlord and an assignation of them to the landlord in security of advances has been held to amount to renunciation of the right of removal so long as the debt was outstanding.[5] A tenant entitled at the expiry of his lease to remove buildings erected by him cannot do so when he has not implemented his obligations under the lease.[6]

Relationship between parties

The attitude of the court in determining what is fixture and what removeable depends also on the relationships of the contending parties.[7] As between heir (or legatee of heritage) and executor of a common ancestor, the court leans in favour of the fixture going with the heritage.[8]

As between seller and purchaser of heritage, failing indication in the contract of sale, the question is mainly one of the degree of permanence of the fixture[9] and the court leans in favour of the fixture going with heritage.[10]

As between a heritable creditor and the general creditors or a trustee in bankruptcy, the same principle applies.[11]

As between fiar and a liferenter's representatives, the law is more favourable to the limited owner attaching articles to the heritage with liberty to remove them when his right expires.[12]

Similarly as between landlord and tenant the latter is more readily allowed to remove attachments, particularly those made for the purposes of his business[13] or for the better enjoyment of the articles

---

[3] *Nisbet v. Mitchell-Innes* (1880) 7 R. 575.
[4] *Dowall v. Miln* (1874) 1 R. 1180; *Brand's Trs. v. B's Trs.* (1876) 3 R. (H.L.) 16; *Miller v. Muirhead* (1894) 21 R. 658; *Edinburgh Gas Commrs. v. Smart*, 1918, 1 S.L.T. 80.
[5] *Miller, supra.*
[6] *Smith v. Harrison & Co's Tr.* (1893) 21 R. 330.
[7] *Howie's Trs. v. McLay* (1902) 5 F. 214.
[8] *Elwes v. Maw* (1802) 3 East 38; *Dowall, supra; Brand's Trs., supra; Reid's Exors. v. R.* (1890) 17 R. 519.
[9] *Tod's Trs. v. Finlay* (1872) 10 M. 422; *Nisbet v. Mitchell-Innes* (1880) 7 R. 575; *Cochrane v. Stevenson* (1891) 18 R. 1208; *Edinburgh Gas Commrs. v. Smart*, 1918, 1 S.L.T. 80; *Jamieson v. Welsh* (1900) 3 F. 176.
[10] *Graham v. Lamont* (1875) 2 R. 438; *Christie v. Smith's Exrx.*, 1949 S.C. 572.
[11] *Arkwright v. Billinge*, 3 Dec. 1819, F.C.; *Reynolds v. Ashby* [1904] A.C. 466; *Howie's Trs. v. McLay* (1902) 5 F. 214; see also *Miller v. Muirhead* (1894) 21 R. 658; *Luke v. Smith* (1894) 1 S.L.T. 545.
[12] *Fisher v. Dixon* (1845) 4 Bell 286; *Graham v. Lamont* (1875) 2 R. 438; *In re Hulse* [1905] 1 Ch. 406.
[13] *Dowall v. Miln* (1874) 1 R. 1180; *Brand's Trs. v. B's Trs.* (1876) 3 R. (H.L.) 16.

themselves, so long always as he has implemented his obligations under the lease.[14] The principles applicable as between landlord and tenant apply also to cases of superior and vassal.[15]

The matter may also arise in valuation cases[16] where the principles applicable as between heir and executor apply, and in relation to the diligence which is appropriate.

Modification of position by contract

Parties may by contract modify or exclude the inference which the court might otherwise draw as to fixity or removability, but such a contract will not affect the rights of persons not parties to it, such as a *bona fide* purchaser of the heritage, or the holder of a security over the heritage.[17]

Moveable objects becoming heritable destinatione

Objects originally moveable may become heritable for purposes of succession only, not of diligence, by the creditor or proprietor disclosing the intention that the objects shall fall to himself or his heir.[18] Thus the collection of materials for a building makes them heritable *destinatione* as soon as they are assembled at the site or incorporated in the fabric,[19] and the funds required to complete a building have been held heritable in succession *destinatione*.[20] Dung made on a farm has been held to belong to the tenant's heir, the tenant being obliged to apply it to the land.[21] Shrubs and gravel in a garden have been held heritable.[22] Fixed machinery erected by a tenant for working minerals or for farming purposes is also heritable *destinatione* as between the tenant's heir and his executor.[23] Books, silver-plate, jewels, and furniture may by destination be made heritable in succession.[24]

[14] *Smith* v. *Harrison's Tr.* (1893) 21 R. 330; *Cowans* v. *Forfarshire Assessor*, 1910 S.C. 810.

[15] *Marshall* v. *Tannoch Chemical Co.* (1886) 13 R. 1042.

[16] e.g. *Cowan* v. *Midlothian Assessor* (1894) 21 R. 812; *Dundee Assessor* v. *Carmichael* (1902) 4 F. 525; *Weir* v. *Glasgow Assessor*, 1924 S.C. 670.

[17] *Hobson* v. *Gorringe* [1897] 1 Ch. 182; cf. *Ryenolds* v. *Ashby* [1904] A.C. 466; *Ellis* v. *Glover & Hobson* [1908] 1 K.B. 388.

[18] Ersk. II, 2, 14; Bell, *Comm.* II, 2; *Prin.* §1475; *Robertson* v. *Seton* (1637) Mor. 5489; cf. McLaren, I, 198.

[19] *Johnstone* v. *Dobie* (1783) Mor. 5443; *Gordon* v. *G.* (1806) Hume 188; cf. *Stewart* v. *Watson's Hosp.* (1862) 24 D. 256.

[20] *Malloch* v. *McLean* (1867) 5 M. 335; *B. of Scotland* v. *White's Trs.* (1891) 28 S.L.R. 891; but see *Fairlie's Trs.* v. *Fairlie's C.B.*, 1932 S.C. 216.

[21] *Reid's Exors.* v. *R.* (1890) 17 R. 519.

[22] *Burns* v. *Fleming* (1880) 8 R. 226.

[23] *Brand's Trs.* v. *B's Trs.* (1876) 3 R. (H.L.) 16; *Miller* v. *Muirhead* (1894) 21 R. 658.

[24] Bell, *Prin.* §1475; *Baillie* v. *Grant* (1859) 21 D. 838.

*Rights heritable or moveable by destination—conversion and recon-
version*

The quality of a right in succession as heritable or moveable depends
primarily on the quality of the object as at the date of the owner's
death.[25] But this quality may be altered by destination, express or
implied, depending on the intention of the creditor or proprietor.[26]
Thus the express exclusion of executors in a personal bond will make it
heritable.[27] Conversion of a right may also be effected by contract, as
by selling land for money,[28] or laying out money on the purchase of
heritage.[29] Under the principle *quoad fieri debet infectum valet* land
contracted to be sold is accounted already moveable, the price falling
to the executor,[30] and conversely.[31] The same rule applies to involuntary sales.[32] A judicial sale also effects conversion,[33] as does sale
by a heritable creditor.[34] A trustee or administrator has no implied
authority to alter the succession to the estate in his charge and acts of
investment or administration do not effect conversion.[35]

Constructive conversion

Conversion may be deemed effected constructively under the principle *quod fieri debet infectum valet* where trustees are directed to buy
or sell heritage, in which case the direction is deemed at once implemented, and the beneficiary's right converted even though the direction has not in fact yet been implemented. The beneficiary's right is
then of the kind intended by the truster, though the property held by
the trustees may still be in fact of the other kind.[36] A direction to 'pay'
beneficiaries normally constructively converts heritage.[37] But if the

[25] *Pringle's Trs.* v. *Hamilton* (1872) 10 M. 621; cf. *McLellan* v. *McL.*, 1960 S.C. 348.
[26] Ersk. II, 2, 14; Bell, *Comm.* II, 2; *Prin.* §1491; *Baird* v. *Watson* (1880) 8 R. 233.
[27] Titles to Land Consolidation (Sc.) Act, 1868, S. 117.
[27] *McAdam's Exor.* v. *Souters* (1904) 7 F. 179.
[29] *Robson* v. *Macnish* (1861) 23 D. 429.
[30] *Chiesly* v. *C.* (1704) Mor. 5531; *Macfarlane* v. *Greig* (1895) 22 R. 405.
[31] *Malloch* v. *McLean* (1867) 5 M. 335; *Ramsay* v. *R.* (1887) 15 R. 25; *Bank of Scotland* v.
White's Trs. (1891) 28 S.L.R. 891; *Brown's Trs.* v. *Smith* (1900) 2 F. 817; *Fairlie's Trs.* v. *F's
C.B.*, 1932 S.C. 216.
[32] *Heron* v. *Espie* (1856) 18 D. 917; *Macfarlane, infra.*
[33] *Macfarlane* v. *Greig* (1895) 22 R. 405; *Royal Bank* v. *Maxwell's Exors.*, 1916, 2 S.L.T. 175.
[34] *Howden*, 1910, 2 S.L.T. 250; see also *Rossborough's Trs.* v. *R.* (1888) 16 R. 157.
[35] *Macfarlane, supra*, 409; *McLellan* v. *McL.*, 1960 S.C. 348.
[36] Bell, *Prin.* §1492; *Advocate-General* v. *Blackburn's Trs.* (1847) 10 D. 166, 185;
Buchanan's Trs. v. *Angus* (1862) 4 Macq. 374; *McGilchrist's Trs.* v. *McG.* (1870) 8 M. 689;
McGregor (1876) 13 S.L.R. 450; *Sheppard's Trs.* v. *S.* (1885) 12 R. 1193; *Playfair's Trs.* v. *P.*
(1894) 21 R. 836; *Watson's Trs.* v. *W.* (1902) 4 F. 798; *Bryson's Trs.* v. *B.*, 1919, 2 S.L.T. 303;
Taylor's Trs. v. *Tailyour*, 1928 S.C. 288.
[37] *Cowan* v. *C_t* (1887) 14 R. 670; *Kippen's Trs.* (1889) 16 R. 668; *Brown's Trs.* v. *B.* (1890) 18
R. 185; *Playfair's Trs.* v. *P.* (1894) 21 R. 836; *Anderson's Exor.* v. *A's Trs.* (1895) 22 R. 254;
McCall's Trs. v. *Murray* (1901) 3 F. 380; *Watson's Trs., supra; Steel's Trs.* v. *Steedman* (1902) 5
F. 239; *Bannerman* v. *B's Trs.* (1906) 13 S.L.T. 754.

trustees have merely a power to buy or sell heritage, there is no conversion until or unless the power is exercised, or unless realization is necessary to give effect to the trust purposes and it is effected, or if they have a power exercisable only in certain contingencies or for certain purposes, and the contingency has arisen and the power been exercised.[38] Where conversion operates in consequence of the exercise of a power, it operates only to the extent that is necessary for the execution of the trust purposes and no further.[39] Mere investment by trustees for the preservation of the estate does not effect conversion,[40] nor does the grant by the court of a power of sale, as being necessary for the execution of the trust.[41] In general, where intestacy has resulted, even an express direction to convert will not operate conversion to the prejudice of the heir in heritage.[42] A sale of heritage by a *curator bonis* under authority of the court has been held to effect conversion where the sale was forced or arose from actual necessity,[43] but does not where it has been merely an act of administration.[44]

Reconversion

If the effect of a direction in a trust deed is constructively to convert heritage to moveables, or vice versa, the beneficiaries, if capable of electing, may, before conversion has actually been effected, elect to take the property destined to them unconverted (since, were conversion effected, the benefit could at once be reconverted).[45] The

[38] Bell, *Prin.* §1493; *Buchanan v. Angus* (1862) 4 Macq. 374; *Duncan's Trs. v. Thomas* (1882) 9 R. 731; *Swain v. Benzie's Trs.*, 1960 S.C. 357. See also *Auld v. Anderson* (1876) 4 R. 211; *Hogg v. Hamilton* (1877) 4 R. 845; *Aitken v. Munro* (1883) 10 R. 1097; *Sheppard's Tr. v. S.* (1885) 12 R. 1193; *Seton's Tr. v. S.* (1886) 13 R. 1047; *Bank of Scotland v. White's Trs.* (1891) 28 S.L.R. 891; *Anderson's Exrx. v. Anderson's Trs.* (1895) 22 R. 254; *Sim v. S.* (1895) 22 R. 921; *Peterkin v. Harvey* (1902) 9 S.L.T. 434. Conversion was held operated in *Boag v. Walkinshaw* (1872) 10 M. 872; *Fotheringham's Trs.* (1873) 11 M. 848; *Nairn's Trs. v. Melville* (1877) 5 R. 128; *Baird v. Watson* (1880) 8 R. 233; *Galloway's Trs. v. G.* (1897) 25 R. 28; *McCall's Trs. v. Murray* (1901) 3 F. 380; *Henderson's Trs. v. H.*, 1907 S.C. 43; *Campbell's Trs. v. Dick*, 1915 S.C. 100.
[39] *Advocate General v. Smith* (1852) 14 D. 585; *Cowan v. C.* (1887) 14 R. 670; *Moon's Trs. v. M.* (1899) 2 F. 201; *McConochie's Trs. v. McC.*, 1912 S.C. 653.
[40] *Carfrae v. C.* (1842) 4 D. 605; *White v. W.* (1860) 22 D. 1335; *Melrose v. M's Trs.* (1869) 7 M. 1050; *Baird v. Watson* (1880) 8 R. 233; *Cathcart's Trs. v. Heneage's Trs.* (1883) 10 R. 1205; *Campbell's Trs. v. C's Trs.* (1900) 8 S.L.T. 232; see also *Dundas v. D.* (1869) 8 M. 44.
[41] *Taylor's Trs. v. Tailyour*, 1927 S.C. 288.
[42] *Thomas v. Tennent's Trs.* (1868) 7 M. 114; *Smith v. Wighton's Trs.* (1874) 1 R. 358; *Cowan v. C.* (1887) 14 R. 670; *Brown's Trs. v. McIntosh* (1905) 13 S.L.T. 72; *Swain v. Benzie's Trs.*, 1960 S.C. 357.
[43] *Macfarlane v. Greig* (1895) 22 R. 405; *McAdam's Exor. v. Souters* (1904) 7 F. 179; *Dick v. D.*, 1925 S.L.T. 337.
[44] *Moncrieff v. Miln* (1856) 18 D. 1286; *Brown's Tr. v. B.* (1897) 24 R. 962.
[45] *Grindlay v. G's Trs.* (1853) 16 D. 27; *Hogg v. Hamilton* (1877) 4 R. 845.

election to reconvert may be exercised expressly, as by overt act or request, or impliedly, as by such conduct as, together with the lapse of time, indicates a clear intention to accept the property unconverted.[46] Inaction does not evidence intention to reconvert.[47]

---

[46] McLaren, I, 237; *Macgregor* (1876) 13 S.L.R. 450; *Hogg* v. *Hamilton* (1877) 4 R. 845; *Peterkin* v. *Harvey* (1902) 9 S.L.T. 434; *Bryson's Tr.* v. *B.*, 1919, 2 S.L.T. 303; *Mackintosh's Exor.* v. *M.*, 1925 S.L.T. 674.

[47] *Macgregor* (1876) 12 S.L.R. 450; *Bryson's Tr., supra.*

PART 2

RIGHTS IN CORPOREAL HERITABLE OBJECTS OF PROPERTY

CHAPTER 5.2

LANDHOLDING GENERALLY—THE FEUDAL SYSTEM

The category of objects of property which are both corporeal and deemed heritable consists only of tracts of land and things annexed thereto. Land differs from all other objects of property in that it is permanent and physically fixed, and in that every piece and tract thereof is unique and distinct from every other.

Original acquisition of rights in lands

Rights in land were originally doubtless acquired by occupation but this mode of acquisition has long since been exhausted, not least by the adoption in Scotland of the principles of feudalism, including the rule thereof that all land with a few exceptions ultimately belongs to the Crown and that all rights in land enjoyed by subjects must be held, immediately or mediately, of and under the Crown.[1]

Rights may also be acquired by natural accession, as where soil is washed down by a river and accrues naturally by alluvio to the land which receives the addition, though if ground is carried off by a sudden torrent and deposited on the lands of another (avulsio) it is deemed to continue to belong to the former owner, notwithstanding its being joined to another's land.[2] Similarly if a river gradually changes course land accresces to one riparian owner[3] but if the change is rapid or violent ownership of the soil transferred is deemed unchanged.[4] Or rights may be acquired by artificial accession, as where trees and plants root in land and are deemed to belong to that land. This principle extends to persons building or planting on another's land, when the

---

[1] Ersk. II, 1, 9–11.
[2] Stair II, 1, 34; Ersk. II, 1, 14. cf. the great Moray floods of 1829.
[3] *M. Tweeddale* v. *Kerr* (1822) 1 S. 397; Bell, *Prin.* §936.
[4] See *Pool* v. *Dirom* (1823) 2 S. 466; *E. Zetland* v. *Perth Glovers' Incorpn.* (1870) 8 M. (H.L.) 144.

building or planting accrues to the owner of the land.[5] By artificial accession also fixtures to or in buildings may become the property of the owner of the building.[6]

The rights of property in all lands in Scotland are either allodial or udal or feudal.[7]

Allodial land

Lands held allodially are owned outright and absolutely. Only exceptionally is land so held; allodial land includes the Crown's paramount superiority,[8] the sovereign's own property, lands belonging to the sovereign's eldest son as Prince and High Steward of Scotland, superiority rights reserved by the Crown in the lands of subjects, and churches, churchyards, manses, and glebes.[9] Lands acquired compulsorily under certain statutes are akin to allodial land.[10]

Udal land

In Orkney and Shetland land might formerly be held by possession without any written title, and some land there is still so held, though other land has been feudalized and is held feudally by charter and sasine.[11] Udal land was and is free of all burdens of services or periodical payments.

Feudal land

The great bulk of land in Scotland is held by feudal tenure. This mode of landholding was introduced into Scotland in the eleventh and twelfth centuries.[12] The main feature was that land was held from a

---

[5] Ersk. II, 1, 15; *Beattie* v. *L. Napier* (1831) 9 S. 639; *Ritchie* v. *Robertson* (1832) 10 S. 621; *Begbie* v. *Boyd* (1837) 16 S. 232; *Paul* v. *Cuthbertson* (1840) 2 D. 1286; *Syme* v. *Harvey* (1861) 24 D. 202. See also *Barbour* v. *Halliday* (1840) 2 D. 1279.

[6] Chap. 5.1, *supra*.

[7] See generally Craig, *J.F.* I, 8; Stair II, 3–12; Bankt. II, 3–III, 2; Ersk. II, 3–12; Bell, *Prin.* Bk. II; Ross, *Lect.* II, 23; Bell, *Conv.*, I, 561 *et seq.*; Menzies, 456 *et seq.*; Wood, 119 *et seq.*; Farran, *Principles of Scots and English Land Law*; *L.A.* v. *M. Zetland*, 1920 S.C. (H.L.) 1, 9.

[8] Stair II, 4, 2.

[9] Stair II, 3, 4; Ersk. II, 3, 8; Menzies, 472. Certain churches and manses are now vested in the Church of Scotland General Trustees in free blench holding from the Crown: Church of Scotland (Property and Endowments) Act, 1925, S. 28(3).

[10] Lands Clauses Consolidation (Sc.) Act, 1845, Ss. 80, 126; Burgh Police (Sc.) Act, 1892, Ss. 196–200; *Macfarlane* v. *Monkland Ry.* (1864) 2 M. 519; *Elgin Mags.* v. *Highland Ry.* (1884) 11 R. 950; *Inverness Mags.* v. *Highland Ry.* (1893) 20 R. 551; 1909 S.C. 943; *Young's Trs.* v. *Grainger* (1904) 7 F. 232; *Heriot's Trust* v. *Caledonian Ry.*, 1915 S.C. (H.L.) 52; *D. Argyll* v. *L.M.S. Ry.*, 1931 S.C. 309.

[11] Stair II, 3, 11; Bankt. II, 3, 10; Ersk. II, 3, 18; Bell, *Prin.* §932; Menzies, 473; *Sinclair* (1624) Mor. 16393; *Beatton* v. *Gaudie* (1832) 10 S. 286. See also *Bruce* v. *Smith* (1890) 17 R. 1000; *Spence* v. *Union Bank* (1894) 1 S.L.T. 648; *Smith* v. *Lerwick Harbour Trs.* (1903) 5 F. 680; *L.A.* v. *Balfour*, 1907 S.C. 1360; *L.A.* v. *Aberdeen University*, 1963 S.C. 533.

[12] Ersk. II, 3, 1; See generally Ganshof, *Feudalism*; Vinogradoff, 'Origins of Feudalism'. 2 Camb. Med. Hist., Ch. 20; 'Feudalism', 3 Camb. Med. Hist., Ch. 18; Barrow, *Feudal Britain*, 1066–1314; Ritchie, *Normans in Scotland*; Innes, *Scotland in the Middle Ages*, Ch. 4; Farran, *Principles of Scots and English Land Law*; *Introd. to Scottish Legal History*, Ch. 1.

superior in return for certain periodical services or payments; the superior owed the duty of maintaining and protecting his vassal, the vassal owed homage and fealty to his superior, and there was a mutual relation of rights and duties betwen superior and vassal.

Originally land was granted only for the vassal's lifetime but later it became, subject to certain conditions, a perpetual and heritable grant, but alienable only with the superior's consent.

A collateral element of feudal tenure was that the grant of lands to superiors commonly carried rights to hold courts and do justice and imposed duties on the vassals to attend those courts.[13] Feudal jurisdictions were abolished by the Heritable Jurisdictions Act, 1747.

Essential features of feudal landholding

The essential feature of the feudal system of landholding is that no proprietor below the Crown owns any piece of land absolutely. The sovereign as paramount superior of all the land in the country, except allodial and udal land, has granted tracts of lands to subjects to hold of and under him for specified returns; these subjects have in turn granted or may grant smaller areas to others, who have in turn granted or may grant smaller pieces to others, and so on. Feudal landholding thus involves the grant of lands to another on conditions and subject to the performance of services, and a continuing relationship between granter and grantee.[14]

There is no legal limit to the amount of subfeuing which may be effected[15] nor to the number of subject-superiors there may be in the chain between the sovereign and the vassal who actually possesses the land.

Interests in the land

Accordingly in the feudal system of landholding a number of persons, the Crown, possibly several subject-superiors, and the vassal, all simultaneously have certain interests in any given piece of land; no one of them owns the land outright but each has simultaneously a defined interest or estate in the land conferring rights defined partly by general law and partly by the terms of the grant to him from his superior.[16] The superior retains an interest in land granted and may intervene to prevent it being diminished in value.

The recognized interests which may simultaneously subsist in any piece of land are:

[13] Stair II, 4, 9.
[14] Stair, II, 3, 7; Ersk. II, 3, 10.
[15] Ersk. II, 3, 13. Prior to the Conveyancing (Sc.) Act, 1874, S. 22, subinfeudination could be validly prohibited but only by an express condition in a grant of lands. Scotland has never had the general prohibition of subinfeudation introduced into England by the Statute *Quia Emptores*, 1290.
[16] Craig, I, 9, 7; Ersk. II, 3, 1.

The interest of the Crown or dominium eminens

The interest of the Crown is that of ultimate and absolute owner-ship, except in so far as rights in and to a particular tract of land have been granted to a vassal-in-chief. But any and every right not so granted remains to the Crown. By virtue of this *dominium eminens* the Crown may compel any proprietor to surrender his property for public necessity.[17]

The interests of superiority or dominium directum

There may be several, or many, interests of superiority, one vested in a vassal-in-chief, who holds directly of the Crown, and each other vested in one who as vassal holds of a superior higher in the chain but is himself superior of one or more vassals. The interest which each superior retains to himself in lands is called *dominium directum*, as the highest and most eminent right,[18] and in questions with the over-superior he is the *dominus*.[19] His title bears to be of the whole lands, not only of the superiority.[20]

The interest of property or dominium utile

The property or *dominium utile* is vested in the vassal who has nobody below him in the feudal pyramid and enjoys the actual posses-sion and use of the piece of land.[21] Thus the vassal and not the superior is entitled to possess the lands and draw the rents,[22] and to be deemed the heritor.[23] For practical purposes he is the owner.

Interests may also be distinguished into fee, which is an interest granted to a person and his heirs generally, and accordingly passes on death to whoever may be heir in heritage of the grantee;[24] tailzied fee or entail, which is an interest granted to a person and a defined series of his heirs only; and liferent, which is an interest held by the grantee for his own life only.

Tenure

Each person having an estate or feudal interest in any land holds it of and under a superior, who similarly holds it of and under another, up

[17] Ersk. II, 1, 2.
[18] Ersk. II, 3, 10.
[19] Ersk. II, 5, 1.
[20] Stair II, 4, 1; Bell, *Prin.* §675; *Hay* v. *Aberdeen Corpn.*, 1909 S.C. 554, 559.
[21] Ersk. II, 3, 10. He may possess personally or mediately, through tenants.
[22] Bell, *Conv.* I, 563.
[23] Bell, *Conv.* I, 642; *Dundas* v. *Nicolson* (1778) Mor. 8511.
[24] The term fee is used both for the right and for the thing affected with the right, and also both of estates granted and reserved, and is consequently applicable both to *dominium directum* and to *dominium utile*. One can speak of the fee of superiority or of property: Ersk. II, 3, 10.

to the superior who holds directly of the Crown, each in turn owing certain prestations to his superior and entitled to certain dues and duties from the vassal who holds of and under him. There is accordingly a relation of tenure between each proprietor and his immediate superior, defining the terms on which he holds the land and what return he owes to his superior, and a chain of tenure between the Crown, the intermediate superiors and the ultimate vassal of lands.

The terms superior and vassal are not absolute but relative to one another, as a superior of lands will himself be vassal of the Crown or an over-superior, and a vassal may, by subfeuing, make himself superior of a new vassal. So too a person may be simultaneously over-superior, superior, and vassal in respect of different pieces of land, or be vassal of different superiors in respect of different pieces of land, or superior of different vassals and sub-vassals in respect of various pieces of land.

The recognized tenures

Various forms of feudal tenure were recognized, according to the conditions under which vassals held their lands. During the military period of feus, if the grant were ambiguous, ward-holding was presumed; after 1746 feu-holding is presumed.[25]

Ward-holding

Ward-holding or military service was the most ancient,[26] deriving its name from the fact that during the minority of a vassal the superior was entitled to the guardianship of his person and management of his estate. By this tenure vassals were obliged to serve their superior in war as often as he called for it, or to give other special services.

In addition to the obligation of military service the superior was entitled to certain incidents or casualties exigible where required. These were Aids or payments which the lord could demand from his vassal, at first for undefined purposes but latterly settled as for three purposes only, viz: (a) to ransom the lord from imprisonment, (b) for the knighting of his eldest son, and (c) for the dowry of his eldest daughter on marriage; and the superior was also entitled to certain Casualties or casual payments: these were

(a) Ward: If the heir were under twenty-one, if male, or under fourteen, if female, the ward or guardianship of the heir belonged to the superior and he had full control of all lands held by military tenure, without at first any liability to account, on the heir's attaining full age. for his stewardship.[27] The right of wardship was often compounded

[25] Bell, *Prin.* §684.
[26] Stair II, 3, 32; Ersk. II, 4, 1–4; Bell, *Prin.* §681; Menzies, 477; see also D. *Argyll* v. *Campbell*, 1912 S.C. 458.
[27] Stair, II, 4, 33 and 56; Ersk. II, 5, 5–9; Menzies, 482.

for by a regular annual payment during the heir's minority, known as taxed ward. When the vassal came of age he might sue for his lands from the lord on doing service as heir and paying relief.[28]

(b) Marriage: The lord also had the right to determine the marriage of the heir, originally in the case of heiresses only.[29] If the heir refused the marriage offered he or she was liable for the 'avail' or market value of the match offered. Latterly avail became payable in every case even if the ward married with the superior's consent,[30] or though the lord failed to procure a spouse.[31] Single avail was originally three years' and later two years' free rent of the vassal's lands.[32] In the case of refusal to marry the bride offered and marriage with another without consent a double avail was payable.[33] By some charters the avail of marriage was a fixed sum, known as taxed avail.

(c) Non-entry was the casualty payable on succession of an heir to a vassal.[34] If by death there was no vassal from whom the superior could exact performance of the services due, he could possess the lands until the vassal's heir entered, did homage to the superior and was accepted by him. Originally if the vassal neglected for a year and a day to enter with the superior he forfeited the holding but later he was allowed to enter with the superior at any time on payment of the casualty of non-entry, measured by the annual value of the lands from the late vassal's death.

(d) Relief was the casualty payable on the succession of an heir to a vassal; it was latterly settled at one year's value of the land.[35]

Wrongs inferring forfeiture of the lands

Wrongful acts of the vassal towards his superior were punishable by recognition, disclamation, purpresture and escheat.

Recognition was the penalty for a vassal holding by ward who alienated more than half of the lands held by this tenure of one superior without that superior's consent. If he alienated to a substitute vassal, the deed was void and he forfeited the whole of his interest in the fee.[36] If he alienated to a sub-vassal to hold of and under him, it was alienation if the subfeu were to be held by ward, blench, mortification or for an illusory service, but not if to be held in feu farm for a real return.[37]

[28] Craig, J.F., II, 20, 10; Bell, *Conv.* I, 564.
[29] Stair II, 4, 37; Ersk. II, 5, 18; Menzies, 482.
[30] *Campbell* v. *McNaughton* (1677) Mor. 8535; *Arbuthnot* v. *Keith* (1662) Mor. 8528.
[31] *Darcie's Case* (1607) 6 Co. Rep. 706; Menzies, 467.
[32] Ersk. II, 5, 20; Bell, *Convg.* I, 565.   [33] Ersk. II, 5, 21.
[34] Stair, II, 4, 18; Ersk. II, 5, 29; Menzies, 484.
[35] Craig J.F. II, 20, 30; Stair II, 4, 26; Ersk. II, 5, 47; Menzies, 486; *Commercial Union Assce. Co.* v. *Waddell*, 1919 S.C. (H.L.) 38, 51.
[36] Stair II, 11, 17; Ersk. II, 5, 10–17; *Hay* v. *Muiries' Creditors* (1631) Mor. 6513.
[37] Craig, III, 3, 8; Stair II, 11, 13; Bell, *Conv.* I, 566.

Disclamation meant a denial of the superior's title, and involved forfeiture of the whole fee.[38] It is now long obsolete.

Purpresture was an encroachment on the superior's lands or rights, and likewise involved forfeiture of the fee.[39] It is now also long obsolete.

Escheat was the forfeiture to the superior of the annual profits of land while the vassal was in a state of rebellion against the Crown or his superior. Escheat might be single escheat, whereby the rebel's moveables fell to the Crown as *bona vacantia*, the Crown or a grantee of the escheat having a year in which to exact the moveables and which formed a burden on the superior's right of liferent escheat and was compounded for by a year's rent; the liferent escheat gave the superior the right to possess the feu while the vassal lived and persisted in rebellion but only in liferent, the fee remaining in the rebel. Liferent escheat was burdened with the vassal's debts, if real and attaching to the lands, but not if merely personal, or subsequent to the escheat. It fell by sentence of death and escape, or by denunciation of the vassal for a criminal cause unrelaxed for a year.[40]

The tenure of ward-holding and the casualties of ward, marriage, and recognition were abolished by the Tenures Abolition Act, 1746. Existing tenures by ward were converted into blench holdings if held of the Crown and into feu-holding if held of a subject superior.

Feu-farm

Feu-farm (or soccage) is the perpetual tenure of land in return for a fixed annual farm or rental, in agricultural services, produce of land, or money, and having analogies with the Roman *emphyteusis*. Originally ignoble, it is now the prevailing tenure.[41]

From 1457[42] the king and lords were allowed to make grants of lands in feu, and there was a continuing tendency to substitute feus for ward-holding. Services tended in time to be commuted into money,[43] and any not so commuted have now been extinguished.[44]

Feu-duty might be in money or in kind down to 1925[45] but all feu-duties in kind in feus granted after the 1874 Act must be of fixed amount or quantity,[46] and in all feus granted after 1924 the feu-duty must be in sterling money.[47] Feu-duties may not be imposed in feus

[38] Craig III, 5, 1; Stair II, 11, 29; Ersk. II, 5, 51; Bell, *Prin.* §730.
[39] Craig, Stair, *supra*; Ersk. II, 5, 52.
[40] Stair II, 4, 61; Ersk. II, 5, 53 and 66; Bell, *Prin.* §731; Menzies, 467.
[41] Stair II, 3, 34; Ersk. II, 4, 5; Bell, *Prin.* §683; Bell, *Conv.* I, 560; Menzies, 478.
[42] Act, 1457, c. 71 (A.P.S. II, 49).
[43] Conveyancing (Sc.) Act, 1874, Ss. 20, 21, and 1924, S. 12.
[44] 1924 Act, S. 12.
[45] 1924 Act, S. 12(1).
[46] 1874 Act, S. 23.
[47] 1924 Act, S. 12; see *L.A. v. Cumming*, 1942 S.C. 25.

granted after 31 July 1974,[48] and existing feu-duties may be extinguished by lump sum payment.[49]

The casualties exigible in feu-holding were (a) non-entry, measured by the feu-duty, unless the superior brought an action for declarator of non-entry; non-entry was abolished in 1874[50] but the superior was entitled to bring an action of declarator and for payment of any casualty due: (b) relief, payable to the superior for granting the heir investiture in the lands measured by an additional year's feu-duty:[51] (c) composition,[52] payable to the superior by a purchaser or other singular successor of the last vassal to obtain recognition as vassal; alienation of a feu was not originally permitted without the superior's consent but after the Tenures Abolition Act, 1746, superiors had to enter purchasers or disponees on payment of a composition; it was measured by a year's rent on the lands as then let:[53] to avoid the uncertainty of incidence of such payments it became customary to provide for payment, at definite and stated intervals, of a further sum in lieu of relief and composition, known as a duplicand, because it was a double feu-duty, payable commonly every nineteenth year;[54] (d) disclamation and (e) purpresture applied as in ward-holding: (f) liferent escheat, entitling the superior to a liferent of the fruits of the lands if the vassal were put to the horn and remained so for a year and a day; in 1746 this casualty was abolished where the denunciation for crime was in respect of civil debt only.[55]

Blench-holding

Blench-holding is the tenure of land in return for services or tributes of various kinds, some valuable and some illusory, and frequently stipulated more in acknowledgment of the superior's right than as profit to him.[56] In modern cases the tribute in blench holding is usually a penny Scots, *si petatur tantum*.

The casualties were the same as in feu-farm tenure. Lands originally held by ward of the Crown or of the Prince of Scotland were later converted into blench-holding by statute.[57]

---

[48] Land Tenure Reform (Sc.) Act, 1974, S. 1.

[49] 1974 Act, Ss. 4–6.

[50] Conveyancing (Sc.) Act, 1874, S. 4; *M. Bute's Trs.* v. *Crawford*, 1914 S.C. 459.

[51] Ersk. II, 5, 47.

[52] See *Heriot's Trust* v. *Paton's Trs.*, 1912 S.C. 1123.

[53] Act, 1469, c. 36; see also *Heriot's Trust, supra; Edinburgh Mags.* v. *Leith School Board*, 1915 S.C. 137; *Mason* v. *Ritchie's Trs.*, 1918 S.C. 466; *L.A.* v. *M. Zetland*, 1918 S.C. 544.

[54] See *E. Zetland* v. *Carron Co.* (1841) 3 D. 1124; *Heriot's Tr.* v. *Lawrie's Trs.*, 1912 S.C. 875; *Adam* v. *Finlay*, 1917 S.C. 464; *Commercial Union Assce. Co.* v. *Waddell*, 1919 S.C. (H.L.) 38, 39.

[55] Bell, *Conv.* I, 622; Menzies, 482.

[56] Craig I, 11, 5; Stair II, 3, 33; Ersk. II, 4, 7; Bell, *Prin.* §682, 692; Menzies, 478; 41 J.R. 331; 42 J.R. 150. But see also *D. Richmond* v. *Countess of Seafield*, 1927 S.C. 833.

[57] Tenures Abolition Act, 1746, S. 2; Admission of Vassals (Sc.) Act, 1751.

Burgage

Burgage was the tenure by which royal burghs, burghs of barony and burghs of regality held lands of the Crown or the subject-superior of the burgh; the usual tribute was the duty of watching and warding. The vassal was truly the burgesses as a group. Burgage tenants normally paid no relief and their land did not fall into non-entry or ward.[58] For all practical purposes burgage was equated with feu-farm tenure in 1874.[59]

A special case of burgage was the tenure by booking in Paisley. The tenure was from the burgh and transfer was by resignation in presence of the town council, the proceedings being recorded by the Town Clerk and a copy delivered to the new tenant.[60] After 1868 conveyances could be recorded in the Register of Booking[61] and even since 1874 lands held prior thereto by booking must be so recorded.[62]

Mortification

Mortification was the tenure whereby were held feudal subjects given to churches, monasteries or other corporations, ecclesiastical or law, for religious, charitable or public uses.[63] The only return was *preces et lacrymae*. No services were due and there were no casualties. At the Reformation lands mortified to religious corporations were forfeited and annexed to the Crown.[64]

Since the final abolition of episcopacy in 1690 the only lands remaining mortified to the churches were the manses and glebes of parish ministers.[65] Lands held for religious or charitable purposes may now be held by feu or blench-holding.

Later simplification of tenures

Ward-holding and the casualties of ward, both simple and taxed ward, marriage, and recognition were abolished in 1746, and lands so held were converted, if held of the Crown, to blench-holdings and if held of a subject-superior, to feu-holdings.[66] The casualties of single and liferent escheat were also abolished.[67]

In 1874 blench tenure became virtually a form of feu-farm and the

[58] Craig I, 10, 21; Stair II, 3, 38; Ersk. II, 4, 8; Bell, *Prin.* §685, 838; Menzies, 479, 846.
[59] Conveyancing (Sc.) Act, 1874, S. 25.
[60] See *Chalmers* v. *Paisley Mags.* (1829) 7 S. 718; Conveyancing (Sc.) Act, 1874, S. 26; *McCutcheon* v. *McWilliam* (1876) 3 R. 565.
[61] Discontinued under Burgh Registers (Sc.) Act, 1926.   [62] 1874 Act, S. 25.
[63] Stair II, 3, 39–40; Ersk. II, 4, 10; Menzies, 478.
[64] See Acts, 1587, c. 29 (A.P.S. III, 431); 1633, c. 10 (A.P.S. V, 27); Stair II, 3, 39–40; Ersk. II, 4, 10, and 11; Bell, *Prin.* §686; Bell, *Convg.* I, 570; Menzies, 521.
[65] Bankt. II, 8, 6; Stair, II, 3, 40 and Ersk. II, 1, 7, tend to treat these lands as *res sacrae*.
[66] Tenures Abolition Act, 1746, Ss. 1–9; see *D. Argyll* v. *Campbell*, 1912 S.C. 458.
[67] Ibid., S. 11.

tenure of lands held burgage was assimilated for nearly all purposes to
that of feu-farm.[68]

The Conveyancing (Sc.) Act, 1874, prohibited the creation of
casualties in new forms and provided for the commutation or redemption of casualties in existing feus, though it remained competent to
stipulate for duplications of feu-duty at fixed intervals, commonly
every nineteenth year.[69] The Feudal Casualties (Sc.) Act, 1914,
abolished casualties, unless they were redeemed or commuted into an
extra feu-duty within a limited time,[70] and made it incompetent in new
feus to stipulate for casualties, duplicands or sums payable at intervals
of more than one year, though it is still competent to stipulate for a
permanent increase or decrease of feu-duty, if certain both as to time
and amount. The Land Tenure Reform (Sc.) Act, 1974, prohibited the
creation of new feu-duties and permitted the redemption of feu-duties
for lump sums.

Crownhold

The Land Commission Act, 1967, established the Land Commission
to acquire land suitable for material development and authorized it (S.
17) to dispose of land by way of feu, sale, or lease, the disposition
stating that the interest conveyed is to be held by way of crownhold,
and containing such conditions restricting development as were necessary to retain for the Crown any element of value which might be or
become attributable to the prospect of any development of that land
for any other purpose. The Commission was dissolved by the Land
Commission (Dissolution) Act, 1971, and lands held were transferred
to the Secretary of State for Scotland. The provisions as to crownhold
disappeared.

Kindly tenants

A few cases survive in villages near Lochmaben of kindly tenancy, of
landholders on former demesne lands of the monarch, who have full
proprietorship but yet hold neither feudally or allodially.[71] Rentallers

---

[68] Conveyancing (Sc.) Act, 1874, Ss. 3 and 25; cf. *McCutcheon* v. *McWilliam* (1876) 3 R. 565.

[69] cf. *Commercial Union Assce. Co.* v. *Waddell*, 1919 S.C. (H.L.) 38, 39.

[70] See *Heriot's Trust* v. *Paton's Trs.*, 1912 S.C. 1123; *Mason* v. *Ritchie's Trs.*, 1918 S.C. 466;
L.A. v. *M. Zetland*, 1920 S.C. (H.L.) 1; *Smith-Shand's Trs.* v. *Forbes*, 1922 S.C. 351; *D.
Richmond* v. *Seafield*, 1927 S.C. 833; *Macdonald* v. *Small's Trs.*, 1928 S.L.T. 321; *Edinburgh
Mags.* v. *Howling's Trs.*, 1921 S.C. 284; *D. Argyll* v. *L.M.S. Ry.*, 1931 S.C. 309; *Smith* v.
Warner's Trs., 1931 S.C. 459; *Dowell's Ltd.* v. *Heriot's Trust*, 1941 S.C. 13; *L.A.* v. *Cumming*,
1942 S.C. 25.

[71] See Stair II, 9, 21; III, 9, 15; Ersk. II, 6, 37; Ross, *Lect.* II, 179, 474; Hunter, *L. & T.* I, 423; II,
122; Rankine, *L.*, 152; *Cassilis' Tutor* v. *Lochinvar* (1581) Mor. 15183; 1 Pat. 77;*Craigie
Wallace* (1623) Mor. 7191; *Kindly Tenants of Lochmaben* v. *Stormonth* (1726) Mor. 15195;
Mounsey v. *Kennedy*, 30 Nov. 1808, F.C.; *M. Queensberry* v. *Wright* (1838) 16 S. 439; *Royal
Four Towns Fishing Assoc.* v. *Dumfriesshire Assessor*, 1956 S.C. 379; Carmont, 'Kindly
Tennants' (1910) 21 J.R. 324; 51 J.R. 201; Farran, *Scots and English Land Law*, 60–4.

have no charter or feudal title, but are enrolled in the landlord's rent books.

Tenancy-at-will

A tenancy-at-will is an anomalous type of holding occasionally found in some rural areas. Generally land is rented for building a house without formal title but subject to payment of a rent. The holding is transferable by obtaining a receipt for the price and intimating the change of tenant to the landlord or his factor. The tenant has no recorded title. He may now acquire from the landlord the interest which enabled the landlord to grant the tenancy-at-will, usually the *dominium utile*, by statutory procedure.[72]

Leasehold

Leasehold is not a feudal tenure but a mode of holding land from a feudal proprietor for a longer or shorter time as defined by the contract of lease.[73]

Rights in land

The proprietary rights which may exist in tracts of land are ownership or property and possession. Under the feudal system a distinctive feature is that several persons, the Crown, an over-superior, a superior, and the vassal, may simultaneously and concurrently have interests or elements of ownership in one piece of land.

Possession is one of the rights which in aggregate make up ownership or property. It consists in the right actually to occupy, control, and use a particular tract of land or a building accessory thereto or a part thereof. It may be enjoyed by the vassal, or granted by him to another as licensee or tenant. No presumption of property is raised by possession, and it is only in particular circumstances that long continued possession can ripen into ownership.[74]

THE REGISTER OF SASINES

The Register of Sasines is a public register of deeds, established in 1617, in which deeds creating, transferring or extinguishing rights in land, or burdening these rights, may be recorded.[75] Deeds recorded have priority by date of recording, not date of granting.[76] Without

---

[72] Land Registration (Sc.) Act, 1979, Ss. 20–2.

[73] See further Ch. 5.15, *infra*.

[74] cf. *Sinclair* v. *S.* (1829) 7 S. 342.

[75] The Registration Act, 1617, specifies reversions, regresses, bonds for making reversions and regresses, assignations and discharges thereof, renunciations of wadsets, grants of redemption and instruments of sasine.   [76] Act, 1693; Ersk. II, 3, 42.

registration deeds create personal rights only against the granter and his heirs. On being recorded they create real rights effective against everyone. But the validity of the title recorded depends on the sufficiency of the progress of title deeds evidencing the right and title of the granter of the deed recorded and of the soundness of the recorded deed itself. Accordingly before any deed is granted or recorded the validity of the prior titles must be examined. Recording carries no guarantee of the soundness of the title. Deeds recorded are photo-copied and the originals returned to the grantee, marked as registered. Extracts (photocopies) of deeds may be obtained; an extract is as probative as the principal unless challenged on the ground of forgery.[77] When dealing with land it is accordingly necessary to search the Register to ascertain what deeds affecting the land are recorded.

Not all real rights affecting land are embodied in deeds recorded; exceptions are servitudes and rights of way, which may be created by possession for the prescriptive period, long leases made real by possession, non-long leases, floating charges, and all merely personal claims against the owner. Search of the Register will not disclose these rights and separate inquiry mist be made to discover them.

Once the Land Register of Scotland has been operational in an area for some time, interests remaining unregistered may be required to be registered and the Register of Sasines for that area will then be closed.[78]

LAND REGISTRATION

The Land Registration (Sc.) Act, 1979, established the Land Register of Scotland as a public register of interests in land, i.e. of estates, interests, servitudes or other heritable rights in or over land, including heritable securities and long leases, i.e. probative leases exceeding twenty years or including an obligation on request to extend so as to last for more than twenty years, but excluding leases which are not long leases.[79] Land includes buildings and land covered with water.[79] An interest in land is registrable (i) on the grant of an interest in feu, long lease or security by contract of ground annual; (ii) on the transfer of the interest for value, except where it is absorbed into another unregistered interest; (iii) on the transfer of the interest in consideration of marriage;[80] (iv) on the transfer of the interest whereby it is absorbed into a registered interest;[81] (v) on any transfer where it is held

[77] Ersk. II, 3, 43.
[78] Land Registration (Sc.) Act, 1979, S. 2(5).
[79] 1979 Act, Ss. 1, 28.
[80] The transfer must be conditioned to take effect only on the marriage taking place; it is not sufficient that it takes place on the occasion of marriage.
[81] E.g. when a vassal surrenders the *dominium utile* to the superior, or a long lease expires.

under long lease, udal tenure or kindly tenancy; or in other circumstances on application if the Keeper of the Registers considers it expedient. The creation over a registered interest in land of a heritable security, a liferent, or an incorporeal heritable right[82] is registrable and on registration it will become a registered interest in land. There are also registrable any transfer of a registered interest in land, any absorption by a registered interest in land of another registered interest, and any other transaction or event which is capable of affecting the title to a registered interest in land, except one creating or affecting an overriding interest.[83] Registration is being introduced in successive operational areas and ultimately in each area the Register of Sasines will be closed so far as relating to that area. On being first registered a title will be examined by the Keeper and in effect guaranteed by him,[84] backed by a state guarantee.[85] The title sheet will disclose all relevant information concerning the registered interest and burdens affecting it other than overriding interests and the land certificate or charge certificate will evidence the interest of the person whose interest is registered. It will become unnecessary to examine prior titles, and only the land or charge certificate will need to be produced on the occasion of any dealing with the interest.

Registration in operational areas is not compulsory, but will be the only means whereby the owner of an interest in land can obtain a real right thereto; without registration he would have only a personal claim against the granter to him of his right.

Once an area has become operational for registration of interest in the Land Register recording of a deed in the Register of Sasines will be competent only in limited circumstances. Without prejudice to creating real rights or obligations otherwise than by registration, such recording will be the only means of creating or effecting a real right or obligation in the cases of (a) an interest in land which is to be transferred or otherwise affected by an instrument which was recorded before the commencement of the 1979 Act in the Register of Sasines with an error or defect, or a deed which was previously recorded with an error or defect in the recording, and has not been re-presented for recording afresh; or (b) where a registered interest in land has been absorbed otherwise than by prescription into another interest in land the title to which is governed by a deed recorded in the Register of Sasines; or (c) anything which is not registrable under the 1979 Act, S. 2(1)–(4) and in respect of which, prior to the 1979 Act, a real right or obligation

---

[82] Excluding salmon-fishings; S. 28. Salmon-fishings are not subordinate rights but distinct praedial interests which can be owned separately from land and rivers.
[83] 1979 Act, S. 2.
[84] 1979 Act, S. 12.
[85] 1979 Act, S. 24.

could be created or affected by recording a deed in the Register of Sasines.[86]

Overriding interests

An overriding interest is in general one which can exist as a real right, without having been recorded in the Register of Sasines. It is,[87] in relation to any interest in land, the right or interest over it of (a) the lessee under a non-long lease; (b) the lessee under a long lease who, prior to the Act, had acquired a real right in the subjects of lease by possession; (c) a crofter, cottar, landholder or statutory small tenant under the legislation relevant thereto;[88] (d) the proprietor of the dominant tenement in a servitude;[89] (e) the Crown or any Government or public department or any public or local authority, under any enactment or rule of law;[90] (f) the holder of a floating charge, whether or not it has attached to the interest;[91] (g) a member of the public in respect of any public right of way or any right held inalienably by the Crown in trust for the public; [92] (h) any person, being a right which has been made real otherwise than by recording in the Register of Sasines or by registration;[93] (i) any other person under any rule of law relating to common interest or joint or common property,[94] not being a right or interest constituting a real right, burden or condition entered in the title sheet of the interest in land under S. 6(1) (e) or having effect by virtue of a deed recorded in the Register of Sasines; or (j) the interest of a person under the Matrimonial Homes (Family Protection) (Scotland) Act, 1981. It does not include any subsisting burden or condition enforceable against the interest in land and entered in its title sheet under S. 6(1). Overriding interests are not in themselves registrable but, under S. 6 (4), may but will not necessarily be entered in the title sheet of the interest affected, so that independent inquiry must be made in relation to their existence.

Application for registration

Application for registration is made on a form prescribed under S. 27 and must be accepted by the Keeper unless (a) it relates to land not sufficiently described to be identifiable; (b) it relates to a merely souvenir plot of land; (c) it is frivolous or vexatious; (d) a deed which

---

[86] 1979 Act, S. 8. The last heading will cover gratuitous dispositions.
[87] 1979 Act, S. 28(1).
[88] See Ch. 5.15, infra.
[89] See Ch. 5.13, infra.
[90] E.g. a wayleave in favour of an Electricity Board.
[91] These are registered in the Companies Register.
[92] See Ch. 5.3.
[93] E.g. an agricultural charge under the Agricultural Credits (Sc.) Act, 1929.
[94] See Ch. 5.7, infra.

accompanies the application, relates to the registered interest in land, and is executed after that interest has been registered, does not bear a reference to the number of the title sheet of that interest. The date of receipt of an application is the date of registration unless the application is rejected on grounds (b) or (c).[95]

Registration: land certificate: charge certificate

Registration is effected by making up a title sheet for the interest in land, or amending the title sheet of an interest previously registered, or, in the case of a heritable security, liferent or incorporeal heritable rights, amending the title sheet of the interest in land to which the heritable security etc, relates. The Keeper issues to the applicant a copy of the title sheet known as a land certificate, or in the case of a heritable security, a charge certificate. Each certificate is authenticated by the seal of the register and is to be accepted for all purposes as sufficient evidence of the contents of the title sheet, or of the facts stated in the charge certificate, as the case may be. Every land certificate and charge certificate contains a statement as to indemnity by the Keeper under Part II (Ss. 12–14) of the Act.[96] The Keeper may, and may be ordered by a court having jurisdiction in questions of heritable right or title or by the Lands Tribunal for Scotland to, rectify any inaccuracy in the Register.[97]

Indemnity in respect of registered interests in land

A person who suffers loss as a result of rectification of the Register, or the Keeper's refusal or omission to rectify, or the loss or destruction of any document while lodged with the Keeper, or an error or omission in any land or charge certificate or in any information given by the Keeper in writing or in another manner prescribed by rules, is entitled to be indemnified by the Keeper in respect of that loss. But the Keeper may exclude in whole or in part any right to indemnity, in respect of anything appearing in or omitted from the title sheet of that interest. There is no entitlement to indemnity in respect of loss arising in various specified circumstances.[98]

Title Sheet

The title sheet for an interest in land discloses:[99] (a) a description of the land consisting of or including a description based on the Ordnance Map and in certain cases its area; (b) the name and designation

---

[95] 1979 Act, S. 4. See Land Registration (Sc.) Rules, 1980 (S.I. 1980, No. 1413) on procedure for application and rectification of the Register.
[96] 1979 Act, S. 5.
[97] 1979 Act, S. 9.
[98] 1979 Act, Ss. 12–13.
[99] 1979 Act, S. 6.

of the person entitled to the interest and the nature of his interest;[1] (c)
any subsisting entry in the Register of Inhibitions and Adjudications
adverse to the interest; (d) any heritable security over the interest; (e)
any enforceable real right pertaining to the interest or subsisting real
burden or condition affecting the interest; (f) any exclusion of indemnity in respect of the interest; (g) such other information as the Keeper
thinks fit to enter in the register. Over-feu-duty or over-rent may, but
need not, be entered. Real rights, real burdens or conditions are
entered by giving their terms or a summary thereof, and unless a
summary contains reference to a further entry in the title sheet wherein
the terms are set out in full the summary is presumed to be a correct
statement of the terms of the right, burden or condition. Overriding
interests, except leases not exceeding twenty years, which affect an
interest in land are to be noted in the title sheet of that interest if
disclosed in any document accompanying an application for registration in respect of that interest, and may be noted on application or if
otherwise disclosed. Any person may obtain an office copy of any title
sheet, part thereof or any document referred to therein.

The effect of registration

Registration has the effect of (a) vesting in the person registered a
real right in and to the interest and to any right, pertinent or servitude,
express or implied, forming part of the interest, subject only to any
adverse interest entered in the title sheet, and to any overriding interest
whether noted therein or not; (b) making any registered right or
obligation relating to the registered interest a real right or obligation;
(c) affecting any registered real right or obligation relating to the
registered interest so far as the right or obligation is capable of being
vested as a real right or being made real or being affected as a real
right.[2] Registration supersedes the recording of a deed in the Register
of Sasines but is without prejudice to other means of creating or
affecting real rights or obligations.[3] A lessee under a long lease,
proprietor under udal tenure, or kindly tenant can obtain a real right to
his interest only by registration and it is the only means of making
rights or obligations relating to such a registered interest in land real
rights or obligations or of affecting them.[4] The date at which rights
become real is the date of registration.[5] The date of entry of a feuar of a

---

[1] E.g. proprietor of the *dominium utile*, superior, lessee under a long lease, creditor in a contract
of ground annual. There may accordingly be more than one title sheet in respect of one piece of
land, each disclosing a distinct interest.
[2] 1979 Act, S. 3(1). E.g. right of salmon fishing can be owned separately from the land; rights
of trout fishing and shooting cannot be subjects of ownership separate from the land.
[3] 1979 Act, S. 3(2). E.g. creation of a servitude by prescription.
[4] 1979 Act, S. 3(3). Udal tenure and kindly tenancy were not previously recordable in the
Register of Sasines or elsewhere.   [5] 1979 Act, S. 3(4).

registrable interest with his superior is the date of registration.[5] Once
an interest has been registered any obligation to assign title deeds or
searches relating to that interest or to deliver them or make them
forthcoming, or any related obligation becomes ineffective in relation
to that interest or any other registered interest. But this does not apply
to a land or charge certificate issued under S. 5, nor where the Keeper
has excluded indemnity under Part II of the 1979 Act.[6]

Ranking

Subject to any express provision as to ranking in any deed or
in or having effect by virtue of an enactment or rule of law, titles to
registered interests in land rank according to the date of registration
and as between a title to a registered interest and a title governed by a
deed recorded in the Register of Sasines rank according to the respective dates of registration and recording. If the dates are the same the
interests concerned rank equally.[7]

[6] 1979 Act, S. 3(5).   [7] 1979 Act, S. 7.

CHAPTER 5.3

THE SOVEREIGN'S PARAMOUNT SUPERIORITY

The rights reserved to the Crown in respect of the feudal lands[1] of the kingdom are the regalia, and no right in lands appropriated by feudal customs to the Crown and *inter regalia* is conveyed by any grant to a subject unless expressed.

The regalia are distinguished into *regalia majora* and *regalia minora*. The former, such as the royal prerogative and the king's paramount superiority over all feudal lands, are inseparable from the royal dignity and cannot be communicated to any subject, or at least cannot be communicated without the consent of parliament, as in the case of annexed estates of the Crown. The latter are communicable to a subject but only by express grant, or grant in terms habile to convey the right, followed by possession thereof for the prescriptive period, and fall into two groups, rights of the nature of *re publicae* deemed by feudal theory to be held by the sovereign in trust for the public, and rights naturally pertinents of land but reserved by feudal custom to the Crown though capable of being granted by it to subjects.[2]

PROPERTY HELD IN TRUST FOR THE PUBLIC

Seas and seashore

While the high-seas are common to all nations and persons, the sovereign has a right of property over the seas and the seabed[3] within the limits of territorial waters, for the purposes of national defence and the trade of the lieges.[4] This right comprises the rights of free navigation, and of fishing, the right to forbid passage to enemies, the rights of jurisdiction,[5] of search, and of levying tolls or duties.[6] The Crown cannot permit a use which interferes with the rights of the public.[3]

---

[1] Salmon-fishings in udal lands are not *inter regalia*: L.A. v. *Balfour*, 1907 S.C. 1360.
[2] Craig, I, 16; Stair II, 3, 60; Ersk. II, 1, 5, and 6; II, 3, 14; II, 6, 13; Bell, *Prin.* §638.
[3] *Crown Estates Commrs.* v. *Fairlie Yacht Slip Ltd.*, 1976 S.C. 161.
[4] Craig I, 15, 3; Stair II, 1, 5; Ersk. II, 1, 6; Bell, *Prin.* §639–40; L.A. v. *Clyde Nav. Trs.* (1891) 19 R. 174; *Crown Estates, supra.*
[5] R. v. *Keyn* (1878) L.R. 2 Ex. D. 63; Territorial Waters Jurisdiction Act, 1878.
[6] Bell, *Prin.* §654–5.

The shore or foreshore includes all land lying between high- and low-water mark.[7] Subject to the Crown's rights as trustee for public uses, the foreshore may be alienated by express grant,[8] or acquired by prescriptive possession on a crown title,[9] particularly a barony title, to lands adjoining the seashore, though without express grant or boundary which indicates an intention to convey the seashore.[10]

A right to the shore implies right to rocks and islets occasionally covered by water, seaweed, and the right to prevent persons making any use of the foreshore other than those reserved to the public.[11]

Minerals in the bed of the sea below low-water mark but within territorial waters belong to the Crown,[12] though they may be acquired by prescription on a barony title.[13]

The public have a right, held in trust by the crown, to use the foreshore for purposes of navigation,[14] and, even where the foreshore has been alienated, may have by prescriptive custom a liberty to use the foreshore for recreation.[15] Recreation may include shooting wild-fowl.[16] But provision for the creation of a nature reserve, may abridge public rights to use the foreshore.[16] A proprietor who, without a grant of harbour, has formed a harbour, may not exclude the public from that part of the shore.[17]

Where lands are bounded by the sea or the seashore the grant includes the shore to the point of lowest ebb,[18] but so far as the shore is

[7] Stair II, 1, 5; Ersk. II, 6, 17; Bell, *Prin.* §641; *Bowie* v. *M. Ailsa* (1887) 14 R. 649; *Musselburgh Real Estate Co.* v. *Musselburgh Mags.* (1905) 7 F. (H.L.) 113; cf. *Officers of State* v. *Smith* (1846) 8 D. 71; 6 Bell, 487; *Agnew* v. *L.A.* (1873) 11 M. 309. As to foreshore in lands held udally, see *Smith* v. *Lerwick Harbour Trs.* (1903) 5 F. 680.

[8] *Duchess of Sutherland* v. *Watson* (1868) 6 M. 199; *Agnew, supra.* The seabed may also be alienable: *Crown Estates, supra.*

[9] *Young* v. *N.B. Ry.* (1887) 14 R. (H.L.) 53; *M. Ailsa* v. *Monteforte*, 1937 S.C. 805.

[10] *Agnew, supra; L.A.* v. *Lord Blantyre* (1879) 6 R. (H.L.) 72; *Buchanan* v. *L.A.* (1882) 9 R. 1218; *L.A.* v. *Wemyss* (1899) 2 F. (H.L.) 1. See also *Scrabster Harbour Trs.* v. *Sinclair* (1864) 2 M. 884; *Baillie* v. *Hay* (1866) 4 M. 625; *L.A.* v. *Maclean* (1866) 38 S. Jur. 584; *Officers of State* v. *Smith, supra; Gammell* v. *Commrs. of Woods* (1854) 13 D. 854; 3 Macq. 419; *Duchess of Sutherland* v. *Watson* (1868) 6 M. 199; *Keith* v. *Smyth* (1884) 12 R. 66; *Aitken's Trs.* v. *Caledonian Ry.* (1904) 6 F. 465; *Musselburgh Real Estate Co.* v. *Musselburgh Mags.* (1905) 7 F. (H.L.) 113; *Mather* v. *Alexander*, 1926 S.C. 139.

[11] Ersk. II, 6, 17; Bell, *Prin.* §644; *Paterson* v. *M. Ailsa* (1846) 8 D. 752; *L. Saltoun* v. *Park* (1857) 20 D. 89; *Nicol* v. *Blaikie* (1859) 22 D. 335; *Colquhoun* v. *Paton* (1859) 21 D. 996; *Baird* v. *Fortune* (1859) 21 D. 848; revd. 4 Macq. 127; *Pirie* v. *Rose* (1884) 11 R. 490.

[12] *Cuninghame* v. *Ayrshire Assessor* (1895) 22 R. 596.

[13] *Wemyss' Trs.* v. *L.A.* (1896) 24 R. 216.

[14] *Agnew* v. *L.A.* (1873) 11 M. 309.

[15] *Smith* v. *Officers of State* (1846) 8 D. 711; (1849) 6 Bell 487; *Scott* v. *Dundee Mags.* (1886) 14 R. 191; cf. *Keiller* v. *Dundee Mags.* (1877) 4 R. 191; *Fergusson* v. *Pollok* (1900) 3 F. 1140; *Hope* v. *Bennewith* (1904) 6 F. 1004; *M. Bute* v. *McKirdy & McMillan*, 1937 S.C. 93.

[16] *Hope, supra; Burnet* v. *Barclay*, 1955 J.C. 34.

[17] *E. Stair* v. *Austin* (1880) 8 R. 183.

[18] *Campbell* v. *Brown*, 18 Nov. 1813, F.C.; *Boucher* v. *Crawford*, 30 Nov. 1814, F.C.; *Blyth's Trs.* v. *Shaw Stewart* (1883) 11 R. 99.

covered at high water it is subject to public uses.[19] If the grantee of lands gains by reclamation of lands from the sea he acquires right to the reclaimed land, but subject to public use.[20]

Trust purposes of sea and seashore

The public uses for which the sea and seashore are held in trust are navigation and fishing.

Navigation is an inalienable right and cannot be encroached on by any grant of ferry, or long exercise of right of ferry, though it must be so exercised as not to interfere with any right of ferry.[21] It does not include the right to fix semi-permanent moorings in the seabed or foreshore without the consent of the owner of the *solum*,[22] nor to anchor boats on private property without consent, save in course of passage.[22]

Fishing is a secondary use of the sea and shore,[23] and, in the case of salmon-fishing, alienable, by an express grant of sea-fishing for salmon, or a grant *cum piscationibus* followed by possession of salmon-fishings.[24] It is questionable whether a grant of white-fishing can be made.[25] Lobster fishing can be granted.[26] A grant of taking oysters, mussels, etc. is competent,[27] but the taking of small shellfish and bait is, if not open to the public, not barred by a general grant of salmon and other fishings without exclusive possession.[28]

Recreation, bathing and other subsidiary uses of the shore are not held in trust but pass with an express or implied grant, so long as the

---

[19] Bell, *Prin.* §643; *Culross Mags.* v. *E. Dundonald* (1769)Mor. 12810; 5 B.S. 556; *Culross Mags.* v. *Geddes* (1809) Hume 554; *Leven* v. *Burntisland Mags.* (1812) Hume 554; *Campbell, supra; Cameron* v. *Ainslie* (1848) 10 D. 446; but where the charter is of land bounded by the 'sea-flood' or the 'full sea' it has been held a bounding charter preventing the grantee from acquiring the seashore by prescription: *Berry* v. *Holden* (1840) 3 D. 205; *St. Monance Mags.* v. *Mackie* (1845) 3 D. 852; see also *Musselburgh Mags.* v. *Musselburgh Real Estate Co.* (1904) 7 F. 308. In this case the superior cannot, if his own lands are so bounded, acquire land from the sea between the vassal's land and high water mark; *Hunter* v. *L.A.* (1869) 7 M. 899; *Montrose Mags.* v. *Commercial Bank* (1886) 13 R. 947.

[20] Bell, *Prin.* §643.

[21] Ersk. II, 1, 6; Bell, *Prin.* §645; *Campbell* v. *C.* (1815) 6 Pat. 417; *Grant* v. *Goodson* (1781) Mor. 12820; 3 Pat. 679; *Colquhoun* v. *D. Montrose* (1804) Mor. 12827, 14283; 4 Pat. 221; *Agnew* v. *L.A.* (1873) 11 M. 309.

[22] *Crown Estates Commrs.* v. *Fairlie Yacht Slip Ltd.*, 1976 S.C. 161.

[23] Bell, *Prin.* §646; As to extent of protected rights to fish see Fishery Limits Act, 1964.

[24] Craig I, 16, 38; Stair II, 3, 69; Ersk. II, 6, 15; Bell, *Prin.* §646. *D. Sutherland* v. *Ross* (1836) 14 S. 960. See also *Commrs. of Woods and Forests* v. *Gammell* (1851) 13 D. 854; 3 Macq. 419; *Anderson* v. *A.* (1867) 6 M. 117.

[25] Stair II, 1, 5; Ersk. II, 6, 17; Bell, *Prin.* §646; *Duchess of Sutherland* v. *Watson* (1868) 6 M. 199; *Nicol* v. *L.A.* (1868) 6 M. 972; *L.A.* v. *McDouall* (1875) 2 R. (H.L.) 49, 55; *Gilbertson* v. *Mackenzie* (1878) 6 R. 610, 1322; *Mackenzie* v. *Murray* (1881) 9 R. 186.

[26] *D. Portland* v. *Gray* (1832) 11 S. 14.

[27] *Ramsay* v. *Kellies* (1776) 5 B.S. 445; *Maitland* v. *McClelland* (1860) 23 D. 216; *D. Sutherland* v. *Watson* (1868) 6 M. 199; *Lindsay* v. *Robertson* (1868) 7 M. 239; *St. Andrews Mags.* v. *Wilson* (1869) 7 M. 1105, but see *Parker* v. *L.A.* (1904) 6 F. (H.L.) 37.

[28] *Hall* v. *Whillis* (1852) 14 D. 324.

uses for navigation and fishing are not impaired.[29] A right to use the foreshore in connection with fishing[30] does not give a right to live there.[31] Fishermen have the use of waste land above high-water mark to dry nets[32] and to use the shore for loading, unloading, drying and pickling white fish.[33]

Navigable rivers

Navigable rivers are vested in the Crown for public use and passage, not merely in tidal reaches but so far upstream as they are fit to transport goods, even though only down-stream.[34] So far as the river is tidal the *alveus* belongs to the Crown, but higher up it belongs to the riparian proprietors though the public has an interest to prevent constructions in the channel which interfere with navigation.[35] The flowing water is public for use of navigation. The banks of public rivers belong to the riparian proprietors and they may exclude the public,[36] save from the use of a tow path, the use of which has been acquired by custom,[37] and so long as the right of navigation is not interfered with.[38] Mooring boats may be done as incidental to navigation, but to keep a raft moored in a public river, or to attach thereto or to the bank pleasure boats, are not incidents of navigation and not permitted.[39]

In some cases the Crown rights of navigation have been granted to statutory trustees to be maintained and improved, as by dredging.[40]

Navigable lochs

A navigable loch, if wholly within the lands of an adjacent proprietor, is a pertinent of those lands, and if touching the lands of

[29] Bell, *Prin.* §647; *Officers of State* v. *Smith* (1849) 6 Bell 487; *Cameron* v. *Ainslie* (1848) 10 D. 446; *Hagart* v. *Fife* (1870) 9 M. 127; *Keiller* v. *Dundee Mags.* (1886) 14 R. 191.
[30] *McDouall* v. *L.A.* (1875) 2 R. (H.L.) 49.
[31] *McCallum* v. *Patrick* (1868) 7 M. 163.
[32] Fisheries Act, 1705; *McDouall, supra.*
[33] White Herring Fisheries Act, 1771, S. 11; *Scott* v. *Gray* (1887) 15 R. 27; *Campbeltown Shipbuilding Co.* v. *Robertson* (1898) 25 R. 922.
[34] *Grant* v. *D. Gordon* (1776) 3 Pat. 679; *Colquhoun* v. *D. Montrose* (1804) 4 Pat. 221; *Wills's Trs.* v. *Cairngorm School Ltd.,* 1976 S.C. (H.L.) 30. See also *Bowie* v. *M. Ailsa* (1887) 14 R. 649.
[35] *Colquhoun's Trs.* v. *Orr Ewing* (1877) 4 R. (H.L.) 116; *E. Breadalbane* v. *Colquhoun's Trs.* (1881) 18 S.L.R. 607; cf. *N.B. Ry.* v. *Perth Mags.* (1885) 13 R. (H.L.) 37.
[36] Stair II, 1, 5; *McIntyre's Trs.* v. *Cupar Mags.* (1867) 5 M. 780; *Gibson* v. *Bonnington Sugar Co.* (1869) 7 M. 394; *L.A.* v. *L. Blantyre* (1879) 6 R. (H.L.) 72; cf. *Hagart* v. *Fyfe* (1870) 9 M. 127.
[37] *Carron Co.* v. *Ogilvie* (1806) 5 Pat. 61.
[38] *C.N. Trs.* v. *Greenock Harbour Trs.* (1875) 12 S.L.R. 595; this does not entitle the public to fish for trout: *Grant* v. *Henry* (1894) 21 R. 358.
[39] *Campbell's Trs.* v. *Sweeney,* 1911 S.C. 1319.
[40] *Lord Blantyre* v. *Clyde Nav. Trs.* (1868) 5 S.L.R. 552; (1871) 9 M. (H.L.) 6; (1881) 8 R. (H.L.) 47; *C.N. Trs.* v. *L. Blantyre* (1883) 10 R. 910; *Carswell* v. *Nith Navigation Trs.* (1878) 6 R. 60.

several proprietors belongs to them in common and may be used by all
for fishing and boating.[41] The *solum* belongs to each in proportion to
and so far as *ex adverso* of his lands,[42] but the water is held in common
for boating, fishing, and fowling. The public have a right of navigation,
but not to beach or moor boats on private land in connection with a
boat-hirer's business, nor can the public by prescription acquire the
right to embark and disembark on private grounds.[43] Where, however,
a navigable loch is a main means of communication, it may be deemed
governed by the same rules as a navigable river.[44] The Crown has a
right in the water and *solum*[45] of sea-lochs *intra fauces terrae* below
low-water mark which entitles it to prevent anyone from using them
for other than recognized public uses.[46]

Port and harbour

The right of making a safe landing-place into a port or harbour
belongs to the Crown, but may be granted by Crown or Parliament to
burghs or subjects, expressly,[47] or by charter as a royal burgh followed
by prescriptive exercise[48] or even by a barony title followed by prescriptive exercise.[49] Grants of port and harbour are subject to the
Crown's rights as trustee for the public, but confer a monopoly within
the limits of the grant.[50]

The right implies a further right to exact harbour dues, and a duty to
make and maintain the harbour and relative works in a state fit for
navigation.[51] The dues are such as are sanctioned by long usage, and
are to be used for the repair and maintenance of the harbour, any

[41] Stair II, 3, 73; Bankt. II, 3, 12; Bell, *Prin.* §651.
[42] *Cochrane* v. *E. Minto* (1815) 6 Pat. 159; *MacDonald* v. *Farquharson* (1836) 15 S. 259; *Baird* v. *Robertson* (1839) 1 D. 1051; *Menzies* v. *Macdonald* (1857) 19 D. (H.L.) 1; *Scott* v. *Napier* (1869) 7 M. (H.L.) 35; *Stewart's Trs.* v. *Robertson* (1874) 1 R. 334; *Mackenzie* v. *Bankes* (1878) 4 R. (H.L.) 192.
[43] *Leith-Buchanan* v. *Hogg*, 1931 S.C. 204.
[44] *Macdonald* v. *Caledonian Canal Commrs.* (1830) 8 S. 881; *Swan's Trs.* v. *Muirkirk Iron Co.* (1850) 12 D. 622; *Colquhoun's Trs.* v. *Orr Ewing* (1877) 4 R. 344, 350.
[45] Including subjacent minerals: *Cunninghame* v. *Ayrshire Assessor* (1895) 22 R. 596.
[46] *L.A.* v. *Clyde Nav. Trs.* (1891) 19 R. 174.
[47] Stair II, 3, 61; Ersk. II, 6, 17; Bell, *Prin.* §654; *Dundee Harbour Trs.* v. *Dougall* (1848) 11 D. 6, 1464; 15 D. (H.L.) 3. cf. *Burghead Harbour Co.* v. *George* (1906) 8 F. 982; *Firth Shipping Co.* v. *Morton's Trs.*, 1938 S.C. 177.
[48] *Macpherson* v. *Mackenzie* (1881) 8 R. 706; cf. *Ayr Harbour Trs.* v. *Weir* (1876) 4 R. 79.
[49] Ersk. II, 6, 18; Bell, *Prin.* §755; *E. Stair* v. *Austin* (1880) 8 R. 183.
[50] *Edinburgh Mags.* v. *Scott* (1836) 14 S. 922; *McFarlane* v. *Edinburgh Mags.* (1827) 5 S. 665; 4 W. & S. 76; *Campbeltown Mags.* v. *Galbreath* (1845) 7 D. 220, 255, 482; *Leith Dock Commrs.* v. *Colonial Life Assce. Co.* (1861) 24 D. 64; *Musselburgh Real Estate Co.* v. *Musselburgh Mags.* (1905) 7 F. (H.L.) 113.
[51] Craig I, 15, 15; Ersk. II, 6, 17; *McFarlane, supra; Bruce* v. *Sandeman* (1827) 5 S. 668; *Campbeltown Mags.* v. *Galbreath* (1845) 7 D. 220, 255, 482; *Bruce* v. *Aiton* (1885) 13 R. 358; *Cormack* v. *Dundee Harbour Trs.*, 1930 S.C. 112; *Firth Shipping Co., supra.*

surplus belonging to the grantee.[52] The grantee is not bound to improve the harbour from his own funds,[53] and is not entitled to levy additional dues for this purpose without Parliamentary sanction.[54] A proprietor of a private harbour has been held bound to give fishermen ground for beaching boats for the winter, as the counterpart of a right to levy dues.[55]

Harbours are commonly now regulated by private legislation frequently incorporating the Harbours, Docks and Piers Clauses Act, 1847.[56] The Burgh Harbours Act, 1853, enabled any royal burgh having a harbour to fix a schedule of rates and apply the revenue in extending and improving the harbour. Harbour authorities are under a general duty to make the harbour reasonably safe for vessels coming thereto, and are liable for negligence, as in buoying the channel or maintaining safe berths.[57] If not bound themselves to supply labour and facilities for loading and unloading, harbour authorities must allow shipowners to employ their own labour and equipment or be liable to shipowners in damages for detention of their ships.[58]

The Harbours, Piers and Ferries (Sc.) Act, 1937, provides for the voluntary or compulsory acquisition by local authorities of any harbour, pier, ferry or boatslip, their maintenance, and the fixing of dues and their application to the expenses of the undertaking.[58a]

Ferry

The right of ferry across public rivers and straits or inlets of the sea belongs to the Crown for the benefit of the public.[59] The right imports the monopoly privilege or carrying travellers, their luggage, and, possibly, vehicles.[60] Its exercise may not interfere with the general liberty of navigation on the same waters, so long as not done to avoid the ferry;[61]

---

[52] *Girdwood* v. *Campbell* (1827) 6 S. 124; (1830) 9 S. 170; *Cowan* v. *Edinburgh Mags.* (1828) 6 S. 586; *Christie* v. *Landale* (1828) 6 S. 813; *Edinburgh Mags.* v. *Leith Shipowners* (1838) 16 S. 1171; *Renfrew Mags.* v. *Hoby* (1854) 16 D. 348; 19 D. (H.L.) 2; *Officers of State* v. *Christie* (1854) 16 D. 454; 18 D. 727.   [53] *Firth Shipping Co., supra.*

[54] *Christie, supra; Home* v. *Allan* (1868) 6 M. 189.

[55] *Aiton* v. *Stephen* (1876) 3 R. (H.L.) 4.

[56] e.g. *Glebe Sugar Refining Co.* v. *Greenock Harbour Trs.*, 1921 S.C. (H.L.) 72.

[57] *Thomson* v. *Greenock Harbour Trs.* (1875) 3 R. 1194; *Buchanan* v. *Clyde Trs.* (1884) 11 R. 531; *Renney* v. *Kirkcudbright Mags.* (1892) 19 R. (H.L.) 11; *Parker* v. *N.B. Ry. Co.* (1898) 25 R. 1059; *Niven* v. *Ayr Harbour Trs.* (1898) 25 R. (H.L.) 42; *Fulwood* v. *Dumfries Harbour Commrs.*, 1907 S.C. 456; *Mackenzie* v. *Stornoway Pier Commission*, 1907 S.C. 435; *Mair* v. *Aberdeen Harbour Commrs.*, 1909 S.C. 721. *A/S Forto* v. *Orkney Harbour Commrs.*, 1915 S.C. 743; *Walker* v. *D. Buccleuch*, 1918, 1 S.L.T. 223; *Robertson* v. *Portpatrick Joint Committee*, 1919 S.C. 293; *Anchor Line* v. *Dundee Harbour Trs.*, 1922 S.C. (H.L.) 79.

[58] *Milligan* v. *Ayr Harbour Trs.*, 1915 S.C. 937.

[58a] See also Harbours Act, 1964, Harbours Development (Sc.) Act, 1972, and Harbours (Sc.) Act, 1982.   [59] Craig I, 15, 15; Stair II, 3, 60; Ersk. II, 2, 17; Bell, *Prin.* §652.

[60] *Ferguson* v. *Dowall*, 18 Jan. 1815, F.C.; 6 Pat. 417; *Baillie* v. *Hay* (1866) 4 M. 625; *Stirling Crawfurd* v. *C.N. Trs.* (1881) 8 R. 826; *L.M.S. Ry.* v. *McDonald*, 1924 S.C. 835.

[61] cf. *Mearns* v. *Myers* (1872) 44 S. Jur. 458; 9 S.L.R. 531.

nor conversely, may the liberty of navigation be exercised to encroach on the privilege of ferry.[62]

A right of private ferry is a monopoly grant by the sovereign to an individual for the public benefit,[63] implying a duty to provide a service and a right to levy fair and reasonable rates,[64] though not excluding neighbouring heritors from transporting themselves in their own boats. It may be conveyed to a third party or leased to a tenant.[65] It excludes any member of the public from operating a ferry for the public.[65]

The Harbours, Piers and Ferries (Sc.) Act, 1937, authorizes local authorities to acquire, maintain, and operate certain ferries.[66]

Highways

A right of highway is vested in the Crown for the public benefit and confers on members of the public liberty to use the surface of the ground along the defined track for the purpose of passage.[67] The right of property in the soil is vested in the owners of adjacent lands, unless expressly acquired from them.[68] Highways may not be encroached on by individuals or communities.[69]

Under the Roads and Bridges (Sc.) Act, 1878, the management and maintenance of highways and bridges in counties was vested in county road trustees, and in burghs in the town council. The county road trustees were superseded by the county councils in 1889[70] and by regional and islands councils in 1975.[71]

Trunk roads, designated by statute, are subject to the Secretary of State for Scotland.[72]

[62] *Agnew* v. *L.A.* (1873) 11 M. 309.
[63] *Campbell* v. *C.*, 18 Jan. 1815, F.C.; *Hunter* v. *Moir* (1830) 9 S. 86; *Moir* v. *Hunter* (1832) 11 S. 32; *D. Montrose* v. *MacIntyre* (1848) 10 D. 896; *Greig* v. *Kirkcaldy Mags.* (1851) 13 D. 975; *Weir* v. *Aiton* (1858) 20 D. 968; *L.M.S. Ry., supra.*
[64] *Montrose Mags.* v. *Scott* (1755) Mor. 4167; *Cumming* v. *Smollett* (1852) 14 D. 855.
[65] *L.M.S. Ry., supra.*
[66] As to rates see *Ross-shire C.C.* v. *Macrae-Gilstrap*, 1930 S.C. 808.
[67] Ersk. II, 6, 17; *Waddell* v. *E. Buchan* (1868) 6 M. 690; *Hope Vere* v. *Young* (1887) 14 R. 425; *McRobert* v. *Reid*, 1914 S.C. 633. For the distinction between a highway and a public right of way see *Sutherland* v. *Thomson* (1876) 3 R. 485; *Donington* v. *Mair* (1894) 21 R. 829; *Reilly* v. *Greenfield Coal Co.*, 1909 S.C. 1328.
[68] *Galbreath* v. *Armour* (1845) 4 Bell 374; *M. Breadalbane* v. *McGregor* (1848) 7 Bell 43; *Wishart* v. *Wyllie* (1853) 1 Macq. 389; *Thomson* v. *Murdoch* (1862) 24 D. 975; *Campbell* v. *Walker* (1863) 1 M. 825; *Waddell* v. *E. Buchan* (1868) 6 M. 690; *Kelvinside Estate Co.* v. *Donaldson's Trs.* (1879) 6 R. 995; *Stewartry Dairy Assocn.* v. *Kirkcudbright Mags.*, 1956 S.C. 488.
[69] But a landowner may erect an openable gate across a public footpath: *Kirkpatrick* v. *Murray* (1856) 19 D. 91; *Hay* v. *Morton's Trs.* (1861) 24 D. 116; *Sutherland* v. *Thomson* (1876) 3 R. 485.
[70] Local Govt. (Sc.) Act, 1889, S. 11.
[71] Local Govt. (Sc.) Act, 1973, S. 133.
[72] Trunk Roads Acts, 1936 and 1946; see also Roads (Sc.) Act, 1970.

Special roads may be provided by the Secretary of State for Scotland or a local highway authority for special classes of traffic only.[73]

Streets

Streets in burghs are similarly held by the district council under the Crown for the public benefit and public right of passage,[74] and can neither be encroached on by private individuals,[75] nor appropriated for public building or feuing.[76] Only statutory authority permits encroachment on adjacent lands for street improvements.[77]

Fairs and Markets

The right of holding fairs and markets is vested in the Crown for the use of the subjects, but is commonly granted to a burgh or an individual for the benefit of the inhabitants of the district. No market or fair can be held without a grant from the Crown, or grant implied in a charter of regality or barony, or inferred from prescriptive exercise or statute.[78] All grants of fair or markets are made subject to any rights already conferred, and these are exempt from interference.[79] Where a right of fair has been granted by royal charter, that grant may be extended by prescriptive usage.[80] Save as authorized by statute or usage, no market dues can be levied.[81]

RIGHTS RESERVED TO THE CROWN

Certain rights in land are deemed *inter regalia*, reserved to the Crown, and impliedly withheld from any grant of lands to subjects but capable of being granted expressly, or tacitly when lands granted are erected into a barony or higher dignity.[82]

---

[73] Special Roads Act, 1949; see also Roads (Sc.) Act, 1970.

[74] *Threshie* v. *Annan Mags.* (1846) 8 D. 276.

[75] *Forbes* v. *Ronaldson* (1783) Mor. 13185; *Gordon* v. *Royal Bank* (1819) 1 Sh. App. 452; *Donald* v. *Esslemont & MacIntosh*, 1923 S.C. 122.

[76] *Miller* v. *Swinton* (1740) Mor. 13527; *Montrose Mags.* v. *Scott* (1762) Mot. 13175; *Young* v. *Dobson*, 2 Feb. 1816, F.C.

[77] *Galashiels Mags.* v. *Schulze* (1894) 21 R. 682. See also Local Government (Footpaths and Open Spaces) (Sc.) Act, 1970.

[78] Bell, *Prin.* §664; *Henderson* v. *E. Minto* (1860) 22 D. 1126; *Blackie* v. *Edinburgh Mags.* (1886) 13 R. (H.L.) 78.

[79] *Falconar* v. *L. Glenbervie* (1642) Mor. 4146; *Farquaharson* v. *E. Aboyne* (1619) Mor. 4147; *Stirling Mags.* v. *Murray* (1706) Mor. 4148.

[80] *Central Motors (St. Andrews) Ltd.* v. *St. Andrews Mags.*, 1961 S.L.T. 290.

[81] Bell, *Prin.* §666; *Lochmaben Mags.* v. *Beck* (1841) 4 D. 16; *Boyd & Latta* v. *Haig* (1848) 10 D. 1433; *Linlithgow Mags.* v. *Edinburgh Ry.* (1859) 21 D. 1215; 3 Macq. 691; *Kerr* v. *Linlithgow Mags.* (1865) 3 M. 370; *Maxwell* v. *Dumfries Mags.* (1866) 4 M. 764; *Kilmarnock Mags.* v. *Mather* (1869) 7 M. 548.

[82] Stair II, 3, 60–1; Ersk. II, 6, 13.

Jurisdiction and courts: fortalices

Rights to hold courts and exercise jurisdiction over feudal vassals might formerly be granted, but all such grants have been abolished.[83] Fortalices or castles built for public defence are also *inter regalia*.[84]

Gold and silver mines

All mines of gold, and mines yielding silver of specified fineness are *inter regalia*.[85] Though formerly deemed inalienable they were later allowed to be feued to the landowner, or other parties if he refused.[86] The permission has been deemed to give a heritable proprietor, as owner of the soil, a *jus quaesitum* to demand such a feu.[87]

This right extends to all proprietors though holding of subject-superiors.[88] Such a grant unites the mines with the lands,[89] though if not expressly mentioned in a later conveyance, they do not pass as parts and pertinents.[90]

Petroleum and natural gas

Under the Petroluem (Production) Act, 1934, petroleum and natural gas existing in their natural conditions in strata in Great Britain are vested in the Crown, together with the exclusive rights of searching and boring for and getting them.[91]

Oil and natural gas

Within territorial waters and, outside them, on the continental shelf all rights as to the exploration and exploitation of the seabed and subsoil thereof and natural resources, except in relation to coal, are vested in the Crown which may grant licences to exploit those rights.[92] The Offshore Petroleum Development (Sc.) Act, 1975, authorizes the Secretary of State for Scotland to acquire land for purposes relating to exploitation of offshore petroleum and regulates operations there and in certain sea areas.

[83] Heritable Jurisdictions Abolition (Sc.) Act, 1747. The office of High Constable of Scotland was excepted.

[84] Stair II, 3, 65.

[85] Royal Mines Act, 1424, c. 13; Mines and Metals Act, 1592, c. 31.

[86] Stair II, 3, 60; Ersk. II, 6, 16; Bell, *Prin.* §669; *E. Hopetoun* v. *Officers of State* (1750) Mor. 13527.

[87] *D. Argyle* v. *Murray* (1739) Mor. 13526.

[88] *D. Argyle, supra.*

[89] *Oughterlony* v. *E. Selkirk* (1755) Mor. 164; *E. Breadalbane* v. *Jameson* (1875) 2 R. 826.

[90] *L.A.* v. *Sinclair* (1868) 5 M. (H.L.) 97; *L.A.* v. *McCulloch* (1874) 2 R. 27; *E. Breadalbane, supra.*

[91] Licences to drill for them are granted by the Crown.

[92] Continental Shelf Act, 1964. The operation of installations is controlled by the Mineral Workings (Offshore Installations) Act, 1971. See also Petroleum and Submarine Pipelines Act, 1975.

Forests

Forests are tracts of land enclosed for the keeping of deer; formerly the privilege of killing deer not privately enclosed was reserved to the Crown, and ground kept for deer hunting was also reserved. A grant of forestry conferred on the grantee the same rights as if his lands had been originally a royal forest and was always deemed oppressive, such that the Session stated that petition should be made to the Crown against such grants for the future. A grant of lands in a royal forest does not carry the right of forest without express words.[93] It was later held[94] that the right of killing deer is not *inter regalia*, so that forestry rights do not now differ from the rights of any proprietor to kill deer on his lands.[95]

Royal fish and fowl

Royal fish belong to the Queen *jure coronae*, not to the taker, nor the owner of the lands on which they are cast.[96] The only royal fish appear to be whales, and not whales taken on the high seas.[97] There is no authority for sturgeon being deemed royal fish in Scotland. Swans may be *inter regalia*.[98]

Salmon-fishing

The right of salmon-fishing is *jus regale*, vested in the Crown unless granted out. It is a separate interest in lands.[99] It may be granted with lands, or separately, but does not pass by implication with a grant of lands.[1] The grant may be express,[2] or be of lands *cum piscationibus* followed by prescriptive possession of salmon-fishings,[3] or be of a

[93] Stair II, 3, 68; Ersk. II, 6, 14; Bankt. II, 3, 110; Bell, *Prin.* §670; *M. Athole v. L. Faskalie* (1680) Mor. 4653; *Robertson v. D. Athole*, 22 May 1810, F.C.

[94] *D. Athole v. McInroy* (1862) 24 D. 673.

[95] See also *Hemming v. D. Athole* (1883) 11 R. 93.

[96] Stair II, 1, 5; Ersk. II, 1, 10.

[97] Bell, *Prin.* §1289; *Suttie v. Aberdeen Arctic Co.* (1861) 23 D. 465; (1862) 4 Macq. 355. See also *Bruce v. Smith* (1880) 17 R. 1000.

[98] Stair II, 3, 60, and 76; *secus*, Ersk. II, 6, 15; see also Bell, *Prin.* §1290; *D. Athole v. Macinroy* (1862) 24 D. 673, 682. cf. Wild Creatures and Forest Laws Act, 1971.

[99] Stair II, 3, 69; *Ogston v. Stewart* (1896) 23 R. (H.L.) 16; *E. Kintore v. Pirie* (1903) 5 F. 818. Contrast trout-fishing: *E. Galloway v. D. Bedford* (1902) 4 F. 851.

[1] Craig I, 16, 38; Stair II, 3, 69; Ersk. II, 6, 11; Bell, *Prin.* §646, 671, 754; *D. Sutherland v. Ross* (1836) 14 S. 960; *Commrs. of Woods and Forests v. Gammell* (1851) 13 D. 854; 3 Macq. 419; *Anderson v. A.* (1867) 6 M. 117; *Ogston v. Stewart's Trs.* (1896) 23 R. (H.L.) 16. It is questionable whether sea trout are salmon at common law: *L.A. v. Balfour*, 1907 S.C. 1360.

[2] Ersk. II, 6, 6, and 15; *L. Gray v. Richardson* (1877) 4 R. (H.L.) 76; *D. Argyll v. Campbell* (1891) 18 R. 1094; *Maxwell v. Lamont* (1903) 6 F. 245.

[3] Ersk. II, 6, 15; *Pool v. Dirom* (1823) 2 S. 466; *L.A. v. Sinclair* (1876) 5 M. (H.L.) 97; *Gordon v. Gordon Wolridge* (1868) 6 S.L.R. 156; *Stuart v. McBarnet* (1868) 6 M. (H.L.) 123; *E. Zetland v. Glover Incorpn. of Perth* (1870) 8 M. (H.L.) 144; *Farquharson v. L.A.*, 1932 S.N. 28. The prescriptive period is now 20 years: *Ogston, supra*. Prescription can run only on fishing by a legal mode: *Maxwell, supra*.

barony title, without mention of fishings, followed by prescriptive possession of salmon-fishings.[4] A specific grant, or lease, of the royal right must include the right to fish by all lawful means, unless specifically limited.[5]

The extent of salmon-fishing so acquired is measured by the possession.[6] A lease of salmon-fishings in the sea does not carry any right to use part of the land for ancillary purposes[7] but a Crown grantee is entitled to access to, and the use of, the foreshore in connection with the fishings.[8]

But the right of salmon-fishing within or *ex adverso* of lands in Orkney or Shetland is not *inter regalia*, this incident of the feudal system being inapplicable to udal lands.[9]

Salmon fishing has long been elaborately regulated by statute with provisions for annual and weekly close times, modes of fishing and penalties for illegal fishing.[10] Where fishing is by net the only legal method is by net and coble.[11] Any *opus manufactum* erected in or about a river which impedes the passage of salmon is illegal, if not protected by prescription.[12]

Wreck

At common law all wrecks became Crown property,[13] unless some living creature were found on board, in which case the owner would claim the wreck within a year and a day.[14] This rule was later obsolete.[15] All unclaimed wreck now belongs to the Crown or its

[4] Ersk. II, 6, 18; *Nicol* v. *L.A.* (1868) 6 M. 972; *D. Richmond* v. *E. Seafield* (1870) 8 M. 530; *L.A.* v. *Cathcart* (1871) 9 M. 744; *L.A.* v. *N. Lighthouses Commrs.* (1874) 1 R. 950; *L.A.* v. *McCulloch* (1874) 2 R. 26; *L.A.* v. *McDouall* (1875) 2 R. (H.L.) 49; see also *L.A.* v. *Hall* (1873) 11 M. 967.

[5] *Johnston* v. *Morrison*, 1962 S.L.T. 322.

[6] *L.A.* v. *Cathcart, supra; E. Zetland* v. *Tennent's Trs.* (1873) 11 M. 469; *L.A.* v. *L. Lovat* (1880) 7 R. (H.L.) 122; *E. Moray* v. *Forres Mags.* (1886) 23 S.L.R. 279. As to possession see *Milne's Trs.* v. *L.A.* (1869) 11 M. 966; *L.A.* v. *Hall* (1869) 11 M. 967; *D. Richmond* v. *E. Seafield* (1870) 8 M. 530; *L.A.* v. *McCulloch* (1874) 2 R. 27; *McDouall* v. *L.A.* (1875) 2 R. (H.L.) 49; *Richardson* v. *Baroness Gray* (1877) 4 R. (H.L.) 76; *D. Roxburghe* v. *Waldie's Trs.* (1879) 6 R. 663; *L.A.* v. *L. Lovat* (1880) 7 R. (H.L.) 122; *Sinclair* v. *Threipland* (1890) 17 R. 507; *Warrand's Trs.* v. *Mackintosh* (1890) 17 R. (H.L.) 13. As to boundaries between fishings see *E. Zetland* v. *Tennent's Trs.* (1873) 11 M. 469; *E. Zetland* v. *Glover Incorpn. of Perth* (1870) 8 M. (H.L.) 144; *Keith* v. *Smyth* (1884) 12 R. 66; *Stuart Gray* v. *Fleming* (1885) 12 R. 530; *Tain Mags.* v. *Murray* (1887) 14 R. 83; *Campbell* v. *Muir*, 1908 S.C. 387.

[7] *Mackinnon* v. *Ellis* (1878) 5 R. 832.

[8] *L.A.* v. *Sharp* (1878) 6 R. 108.

[9] *L.A.* v. *Balfour*, 1907 S.C. 1360.

[10] Salmon Act, 1696 (c. 35); Salmon Fisheries (Sc.) Acts, 1828–70; Salmon and Freshwater Fisheries (Protection) (Sc.) Act, 1951.

[11] *Maxwell* v. *Lamont* (1903) 6 F. 245.

[12] *E. Kintore* v. *Pirie* (1903) 5 F. 818.

[13] Stair III, 3, 27; Ersk. II, 1, 13; Bell, *Prin.* §1292.

[14] *Hamilton* v. *Cochran* (1622) Mor. 16791.

[15] *Montier* v. *Agnew* (1725) Mor. 16796.

grantee.[16] The local receiver of wreck, must, within forty-eight hours, give notice to the grantee of any wreck taken into his possession. If it is not claimed by an owner within a year it must be delivered to the grantee, or sold and the proceeds paid to the Crown. The sites of historic wrecks needing protection may be made restricted areas and prohibitions may be imposed on approaching dangerous wrecks.[17]

OTHER CROWN RIGHTS

Certain other Crown rights are aspects of the prerogative rather than incidents of its paramount superiority of lands.[18]

It is by virtue of the Crown's *dominium eminens* that it may require any proprietor to surrender his right for public purposes, by virtue of compulsory purchase powers conferred on various authorities,[19] and may destroy it if necessary to deny its use to an enemy.[20]

Ownerless subjects

Things abandoned by their owners fall to the Crown: *quod nullius est, fit domini regis*.[21] Till such a thing can be deemed abandoned, it must be handed to the police for custody,[22] but if unclaimed after a period may be awarded to the finder, or sold.[22]

Treasure

Treasure hidden in the earth, the proper owner of which cannot be ascertained, belongs to the Crown, under the principle *quod nullius est, fit domini regis*, but the right may be granted to a subject expressly.[23] To amount to treasure the articles must be precious, appear to have been concealed in the ground or a building rather than merely abandoned or lost, and the owner be unknown or unascertainable.

Bona Vacantia

Property left by a deceased person, not disposed of by his will, and to whom no heir on intestacy can be found, is *inter regalia minora*, and

---

[16] Merchant Shipping Act, 1894, Ss. 510–37; see also *Commrs. of Customs v. L. Dundas*, 25 May 1810, F.C.; *M. Breadalbane v. Smith* (1850) 12 D. 602; *L.A. v. Hebden* (1868) 6 M. 489.

[17] Protection of Wrecks Act, 1973.

[18] *L.A. v. Aberdeen University*, 1963 S.C. 533.

[19] Ersk. II, 1, 2.

[20] *Burmah Oil Co. v. Lord Advocate*, 1964 S.C. (H.L.) 117, 127.

[21] Stair II, 1, 5; III, 3, 27; Ersk. II, 1, 12; Bell, *Prin.* §1288, 1291; *Sands v. Bell & Balfour*, 22 May 1810, F.C.; *L.A. v. Aberdeen University*, 1963 S.C. 533, 549.

[22] Burgh Police (Sc.) Act, 1892, S. 412; Lost Property (Sc.) Act, 1965.

[23] Craig I, 16, 40; Stair II, 1, 5; II, 1, 5; II, 3, 60; III, 3, 27; Bankt. I, 3, 16; I, 8, 9; II, 1, 8; Ersk. II, 1, 11–12; Bell, *Prin.* §1293; *Cleghorn and Bryce v. Baird* (1696) Mor. 13522; *Gentle v. Smith* (1788) 1 Bell *Ill.* 375.

falls to the Crown as *ultimus haeres*,[24] by way of caduciary right and not by inheritance, under the rule *quod nullius est fit domini regis*. It falls to be delivered to the Queen's and Lord Treasurer's Remembrancer.[25]

By analogy property of unincorporated bodies and juristic persons left undisposed of falls to the Crown.[26]

---

[24] Stair III, 3, 47; IV, 13, 1; Bankt. III, 3, 91; Ersk. III, 10, 2; Bell, *Prin.* §1294; McLaren, *Wills*, I, 80; Succession (Sc.) Act, 1964, S. 7.

[25] *Rutherford* v. *L.A.*, 1932 S.C. 674.

[26] *Caledonian Employers Benevolent Socy.*, 1928 S.C. 633.

CHAPTER 5.4

CREATION OF A NEW FEUDAL ESTATE

1 CHARTER

A new feudal estate in lands was originally created by the Crown or a subject superior personally, on the lands and in presence of at least two vassals (*pares curiae*) delivering to the grantee a symbolical portion of the lands, earth and stone, as respresenting the whole, and the grantee thereupon swearing fealty to the superior. It subsequently became the practice to give a written testimony of the grant (*breve testatum*) sealed by granter and witnesses, or a certificate from a notary public, or of two witnesses to the investiture.[1] This constituted proper investiture.

Improper investiture consisted of the granter first executing the *breve testatum* and directing it to his bailie as a warrant to him to give possession to the grantee; the bailie having done so on the lands sealed the *breve testatum*, or sealed a separate decalaration of the fact. This became the basis of the later instrument of sasine. Infeftment of infeudation is synonymous with investiture.

Introduction of charters

Subsequently a charter based on the *breve testatum* was introduced and since then solemnly authenticated writ has always been recognized as necessary for the constitution and not only for the proof of infeftment or infeudation. At first a separate precept authorizing infeftment accompanied the charter but later the precept of sasine came to be embodied in the charter.[2]

Original charters and charters by progress

An original charter was one by which a feu was first granted, and all subsequent charters are, in case of ambiguity, to be interpreted conformably to the original charter, and, if there be no express alteration, all clauses in the original charter were to be implied in later renewals thereof.[3]

---

[1] Stair II, 3, 12; Ersk. II, 3, 17; Bell, *Prin.* §757, 769; Ross, *Lect.* II, 117; Bell, *Convg.* I, 577; Menzies, 493. On this see Robertson, in *The Scottish Tradition*, 84.

[2] Ersk. II, 3, 33.

[3] Ersk. II, 3, 30; Bell, *Prin.* §757.

Charters by progress were renewed dispositions or transmissions of a feu formerly granted, proceeding on the vassal's resignation, or confirmation of his disponee, or the inheritance of his heir, or an apprising and adjudication.[4]

Charter of novodamus

A charter of novodamus is an original grant but replacing a previous grant of the same subjects, and granted to release the grantee from or modify burdens and conditions previously affecting the grant, or to remedy a defect in the former title or modify the conditions on which the subjects are held. A charter of novodamus may be a first grant as well as a renewal of a former grant, and convey subjects to which the grantee was not previously entitled.[5] It may not be used to increase feu-duties.[6]

2 SASINE

Sasine

Sasine[7] is the taking of legal possession of land, which completes the grantee's title to the land independently of actual possession thereof and without which physical occupation and possession is of no avail. By taking sasine the vassal becomes infeft in the lands. Only sasine confers a real right in the land.[8]

Originally legal possession of the land was delivered to the grantee by investing him on the ground with symbols thereof, and later along with the charter by the superior's bailie sealing the charter in testimony that possession was given, or subscribing a declaration, even 'in a separate writing, that he had done so.

Precept of sasine

In the fifteenth century the practice developed of the superior delivering along with the charter a precept of sasine which later, by the Act of 1672, c. 7, was ordered to be engrossed in the charter, before the testing clause. This was a command by the superior to his bailie to give sasine of the subject disponed to the vassal or his attorney by delivery of the appropriate symbols. The person to be infeft had to be identified. Precepts might be general, or special (authorizing infeft-ment only in security, or in liferent, or in fee subject to an entail).

---

[4] Stair II, 3, 15; Ersk. II, 3, 20; Bell, *Prin.* §775.
[5] Stair II, 3, 15; Ersk. II, 3, 23; *Scott* v. *Archbishop of Glasgow* (1680) Mor. 9339.
[6] Land Tenure Reform (Sc.) Act, 1974, S. 3.
[7] See generally Bell, *Conv.* I, 648; Menzies, 538.
[8] Stair II, 3, 16.

Though the name of the bailie to whom the precept was directed was commonly left blank and the precept could be executed by any person giving sasine to the vassal, it had to contain a special mandate to infeft the vassal. Whoever had possession of the precept was presumed to be the vassal's attorney to receive possession in his name.[9]

Instrument of sasine

Sasine was given on the lands by the superior or his bailie delivering the precept, in the presence of witnesses and of the vassal or his attorney, to a notary who read it, after which the superior or his bailie delivered to the vassal or his attorney the appropriate symbols.[10] Then, the vassal or his attorney put a piece of money in the notary's hands and declared that he took instruments in the hands of the notary, before the witnesses, that he had received sasine of the lands in due form.[11] The notary then extended a written Instrument of Sasine, narrating the precept of sasine and so much of the charter as was necessary for understanding the precept, and subjoined his own attestation, that he, having been specially called for the purpose knew, saw, and heard that these facts were done as are recited in the instrument to which he and the witnesses attached their signatures.[12] Great particularity was required in the instrument and the courts frequently held blunders and omissions fatal to the sasine.[13] An instrument of sasine was the only competent evidence of symbolic delivery of possession.[14]

Where sasine not taken

A charter or disposition not followed by sasine created only a personal right in the grantee and did not vest in him a real or feudal right in the lands, and consequently left the lands subject to the diligence of the granter's creditors, and liable to be defeated by any later disposition of the lands, sasine on which was registered first.[15] An instrument of sasine, evidencing delivery of sasine, and duly recorded in the appropriate Register of Sasines, alone created a real right in the lands in the grantee.

---

[9] Stair II, 3, 16; Ersk. II, 3, 33; Bell, *Prin.* §876–9.

[10] The symbols differed according to the nature of the subjects granted by the superior: the customary ones were earth and stone for lands, clap and happer for mills, net and coble for fishings, a sheaf of corn for parsonage tithes, hasp and staple for houses within burghs, a psalm book and the keys of the church for the patronage of a living, the book of court for a heritable jurisdiction, a penny or a handful of grain for a right of annual rent: Ersk. II, 3, 36; Duff, 100; Bell, *Convg.* I, 655; Menzies, 573.

[11] Bell, *Convg.* I, 650; Menzies, 570.

[12] Stair II, 3, 16–17; Ersk. II, 3, 34–7; Bell, *Convg.* I, 649, Menzies, 569.

[13] Stair II, 3, 18.

[14] Stair II, 3, 16.

[15] Stair II, 3, 16; Ersk. II, 3, 48.

When sasine not required

Exceptionally sasine was not required, in the case of crown lands, royal burghs holding lands burgage,[16] and the former legal liferents of terce and courtesy.

Sasine of contiguous or discontiguous subjects

One sasine might suffice for several parcels of land if contiguous, unless held from different superiors, or by different tenures, or where the vassal of one became proprietor of the other by purchase, there being separate titles to each.[17] Discontiguous lands required separate sasine unless they had been united by a crown charter of union, in which case sasine on a place specified or, if none specified, on any of the lands would serve for the whole.[18] Lands held of different superiors, or by different tenures are incapable of union, but subjects of different kinds may be covered by a charter of union and transferred by one sasine.

If lands have been errected by the Crown into a barony, lands spatially separated, and subjects, however different in nature, may be transferred by one sasine as if united by a charter of union.[19]

Sasine of separate heritable subjects

Separate symbolical deliveries were necessary when the charter conveyed other subjects, such as salmon-fishings, for which earth and stone were not appropriate symbols.[20]

Warrant for sasine essential

An instrument of sasine is relative to the precept on which it proceeds as its warrant, and was not evidence unless the precept were produced, save in special cases.[21]

3 REGISTRATION

Registration

Publication of sasines was required by several sixteenth-century statutes, but these were superseded by the Registration Act, 1617 (c. 16) which established the Register of Sasines and required instruments

---

[16] Stair II, 3, 38; Ersk. II, 3, 34; Bell, *Prin.* §839.
[17] Ersk. II, 3, 44.
[18] Stair II, 3, 44; Ersk. II, 3, 45.
[19] Stair II, 3, 45; Ersk. II, 3, 46.
[20] Ersk. II, 3, 44; Bell, *Convg.* I, 660.
[21] Stair II, 3, 19; Mack. II, 3, 15; Ersk. II, 3, 38.

of sasine and other similar deeds affecting land to be registered within sixty days after their dates, failing which the sasine was ineffectual, save against the granter and his heirs, and successors.[22] Sasine of burgage-lands were included by an Act of 1681.[23]

Sasines have priority according to the date of registration, not according to the date of the sasines themselves.[24]

An unrecorded sasine is null for all purposes,[25] except against the granter and his heirs,[26] and a recorded sasine with an omission *in essentialibus* is also invalid;[27] such nullities cannot be cured by prescriptive possession.

The instrument was entered in the minute book of the Registers, and subsequently transcribed *ad longum* into the register; any error in essentials, or erasure or other vitiation, was fatal. A certificate of registration was endorsed on the instrument of sasine by the keeper of the register.[28]

Registration in the sasine register being for publication, the original deed is returned to the grantee after registration, marked as registered, but extracts (now photostat copies) of deeds may be obtained; an extract is as probative as the principal itself, unless there is challenge on the ground of forgery.[29]

Sasine and infeftment after 1845

After 1845[30] symbolic delivery on the lands was unnecessary and infeftment could be obtained by producing to a notary public the warrants of sasine and relative writs and expeding and recording in the Register of Sasines an abbreviated instrument of sasine setting forth that sasine had been given, such sasine to be effectual whether the lands were contiguous or discontiguous, held by the same or different titles, of one or more superiors; the instrument of sasine, if in the revised form permitted by the Act, could be recorded at any time during the grantee's life, and on being recorded had the same effect as if sasine had been taken and an instrument of sasine recorded according to the previous law and practice.

The Lands Transference Act, 1847, permitted short statutory forms of the principal clauses, and the Titles to Land Act, 1858, permitted a

---

[22] Bell, *Conv.* I, 662; Menzies, 556.
[23] Stair II, 3, 20; Ersk. II, 3, 39–41.
[24] Act of 1693, c. 13.
[25] *Paterson* v. *Douglas* (1714) Rob. App. 99; *Young* v. *Leith* (1847) 9 D. 932; (1848) 2 Ross. L.C. 103.
[26] *Gray* (1626) Mor. 13540; *Simpson* v. *Blackie* (1678) Mor. 13553.
[27] *Mackintosh* v. *Weir* (1825) 2 Ross L.C. 75; *Davidson* v. *McLeod* (1827) 6 S. 8.
[28] See *Cowper* (1885) 12 R. 415; *Elgin Mags.* (1885) 12 R. 1136; *Hepburn* (1905) 7 F. 484.
[29] Stair II, 3, 24; Ersk. II, 3, 43.
[30] Infeftment Act, 1845.

short description of the lands in statutory form, rendered the precept
of sasine and instrument of sasine unnecessary, and made it competent
to record the charter itself, with a warrant of registration thereon, in
the Register of Sasines.

The Titles to Land Consolidation (Sc.) Act, 1868 (amended in 1869)
and the Conveyancing (Sc.) Act, 1874, established the modern system,
which was further developed by the Conveyancing (Sc.) Act, 1924, the
Conveyancing Amendment (Sc.) Act, 1938, and the Land Registration
(Sc.) Act, 1979.

Rights of barony and regality

A royal grant might erect lands *in liberam baroniam*, as one feudal
tenement, designated by a general name, though consisting of separate
lands, having also extensive rights of jurisdiction within appointed
limits and accompanied by pertinents and privileges not attendant on
ordinary estates. A charter, or subsequent disposition, of the barony,
its name being *nomen universitatis*, conveyed all the lands and separate portions of the barony lands, and all pertinents belonging to it.[31] A
royal grant might similarly erect lands *in liberam regalitatem*, where
even wider jurisdiction, civil, and criminal, was exercised by the Lord
of Regality. Regality jurisdiction has been abolished.[32]

Burghs of barony and regality were erected by the crown to be held
of barons of lords of regality.[33]

MODERN CREATION OF NEW FEUDAL ESTATE

The creation may be by a feu-charter, feu-disposition or feu-
contract. The former two are identical in form and are unilateral
grants giving execution to an intent to give lands in feu. The feu-
contract is bilateral, the deed executive of a contract to grant and take
land on feu,[34] and appropriate where the parties wish to be able to
enforce by personal diligence the obligations undertaken thereby. In
addition to the clauses common to all three forms of grant, it contains
an express obligation by the vassal to pay and perform the duties
undertaken to the superior, and a clause of registration for preservation and execution by virtue of which the superior may use summary

[31] Stair II, 3, 45, and 60; Ersk. I, 4, 25; II, 3, 46; II, 6, 18; Bell, *Prin.* §749–54.
[32] Stair II, 3, 45; Ersk. II, 3, 46; Bell, *Prin.* §749; Heritable Jurisdictions Abolition (Sc.) Act, 1746, Ss. 1, 24.   [33] Bell, *Prin.* §848.
[34] The normal rules of contract apply to the capacity of parties, creation, proof, enforceability and breach of the prior contract to grant a feu: see *L. Clinton* v. *Brown* (1874) 1 R. 1137; *Stodart* v. *Dalzell* (1876) 4 R. 236; *Tayport Land Co.* v. *Dougall's Trs.* (1895) 23 R. 287; *Kerr* v. *Forrest's Tr.* (1902) 10 S.L.T. 67; *Alston* v. *Nellfield Manure Co.,* 1915 S.C. 912; *Mitchell* v. *Stornoway Trs.,* 1936 S.C. (H.C.) 56.

diligence to enforce performance of the obligations of the contract. In a feu-charter or feu-disposition the vassal accepts personal liability by acceptance of the deed.[35]

Clauses of modern feu-charter, feu-disposition or feu-contract

The clauses and their scope and purposes have been carried on from mediaeval charters and some still bear the names they did in Latin charters. But by statute it is now frequently possible to abbreviate the clauses, though they may bear the same connotations as the older long clauses.

(1) NARRATIVE CLAUSE

The narrative clause sets out the names and designations of the parties, who must be sufficiently identified.[36] The expression 'heritable proprietor' used of the granter implies that he is himself infeft in the lands disponed;[37] if he has no title or only a personal title his grant is validated by accretion if he later obtains infeftment.[38] If not himself infeft he may not deduce his own title from his author in the deed so as to make his deed a warrant for infeftment of the grantee.[39]

An effectual grant may be made by a party having an interest in the lands less than fee, e.g. in liferent, if with the consent of the true owner,[40] or even by a person having no interest if such consent be taken.[41]

The narrative clause also sets out the cause or consideration for the grant, whether gratuitous, as from love, favour and affection, or onerous, for a price or other valuable consideration.[42] It commonly also acknowledges receipt of the price.

(2) DISPOSITIVE CLAUSE

The dispositive clause is the principal clause;[43] it contains the words

[35] *Hunter* v. *Boog* (1834) 13 S. 205.

[36] Ersk. II, 3, 21; *Guthrie* v. *Munro* (1833) 11 S. 465; *Scottish Union Ins. Co.* v. *Calderwood* (1836) 14 S. 667.

[37] Duff, 59; Bell, *Convg.* I, 580; Menzies, 166, 499.

[38] Stair III, 2, 1; Ersk. II, 7, 2; Bell, *Prin.* §881; *Lockhart* v. *Ferrier* (1837) 16 S. 76; *Innes* v. *Gordon* (1844) 7 D. 141; *McGibbon* v. *McG.* (1852) 14 D. 605; *E. Fife* v. *Duff* (1863) 1 M. (H.L.) 19; *Swans* v. *Western Bank* (1866) 4 M. 663; *Smith* v. *Wallace* (1869) 8 M. 204.

[39] Conveyancing (Sc.) Act, 1924, S. 3, does not apply to original feudal grants. See also 1979 Act, S. 15 (3).

[40] *Sorley's Trs.* v. *Grahame* (1832) 10 S. 319.

[41] Ersk. II, 3, 21; *Mounsey* v. *Maxwell* (1808) Hume 237; *Stirling* v. *Tenants* (1830) Hume 238.

[42] Ersk. II, 3, 22. This is essential under the Stamp Act, 1891, S. 5.

[43] Bell, *Convg.* I, 582; Menzies, 502.

of conveyance, the word 'dispone' being no longer essential;[44] the name of the grantee and the destination; a description of the lands granted; and the reservations, burdens, qualifications and other conditions of the grant.

The dispositive clause is the ruling clause[45] and, unless ambiguous, cannot be modified by the narrative[46] or executive clauses;[47] if ambiguous or deficient other clauses may be invoked to clarify the ambiguity or supply the omission.[48]

Destination

The grant is normally in favour of the grantee and his heirs and assignees whomsoever, but fees being both heritable and transmissible a grant to the grantee alone has the same effect.[49] It may, however, be to the grantee and a special series of heirs, such as his heirs male, or to one person in liferent and another in fee, or to one person, whom failing, to another, or to several persons in common. In the absence of a clause of return, lands granted do not revert to the granter on the failure of heirs.[50] The clause normally concludes with the words 'heritably and irredeemably' but these are redundant.

Description

The lands must be described sufficiently to make them identifiable with certainty and accurately delimitable.[51] A description may be by general name, as by the name of the lands, particularly if an old estate or lands erected into a barony.[52] It may be particular, by boundaries, by measurement, or by reference to a plan,[53] and normally including reference to the parish and county in which the lands lie. Such a description may be general followed by an enumeration of particulars, or a list of particular pieces of land.

[44] Prior to the 1868 Act, S. 20, 'dispone' was essential in conveyances of heritage *mortis causa*, and prior to the 1874 Act, S. 27, that word was deemed essential in *inter vivos* deeds. It is still the word normally used. The phrase appropriate to an original grant is: 'sell and in feu-farm dispone'.

[45] Ersk. III, 8, 47; Bell, *Prin.* §760.

[46] *Chancellor* v. *Mosman* (1872) 10 M. 995; *Brownlie* v. *Miller* (1880) 7 R. (H.L.) 66; *Orr* v. *Mitchell* (1893) 20 R. (H.L.) 27; *Inglis* v. *Gillanders* (1895) 22 R. (H.L.) 51; *D. Sutherland's Trs.* v. *C. Cromarty* (1896) 23 R. (H.L.) 32; *Cooper Scott* v. *Gill Scott*, 1924 S.C. 309.

[47] *Forrester* v. *Hutchison* (1826) 4 S. 824.

[48] *Kerr* v. *Innes* (1810) 5 Pat. 320, 444; *L.A.* v. *Sinclair* (1865) 5 M. (H.L.) 97; *L.A.* v. *McCulloch* (1874) 2 R. 27; *Orr* v. *Mitchell* (1893) 20 R. (H.L.) 27; *Dick-Lauder* v. *Leather-Cully*, 1920 S.C. 48.

[49] Bell, *Convg.* I, 585; Menzies, 504; *Reid* v. *Young* (1838) 16 S. 383.

[50] Ersk. III, 10, 1.   [51] Ersk. II, 3, 23; Bell, *Convg.* I, 588; Menzies 506.

[52] Bell, Convg. I, 589; Menzies 541; cf. *E. Argyle* v. *Campbell* (1668) Mor. 9631. The Keeper of the Registers may reject a deed containing a description too general: *Macdonald* v. *Keeper of Sasine Register*, 1914 S.C. 854. See also *Macdonald* v. *Newall* (1898) 1 F. 68 (parole evidence competent): *Houldsworth* v. *Gordon Cumming*, 1910 S.C. (H.L.) 49.

[53] N.B. Ry. Co. v. Hawick Mags. (1862) 1 M. 200.

Bounding title

The description may or may not constitute a bounding charter or bounding title,[54] i.e. one which sets limits to the lands granted so that even prescriptive possession beyond the limits will not establish ownership thereof,[55] though the grantee may, by prescriptive possession, acquire a right in incorporeal objects, such as a servitude or right to salmon-fishings, beyond his boundaries.[56]

A bounding title may be constituted by specific boundaries, such as a wall or street,[57] or the lands of another,[58] by boundaries and demonstrative measurements,[59] by taxative measurements or measurements which are an essential of the bargain,[60] by measurements and certain boundaries, sufficient to make the area certain,[61] by a general name together with an enumeration of lands possessed by named persons, which enumeration is presumed to be taxative,[62] by a statement that the lands lie within a certain parish or county,[63] by a reference to boundaries on a plan.[64]

If the limits set by a bounding charter are vague or ambiguous, extrinsic evidence may be adduced to fix them.[65]

Where a plan and also a description are used, it is a question of circumstances which will rule.[66] Boundaries, if clearly stated, prevail against plan or measurements,[67] unless measurements are an essential part of the contract.[68]

---

[54] Stair II, 3, 26; Ersk. II, 6, 2; Bell, *Prin.* §738; Duff, 63; Bell, *Convg.* I, 596; Menzies 511.

[55] Stair II, 3, 26; Ersk. II, 6, 3; Bell, *Prin.* §738; *N.B. Ry.* v. *Moon's Trs.* (1879) 6 R. 640; *Reid* v. *McColl* (1879) 7 R. 74; *N.B. Ry.* v. *Hutton* (1896) 23 R. 522; *Houston* v. *Barr*, 1911 S.C. 134; *Troup* v. *Aberdeen Heritable Sec. Co.*, 1916 S.C. 918; *Nisbet* v. *Hogg*, 1950 S.L.T. 289.

[56] *Liston* v. *Galloway* (1835) 14 S. 97; *Beaumont* v. *Glenlyon* (1843) 5 D. 1337; *E. Zetland* v. *Tennents' Trs.* (1873) 11 M. 469; cf. *E. Dalhousie* v. *McInroy* (1865) 3 M. 1168.

[57] *Kerr* v. *Dickson* (1842) 1 Bell 490; *D. Buccleuch* v. *Edinburgh Mags.* (1864) 2 M. 1114.

[58] *Reid* v. *McColl* (1879) 7 R. 84; but see *Troup* v. *Aberdeen Heritable Soc. Co.*, 1916 S.C. 918.

[59] *Gibson* v. *Bonnington Sugar Co.* (1869) 7 M. 394; *Blyth's Trs.* v. *Shaw Stewart* (1883) 11 R. 99; *Currie* v. *Campbell's Trs.* (1888) 16 R. 237.

[60] *Darroch* v. *Ranken* (1841) 4 D. 219; *Hunter* v. *L. Adv.* (1869) 7 M. 899; cf. *Brown* v. *N.B. Ry. Co.* (1906) 8 F. 534.

[61] *Stewart* v. *Greenock Harbour Trs.* (1866) 4 M. 283.

[62] *Murray* v. *Oliphant's Wife* (1634) Mor. 2262; *Gardner* v. *Scott* (1843) 2 Bell 129; *Critchley* v. *Campbell* (1884) 11 R. 475.

[63] *Gordon* v. *Grant* (1850) 13 D. 1; Bell, *Convg.* I, 597.

[64] *N.B. Ry.* v. *Hawick Mags.* (1862) 1 M. 200.

[65] *Davidson* v. *Anstruther-Easter Mags.* (1843) 7 D. 342; *Dalhousie's Tutors* v. *Minister of Lochlee* (1890) 17 R. 1060; *Hetherington* v. *Galt* (1905) 7 F. 706. *Boyd* v. *Hamilton*, 1907 S.C. 912.

[66] *Paterson* v. *Carnegie* (1851) 13 D. 997; *N.B. Ry.* v. *Moon's Trs.* (1879) 6 R. 640; *Currie* v. *Campbell's Trs.* (1888) 16 R. 237.

[67] *Ure* v. *Anderson* (1834) 12 S. 494; *Gibson* v. *Bonnington Sugar Co.* (1869) 7 M. 394. *Currie, supra.*

[68] *Hepburn & Somerville* v. *Campbell* (1781) Mor. 14168.

In general if lands are described as bounded 'by' a feature, that is excluded from the lands,[69] but walls or a road may be common property, the boundary running down the centre line,[70] and if lands are 'enclosed by' walls, the subjects granted include the walls,[72] and where lands are bounded by a non-navigable river they include the *alveus* of the river *ad medium filum*.[72]

Statutory description by general name

It may be a statutory description by general name,[73] which is competent where a previous recorded disposition has specified that lands conveyed and particularly described therein are to be designed and known in future by one general name therein specified. The future deeds must contain the general name, the county, the burgh (if within burgh, a reference to the recorded deed and a statement that that deed prescribed the general name).

Description by reference in statutory forms

The description may be a description by reference in statutory form[74] to a full particular description of the lands (which may be part of a larger description) contained in a prior conveyance recorded in the Register of Sasines to which a reference is given.

Land in respect of which an interest has been registered in the Land Register is sufficiently described if described by reference to the number of the title sheet of that interest.[75]

Description by reference

It may be a description by reference not in statutory form, such as the lands contained in a deed adequately identified,[76] though not identified in accordance with the requirements of statutory reference.[77] Reference may be made to a plan, a copy of which since 1924[78] may be ingiven and is retained in the Register of Sasines. Identification of an

---

[69] *Smyth* v. *Allan* (1813) 5 Pat. 669; *Fleming* v. *Baird* (1841) 3 D. 1015; *St. Monance Mags.* v. *Mackie* (1845) 7 D. 582; *Ewing* v. *York* (1857) 20 D. 351; *D. Buccleuch* v. *Edinburgh Mags.* (1864) 2 M. 1114; *Lockhart* v. *N. Berwick Mags.* (1902) 5 F. 136; *Logie* v. *Reid's Trs.* (1903) 5 F. 859; *Musselburgh Mags.* v. *Musselburgh Real Estate Co.* (1904) 7 F. 308; *Houstoun* v. *Barr*, 1911 S.C. 134.
[70] *Ayr Mags.* v. *Dobbie* (1898) 25 R. 1184.
[71] *Wilson* v. *Laing* (1844) 7 D. 113.
[72] *Wishart* v. *Wylie* (1853) 1 Macq. 389; *Hamilton Mags.* v. *Bent Colliery Co.*, 1929 S.C.686.
[73] 1868 Act, S. 13 and Sched. G,.
[74] 1874 Act, S. 61; 1924 Act, S. 8 and Sched. D, amd. 1938 Act, S. 2; cf. *Cattanach's Tr.* v. *Jamieson* (1884) 11 R. 972; *Murray's Tr.* v. *Wood* (1887) 14 R. 856; *Matheson* v. *Gemmell* (1903) 5 F. 448.
[75] 1979 Act, S. 15(1).
[76] e.g. 'the house in High Street, Middelburgh, bought by me from XY'.
[77] *Matheson* v. *Gemmell* (1903) 5 F. 448.
[78] Conveyancing (Sc.) Act, 1924, S. 48; see also *Johnston's Trs.* v. *Kinloch*, 1925 S.L.T. 124.

earlier recorded deed may be aided by mentioning the Register volume and folio.[79]

Agreement as to common boundary

Where titles to adjoining lands disclose a discrepancy as to the common boundary and the proprietors of those lands have agreed to, and have executed a plan of, that boundary, if either or both holds his interest in the lands by a deed recorded in the Register of Sasines, the agreement and plan may be recorded therein and is then binding on the singular successors of the parties and on all other persons having an interest in the land. If one or both of the interests are registered interests the plan is registrable and binding on all parties.[80]

Parts and pertinents

A grant of lands carries by implication the parts and pertinents thereof;[81] it conveys not only the surface but the airspace above and the earth below, *a caelo usque ad centrum*,[82] buildings on the land,[83] and things annexed actually or constructively to the soil,[84] trees, woods and orchards,[85] mines and minerals,[86] the right of trout-fishing in rivers running through the lands,[87] servitudes attaching to the lands over other lands,[88] seats in the parish church,[89] and parts of the church-yard which have become an adjunct of the lands,[90] and the right to light from the street as laid out or as immemorially existing.[91]

There do not pass as parts and pertinents any rights incapable of alienation, namely, the *regalia majora*, the royal sovereignty and the paramount superiority of the Crown, certain *regalia minora*, namely navigable rivers and highways,[92] and water rights in favour of non-riparian owners where a third party has a title to object.[93]

Nor do there pass as parts and pertinents of lands any of the *regalia minora*,[94] which must be expressly conveyed[95] or may be acquired by

[79] 1924 Act, S. 8.
[80] 1979 Act, S. 19.
[81] Bell, *Conv.* I. 600; Menzies, 514; *Gordon* v. *Grant* (1850) 13 D. 1.   [82] Bell, *Prin.* §737.
[83] Ersk. II, 6, 4; Bell, *Prin.* §743; *Rose* v. *Ramsay* (1777) Mor, 9645; *Downie* v. *Wallace* (1777) Mor. Appx. Implied Assignation, 16.
[84] *Graham* v. *Lamont* (1875) 2 R. 438; *Nisbet* v. *Mitchell-Innes* (1880) 7 R. 575.
[85] Stair II, 3, 73; *Bruce* v. *Dalrymple* (1709) Mor. 9638; *Paul* v. *Cuthbertson* (1840) 2 D. 1286.
[86] Ersk. II, 6, 1; Bell, *Prin.* §669; *Addie* v. *Gillies* (1848) 10 D. 836.
[87] *Mackenzie* v. *Rose* (1832) 6 W. & S. 31; see also *Patrick* v. *Napier* (1867) 5 M. 683; *E. Galloway* v. *D. Bedford* (1902) 4 F. 851; *Beckett* v. *Bisset*, 1921, 2 S.L.T. 33; *Kilsyth Fish Protn. Assoc.* v. *McFarlane*, 1937 S.C. 757.
[88] Bell, *Prin.* §745; *Borthwick* v. *B.* (1668) Mor. 9632.
[89] *Stephen* v. *Anderson* (1887) 15 R. 72.
[90] Ersk. II, 6, 11; *D. Roxburgh* v. *Miller* (1877) 4 R. (H.L.) 76.
[91] *Donald* v. *Esslemont & Macintosh*, 1923 S.C. 122.   [92] Ersk. II, 6, 17.
[93] *Patrick* v. *Napier* (1867) 5 M. 683.
[94] See Ch. 5.3, *supra*; Bell, Prin. §748.
[95] Ersk. II, 6, 13; Bell, *Prin.* §748; Bell, *Convg.* I, 606.

prescription on a habile title.[96] In particular rights of salmon-fishing
need express grants from the Crown, or Crown grant of lands *cum
piscationibus* followed by possession of salmon-fishings for the prescriptive period,[97] or prescriptive possession of salmon-fishings on a
barony title,[98] or a title from a subject-superior *cum piscationibus*
followed by prescriptive possession, if the salmon-fishings were originally granted by the Crown.[99] Trout-fishing on the other hand is a
pertinent of lands, and may be reserved on a sale or even conveyed to a
third party.[1]

Nor do obligations and rights of relief against parties other than the
granter pass, unless specially assigned or made real burdens.[2]

It is common, though unnecessary, to conclude the grant of the lands
with the phrase 'and my whole right, title and interest in the *dominium
utile* of the said subjects'.

The dispositive clause concludes with any reservations, burdens,
qualifications and conditions (other than feu-duty) affecting the grant.

Conditions of grant of feu

The dispositive clause contains also the conditions attached by the
superior to the grant of the feu. These are distinguished as essential to a
feu, without which it cannot exist, such as the reserved superiority, the
written charter, and sasine, natural incidents of a feu, which are
implied in the grant unless expressly negatived, such as warrandice,
and accidentals which must be expressly provided for.[3] These include
various kinds of express conditions, some of which may be inherent
and others merely personal.[4] Inherent conditions do but personal
conditions do not transmit with the lands to successors of the original
parties.[4]

(a) Inherent conditions of grant

Inherent conditions of a feudal grant attach to the lands themselves,
not merely to the grantees personally, and transmit with them.[5] Any
term which is permanent, inherently connected with the lands, and
naturally connected with the grant made, is an inherent condition of
the feudal grant.[6] They do not need to be declared real burdens, nor to

[96] Bell, *Convg.* I, 606.
[97] *Stuart* v. *McBarnet* (1868) 6 M. (H.L.) 123.
[98] *L.A.* v. *Sinclair* (1867) 5 M. (H.L.) 97; *McDouall* v. *L.A.* (1875) 2 R. (H.L.) 49.
[99] *L.A.* v. *Sinclair, supra; E. Zetland* v. *Glover Incorpn.* (1870) 8 M. (H.L.) 144; *Smith* v.
Lerwick Harbour Commrs. (1903) 5 F. 680; *McKendrick* v. *L.A.* 1970 S.L.T. (Sh. Ct.) 39.
[1] *Don District Board* v. *Burnett*, 1918 S.C. 37.
[2] *Spottiswoode* v. *Seymer* (1853) 15 D. 458.   [3] Ersk. II, 3, 11.
[4] e.g. *Jolly's Exrx.* v. *Visct. Stonehaven*, 1958 S.C. 629.
[5] Ersk. II, 3, 11; Bell, *Prin.* §861; *Stewart* v. *D. Montrose* (1861) 4 Macq. 499; *Hope* v. *Hope*
(1864) 2 M. 670.
[6] *Tweeddale's Trs.* v. *E. Haddington* (1880) 7 R. 620; *Robertson* v. *N.B. Ry.* (1874) 1 R. 1213.

appear on the Register of Sasines. An example is a clause of relief by the superior in favour of the vassal from minister's stipend and future augmentations, which passes to a disponee from the vassal without special assignation.[7]

Real burdens

Real burdens are conditions which do not only attach to the grantee and his heirs personally, but affect the lands themselves and pass with the lands on their transfer.[8] In the strict sense a real burden is a reserved money payment, contained in an original grant or a transmission, due from the lands and enforceable only by real diligence against the lands, unless there is also a personal undertaking enforceable by personal action. A real condition is a condition, such as one regarding the errection of buildings, which is an integral part of an original grant of lands, which can be enforced by personal action and diligence.[9] But the term real burden is applied to both burdens and conditions.

To constitute a real burden no *voces signatae* or particular words are necessary; it is unnecessary to declare the obligation a real burden or *debitum fundi*, to provide that it shall attach to singular successors or that it shall be inserted in future dispositions of the fee, though all such provisions are common, but it must be clear that the lands are affected and not only the grantee and his heirs. This is more apparent where the obligation is a continuing one than where it is one discharged at once.[10]

The burden must be imposed in the dispositive clause of the constitutive deed[11] and express or imply clearly that not only the grantee and his heirs are to be affected but that the burden is to attach to the lands themselves,[12] which must be clearly identified;[13] the condition must appear in full in the grantee's infeftment and the deed constituting the burden must be recorded in the Register of Sasines, unless the burden is an inherent condition of the grant.[14] A real burden, if for

[7] *Lennox v. Hamilton* (1843) 5 D. 1357; *Stewart, supra; Hope, supra.*

[8] A real burden may also be constituted by separate deed, as by a contract of ground annual.

[9] *Tweeddale's Trs. v. E. Haddington* (1880) 7 R. 620; *Anderson v. Dickie*, 1915 S.C. (H.L.) 79. It is questionable whether a right of rod-fishing can be made a real burden: *Harper v. Flaws*, 1940 S.L.T. 150.

[10] *Clark v. City of Glasgow Life Assce. Co.* (1854) 1 Macq. 668; contrast *Edinburgh Mags. v. Begg* (1883) 11 R. 352; *Jolly's Exrx. v. Viscount Stonehaven*, 1958 S.C. 635.

[11] Bell, *Prin.* §920; *Cowie's Tr. v. Muirden* (1893) 20 R. (H.L.) 81, 87; *Kemp v. Largs Mags.*, 1939 S.C. (H.L.) 6.

[12] *Tailors of Aberdeen v. Coutts* (1840) 1 Rob. 296; *Baird's Trs. v. Mitchell* (1846) 8 D. 464; *Arbroath Mags. v. Dickson* (1872) 10 M. 630; *Davidson v. Dalziel* (1881) 8 R. 990; *Kemp, supra.*

[13] *Cowie's Tr., supra; Anderson, supra.*

[14] *Tailors of Aberdeen, supra; Stewart v. D. Montrose* (1861) 4 Macq. 499; *Croall v. Edinburgh Mags.* (1870) 9 M. 323; *Liddall v. Duncan* (1898) 25 R. 1119; *Anderson, supra.*

payment of money, must be definite in amount,[15] but may be *ad factum praestandum*, even though performance thereof requires outlay of money;[16] the creditor must be identified, though he may be a party to the deed or a third party or unnamed but identifiable.[17] If the burden is not for payment of money the superior, or party in whose favour it is constituted, must have both title and interest to enforce the obligation,[18] and it must be specific,[19] not be contrary to law, inconsistent with the nature of the property disponed, useless or vexatious or contrary to public policy.[20] Whether a co-feuar or other third party has title to enforce a real condition depends on whether he has a *jus quaesitum tertio*,[21] and such a party must prove a real and substantial interest to enforce.[22] A vassal's tenant has no title to challenge enforcement by the superior.[23]

A real condition must be specific and precise;[24] it is construed strictly and *contra proferentem*,[25] the presumption is for freedom[26] and an obligation will not readily be held to imply a restriction,[27] nor a restriction on construction to imply a restriction in use.[28]

Since 1874 real burdens and conditions may be validly imposed by reference to a prior writ in which they are set out *ad longum*.[29]

It is common to fence a real burden with irritant and resolutive

[15] *Tailors of Aberdeen, supra; Erskine* v. *Wright* (1846) 8 D. 863; *Edinburgh Mags.* v. *Begg* (1883) 11 R. 352; *Forbes* v. *Welsh & Forbes* (1894) 21 R. 630.

[16] *Clark* v. *Glasgow Life Assce. Co.* (1854) 17 D. (H.L.) 27; *Edmonstone* v. *Seton* (1888) 16 R. 1.

[17] Bell, *Comm.* I. 730; *Erskine, supra.*

[18] *Tailors of Aberdeen, supra; E. Zetland* v. *Hislop* (1882) 9 R. (H.L.) 40; *Waddell* v. *Campbell* (1898) 25 R. 456; *Menzies* v. *Caledonian Canal Commrs.* (1900) 2 F. 953; *Macdonald* v. *Douglas,* 1963 S.C. 374.

[19] *Anderson* v. *Valentine,* 1957 S.L.T. 57.

[20] *Tailors of Aberdeen, supra; Orrock* v. *Bennett* (1762) Mor. 15009; *Yeaman* v. *Crawford* (1770) Mor. 14537; *Aberdeen Varieties* v. *Donald,* 1939 S.C. 788; contrast *E. Zetland* v. *Hislop* (1882) 9 R. (H.L.) 40; *Beckett* v. *Bisset,* 1921, 2 S.L.T. 33.

[21] *Hislop* v. *MacRitchie's Trs.* (1881) 8 R. (H.L.) 95; *Turner* v. *Hamilton* (1890) 17 R. 494; *Johnston* v. *Walker trs.* (1897) 24 R. 1061; *Murray's Trs.* v. *St. Margaret's Convent,* 1907 S.C. (H.L.) 8; *Braid Hills Hotel* v. *Manuel,* 1909 S.C. 120; *Nicholson* v. *Glasgow Blind Asylum,* 1911 S.C. 391; *Macdonald, supra.*

[22] *Maguire* v. *Burges,* 1909 S.C. 1283; *Low* v. *Scottish Amicable Bldg. Socy.,* 1940 S.L.T. 295; *Williamson & Hubbard* v. *Harrison,* 1970 S.L.T. 346.

[23] *Eagle Lodge, Ltd.* v. *Keir & Cawder Estates, Ltd.,* 1964 S.C. 30.

[24] *Murray's Trs.* v. *St. Margaret's Convent,* 1907 S.C. (H.L.) 8; *Kirkintilloch Kirk Session* v. *Kirkintilloch School Board,* 1911 S.C. 1127; *Anderson* v. *Dickie,* 1915 S.C. (H.L.) 79; *Scottish Temperance Life Assce. Co.* v. *Law Union & Rock Ins. Co.,* 1917 S.C. 175; *Ewing's Trs.* v. *Crum Ewing,* 1923 S.C. 569; *Kemp* v. *Largs Mags.,* 1939 S.C. (H.L.) 6; *Hunter* v. *Fox,* 1964 S.C. (H.L.) 95.

[25] *Heriot's Hospital* v. *Ferguson* (1773) 3 Paton 674; *Wyllie* v. *Dunnett* (1899) 1 F. 982; *Walker's Trs.* v. *Haldane* (1902) 4 F. 594; *Bainbridge* v. *Campbell,* 1912 S.C. 92.

[26] *Bainbridge* v. *Campbell,* 1912 S.C. 92.

[27] *Fleming* v. *Ure* (1896) 4 S.L.T. 26; *Kemp* v. *Largs Mags.,* 1939 S.C. (H.L.) 6.

[28] *Buchanan* v. *Marr* (1883) 10 R. 936; *Miller* v. *Carmichael* (1888) 15 R. 991; *Mathieson* v. *Allan's Trs.,* 1914 S.C. 464; *Porter* v. *Campbell's Trs.,* 1923 S.C. (H.L.) 94.

[29] 1874 Act, S. 32 and Sched. H, 1924 Act, S. 9 and Sched. E, 1938 Act, S. 2(1).

clauses, designed to rescind the grant if the burden is not implemented; but such clauses are not necessary, and will not make a personal burden into a real burden;[30] but may favour the interpretation that an ambiguous condition is intended to be real. They also provide a powerful sanction for non-implement.

Loss of title or interest to enforce real burden or condition

A superior must have a legitimate interest to enforce the restriction; this is normally patrimonial or financial.[31] An interest merely useless and burdensome to the vassal is not legitimate. The superior is presumed to have a legitimate interest.[32] A superior may lose the right to enforce real conditions against one feuar by long acquiescence in contravention by that feuar,[33] or against all in a district by contravention by some of the feuars in the district, but not merely by one.[34] A superior is more readily barred by acquiescence than is a co-feuar with a title to object.[35]

If a superior has undertaken in one feu contract to insert similar conditions in other feu contracts and has not done so the later feuars cannot enforce the conditions in the first case[36] but may claim damages from the superior for breach of contract.[37]

The superior may expressly waive or discharge any conditions, but such does not affect the right of co-feuars to enforce unless they consented to the waiver or discharge.[38]

Effect of alienation of feu by vassal

When a valid real burden or condition has become enforceable by the superior the vassal, even if he alienates the feu, remains liable under his personal obligation for obligations becoming prestable before the change of ownership, while the new vassal incurs liability under the real obligation which transmits with the lands.[39]

---

[30] *Allan* v. *Cameron's Trs.* (1781) 2 Pat. 572.

[31] *Stewart* cv. *Bunten* (1878) 5 R. 1108; *Menzies* v. *Caledonian Canal Commrs.* (1900) 2 F. 953.

[32] *E. Zetland* v. *Hislop* (1882) 9 R. (H.L.) 40.

[33] *Ben Challum, Ltd.* v. *Buchanan*, 1955 S.C. 348.

[34] *Campbell* v. *Clydesdale Bank* (1868) 6 M. 943; contrast *Ewing* v. *Campbell* (1877) 5 R. 230; *Stewart* v. *Bunten* (1878) 5 R. 1108; *Howard de Walden Estates* v. *Bowmaker*, 1965 S.C. 163.

[35] *Liddall* v. *Duncan* (1898) 25 R. 1119; *Mactaggart* v. *Roemmele*, 1907 S.C. 1318.

[36] *Calder* v. *Edinburgh Merchant Co.* (1886) 13 R. 623; *Walker & Dick* v. *Park* (1888) 15 R. 477.

[37] *Dixon's Trs.* v. *Allan's Trs.* (1870) 8 M. (H.L.) 182.

[38] *Dalrymple* v. *Herdman* (1878) 5 R. 847.

[39] *Macrae* v. *Mackenzie's Trs.* (1891) 19 R. 138; *Marshall* v. *Callander Hydro Co.* (1895) 23 R. (H.L.) 55; *Rankine* v. *Logie Den Land Co.* (1902) 4 F. 1074.

Modification or discharge of real burdens and conditions

Such changes may be effected by minute of waiver or charter of
novodamus granted by the superior, by his acquiescence in contraven-
tions, or under statute.[40]

(b) Reservation of minerals

A superior in granting lands may and commonly does reserve minerals to himself;[41] if he does he may work them himself[42] or form roads
therein for carriage of minerals between mines in other properties.[43] A
conveyance of lands reserving right to work minerals is construed as a
conveyance reserving property in the minerals.[44] General terms such as
'mines' and 'minerals' are open to interpretation, having regard to the
circumstances.[45] He may in such a case grant the minerals separately,[46]
or convey them with a subsequent disposition of the superiority.[47] A
reservation not made in the original charter but later is ineffective
without reinvestiture of the vassal.[48]

Whether a particular substance is or is not a mineral depends on the
circumstance of each particular case,[49] but a mineral is something
other than the ordinary subsoil of the area and exceptional in character, use or value,[50] and it is material to ascertain what the parties
contemplated at the time, which may be determined by reference to
whether the substance was or was not called a mineral by mining or
commercial persons or by landowners at that time.[51]

If minerals are reserved, there should also be reserved power to enter
on the lands, to work the minerals, and other rights necessary for so
doing. Reservations of the minerals probably implies right to work
only by underground workings, but a right to work probably implies
right to the minerals.[52]

A grant of land for a specified purpose, such as a railway, carries by

[40] e.g. Housing (Sc.) Act, 1966, S. 189.
[41] Bell, *Conv.* I, 609; Menzies, 571.
[42] *Buchanan* v. *Andrew* (1873) 11 M. (H.L.) 13.
[43] *D. Hamilton* v. *Graham* (1871) 9 M. (H.L.) 98.
[44] *D. Hamilton* v. *Dunlop* (1885) 12 R. (H.L.) 65.
[45] See further Ch. 5.6, *infra*.
[46] *White* v. *Dixon* (1883) 10 R. (H.L.) 45.
[47] Bell, Convg. I, 611; *Orr* v. *Mitchell* (1893) 20 R. (H.L.) 27.
[48] *Kerse Estates, Ltd.* v. *Welsh*, 1935 S.C. 387.
[49] *Caledonian Ry.* v. *Glenboig Union Fireclay Co.*, 1911 S.C. (H.L.) 72; *Caledonian Ry.* v. *Symington*, 1912 S.C. (H.L.) 9.
[50] *Glasgow Mags.* v. *Farie* (1888) 15 R. (H.L.) 94; *Caledonian Ry., supra; Borthwick Norton* v. *Paul*, 1947 S.C. 659.
[51] *Caledonian Ry., supra; M. Linlithgow* v. *N.B. Ry.*, 1912 S.C. 1327. See also *D. Hamilton* v. *Bentley* (1841) 3 D. 1121; *N.B. Ry.* v. *Budhill Coal Co.*, 1910 S.C. (H.L.) 1; *Forth Bridge Ry.* v. *Dunfermline*, 1910 S.C. 316.
[52] *D. Hamilton* v. *Dunlop* (1885) 12 R. (H.L.) 65.

implication a right to necessary support, whether the subjacent strata still belong to the granter or are subsequently conveyed by him to another.[53]

(c) Prohibition of subinfeudation

A condition forbidding subinfeudation made before the Conveyancing Act, 1874, was valid; if made thereafter it is invalid,[54] and all such provisions are now invalid.[55]

(d) Prohibition of alienation

Clauses prohibiting alienation save by leave of the superior were abolished by the Tenure Abolition Act, 1746, S. 10. A clause in a *mortis causa* disposition prohibiting alienation without certain consents is valid.[56]

(e) Superior's right of pre-emption

It is competent to reserve to the granter the right to have the subjects offered to him first if they should be for sale.[57] Such a clause is narrowly construed and must appear on the Register of Sasines if it is to be effectual against singular successors.[58] Intention to exercise the right must be intimated within forty days, or any shorter period prescribed in the grant, after an offer has been made by the vassal.[59] This has been extended to any right of pre-emption created in a deed or writing executed after 1st September 1974 in favour of any person of an interest in land in the event of sale thereof.[60]

(f) Superior's right of redemption

The superior may validly reserve the right to redeem the feu with buildings, even if the vassal is not anxious to sell.[61]

(g) Superior's reservations of right to divide superiority

At common law a superior cannot interject a mid-superior between himself and his vassal, nor divide the superiority (though this does not prevent a superiority becoming vested in *pro indiviso* owners[62]), but a right to do so may validly be reserved.

[53] *N.B. Ry. Co.* v. *Turners* (1904) 6 F. 900.

[54] 1874 Act, S. 22; Bell, *Prin.* §866; but see *Colquhoun* v. *Walker* (1867) 5 M. 773; *Inglis* v. *Wilson*, 1909 S.C. 1393.

[55] Conveyancing Amdt. Act, 1938, S. 8.   [56] *Burnett's Trs.* v. *B.*, 1909 S.C. 223.

[57] Bell, *Prin.* §861, 865; Bell, *Convg.* I, 612; *E. Mar* v. *Ramsay* (1838) 1 D. 116; *Christie* v. *Jackson* (1898) 6 S.L.T. 245.

[58] *E. Mar, supra; Lumsden* v. *Stewart* (1843) 5 D. 501; *McLean* v. *Kennaway* (1904) 12 S.L.T. 117.   [59] Conveyancing Amdt. Act, 1938, S. 9.

[60] Land Tenure Reform (Sc.) Act, 1974, S. 13.

[61] Menzies, 575; *McElroy* v. *D. Argyll* (1902) 4 F. 885.

[62] *Cargill* v. *Muir* (1837) 15 S. 408.

(h) Irritancy clause

The Feu-Duty Act, 1597, c. 17,[63] provides by analogy with *emphyteusis*, that if a vassal fails to pay his feu-duty for five complete years he will forfeit his feu. It is, however, common to include an express irritancy clause *ob non solutum canonem*.[64]

(j) Clause requiring registration within limited period

The superior has an interest that the vassal record his grant quickly so that the superior has an entered vassal and the conditions of the grant are made real burdens on the lands. It is competent to require the grant to be recorded within a limited period on pain of ceasing to be a valid warrant for infeftment thereafter.

(k) Clause conferring monopoly on superior's agents

A clause conferring on an agent chosen by the superior a monopoly of preparing deeds relating to the feu is now void.[65]

(l) Building conditions

The charter commonly includes conditions requiring buildings to be erected,[66] and prescribing the permitted and prohibited uses thereof and of the feu generally. Such conditions may be personal between granter and grantee only[67] or real, binding the successors of the parties to the relationship.[68] Except so far as qualified by his feu-charter itself,[69] a vassal has liberty in the use of his feu. Any such condition must not be illegal, inconsistent with the nature of the property, or too vague,[70] or merely vexatious,[71] and restrictions are strictly interpreted.[72] The superior must have an interest to enforce the condition but there is a strong presumption that he has such interest;[73] it need not be patrimonial.[74] There is a distinction between restrictions on construction or structure, and restrictions on use, which is important in

---

[63] Amended by Land Tenure Reform (Sc.) Act, 1974, S. 15.

[64] See further Chs. 4.6, *supra*, and 5.18, *infra*.

[65] 1874 Act, S. 22.

[66] e.g. *Glasgow Mags.* v. *Hay* (1883) 10 R. 635; *Carswell* v. *Goldie*, 1967 S.L.T. 339.

[67] *Corbett* v. *Robertson* (1872) 10 M. 329; *Walker* v. *Church of Scotland Trs.* 1967 S.L.T. 297.

[68] *Glasgow Mags.*, *supra*.

[69] *Shearer* v. *Peddie* (1899) 1 F. 1201; *Campbell's Trs.* v. *Glasgow Mags.* (1902) 4 F. 752.

[70] *Kirkintilloch Kirk Session* v. *Kirkintilloch School Board*, 1911 S.C. 1127; *Anderson* v. *Dickie*, 1915 S.C. (H.L.) 79; *Scottish Temperance Life Assce Co.* v. *Law Union & Rock Ins. Co.*, 1917 S.C. 175.

[71] *Tailors of Aberdeen* v. *Coutts* (1840) 1 Rob. 296.

[72] *Cowan* v. *Edinburgh Mags.* (1887) 14 R. 682; *Walker Trs.* v. *Haldane* (1902) 4 F. 594; *Porter* v. *Campbell's trs.*, 1923 S.C. (H.L.) 94.

[73] *E. Zetland* v. *Hislop* (1882) 9 R. (H.L.) 40.

[74] *Howard de Walden Estates* v. *Bowmaker*, 1965 S.C. 163.

relation to alleged contravention.[75] Such conditions may be declared real burdens, particularly if there are obligations to pay the cost, in whole or in part, of buildings or works erected or to be erected by the superior.[76] The presumption is for freedom of use, and if restrictions are to be real conditions, effective against singular successors, this must be made plain.[77] It is a question of fact whether a building satisfies the superior's conditions; if it does not, irritancy of the feu may be granted.[78] Conditions are strictly construed and a restriction on structural changes is not infringed by a change of use.[79]

Reference to conditions stated elsewhere

Real burdens, conditions, provisions or limitations may be imported into a charter by reference therein to another recorded deed in which they are set out in length.[80]

Where there has been in an earlier deed relating to the same subjects a clause directing insertion of conditions in all subsequent deeds, the omission thereof subsequently does not affect the title, unless the direction to refer is fenced with an irritant or resolutive clause. If the lands were possessed for the prescriptive period on a title omitting the conditions these become unenforceable, unless they are of the nature of inherent conditions of the feudal grant.[81] Even if they are omitted from any deed but the then proprietor's recorded title contains a reference, this now cures any previous omission retrospectively, and if the then proprietor's title omits refererence, he may cure the defect by executing a recording deed of acknowledgment.[82]

Alternatively the superior may record in the appropriate register of sasines a unilateral Deed of Declaration of Conditions setting out standard feuing conditions and include a reference thereto in all future charters to individual vassals.[83]

A land obligation specified in a deed executed after the commencement of the 1979 Act becomes a real obligation affecting the land to which it relates on the recording of the deed in the Register of Sasines or on the obligation being registered in the Land Register, unless the deed contains an express statement that the statutory section is not to apply.[84]

---

[75] *Mathieson* v. *Allan's Trs.*, 1914 S.C. 464.
[76] *Edinburgh Mags.* v. *Begg* (1883) 11 R. 352; *Macdonald* v. *Douglas*, 1963 S.C. 374.
[77] *Kemp* v. *Largs. Mags.* 1939 S.C. (H.L.) 6.
[78] *Ardgowan Estates* v. *Lawson*, 1948 S.L.T. 186.
[79] *Mathieson, supra; Fettes Trust* v. *Anderson*, 1947 S.N. 167.
[80] 1868 Act, S. 10, 146 and Sched. D.
[81] *Hope* v. *H.* (1864) 2 M. 670.
[82] 1924 Act, S. 9.
[83] 1874 Act, S. 32. cf. *Gorrie & Banks Ltd.* v. *Musselburgh*, 1973 S.C. 33.
[84] 1979 Act, S. 17.

It is not necessary in any deed relating to a registered interest in land to insert or refer to any real burden, condition, provision or other matter affecting that interest if it has been entered on the title sheet of that interest in the Land Register under S. 6(1) of the 1979 Act. Such a deed imports for all purposes a full insertion of the real burden or other matter.[85]

Questions have frequently arisen of enforceability; if expressed in the title they are enforceable by the superior but whether a co-feuar also may enforce them depends on whether there is express statement to that effect, or it is implied by the terms of the grants or there is mutual agreement among the co-feuars or there is mutuality of rights and obligations among them.[86]

Irritant and resolutive clauses

An irritant clause may be added to annul any act or deed done or made in contravention of the conditions. Such a clause is not essential to make feuing conditions permanently enforceable but may help to show that conditions are so intended.[87] A resolutive clause may be added to forfeit the grantee's right and title in the event of contravention, and cause the property to revert to the granter.

It is common to provide that all conditions shall be engrossed *ad longum* in the first infeftment and repeated or validly referred to in all transmissions under pain of irritancy.[88]

Variation and discharge of land obligations

A superior may, on any conditions which satisfy him, vary or discharge any conditions or land obligations, by granting a Minute of Waiver. The terms of any deed recorded in the Register of Sasines, whereby a land obligation[89] is varied or discharged or a registered variation or discharge of a land obligation, is binding on the singular successors of the person entitled to enforce the land obligation and of the person on whom the land obligation was binding.[90]

By the Conveyancing and Feudal Reform (Sc.) Act, 1970 any land obligation[89] with certain exceptions[91] may, on the application of a

[85] 1979 Act, S. 15(2), excluding application of 1868, 1874 and 1924 Acts from such deeds.

[86] *Hislop* v. *MacRitchie's Trs.* (1882) 8 R. (H.L.) 95; *MacTaggart* v. *Harrower* (1906) 8 F. (H.L.) 1101; *Murray's Trs.* v. *St. Margaret's Convent,*. 1907 S.C. (H.L.) 8; *Macdonald* v. *Douglas,* 1963 S.C. 374.

[87] *Tailors of Aberdeen* v. *Coutts* (1840) 1 Rob. 296; *Glasgow Mags.* v. *Hay* (1883) 10 R. 635.

[88] cf. *Welsh* v. *Jack* (1882) 10 R. 113.

[89] Defined, S. 1(2). It applies generally to conditions of tenure, real burdens, servitudes, and similar burdens.   [90] 1979 Act, S. 18.

[91] Sched. I excepts the obligations to pay feu-duty, ground annual, rent and similar payments, obligations relating to the right to work minerals, obligations imposed by or on behalf of the Crown for certain purposes, obligations created or imposed for naval, military, air force or civil aviation purposes, and obligations created or imposed in relation to leases of agricultural holdings, smallholdings and crofts.

burdened proprietor, be varied or discharged by the Lands Tribunal for Scotland if satisfied that in all the circumstances (a) by reason of changes in the character of the land affected or its neighbourhood or other circumstances which the Tribunal may deem material, the obligation is or has become unreasonable or inappropriate; or (b) it is unduly burdensome compared with any benefit resulting or which would result from its performance; or (c) the existence of the obligation impedes some reasonable use of the land.[92] The Lands Tribunal may order a payment (i) in compensation for any substantial loss or disadvantage suffered by the proprietor as benefited proprietor in consequence of the variation or discharge; or (ii) to make up for any effect which the obligation produced at the time when it was imposed in reducing the consideration then paid or made payable for the interest in land affected by it.[93] The Tribunal may refuse to vary or discharge a land obligation on ground (c) if of the opinion that, due to exceptional circumstances related to amenity or otherwise, money would not be an adequate compensation for any loss or disadvantage to a benefited proprietor.[94] The power to vary or discharge includes power to add or substitute a provision which seems reasonable as a result of the variation or discharge of the obligation and may be accepted by the applicant.[95] Irritant or resolutive clauses are to be effective only in so far as they would have been if the obligation had been varied by the person entitled to enforce the obligation.[96] Any such order which has taken effect if recorded in the Register of Sasines is to be binding on all persons having interest.[97] It is incompetent by contract to exclude or modify Ss. 1–2.[97] Only a burdened proprietor may apply under S. 1(3).[99]

Under these powers the Lands Tribunal has discharged a servitude of access and egress,[1] allowed a limited use of a house basement as a nursery school[2] discharged feuing conditions which prevented the use of the premises as a factory,[3] discharged on compensation feuing conditions which prevented a boarding house from being extended and used as a licensed hotel[4] discharged a restrictive condition in a long lease which prevented assignation except as a whole,[5] discharged a

---

[92] S. 1(1)–(3).
[93] cf. *McVey* v. *Glasgow Corpn.*, 1973 S.L.T. (Lands Tr.) 15.
[94] S. 1(4).
[95] S. 1(5).
[96] S, 1(6).
[97] S. 2(4).   [98] S. 7.
[99] *Reid* v. *Stafford*, 1979 S.L.T. (Lands. Tr.) 16.
[1] *Devlin* v. *Conn*, 1972 S.L.T. (Lands Tr.) 11.
[2] *Main* v. *Lord Doune*, 1972 S.L.T. (Lands Tr.) 14.
[3] *West Lothian Coop Socy.* v. *Ashdale Land Co.*, 1972 S.L.T. (Lands Tr.) 30.
[4] *Smith* v. *Taylor*, 1972 S.L.T. (Lands Tr.) 34.
[5] *McQuiban* v. *Eagle Star Ins. Co.*, 1972 S.L.T. (Lands Tr.) 39.

prohibition on selling liquor,[6] varied conditions to allow a house to be
built.[7]

It has refused discharge of feuing conditions to permit an ice rink to
be used for trade,[8] a grocer's shop to be converted into a betting shop.[9]

It is incompetent to seek discharge of what is not a separate land
obligation but only a qualification attached to a land obligation.[10]

The power to vary or discharge a land obligation does not extend to
an obligation imposed directly by statute.[11]

(3) TERM OF ENTRY

The date of entry to the lands is expressed, normally in short
statutory form.[12] If not expressed it is implied[13] that entry is at the first
term of Whitsunday or Martinmas after the last date of the conveyance, unless it appears that another date is intended. Immediate
entry means entry as soon as possible,[14]

(4) TENENDAS

This clause[15] sets out the superior of whom the lands are to be held,
and the tenure by which they are held.[16] Under a new grant the holding
is always *de me*, of and under the granter and his successors.

(5) REDDENDO

This clause[17] specifies the payments due by the vassal to the superior.
Since the 1874 Act the annual feu-duty must be of fixed amount or
quantity,[18] and since 1924 must be in sterling money.[19] Interest does
not run on feu-duty *ex lege*, but interest is normally stipulated for, and
in any event it runs from a judicial demand for payment.[20] No

---

[6] *Owen* v. *Mackenzie*, 1974 S.L.T. (Lands Tr.) 11.

[7] *Robinson* v. *Hamilton*, 1974 S.L.T. (Lands Tr.) 2; *Gorrie & Banks* v. *Musselburgh*, 1974
S.L.T. (Lands Tr.) 5.

[8] *Murrayfield Ice Rink* v. *Scottish Rugby Union*, 1972 S.L.T. (Lands Tr.) 20; 1973 S.L.T. 99.

[9] *Bolton* v. *Aberdeen Corpn.*, 1972 S.L.T. (Lands Tr.) 26.

[10] *Reid, supra.*

[11] *Macdonald*, 1973 S.L.T. (Lands Tr.) 26.

[12] Bell, *Conv.* I, 631; 1868 Act, S. 5 and Sched. B, No. 1.

[13] 1874 Act, S. 28.

[14] *Heys* v. *Kimball & Morton* (1890) 17 R. 381.

[15] Called from the corresponding clause in the Latin charter: *tenendas praedictas terras de me.*

[16] Bell, *Conv.* I, 632; Menzies, 520.

[17] Called from the corresponding clause in the Latin charter: *reddendo inde annuatim*; Bell,
Conv. I, 632; Menzies, 521.

[18] 1874 Act, S. 23.

[19] 1924 Act, S. 12; see *L.A.* v. *Cumming*, 1942 S.C. 25.

[20] *M. Tweeddale* v. *Aytoun* (1842) 4 D. 862; *M. Tweeddale's Trs.* v. *E. Haddington* (1880)
7 R. 620.

casualties are now due *ex lege*, but, though no casualty might be stipulated for on the succession of an heir or the transfer to a singular successor, other casualties of a periodical fixed sum or quantity might be stipulated for, provided the sum or quantity was certain and the time or times when it should be exigible was also certain and not dependent on any event or occasion except the occurrence of the time at which it was exigible.[21]

Under the Land Tenure Reform (Sc.) Act, 1974, new feu-duties may not be created after 31 July 1974, and an existing feu-duty may be redeemed on notice for a payment of the sum which would purchase 2½ per cent. Consols yielding an annual sum equivalent to the feu-duty. On a transfer of land feu-duty is deemed to have been redeemed, the seller being obliged to pay the redemption money to the superior.[22]

Under the Feudal Casualties Act, 1914, it is incompetent now to stipulate for casualties, duplicands or sums payable at intervals of more than one year, and provision was made for the compulsory extinction of existing casualties and duplicands before 1930 on terms of a proportionate increase in the annual feu-duty. But it is still permissible to stipulate for a permanent increase or reduction in feu-duty, if certain both as to time and amount. The 1924 Act provided that in all prior feus feu-duty not expressed in money must be converted to money, and in future feus feu-duty must be expressed in sterling money. Rights to carriages and services stipulated for under old feu-charters, if not commuted under the 1874 Act, Ss. 20–1, must have commuted before 1935 or else have been extinguished (S. 12(7)).

(6) ASSIGNATION OF WRITS

This clause assigns the writs constituting the granter's title to the lands to the effect only of maintaining and defending the grantee's right, with an obligation to make them forthcoming to the grantee on all necessary occasions.[23] An inherent condition of the grant needs no assignation but a collateral condition, such as an obligation of relief by a vassal in favour of his disponee, does not transmit in favour of a purchaser from the disponee unless specially assigned.[24] In deeds executed after the commencement of the 1979 Act granting land in feu this clause is unnecessary and such a deed unless specially qualified imports an assignation to the grantee of the title deeds and searches to the effect of maintaining and defending the right of the grantee in the

---

[21] 1874 Act, S. 23.
[22] Ss. 1, 4–6.
[23] Bell, *Conv.* I, 637; Menzies, 530; 1868 Act, Ss. 5, 8 and Sched. B.
[24] *Home* v. *Breadalbane's Trs.* (1842) 1 Bell 1; *Sinclair* v. *M. Breadalbane* (1846) 5 Bell 353; *Spottiswoode* v. *Seymer* (1853) 15 D. 458.

feu; and the superior is held obliged to make the title deeds and searches forthcoming to the grantee on all necessary occasions.[25]

(7) ASSIGNATION OF RENTS

Apart from express provision, the grantee becomes entitled to the rents of the land for possession following his term of entry.[26] The short statutory clause 'and I assign the rents', unless qualified, imports an assignation to the rents to become due for the possession following the terms of entry, according to the legal and not the conventional terms, unless in the case of forehand rents, in which case it imports an assignation of the rents payable at the conventional terms subsequent to the date of entry.[27] It is unnecessary to intimate to tenants the assignation of rents after the vassal has taken infeftment,[28] but if infeftment is not taken intimation is necessary to preclude the tenants from paying to the assignor.[29] In deeds executed after the commencement of the 1979 Act it is not necessary to insert a clause of assignation of rents and any such deed, unless specially qualified, imports an assignation of the rents payable (i) in the case of backhand rents, at the legal terms following the date of entry, and (ii) in the case of forehand rents, at the conventional terms following that date.[30]

(8) OBLIGATION OF RELIEF

The clause of relief[31] is an obligation of indemnity which binds the granter to free and relieve the grantee of feu-duties and casualties, or money in lieu thereof, payable to the granter's superior now and in all time coming, and of all public, parochial and local burdens exigible prior to the term of entry. Such a clause may, if clearly expressed, give relief from even burdens imposed subsequently to the deed, but this is not presumed from general words;[32] it certainly covers burdens merely

[25] 1979 Act, S. 16(2).

[26] Bell, *Conv.* I, 638; Menzies, 532; *Lord Glasgow's Trs.* v. *Clark* (1889) 16 R. 545.

[27] 1868 Act, Ss. 5, 8, Sched. B. For rent purposes farms are arable or pastoral, according to which element predominates in the income thereof: *Mackenzie's Trs.* v. *Somerville* (1900) 2 F. 1278. The legal terms for rent are, if arable, at Whitsunday (after sowing) and Martinmas (after reaping); if pastoral, at Whitsunday, on entry, and Martinmas. The conventional terms are such as the parties may fix; a common arrangement is some postponement. A forehand rent is one payable sooner than law implies, a backhand rent one payable later. See also *Butter* v. *Foster*, 1912 S.C. 1218.

[28] *Webster* v. *Donaldson* (1780) Mor. 2902.

[29] *Flowerdew* v. *Buchan* (1835) 13 S. 615.

[30] 1979 Act, S. 16(3).

[31] Bell, *Conv.* I, 641; Menzies, 532.

[32] *Scott* v. *Edmond* (1850) 12 D. 1077; *N.B. Ry. Co.* v. *Edinburgh Mags.*, 1920 S.C. 409; cf. *Welwood's Trs.* v. *Mungall*, 1921 S.C. 911; *Stenhouse's Trs.* v. *St. Andrew's Mags.*, 1933 S.C. 373.

later reimposed, the incidence of which is the same as under the former law,[33] but not burdens the incidence or application of which is changed so as to become a new burden.[34] It may cover burdens on buildings subsequently erected if contemplated when the feu was granted.[35] The presumption that relief covers only existing burdens and new burdens similar in character and incidence may, however, be overcome by long contrary usage.[36] The obligation does not extend to any personal tax,[37] nor to costs of maintenance and repair, unless clearly expressed.[38] The superior's liability may extend to burdens on occupiers as well as on owners.[39] The obligation is probably not available to a vassal who has subfeued and is not himself liable for the burden, nor can he assign it to his sub-vassal because it attaches to his feu.[40] It binds a singular successor in the superiority but not his personal representatives unless the intention to do so is apparent.[41]

A superior has been held liable in damages where he bound himself to take feuars on the opposite side of a road bound to relieve the present feuars of half of the annual liability for upkeep of the road but the opposite side was acquired compulsorily and no clause of relief inserted in the statutory disposition.[42]

It is not necessary in any deed conveying an interest in land executed after the commencement of the 1979 Act to insert a clause of obligation of relief and any such deed, unless specially qualified, imports an obligation on the granter to free and relieve the grantee of all feu-duties, ground annuals, annuities and public, parochial and local burdens exigible in respect of the interest prior to the date of entry and, in the case of a grant of land in feu, of all feu-duties payable by the granter to his superiors from and after the date of entry.[43]

It is not necessary in any deed relating to a registered interest in land to include an assignation of any obligation or right of relief or to narrate the writs by which the granter became entitled to enforce the obligation or exercise that right if the obligation or right has been entered in the title sheet of that interest in the Land Register. The deed

[33] *Dunbar's Trs.* v. *British Fisheries Soc.* (1878) 5 R. (H.L.) 221; *Lindsay* v. *Bett* (1898) 25 R. 1155; cf. *Lees* v. *Mackinlay* (1857) 20 D. 6; *Hunter* v. *Chalmers* (1858) 20 D. 1311; *Paterson's Trs.* v. *Hunter* (1863) 2 M. 234; *Wilson* v. *Musselburgh Mags.* (1868) 6 M. 483; *Nisbet* v. *Lees* (1869) 7 M. 881; *Preston* v. *Edinburgh Mags.* (1870) 8 M. 502; *Jopp's Trs.* v. *Edmond* (1888) 15 R. 271; *N.B. Ry. Co.* v. *Edinburgh Mags.*, 1920 S.C. 409.
[34] *Stewart* v. *E. Seafield* (1876) 3 R. 518; *Dunbar's Trs., supra.*
[35] *Preston* v. *Edinburgh Mags.* (1870) 8 M. 502; *Latto* v. *Aberdeen Mags.* (1903) 5 F. 740.
[36] *N.B. Ry.* v. *Edinburgh Mags.*, 1920 S.C. 409.
[37] *Lindsay, supra; Edinburgh Corpn.* v. *L.A.*, 1923 S.C. 112.
[38] *Duncan* v. *Church of Scotland General Trs.*, 1941 S.C. 145.
[39] *N.B. Ry., supra.*
[40] *Latto, supra.*
[41] *Hope* v. *Hope* (1864) 2 M. 670; *McCallum* v. *Stewart* (1870) 8 M. (H.L.) 1.
[42] *Leith School Board* v. *Rattray's Trs.*, 1918 S.C. 94.
[43] 1979 Act, S. 16(3).

for all purposes imports a valid and complete assignation of the obligation or right.[44]

(9) WARRANDICE CLAUSE

By the clause of warrandice[45] the granter binds himself that the deed and right thereby granted shall be effectual to the vassal, and that he shall not be evicted therefrom or suffer loss by reason of any defect in the granter's title or fact or deed of his. Warrandice is implied in all deeds in a degree varying with the nature of the deed. In donations and gratuitous deeds the obligation is that the granter will not grant any contrary deed, which would render the grant ineffectual, but without prejudice to past deeds granted or to future deeds which the granter may be compelled to grant in fulfilment of a prior undertaking or promise. In deeds granted for consideration less than the true value, warrandice is implied against the granter's past and future deeds. In deeds granted for full and fair consideration, such as on sale, absolute warrandice is implied, against the granter's own acts, past or future, and against all defects that may appear to have been in his right to it prior to the grant.[46]

Express warrandice supersedes implied warrandice.

Warrandice was formerly personal or real. Personal warrandice binds the granter personally only, and either generally or specially. By a general clause of warrandice the granter binds himself personally, without specifying by what kind or degree of warrandice, in which case the degree due by implied warrandice attaches. Special warrandice is either simple warrandice, that the granter shall do no act inconsistent with the grant;[47] or warrandice from fact and deed, that the granter has not granted, and will not grant, any contrary deed;[48] and absolute warrandice, by which the granter becomes liable if, through any defect in the right, the grantee be evicted from the subject, in whole or in part, by a third party, even though neither granter nor his authors have done any deed conflicting with the warrandice.[49]

Real warrandice was secured warrandice and existed where some lands were made over to a purchaser and other lands, warrandice-lands, were disponed subsequently in security of the principal lands, enabling the purchaser to have recourse to the warrandice-lands if the principal lands were taken from him; and also where one piece of land

---

[44] 1979 Act, S. 15(4).
[45] Stair II, 3, 46; Ersk. II, 3, 25–32; Bell, *Conv.* I, 642; Menzies, 526.
[46] Bell, *Prin.* §894.
[47] This is implied in donations.
[48] This is implied in compromises.
[49] This is implied in sales at a fair price.

was exchanged for another, in which case the purchaser, if evicted from the lands received, had recourse against his lands originally given in exchange, both against the other party, his heirs and singular successors. Real warrandice of the second kind was implied by law in deeds expressly bearing to be excambions. The Conveyancing (Sc.) Act, 1924, S. 14 prohibited future grants of express real warrandice and negatived any implication of real warrandice in future transactions.

Statutory clause of warrandice

The statutory clause 'and I grant warrandice' unless qualified, implies absolute warrandice as regards the lands and writs and evidents, and warrandice from fact and deed as regards the rents.[50] In any event absolute warrandice is implied in a conveyance of heritage for a full price. The clause has effect whether the deed is onerous or gratuitous.[51]

Trustees granting a feu normally grant warrandice from their own facts and deeds only and bind the trust estate and the beneficiaries thereunder in absolute warrandice.[52]

Absolute warrandice guarantees peaceable possession of the subjects conveyed, and warrants the assignation of writs for the purpose of maintaining the grantee in possession of what the grant conveys,[53] but not against disappearance of the property,[54] losses or burdens natural to the right,[55] nor any arising from the nature or legal effects of ownership,[56] nor from servitudes, unless exceptional or very burdensome,[57] nor against losses or burdens caused by supervenient happenings or legislation.[58]

In the event of eviction or other loss a grantee in right of absolute warrandice can recover the full damage thereby sustained.[59] Action founded on the obligation of warrandice is competent when eviction is threatened on an unanswerable ground arising from the granter's fault,[60] or if the granter disputes liability to relieve in the event of eviction,[61] or when eviction has taken place.[62] Threat of eviction

[50] 1868 Act, S. 5, 8, and Sched. B, No. 1.
[51] Macalister v. M's Exors. (1866) 4 M. 495.
[52] cf. Horsburgh's Trs. v. Welch (1886) 14 R. 67.
[53] Brownlie v. Miller (1880) 7 R. (H.L.) 66.
[54] Bell, Prin. §122.
[55] Bell, Prin. §895; MacRitchie's Trs. v. Hope (1836) 14 S. 578.
[56] Plenderleath v. E. Tweeddale (1800) Mor. 16639; Brownlie, supra.
[57] Urquhart v. Halden (1835) 13 S. 884.
[58] Muirhead v. Lord Colvil (1715) 5 B.S. 125; Tay Salmon Fisheries v. Speedie, 1929 S.C. 593; Mackeson v. Boyd, 1942 S.C. 56.
[59] Carmichael v. Anstruther (1821) 1 S. 25; Galloway v. Gardner (1838) 1 D. 74; Cairns v. Howden (1870) 9 M. 284.
[60] Ersk. II, 3, 30; Bell, Prin. §895; Smith v. Ross (1672) Mor. 16596.
[61] Melville v. Erskine's Trs. (1842) 4 D. 385; Leith Heritages Co. v. Edinburgh and Leith Glass Co. (1876) 3 R. 789.　　　　[62] Bell. Prin. §895.

should be intimated to the party liable in warrandice. The grantee is not bound to defend, if his right is untenable.[63] If there is partial eviction the grantee may recover indemnity for the actual loss sustained; he cannot claim to reconvey the property and recover its value.[64]

If the grantee successfully defends his right against threatened eviction, he cannot claim his expenses under warrandice,[65] if he defends unsuccessfully, having utilized all competent defences, he is entitled to his expenses as well as compensation for the loss caused by eviction,[66] but not if he omitted a competent defence.[67]

Warrandice is a personal obligation and transmits against the granter's executor, unless granted in terms which bind heirs generally, or heirs of entail.[68]

(10) CLAUSE OF REGISTRATION

A feu-charter or feu-disposition may be registered for preservation only. A feu-contract may be registered for preservation and execution.

The short statutory clause 'and I consent to registration hereof for preservation', unless qualified, imports consent to registration in the Books of Council and Session, or other judges' books, for preservation.[69] If presented for registration in the Register of Sasines with a warrant specifying that the writ is to be registered for preservation as well as for publication, such registration is equivalent to registration also in the Books of Council and Session for preservation.[70]

(11) TESTING CLAUSE

This clause in ordinary form narrates the authentication of the deed.[71]

COMPLETION OF GRANTEE'S TITLE

The granter is not divested of property in the subjects of the grant until he delivers the feu-charter, feu-disposition or feu-contract, even if

[63] *Downie* v. *Campbell*, 31 Jan. 1815, F.C.
[64] *Welsh* v. *Russell* (1894) 21 R. 769.
[65] Stair II, 3, 46; Ersk. II, 3, 32; Bell, *Convg.* I, 219; *Inglis* v. *Anstruther* (1771) Mor. 16633.
[66] Bell, *Convg.* I, 219; *Dougall* v. *Dunfermline Mags.*, 1907 S.C. 151.
[67] Bell, *Prin.* §895; *Clerk* v. *Gordon* (1681) Mor. 16605.
[68] *D. Montrose* v. *Stuart* (1887) 15 R. (H.L.) 19; *D. Bedford* v. *E. Galloway's Tr.* (1904) 6 F. 971.
[69] 1868 Act, S. 138, and Sch. B, No. 1. Feu-charters by subject superiors may be recorded in the Books of Council and Session: Bell, *Convg.* I, 645.
[70] Land Registers (Sc.) Act, 1868, S. 12, amd. Conveyancing (Sc.) Act, 1924, S. 10.
[71] See Ch. 1.6, *supra*.

the grantee has paid the price and taken actual occupation of the subjects of grant.[72] He has only a *jus crediti* until delivery of the deed.[73] Hence if the granter is sequestrated or put into liquidation the subjects are part of the sequestrated estates.[73] Nor is the granter a trustee for the grantee.[73] The delivery of a feu-charter, feu-disposition or feu-contract creates only a personal right in the vassal, but is a warrant for his obtaining a real right in the lands, formerly by taking sasine on the lands, the expeding of an Instrument of Sasine, and registration of it in the Register of Sasines,[74] and now by recording of the deed in the appropriate division of the General Register of Sasines. To permit registration the grantee must be identified and registration must be effected while he is still alive. Recording implies entry with the superior.[75] The date of recording is the criterion of preference in competition.[76]

Warrant of registration

If the feu-charter contains a general description of the lands, or a particular description of them, or a description by statutory reference, or a description by general name under the 1868 Act, S. 13, the grantee completes title by endorsing at the end of the deed a warrant of registration, signed by the grantee, or his agent, in the form of Schedule F to the Conveyancing Act, 1924, and forwarding the charter to the Keeper of the Registers of Scotland to be recorded in the appropriate division(s) of the General Register of Sasines, and thereafter returned to the grantee for retention, or, formerly, by expeding and sending for recording, with a warrant of registration in his favour, in the form of Schedule H, No. 1, to the 1924 Act, in the appropriate division(s) of the General Register of Sasines, and for later return to the grantee, a notarial instrument in the form of Schedule J of the 1868 Act, and now by expeding a Notice of Title under the Conveyancing Act, 1924, to the same effect and sending it for recording with a warrant of registration in his favour in the form of Schedule F to the 1924 Act thereon.

If, on the other hand, the description of the lands is either in general terms or by reference not in statutory form, the grantee cannot register the deed, but may expede and record in the General Register of Sasines a notarial instrument in the form of Schedule L of the 1868 Act, the feu-charter being used as a midcouple linking the titles of the granter and grantee.

Survivorship in a destination is imported into the warrant and a survivor is infeft and needs no further completion of title.

[72] Hence payment of the price and delivery of the deed should be contemporaneous.
[73] *Gibson and Hunter Home Designs Ltd*, 1976 S.C. 23.
[74] Bell, *Conv.* I, 648; Menzies, 538.
[75] Conveyancing (Sc.) Act, 1874, S. 4.
[76] Titles to Land Consolidation (Sc.) Act, 1868, S. 142.

It is still competent for a feu-charter to contain a precept of sasine, and an Instrument of Sasine may be expede and recorded.

Clause of direction

A clause of direction may be inserted before the testing clause, directing registration of specified parts of the deed, or of the deed with specified exceptions.[77] The warrant of registration then bears to request registration in terms of the clause of direction contained in the deed.

Registration

In areas in which the Land Register is operational the deed must, instead of being recorded in the Register of Sasines, be registered in the Land Register.[78] This has the effect of vesting in the person registered a real right in and to the interest conveyed and to any right, pertinent or servitude, express or implied, forming part of that interest, subject only to any matter entered adverse to the person's interest and to any overriding interest noted or not. It also implies entry with the superior.[79] The date of registration is the criterion of preference in competition.[79]

Continuity of trust infeftment

If property of a religious or educational body is taken in the name of office-bearers or trustees,[80] or the office of trustee conferred on the holder of an office, or proprietor of an estate, and his successors therein,[81] successors in office are deemed to have a valid and complete title by infeftment as if named in the completed title, without need for conveyance to them.

LAPSE OF TIME FORTIFYING TITLE: THE POSITIVE PRESCRIPTION

To fortify a grantee's title to lands and obviate challenge after a substantial time the rules of the positive prescription secure a possessor his right against all challenge after the lapse of a stated time, subject to certain conditions.

No amount of possession of heritage can by itself create a title thereto, as the ultimate dominion of all lands is vested in the Crown

---

[77] 1868 Act, S. 12.
[78] Land Registration (Sc.) Act, 1979, S. 2(1)(a)(i).
[79] Ibid., S. 3(1) and (4).
[80] 1868 Act, S. 26.
[81] 1874 Act, S. 45; *Mailler's Trs.* v. *Allan* (1904) 6 F. 326.

and any land not covered by the title of a vassal belongs to his superior, and if not covered by the title of a superior belongs to the Crown. Still less can any bare possession avail against a person producing a charter to the lands in question: *nulla sasina, nulla terra.* Possession may, however, fortify a defective title. Thus if a tenant procures a grant of the land *a non domino* and possesses in reliance thereon, without paying rent, for the prescriptive period, he acquires a title good against landlord and third parties.[82] If he obtains an *ex facie* valid grant of feu prescription fortifies the grant though it was originally made *ultra vires.*[83] The Prescription Act, 1594, enacted that where a proprietor's charter and sasine were extant and there had been possession for forty years he should not be required to produce other title. The Prescription Act, 1617 (c. 12), enacted that forty years' peaceable possession without lawful interruption by virtue of heritable infeftment by the Crown or other superior should constitute an unchallengeable title, provided that the possessor could produce a charter with the instrument of sasine following thereon; or where there was no charter extant, one or more instruments of sasine covering forty years, either proceeding upon retours or upon precepts of *clare constat.*[84]

The Conveyancing (Sc.) Act, 1874, S. 34, restated the rule and, as amended and restated by the Conveyancing (Sc.) Act, 1924, S. 16, it was provided that 'Any *ex facie* valid irredeemable title to an estate in land [defined by the 1874 Act, S. 16, and the 1924 Act, S. 2] recorded in the appropriate Register of Sasines shall be sufficient foundation for prescription [under the Act of 1617] and possession following on such recorded title for the space of twenty years continually, and together and that peaceably without any lawful interruption; should be equivalent to possession for forty years under the 1617 Act. No deduction or allowance was now to be made for any period of minority or of legal disability on the part of those against whom prescription is used. The changes made did not affect the character or period of possession, use or enjoyment necessary to constitute or prove the existence of servitudes, public rights of way or other public rights.[85] By the Conveyancing and Feudal Reform (Sc.) Act, 1970, S. 8, the period was reduced to ten years.[86] This rule was restated in the Prescription and Limitation (Sc.) Act, 1973, S. 1, which provided that if an interest in land has been possessed by a person, or a person and his successors, for

---

[82] *Grant* v. *G.* (1677) Mor. 10876; *Hilson* v. *Scott* (1895) 23 R. 241; *Fraser* v. *L. Lovat* (1898) 25 R. 603; cf. *Hamilton* v. *Scotland* (1807) Hume 461; *Macdonald* v. *Lockhart* (1853) 1 Macq. 790; *Mackie* v. *M.* (1896) 34 S.L.R. 34; *Edinburgh Mags.* v. *St. John's Church*, 1915 S.C. 249; *Stobie* v. *Smith*, 1921 S.C. 894, 904.

[83] *Edinburgh Mags., supra.*

[84] Bell, *Prin.* §2002.

[85] 1924 Act, S. 16.

[86] e.g. *Lock* v. *Taylor*, 1976 S.L.T. 238.

a continuous period of ten years openly, peaceably[87] and without any judicial interruption,[88] and the possession was founded on, and followed the recording of, a deed sufficient in its terms to constitute in favour of that person a title to that interest in that land, or land of a description liable to include the land, the validity of the title is exempt from challenge except on the ground that the deed is invalid *ex facie*[89] or forged. The prescriptive period remains twenty years in relation to an interest in any foreshore or salmon-fishings as against the Crown.[90] Subjects which may be transmitted without sasine, such as leases, allodial land and servitudes, are within the Act of 1617, and titles thereto may be fortified by prescription.[91]

Title and possession both requisite

The operation of the positive prescription depends on the coexistence of title and possession, and neither will suffice alone to found prescription.[92] Where both elements coexist, the lapse of time fortifies the title against all challenge,[93] even by the Crown,[94] save only on the grounds of intrinsic nullity,[95] and forgery. Thereafter it is unavailing to inquire whether the title was originally good or bad or whether the granter had or had not right to grant the title.[96]

Requisite title

The title requisite to found prescription was originally a charter of the lands and also the instrument of sasine following thereon,[97] or the sasine of an heir. In modern practice the title requisite is a deed sufficient to create title to an interest in land, recorded in the Register of Sasines. This includes a charter or disposition, and a decree of adjudication with infeftment thereon followed by decree of declarator of expiry of the legal,[98] but not a decree of adjudication with infeft-

---

[87] cf. Ersk. II, 1, 23.

[88] Defined, 1973 Act, S. 4.

[89] This excludes a deed, informality of execution of which has been cured under the 1874 Act, S. 39; 1973 Act, S. 5.   [90] 1973 Act, S. 1(4).

[91] Bell, *Prin.* §2003. Such subjects are probably not within the category of 'estates in land' as defined by the 1874 and 1924 Acts, but are within the 1973 Act, Ss. 2 and 3.

[92] *Fergusson* v. *Shirreff* (1844) 6 D. 1363; *Lick* v. *Chalmers* (1859) 21 D. 408; *Montgomery* v. *Watson* (1861) 23 D. 635; *Andersons* v. *Lows* (1863) 2 M. 100; *Copland* v. *Maxwell* (1871) 9 M. (H.L.) 1; *Grant* v. *Henry* (1894) 21 R. 358.

[93] *Millers* v. *Dickson* (1776) Mor. 10937; *Forbes* v. *Livingstone* (1827) 1 W. & S. 657.

[94] *L.A.* v. *Dundas* (1831) 5 W. & S. 723.

[95] *Cooper Scott* v. *Gill Scott*, 1924 S.C. 309; as to intrinsic nullities see *Shepherd* v. *Grant's Trs.* (1844) 6 D. 464; 6 Bell 173.

[96] *L.A.* v. *Graham* (1844) 7 D. 183; *Auld* v. *Hay* (1880) 7 R. 663; *Glen* v. *Scale's trs.* (1881) 9 R. 317; *Fraser* v. *L.A.* (1898) 25 R. 603; *Ramsay* v. *Spence*, 1909 S.C. 1441.

[97] Prescription Act, 1617 (c. 12); *Fraser* v. *Hogg* (1679) Mor. 10784; *Ochterlony* v. *Officers of State* (1825) 1 W. & S. 533; *Glen* v. *Scale's Tr.* (1881) 9 R. 317.

[98] *Robertson* v. *D. Atholl* (1815) 3 Dow 108; *McKenzie* v. *Robertson* (1827) 5 S. 694; see also Prescription and Limitation (Sc.) Act, S. 1973, 1 (3).

ment thereon but without a declarator of expiry of the legal, which is not *ex facie* irredeemable and requires twenty years for prescription to operate,[99] nor any redeemable title, such as a disposition *ex facie* in security only. It now includes a notarial instrument or notice of title without their warrants.[1]

The deeds founded on must be *ex facie* valid and free from intrinsic nullity, such as absence of subscription,[2] but prescription precludes extrinsic objections,[3] except forgery.[4]

An infeftment with its warrant, such as a charter and sasine or, now, a recorded feu-charter or disposition, is a good title for prescriptive purposes though proceeding *a non domino* and though subject to a latent nullity.[5]

The title must be definite[6] and bear to cover the lands in question; if it does not it is not habile to found prescription.[7] Subjects excepted in a disposition describing lands by a bounding title cannot be acquired by prescription.[8] But it is sufficient that the subjects would pass as part and pertinent of lands expressly conveyed.[9]

Requisite possession

The possession relied on must be referable exclusively to the title founded on.[10] It must be specifically and unequivocally related to the subject claimed, as by occupying and using lands. Possession of subjects as part and pertinent of subjects covered by the title suffices, the onus of proof being on the claimant[11] and such possession will prevail even against an express title to the same subjects not followed by possession.[12] Possession may be of a particular storey of a house, or of

[99] *Hinton* v. *Connell's Trs.* (1883) 10 R. 1110.

[1] 1973 Act, S. 5(1), altering *Sutherland* v. *Garrity*, 1941 S.C. 196. As to disconformity between warrant and notarial instrument see *Simpson* v. *Marshall* (1900) 2 F. 447.

[2] *Shepherd* v. *Grant's Trs.* (1847) 6 Bell 153; *Kinloch* v. *Bell* (1867) 5 M. 360; *Glen, supra.*

[3] *Thomson* v. *Stewart* (1840) 2 D. 564; *L.A.* v. *Graham* (1845) 7 D. 183; *Fraser* v. *L. Lovat* (1898) 25 R. 603; *Simpson* v. *Marshall* (1900) 2 F. 447; *Troup* v. *Aberdeen Heritable Securities Co.*, 1916 S.C. 918; *Cooper Scott* v. *Gill Scott*, 1924 S.C. 309.

[4] *Auld* v. *Hay* (1880) 7 R. 663; *D. Buccleuch* v. *Boyd* (1890) 18 R. 1; *D. Roxburgh* v. *Scott* (1890) 18 R. 8; Prescription and Limitation (Sc.) Act, 1973, S. 1.

[5] Stair II, 12, 20; Ersk. III, 7, 4; Bell, *Prin.* §2010; *Hilson* v. *Scott* (1895) 23 R. 241; *Tayport Land Co.* v. *Dougall's Trs.* (1895) 23 R. 287; *Fraser* v. *L. Lovat* (1898) 25 R. 603.

[6] *Brown* v. *N.B. Ry. Co.* (1906) 8 F. 534; *Hay* v. *Aberdeen Corpn.*, 1909 S.C. 554.

[7] *Education Trust Governors* v. *Macalister* (1893) 30 S.L.R. 818; *Caledonian Ry.* v. *Jamieson* (1899) 2 F. 100. cf. *Borthwick-Norton* v. *Gavin Paul*, 1947 S.C. 659.

[8] *N.B. Ry.* v. *Hutton* (1896) 23 R. 522.

[9] Ersk. III, 7, 4; Bell, *Prin.* §2008; *Baird* v. *Fortune* (1861) 4 Macq. 127; *L.A.* v. *Hunt* (1867) 5 M. (H.L.) 1.

[10] *Agnew* v. *Stranraer Mags.* (1822) 2 S. 42; *Officers of State* v. *Haddington* (1830) 8 S. 867; *Ross* v. *Milne, Cruden & Co.* (1843) 5 D. 648; *D. Buccleuch* v. *Edinburgh Mags.* (1843) 5 D. 846; *Milne's Trs.* v. *L.A.* (1873) 11 M. 966; *Edmonstone* v. *Jeffrey* (1886) 13 R. 1038; *Houston* v. *Barr*, 1911 S.C. 134; *D. Argyll* v. *Campbell*, 1912 S.C. 458.

[11] *L.A.* v. *Hunt* (1867) 5 M. (H.L.) 1; *Scott* v. *Napier* (1869) 7 M. (H.L.) 35; *D. Argyll, supra.*

[12] *Perth Mags.* v. *Wemyss* (1828) 8 S. 82; *E. Fife's Trs.* v. *Cumming* (1830) 8 S. 326.

a part above or below the surface. In the case of an express grant of minerals possession of the surface is sufficient, but if minerals are claimed as part and pertinent of lands possession of the actual minerals by working them, sufficient to indicate to other parties that the minerals were being claimed, is necessary.[13] The sufficiency of the possession depends on the subject in question; thus fishing by net and coble is the normal mode of possessing salmon-fishings, but this is not invariable, and possession by rod and line may suffice.[14]

If two parties have competing titles, their rights must be determined by the state of possession.[15]

The possession must be continuous, peaceable and uninterrupted. Continuous possession requires regular exercise, though acts of possession may be separated by intervals.[16] Interruption cancels any period of time which has run. It may be effected judicially by calling the case in court, when the interruption lasts forty years.[17] It might formerly also be effected judicially by mere citations on a summons under the signet, recorded, if to be valid against singular successors, within sixty days, in the General Register of Sasines and renewed every seven years,[18] for extrajudicially (*via facti*) by actual dispossession or notarial protest, similarly recorded in the Register of Sasines,[19] but these are ineffective after 1976.[20]

Possession must be exclusive,[21] but does not cease to be so by reason of occasional encroachments by the public, though repetition of such invasions might eventually render possession no longer exclusive.[22]

The possession must also be lawful[23] and peaceable, but need not have been bona fide.[24]

The possession may be natural or civil, i.e. enjoyed personally and directly, or mediately, as by vassal[25] or tenant,[26] so long as the latter's

---

[13] *Forbes* v. *Livingstone* (1827) 6 S. 167; *L.A.* v. *Wemyss* (1899) 2 F. (H.L.) 1.

[14] *Ramsay* v. *D. Roxburgh* (1848) 10 D. 661; *Stuart* v. *McBarnet* (1868) 6 M. (H.L.) 123; *Warrand's Tr.* v. *Mackintosh* (1890) 17 R. (H.L.) 13.

[15] *Stuart* v. *McBarnet* (1868) 6 M. (H.L.) 123; *L.A.* v. *Lovat* (1880) 7 R. (H.L.) 122; *Heriot's Hosp.* v. *Cormack* (1883) 11 R. 320; *McArly* v. *French's Trs.* (1883) 10 R. 574; *Cooper's Trs.* v. *Stark's Trs.* (1898) 25 R. 1160.

[16] Stair IV, 40, 20; *Macdonnell* v. *D. Gordon* (1828) 6 S. 600.

[17] Ersk. III, 7, 43; Bell, *Prin.* §2007; *D. Buccleuch* v. *Edinburgh Mags.* (1843) 5 D. 847; Prescription and Limitation (Sc.) Act, 1973, S. 4.

[18] Interruptions Act, 1669, repealed by 1973 Act.

[19] Ersk. III, 7, 40.   [20] 1973 Act, S. 4.

[21] *D. Portland* v. *Gray* (1832) 11 S. 14; *E. Fife's Trs.* v. *Sinclair* (1849) 12 D. 223; *Lindsday* v. *Robertson* (1867) 6 M. 889.

[22] *Young* v. *N.B. Ry.* (1887) 14 R. (H.L.) 53.

[23] *Mackenzie* v. *Renton* (1840) 2 D. 1078; *Ramsay* v. *D. Roxburgh* (1850) 7 Bell 248; *D. Richmond* v. *E. Seafield* (1870) 8 M. 530; *Maxwell* v. *Lamont* (1903) 6 F. 245.

[24] Ersk. III, 7, 15.   [25] *L.A.* v. *McCulloch* (1874) 2 R. 27.

[26] *L.A.* v. *Hall* (1873) 11 M. 967. See also possession by liferenter by constitution: *Shepherd* v. *Grant's Trs.* (1847) 6 Bell 153; liferenter by reservation: *M. Clydesdale* v. *E. Dundonald* (1726) M. 1262.

possession is ascribed to the superior's or landlord's grant as evidenced by payment of feu-duty or rent.

Possession against title

No kind or amount of possession will establish any right contradictory of or inconsistent with the grant to which it is referred.[27] In particular no possession will confer title to any ground outwith the limits defined in a bounding charter.[28]

Computation of time

The ten (formerly forty and later twenty) years run from the end of the day on which infeftment took place[29] and must run to the very end of this period. Interruption on even the last day of the period cancels all the prior possession and the period must commence running again. A true owner of lands is not barred by delay from challenging an invalid right to lands not yet fortified by prescription.[30]

Prescriptive progress

To ascertain whether a title granted is unchallengeable by virtue of prescription it is accordingly necessary to find the first *ex facie* valid irredeemable title to the lands in question in favour of the granter, or one from whom he has derived title, which is at least ten years back from the grant now in question, and to be satisfied as to its validity, and to the unbroken and unchallengeable transmission of the lands from that writ to the present granter.

Connection with granter

Unless the title which is the basis for the operation of prescription is in favour of the present granter himself there must be connecting links between that foundation writ and the granter's own title. *Ex facie* valid irredeemable dispositions by way of gift or on sale are good links. A declarator of irritancy of lands, whereby they came into the granter's ownership, but granted in absence, is not a good connecting link.[31] A decree of adjudication followed by infeftment is good only if followed by declarator of expiry of the legal.[32]

In the case of deaths prior to the Succession (Sc.) Act, 1964, the title of a legatee completed by notice of title proceeding on a valid will, or

[27] *Officers of State* v. *E. Haddington* (1831) 5 W. & S. 570; *Fleeming* v. *Howden* (1868) 6 M. 782.
[28] *N.B. Ry.* v. *Hutton* (1896) 23 R. 522; *Logie* v. *Reid's Trs.* (1903) 5 F. 859.
[29] *Simpson* v. *Marshall* (1900) 2 F. 447; *Buchanan* v. *Geils* v. *L.A.* (1882) 9 R. 1218; *Ogston* v. *Stewart* (1896) 23 R. (H.L.) 16.
[30] *Mackie* v. *M.* (1896) 4 S.L.T. 3.
[31] *Bruce* v. *Stewart* (1900) 2 F. 948.
[32] *Hinton* v. *Connell's Trs.* (1883) 10 R. 1110.

the title of an heir, established as such by decree of general service, followed by notice of title, form good connecting links.[33]

In the case of deaths since the Succession (Sc.) Act, 1964, confirmation of an executor, if it contains a description of the property, gives him a valid title to the property and he may transmit it to a person entitled by will or under that Act by docket endorsed on the confirmation or certificate of confirmation, and such a docket is a valid link.[34]

Operation of prescription

The object of the positive prescription is to fortify bad or doubtful titles and place them beyond challenge. It excludes all objections to the title founded on latent nullities or extrinsic objections, but not against instrinsic nullities.[35] A vassal may obtain a fresh title if he fails to pay feu-duty and having obtained a charter from another person, possesses thereon for the prescriptive period,[36] or a tenant may acquire a title to the lands good against the landlord if he does not pay rent, obtains a disposition from another party and possesses thereon for the prescriptive period.[37] Good faith is not a prerequisite for prescription.

Operation of long negative prescription

The operation of the long negative prescription of twenty[38] (formerly forty[39]) years may also operate indirectly to fortify a vassal's right, by cutting off claims which challenge his right of property, such as under an alleged will or disposition in favour of the claiment, if not insisted on within twenty years.[40]

Prescription in cases of interests registrable in the Law Register

S. 1 of the 1973 Act, rendering an interest possessed continuously for ten years exempt from challenge, is amended by the Land Registration (Sc.) Act, 1979, S. 10, in relation to registered interests to continue to render a title unchallengeable in the only case where that may still be useful, viz. where the registration has been made subject to an exclusion of indemnity, but this does not apply where possession was founded on the recording of a deed which is invalid *ex facie* or was forged, or possession was founded on registration in respect of an

---

[33] *Mackay's Exrx* v. *Schonbach*, 1933 S.C. 747; *Sibbald's Heirs* v. *Harris*, 1947 S.C. 601.

[34] Succession (Sc.) Act, 1964, S. 15 and Sched. 1, amd. Law Reform (Misc. Prov.) (Sc.) Act 1968, S. 19.

[35] Ersk. III, 7, 9; Bell, *Prin.* §2015; *Shepherd* v. *Grant's Trs.* (1844) 6 Bell, 153; *Kinloch* v. *Bell* (1867) 5 M. 360; *Cooper Scott* v. *Gill Scott*, 1924 S.C. 309.

[36] *Hamilton* v. *Scotland* (1807) Hume 461; *Macdonald* v. *Lockhart* (1853) 1 Macq. 790.

[37] *Grant* v. *G.* (1677) Mor. 10876.

[38] Conveyancing (Sc.) Act, 1924, S. 17; Prescription and Limitation (Sc.) Act, 1973, S. 7.

[39] Prescription Acts, 1469, c. 29; 1474, c. 55; and 1617, c. 12.

[40] *Pettigrew* v. *Harton*, 1956 S.C. 67.

interest in land in the Land Register of Scotland proceeding on a forged deed and the person appearing from the Register to be entitled to the interest was aware of the forgery at the time of registration in his favour.

CHAPTER 5.5

THE ESTATE OF THE SUPERIOR

An estate of superiority is created by any feudal landholder under the Crown when he grants a feu of any part of his lands to be held in fee by a vassal of and under him. He thereby retains certain rights in the lands, known collectively as the *dominium directum*, which he himself holds of the Crown or of an over-superior, but conveys others to the vassal. All rights in the lands not reserved to the Crown or any over-superior, nor conveyed to the vassal and which do not pass by implication as parts and pertinents of the lands conveyed, are reserved to the superior.[1] He also normally stipulates expressly for feu-duty or blench-duty, and formerly for casual payments also, and may impose express conditions on the use of the lands granted.

The estate of superiority is higher and more important than the estate of the vassal.[2] It is also the radical right and the vassal's rights revert to it if they should be suspended or fail.

An estate of superiority can be sold without the vassals' consent, thereby substituting a new superior for the old,[3] but it is indivisible and ʾannot be split in parts,[4] as such would inconvenience the vassals, ɔugh a person's superiority of certain lands can be sold to one and ...at of other lands to another, the right to feu-duties may be assigned, reserving the other rights of superiority,[5] and a superiority may be divided among creditors or between superior and creditor.[6]

Nor can a superior, unless he has reserved power to do so, or has the vassals' consent, interpose a new mid-superior between himself and his vassals.[7] The right to object is personal to the vassal and may be lost by lapse of the prescriptive period.[8]

---

[1] Bell, *Prin.* §687–8.
[2] Ersk. II, 3, 10.
[3] Bell, *Prin.* §855; *Dreghorn* v. *Hamilton* (1774) Mor. 15015.
[4] Ersk. II, 3, 12; *Montrose* v. *Colquhoun* (1782) 6 Pat. 805.
[5] Stair II, 4, 10; Bell, *Prin.* §688, 703; *Douglas* v. *Vassals* (1671) Mor. 9306.
[6] *Home* v. *Smith* (1794) Mor. 15077.
[7] Bell, *Prin.* §678; *Douglas, supra; Argyle* v. *McLeod* (1672) Mor. 15013; *Archbp. of St. Andrews* v. *M. Huntly* (1682) Mor. 15015; *Hotchkis* v. *Walker's Trs.* (1822) 2 S. 70.
[8] Bell, *Prin.* §857; Bell, *Convg.* II, 753; *Hotchkis, supra.*

Superior's rights

The superior's rights against the vassal comprise essential or fixed rights, namely the radical right of property in the lands and the right to some service or payment from the vassal in acknowledgment of the relationship; natural rights, such as arise from the nature of the feudal relationship itself, including formerly, casualties; and accidental rights, such as real burdens, reservations and conditions of the particular grant, depending in every case on the feu-charter or contract.[9]

(1) ESSENTIALS OF A FEU

Radical right of superior

The superior is not divested of any rights in the land, by his grant to the vassal of the *dominium utile*, except in so far as these are thereby conveyed. His infeftment subsists in all other respects, both in questions with his own superior and with third parties. Thus the superior may pursue real actions concerning the lands against any person other than his vassal or persons deriving right from him, such as to eject a squatter.[10]

Right to feu-duty

The feu-duty unless redeemed may be any sum in sterling money agreed by the parties.

The superior has various means for compelling payment of feu-duties. Where feu-duty has been redeemed none of these will in practice be invoked.

(1) *Personal action*

A personal action for payment is competent against the original vassal *ex contractu*, the vassal by acceptance of the feu making himself personally liable for the feu-duties and other obligations of the feu until a purchaser from him has become infeft and notice of change of ownership been given to the superior under the Conveyancing (Sc.) Act, 1874, S. 4.[11] It is also competent against the original vassal and his representatives if he undertook a personal obligation for feu-duties, even after a purchaser from him had entered with the superior.[12]

[9] Ersk. II, 3, 11; II, 5, 1.
[10] *Lagg* (1624) Mor. 13787.
[11] Bell, *Prin.* §700; *Tweeddale's Trs.* v. *E. Haddington* (1880) 7 R. 620; *Scottish Drainage Co.* v. *Campbell* (1889) 16 R. (H.L.) 16; *Macrae* v. *Mackenzie's Tr.* (1891) 19 R. 138.
[12] *Royal Bank* v. *Gardyne* (1853) 1 Macq. 358; *King's College* v. *Hay* (1854) 1 Macq. 526; *Brown's Trs.* v. *Webster* (1855) 2 Macq. 40; *Dundee Police Commrs.* v. *Straton* (1884) 11 R. 586; *Burns* v. *Martin* (1887) 14 R. (H.L.) 20. See also *Marshall's Tr.* v. *Macneill* (1888) 15 R. 762.

Personal action is also competent against singular successors who enter as vassals, for the feu-duties for their period as vassals,[13] against sub-vassals to the extent of their sub-feu-duties,[14] possibly against tenants while in possession of the lands,[15] or against intromitters with the profits of the lands during their intromissions.[16]

If there is no continuing personal obligation on the vassal's representatives, his heir may renounce the feu, and the vassal's representatives will be liable only for obligations due at his death.[17] Nor is a disponee in security liable to implement an obligation incumbent only on the vassal.[18]

But the annual feu-duty is not only a personal debt, but is a *debitum fundi*, or debt forming a charge on the lands feued and a real right reserved to the superior out of the lands feued.

(2) Hypothec

The superior also has a hypothec over the crop and *invecta et illata* on the lands in security of the last or current feu-duty, similar but preferable to a landlord's hypothec for his rent,[19] and enforced by sequestration.[20]

(3) Real security over lands

The superior, having a real right in the lands, has a preference over purchasers and creditors in voluntary or judicial sales, and in the ranking of creditors in bankruptcy.[21] This extends to the whole lands feued, though divided by sale or subfeuing, any vassal or subfeuar who pays having a right of relief against the others for payment in excess of his *pro rata* share.[22]

(4) Poinding of the ground

An action for poinding of the ground is a remedy available for attaching goods brought on the land by the vassal, and by his tenants,

[13] *Rollo* v. *Murray* (1629) Mor. 4185.

[14] *Hyslop* v. *Shaw* (1863) 1 M. 535; *Tweeddale's Trs., supra; Sandeman* v. *Scottish Property Investment Co.* (1881) 8 R. 790.

[15] Bell, *Prin.* §700; but see *Prudential Assce. Co.* v. *Cheyne* (1884) 11 R. 871; *Nelson's Trs.* v. *Tod* (1896) 23 R. 1000.

[16] *Biggar* v. *Scott* (1738) Mor. 4191; *Prudential Assce. Co., supra.*

[17] *Aiton* v. *Russell's Exors.* (1889) 16 R. 625; *Macrae* v. *Mackenzie's Tr.* (1891) 19 R. 139; *Marshall* v. *Callander Hydro Co.* (1896) 23 R. (H.L.) 55.

[18] *Patterson* v. *Robertson*, 1912, 2 S.L.T. 494.

[19] Stair II, 4, 7; Mack. II, 6, 12; Ersk. II, 6, 63; Bell, *Comm.* II, 27; *Prin.* §698; Ross II, 392; *Yuille* v. *Lawrie* (1823) 2 S. 155; *Athole Hydropathic Co., Ltd.* (1886) 13 R. 818; *Anderson's Trs.* v. *Donaldson & Co.*, 1908 S.C. 38. It is unaffected by the Hypothec Abolition Act, 1880.

[20] e.g. *Anderson's Trs., supra.*   [21] Bankruptcy (Sc.) Act, 1913, S. 97(2).

[22] Bell, *Prin.* §697; *Wemyss* v. *Thomson* (1836) 14 S. 233; *Little Gilmour* v. *Balfour* (1839) 1 D. 4034; *Knight* v. *Cargill* (1846) 8 D. 991; *Nisbet* v. *Smith* (1876) 3 R. 781; *Sandeman* v. *Sc. Property Investment Co.* (1885) 12 R. (H.L.) 67.

to the extent of their year's unpaid rent.[23] It covers all arrears of feu-duties. The action is not affected by sequestration,[24] though decree taken after sequestration gives preference for one year's arrears and the current term's feu-duty only.[25] It may be competent to a divested superior for feu-duty due down to the date of his divestiture.[26] A superior cannot bring an action of maills and duties against the tenants or take possession thereunder in view of his vassal's infeftment.[27] He cannot attach the rents of the vassal's tenants for recovery of feu-duty.[28]

(5) Adjudication

Adjudication is competent, as on other *debita fundi*.[29]

(6) Tinsel of the feu

The superior may, lastly, seek tinsel of the feu, or declarator of irritancy of the feu *ob non solutum canonem*[30] which infers forfeiture of the vassal's right for breach of the feudal contract by failure to pay feu-duty and returns the land and all on it to the superior.[31] This irritancy exists under statute[32] when five[33] years' feu-duties are unpaid, and is frequently also stipulated for conventionally. Declarator is required in all cases that it has been incurred, and the irritancy may be purged by payment before decree is obtained, even if the irritancy is expressed as a conventional one.[34] The superior cannot both claim irritancy of the feu and recover the unpaid arrears of feu-duty.[35] Where feu-duty has not been allocated it is incompetent to irritate part of the feu.[36]

[23] Stair IV, 23, 5, and 10; Ersk. IV, 1, 11; Bell, *Prin.* §699.

[24] Bankruptcy (Sc.) Act, 1913, S. 97(2).

[25] *Campbell* v. *Edinburgh Parish Council*, 1911 S.C. 280; cf. *Aberdeen Corpn.* v. *B.L. Bank*, 1911 S.C. 239.

[26] *Scottish Heritages Co.* v. *N.B. Property Inv. Co.* (1885) 12 R. 550; *Maxwell's Trs.* v. *Bothwell School Board* (1893) 20 R. 958; *Campbell* v. *Edinburgh Parish Council*, 1911 S.C. 280.

[27] *Prudential Assce. Co.* v. *Cheyne* (1884) 11 R. 871.

[28] *Aberdeen Corpn.*, *supra*.

[29] Bell, *Prin.* §699A; *Sandeman* v. *Scottish Property Investment Co.* (1885) 12 R. (H.L.) 67, 71.

[30] By analogy with the Roman relationship of *emphyteusis*.

[31] Ersk. II, 5, 25–7; Bell, *Prin*, §701; Bell, *Convg.* II, 754.

[32] Feuduty Act, 1597 (c. 17).

[33] Land Tenure Reform (Sc.) Act, 1974, S. 15.

[34] *Lockhart* v. *Shiells* (1770) Mor. 7244; *Rait* v. *Spence* (1848) 11 D. 126; *Hope* v. *Aitken* (1872) 10 M. 347; *Maxwell's Trs.* v. *Bothwell School Board* (1893) 20 R. 958. By the Conveyancing Acts Amdt. Act, 1887, S. 4, no such declarator is deemed final until an extract has been recorded in the appropriate Register of Sasines. See also Conveyancing Amdt. (Sc.) Act, 1938, S. 6.

[35] Bell, *Prin.* §701; *Edinburgh Mags.* v. *Horsburgh* (1834) 12 S. 593; *Malcolm* v. *Donald*, 1956 S.L.T. (Sh. Ct.) 101.

[36] *Fothringham* v. *Anderson*, 1950 S.L.T. (Sh. Ct.) 25.

The annulment of the vassal's right does not avoid securities granted by him, but the superior takes the lands free of the security-rights unless the holders thereof purge the irritancy.[37] The annulment, however, avoids all subfeus granted by the vassal, and the lands revert to the superior unaffected by any such rights.[38] The superior, however, recovers the lands subject to any statutory real burdens imposed on them.[39]

Vassal's right of retention of feu-duty

The vassal may withhold payment of feu-duty if the superior, acting as such, has failed to perform any essential condition of the feu-contract.[40]

Allocation of feu-duty

The feu-duty attached by a superior to lands feued attaches to every part thereof, notwithstanding that the vassal may have subfeued parts of the lands. The vassal may, however, obtain the superior's consent in his feu-contract to the allocation of a proportion of the total feu-duty to each part of the lands in the event of the vassal subfeuing,[41] or the superior may subsequently agree to allocation. Allocation is effected by a memorandum of allocation of feu-duty endorsed on the original grant.[42] Alternatively a separate memorandum may be recorded, and this binds heritable creditors and all having interest other than existing heritable creditors who are not parties to it.[43] A charter of novodamus or a charter by progress may also be granted by the superior containing an allocation of feu-duty. A vassal may be authorized by his charter to allocate feu-duty in certain terms. If a vassal allocates feu-duty in a way not authorized it is invalid and each feuar is jointly and severally liable for the cumulo feu-duty, though the superior may be barred by acquiescence from objecting.[44]

Compulsory allocations of feu-duty

Without prejudice to other methods of allocation, any proprietor of part of a feu burdened with a cumulo feu-duty may serve on his superior or other recipient of the cumulo feu-duty a notice of allocation of the portion of the cumulo feu-duty which has been apportioned

---

[37] Ersk. II,. 5, 79; *Drummond* v. *Hamilton's Crs.* (1686) Mor. 7235.

[38] *Cassels* v. *Lamb* (1885) 12 R. 722; *Sandeman* v. *Sc. Property Investment Co.* (1885) 12 R. (H.L.) 67.

[39] *Pickard* v. *Glasgow Corpn.*, 1970 S.L.T. (Sh. Ct.) 63.

[40] Bell, *Prin.* §702; *Gibson* v. *Heriot's Hospital* (1811) Hume 15; *Ainslie* v. *Edinburgh Mags.* (1842) 4 D. 639; *Arnott's Trs.* v. *Forbes* (1881) 9 R. 89; *Thom* v. *Chalmers* (1886) 13 R. 1026.

[41] cf. *Mitchell's Trs.* v. *Galloway's Trs.* (1903) 5 F. 612.

[42] 1874 Act, S. 8 and Sched. D.

[43] 1924 Act, S. 13.

[44] *Nelson's Trs.* v. *Tod* (1904) 6 F. 475; *Pall Mall Trust* v. *Wilson*, 1948 S.C. 232.

by disposition or other document or by any other method, formal or informal, on the part of the feu of which he is proprietor. Such notice, in the form prescribed by regulations, is effective to allocate the feu-duty.[45] If the superior wishes to object to the amount which the proprietor seeks to have allocated he may apply to the Lands Tribunal which must by order allocate the cumulo feu-duty, in such manner as they consider reasonable, on the applicant's and on every other part of the feu held by a separate proprietor.[46] Once allocation has been made that part of the feu is to be treated as if it never had been part of the whole feu. Nothing in these provisions empowers the Lands Tribunal to alter the total amount of feu-duty exigible in respect of the feu. Any order under S. 4 supersedes any existing apportionment.[47] It is incompetent to contract out of or limit the operation of Ss. 3–6.[48]

Superior's sale of feu-duties

Without selling his superiority a superior may sell and convey to the purchaser the right, held blench of the superior, to receive the feu-duties, and this constitutes a real right to them.[49]

(2) NATURAL RIGHTS

Natural incidents of the feudal relationship differ from essentials in that they may be modified without infringing the feudal relationship, if expressly done in the contract itself. They include the implied obligation of warrandice, which may be modified or excluded by the contract, and formerly the superior's right to casualties.[50]

(3) ACCIDENTAL OR CONVENTIONAL RIGHTS

The existence and scope of such rights depends entirely on the agreement of parties; they are never presumed but must be matters of express stipulation,[51] and must appear on the recorded title.

Reservations

The superior's grant may reserve to him certain rights, such as to mines and minerals. The extent of the reservation depends on the interpretation of the particular clause.[52] A reservation of the right to

---

[45] Conveyancing and Feudal Reform (Sc.) Act, 1970, S. 3.
[46] Ibid., S. 4. See e.g. *Moray Estates Development Co.*, 1971 S.C. 306; *Barr v. Bass*, 1972 S.L.T. (Lands Tr.) 5.
[47] Ibid., S. 5.   [48] Ibid., S. 7.
[49] Bell, *Prin.* §703; *Douglas v. Vassals* (1671) Mor. 9306.
[50] Ersk. II, 3, 11.   [51] Ersk. II, 3, 11.
[52] e.g. *Harvie v. Stewart* (1870) 9 M. 129; *Orr v. Mitchell* (1893) 20 R. (H.L.) 27; *Cadell v. Allan* (1905) 7 F. 606.

work minerals implies reservation of property in the minerals.[53] Reservation has been held to include the right to form in the reserved mineral strata roads for the underground conveyance of minerals extracted from under other properties,[54] but not the right to mine in strata not expressly reserved nor to use them for conveying coal from other lands.[55]

It is a question of interpretation whether particular mineral substances are covered by the clause of reservation. Whether a substance is covered by a general reservation of 'minerals' depends on whether at the time of the conveyance the substance was called a mineral by landowners and mining engineers in the locality, and whether it was distinct from the ordinary subsoil of the district.[56]

Where the superior has effectively reserved property in the minerals he may work them himself or let the right of extraction to a mineral tenant for a periodical payment or a royalty on the minerals extracted.[57]

It is implied that the mineral working will not remove support from the surface lands,[58] but express provision may be made in the reservation of minerals for the superior withdrawing support from the lands granted to the vassal,[59] with[60] or without[61] liability to compensate for damage done thereby, and liberty to withdraw support may even be held to have been impliedly reserved.[62]

Under the Coal Industry Nationalisation Act, 1946, S. 64(3) there was vested in the National Coal Board all the rights of superiority, other than that of the Crown, in coal-bearing strata.[63]

Personal burdens

The superior may take the grantee bound by acceptance of the grant to pay money to him or to a third party. Such a burden is binding on the grantee personally and his representatives, but does not attach to the lands, nor affect a disponee thereof.[64] It is enforceable as an ordinary debt.

[53] *D. Hamilton* v. *Dunlop* (1885) 12 R. (H.L.) 65.
[54] *D. Hamilton* v. *Graham* (1871) 9 M. (H.L.) 98.
[55] *Ramsay* v. *Blair* (1876) 3 R. (H.L.) 41.
[56] *Caledonian Ry.* v. *Glenboig Union Fireclay Co.*, 1911 S.C. (H.L.) 72; *Borthwick-Norton* v. *Gavin Paul*, 1947 S.C. 659.
[57] cf. *Dalgleish* v. *Fife Coal Co.* (1892) 30 S.L.R. 58.
[58] *White* v. *Dixon* (1883) 10 R. (H.L.) 45.
[59] *White* v. *Dixon* (1883) 10 R. (H.L.) 45.
[60] *Anderson* v. *McCracken* (1900) 2 F. 780.
[61] *Buchanan* v. *Andrew* (1873) 11 M. (H.L.) 13.
[62] *B. of Scotland* v. *Stewart* (1891) 18 R. 957.
[63] cf. *Wauchope Settlement Trs.* v. *N.C.B.*, 1947 S.N. 185.
[64] *Mackenzie* v. *L. Lovat* (1721) Robertson's App. 607; *Martin* v. *Paterson* (1808) Mor. Personal and Real, No. 5; *Macintyre* v. *Masterton* (1824) 2 S. 664; *Forbes' Trs.* v. *Gordon's Assignees* (1833) 12 S. 219; *Mackenzie* v. *Clark* (1903) 11 S.L.T. 428.

Real burdens

A real burden not only binds the grantee, but attaches to and runs with the lands, and affects singular successors of the grantee, but not personal representatives who do not take up the subjects burdened.[65] It may be created by reservation in a grant of lands in favour of the granter, or by express constitution in favour of the granter or a third party, and it requires a payment by the grantee.

To be a valid real burden no *voces signatae* are necessary, but it must clearly appear that the lands are to be burdened, and not merely the grantee personally.[66] The creditor must be named or clearly identified,[67] the sum due must be definite in amount,[68] it must appear in the dispositive clause of the feu-charter,[69] and it must appear in the Register of Sasines.[70]

In the absence of a personal obligation for payment a real burden is enforceable only by real diligence against the lands.

The term real burden frequently extends to cover what are strictly real conditions of the grant, which similarly attach to and run with the lands, but do not require payment of money but the performance of some other obligation, such as to build.[71] A real condition can be enforced by personal action against the vassal for the time being.[72] To be a valid real condition it must be expressed or clearly implied that the condition is to affect the lands themselves and not merely the grantee and his heirs.[73] The superior, or party in whose favour the condition is created, must have an interest to enforce it,[74] the condition must not be contrary to law, inconsistent with the nature of the species of property disponed, useless or vexatious, nor contrary to public policy,[74] and the clause constituting the condition must appear in the charter and in the appropriate Register of Sasines.[75]

Obligation to build

In urban feus the superior commonly binds the vassal to build and maintain a dwelling house or other specified premises to a stated

[65] *Macrae v. Mackenzie's Trs.* (1891) 19 R. 138.
[66] *Tailors of Aberdeen v. Coutts* (1840) 1 Rob. App. 296; *Williamson v. Begg* (1887) 14 R. 720.
[67] *Erskine v. Wright* (1846) 8 D. 863.
[68] *Edinburgh Mags. v. Begg* (1883) 11 R. 352.
[69] Bell, *Prin.* §920; *Cowie's Tr. v. Muirden* (1893) 20 R. (H.L.) 81.
[70] *Tailors of Aberdeen, supra; Stewart v. D. Montrose* (1861) 4 Macq. 499.
[71] cf. *Edmonstone v. Seton* (1888) 16 R. 1.
[72] *Tweeddale's Trs. v. E. Haddington* (1880) 7 R. 620.
[73] *Tailors of Aberdeen, supra; Sc. Temperance Life Assce. Co. v. Law Union Ins. Co.,* 1917 S.C. 175; *Hunter v. Fox,* 1964 S.C. (H.L.) 95.
[74] *Tailors of Aberdeen, supra; Sc. Temperance Life Assce. Co. v. Law Union Ins. Co.,* 1917 S.C. 175; *Hunter v. Fox,* 1964 S.C. (H.L.) 95.
[75] *Tailors of Aberdeen, supra.*

value,[76] and this may be declared a real burden and fenced by
an irritancy clause. On the vassal's failure the superior may obtain
declarator of that fact and obtain an order ordaining the defender to
erect the buildings within a specified time. Such an irritancy can be
allowed, if the court exercised its discretion, to be purged at any time
before decree of declarator that it has been incurred.[77]

Building restrictions

In respect of building restrictions there is a presumption in favour of
freedom of ownership and a restriction not expressed is not readily
implied,[78] while a restriction is invalid if vague and affecting merely a
question of taste[79] or deemed too vague and indefinite as a restraint on
the use of property.[80] *In dubio* a restriction is construed *contra proferentem*, [81] but a restriction clearly expressed is enforceable in its
terms.[82] To be effectual a restriction must be a real burden and not
merely a personal right against the grantee.[83]

A restriction validly imposed as a real condition binds singular
successors of superior and vassal. In considering whether singular
successors are bound the intention of the parties to the original deed is
irrelevant, and singular successors are not bound by a clause which
admits of doubt in interpretation.[84]

Restrictions may be imported by reference to a plan, provided it is
clear that the plan is intended to be a part of the contract,[85] which
appears if it is attached to the charter and signed by the superior.[86] The
exhibition of a plan before contract does not bind parties to conform
thereto,[87] nor is a reference to a feuing-plan for identification of the

---

[76] As to valuation, see *Brechin Mags.* v. *Guthrie, Craig, Peter & Co.*, 1926 S.N. 106.

[77] *Anderson* v. *Valentine*, 1957 S.L.T. 57; *Precision Relays* v. *Beaton*, 1980 S.L.T. 206.

[78] *Middleton* v. *Leslie* (1894) 21 R. 781; *Walker Trs.* v. *Haldane* (1902) 4 F. 594.

[79] *McNeill* v. *Mackenzie* (1870) 8 M. 520.

[80] *Murray's Trs.* v. *St. Margaret's Convent*, 1907 S.C. (H.L.) 8.

[81] *Dennistoun* v. *Thomson* (1872) 11 M. 121; *Banks* v. *Walker* (1874) 1 R. 981; *Moir's Trs.* v.
McEwan (1880) 7 R. 1141; *Hood* v. *Traill* (1884) 12 R. 362; *Miller* v. *Carmichael* (1888) 15 R.
991; *Middleton* v. *Leslie* (1894) 21 R. 781; *Assets Co.* v. *Lamb & Gibson* (1896) 23 R. 569;
Assets Co. v. *Ogilvie* (1897) 24 R. 400; *Wylie* v. *Dunnett* (1899) 1 F. 982; *Graham* v. *Shiels*
(1901) 8 S.L.T. 368; *Walker Trs.* v. *Haldane* (1902) 4 F. 594; *Kerridge* v. *Gray* (1902) 5 F. 283;
Street v. *Dobbie* (1903) 5 F. 941; *Minister of Prestonpans* v. *The Heritors* (1905) 13 S.L.T. 463;
Shand v. *Brand* (1907) 14 S.L.T. 704; *Bainbridge* v. *Campbell*, 1912 S.C. 92; *Dykehead Co-op
Socy.* v. *Public Trustee*, 1926 S.C. 157.

[82] *Morrison* v. *McLay* (1874) 1 R. 1117; *Naismith* v. *Cairnduff* (1876) 3 R. 863; *Partick Police
Commrs.* v. *G.W. Steam Laundry Co.* (1886) 13 R. 500; *Sandeman's Trs.* v. *Brown* (1892) 20 R.
210; *Millar* v. *Church of Scotland Endowment Cttee. Trs.* (1896) 23 R. 557; *Lawson* v. *Wilkie*
(1897) 24 R. 649; *Walker Trs., supra; Montgomerie-Fleming's Trs.* v. *Kennedy*, 1912 S.C. 1307.

[83] *Scottish Temperance Life Assce. Co.* v. *Law Union and Rock Ins. Co.*, 1917 S.C. 175.

[84] *Walker* v. *Church of Scotland General Trs.*, 1967 S.L.T. 297.

[85] *Sim* v. *Stewart* (1827) 5 S. 841; *Barr* v. *Robertson* (1854) 16 D. 1049; *Free St. Mark's
Church Trs.* v. *Taylor's Trs.* (1869) 7 M. 415; *Assets Co.* v. *Lamb & Gibson* (1896) 23 R. 569.

[86] *Crawford* v. *Field* (1874) 2 R. 20.

[87] *Heriot's Hospital* v. *Gibson* (1814) 2 Dow 301; *Croall* v. *Edinburgh Mags.* (1870) 9 M.
323.

subjects sufficient to bind grantees to conform thereto.[88] If a feu-contract binds the vassal to build according to a plan and buildings have been erected, but the plan is subsequently lost, the onus is on the vassal to show that alterations proposed are not disconform to the plan.[89]

Restrictions on use

Restrictions on the mode of use of property are competent but are strictly controlled.[90] They should be express, or carry the clearest implication,[91] but if clear will be given effect to.[92]

Objections to restrictions

Restrictions imposed may be open to challenge as being repugnant to the nature of the estate taken by the vassal, contrary to law, too vague,[93] or as being contrary to public policy, being, e.g. in unreasonable restraint of trade.[94] Prohibitions on the use of houses as licensed premises are lawful.[95]

Enforcement of restrictions

Enforcement is commonly by a clause of irritancy,[96] but failing such provision interdict against contravention is competent.

Title and interest to enforce restrictions

The superior who imposes the restrictions has a clear title to enforce them so long as he has a legitimate interest, as have his successors as such[97] and the vassal, in consenting to be bound thereby, prima facie concedes the superior's interest to do so.[98] A vassal in seeking release must seek to prove that, by some change of circumstances, any interest which the superior may have had in maintaining the restriction has ceased to exist.[99] What is a sufficient interest depends on the case; it

---

[88] *Gordon v. Marjoribanks* (1818) 6 Dow 87; *Walker v. Renton* (1825) 3 S. 650; *Barr, supra*; *Free St. Mark's Ch. Trs., supra.*

[89] *Sutherland v. Barbour* (1887) 15 R. 62.

[90] *Heriot's Hospital v. Ferguson* (1773) Mor. 12187; 3 Pat. 674.

[91] *Hood v. Traill* (1885) 12 R. 362.

[92] *Colquhoun's C.B. v. Glen's Tr.*, 1920 S.C. 737.

[93] *Kirkintilloch Kirk Session v. Kirkintilloch Parish Council*, 1911 S.C. 1127.

[94] *E. Zetland v. Hislop* (1882) 9 R. (H.L.) 40, 47.

[95] *Lauder*, 16 June 1815, F.C.; *Ewing v. Campbell* (1878) 5 R. 230; *Ewing v. Hastie* (1878) 5 R. 439; *E. Zetland, supra; Menzies v. Caledonian Canal Commrs.* (1900) 2 F. 953; cf. *Gold v. Houldsworth* (1870) 8 M. 1006 (long lease).

[96] *Carswell v. Goldie*, 1967 S.L.T. 339.

[97] *Macdonald v. Douglas*, 1963 S.C. 374.

[98] *Tailors of Aberdeen v. Coutts* (1840) 1 Rob. App. 26; *E. Zetland v. Hislop* (1882) 9 R. (H.L.) 40, 47; *S.C.W.S. v. Finnie*, 1937 S.C. 835; *Macdonald, supra.*

[99] *Campbell v. Clydesdale Bank* (1868) 6 M. 943; *Macdonald, supra.*

need not be a direct patrimonial interest,[1] nor need it be necessarily beneficial.[2] A contravening vassal may not contend that the superior has no interest in respect of a particular contravention.[3] Only a vassal has a title to sue the superior for declarator that he may do some act which appears to contravene; the vassal's tenant has no such title, not even if the vassal consents.[4]

The onus on a vassal denying the superior's interest is very heavy where the vassal is the original grantee, who is personally bound contractually as well as subject to a real burden, but less so in the case of a singular successor to him.[5]

Enforceability by co-feuars

Prima facie only the superior, who alone is a party to the feu-contract, can seek to enforce the restrictions. But another vassal holding an adjacent feu of the same superior may also have a title to enforce the restrictions, having a *jus quaesitum tertio* under the contract between superior and contravening vassal,[6] but only if there is some mutuality and community of rights and obligations between the feuars, which arises (1) if the superior makes it an express condition of his feu-contract that he will insert the same general restrictions in all feus granted by him in the same street or locality, or (2) by reasonable implication from a reference in all the feu-contracts to a common plan or scheme of building prepared and adopted by the superior; or (3) by mutual agreement between the feuars themselves. It is not sufficient to confer a title that the other vassal will be prejudiced by the contravention.[7] An adjacent feuar who has no title to object cannot overcome the objection by obtaining the consent and concurrence of the superior.[8] The whole of the titles of the property must be looked at for indication whether conferment of *jus quaesitum tertio* was intended; identity of restriction between one vassal's title and that of the

---

[1] *Stewart* v. *Bunten* (1878) 5 R. 1108; *Menzies* v. *Caledonian Canal Commrs.* (1900) 2 F. 953; *Forrest* v. *Watson's Hospital* (1905) 8 F. 341; cf. *Beattie* v. *Ure* (1876) 3 R. 634; *Naismith* v. *Cairnduff* (1876) 3 R. 863.

[2] *Menzies, supra.*

[3] *Waddell* v. *Campbell* (1898) 25 R. 456; *Calder* v. *North Berwick Police Commrs.* (1899) 1 F. 491; *Hill* v. *Millar* (1900) 2 F. 799; *Moyes* v. *McDiarmid* (1900) 2 F. 918.

[4] *Eagle Lodge, Ltd.* v. *Keir and Cawder Estates, Ltd.,* 1964 S.C. 30.

[5] *Waddell, supra; Menzies, supra.*

[6] In *Lawrence* v. *Scott,* 1965 S.C. 403, *jus quaesitum* was expressly conferred.

[7] *Hislop* v. *MacRitchie's Trs.* (1881) 8 R. (H.L.) 95; see also *Heriot's Hospital* v. *Cockburn* (1826) 2 W. & S. 302; *Edinburgh Mags.* v. *Macfarlane* (1858) 20 D. 156; *McGibbon* v. *Rankin* (1871) 9 M. 423; *Robertson* v. *N.B. Ry.* (1874) 1 R. 1218; *Maguire* v. *Burges,* 1909 S.C. 1283. A similar right may be conferred on co-disponees as well as on co-feuars: *Braid Hills Hotel* v. *Manuel,* 1909 S.C. 120; *Nicholson* v. *Glasgow Blind Asylum,* 1911 S.C. 391; *Botanic Gardens Picture Ho.* v. *Adamson,* 1924 S.C. 549; *Macdonald* v. *Douglas,* 1963 S.C. 374; *Lawrence* v. *Scott,* 1965 S.C. 403; A vassal's tenant has probably no *jus quaesitum*: see *Eagle Lodge Ltd.* v. *Keir and Cawder Estates Ltd.,* 1964 S.C. 30.

[8] *Hislop, supra.*

contravener is not in itself sufficient.[9] Restrictions need not be absolutely identical to be mutually enforceable so long as the restrictions
which anyone can enforce against any other are clearly ascertainable
from his title.[10]

The superiors' failure to impose the restrictions contained in one
grant in another granted later destroys the community of interest, and
cannot subsequently be cured.[11] Power reserved to the superior to
dispense with a restriction also destroys the mutuality requisite for
enforcement.[12]

The superior cannot discharge one vassal from the restrictions without the consent of the rest.[13]

The superior's consent to discharge the restrictions cannot affect the
right to object of a co-feuar, and still less when the co-feuar's renunciation impairs the superior's right to enforce the condition.[14]

The superior may be disentitled to enforce a restriction by his own
failure to perform his duties under the feu-contract.[15]

Acquiescence

A superior may be barred from enforcing building restrictions if he
has knowingly allowed material breaches to take place and to subsist
for some substantial time.[16] To infer acquiescence it must be shown
that the superior knew or had full means of knowledge that the
restriction was being disregarded. Silence does not by itself imply
consent, particularly if it is only unauthorized use rather than unauthorized building which is in issue.

Acquiescence is rather more readily inferred where the contravention involves not merely change of use but structural alterations involving considerable expense.[17]

Acquiescence, if established, extends only to the things acquiesced
in, or things *ejusdem generis*, and does not infer abandonment of all
the restrictions.[18]

[9] *Nicholson* v. *Glasgow Blind Asylum*, 1911 S.C. 391.

[10] *Botanic Gardens Picture Ho.* v. *Adamson*, 1924 S.C. 549.

[11] *Walker & Dick* v. *Park* (1888) 15 R. 477; *Botanic Gardens Picture Ho.* v. *Adamson*, 1924
S.C. 549; cf. *Carson* v. *Miller* (1863) 1 M. 604; *Calder* v. *Edinburgh Merchant Co.* (1886) 13 R.
623; *Johnston* v. *MacRitchie* (1893) 20 R. 539; *Bannerman's Trs.* v. *Howard & Wyndham*
(1902) 39 S.L.R. 445; *Thomson* v. *Mackie* (1903) 11 S.L.T. 562; *Murray's Trs.* v. *St. Margaret's
Convent*, 1907 S.C. (H.L.) 8.

[12] *Turner* v. *Hamilton* (1890) 17 R. 494.

[13] *Dalrymple* v. *Herdman* (1878) 5 R. 847.   [14] *Hislop, supra*, 102.

[15] *Stevenson* v. *Steel Co. of Scotland* (1899) 1 F. (H.L.) 91; *Cheyne* v. *Taylor* (1899) 7 S.L.T.
276.

[16] *Browns* v. *Burns* (1824) 2 S. 298; *Campbell* v. *Clydesdale Bank* (1868) 6 M. 943; *Ben
Challum Ltd.* v. *Buchanan*, 1955 S.C. 348.

[17] *Johnston* v. *Walker Trs.* (1897) 24 R. 1061, 1074; *Ben Challum, supra; Howard de Walden
Estates* v. *Bowmaker*, 1965 S.C. 163.

[18] *Stewart* v. *Bunten* (1878) 5 R. 1108, 1116; *Johnston, supra; Mactaggart* v. *Roemmele*, 1907
S.C. 1318.

Acquiescence by the superior does not bar a co-feuar, if he has *jus quaesitum tertio*, who can object only if he has a proper interest to do so. Hence a co-feuar is much less readily barred than is a superior from objecting to one breach by failure to object to a prior breach.[19]

Discharge of land obligations

Under the Conveyancing and Feudal Reform (Sc.) Act, 1970, S. 1, the Lands Tribunal for Scotland may on the application of a vassal discharge restrictive conditions in a feu-grant[20] and in doing so decide on whether neighbouring proprietors and parties benefited by the restriction as well as the superior.[21] But it cannot vary land obligations and substitute new ones altering the burden on burdened proprietors who did not consent.[22]

Superior's duties to vassals

The superior's main duties to his vassal, on granting the latter a feu, are to warrant his grant, and to relieve from public burdens in terms of his undertaking in the feu-charter. Such obligations run with the lands though not declared real burdens.[23] The superior's duties are the counterpart of the vassal's to him, and he cannot enforce the contract against the vassal if he is unwilling to perform his own part of the contract.[24]

---

[19] *Gould* v. *McCorquodale* (1869) 8 M. 165; *Stewart* v. *Bunten* (1878) 5 R. 1108; *Liddall* v. *Duncan* (1898) 25 R. 1119; *Mactaggart* v. *Roemmele*, 1907 S.C. 1318.

[20] *Robinson* v. *Hamilton*, 1974 S.L.T. (Lands Tr.) 2; *Owen* v. *Mackenzie*, 1974 S.L.T. (Lands Tr.) 11; *Sinclair* v. *Gillon*, 1974 S.L.T. (Lands Tr.) 18.

[21] *Smith* v. *Taylor*, 1972 S.C. 258. cf. *Crombie* v. *Heriot's Tr.*, 1972 S.L.T. (Lands Tr.) 40; *Bachoo* v. *Wimpey*, 1977 S.L.T. (Lands Tr.) 2.

[22] *Young*, 1978 S.L.T. (Lands Tr.) 28.

[23] *Stewart* v. *D. Montrose* (1863) 4 Macq. 499; *Dunbar* v. *British Fisheries Co.* (1878) 5 R. (H.L.) 221; *E. Zetland* v. *Hislop* (1882) 9 R. (H.L.) 40, 48.

[24] *Stevenson* v. *Steel Co. of Scotland* (1899) 1 F. (H.L.) 91.

THE ESTATE OF THE VASSAL

The grant of a feudal charter in favour of a vassal confers on him the *dominium utile* or actual beneficial rights in the whole tract of ground comprehended in the description of the lands conveyed, or held to be carried by the conveyance though not specially mentioned, together with all parts and pertinents of the land on the surface, such as buildings, woods and waters, or under it such as minerals, *a caelo usque ad centrum,*[1] but under exception of *regalia,* unless expressly granted,[2] and of any heritable subjects expressly reserved by the superior.

Barony privileges

The vassal was formerly entitled to additional right, by the erection of his lands into a barony by a general designation. A barony title included all the different rights of which it consisted, though not separately expressed. Thus the conveyance of a barony carries all that belongs to it, or has been possessed as part and pertinent of it, though not specially enumerated; possession of any part of the barony is reputed possession of the whole, and where the baron has a right to any of the *regalia,* a grant of the barony transmits them though not expressly mentioned.[3] A warrant to infeft in a barony has been found sufficient to authorize infeftment in lands described as part of the barony.[4]

But a barony title to lands with parts and pertinents may not be sufficient to give a right to submarine minerals without possession of them.[5]

Parts and pertinents

Among the heritable things rights to which pass as part and pertinent of lands, though not expressly mentioned, are buildings and other things attached to the soil, trees and growing plants, minerals under

---

[1] Stair II, 3, 75; Ersk. II, 6, 1–5; Bell, *Prin.* §737.
[2] Ersk. II, 6, 13; e.g. *Scott* v. *Dundee Mags.* (1886) 14 R. 191.
[3] Stair II, 3, 60; Mack. II, 3, 3; Ersk. II, 3, 46; II, 6, 18; see also *L.A.* v. *Hebden* (1868) 6 M. 489; *Mather* v. *Alexander,* 1926 S.C. 139.
[4] *Hill* v. *D. Montrose* (1833) 11 S. 958.
[5] *L.A.* v. *Wemyss* (1899) 2 F. (H.L.) 1.

the surface, water on or under the surface, and such privileges as go
with the occupation and use of the lands, or have been enjoyed along
with it for the prescriptive period.[6] What are parts and pertinents are
defined by possession for the prescriptive period along with, and under
the title of, the lands.[7]

Possession of heritage

Possession of heritage is constituted by actual occupation and use of
subjects, such occupation and use as is capable of being exercised in
relation to the particular subjects, and as evidences the other requisite
of possession, an intention to claim and hold the subjects against other
claimants.[8] Neither bare occupancy nor intention to claim is sufficient
by itself to constitute legal possession.

Possession may be exercised with different intentions according to
the capacity in which the possessor claims the right of occupancy and
use. A proprietor in possession claims for himself against everyone else
(natural possession); if he lets the lands to a tenant he exercises
possession mediately through his tenant (civil possession) and claims
possession against all, saving the tenant's rights, while the tenant
exercises natural possession and claims it against all, saving the landlord's radical right.

Possession as evidence of extent of lands conveyed

Possession of lands may be evidence of the extent of lands conveyed
by a charter or disposition.[9] No possession beyond it can avail against
a bounding title or boundary adequately described.[10] Thus a general
description containing lands possessed by named persons has been
held to limit the conveyance to the lands possessed, though other lands
were known as part of the lands generally described.[11]

But where lands were described by plan and measurements, neither
being strictly accurate, and the boundary was marked by a line of trees
planted by agreement, possession thereunder made the arranged
boundary binding on a singular successor.[12]

---

[6] Stair II, 3, 73; Ersk. II, 6, 4; Bell, *Prin.* §739–48; *Gordon* v. *Grant* (1850) 13 D. 1; *Baird* v. *Fortune* (1861) 4 Macq. 127; *L.A.* v. *Hunt* (1867) 5 M. (H.L.) 1; *N.B. Ry.* v. *Hutton* (1896) 23 R. 522.
[7] *Scott* v. *Lord Napier* (1869) 7 M. (H.L.) 35; *Agnew* v. *L.A.* (1873) 11 M. 309; *Stewart's Trs.* v. *Robertson* (1874) 1 R. 334; *Keith* v. *Smyth* (1884) 12 R. 66; *Cooper's Trs.* v. *Stark's Trs.* (1898) 25 R. 1160; *Meacher* v. *Blair-Oliphant*, 1913 S.C. 417.
[8] Stair II, 1, 9; Ersk. II, 1, 20; Bell, *Prin.* §1311.
[9] *Agnew* v. *L.A.* (1873) 11 M. 309; *Girdwood* v. *Paterson* (1873) 11 M. 647; *Keith* v. *Smyth* (1884) 12 R. 66; *Caledonian Canal Commrs.* v. *Smith* (1900) 8 S.L.T. 124.
[10] *N.B. Ry.* v. *Moon's Trs.* (1879) 6 R. 640; *Reid* v. *McColl* (1879) 7 R. 84; *Dalhousie's Tutors* v. *Minister of Lochlee* (1890) 17 R. 1060; 18 R. (H.L.) 72.
[11] *Murray* v. *Oliphant* (1634) Mor. 2262; see also *Mansfield* v. *Walker's Trs.* (1855) 1 S. & McL. 203.   [12] *Hetherington* v. *Galt* (1905) 7 F. 706.

Bona fide *and* mala fide *possession*

Possession may be bona fide or mala fide; a bona fide possessor is one who, whether rightly or wrongly, honestly believes himself proprietor of the lands on probable grounds and with a good conscience, such as a purchaser in good faith from one who had no title to sell the lands;[13] any other possessor is a mala fide possessor. A bona fide possessor is put in mala fide if another party produces clear and convincing evidence of his right of property and consequent right to possess, or by decree of court, it being a question of circumstances whether a judgment at first instance or only a final judgment on appeal has that effect. In either case he is bound to yield possession, with the whole fruits and profits of the lands during his possession.

Effects of bona fide *possession*

So long as a possessor possesses *in bona fide* he is entitled to keep the fruits that the subjects yielded while he had reason to think his title good, crops produced from seed sown by the bona fide possessor, and rents falling legally due during his possession, but not fruits not yet separated from the subject which produced them, such as growing timber.[14]

Possession as basis for prescription

Possession on an *ex facie* valid irredeemable title is essential for the fortification of the title by the positive prescription.[15]

Protection and recovery of possession

The actual possessor of heritage, who has some prima facie lawful title to possess the lands,[16] such as infeftment or tenancy,[17] or even a personal title, such as charter without infeftment thereon,[16] or at least a title prima facie applicable to the lands, even of servitude,[18] is entitled to protect his possession by interdict against threatened or actual encroachment, or, in case of actual dispossession, by action of ejection.[19] No amount of possession avails if contrary to the title under which the right of possession is claimed.[20] The requisite possession

[13] Ersk. II, 1, 25; *Huntly's Trs. v. Hallyburton's Trs.* (1880) 8 R. 50; cf. *Menzies v. M.* (1863) 1 M. 1025.

[14] Stair II, 1, 121; Ersk. II, 1, 26; cf. *Morrison v. St. Andrew's School Board*, 1918 S.C. 51.

[15] Ch. 5.4, *supra*.

[16] *Knox v. Brand* (1827) 5 S. 714; *Carson v. Miller* (1863) 1 M. 604, 611; see also *Dickson v. Dickie* (1863) 1 M. 1157; *Brown's Trs. v. Fraser* (1870) 8 M. 820.

[17] *Macdonald v. Dempster* (1871) 10 M. 94; *Galloway v. Cowden* (1885) 12 R. 578.

[18] *Liston v. Galloway* (1835) 14 S. 97; *Carson v. Miller* (1863) 1 M. 604; *Drummond v. Milligan* (1890) 17 R. 316.

[19] Stair IV, 26, 3; Bankt. II, 1, 33; Ersk. IV, 1, 50; *Mather v. Alexander*, 1926 S.C. 139.

[20] *Haigues v. Halyburton* (1705) Mor. 10623; *Lockhart v. Sinclair* (1724) Mor. 10625; *Bridges v. Elder* (1822) 1 S. 373.

must be bona fide,[21] have lasted uninterrupted for at least seven years,[22] have been exercised *nec vi nec clam nec precario*,[23] and have been prima facie attributable to some written title, and not merely to contract.[24]

The decision in a possessory action proceeds on the basis *spoliatus ante omnia restituendus* and the judgment does not decide any issue of heritable title. But standing a possessory judgment the possessor of lands is entitled to hold them as a bona fide possessor until ousted by an action in which his title is challenged and found inadequate to justify his possession.[25]

Right of exclusive occupation and use

The proprietor of lands has the exclusive right to occupation and use of the lands *a caelo usque ad centrum*. Thus he may prevent a neighbour from allowing his building[26] to project over the land[27] or from discharging rainwater therefrom on to the land,[28] or allowing his trees to overshadow the land.[29] But he may not object to the flight over his land of aircraft at a height which is reasonable in the circumstances.[30]

Right to exclude trespassers

Trespass is any temporary intrusion or entering upon the lands or heritages of another without his permission or legal justification.[31] Trespass may be committed by an individual, on foot, animal, boat or vehicle, or by allowing his animal to stray on to the proprietor's lands,[32] by picketing on a private road,[33] or entering premises without entitlement.[34]

The proprietor may prevent trespass by warning trespassers off his lands[35] but may not eject them forcibly unless the trespasser uses or threatens violence to the proprietor or is doing actual damage to

---

[21] *Montgomery* v. *Home* (1664) Mor. 10627; *Dunfermline* v. *Pitmedden* (1698) Mor. 10630.

[22] *Colquhoun* v. *Paton* (1859) 21 D. 429.

[23] *Calder* v. *Adam* (1870) 8 M. 645; *McKerron* v. *Gordon* (1876) 3 R. 429.

[24] *Neilson* v. *Vallance* (1828) 7 S. 182; *Carson, supra; Calder* v. *Adam* (1870) 8 M. 645.

[25] Stair IV, 17, 2; IV, 45, 17; Bankt. II, 1, 33; IV, 24, 49.

[26] Or even a cornice thereof: *Milne* v. *Mudie* (1828) 6 S. 967.

[27] *Hazle* v. *Turner* (1840) 2 D. 886; *Urquhart* v. *Melville* (1853) 16 D. 307; *McIntosh* v. *Scott* (1859) 21 D. 363.

[28] *Garriochs* v. *Kennedy* (1769) Mor. 13178.

[29] *Halkerston* v. *Wedderburn* (1781) Mor. 10495; *Lemmon* v. *Webb* [1895] A.C. 1.

[30] Civil Aviation Act, 1982, S. 76; *Steel-Maitland* v. *British Airways*, 1981 S.L.T. 110.

[31] cf. *McAdam* v. *Laurie* (1876) 3 R. (J.) 20.

[32] *Robertson* v. *Wright* (1885) 13 R. 174; *McLeod* v. *Davidson* (1886) 14 R. 92; *Thurlow* v. *Tait* (1893) 1 S.L.T. 62; *Arneil* v. *Paterson*, 1931 S.C. (H.L.) 117; cf. *Winans* v. *Macrae* (1885) 12 R. 1051.

[33] *Merry* v. *Cuninghame* v. *Aitken* (1895) 22 R. 247.

[34] *Merryton Coal Co.* v. *Anderson* (1890) 18 R. 203.

[35] *Mather* v. *Alexander*, 1926 S.C. 139.

property[36] and even then may use only the force reasonably necessary in the circumstances. An intruder into a private house may more readily be forcibly ejected. The proprietor may obtain interdict if there is threat or probability of continuance or repetition of the trespass,[37] unless it were done in good faith[38] or with no intention to claim a right,[39] or no harm was done.[40] Damages may be recovered only if the trespasser has done actual damage.[41] Interdict is not justified by mere assertion of a right without actual trespass.[42]

Trespass is elided if authorized by the proprietor,[43] or justified by the public interest,[44] in case of emergency, to escape from pressing danger or peril apprehended, to recover goods or animals straying on to the lands or being taken there,[45] in pursuit of foxes, which have been preying on sheep or poultry,[46] to investigate or prevent threatened or reasonably suspected crime[47] or in other circumstances of necessity. A person may not, however, enter the lands of another to hunt, save by permission.[48]

Many statutes authorize entries which would otherwise be trespasses,[49] and judicial warrant may authorize entry.[50]

Trespass is a criminal offence only in the case of a person who lodges in any premises, or occupies or encamps on any land which is private property without the consent and permission of the owner or legal occupier[51] and in cases of trespass in quest of fish or game.[52]

---

[36] *Bell* v. *Shand* (1870) 7 S.L.R. 267; *Aitchison* v. *Thorburn* (1870) 7 S.L.R. 347; *Wood* v. *N.B. Ry.* (1899) 2 F. 1; cf. *Geils* v. *Thompson* (1872) 10 M. 327. The landowner may be criminally liable for assault: *E. Eglinton* v. *Campbell* (1770) McLaurin 505; *Craw* (1827) Syme 188, 210; *Reid* (1837) 2 Swin. 236; *Kennedy* (1838) 2 Swin. 213.

[37] *Baird* v. *Thomson* (1825) 3 S. 448; *Jolly* v. *Brown* (1828) 6 S. 872; *McKerron* v. *Gordon* (1876) 3 R. 429; *Hay's Tr.* v. *Young* (1877) 4 R. 398; *Steuart* v. *Stephen* (1877) 4 R. 873; *Macleod* v. *Davidson* (1886) 14 R. 92; *Merryton Coal Co.* v. *Anderson* (1890) 18 R. 203; *Warrand* v. *Watson* (1905) 8 F. 253; *Inverurie Mags.* v. *Sorrie*, 1956 S.C. 175; see also *Johnson* v. *Grant*, 1923 S.C. 789; *Macleay* v. *Macdonald*, 1928 S.C. 776; 1929 S.C. 371.

[38] *Hay's Tr.*, *supra*; *Macleod*, *supra*.

[39] *Steuart* v. *Stephen* (1877) 4 R. 873.   [40] *Winans* v. *Macrae* (1885) 12 R. 1051.

[41] *Graham* v. *D. Hamilton* (1868) 6 M. 965; *Scott's Trs.* v. *Moss* (1889) 17 R. 32; *L.A.* v. *Glengarnock Iron Co.*, 1909, 1 S.L.T. 15; *Lock* v. *Taylor*, 1976 S.L.T. 238.

[42] *Warrand* v. *Watson* (1905) 8 F. 253; *Inverurie Mags.*, *supra*.

[43] cf. *Steuart* v. *Stephen* (1877) 4 R. 873; *Inland Revenue* v. *Anderson*, 1922 S.C. 284.

[44] Bell, *Prin.* §956; Hume, *Lect.* III, 206.

[45] *E. Morton* v. *McMillan* (1893) 1 S.L.T. 92.

[46] *Colquhoun* v. *Buchanan* (1785) Mor. 4997.

[47] *Shepherd* v. *Menzies* (1900) 2 F. 443; *Southern Bowling Club* v. *Ross* (1902) 4 F. 405.

[48] *Watson* v. *Errol* (1763) Mor. 4991; *M. Tweeddale* v. *Dalrymple* (1778) Mor. 4992; *E. Breadalbane* v. *Livingstone* (1780) Mor. 4999.

[49] See e.g. Burgh Police (Sc.) Act, 1892; Public Health (Sc.) Act, 1897, Ss. 26, 28, 45, 82, 98, 109, 114; Rights of Entry (Gas and Electricity Boards) Act, 1954, S. 1; Mines and Quarries Act, 1954, S. 145; Agriculture (Safety, Health & Welfare Prov.) Act, 1956, Ss. 10(2), 11; Factories Act, 1961, S. 146; Offices, Shops and Railway Premises Act, 1963, S. 53.

[50] *Stewart* v. *Roach*, 1950 S.C. 318.

[51] Trespass (Sc.) Act, 1865, S. 3; *Paterson* v. *Robertson*, 1944 J.C. 166 (squatters).

[52] See further, *infra*, and *Ward* v. *Robertson*, 1938 J.C. 32.

Under the Winter Herding Act, 1686, possessors of lands are ordained to have their horses, nolt, sheep, swine and goats herded the
whole year and enclosed at night. If they contravene they are liable to a
penalty of half a mark per beast as well as for the damage done to the
planting.[53] The aggrieved neighbour may detain the straying beasts
until paid the penalty and his expenses in keeping them, but not if they
had ceased to trespass before being detained.[54] Restitution of a
poinded animal must be refused if the statutory penalty has not been
rendered.[54] If animals are unlawfully detained, there is liability in
damages if they are lost.[56] Interdict against allowing animals to
trespass has been refused where it was not proved that the owner had
failed to take reasonable precautions to prevent the cattle from
trespassing.[57]

A proprietor must take reasonable care for the safety of even
trespassers who come on his lands[58] which imports a limited duty to
fence and warn of dangers.[59] He may not set man-traps or spring-guns
against trespassing persons or animals.[60]

Encroachment

Encroachment in the permanent usurpation by another of some
portion of a man's lands,[61] as by trees overhanging his land,[62] a
building projecting over it,[63] a crane jib swinging over it,[64] dumping
rubbish on another's lands[65] attaching a flue to the outside of a gable,[66]
attaching a sign to another's building,[67] or to a common entrance,[68]
erecting a shop signboard above the centre line of the joists between
shop and first floor,[69] constructing a road through another's lands,[70]

[53] cf. *Shaw & Mackenzie v. Ewart*, 2 March 1809, F.C.; *Farquharson v. Walker*, 1977 S.L.T.
(Sh. Ct.) 22.
[54] *McArthur v. Jones* (1878) 6 R. 41.
[55] *McArthur v. Miller* (1873) 1 R. 248.
[56] *Fraser v. Smith* (1899) 1 F. 487.
[57] *Robertson v. Wright* (1885) 13 R. 174.
[58] Occupiers' Liability (Sc.) Act, 1960, S. 2.
[59] *Black v. Cadell* (1812) 5 Paton 567; *Hislop v. Durham* (1842) 4 D. 1168; *Prentice v. Assets
Co.* (1889) 17 R. 484; *McGlone v. B.R. Board*, 1966 S.C. (H.L.) 1.
[60] *H.M.A. v. Craw* (1827) Syme 188, 210.   [61] Hume, Lect. III, 202.
[62] *Halkerston v. Wedderburn* (1781) Mor. 10495; *Lemmon v. Webb* [1895] A.C. 1.
[63] Ersk. II, 9, 9; Bell, *Prin.* §941, 967; *Graham v. Greig* (1838) 1 D. 171; *McIntosh v. Scott*
(1859) 21 D. 363; *Leonard v. Lindsay* (1886) 13 R. 958; *Wilson v. Pottinger*, 1908 S.C. 580;
Brown v. Barry, 1957 S.C. 351.
[64] *Brown v. Lee Constructions*, 1977 S.L.T. (Notes) 61.
[65] cf. *Whitwham v. Westminster Brymbo Coal Co.* [1896] 1 Ch. 894; Deposit of Poisonous
Waste Act, 1972.
[66] *Walker v. Braidwood* (1797) Hume 512; cf. *Gellatly v. Arroll* (1863) 1 M. 592.
[67] *Thomson v. Crombie* (1776) Mor. 13182; *Drysdale v. Lowrie*, 13 May 1812, F.C.
[68] *Mackenzie v. Murray* (1812) Hume 520.
[69] *Alexander v. Butchart* (1875) 3 R. 156; *McArly v. French's Trs.* (1883) 10 R. 574; *Birrell v.
Lumley* (1905) 12 S.L.T. 719. cf. *Girdwood v. Paterson* (1873) 11 M. 647.
[70] *Fergusson Buchanan v. Dunbartonshire C.C.*, 1924 S.C. 42.

laying a pipe through another's land,[71] letting the roots of trees penetrate another's land,[72] carrying a quarry or mine into a neighbour's lands and extracting the minerals therefrom. A person is, in general, not barred from objecting by the acquiescence of a predecessor in title in the encroachment.[73]

Encroachments underground

The proprietor of lands may object to pipes laid without authority under the surface of his lands,[74] or the roots of trees penetrating through the soil.[75] In so far as he is entitled to the minerals he may interdict another from mining underneath his lands and abstracting the minerals thereunder. Where minerals under his lands have been wrongfully abstracted by another, damages are recoverable for the loss, measured, in the case of inadvertent or mistaken encroachment, by the value of the minerals less the cost of winning and raising them,[76] but in the case of deliberate, fraudulent, furtive or wholly unauthorized encroachment, by the value of the minerals less the cost of raising only.[77] Occasionally other methods of measuring damages have been adopted.[78]

Right to support

A landowner is entitled as a natural right of property to have his land maintained in its natural state and not affected by operations on adjacent or subjacent land which cause damage by withdrawal of support therefrom.[79] The right entitles him to complain of operations, such as mining or quarrying, only if they cause subsidence or otherwise

[71] Galbreath v. Armour (1845) 4 Bell 374; cf. Hazle v. Turner (1840) 2 D. 886.
[72] Lemmon v. Webb [1895] A.C. 1; McCombe v. Reid [1955] 2 Q.B. 429; Davey v. Harrow Corpn. [1958] 1 Q.B. 60.
[73] Brown v. Barry, 1957 S.C. 351.
[74] Bell, Prin. §942; Galbreath v. Armour (1845) 4 Bell 374; cf. Hazle v. Turner (1840) 2 D. 886.
[75] Hume, Lect. III, 203; Butler v. Standard Telephones [1940] 1 All E.R. 121; Davey v. Harrow Corpn. [1958] 1 Q.B. 60.
[76] Hilton v. Woods (1867) L.R. 4 Eq. 432; Jegon v. Vivian (1871) L.R. 6 Ch. 742; Re United Merthyr Coal Co. (1872) L.R. 15 Eq. 46; Ashton v. Stock (1877) 6 Ch. D. 719; Trotter v. Maclean (1879) 13 Ch. D. 574; Houldsworth v. Brand's Trs. (1877) 4 R. 369; Whitwham v. Westminster Brymbo Coal Co. [1896] 2 Ch. 538.
[77] Durham v. Hood (1871) 9 M. 474; Ramsay v. Blair (1876) 3 R. (H.L.) 41; Wilsons v. Waddell (1876) 4 R. (H.L.) 29; Livingstone v. Rawyards Coal Co. (1880) 7 R. (H.L.) 1; Llynvi Co. v. Brogden (1870) L.R. 11 Eq. 188; Phillips v. Homfray (1871) L.R. 6 Ch. 770; Taylor v. Mostyn (1886) 33 Ch. D. 226; Bulli Co. v. Osborne [1889] A.C. 351.
[78] Livingstone, supra; Davidson's Trs. v. Caledonian Ry. (1898) 23 R. 45; see also D. Portland v. Wood's Trs., 1927 S.C. (H.L.) 1.
[79] Bell, Prin. §970; Humphries v. Brogden (1848) 12 Q.B. 739; Caledonian Ry. v. Sprot (1856) 2 Macq. 449; Bonomi v. Backhouse (1861) 9 H.L.C. 503; Elliott v. N.E. Ry. (1863) 10 H.L.C. 333; Buchanan v. Andrew (1873) 11 M. (H.L.) 13; Livingstone v. Rawyards Coal Co. (1880) 7 R. (H.L.) 1; Dalton v. Angus (1881) 6 App. Cas. 740; White v. Dixon (1883) 10 R. (H.L.) 45; Angus v. N.C.B., 1955 S.C. 175; L.A. v. Reo Stakis Organisation, 1980 S.L.T. 237.

appreciably damage or interfere with the use of the complainer's lands.[80] Each distinct subsidence causing damage is a separate ground of action, even though caused by one mining operation.[81]

The landowner may seek interdict against operations under or alongside his land likely to produce injury or which will necessarily result in subsidence.[82] Alternatively, or additionally, he may recover damages for any actual and appreciable damage caused by subsidence.[83] Negligence need not be proved.[84]

Where the support is afforded in part by underground water or running sand an adjacent proprietor may be entitled, without liability for subsidence, to drain it or appropriate it.[85]

Support to lands already built on

Where buildings had been erected on the surface before the adjacent or subjacent ground was granted to another, the other is prima facie bound to continue to afford to the granter's lands the support which they were being afforded at the time of severance. A contractual obligation to pay for damage to buildings may supersede the common law obligation, but may not apply to new buildings on the site of buildings existing at the date of the contract.[86]

Support to lands subsequently built on

Where, however, after the adjacent or subjacent ground had been granted to one person buildings are erected on the surface by the granter or his successors, the latter has no claim for subsidence so far as caused by the additional loading on the surface, and similarly where the surface is granted, the subjacent strata being reserved.[87]

A contractual obligation to pay for surface damages has been held not restricted to the state of the ground at the date when surface and mineral estates were separated, but to cover damage to a house subsequently built, though opinions were reserved as to the rights of parties if the ground became covered with streets and buildings.[88]

---

[80] *Bonomi, supra; Darley Main Colliery Co.* v. *Mitchell* (1886) 11 App. Cas. 127; *Gray* v. *Burns* (1894) 2 S.L.T 187.

[81] *Darley Main, supra; Geddes* v. *Haldane* (1906) 13 S.L.T. 707; *D. Abercorn* v. *Merry & Cuninghame,* 1909, 1 S.L.T. 321.

[82] *Buchanan, supra; White* v. *Dixon* (1881) 9 R. 375; *Shawrigg Fireclay Co.* v. *Mitchell Collieries Ltd.* (1903) 5 F. 1131.

[83] *Darley Main, supra; West Leigh Colliery Co.* v. *Tunnicliffe* [1908] A.C. 27.

[84] *Angus* v. *N.C.B.,* 1955 S.C. 175, 181.

[85] *Bald* v. *Alloa Coal Co.* (1854) 16 D. 870; *Elliott, supra; Popplewell* v. *Hodkinson* (1869) L.R. 4 Ex. 248; *Jordeson* v. *Sutton Gas Co.* [1899] 2 Ch. 217.

[86] *Barr* v. *Baird* (1904) 6 F. 524.

[87] *Hamilton* v. *Turner* (1867) 5 M. 1086; *Dryburgh* v. *Fife Coal Co.* (1905) 7 F. 1083; *Geddes's Trs.* v. *Haldane* (1906) 14 S.L.T. 328.

[88] *Neill's Trs.* v. *Dixon* (1880) 7 R. 741.

Where the owner of lands grants the surface for a specified purpose which involves loading the surface, the grant, in the absence of evident contrary intention, carries by implication a right to reasonable and necessary support for the works from the granter's adjacent lands and subjacent strata, and this obligation transmits with the lands to a successor of the granter.[89]

The same principles apply in respect of land burdened by railways, roads, pipelines, sewers, or other structures.[90] The Railways Clauses Consolidation (Sc.) Act, 1845, Ss. 70–8, reserves the minerals under a railway line to the landowner, but gives the railway authority power to prevent working within a limited distance on paying compensation.[91]

Variation by right of contract

The right to be supported or to recover compensation for damage caused by withdrawal of support may be modified by contract, particularly when ownership of surface and of subjacent strata are separated, or mineral leases granted. Thus a superior may feu lands, reserving the minerals and excluding liability for damage to the vassal by working the minerals,[92] or reserving right to work in a manner injurious to the surface,[93] or right to bring down the surface on payment of damages.[94]

Many cases turn on the interpretation of particular phrases in the light of their circumstances.[95]

Statutory provisions

The Coal-Mining (Subsidence) Act, 1950, imposed on the National Coal Board the duty to carry out repairs or make payments in respect of subsidence damage after 1st January, 1947, and affecting any dwelling house. There was power also to effect preventive works. The statutory right was alternative to any other rights in respect of the damage.

[89] *Caledonian Ry.* v. *Sprot* (1856) 2 Macq. 449; *Dalton* v. *Angus* (1881) 6 App. Cas. 740; *N.B. Ry.* v. *Turner* (1904) 6 F. 900.

[90] *Caledonian Ry.* v. *Sprot* (1856) 2 Macq. 449; *Caledonian Ry.* v. *L. Belhaven* (1857) 3 Macq. 56; *Caledonian Ry.* v. *Henderson* (1876) 4 R. 140; *Caledonian Ry.* v. *Dixon* (1880) 7 R. (H.L.) 117; *Aitken's Trs.* v. *Rawyards Coal Co.* (1894) 22 R. 201; *N.B. Ry.* v. *Turners* (1904) 6 F. 900; *Clippens Oil Co.* v. *Edinburgh Water Trs.* (1904) 6 F. (H.L.) 7; *Midlothian C.C.* v. *N.C.B.*, 1960 S.C. 308; see also *Mid and East Calder Gas Light Co.* v. *Oakbank Oil Co.* (1891) 18 R. 788.

[91] *D. Hamilton's Trs.* v. *Caledonian Ry.* (1905) 7 F. 847; *N.B. Ry.* v. *Forth Bridge Ry. Co.* 1922 S.C. 215. See also Harbours, Docks and Piers Clauses Act, 1847.

[92] *Buchanan* v. *Andrew* (1873) 11 M. (H.L.) 13; *White* v. *Dixon* (1883) 10 R (H.L.) 45.

[93] *Bank of Scotland* v. *Stewart* (1891) 18 R. 957.

[94] *Anderson* v. *McCracken Bros.* (1900) 2 F. 780; *Pringle* v. *Carron Co.* (1905) 7 F. 820; see also *Gray* v. *Burns* (1894) 2 S.L.T. 187.

[95] *Galbraith's Tr.* v. *Eglinton Iron Co.* (1868) 7 M. 167; *Hallpenny* v. *Dewar* (1898) 25 R. 889; *Taylor* v. *Auchinlea Coal Co.*, 1912, 2 S.L.T. 10; *Dryburgh* v. *Fife Coal Co.* (1905) 7 F. 1083.

The Coal-Mining (Subsidence) Act, 1957, applies to subsidence damage caused after its date by the withdrawal of support in connection with the mining of coal. The National Coal Board must execute remedial works or pay the cost of execution of remedial works, and may execute preventive works. It must also pay damages for death or disablement resulting from injury caused by subsidence damage.

The Mines (Working Facilities and Support) Act, 1966, empowers the Court of Session, if satisfied that it is expedient in the national interest and that it is not reasonably practicable to obtain the right by private arrangement, to grant any person a right to search or work any specified minerals, together with certain ancillary rights including a right to let down the surface. Restrictions may be imposed on working minerals required for support.

Rights in buildings

Buildings already on lands are conveyed by feudal grant as part and pertinent of the lands and the proprietor of lands is prima facie entitled to erect or demolish buildings on his land, subject to any restrictions in his feu-charter and to obtaining planning and other necessary permission.

Buildings must be erected entirely on the proprietor's lands save that where an implied contract can be inferred from a feuing plan or other circumstances the owner of one of several adjoining lots may erect a gable half on the adjacent land without the other proprietor's consent, and reclaim half of the cost when the other proprietor comes to use the common gable.[96]

The proprietor of buildings is entitled to have them supported by any adjoining buildings with which he has such common[97] gables or walls and may object to interference with the common gable if likely to harm his building.[98] The proprietor of an upper floor is entitled to support from lower storeys.[99]

A servitude right of support is recognized in two cases. By the servitude *tigni immittendi* the owner of one building has the right to insert a beam or other structural member of his building into the wall of another building, keep it there, and renew it as necessary.[1] By the servitude *oneris ferendi* the owner of the one building has the right to

[96] *Rodger* v. *Russell* (1873) 11 M. 671; *Jack* v. *Begg* (1875) 3 R. 35; *Sinclair* v. *Brown* (1882) 10 R. 45; *Robertson* v. *Scott* (1886) 13 R. 1127; *Berkeley* v. *Baird* (1895) 22 R. 372; *Fraser* v. *Campbell* (1895) 22 R. 558; *Baird* v. *Alexander* (1898) 25 R. (H.L.) 35; *Roberts* v. *Galloway* (1898) 6 S.L.T. 25; *Calder* v. *Pope* (1900) 8 S.L.T. 149; *Stark's Trs.* v. *Cooper's Trs.* (1900) 2 F. 1257; *Wilson* v. *Pottinger*, 1908 S.C. 580.
[97] Usually miscalled 'mutual' gables.
[98] *Lamont* v. *Cumming* (1875) 2 R. 784; *Leonard* v. *Lindsay & Benzie* (1886) 13 R. 968.
[99] *MacNab* v. *McDevitt*, 1971 S.L.T. (Sh. Ct.) 41.
[1] Inst. II, 1, 29; Dig. 8, 2, and 3; 50, 16, 62; Stair II, 7, 6; Forbes, II, 4, 3, 2; Mack. II, 9, 6, 7; Bankt. II, 7, 7; Ersk. II, 9, 7; Bell, *Prin.* §1003.

have his building supported by another's building underneath. In this case it implies an obligation on the other to maintain his building.[2]

A proprietor of buildings is also entitled to have light from the street for his building.[3]

A burden on property in favour of another part of it must either enter the titles or be created as one of the recognized servitudes.[4]

Whether the proprietor of a part of a building can alter or extend it against the wishes of the proprietor of other parts of the building depends on the titles, any restrictions therein, the existence or not of common property in the part to be altered and any injury likely to result from the change.[5]

Rights to minerals

Save in so far as minerals have been reserved by the Crown or superiors, or been statutorily expropriated,[6] the proprietor has the right to all minerals below the surface of his lands[7] or under highways,[8] lochs[9] and rivers[10] and he may work them, or lease them to another to work.[11]

Timber

Apart from private ownership and development of woodlands the Forestry Commission has the duty of promoting the development of the afforestation and the production and supply of timber, including the establishment asnd maintenance of adequate reserves of growing trees.[12] The Commission may manage, plant and use land put at their disposal by the Secretary of State for Scotland.[13] He may acquire by purchase, lease or exchange, land suitable for afforestation, or acquire it compulsorily; certain categories of land are excepted.[14]

Proprietors of land may make forestry dedication agreements with

[2] Dig. 8, 5, 6–8; *Murray* v. *Brownhill* (1715) Mor. 1452; *Troup* v. *Aberdeen Heritable Securities Co.*, 1916 S.C. 918.

[3] *Glasgow Union Ry. Co.* v. *Hunter* (1870) 8 M. (H.L.) 156; *Donald* v. *Esslemont & Macintosh*, 1923 S.C. 122.

[4] *Alexander* v. *Buchart* (1875) 3 R. 156.

[5] *Johnston* v. *White* (1877) 4 R. 721; *Barclay* v. *McEwen* (1880) 7 R. 792; *Boswell* v. *Edinburgh Mags.* (1881) 8 R. 986; *Arrol* v. *Inches* (1887) 14 R. 394; *Turner* v. *Hamilton* (1890) 17 R. 494; *Todd* v. *Wilson* (1894) 22 R. 172.

[6] Petroleum (Production) Act, 1934, S. 1; Coal Industry Nationalisation Act, 1946, Ss. 5, 64(3), and Sched. 1.

[7] *Bruce* v. *Erskine* (1716) Mor. 9642; *Mitchell* v. *York Buildings Co.* (1777) 6 Pat. 795.

[8] *Wishart* v. *Wyllie* (1853) 1 Macq. 389.

[9] *Baird* v. *Robertson* (1839) 1 D. 1051; *Scott* v. *L. Napier* (1869) 7 M. (H.L.) 35.

[10] *Wishart, supra; Bicket* v. *Morris* (1866) 4 M. (H.L.) 44; *Orr Ewing* v. *Colquhoun's Trs.* (1877) 4 R. (H.L.) 116.

[11] *Borthwick-Norton* v. *Gavin Paul*, 1947 S.C. 659.

[12] Forestry Act, 1967 Ss. 1–2. See also Forestry Act, 1979.

[13] 1967 Act, S. 3.

[14] Ibid., S. 39–40.

the Forestry Commissioners, which may be recorded in the Register of Sasines and are then enforceable by the Commissioners against any person having an interest in the land and any person deriving title from him, but not against a bona fide purchaser for value of the land prior to the recording of the agreement.[15] If the Commission is satisfied that trees are being damaged by rabbits, hares, or vermin by reason of the occupier of the land's failure to destroy them, it may authorize any competent person to do so, and charge the occupier.[16]

Save in excepted cases a felling licence from the Commission is required for the felling of growing trees[17] and the Commission may give felling directions to the owner of trees requiring him to fell them within a stated period.[18]

Rights in lochs

A sea-loch is an extension of the sea and seashore and no landed proprietor acquires right to the *solum* or the water thereof.

An inland loch surrounded entirely by the lands of one proprietor belongs entirely to him, both as to the *solum* and the water,[19] and he has exclusive rights of fishing.[20] If however a stream runs out of it he may not so use the loch as to infringe the rights of riparian owners in the stream.[21]

If the lands of more than one landowner front on the loch, the titles, or the titles supplemented by evidence of possession, may indicate that one owner has exclusive property in the whole loch,[22] but otherwise each proprietor has an exclusive right in the *solum ex adverso* of his lands out to the middle of the loch[23] and all have a right of property in the water in common, with liberty to sail or fish on the surface and to use it for primary purposes.[24] The Court may regulate or limit the number of boats each proprietor may put on the loch.[25]

If an inland loch is used for navigation, the principles applicable to navigable rivers probably apply.[26]

[15] Ibid., S. 5.
[16] Ibid., S. 7.
[17] Ibid., S.s 9–17.
[18] Ibid., S.s 18–35.
[19] Stair II, 3, 7, 3; Bankt. II, 3, 12; Bell, *Prin.* §651; *Macdonnell* v. *Caledonian Canal Commrs.* (1830) 8 S. 881.
[20] *Montgomerie* v. *Watson* (1861) 23 D. 635.   [21] Bell, *Prin.* §1110.
[22] *Scott* v. *Lord Napier* (1869) 7 M. (H.L.) 35; *Stewart's Trs.* v. *Robertson* (1874) 1 R. 334; *Meacher* v. *Blair Oliphant*, 1913 S.C.417.
[23] *Cochrane* v. *E. Minto* (1815) 6 Pat. 139.
[24] Bell, *Prin.* §1111; *Menzies* v. *MacDonald* (1854) 16 D. 827; 2 Macq. 463; *Stewart's Trs.*, *supra*; *Mackenzie* v. *Bankes* (1878) 5 R. (H.L.) 192; *Menzies* v. *Wentworth* (1901) 3 F. 941. As to reservoirs see *Kilsyth* v. *Fish Assocn.* v. *McFarlane*, 1937 S.C. 757.
[25] *Mackenzie* v. *Bankes* (1878) 5 R. (H.L.) 192; *Menzies* v. *Wentworth* (1901) 3 F. 941.
[26] *Macdonell* v. *Caledonian Canal Commrs.* (1830) 8 S. 881; *Colquhoun's Trs.* v. *Orr Ewing* (1877) 4 R. 344; *Leith Buchanan* v. *Hogg*, 1931 S.C. 204.

Rights in surface and percolating water

Surface and percolating water are *partes soli*. A landowner is entitled to appropriate and use water which gathers on the surface as in a bog, or percolates through the soil of his land, and to abstract it by well, even to the detriment of a neighbour's well enjoyed for the prescriptive period.[27] He may drain the water into a stream, but this gives him no greater rights in the water of the stream.[28] Water on or in land, and pipes and drains, cannot be conveyed to other than the owner of the soil, but another party may have a servitude right to draw water from a landowner's land.[29]

Surface water may be discharged on to an inferior neighbour's land if flowing naturally that way,[30] but surface water may not be drained in a direction other than its natural flow, nor water pumped to the surface or channelled from a stream.[31] An inferior proprietor cannot do anything to prevent the water coming on his land or to cause it to flow back.[32] Nor can he insist on a continuance of a flow of water from higher lands.[33]

Land drainage

Under the Land Drainage (Sc.) Act, 1930, an owner or occupier of agricultural land may get the sheriff to ordain an adjacent owner or occupier to maintain the banks and cleanse the channel of a watercourse, or obtain authority to make underground main drains through the land of another owner.

Under the Land Drainage (Sc.) Act, 1958, the owner of any agricultural land may apply to the Secretary of State for Scotland for an improvement order authorizing the execution of such drainage works as will improve the drainage of the land or prevent or mitigate flooding or erosion. The order may provide for an improvement committee of the owners of land affected discharging functions under the order (Ss. 1–3). The authorized persons must make good damage to land consequential on their operations, and compensate the owners of non-agricultural land and the occupiers of any land, for damage suffered (Ss. 4–5). An owner may increase the rent of an agricultural holding

---

[27] *Linlithgrow Mags.* v. *Elphinstone* (1768) Mor. 12805; *Chasemore* v. *Richards* (1859) 7 H.L. Cas. 349; *Mayor of Bradford* v. *Pickles* [1895] A.C. 587; *Milton* v. *Glen Moray Glenlivet Distillery Co.* (1898) 1 F. 135.

[28] *Cowan* v. *L. Kinnaird* (1865) 4 M. 236; *Stevenson* v. *Hogganfield Bleaching Co.* (1892) 30 S.L.R. 86.

[29] *Crichton* v. *Turnbull,* 1946 S.C. 52.

[30] *Campbell* v. *Bryson* (1865) 3 M. 254; *Anderson* v. *Robertson,* 1958 S.C. 367.

[31] Ersk. II, 9, 2; *Campbell* v. *Bryson* (1864) 3 M. 254; *Young* v. *Bankier Distillery* (1893) 20 R. (H.L.) 76; *Anderson, supra.*

[32] *Montgomerie* v. *Buchanan's Trs.* (1853) 15 D. 853.

[33] *L. Blantyre* v. *Dunn* (1848) 10 D. 509; *Ardrossan Mags.* v. *Dickie* (1906) 14 S.L.T. 349.

equal to the increase in rental value attributable to the drainage (S. 6).
The Secretary of State may require the execution or maintenance of
protective works, and may make grants towards improvement expenditure (Ss. 8–9).

Flood prevention

The Flood Prevention (Sc.) Act, 1961, empowers local authorities,
alone or in combination, to carry out works for the prevention or
mitigation of flooding of non-agricultural land, on both land within
and on land outwith their areas (Ss. 1–3). Flood prevention operations
must be carried out under a flood prevention scheme made by the local
authority and confirmed by the Secretary of State (S. 4). They may be
authorized to acquire compulsorily any land required for the exercise
of their powers under the Act (S. 7). Claims are competent for depreciation in the value of any interest in land by the operations (S. 11).

Drainage from mines

In mines a mine-owner may work his minerals to the boundary of his
lands, though he may thereby drain water into adjacent workings.[34]
The inferior mine-owner must receive the water or leave a barrier of
minerals on his side of the boundary.[35] But the superior mine-owner
may not pump or otherwise artificially direct water which would not
have naturally flowed there into an inferior mine-owner's strata,[36] nor
pump it into a stream with the effect of polluting it.[37]

Rights in navigable rivers

Where a river is tidal and navigable,[38] it is subject to public rights of
navigation. The *alveus* is vested in the Crown in trust for public
purposes[39] and the Crown, or a statutory body in its place, may
improve the channel and prevent encroachment.[40] The foreshore,
unless conveyed by grant, is also vested in the Crown.[41] Subject to the
public rights the banks belong to the owner of the adjacent lands, and
the public have the use of the banks only by custom, grant or use for

[34] *Baird* v. *Monkland Iron Co.* (1862) 24 D. 1418.
[35] *Blair* v. *Hunter Finlay & Co.* (1870) 9 M. 204; *Durham* v. *Hood* (1871) 9 M. 474.
[36] *Turner* v. *Ballandene* (1834) 7 W. & S. 163; *Blair, supra; Bankier Distillery* v. *Young* (1892)
19 R. 1083; affd. 20 R. (H.L.) 76.
[37] *D. Buccleuch* v. *Gilmerton Coal Co.* (1894) 1 S.L.T. 576.
[38] This is a question of fact: see *Bowie* v. *M. Ailsa* (1887) 14 R. 649.
[39] *L.A.* v. *Clyde Nav. Trs.* (1852) 1 Macq. 46; *Colquhoun's Trs.* v. *Orr Ewing* (1877) 4 R.
(H.L.) 116.
[40] *Colquhoun's Trs., supra;* see also *L. Blantyre* v. *Clyde Nav. Trs.* (1881) 8 R. (H.L.) 47.
[41] *L.A.* v. *Lord Blantyre* (1879) 6 R. (H.L.) 72; *Buchanan* v. *L.A.* (1882) 9 R. 1218.

the prescriptive period.[42] The right to fish, unless conveyed by grant, is in the Crown.[43]

Where a river is non-tidal but navigable both *alveus* and banks belong to the riparian proprietors but the public have liberty of use of the water for purposes of navigation by any vessel which can be described as a boat, including canoes,[44] and probably also the right to moor and anchor.[45] Hence the proprietors cannot alter the *alveus* so as to interfere with the right of navigation. The right to fish belongs to the riparian proprietors.[46]

Rights in private (non-navigable) rivers and streams—the alveus

Where water flows in a definite channel of any size on or under the surface the bed and banks of the stream or river belong to the proprietor of the adjacent lands or, where the stream is the boundary, each owns the bed of the stream, so far as *ex adverso* of his lands, *ad medium filum*.[47] But no proprietor may interfere with the bed of the river, even within his own portion of the *alveus*, so as to interfere with the flowing water or to cause real apprehension of resulting injury,[48] nor obstruct the channels through which the river flows when in spate.[49] Nor may a proprietor erect anything which will hinder the flow of the river higher up,[50] or accelerate it.[51]

He may strengthen the banks on his side to prevent his lands being flooded so long as this does not result in the opposite proprietor's land being further inundated.[52] Nor may he do anything in the bed of the stream which will change the level or direction of the flow, or augment its force.[53]

[42] Ersk. II, 1, 5; Bell, *Prin.* §650; *Colquhoun v. D. Montrose* (1801) 4 Paton 221; *Carron Co. v. Ogilvie* (1806) 5 Paton 61.

[43] *Lindsay v. Robertson* (1868) 7 M. 239.

[44] *Colquhoun's Trs v. Orr Ewing* (1877) 4 R. 344; 4 R. (H.L.) 116; *E. Breadalbane v. Colquhoun's Trs.* (1881) 18 S.L.R. 607; *Will's Trs. v. Cairngorm Canoeing School Ltd.*, 1976 S.C. (H.L.) 30; see also *Grant v. D. Gordon* (1776) 3 Paton 679; (1782) 2 Paton 582.

[45] *Campbell's Trs. v. Sweeney*, 1911 S.C. 1319.

[46] *Will's Trs., supra.*

[47] Ersk. II, 1, 5; Bell, *Prin.* §1101; *Wishart v. Wylie* (1853) 1 Macq. 389; *McIntyre's Trs. v. Cupar Mags.* (1867) 5 M. 780; *Gibson v. Bonnington Sugar Co.* (1869) 7 M. 394; *Menzies v. M. Breadalbane* (1901) 4 F. 55.

[48] *Morris v. Bicket* (1866) 4 M. (H.L.) 44; *Jackson v. Marshall* (1872) 10 M. 913; *D. Roxburghe v. Waldie's Trs.* (1879) 6 R. 663; *Orr Ewing v. Colquhoun's Trs.* (1877) 4 R. (H.L.) 116; *McGavin v. McIntyre* (1890) 17 R. 818; 20 R. (H.L.) 49; *Ross v. Powrie and Pitcaithley* (1891) 19 R. 314; *Gay v. Malloch*, 1959 S.C. 110.

[49] *Menzies v. E. Breadalbane* (1828) 3 W. & Sh. 235; *Jackson, supra.*

[50] *Morris, supra*; cf. *Hope v. Heriot's Hospital* (1878) 15 S.L.R. 400.

[51] *D. Roxburghe v. Waldie* (1821) Hume 524.

[52] *Farquharson v. F.* (1741) Mor. 12779; *Menzies, supra; Morris, supra; Jackson v. Marshall* (1872) 10 M. 913; *Murdoch v. Wallace* (1881) 8 R. 855.

[53] *Farquharson, supra; Menzies, supra; Morris, supra; Orr-Ewing, supra.*

Rights in private (non-navigable) rivers and streams—the water

All riparian proprietors have a common interest in the water of a stream but no one has exclusive right of property therein.[54] A proprietor not having lands fronting on the stream has probably no interest in it.[55] Hence no proprietor may use or affect the flow of the water to the prejudice of others. One may, at least in a question with an opposite proprietor, divert part of the stream through a mill-lade, returning the water to the river undiminished,[56] but not to an extent which interferes with the passage of salmon,[57] nor may he divert the flow for agricultural or manufacturing purposes.[58] Still less can water be impounded and stored, save by statutory authority.[59]

Every riparian proprietor is entitled to take water from the stream for primary uses, for drinking by men and animals, and for ordinary domestic purposes, such as cooking, washing and even home brewing,[60] even though this diminishes or even exhausts the supply available for inferior proprietors.[61] The surplus must be returned to the stream within the proprietors' own lands.[62]

But no proprietor may take water for other purposes, such as irrigation or manufacture, if by so doing he infringes the reasonable rights of any inferior proprietor.[63]

A proprietor may also prevent operations by a superior proprietor which result in appreciable change in the quality of the water coming down, such as pollution unfitting the water for primary uses, or for any special use for which an inferior proprietor requires it, such as distilling,[64] but not operations of the character of ordinary estate management even if resulting in temporary fouling.[65] A mine-owner may not, save

[54] *Morris* v. *Bickwt* (1864) 2 M. 1082; 4 M. (H.L.) 44.

[55] *L. Melville* v. *Denniston* (1842) 4 D. 1231; *Bonthrone* v. *Downie* (1878) 6 R. 324; *M. Breadalbane* v. *West Highland Ry.* (1895) 22 R. 307.

[56] *Hamilton* v. *Edington* (1793) Mor. 12824; *Cowan* v. *Kinnaird* (1865) 4 M. 236; *E. Kintore* v. *Pirie* (1903) 5 F. 818.

[57] *E. Kintore, supra.*

[58] *Bannatyne* v. *Cranston* (1624) Mor. 12769; *M. Abercorn* v. *Jamieson* (1791) Hume 510; *Hamilton, supra; Cowan, supra.*

[59] *Hunter and Aitkenhead* v. *Aitken* (1880) 7 R. 610; *Willoughby d'Eresby* v. *Wood* (1884) 22 S.L.R. 471.

[60] *Johnstone* v. *Ritchie*, 15 Feb. 1822, F.C.; as to water closets see *Bonthrone* v. *Downie* (1878) 6 R. 324.

[61] *Bell, Prin.* §1104–5; *Russel* v. *Hasig* (1791) Bell's Oct. Cas. 338; *Hood* v. *Williamsons* (1861) 23 D. 496; *D. Buccleuch* v. *Cowan* (1876) 4 R. (H.L.) 14.

[62] *Hood* v. *Williamson* (1861) 23 D. 496.

[63] *Hamilton* v. *Edington* (1793) Mor. 12824; *Macenzie* v. *Woddrop* (1854) 16 D. 381; *Young* v. *Bankier Distillery Co.* (1893) 20 R. (H.L.) 76.

[64] *Bell, Prin.* §1106; *Rigby and Beardmore* v. *Downie* (1872) 10 M. 568; *Caledonian Ry.* v. *Baird* (1876) 3 R. 839; *Young* v. *Bankier Distillery* (1893) 20 R. (H.L.) 76; *C. Seafield* v. *Kemp* (1899) 1 F. 402; *Fleming* v. *Gemmill*, 1908 S.C. 340.

[65] *Armistead* v. *Bowerman* (1888) 15 R. 814.

by contract or prescriptive right, discharge into a stream water pumped from a mine.[66]

But in the case of some streams the water may have for long been devoted to secondary purposes and a riparian proprietor may have acquired by prescription the right to pollute water.[67] If so he may not take it in any other way or at any other place with the effect of increasing pollution.[68]

The Rivers (Prevention of Pollution) (Sc.) Acts, 1951 and 1965, and the Border Rivers (Prevention of Pollution) Act, 1951, seek to prevent pollution and to require preventive measures.

Rights of fishing

The right to fish for salmon is *inter regalia*[69] and does not belong to a proprietor of lands unless expressly granted to him by the Crown with the lands[70] or separately,[71] or there be at least a grant of fishings followed by possession of salmon-fishings for the prescriptive period,[72] or a barony title followed by prescriptive possession of salmon-fishings.[73] The requisite possession must be for the benefit of the person claiming the right, attributable to the grant and in accordance with it.[74] It must also be exclusive and exercised by a legal method.[75]

The only lawful modes of fishing for salmon are by rod, by net and coble[76] and by cruives.[77] In the sea fixed engines, such as stake nets, are lawful.[78] Unless a proprietor owns both banks he may not fish beyond

---

[66] *Young* v. *Bankier Distillery Co.* (1893) 10 R. (H.L.) 76.

[67] *Portobello Mags.* v. *Edinburgh Mags.* (1882) 10 R. 130; *McIntyre* v. *McGavin* (1893) 20 R. (H.L.) 49; cf. *Moncrieffe* v. *Perth Police Commrs.* (1886) 13 R. 921.

[68] *McIntyre, supra.*

[69] Stair II, 3, 69; Ersk. II, 6, 15; Bell, *Prin.* §671; *Commrs. of Woods and Forests* v. *Gammell* (1859) 5 Macq. 419; see also *L.A.* v. *Sharp* (1878) 6 R. 108; There is an exception in Orkney and Shetland: *Smith* v. *Lerwick Harbour Trs.* (1903) 5 F. 680; *L.A.* v. *Balfour*, 1907 S.C. 1360.

[70] *Mackenzie* v. *Davidson* (1841) 3 D. 646; *E. Galloway* v. *Birrel* (1868) 5 S.L.R. 113; *Gray* v. *Richardson* (1877) 4 R. (H.L.) 76; *L.A.* v. *Lovat* (1880) 7 R. (H.L.) 122; *D. Argyll* v. *Campbell* (1891) 18 R. 1094; *Maxwell* v. *Lamont* (1903) 6 F. 245.

[71] *Hogarth* v. *Grant* (1901) 8 S.L.T. 324.

[72] *Sinclair* v. *L.A.* (1867) 5 M. (H.L.) 97; *Stuart* v. *McBarnet* (1868) 6 M. (H.L.) 123; *McCulloch* v. *L.A.* (1874) 2 R. 27; *Sinclair* v. *Threipland* (1890) 17 R. 507; *Ogston* v. *Stewart* (1896) 23 R. (H.L.) 16.

[73] *Nicol* v. *L.A.* (1868) 6 M. 972; *D. Richmond* v. *E. Seafield* (1870) 8 M. 530; *L.A.* v. *Cathcart* (1871) 9 M. 744; *McDouall* v. *L.A.* (1875) 2 R. (H.L.) 49. See also *L.A.* v. *Northern Lighthouses Commrs.* (1874) 1 R. 950.

[74] *Milne's Trs.* v. *L.A.* (1869) 11 M. 966; *D. Argyll, supra; Ogston, supra.*

[75] *Ramsay* v. *D. Roxburghe* (1848) 10 D. 661; *Milne* v. *Smith* (1850) 13 D. 112; *Anderson* v. *A.* (1867) 5 M. 499; 6 M. 117; *Maxwell* v. *Lamont* (1913) 6 F. 245.

[76] *Hay* v. *Perth Mags.* (1863) 1 M. (H.L.) 41; *Wedderburn* v. *D. Atholl* (1900) 2 F. (H.L.) 57; *Maxwell* v. *Lamont* (1903) 6 F. 245; *Oswald* v. *McCall*, 1919 S.C. 584.

[77] Stair II, 3, 70; Ersk. II, 6, 15; Bell, *Prin.* §1118; *Halkerston* v. *Scott* (1769) Mor. 14276; *E. Kintore* v. *Forbes* (1828) 3 W. & S. 261; *D. Fife* v. *George* (1897) 24 R. 549.

[78] Paidle nets in the Solway are illegal: *E. Mansfield* v. *Parker*, 1914 S.C. 997.

the *medium filum* of the river,[79] and he may not interfere with the *alveus*.[80] He may object to interference with the *alveus*,[81] pollution of the river[82] or excessive abstraction of water by an inferior riparian proprietor.[83] Salmon-fishing in the sea *ex adverso* of lands may be granted; in the absence of clear boundaries or possession the boundary is a line perpendicular to the average line of the coast.[84] If not so granted the Crown or persons in its right are entitled to access to the shore for fishing, and to use the shore for drawing and drying salmon nets.[85] Salmon-fishings may be let on lease.[86] The public have no right to fish in a tidal river within the bounds of an express grant of salmon-fishing.[87] The mode of exercising salmon-fishing is extensively controlled by statute, penalizing illegal modes. Weekly and annual close times are prescribed.[88] Special legislation applies to the Tweed and the Solway.[89]

The right of fishing for trout in private, i.e. non-tidal and non-navigable, waters is part and pertinent of the lands fronting the loch or river, unless reserved or disponed separately to one other than the proprietor thereof. A grant without possession of land is personal only and will not affect singular successors.[90] It cannot be held separately from property in the loch, stream or adjacent lands.[91] A bare right of access to a private stream or loch does not confer any right of fishing,[92] so that the public cannot acquire a right against a proprietor of the lands or water,[93] nor may an agricultural tenant fish, unless authorized

---

[79] *Milne, supra; Fraser* v. *Grant* (1866) 4 M. 596; *Stuart* v. *McBarnet* (1868) 6 M. (H.L.) 123; E. *Zetland* v. *Tennent's Trs.* (1873) 11 M. 469; *Campbell* v. *Muir*, 1908 S.C. 387. If this cannot be done the court may regulate the rights of parties: *Gray* v. *Perth Mags.* (1757) 1 Pat. 645; *Gay* v. *Malloch*, 1959 S.C. 110.

[80] *Bicket* v. *Morris* (1867) 4 M. (H.L.) 44; *Mather* v. *Macbraire* (1873) 11 M. 522; *Orr Ewing* v. *Colquhoun's Trs.* (1877) 4 R. (H.L.) 116; *D. Sutherland* v. *Ross* (1878) 5 R. (H.L.) 137; *D. Roxburghe* v. *Waldie's Trs.* (1879) 6 R. 663; *Robertson* v. *Foote* (1879) 6 R. 1290; *Ross* v. *Powrie & Pitcaithley* (1891) 19 R. 314; *Gay* v. *Malloch*, 1959 S.C. 110.

[81] *Gay, supra.*

[82] *Moncrieff* v. *Perth Police Commrs.* (1886) 13 R. 921; *Armistead* v. *Bowerman* (1888) 15 R. 814; *C. Seafield* v. *Kemp* (1899) 1 F. 402.

[83] *D. Roxburghe, supra; Pirie* v. *E. Kintore* (1906) 8 F. (H.L.) 16.

[84] *McTaggart* v. *McDouall* (1867) 5 M. 534; *Tain Mags.* v. *Murray* (1887) 15 R. 83.

[85] *L.A.* v. *Sharp* (1889) 6 R. 108.

[86] Stair I, 13, 15; Bankt. I, 17, 10; *Gemmill* v. *Riddell* (1847) 9 D. 727; E. *Fife* v. *Wilson* (1864) 3 M. 323; *Mackintosh* v. *May* (1895) 22 R. 345.

[87] *Anderson* v. *A.* (1867) 6 M. 117.

[88] See Salmon Act, 1696, (c. 35); Salmon Fisheries (Sc.) Acts, 1828, 1862, 1863, 1864, 1868, and 1870; Salmon and Freshwater Fisheries (Protection) (Sc.) Act, 1951, Freshwater and Salmon Fisheries (Sc.) Act, 1976.

[89] Solway Act, 1804; Tweed Fisheries Acts 1857 and 1859.

[90] E. *Galloway* v. *D. Bedford* (1902) 4 F. 851.

[91] *Menzies* v. *Macdonald* (1854) 16 D. 827; *Patrick* v. *Napier* (1867) 5 M. 683; E. *Galloway* v. *D. Bedford* (1902) 4 F. 857.

[92] *Ferguson* v. *Shireff* (1844) 6 D. 1363; *Montgomery* v. *Watson* (1861) 23 D. 635.

[93] *Montgomery, supra; Arthur* v. *Aird*, 1907 S.C. 1170.

by his lease.[94] Each riparian proprietor may fish *ex adverso* of his own lands[95] and in the case of small streams is not restricted to his own side of the *medium filum*.[96] A proprietor may licence others to fish,[97] or let the fishing rights on lease. A right to fish might be acquired as a real burden[98] but can be a servitude only in favour of lands adjacent to the river.[99] The public right to be at or on a non-tidal river for navigation or recreation does not imply liberty to fish there, nor can such a right be acquired by prescription.[1] Trout-fishing is also regulated by statute.[2] The Secretary of State may make a protection order in relation to the catchment area, or part thereof, of any river, prohibiting fishing or taking freshwater fish in the prescribed area save on specified conditions. Wardens may be appointed to ensure compliance with protection orders.[3]

Rights of game

The right of property on land includes as a pertinent the exclusive right to take or kill game[4] on the lands.[5] A proprietor may accordingly exclude from his lands as trespassers persons entering thereon to kill game.[6] Sporting rights dissociated from any right in the lands themselves are not recognized.[7] Various statutes make poaching, i.e. trespass in pursuit of game, criminal.

A proprietor of lands[8] may grant a lease of shootings, which is a true lease[9] and not merely a personal licence,[10] or the exclusive right of shooting game on the lands, saving the agricultural tenant's rights, and this impliedly imposes on the shooting tenant liability to relieve the proprietor of the agricultural tenant's claims for damage arising from an unduly large stock of game.[11]

[94] *Copland* v. *Maxwell* (1871) 9 M. (H.L.) 1.

[95] *Menzies* v. *Wentworth* (1901) 3 F. 941; *Arthur, supra*.   [96] *Arthur, supra*.

[97] *E. Galloway, supra*. This does not give a right to sue for damage to the fishings: *E. Lothian Angling Assocn.* v. *Haddington*, 1980 S.L.T. 213.

[98] *Patrick* v. *Napier* (1867) 5 M. 683; *Harper* v. *Flaws*, 1940 S.L.T. 150.

[99] *Patrick, supra*.

[1] *Grant* v. *Henry* (1894) 21 R. 358.

[2] See Trout (Sc.) Acts, 1902 and 1933; Salmon and Freshwater Fisheries (Protection) (Sc.) Act, 1951.   [3] Freshwater and Salmon Fisheries (Sc.) Act, 1976, Ss. 2–3.

[4] There is no complete legal definition of game; many statutes contain their own definitions.

[5] Ersk. II, 6, 6; *Welwood* v. *Husband* (1874) 1 R. 507. Even a long leaseholder has no right.

[6] *E. Breadalbane* v. *Livingstone* (1791) 3 Pat. 221; *Pollock, Gilmour & Co.* v. *Harvey* (1828) 6 S. 913; *Birkbeck* v. *Ross* (1865) 4 M. 272.

[7] *Johnstone* v. *Gilchrist*, 1934 S.L.T. 271.

[8] cf. *M. Huntly* v. *Nicol* (1896) 23 R. 610.

[9] *Macpherson* v. *M*. (1839) 1 D. 794; *Sinclair* v. *L. Duffus* (1842) 5 D. 174; *Menzies* v. *M*. (1861) 23 D. (H.L.) 16; *Stewart* v. *Bulloch* (1880) 8 R. 381.

[10] *E. Aboyne* v. *Innes*, 22 June 1813, F.C.; *Pollock, Gilmour & Co.* v. *Harvey* (1828) 6 S. 913; *Birkbeck* v. *Ross* (1865) 4 M. 272.

[11] *Bryne* v. *Johnson* (1875) 3 R. 255; *Eliott's Trs.* v. *E*. (1894) 21 R. 858; see also *Inglis* v. *Moir's Tutors* (1871) 10 M. 204; *Kidd* v. *Byrne* (1875) 3 R. 255.

An agricultural tenant has no right implied by his lease to kill game,[12] but may kill rabbits to protect his crops[12] and scare game so long as not scaring it from the lands completely.[14] By the Ground Game Act, 1880,[15] every occupier of land has a right, inseparable from his occupancy, to kill and take rabbits and hares on the land. Agricultural tenants have also rights at common law and under statute to compensation for damage by game.[16]

Conservation and control of deer

The Deer (Sc.) Acts, 1959 and 1967, established a Red Deer Commission to advise the Secretary of State for Scotland and landowners as to red deer. It may authorize the killing of marauding deer, and make control schemes for the reduction of deer where they are damaging agriculture and forestry (Ss. 1–11). The Commission may provide services and equipment for the killing of red deer, and their disposal (Ss. 12–18). The rights of occupiers of land to recover compensation for damages caused by red deer continue unaffected (S. 19). Close seasons are fixed for red deer (S. 21). The poaching of all species of deer is penalized (Ss. 22–5).

LIMITATIONS ON USES OF LAND

Common law and statute both impose material qualifications on a landowner's power to use his lands as he wills. The common law principles apply the maxim *sic utere tuo ut alienum non laedas*.

Use in aemulationem vicini

No proprietor of lands may use them, or act on them, *in aemulationem vicini*, doing what may be legal but with the sole or predominant purpose of inconveniencing or harming his neighbour.[17] The presumption is against such being his purpose,[18] and operations on land cannot be restrained if undertaken for a proprietor's own

---

[12] E. Hopetoun v. Wight, 17 Jan. 1810, F.C.; Wemyss v. Gulland (1847) 10 D. 204; Copland v. Maxwell (1868) 9 M. (H.L.) 1; Welwood, supra.

[13] Moncrieff v. Arnott (1828) 6 S. 530; Inglis v. Moir's Tutors (1871) 10 M. 204; Brown v. Thomson (1882) 9 R. 1183; Fraser v. Lawson (1882) 10 R. 396.

[14] Wemyss, supra.

[15] Amended by Agriculture (Sc.) Act, 1948, Ss. 48, 50, and Crofters (Sc.) Act, 1955, S. 27.

[16] Ch. 5.15, infra.

[17] Bankt. IV, 45, 112; Ersk. II, 1, 2; Bell, Prin. §964; Somerville v. S. (1613) Mor. 12769; Dunlop v. Robertson (1803) Hume 515; Campbell v. Muir, 1908 S.C. 387; More v. Boyle, 1967 S.L.T. (Sh. Ct.) 38. The observations of Lord Watson in Mayor of Bradford v. Pickles [1895] A.C. 587 are obiter and unsound. See also Ch. 4.39, supra.

[18] Bankt., supra.

legitimate purposes or benefit or if only incidentally injuring a neighbour.[19]

Nuisance

At common law nuisance is any use of land which causes substantial inconvenience or injury to an adjacent proprietor in the ordinary use and enjoyment of his property. The conduct complained of need not be illegal, nor any unusual or unnatural use of property. The commoner kinds of nuisance are the emission of noise or fumes, the pollution of air or water. The complainer need not prove intent to harm, nor lack of due care to prevent harm.[20]

Statutory nuisances

Legislation, particularly the Burgh Police (Sc.) Acts and the Public Health (Sc.) Acts, prescribe that large numbers of acts of different kinds, all prejudicial to public health or comfortable enjoyment of life, shall be statutory nuisances, the commission of which are statutory offences.

Poisonous waste

It is an offence to deposit on land waste of a poisonous, noxious or polluting kind where its presence is liable to give rise to environmental hazard. The person depositing it is liable for damage caused thereby unless it is due wholly to the fault of the person who suffered the damage, or was suffered by a person who voluntarily accepted the risk thereof.[21] Authorities must be notified before waste is removed or deposited.

Restrictions imposed by Planning Acts

The Town and Country Planning (Sc.) Act, 1972,[22] replacing most of the earlier legislation on the subject, requires local planning authorities to survey and prepare and revise development plans of their districts, indicating the manner in which they propose land therein should be used. Landowners require permission from the planning authority for any development of land, i.e. building, engineering, mining or other operations in, on, over or under land, or the making of any material change in the use of any buildings or other land,[23] subject

[19] *Somerville, supra; Dunlop, supra.*
[20] Ch. 4.32, *supra.*   [21] Deposit of Poisonous Waste Act, 1972, Ss. 1–2.
[22] See also Town and Country Amenities Act, 1974; Town and Country Planning (Sc.) Act, 1977.
[23] Discontinuance of an existing use is not a material change of use: *Paul v. Ayrshire C.C.,* 1964 S.C. 116. A planning authority has no jurisdiction below low-water mark: *Argyll & Bute D.C.* v. *Secretary of State for Scotland,* 1976 S.C. 248. The Secretary of State in granting planning permission in a case referred to him may accept undertakings by the developer, though unenforceable in law: *Bearsdon Town Council* v. *Glasgow Corpn.* 1971 S.C. 274.

to certain exceptions (Ss. 19–41). Applications for planning permission must be accompanied by a certificate of notice to other owners of land affected, and stating that the land is not an agricultural holding or that notice has been given to every tenant of an agricultural holding affected by the application (Ss. 22–5). Planning permission may be revoked or modified (Ss. 42–3). Compensation may be claimed for the refusal of planning permission or its grant subject only to conditions (Ss. 123–52), or for revocation or modification of planning permission (Ss. 153–68). An owner or lessee may in certain cases require the local planning authority to purchase his interest in the land (Ss. 169–97).

Caravan sites

The Caravan Sites and Control of Development Act, 1960, prohibits the use of land as a caravan site without a local authority licence, subject to certain exemptions (Ss. 1–4). Conditions may be attached to site licences, against which appeal lies to the Sheriff,[24] and altered at any time (Ss. 5–9). A site licence may, with the consent of the local authority, be transferred to a new occupier of the land, and a person acquiring an estate in land by operation of law and thereby becoming occupier is entitled to have the licence endorsed to him (S. 10). Sites in use at the commencement of the Act are exempted from the requirements of a site licence but subject to special provisions (Ss. 13–20). Local authorities may provide caravan sites and for that purpose may acquire land compulsorily (S. 24).

Control of buildings

Local building authorities exercise control over buildings in interests of stability and safety and health by requiring that plans be deposited and authority obtained for building and alteration.[25] A proprietor of adjoining property has a title to object to the grant by the authority of a warrant for building or alteration which infringes his property rights.[26]

Pipelines

The Pipe Lines Act, 1962, provides that cross-country pipelines (as defined in S. 65) may not be constructed without the authority of the Minister of Power, nor a local pipeline (not over ten miles) without notice to the Minister (Ss. 1–8). The Minister may prevent an unnecessary multiplicity of pipelines (Ss. 9–10). A pipeline promoter may

[24] cf. *Clyde Caravans (Langbank) Ltd.* v. *Renfrew C.C.*, 1962 S.L.T. (Sh. Ct.) 20.
[25] Building (Sc.) Act, 1959; and see Building Standards (Sc.) Regs. 1963 (S.I. 1897, 1963); Local Govt. (Sc.) Act, 1973, S. 227.
[26] But see *Park* v. *Blair*, 1961 S.L.T. 397.

apply for compulsory purchase powers (Ss. 11–14). Requirements may be imposed as to the construction of pipelines (Ss. 20–3) and their safety (Ss. 24–6) and the Minister may require demolition of structures or deposits which imperil pipelines (Ss. 27–32).

Public rights of way

A public right of way is a right exercisable by any member of the public as such to pass from one public place to another public place[27] by a definite track.[28] It can probably not be acquired by use over lands held for railway or other public purposes.[29] The foreshore is a 'public place' only if the public actually resort there.[30] It is distinct from a servitude right of way, and from a personal privilege of access.[31] It may be created by grant, but is normally acquired by prescriptive use (twenty years) in a way implying assertion of a public right, openly and without interruption.[32] It may be vindicated by any member of the public or by a society formed to vindicate such rights.[33]

It will be lost by disuse for the prescriptive period (twenty years),[34] or by unchallenged contrary actings by the proprietor though for a lesser period,[35] or may be extinguished by statute.[36]

Access to the countryside

The Countryside (Scotland) Acts, 1967 and 1981, established the Countryside Commission for Scotland with functions for the provision, development and improvement of facilities for the enjoyment of the Scottish countryside, and the conservation and enhancement of its natural beauty (Ss. 1–4). The Commission may (S. 5) make proposals for development projects or schemes, and (S. 6) by agreement acquire land, or acquire it compulsorily, hold and manage it, dispose of it, provide equipment and services, and exercise powers to carry out work or provide services or facilities conferred by the Act on local authorities or local planning authorities, on their own or, with consent, on other persons' land, agreements as to which may be recorded in the Registers of Sasines.

---

[27] *Campbell* v. *Lang* (1853) 1 Macq. 451; *Young* v. *Cuthbertson* (1854) 1 Macq. 455; *Duncan* v. *Lees* (1871) 9 M. 855; *M. Bute* v. *McKirdy & McMillan,* 1937 S.C. 93.

[28] *Mackintosh* v. *Moir* (1871) 9 M. 574; *Norrie* v. *Kirriemuir Mags.,* 1945 S.C. 302.

[29] *Edinburgh Mags.* v. *N.B. Ry.* (1904) 6 F. 620.

[30] *Darrie* v. *Drummond* (1865) 3 M. 496; *M. Bute, supra.*

[31] *Norrie, supra.*

[32] *Burt* v. *Barclay* (1861) 24 D. 218; *Mann* v. *Brodie* (1885) 12 R. (H.L.) 52; *Macpherson* v. *Scottish Rights of Way Socy.* (1888) 15 R. (H.L.) 68; *McInroy* v. *D. Atholl* (1891) 18 R. (H.L.) 46; *Norrie, supra;* Prescription and Limitation (Sc.) Act, 1973, S. 3. Where a new road was substituted for an old one it was held that the years of use of each could be added to make the prescriptive period: *Kinloch* v. *Young,* 1911 S.C. (H.L.) 1.

[33] *Potter* v. *Hamilton* (1870) 8 M. 1064; *Macpherson, supra.*

[34] Prescription and Limitation (Sc.) Act, 1973, S. 8.

[35] Rankine, *Landownership,* 337.   [36] e.g. New Towns (Sc.) Act, 1968, S. 23.

Access agreements may be made (Ss. 10, 12–13, 1981 Act, S. 3) in respect of open country by the local planning authority with any person having an interest in land and (S. 14) a local planning authority may make an access order in respect of any land. A person interested in land comprised in an access agreement or order may not carry out any work substantially reducing the area to which the public may have access. Access agreements and orders have to be recorded in the Register of Sasines and are enforceable against persons having interest in the land and their successors (S. 16). A person entering on land comprised in the agreement or order for open-air recreation without causing damage is not a trespasser, nor under any liability by reason only of so entering or being on the land (S. 11).

Such agreements or orders may (Ss. 17–18) make provision for securing safe and sufficient access for the public to the land, for the improvement or repair of means of access, new means of access, safety measures, and the prevention of impediments or dangers. Compensation is payable for access orders (Ss. 20–3). Local authorities may acquire land for open-air recreations (S. 24), as may the Secretary of State (S. 25).

Local planning authorities may by agreement or by compulsory order create public paths over land (Ss. 30–8), and the Commission may make proposals for long-distance routes which, if approved by the Secretary of State, shall be implemented by the local planning and other authorities concerned (Ss. 39–42).

Local planning authorities may provide country parks, camping sites, caravan sites, accommodation, meals and refreshments, and parking places (Ss. 48–51) and improve waterways for recreation (Ss. 61–2), as may local water authorities (S. 63) and electricity boards (S. 64). The Forestry Commission may also (S. 58) provide tourist, recreational or sporting facilities. In exercising their functions relating to land under any enactment every Minister, department, and public body must have regard to the desirability of conserving the natural beauty and amenity of the countryside (S. 66).

Nature conservation

The Nature Conservancy Council Act, 1973, established the Nature Conservancy Council to establish nature reserves and conserve flora, fauna and other natural features.

Under the National Parks and Access to the Countryside Act, 1949, the Nature Conservancy Council may (Ss. 15–20) enter into agreements with the owners, tenants and occupiers of land to secure that it be managed as a nature reserve, or may acquire land compulsorily for nature reserves, and may make bye-laws for the protection of the reserve.[37] Local authorities may (S. 21) provide nature reserves on any land in their areas. The Nature Conservancy Council must (S. 23) inform local planning authorities of areas of special scientific interest.

The Conservation of Wild Creatures and Wild Plants Act, 1975, penalizes, save in excepted cases, conduct harmful to wild creatures and plants.

Ancient Monuments and historic buildings

The Ancient Monuments and Archaeological Areas Act, 1979, enables the Secretary of State to list, control works affecting, acquire compulsorily, take under guardianship, agree with owners about, and allow the public access to, ancient monuments. Interference with a scheduled ancient monument is an offence. Grants may be made for the preservation of historic buildings, their contents and adjoining land.[38] The Secretary of State may designate areas as areas of archaeological importance, which limits the operations which may be done on land within the area.[39]

A local planning authority may make tree preservation orders for the preservation of trees and woodlands, and building preservation orders restricting the demolition, alteration or extension of buildings of special architectural or historic interest,[40] and the Secretary of State has to compile lists of buildings of such interest.[41]

The Local Authorities (Historic Buildings) Act, 1962, extended to Scotland by the Civic Amenities Act, 1967, enables local authorities to make contributions towards the repair and maintenance of buildings of historic or architectural interest.

Amenities

The Civic Amenities Act, 1967,[42] requires local planning authorities to designate areas of special architectural or historic interest the character or appearance of which it is desirable to preserve or enhance as conservation areas (S. 1), makes further provision for penalizing unauthorized work on buildings listed as of special architectural or historic interest or acts of wilful damage to a listed building (Ss. 2–3). Local planning authorities may execute works necessary for the preservation of an unoccupied listed building, or compulsorily purchase

[37] See *Barnet* v. *Barclay*, 1955 S.C. 34.
[38] Historic Buildings and Ancient Monuments Act, 1953. Functions transferred to Secretary of State for Scotland: Transfer of Functions (Scottish Royal Parks and Ancient Monuments) Order, 1969 (S.I. 383, 1969).
[39] 1979 Act, Part II.
[40] Town and Country Planning (Sc.) Act, 1972, Ss. 52–60; see also Ss. 163, 180; *Tronsite Ltd.* v. *Edinburgh Corpn.*, 1965 S.C. 129.
[41] Ibid., S. 52.
[42] Amended by Town and Country Planning (Sc.) Act, 1972. See also Town and Country Amenities Act, 1974.

any such building which is not being properly preserved (Ss. 6–7) or make building preservation orders (Ss. 10–11). They are empowered to secure the preservation or planting of trees and their replacement (Ss. 12–17).

By the Refuse Disposal (Amenity) Act, 1978, local authorities must provide refuse dumps open to the public (S. 1). Dumping old motor vehicles is an offence (S. 2) and the local authority has the duty of removing and disposing of abandoned vehicles, recovering the expense of so doing (Ss. 3–5) and of disposing of other refuse (S. 6).

Protection of wild life

Numerous statutes seek to protect various kinds of wildlife, notably fish, deer, seals, birds, badgers and other creatures.

Highlands and Islands Development Board

The Highlands and Islands Development (Sc.) Act, 1965, established the Development Board to promote social and economic development in the crofting counties.[43] The Board has power (S. 4) to acquire land by agreement or compulsorily, to hold and manage land and dispose of it (S. 5), to erect buildings and carry out works or other operations on land and provide equipment and services (S. 6), to carry on businesses, and (S. 8) make grants and loans. They also (S. 10) have powers of entry on lands and (S. 11) powers to demand information about land or businesses.

---

[43] Further powers were conferred by a similar Act of 1968.

CHAPTER 5.7

JOINT AND COMMON PROPERTY— COMMON INTEREST

Either the superiority or the fee of heritage may be vested at any time in more than one person, holding the lands undivided, either as joint owners or owners in common.[1].

Joint Property

In the case of joint ownership, of which the main instances are ownership by trustees or partners, the land is possessed undivided, and the owners together have one title to one estate in every part of the lands.[2] All joint owners have equal interests therein, and on the death of any one his interest passes by accretion to the survivors until there remains but one who then has the sole title.[3] No joint owner can alienate or by will dispose of his interest in the land, nor burden it, and it does not pass on his intestacy as part of his estate. Decisions affecting the land must be reached by a majority and actions must be brought by all owners jointly.[4] No one joint owner has any claim to have the subjects divided to give him a title to any individual share thereof.[5] Heritage may be owned by spouses jointly in which case, if there is a special destination to the survivor, neither can dispose of his or her share by *mortis causa* deed but this is the only restriction on disposal of either's share.[6]

Common Property

In the case of ownership in common,[7] of which instances are the rights of heirs portioners on intestacy,[8] and the rights of the houses surrounding a central garden,[9] the land is possessed undivided, but

[1] In the older books and cases the terminology is confused and joint property and common property are not clearly distinguished. See *Banff Mags. v. Ruthin Castle*, 1944 S.C. 36, 68; *Munro v. M.* 1972 S.L.T. (Sh. Ct.) 6.
[2] *Cargill v. Muir* (1837) 15 S. 408; *McNeight v. Lockhart* (1843) 6 D. 128; *Schaw v. Black* (1889) 16 R. 336, 340. [3] *Banff Mags., supra*, 68–9.
[4] *Grozier v. Downie* (1871) 8 M. 826; cf. *Schaw v. Black* (1889) 16 R. 336.
[5] *Banff Mags., supra.*
[6] *Steele v. Caldwell*, 1979 S.L.T. 228.
[7] Stair I, 7, 15; I, 16, 4; Bankt. I, 8, 38; Ersk. III, 3, 56; Bell, *Prin.* §1072.
[8] *Cargill v. Muir* (1837) 15 S. 408; *McNeight v. Lockhart* (1843) 6 D. 128.
[9] *Grant v. Heriot's Trust* (1906) 8 F. 647.

each owner has his own separate title to a fraction of the undivided whole. The interests of owners in common are not necessarily equal. On the death of any one his right does not pass to the others by accretion but passes to his own heirs on intestacy.[10] He may alienate his share, or dispose of it by will, or burden it.[11] Whether a particular piece of land is held in common, or by one proprietor only, as when a building is sold off in parts, depends on the titles.[12] So long as the land is possessed in common decisions affecting it must have the agreement of all and actions must be brought by all proprietors in common,[13] while any one may prevent alteration or extraordinary use of the property,[14] but not necessary repairs.[15]

Division or division and sale

So long as the community of property subsists no one proprietor in common has title to any identifiable parts of the lands, but any one may at any time call for a division of the lands by agreement, or if the others will not agree, bring an action for their division[16] or, if indivisible, or where division would be inequitable to some of the parties,[17] for their sale and division of the realized value: *nemo in communione invitus detineri potest.*[18] This is so notwithstanding the existence of a security over the common property.[19]

It is probably incompetent for a testator to seek to exclude the right of legatees in common to pursue for division, or division and sale,[20] but one *pro indiviso* propietor may by contract bar himself from resorting to an action of division or sale.[21] Division is not precluded by the existence of a bond over the subjects,[22] but may be by the existence of a

[10] *Schaw* v. *Black* (1889) 16 R. 336; *Banff Mags.* v. *Ruthin Castle*, 1944 S.C. 36, 68.

[11] *Cargill* v. *Muir* (1837) 15 S. 408; *Johnston* v. *Crawford* (1885) 17 D. 1023; *Schaw* v. *Black* (1889) 16 R. 336.

[12] *Barclay* v. *McEwen* (1880) 7 R. 792.

[13] *Millar* v. *Cathcart* (1861) 23 D. 743; *Lade* v. *Largs Bakery Co.* (1863) 2 M. 17; *Grozier* v. *Downie* (1870) 9 M. 826; *Aberdeen Station Cttee.* v. *N.B. Ry.* (1890) 17 R. 975, 984; *Grant, supra*; *Price* v. *Watson*, 1951 S.C. 359. But any one can take action to check trespass: *Warrand* v. *Watson* (1905) 8 F. 253.

[14] *Taylor* v. *Dunlop* (1872) 11 M. 25; *Sutherland* v. *Barbour* (1887) 15 R. 62.

[15] *Deans* v. *Woolfson*, 1922 S.C. 221.

[16] *Brock* v. *Hamilton* (1852) 14 D. 701; *Anderson* v. *A.* (1857) 19 D. 700; *Morrison* v. *Kirk* 1912 S.C. 44.

[17] *Thom* v. *Macbeth* (1875) 3 R. 161; *Morrison, supra*, 48.

[18] C. 10, 35, 2; Craig, *J.F.* II, 8, 35 and 41; Bell, *Prin.* §1079; *Milligan* v. *Barnhill* (1782) Mor. 2486; *Bryden* v. *Gibson* (1837) 15 S. 486; *Anderson* v. *A.* (1857) 19 D. 700; *Brock* v. *Hamilton* (1852) 19 D. 701; *Thom* v. *Macbeth* (1875) 3 R. 161; *Grant* v. *Heriot's Trust* (1906) 8 F. 647; *Morrison* v. *Kirk*, 1912 S.C. 44; *Banff Mags., supra*; *Price, supra*. Sale by private bargain is permissible: *Campbell* v. *Murray*, 1972 S.C. 310.

[19] *Morrison, supra*.

[20] *Grant, supra*, 658.

[21] *Morrison, supra*, 47.

[22] *Morrison, supra*.

neccessarily continuing common interest, such as that of flat-dwellers in the common entrance and stair

Common property in common (or 'mutual') gables and walls

A further instance of common property exists where a common gable, or dividing wall between two plots of land, has been built.[23] The first builder of a gable may recover half of the cost when the adjacent proprietor comes to make use of it as common to both buildings.[24] Either proprietor may object to operations by the other on the common gable or wall liable to be injurious to it as his gable or wall,[25] or detrimental to his security, light or air.[26]

Common property—other cases

Other cases of common property include entrances and stairs owned and used in common by two or more properties.[27]

Common interest

A right different from common property exists among the owners of subjects possessed in separate portions, but united by their common interest therein. This right is incorporated with the several rights of individual property. Sale or division cannot resolve any difficulties arising in management, but the exercise of the common interest must, in case of dissension, be regulated by law or equity.[28]

Instances of this arise where a superior feus lands retaining the property of a common square or garden, in which each feuar has no property but a common interest,[29] or where the square or garden is held in common by the feuars, each having a right of property in common and also a common interest in the square, or feuars have a common interest in a passage along the side of their respective feus,[30] or several frontagers in a street have a common interest in the space above the street as an inlet for light and air.[31] Members of the community have a common interest in the streets in a burgh and the airspace above it.[31]

---

[23] *Walker* v. *Sherar* (1870) 8 M. 494; *Trades House* v. *Ferguson,* 1979 S.L.T. 187.

[24] *Jack* v. *Begg* (1875) 3 R. 35; *Robertson* v. *Scott* (1886) 13 R. 1127; *Wilson* v. *Pottinger,* 1908 S.C. 580.

[25] Bell, *Prin.* §1075, 1078; *Warrens* v. *Marwick* (1835) 13 S. 944; *Dow and Gordon* v. *Harvey* (1869) 8 M. 118; *Lamont* v. *Cumming* (1875) 2 R. 785.

[26] *Gray* v. *Macleod,* 1979 S.L.T. (SL. Ct.) 17.

[27] Bell, *Prin.* §1075, 1086; *Brock, supra; Deans* v. *Woolfson,* 1922 S.C. 221; *W.V.S. Office Premises Ltd.* v. *Currie,* 1969 S.C. 170; cf. *Davie* v. *Edinburgh Corpn.* 1977 S.L.T. (Notes) 5.

[28] Bell, *Prin.* §1086; cf. *Johnston* v. *White* (1877) 4 R. 721; *Grant* v. *Heriot's Trust* (1906) 8 F. 647, 658.

[29] *Watson's Hospital* v. *Cormack* (1883) 11 R. 320; *Grant, supra.*

[30] *Mackenzie* v. *Carrick* (1869) 7 M. 419; *Grant, supra.*

[31] *Donald* v. *Esslemont & Macintosh,* 1923 S.C. 122.

Law of the tenement

The chief instances of common interest arise in flatted buildings, where different storeys and houses therein belong to different proprietors. This combines the individual property of each in his own house with a common interest in the rest of the whole, so far as necessary for his support, stability and cover. Apart from express provision in the titles, custom regulates the relative rights of proprietors.[32] The ownership of the *solum*, any garden or basement area in front, and the garden or court at the rear prima facie belong to the owners of the ground floor houses, subject to a common interest of the other owners to be supported and to prevent damage to their houses, as by depriving them of light.[33] The external walls of each house belong to the owner of that house, but the other owners have common interest therein and may prevent operations liable to endanger the security of their houses.[34] Gable walls are the common property of the owners on either side, so far as bounding their respective houses, but all the other owners in the blocks have common interest therein to prevent damage to the stability of the building.[35] The owner of each storey has an interest that storeys below be maintained to support him, and that storeys above be maintained to afford him cover. The floor and roof of each flat are divided along the mid-line of the joists, but neither superior nor inferior proprietor may so act as to weaken the joists or expose them to unusual danger of fire.[36] Hence a shop on the ground floor may not exhibit a signboard extending above such mid-line, unless such a sign has been assented to or allowed to remain for the prescriptive period.[36] A common entrance, passages, staircase and liftshaft and the walls therof are the common property of all the premises to which they give access;[37] the side walls of such entrances are the common property of the proprietors and of the owner of the adjacent house.[38]

[32] Stair II, 7, 6; Bankt. II, 7, 9; Ersk. II, 9, 11; Bell, *Prin.* §1086; *Smith v. Giuliani*, 1925 S.C.(H.L.) 45.
[33] *Johnson v. White* (1877) 4 R. 721; *Boswell v. Edinburgh Mags.* (1881) 8 R. 986; *McArly v. French's Trs.* (1883) 10 R. 574; *Sutherland v. Barbour* (1887) 15 R. 62. A 'right in common' to area or garden ground may be a right of common interest only: *Johnston, supra.*
[34] *Ferguson v. Marjoribanks*, 12 Nov. 1816, F.C.; *Pirie v. McRitchie*, 5 June 1819, F.C.; *McKean v. Davidson* (1823) 2 S. 480; *Murray v. Gullan* (1825) 3 S. 639; *McNair v. McLauchlan* (1826) 4 S. 546; *Brown v. Boyd* (1841) 3 D. 1205; *Gellatly, infra; Johnston v. White* (1877) 4 R. 721.
[35] *Gellatly v. Arrol* (1863) 1 M. 592; see *Morris v. Bicket* (1864) 2 M. 1081, 1089 and *Todd v. Wilson* (1894) 22 R. 172; see also *Watt v. Jamieson*, 1964 S.C. 56.
[36] *Alexander v. Butchart* (1875) 3 R. 156; *McArly v. French's Trs.* (1883) 10 R. 574.
[37] *Taylor v. Dunlop* (1872) 11 M. 25; cf. *Leith Mags. v. Irons*, 1907 S.C. 384.
[38] *Anderson v. Dalrymple* (1799) Mor. 12831; *Reid v. Nicol* (1799) Mor. Property, Appx.1; *Ritchie v. Purdie* (1833) 11 S. 771; *Graham v. Greig* (1838) 1 D. 171; *Gellatly v. Arrol* (1863) 1 M. 592; *Taylor v. Dunlop* (1872) 11 M. 25.

Subject to the titles, the roof belongs to the several owners of the topmost storey, but all proprietors have a common interest that it is maintained in repair for their common benefit and not damaged.[39] The attic space may not be converted into an attic storey without consent,[40] but the topmost proprietors may make rooms in the space.[41] Some parts of a tenement such as the common entrance and staircase are normally common property; one owner cannot carry a flue to the roof through a staircase owned in common.[42] The *solum* and roof may also be expressly made common property.[43]

These rights of common interest are of a proprietary and not of a servitude character,[44] but do not entitle any proprietor to invade another's premises or conduct operations thereon.[45] The duty which one proprietor owes to another whose common interest may be infringed is of taking reasonable precautions only, and he is not liable unless he should have foreseen the danger of damage and taken precautions, or should in the circumstances have examined periodically for signs of damage.[46]

Where repairs to a part of a building held as common property, or in which several proprietors have common interest, if sharing of liability is imposed in the titles of each or imposed by a deed of conditions applicable to all and made real burdens, any one proprietor defraying charges may recover a due proportion from each other.[47] Whether repairs are such as should be defrayed in common or not is a question of fact, having regard to any provision in the titles.[48]

Where alterations are contemplated, such as the conversion of the ground floor into shops, the other proprietors in the building can prevent the change if the part to be altered is common property,[49] but not if they have merely a common interest in it unless that interest is being prejudiced by the change.[50]

[39] *Taylor* v. *Dunlop* (1872) 11 M. 25; *Sanderson's Trs.* v. *Yule* (1897) 25 R. 211; *Smith* v. *Giuliani*, 1925 S.C. (H.L.) 45; *Duncan* v. *Ch. of Scotland Trs.*, 1941 S.C. 145; *Duncan Smith & MacLaren* v. *Heatley*, 1952 J.C. 61.
[40] *Sharp* v. *Robertson* (1800) Mor. Property, Appx. 3; *Watt* v. *Burgess' Tr.* (1891) 18 R. 766.
[41] *Taylor* v. *Dunlop* (1872) 11 M. 25.
[42] *Taylor* v. *Dunlop* (1872) 11 M. 25.
[43] *Turner* v. *Hamilton* (1890) 17 R. 494; *W.V.S. Office Premises Ltd.* v. *Currie*, 1969 S.C. 170; contrast *Johnston* v. *White* (1877) 4 R. 721.
[44] *Smith* v. *Giuliani*, 1925 S.C. (H.L.) 45, 59.
[45] *Smith, supra,* 57; *Duncan Smith & MacLaren, supra,* 64.
[46] *Thomson* v. *St Cuthbert's Coop. Assoc. Ltd.,* 1958 S.C. 380; *Kerr* v. *McGreevy,* 1970 S.L.T. (Sh. Ct.) 7; *Doran* v. *Smith* 1971 S.L.T. (Sh. Ct.) 46.
[47] *Wells* v. *New House Purchases Ltd.* 1964 S.L.T. (Sh. Ct.) 2.
[48] *McNally & Miller Ltd.* v. *Mallinson,* 1977 S.L.T. (Sh. Ct.) 33.
[49] *Boswell* v. *Edinburgh Mags.* (1881) 8 R. 986; *Sutherland* v. *Barbour* (1887) 15 R. 62; *Turner* v. *Hamilton* (1890) 17 R. 494; *Taylor's Trs.* v. *McGavigan* (1896) 23 R. 945; see also *Arrol* v. *Inches* (1887) 14 R. 394.
[50] *Johnston* v. *White* (1877) 4 R. 721; *Barclay* v. *McEwan* (1880) 7 R. 792; *Calder* v. *Edinburgh Merchant Co.* (1886) 13 R. 623; *Birrell* v. *Lumley* (1905) 12 S.L.T. 719.

Similary in 'terrace' or 'semi-detached' houses both proprietors have common interest in the stability of their common gables.

Common[51] Gables

By custom the builder of a tenement or house, into the gable of which he expects that the owner of the adjacent land will wish to dovetail his building, may erect the gable half on either side of the boundary-line and recover half of the cost of erecting it when the adjacent owner comes to make use of the gable.[52] Till then the builder has the property in the whole gable, or possibly property in one half with the right to use the whole till the adjacent owner uses the other half.[53] When the adjacent owner uses it each has a right of common property in the gable. The second builder may insert the ends of the joists therein, and bond in front and rear walls, make fireplaces and vents in the gable and heighten it reasonably, so long as he does not injure the other's property thereby.[54] It is questionable whether the adjacent owner may make any use of the gable without settling with the party in right of the gable.[55]

The rule of common gables may also be founded on implied contract inferred from a feuing plan or other circumstances, and there is no such rule where there is no basis for inferring the contract.[56] Where a common gable has been unjustifiably erected half on the complainer's lands, the court may allow it to stand subject to compensation to the complainer for the encroachment.[57]

Common walls and fences; march-fences

A wall or fence merely forming a division between properties, as between back greens, is intended only to enclose. If erected exclusively on one owner's land, it is his property; if erected along the boundary it is doubtless common property.

For one party to alter such a common wall without the other's consent might well be a breach of the implied contract under which the wall was built.[58] A garden or field division wall cannot be converted into a mutual gable without consent.[59]

---

[51] Frequently miscalled 'mutual' gables.

[52] *Glasgow R.I.* v. *Wylie* (1877) 4 R. 894; *Sinclair* v. *Brown* (1882) 10 R. 45; *Robertson* v. *Scott* (1886) 13 R. 1127; *Berkeley* v. *Baird* (1895) 22 R. 372; *Baird* v. *Alexander* (1898) 25 R. (H.L.) 35; *Stark's Trs.* v. *Cooper's Trs.* (1900) 2 F. 1257.

[53] *Robertson, supra,* 1130–2; cf, *Berkely, supra,* 376.

[54] *Lamont* v. *Cumming* (1875) 2 R. 784; *Robertson, supra; Dow & Gordon* v. *Harvey* (1869) 8 M. 118; *Bryce* v. *Norman* (1895) 2 S.L.T. 471; cf. *Wilson* v. *Pottinger,* 1908 S.C. 580.

[55] *Glasgow R.I., supra,* 897.

[56] *Jack* v. *Begg* (1875) 3 R. 35.

[57] *Sanderson* v. *Geddes* (1874) 1 R. 1198; *Grahame* v. *Kirkcaldy Mags.* (1882) 9 R. (H.L.) 91; *Wilson, supra.*   [58] *Lamont* v. *Cumming* (1875) 2 R. 784, 790.

[59] *Jack* v. *Begg* (1875) 3 R. 35, 42.

March-fences

Adjoining proprietors may by agreement erect a fence or dyke at common expense, and such may by agreement or practice be treated as a march-fence, in which event it must be maintained at common expense.[60]

By the March Dykes Act, 1661 (c. 284)[61] one proprietor may compel the owner of adjoining lands to share equally the expense of erecting, repairing, or, where necessary, rebuilding[62] march dykes or fences between their lands, Application is made to the Sheriff Court or the Court of Session,[63] failing which, or failing consent, the adjoining proprietor cannot be compelled to share the cost of the fence.[64] The court may refuse an application if the pursuer's request is oppressive or unfair.[65] The Act applies only to lands exceeding five or six acres in extent,[66] and not where the boundary is the *medium filum* of a stream.[67] The fence must be beneficial, though not necessarily equally so, to both proprietors.[68]

The March Dykes Act 1669 (c. 38) empowers the sheriff on the application of a landowner where the marches are crooked and unequal to visit the marches,[69] adjudge parts of one estate to the other and if the exchange is not equal, award compensation to the landowner deprived. Under this Act also the Court will refuse an application which would be oppressive or unfair. The sheriff may fix a longer and less direct march if he considers this more convenient for both parties.[70]

Commonty

A commonty is a species of common property but differing from *pro indiviso* rights in common property, being a right to a share in common grounds for the purpose of pasturage, accessory to the commoner's individual lands, and having no existence save as appendages of individually held lands.[71] Commonty only exists where the respective

---

[60] *Strang* v. *Steuart* (1864) 2 M. 1015.

[61] Stair II, 3, 75; Bankt. I, 10, 153; Ersk. II, 6,4.

[62] *Paterson* v. *McDonald* (1880) 7 R. 958.

[63] *Pollock* v. *Ewing* (1869) 7 M. 815.   [64] *Ord* v. *Wright* (1738) Mor. 10479.

[65] E. *Peterborough* v. *Garioch* (1784) Mor. 10497; E. *Cassillis* v. *Paterson*, 28 Feb. 1809, F.C.; E. *Airlie* v. *Farquharson* (1887) 24 S.L.R. 761; *Blackburn* v. *Head* (1904) 11 S.L.T. 521; *Scott* v. *D. Argyll* (1907) 14 S.L.T. 829; *Secker* v. *Cameron*, 1914 S.C. 354.

[66] *Graham* v. *Irving* (1899) 2 F. 29.

[67] *Penman* v. *Douglas* (1739) Mor. 10481; *Secker, supra.*

[68] *Blackburn* v. *Head* (1904) 11 S.L.T. 521.

[69] *L.A.* v. *Sinclair* (1872) 11 M. 137.

[70] E. *Kintore* v. *E. Kintore's Trs.* (1886) 13 R. 997.

[71] Stair I, 7, 15; More's *Notes*, liii; Bankt. II, 7, 32; Ersk. III, 3, 56; Bell, *Prin.*§1072, 1087; Rankine, *L.O.* 600: L. *Blantyre* v. *Jaffray* (1856) 19 D. 167; *Milne* v. *Inveresk Par. Co.* (1899) 2 F. 283; *Macandrew* v. *Crerar*, 1929 S.C. 699.

rights of the commoners have not been defined by feudal grant and are ascertained only by possession. Each commoner may prevent attempts by any other to put the common to other than its ordinary use for pasturing animals

Statute[72] has empowered the Court of Session[73] to value and divide commonties, except property belonging to the King or held in burgage by burghs,[74] according to the value of the rights and interests of the various parties concerned, estimated according to the valuation of their respective lands or properties,[75] and the divisions to be made of the part of the commonty next adjacent to each person's property. Possession in different proportions does not affect the rule of division in proportion to valuation.[76] The Act does not apply where the right is one of servitude,[77] nor a precise and definite share in common grazing,[78] but does where more than one person has title to the property over which the commoners exercised their common interest.[79] Once divided, lots of commonty are held by titles along with other lands.[80]

Common grazing rights

A right of common grazing is not a right of property but a right, of the nature of a servitude, enjoyed by several proprietors or tenants in common, to the pro indiviso use of certain ground for grazing animals.[81] The right may be constituted by grant[82] or by prescription. Where several proprietors have a right of common grazing, none has a right for an indefinite number of animals but their claims are proportioned to the rents of the several lands and to the number of cattle that each can winter on his own lands. the proportions may be fixed by an action of souming and rouming.

Runrig lands

Where lands are divided runrig different proprietors have separate property in adjacent strips or ridges of land.[83] By statute[84] such lands

[72] Division of Commonties Act, 1695 (c. 69).
[73] Now competent in the Sheriff Court: Sheriff Courts (Sc.) Act, 1907, replacing 1877 Act, S. 8(3).
[74] *Hunter* v. *Mailler* (1854) 16 D. 641.
[75] *Macandrew, supra*; see also *Bruce* v. *Bain* (1883) 11 R. 192.
[76] *D. Douglas* v. *Baillie* (1740) Mor. 2474.
[77] *Stewart* v. *Tillicoultry* (1739) Mor. 2469; *Gordon* v. *Grant* (1850) 13 D. 1.
[78] *Macandrew* v. *Crerar*, 1929 S.C. 699.
[79] *Stewart* v. *Mackenzie* (1748) Mor. 2476; *Maitland* v. *Lambert* (1769) Mor. 2483.
[80] *Walker* v. *Miln* (1871) 9 M. 823; *Edmonstone* v. *Jeffray* (1886) 13 R. 1038.
[81] Ersk. II, 9, 14–16.
[82] e.g. *Macandrew* v. *Crerar*, 1929 S.C. 699.
[83] See Ersk. III, 3, 59; Bell, *Prin.* §1098.
[84] Runrig Lands Act, 1695 (c. 36).

may be redivided into consolidated portions according to the rights of the several proprietors,[85] but lands belonging to burghs and incorporations, and patches over four acres, are excluded.[86]

---

[85] *Davidson* v. *Kerr* (1748) Elch. Runridge, No. 1; *Davidson* v. *Heddell* (1829) 8 S. 219; *Lady Gray* v. *Richardson* (1876) 3 R, 1031; affd. 4 R. (H.L.) 76.
[86] Bell, *supra; Burns* v. *Boyle* (1829) 7 S. 415.

CHAPTER 5.8

ENTAILED ESTATE OR TAILZIED FEE

An entail is a disposition of the superiority or the fee of lands containing an express destination thereof to a prescribed series of heirs of the grantee other than the heirs-at-law,[1] clauses prohibiting alienation, contracting of debt affecting the estate, and altering of the order of succession,[2] and clauses irritant, annulling any prohibited act if done, and resolutive ; annulling the right to the estate of an heir contravening the provisions of the entail.[3] Entailing lands was made competent by the Entail Act, 1685, (c. 22), and was competent only of subjects which could be feudalized.[4] The object was to enable landowners to ensure that their lands passed undivided and unburdened down through the family.

Essentials

Entails might be embodied in any deed which could convey, or include, a conveyance of lands, but commonly in a *mortis causa* settlement. The essentials were the destination, the three cardinal prohibitions, the irritant and resolutive clauses, and registration in the Register of Tailzies.

The destination had to be a special class of heirs, different from[5] that of the legal order of succession,[6] who must be designed so as to be

---

[1] *Moubray's Trs. v. M.* (1895) 22 R. 801, 808.

[2] Known as the cardinal prohibitions.

[3] See generally Stair II, 3, 43; Bankt. II, 3, 133; Ersk. III, 8, 21; Bell, *Comm.* I, 43; *Prin.* §1716–74; *Ross, Lect.* II, 503; Menzies, 719; Sandford, *Entails, passim.*

[4] *Dalyell v. D.*, 17 Jan. 1810, F.C.; *Stirling v. Dunn* (1827) 3 W. & S. 462; *Henderson v. Drysdale* (1834) 7 W. & S. 441; *Stewart v. Nicholson* (1859) 22 D. 72; *Howden v. Rocheid* (1869) 7 M. (H.L.) 110; *Brown v. Soutar* (1870) 8 M. 702. Heritable rights which cannot be feudalized, such as of leases by assignation: *E. Dalhousie v. Ramsey-Maule* (1782) Mor. 10963; *Maule v. Maule*, 4 Mar. 1829, F.C.; see also *Chisholm v. Chisholm-Batten* (1864) 3 M. 202, 226; or rights of reversion, can be entailed but bind *inter haeredes* only. Moveables cannot be entailed: *Baillie v. Grant* (1859) 21 D. 838; *Kinnear v. K.* (1877) 4R. 705; *Sandys v. Bain's Trs.* (1897) 25 R. 261; but see *Bute v. B's Trs.* (1880) 8 R. 191; *Adam's Trs. v. Wilson* (1899) 1 F. 1042.

[5] *Leny v. L.* (1860) 22 D. 1272; *Moubray's Trs., supra.*

[6] For this, see Ch. 7.3, *infra*. If under the final branch of a destination entailed property descended to the heirs whomsoever of the maker or the last substitute heir, the estate is held in fee by the last substitute: *E. March v. Kennedy* (1760) 2 Pat. 49. As to fortifying by prescription the right of an heir called by mistake see *Cooper Scott v. Gill Scott*, 1924 S.C. 309.

recognizable as a line of heirs,[7] and transmission had to be without division among heirs-portioners.[8]

Cardinal prohibitions and irritant and resolutive clauses

The 1685 Act required these clauses to be expressed. If the entail was defective in one or more of the cardinal prohibitions, the entail was binding in other respects. The Rutherfurd Act, 1848, S. 43 made an entail invalid in one prohibition, or as to irritant or resolutive clause, invalid as regards all,[9] but a relaxation of the cardinal prohibitions *in gremio* of the entail did not make otherwise valid prohibitions ineffectual.[10] After Acts of 1848, 1858, and 1860[11] express inclusion of any of these clauses was unnecessary, provided the entail contained an express clause authorizing registration in the Register of Entails. On a contravention by the heir in possession the next heir was entitled to seek declarator and have himself served heir to the last heir who did not contravene;[12] the contravening heir might purge the irritancy by reducing the contravening deed.[13] The cardinal prohibitions were formerly interpreted very strictly[14] but latterly less so.[15]

Registration

Deeds of entail had to contain a description of the lands adequate for infeftment, not only to convey the lands, but to make it apparent from the Register of Entails what subjects were fettered.[16] The deed of entail required to be recorded in the Register of Entails under the authority of the court. An unrecorded deed of entail was not protected by the 1685 Act and, though binding on the heirs themselves, was ineffective against onerous creditors of the heir in possession;[17] such an heir might sell[18] and was not obliged to reinvest the price.[19] A feudal title to the lands entailed also required to be duly completed by registration in the Register of Sasines. On the transmission of an

---

[7] *Leny, supra; Gordon* v. *G's Trs.* (1866) 4 M. 501.
[8] Because such inheritance would make the estate liable to subdivision: Bell, *Prin.* §1723; *Farquar* v. *F.* (1838) 1D. 121; *MacDonald* v. *Lockhart* (1842) 5 D. 372; *Collow's Trs.* v. *Connell* (1866) 4 M. 465; *Connell* v. *Grierson* (1867) 5 M. 379. See also *Primrose* v. *P.* (1854) 16 D. 498.
[9] *D. Hamilton* v. *L. Hamilton* (1870) 8M. (H.L.) 48.
[10] *Catton* v. *Mackenzie* (1872) 10 M. (H.L.) 12.
[11] All re-enacted by Titles to Land Consolidation (Sc.) Act, 1868, S. 14.
[12] *Bontine* v. *Graham* (1840) 1 Rob. App. 347.
[13] *Abernethie* v. *Gordon* (1840) 1 Rob. App. 434.
[14] *Lang* v. *L.* (1839) MacL & Rob. 871; *Lumsden* v. *L.* (1843) 2 Bell 104; *Cathcart* v. *C.* (1863) 1 M. 759; *Fraser* v. *F.* (1879) 7 R. 134.
[15] *Wallace* v. *W's Trs.* (1880) 7 R. 902; *Verney* v. *V.*, 1914 S.C. 801.
[16] *King* v. *E. Stair* (1846) 5 Bell 82.
[17] *Wilison* v. *Callender* (1724) Mor. 15369.
[18] *Graham* v. *G.* (1829) 8 S. 231.
[19] *Montgomerie* v. *E. Eglinton* (1843) 2 Bell 149.

entailed interest in an area operational for the purposes of land registration it is probably registrable under the Land Registration (Sc.) Act,
1979.[20]

Special conditions

The maker of an entail might adject further special conditions, such
as provisions for payment of annuities, conditions that heirs of entail
should use a particular surname, arms and designation,[21] or clauses of
devolution providing that in certain circumstances the lands entailed
should descend to another line of heirs.[22]

Reserved powers

Relaxation of the cardinal prohibitions, so long as not contradictory
thereof,[23] could competently be included in an entail, in the form of
reserved powers to such effect as to sell to pay the entailer's debts,[24] to
grant feus within reasonable limits,[25] to sell or to excamb the estate and
to reinvest in land to be entailed on the same heirs,[26] to grant provisions
to the surviving spouse and younger children,[27] and to nominate
heirs.[28]

Contravention

On contravention of an entail by an heir in possession the next heir
was entitled by the Act of 1685 to pursue a declarator thereof and have
himself served heir to the last non-contravening heir infeft in the fee.[29]
A contravening heir is entitled to purge the irritancy by performing the
condition or rescinding the *ultra vires* action.[30] Deeds granted after
contravention but before irritancy was declared are valid in questions
with purchasers or bona fide onerous creditors.[31]

[20] 1979 Act. S. 2(4)(c).

[21] Bell, *Prin.*§1725; Bell, *Convg.* II, 1010; *Moir* v. *Graham* (1794) Mor. 15537; *Munro* v. *M.*
(1828) 3 W. & S. 344; *Cumming's Trs.* v. *C.* (1832) 10 S. 804; *Hunter* v. *Weston* (1882) 9 R.
492.

[22] Bell, *Prin.* §1726; *M. Hastings* v. *Lady Hastings* (1847) 6 Bell 30; *V. Hawarden* v.
Elphinstone's Trs. (1866) 4 M. 353; *Campbell* v. *C.* (1868) 6 M. 1035; *Munro* v. *Butler
Johnstone* (1868) 7 M. 250; *Home* v. *H.* (1876) 3 R. 591; *Nicholson* v. *Arbuthnott* (1878) 5 R.
872.

[23] *Baird* v. *B.* (1844) 6 D. 643, 650.

[24] Bell, *Prin.* §1728; *Scot* v. *His Heirs of Tailzie* (1751) Mor. 15394.

[25] *Cathcart* v. *Schaw* (1755) 1 Pat. 618; *Innes* v. *Kerr* (1812) 5 Pat. 609, 768.

[26] *Baird, supra.*

[27] *Dickson* v. *D.* (1854) 1 Macq. 729; *Catton* v. *Mackenzie* (1872) 10 M. (H.L.) 12; *Chancellor's Trs.* v. *Sharples's Trs.* (1896) 23 R. 435; *Balfour-Melville* v. *Mylne* (1901) 3 F. 421.

[28] Rankine, *L.O.*, 713. As to reserved power to disentail without judicial authority, see *Abbey*
v. *Atholl Properties, Ltd.*, 1936 S.N. 97.

[29] Bell, *Prin.* §1761; *Dundas* v. *Murray* (1774) Mor. 15430; *Bontine* v. *Graham* (1840) 1 Rob.
347.

[30] *Abernethie* v. *Gordon* (1840) 1 Rob. App. 434.

[31] Entail Amdt. Act, 1848, S. 40.

Assignation or attachment of heir's rights

An heir in possession may assign the lands in security, under the qualification that the security shall be *ipso facto* extinguished by the heir's death.[32] The lands may similarly, and under the same qualification, be attached by the heir's creditors.[33] The *spes successionis* of an heir-apparent cannot be attached by creditors.[34]

Prohibition of new entails after 1914

The Entail (Sc.) Act, 1914, S. 2, without prejudice to existing entails, prohibited the making of fresh entails, and provided that where, at its date, any money, land or moveables was held for purchasing land to be entailed but the direction had not been carried into effect, the date when the deed directing such entailing came into operation should be held to be the date of any entail to be made in execution of the direction, whatever its actual date.[35] Attention need now, accordingly, be given only to the powers of heirs of entail in possession under pre-1914 entails, and to the disentail of entailed lands.

Powers of heir of entail in possession at common law

An heir of entail in possession is not a mere liferenter of the lands, but a full fiar, subject, however, to the fetters and restrictions of the entail.[36] In view of the purpose of entailing lands and of the cardinal prohibitions of a strict entail his common law powers were very restricted.

The cardinal prohibition against alienation prevented an heir in possession from selling or granting feus,[37] granting leases of more than ordinary duration,[38] leasing for a grassum in addition to the rent,[39] or letting the mansion-house beyond his lifetime.[40] But the prohibition might be qualified and power to feu or lease given.[41] The power to excamb might be contained in an entail[42] but could be exercised only

---

[32] *Graham v. Hunter* (1828) 7 S. 13; *Grahame v. Alison* (1833) 6 W. & S. 518; *Ferrier v. Gartmore Heritable Creditors* (1835) 13 S. 1121.

[33] *Nairne v. Gray*, 15 Feb. 1810, F.C.; *Bontine v. Graham* (1840) 1 Rob. 347.

[34] *Beaton v. Macdonald* (1821) 1 S. 49.

[35] *Elliot Lockhart's Trs. v. E.L.*, 1927 S.C. 614, 620. See also *Lumsden's Trs. v. L.*, 1917 S.C. 579.

[36] *Gould v. G's Trs.* (1899) 2 F. 130, 139; *E. Galloway v. D. Bedford* (1902) 4 F. 851, 867; *Gillespie v. Riddell*, 1908 S.C. 628; *Somervell's Tr. v. S.*, 1909 S.C. 1125, 1130; see also *E. Breadalbane v. Jamieson* (1877) 4 R. 667; *Campbeltown Coal Co. v. D. Argyll*, 1926 S.C. 126.   [37] *Cathcart v. Schaw* (1756) 1 Pat. 618.

[38] *Queensberry Leases* (1819) 1 Bligh 339; *Eliott v. Pott* (1821) 1 Sh. App. 16, 89.

[39] *Eliott, supra.*

[40] *Cathcart, supra.*

[41] *Innes v. Ker* (1813) 5 Pat. 768; *E. Elgin v. Wellwood* (1821) 1 Sh. App. 44.

[42] *Baird v. B.* (1847) 6 Bell 7.

to such an extent as is consistent with the subsistence of the entail over the bulk of the estate.[43]

The prohibition against charging with debt disentitled an heir in possession, unless the entail specially enabled him to do so, from burdening the estate or succeeding heirs with the expense of improvements made by him on the estate.

Unless it were given him by the entail or by private Act an heir in possession had no power at common law to sell for payment of debts which affected or might be made to affect the estate.

An heir is possession could, however, work minerals even to the point of exhausting them,[44] cut wood, if ready for cutting,[45] and the cutting does not interfere with the amenity of the mansion-house,[46] though the heir cannot transmit to his executors a right to cut timber after his death;[47] he could not let the mansion-house for longer than his lifetime,[48] nor demolish it and sell the materials,[49] though he may demolish and replace by another house equally good.[50]

An heir is not affected by the personal contracts and obligations of his predecessor, since he does not represent the predecessor; he takes his interest in the estate direct from the entailer.[51]

Statutory Powers

The powers of heirs of entail in possession have been greatly extended by various statutes, which have empowered them, within the limits set by the several Acts, to do the following:

(a) to grant leases;[52]

---

[43] *Dalhousie's Trs.* v. *D.* (1878) 6 R. 141.

[44] *Muirhead* v. *Young* (1855) 17 D. 875; (1858) 20 D. 592; *Muirhead* v. *M's Trs.* (1899) 7 S.L.T. 2.

[45] *Bontine* v. *Graham's Trs.* (1827) 6 S. 74.

[46] *Boyd* v. *B.* (1870) 8 M. 637; *Huntley's Trs.* v. *Hallyburton's Trs.* (1880) 8 R. 50; see also *Ker* v. *Graham's Trs.* (1827) 6 S. 73, 270; *Macqueen* v. *Tod* (1899) 1 F. 1069; Entail (Sc.) Act, 1914, S. 7.

[47] *Paul* v. *Cuthbertson* (1840) 2 D. 1286; *Morison* v. *Lockhart;* 1912 S.C. 1017.

[48] *Leslie* v. *Orme* (1780) 2 Paton 533; *Montgomerie* v. *Vernon* (1895) 22 R. 465; modified by Entail (Sc.) Act, 1914, S. 6; see also *Hill* (1851) 14 D. 13; *Spiers* (1854) 17 D. 289.

[49] *Gordon* v. *G.,* 24 Jan. 1811, F.C.

[50] *Moir* v. *Graham* (1826) 4 S. 730; *E. Breadalbane* v. *Jamieson* (1877) 4 R. 667.

[51] *Gillespie* v. *Riddell,* 1908 S.C. 628, 637; 1909 S.C. (H.L.) 3; *Jolly's Exrx.* v. *Visct. Stonehaven,* 1958 S.C. 635.

[52] Entail Improvement Act, 1770, S. 1: *Hamilton* v. *H.* (1846) 9 D. 53; *Campbeltown Coal Co.* v. *Argyll,* 1926 S.C. 126; Entail Powers (Sc.) Act, 1836 S. 2, extended by Entail Act, 1838; see *Forbes* v. *Wilson* (1873) 11 M. 454; *Gould* v. *G's Trs.* (1899) 2 F. 130; *E. Galloway* v. *D. Bedford* (1902) 4 F. 851; (1904) 6 F. 971; *L. Abinger's Trs.* v. *Cameron,* 1909 S.C. 1245; Entail Amdt. Act, 1848, S. 4; Entail Amdt. Act, 1853, S. 5; Entail Amdt. (Sc.) Act, 1868, S. 3; Entail (Sc.) Act, 1882, S. 4.

(b) to grant building leases;[53]
(c) to feu;[54]
(d) to excamb;[55]
(e) to sell;[56]
(f) to charge the estate for expenditure;[57]
(g) to grant family provisions;[58]
(h) to erect cottages.[59]

Termination of entail at common law

An entail comes to an end at common law (a) when all the heirs of entail are dead[60] or the estate comes to be held by the last heir called as heir under the deed. If the estate comes to be held by the heirs whomsoever or heirs general of an institute, such estate is deemed fee-simple estate without judicial procedure;[61] (b) when heirs-portioners have not been

[53] Entail Improvement Act, 1770, S. 4: *Carrick* v. *Miller* (1868) 6 M. (H.L.) 101; *Gordon* v. *Rae* (1883) 11 R. 67; *Carter* v. *Lornie* (1890) 18 R. 353; *Montgomery* v. *Vernon* (1895) 22 R. 465; *McDowel* v. *McD.* (1904) 6 F. 575; Entail Sites Act, 1840, S. 1 (and see also New Parishes (Sc.) Act, 1844, S. 10); Entail Amdt. Act, 1848, S. 4; Entail Amdt. Act, 1853, S. 5; Entail Amdt. (Sc.) Act, 1868, S. 3: *Stewart* v. *Murdoch* (1882) 9 R. 458; Entail (Sc.) Act, 1882, S. 4.
[54] Entail Sites Act, 1840, S. 1 (and see also New Parishes (Sc.) Act, 1844, S. 10); Entail Amdt. Act, 1848, S. 4: *Farquharson* (1870) 9 M. 66; *D. Portland*, 1909 1 S.L.T. 72; Entail Amdt. Act, 1853, S. 5: *E. Kinnoul* (1862) 24 D. 379; Entail Amdt. (Sc.) Act, 1868, S. 3; Entail (Sc.) Act, 1882, S. 4; Entail (Sc.) Act, 1914, S. 4: *Jolly's Exrx.* v. *V. Stonehaven*, 1958 S.C.635.
[55] Entail Improvement Act, 1770, S. 32; Entail Powers (Sc.) Act, 1836, S. 3, extended by Entail Act, 1838; Entail Amdt. Act. 1848, S. 5; Entail Amdt. (Sc.) Act, 1853, S. 5; Entail Amdt. Act, 1868, S. 14.
[56] Tenures Abolition Act, 1746, Ss. 14, 16; Sales to the Crown Act, 1746, Ss. 2–3: *Fleeming* v. *Howden* (1868) 6 M. (H.L.) 113; Land Tax Redemption Act, 1801, S. 61; Entail Powers (Sc.) Act, 1836, S. 7; lands Clauses Consolidation (Sc.) Act, 1845, Ss. 7, 67: *Whitelaw* v. *W's Curator*, 1931 S.L.T. 99; Entail Amdt. Act, 1848, Ss. 4, 25: *McKenzie* v. *McK.* (1849) 11 D. 1115; *Scott Plummer* (1885) 12 R. 1349; *Laurie* (1898) 25 R. 636; *Callender-Brodie* (1904) 12 S.L.T. 474; *L.A.* v. *E. Moray's Trs.* (1905) 7 F. (H.L.) 116; *Kinloch*, 1920, 2 S.L.T. 79; *D. Richmond*, 1929 S.L.T. 441; Entail Amdt. Act, 1853, S. 5; Entail Amdt. (Sc.) Act, 1868, S. 9; Entail Amdt. (Sc.) Act, 1875, S. 6; Entail (Sc.) Act, 1882, Ss. 4, 19: *Ballantine* (1883) 10 R. 1061; *Stirling Stuart*, 1915, 2 S.L.T.260; *E. Rothes*, 1918, 1 S.L.T. 164; *Hope Vere*, 1921, 2 S.L.T. 271; *D. Sutherland*, 1922 S.L.T. 250; *Keck*, 1949 S.C. 462.
[57] Entail Improvement Act, 1770, S. 9; Entail Amdt. Act, 1848, Ss. 4, 13: *M. Bradalbane's Trs.* v. *Campbell* (1868) 6 M. (H.L.) 43; Entail Amdt. Act, 1853, S. 5; Entail Amdt. (Sc.) Act, 1868, S. 11; Entail Amdt. (Sc.) Act, 1875, Ss. 7–8; Entail Amdt. (Sc.) Act, 1878: *E. Kinnoul* v. *Haldane*, 1911 S.C. 1279; *Shepherd's Exors.* v. *Mackenzie*, 1913 S.C. 144; *Campbell's Trs.* v. *Adamson*, 1936 S.C. (H.L.) 31; *Maxwell-Stuart's Tr.* v. *M.S.*, 1947 S.L.T. 59; Entail Act, 1880; Entail (Sc.) Act, 1882, S. 4; War Damage Act, 1939, Ss. 6, 11; War Damage Act, 1941, S. 7; War Damage Act, 1943, S. 66. As to charging succession duty, see *Blythswood's J.F.* v. *Douglas*, 1935 S.C. 511.
[58] Entail Provisions Act, 1824, S. 1: *Callander* v. *C.* (1869) 7 M. 777; see also *Hunter Blair* v. *H.B.* (1899) 1 F. 437; *Somervill's Tr.* v. *S.*, 1909 S.C. 1125: Entail Amdt. Act, 1848, S. 21: *Brodie* v. *B.* (1867) 6 M. 92; *Balfour-Melville* v. *Duncan* (1903) 5 F. 1079; Entail Amdt. Act, 1853, S. 5; Entail Amdt. (Sc.) Act, 1868, S. 6; *E. Haddington*, 1919 S.C. 727; Entail Amdt. (Sc.) Act, 1875, S. 10; Entail Amdt. (Sc.) Act, 1878; Entail (Sc.) Act, 1882, S. 24.
[59] Entail Cottages Act, 1860, S. 1; Entail Amdt. (Sc.) Act, 1868, S. 12; Entail Amdt. (Sc.) Act, 1875, S. 3.   [60] *Henry* v. *Watt* (1832) 10 S. 644.
[61] *E. March* v. *Kennedy* (1760) 2 Paton 49; *Steele* v. *Coupar* (1853) 15 D. 385; *Gordon* v. *G's Trs.* (1882) 9 R. (H.L.) 101; Entail Amdt. Act, 1875, S. 13.

excluded and succeed under the destination;[62] (c) by prescriptive possession of the lands on a fee-simple title or one made up under the entail but in which the fetters of the entail have not been included expressly or by reference;[63] and (d) by prescriptive possession under an entail of later date, though covering the same lands and under the same conditions.[64] Also at common law an entail defective in one or more of the cardinal prohibitions was to that extent ineffective and so might not prevent alienation to an onerous purchaser.[65]

The Entail Amdt. Act, 1848, S. 43, enacted that an entail defective as to one of the cardinal prohibitions was deemed defective as to all of them, and such an entail might be terminated if challenged by an heir.[66]

Disentail

An heir of entail in possession if of full age, *capax*, and not debarred by marriage-contract[67] may, with the authority of the Court, disentail and acquire the estate in fee-simple (a) without consent if he is the only heir of entail in existence;[68] (b) without consent if he was born after 1 August, 1848, (old entail)[69] or after the date of the entail (new entail)[70] (c) with the consent of the heir-apparent if the heir was born before and the heir-apparent born after the date of the entail;[71] (d) with the consents of the three nearest heirs of entail or of the whole heirs of entail, if less than three, in being at the date thereof and the date of the Court's first interlocutor in the application, or the consents of the three nearest heirs who at these dates are entitled next in order to succeed, or the consents of the heir-apparent under the entail and of the heirs, at least two in number, including the heir-apparent, who in order successively would be heirs apparent, provided always that the nearest heir for the time entitled to succeed after the heir in possession is at least twenty-one and not legally incapacitated.[72]

The consent of an heir of entail, if under age or *incapax*, may be given by a *curator ad litem*;[73] the court has power to value an heir's

[62] Bell, *Convg.* II, 1048; *Collow's Trs.* v. *Connell* (1866) 4 M. 465.

[63] *Cathcart* v. *Maclaine* (1846) 8 D. 970; *Holmes and Campbell* v. *Cuninghame* (1851) 13 D. 689.

[64] E. *Eglinton* v. *Montgomerie* (1843) 2 Bell 149; *Stewart* v. S. (1846) 5 Bell 139; *Inglis* v. *I.* (1851) 14 D. 54.

[65] *Carrick* v. *Buchanan* (1844) 3 Bell 342; *Lindsey* v. *Oswald* (1863) 2 M. 249.

[66] *D. Hamilton* v. *L. Hamilton* (1870) 8 M. (H.L.) 48.

[67] 1848 Act, S. 8; 1882 Act, S. 17; Bell, *Prin.* §1774A; *Scott Douglas* (1883) 10 R. 952; *Pringle* v. *P.* (1891) 18 R. 895; *Lockhart*, 1909 1 S.L.T. 36.

[68] 1848 Act, S. 3; 1875 Act, S. 5(3); 1882 Act, S. 3; *Gorden* v. *Mosse* (1851) 13 D. 954; *Bruce Gardyne* v. *B.G.* (1883) 11 R. 60.

[69] 1848 Act, S. 2: an 'old' entail is one dated before 1st August 1848.

[70] 1848 Act, S. 1: a 'new' entail is one dated on or after 1st August 1848.

[71] 1848 Act, Ss, 1, 2; 1882 Act, S. 3.

[72] 1848 Act, S. 3; 1853 Act, S. 19; 1882 Act, S. 3; consent may be given at 21: 1875 Act, S. 4; and in the course of an application to the court: 1875 Act, S. 5(1).   [73] 1882 Act, S. 12.

expectancy and when the value is paid into bank or secured to the satisfaction of the court, to dispense with his consent;[74] it may authorize a factor *loco absentis* to execute an instrument of disentail,[75] and may even force disentail when the heir in possession has, after the 1882 Act, contracted debt.[76]

Money derived from the sale of part of an entailed estate or invested in trust to purchase lands to be settled on the heirs of entail may be aquired by the heir outright by application to the court.[77] Where money has been invested in trust for the purchase of land to be entailed, the person who would have become institute under the intended entail may acquire the funds free of the entail.[78] An heir who seeks to disentail must produce a schedule showing the debts and family provisions affecting the fee and not secured.[79]

Disentail is effected by applying to the Court of Session for authority to execute, and executing and recording in the Register of Entails, an instrument of disentail in the form provided by the 1848 Act,[80] subscribed by the disentailing heir and a notary before two winesses. When recorded, it absolutely frees and relieves the entailed estate of all the restrictions imposed thereby. The disentail only removes the fetters of entail and does not evacuate the destination of the lands.[81] A superior who has been heir of entail in possession retains the right to enforce building restrictions after he has become fee simple proprietor.[82] Disentail proceedings can be reduced where the procedure has not taken account of provisions for younger children,[83] but instruments of disentail and deeds granted under authority of the court under the Entail Acts are final if not appealed.[87] On disentail of lands in an area operational for the purposes of the Land Registration (Sc.) Act 1979, the title is probably registrable.[85]

---

[74] 1875 Act, S. 5(2); 1882 Act, S. 13; *Baird* v. *B.* (1891) 18 R. 1184; *D. Sutherland* v. *M. Stafford* (1892) 19 R. 504; on calculation see *De Virte* v. *Wilson* (1877) 5 R. 328; *E. Kintore*, 1918 S.C. 883. Interest does not run until it is paid or secured: *Pringle* v. *P.* (1892) 19 R. 926.

[75] 1882 Act, S. 14; Presumption of Death (Sc.) Act, 1977, S. 16.

[76] 1882 Act, S. 18; *L. Napier & Ettrick's Trs.* v. *Napier* (1901) 3 F. 579; *Somervell's Tr.* v. *Dawes* (1903) 5 F. 1065; *Somervell's Tr.* (1906) 13 S.L.T. 718; *Somervell's Tr.* v. *S.*, 1907 S.C. 528; 1909 S.C. 1125.   [77] 1848 Act, S. 26.

[78] 1848 Act, S. 27; *Black* v. *Auld* (1873) 1 R. 133; *Craig* v. *Picken's Trs.* (1886) 13 R. 603; *Tireman*, 1930 S.L.T. 561; *Fletcher* v. *F.'s Trs.*, 1934 S.C. 291.

[79] 1848 Act, Ss. 6, 32; 1875 Act, S. 12(5). Third parties, if not secured, may object to disentail: *Irving* v. *I.* (1871) 9 M. 539; *Baikie* v. *Kirkwall Educ. Trust*, 1914 S.C. 860: *Glasgow Corpn.* v. *L. Blythswood*, 1920 S.C. 398; cf. *L. Stonehaven*, 1926 S.L.T. 64.

[80] 1848 Act, S. 32; by the 1853 Act the disentail may be executed and the authority of the Court later applied for. In such a petition the court will not consider whether an irritancy has been incurred: *Inverclyde*, 1953 S.L.T. (Notes) 70.

[81] 1848 Act, S. 32; *Gray* v. *G's Trs.* (1878) 5 R. 820.

[82] *MacDonald* v. *Douglas*, 1963 S.C. 374.

[83] *Nicolson's Trs.* v. *N.*, 1925 S.L.T. 383.

[84] 1882 Act, S. 29; *V. Fincastle* v. *E. Dunmore* (1876) 3 R. 345; *Mackenzie* v. *Catton's Trs.* (1877) 5 R. 313.   [85] 1979 Act, S. 2 (4)(c).

THE LIFERENT ESTATE

Older authorities regarded liferent as a personal servitude, or burden on the fee of land,[1] but it is better to regard proper liferent of heritage (as distinct from improper or beneficiary liferent, where the liferenter is only a beneficiary, the fee being vested in trustees)[2] as a distinct estate in land, limited both in duration and by the concurrent existence of the estate of fee vested in another, the two estates in the land coexisting and mutually limiting each other.[3] Proper liferent is normally concerned with, possibly even confined to, cases where the liferenter is feudally vested in heritage,[4] whereas improper liferent may be, and frequently is, a right attaching to moveables, or to a mixed estate of heritage and moveables.

Nature of proper liferent

A proper liferent is the right to possess, use, and enjoy heritable subjects during the grantee's life, without destroying or wasting their substance, *salva rei substantia*, corresponding to the *usufructus* of the civil law.[5] Liferent is prima facie and normally a right to enjoy the use of heritage for the grantee's lifetime, but it includes also cases where the limited right may terminate before death, on the occurrence of some intervening and uncertain event, such as a daughter's marriage[6] or a widow's second marriage. The fee of the subjects is vested in another person, to whom the rights of actual possession, use and enjoyment revert on the expiry of the liferent. If the fee is not conferred on anyone it remains vested in the granter, and if he has died, in his *haereditas jacens.*[7] A liferent may be made subject to a resolutive condition or to prohibitions on specified uses of the lands, though these may be unenforceable if too vague or otherwise objectionable.[8]

---

[1] Stair II, 6, 4; Bankt. II, 6; Ersk. II, 9, 39: *Patrick* v. *Napier* (1867) 5 M. 683, 699.

[2] On improper liferent, see Ch. 6.2, *infra.*

[3] Ersk. II, 9, 41; Bell, *Comm.* I, 52; Bell, *Prin.* §1037.

[4] *Miller* v. *Inland Revenue*, 1930 S.C. (H.L.) 49, 56; *Fogo's J.F.* v. *Fogo's Trs.*, 1929 S.C. 546, is a case of proper liferent of a mixed estate.   [5] Bell, *Prin.* §1037.

[6] cf. *Carruthers* v. *Crawford*, 1945 S.C. 82.

[7] *Cumstie's Trs.* v. *C.* (1876) 3 R. 921; *Kindness* v. *Bruce* (1902) 4 F. 415; *Carruthers, supra.*

[8] *Chaplin's Trs.* v. *Hoile* (1890) 18 R. 27; *Wemyss* v. *W.*, 1921 S.C. 30; *Balfour's Trs.* v. *Johnston*, 1936 S.C. 137; *Veitch's Exor.* v. *V.*, 1947 S.L.T. 17.

Whether grant of fee or of liferent

It is a question of the granter's intention and of interpretation whether a gift or bequest of heritage is one in liferent only or in fee.[9] A liferent with a power of disposal, if unqualified, amounts to a grant of fee.[10] The fact that the fee is not disposed of and will fall into intestacy if the gift be held to be of liferent only is not at all conclusive in favour of its being interpreted as a gift of fee, but is a factor to be weighed in case of doubt.[11]

Initial gift of the fee later qualified

Words in a deed conferring initially a gift of fee to a beneficiary may be later qualified by expressions which may be held either to abridge the gift or merely to attach conditions to its use or enjoyment. The general principle is that unless the later qualifications in terms purport to abridge the gift itself they relate only to the mode of enjoyment.[12] Qualifications in a later separate deed are more readily held to reduce an initial gift than if in the same deed.[13]

Whether gift of restricted right of fee

In some cases a gift has apparently been made of a fee subject to certain restrictions, but the tendency has been to hold such gifts to be gifts of fee, the restrictions being ineffectual,[14] and there is now no recognized kind of right intermediate between fee and liferent.[15]

Whether grant of liferent or lesser right

It is a question of interpretation whether a right granted, whatever it be called in the deed granting it, is a proper liferent of heritage or a lesser right such as a bare licence to occupy, or personal right of

[9] See e.g. *Henderson's Trs.* v. *H.* (1876) 3 R. 320; *Gibson's Trs.* v. *Ross* (1877) 4 R. 1038; *Anderson* v. *Thomson* (1877) 4 R. 1101; *Houston* v. *Mitchell* (1877) 5 R. 154; *Smith's Trs.* v. *S.* (1883) 10 R. 1144; *Lawson's Trs.* v. *L.* (1890) 17 R. 1167; *Mitchell* v. *Ch. of Scotland* (1895) 2 S.L.T. 629; *Whitehead's Trs.* v. *W.* (1897) 24 R. 1032; *Newall's Trs.* v. *Inglis's Trs.* (1898) 25 R. 1176; *Jamieson's Trs.* v. *J.* (1899) 2 F. 258; *Mackenzie's Trs.* v. *M.* (1899) 2 F. 330; *Sim* v. *Duncan* (1900) 2 F. 434; *Patrick* v. *Fowler* (1900) 2 F. 690; *Crawford's Trs.* v. *Working Boys' Home* (1901) 8 S.L.T. 371; *Brash's Trs.* v. *Phillipson*, 1916 S.C. 271; *Letham* v. *Evans*, 1918 1 S.L.T. 27; *Smart* v. *S.*, 1926 S.C. 392; *Mearns* v. *Charles*, 1926 S.L.T. 118; *Graham* v. *G's Trs.*, 1927 S.C. 388; *Fogo's Trs.*, 1929 S.C. 546; *Duncan* v. *Edinburgh R.I.*, 1936 S.C. 811.
[10] *Rattray's Trs.* v. *R.* (1899) 1 F. 510; *Mickel's J.F.* v. *Oliphant* (1892) 20 R. 172.
[11] *Smith's Trs.* v. *S.* (1883) 10 R. 1144; *Lawson's Trs.* v. *L.* (1890) 17 R. 1167; *Spink's Exors.* v. *Simpson* (1894) 21 R. 551; *Sim* v. *Duncan* (1900) 2 F. 434; *Gillies' Trs.* v. *Hodge* (1900) 3 F. 238; *Milne's Trs.* v. *Milne's Exor.*, 1937 S.C. 149.
[12] *Tweeddale's Trs.* v. *T.* (1905) 8 F. 264.
[13] *Russell* v. *Bell's Trs.* (1897) 24 R. 666; *Tweeddale's Trs.*, *supra*; *Ford's Trs.* v. *F.*, 1940 S.C. 426.
[14] *Johnston* v. *J.* (1903) 5 F. 1039.
[15] cf. *Cochrane's Exrx.* v. *C.*, 1947 S.C. 134; overruling *Denholm's Trs.* v. *D's Trs.*, 1907 S.C. 61; and *Heavyside* v. *Smith*, 1929 S.C. 68; and qualifying *Ironside's Exor.* v. *I.*, 1933 S.C. 116.

occupation, corresponding to the Roman *habitatio*, which is not an
estate in the land, confers no real right, and is but a mere burden on the
fee thereof.[16] A person entitled to occupancy is liable to the burdens
incumbent on an occupier such as local rates, but not for feu-duty or
landlord's repairs,[17] or interest on a bond over the property.[18]

Subjects of liferent

The subjects of proper liferent of heritage are only such heritable
things as are not consumed by use; hence rights to minerals, unless
expressly given in liferent, are excluded. But a liferenter may enjoy the
revenue of mineral-workings opened or let by the granter of the liferent
as much as the rents of farms.[19]

Creation

Liferents of heritage arising by operation of law were formerly
recognized, in the legal rights of terce and courtesy,[20] but all proper
liferents are now conventional, created by constitution, or grant in
favour of a third party,[21] or by reservation, when an owner conveys
land to another in fee, reserving a liferent to himself.[21] Infeftment by
registration in the Register of Sasines, on behalf of the liferenter, is
necessary to confer real rights in the lands,[21] except in liferent by
reservation, which depends on the granter's existing sasine.[22] The
rights and powers of liferenters by reservation have in some cases been
treated as greater, and closer to those of a fiar.[23]

Restrictions on creation of liferents of heritage

By the Entail Amendment (Rutherfurd) Act, 1848, Ss. 47–8, it was
competent to grant a liferent interest in lands in favour only of a party
in life[24] at the date of the grant, and where any land is, by virtue of a
deed dated on or after 1 August, 1848, held in liferent by a party of full

[16] Ersk. II, 9, 39; Bell, *Prin.* §1037; *Clark* v. *C.* (1871) 9 M. 435; *Rodger's Trs.* v. *R.* (1875) 2 R. 294; *Kinloch's Trs.* v. *K.* (1880) 7 R. 596; *Bayne's Trs.* v. *B.* (1894) 22 R. 26; *Cathcart's Trs.* v. *Allardice* (1899) 2 F. 326; *Johnston* v. *J.* (1904) 6 F. 665; *Smart's Trs.* v. *S's Trs.*, 1912 S.C. 87; *Montgomerie-Fleming's Trs.* v. *Carre*, 1913 S.C. 1018; contrast *Morris* v. *Anderson* (1882) 9 R. 952; *Mackenzie's Trs.* v. *Kilmarnock's Trs.*, 1909 S.C. 472; *Johnstone* v. *Mackenzie's Trs.*, 1912 S.C. (H.L.) 106; *Milne's Trs.* v. *M.*, 1920 S.C. 456; see also *Ctess. of Lauderdale*, 1962 S.C. 302.
[17] *Clark, supra; Bayne's Trs., supra; Johnstone, supra; Montgomerie-Fleming's Trs., supra.*
[18] *Cathcart's Trs., supra.*
[19] *Wardlaw* v. *W's Trs.* (1875) 2 R. 368.
[20] See Ch. 7.2, *infra.*
[21] Stair II, 6, 6; Bankt. II, 6, 6; Ersk. II, 9, 41; Bell, *Comm.* I, 53; *Prin.* §1040–1; *Hardie* v. *Mags. of Port Glasgow* (1864) 2 M. 746.
[22] Ersk. II, 9, 42; Bell, *Prin.* §1055.
[23] Bell, *Prin.* §1040.
[24] cf. *Stewart's Trs.* v. *Whitelaw*, 1926 S.C. 701; *Reid's Trs.* v. *Dashwood*, 1929 S.C. 748.

age, born after that date, such party is deemed to be fee simple proprietor and may apply to the court for declarator accordingly.[25] By the Entail Act, 1914, S. 8, this principle was extended to deeds dated before the stated date. It is accordingly incompetent to create a perpetual series of liferents of heritage. The *nobile officium* cannot be invoked to confer a right on persons other than those for whom the statutory right is created, such as a pupil or minor,[26] but the provision does not apply to an annuity.[27] The Law Reform (Misc. Prov.) (Sc.) Act, 1968, S. 18, imposes similar restrictions on the duration of the liferents created by a deed executed after 25 November 1968.

Mode of creation of proper liferent of heritage

A liferent interest is created by a feu-charter or disposition or will or marriage contract bearing to be in favour of the grantee in liferent, or for his liferent use, or words to the same effect,[28] and to another in fee, or by a grant of lands to another in fee, reserving the granter's liferent. Title is completed by recording the feu-contract or disposition in the Register of Sasines, or by expeding a notice of title following on the will or marriage-contract and recording it similarly. In the case of lands in an area operational for the purposes of the Land Registration (Sc.) Act, 1979, the creation over a registered interest in land of a liferent is registrable.[29]

Destinations to parents and children

If the destination in the deed is to one in liferent and his heirs or children *nascituri* in fee the party called is deemed fiar;[30] if to one in liferent only, or liferent allenarly, or in alimentary liferent, and to his heirs in fee, the party called has only a liferent but has also a fiduciary fee, or holds the fee in trust, till they come into existence, for the persons who may be heirs at the date of his death.[31] The fee in such cases cannot be *in pendente* and if not destined to a named fiar, nor

[25] *Middleton*, 1929 S.C. 394; *Earl of Moray*, 1950 S.C. 281; see also *Harvey's Trs. v. H.*, 1942 S.C. 582.
[26] *Crichton-Stuart's Tutrix*, 1921 S.C. 840.
[27] *Drybrough's Tr. v. D's Tr.*, 1912 S.C. 939.
[28] The destination may be to two or more in liferent and to one of them, or the survivor or the heir of the survivor, in fee, or to two or more in conjunct fee and liferent.
[29] 1979 Act, S. 2(3) (ii).
[30] *Frog's Creditors* v. *His Children* (1735) Mor. 4262; *Lillie* v. *Riddell* (1741) Mor. 4267; *Lindsay* v. *Dott* (1807) Mor. Fiar, Appx. 1; *Dewar* v. *McKinnon* (1825) 1 W. & S. 161; *Ferguson's Trs.* v. *Hamilton* (1862) 4 Macq. 397; *McClymont's Exors.* v. *Osborne* (1895) 22 R. 411; *Dalrymple's Trs.* v. *Watson's Trs.*, 1932 S.L.T. 480.
[31] *Newlands* v. *N's Creditors* (1798) 3 Ross L.C. 634; *Miller* v. *M.* (1833) 12 S. 31; *Douglas* v. *Thomson* (1870) 8 M. 374; *Snell* v. *White* (1872) 10 M. 745; *Ferguson* v. *F.* (1875) 2 R. 627; *Cumstie* v. *C's Trs.* (1876) 3 R. 921; *Dawson* (1877) 4 R. 597; *Tristram* v. *McHaffies* (1894) 22 R. 121; *Gifford's Trs.* v. *G.* (1903) 5 F. 723; see also *Studd* v. *Cook* (1883) 10 R. (H.L.) 53, 61; *Lockhart's Trs.* v. *L.*, 1921 S.C. 761; *Devlin* v. *Lowrie*, 1922 S.C. 255.

vested in the liferenter under the doctrine of fiduciary fee, remains with the granter and passes to his heirs. Similarly if the liferenter dies without heirs of the destined class the fee reverts to the granter. If the fiar predeceases the liferenter the right of fee passes to the fiar's heirs under the destination, failing whom it falls into the *haereditas jacens* of the fiar and passes the fiar's heir under the rules of intestacy.[32]

These rules have no application where the fiar is named and in existence, nor where the fee is destined to named children and other children born later, when it vests in the named children for themselves and those subsequently born,[33] nor where the fee is vested in trustees to hold for a parent in liferent and unnamed children in fee,[34] nor where the fiars were other than the children or heirs of the body of the liferenter.[35]

These rules, though applicable originally to heritage, were extended to moveables[36] and to mixed estate,[37] and to cases of improper liferent, with an interposed trust.[37]

The Trusts (Sc.) Act, 1921, S. 8 largely displaces the rule of *Frog's Creditors*;[39] it provides that where in any deed property is conveyed to any person in liferent and in fee to persons who, when the conveyance comes into operation, are unborn or incapable of ascertainment, the person to whom the property is conveyed in liferent is not to be deemed fiar merely because the liferent is not expressed to be a liferent allenarly, but all such conveyances, unless a contrary intention appears, have effect as if it were declared to be a liferent allenarly. This rule, unlike the rule of *Frog's Creditors*,[39] applies whatever the relationship between liferenter and unborn or unascertainable fiars. A fiduciary fiar, at common law or under this provision, may be given by the court the powers of a trustee, or trustees may be appointed, or a judicial factor to hold the property in trust.[40]

Where the destination is governed by the rule of *Frog's Creditors*[41] infeftment in favour of the parent in liferent and the children in fee gives an unqualified right of fee to the parent, but if the destination is governed by the 1921 Act, S. 8, infeftment gives the parent a fiduciary

[32] *Todd* v. *Mackenzie* (1874) 1 R. 1203.
[33] *McGowan* v. *Robb* (1862) 1 M. 141; (1864) 2 M. 943; *Martin's Trs.* v. *Milliken* (1864) 3 M. 326.
[34] *Rait* v. *Arbuthnott* (1892) 19 R. 687; *Gifford's Trs.* v. *G.* (1903) 5 F. 723.
[35] *Ramsay* v. *Beveridge* (1854) 16 D. 764.
[36] *McClymont's Exors.* v. *Osborne* (1895) 22 R. 411.
[37] *Fraser's Trs.* v. *Turner* (1901) 8 S.L.T. 466.
[38] *Lockhart's Trs.* v. *L.*, 1921 S.C. 761.
[39] *Frog's Creditors* v. *His Children* (1735) Mor. 4262; see *Colville's Trs.* v. *Marindin*, 1908 S.C. 911.
[40] 1921 Act, S. 8(2): *Gibson*, 1967 S.C. 161; but see *Cripps's Trs.* v. *C.*, 1926 S.C. 188.
[41] *Frog's Creditors* v. *His Children* (1735) Mor. 4262; see *Colville's Trs.* v. *Marindin*, 1908 S.C. 911.

fee.[42] If infeftment is taken only in favour of the parent in liferent the granter is not divested as fiar.[43]

Where a fiduciary fee is held for children *nascituri*, unless the deed of gift indicates a contrary intention, the fee vests in each child on coming into existence,[44] subject to partial defeasence if other children are born, or if a child does not survive the expiry of the liferent. The fiduciary fee lasts only so long as required to ascertain the fiar.[45]

Destinations to spouses

In this class of cases the main rules of construction are: A destination to spouses in joint or conjunct fee gives an equal right of fee to each; if survivorship be added, the survivor takes the whole fee.[46] A destination in conjunct liferent gives each a liferent of a half and to the survivor liferent of the whole.[47] A destination in conjunct fee and liferent prima facie gives the fee to the husband and a liferent to the wife if she survives,[48] but different interpretations are justified if the husband paid a price for the property,[49] or the property came from the wife or her relatives,[50] or the heirs of one spouse are favoured.[51] If the destination includes mention of survivorship, the survivor will have the fee, whoever had it during the marriage.

Destinations to strangers

The main rules of interpretation in this case are:
If there is a destination to two strangers and the heirs of one, the fee goes to the one having heirs, the other having a liferent only.[52] If to two strangers in conjunct fee and liferent each has a share in the liferent, the survivor a liferent of the whole, and the heirs of each take a half share of the fee.[53] If such a destination mentions survivorship, the survivor has the whole fee.[54]

[42] *McLachlan's Trs.* v. *McL.* (1858) 20 D. 612; *Livingstone* v. *Waddell's Trs.* (1899) 1 F. 831.

[43] *Stewart* v. *Rae* (1883) 10 R. 463; *Livingstone, supra.*

[44] *Beattie's Trs.* v. *Cooper's Trs.* (1862) 24 D. 519; *Robertson* (1869) 7 M. 1114; *Douglas* v. *Thomson* (1870) 8 M. 374; *Turner* v. *Gaw* (1894) 21 R. 563.

[45] *Ferguson* v. *F.* (1875) 2 R. 627; *Maule* (1876) 3 R. 831; *Black* v. *Mason* (1881) 8 R. 497.

[46] *Walker* v. *Galbraith* (1895) 23 R. 347; *Perrett's Trs.* v. *P.,* 1909 S.C. 522. The older view was that the fee was in one, normally the husband; Stair II, 6, 10; Ersk. III, 8, 36; Bell, *Convg.* II, 834.

[47] *Reid's Trs.* v. *R.* (1879) 6 R. 916; *Dick's Trs.* v. *Baird,* 1909 1 S.L.T. 101; *Paull* v. *Forbes,* 1911 1 S.L.T. 29.

[48] Stair, Ersk., *supra; Millar* v. *M. Lansdowne,* 1910 S.C. 618.

[49] *Fisher's Trs.* v. *F.* (1844) 7 D. 129.

[50] *Smith Cuninghame* v. *Anstruther's Trs.* (1872) 10 M. (H.L.) 39; *Brough* v. *Adamson* (1887) 14 R. 858.

[51] *Smith Cuninghame, supra.*

[52] Ersk. III, 8, 35; Bell, *Prin.* §1709.

[53] Ersk. Bell, *supra; Paul* v. *Home* (1872) 10 M. 937.

[54] Craigie, *Herit.,* 558; cf. *Devlin* v. *Lowrie,* 1922 S.C. 255.

Liferenter's powers

The liferenter is *interim dominus* or proprietor for life.[55] Though infeft he cannot alienate the lands *inter vivos*[56] or *mortis causa;*[57] he cannot grant a feu,[58] nor a lease[59] or servitude for any period longer than his own life. As he is not in general entitled to cut timber, he cannot sell trees, but coppice wood may be sold as well as cut,[60] though the purchaser's rights cease on the liferenter's death.[61] Where minerals had been worked by the granter, a liferenter has been held entitled to concur with the fiars in renewing the leases, provided there was no substantial danger of exhaustion of the minerals.[62]

Subject thereto he has the ordinary powers of administration of a proprietor, subject to the overriding consideration that nothing may be done to depreciate the capital value of the fee of the lands.

Liferenter's rights

The liferenter is entitled to all uses of the subjects and their fruits, subject to not destroying the substance of the subjects;[63] he is entitled to possession, and to appropriate all industrial or natural produce separated from the land during his liferent.[64] He may gather brush-wood and windfalls, and timber and extraordinary windfalls necessary for the maintenance and repair of the buildings and fences,[65] but only after intimation to the fiar.[66] The liferenter is also entitled to coppice wood, cut regularly as it ripens,[67] and his rights may be expressly extended.[68]

He may continue to work, and takes the royalties of, any minerals being worked when the liferent opens, but may not open new mines or quarries,[69] and particularly may take minerals necessary for domestic

---

[55] Ersk. II, 9, 41.
[56] cf. *Ferguson* v. *F.* (1875) 2 R. 627; *Chaplin's Trs.* v. *Hoile* (1890) 18 R. 27; *Devlin* v. *Lowrie,* 1922 S.C. 255.
[57] *Carruthers* v. *Crawford,* 1945 S.C. 82.
[58] Bell, *Prin.* §1056; *Redfearn* v. *Maxwell,* 7 Mar. 1816, F.C.
[59] Bell, *Prin.* §1057; *Fraser* v. *Croft* (1898) 25 R. 496.
[60] *Tait* v. *Maitland* (1825) 4 S. 247; *Macalister's Trs.* v. *M.* (1851) 13 D. 1239.
[61] Stair II, 3, 74; Ersk. II, 9, 58; Bell, *Prin.* §1058.
[62] *Wardlaw* v. *W's Trs.* (1875) 2 R. 368.
[63] Ersk. II, 9, 56; Bell, *Prin.* §1044; *Rogers* v. *Scott* (1867) 5 M. 1078.
[64] *Nisbett* v. *N's Trs.* (1835) 13 S. 517.
[65] *Macalister's Trs.* v. *M.* (1851) 13 D. 1239.
[66] *Dickson* v. *D.* (1823) 2 S. 152; *Tait* v. *Maitland* (1825) 4 S. 247.
[67] *Macalister's Trs.* v. *M.* (1851) 13 D. 1239.
[68] *Dingwall* v. *Duff* (1833) 12 S. 216.
[69] Bankt. II, 6, 6; Ersk. II, 9, 57; Bell, *Comm.* I, 61; *Prin.* §1042, 1070; *Wardlaw* v. *W's Trs.* (1875) 2 R. 368; *Dick's Trs.* v. *Robertson* (1901) 3 F. 1021; cf. *Guild's Trs.* v. *G.* (1872) 10 M. 911; *Baillie's Trs.* v. *B.* (1891) 19 R. 220; *Nugent* v. *N's Trs.* (1899) 2 F. (H.L.) 21.

and estate use,[70] and for this purpose may open workings, probably subject to liability to account to the fiar.

He is entitled to feu-duties,[71] and rents,[72] according to the legal terms of payment,[73] and if entitled to the liferent interest in a heritable bond, to the termly payment of interest,[74] but not to casualties, grassums or other extraordinary profits of land.[75]

In the case of a liferent granted for payment, which could extend to more than twenty years, after 31st July 1974, no part of the property is to be used as or part of a private dwelling-house, on pain of being removed.[76]

Liferenter's liabilities

The liferenter is liable for all the annual and periodical burdens attaching to the subjects, such as feu-duty, stipend and annual rates, but not for burdens attaching to heritors only occasionally.[77]

He is not liable for fair wear and tear or natural deterioration of the subjects, but he is bound to preserve the subjects in as good condition as he got them and to meet the expenses necessary for normal repairs.[78] If the fiar executes repairs the liferenter must pay the interest of the expenditure.[79]

In the event of natural decay or accidental destruction of the subjects liferented, neither fiar not liferenter is bound to restore. If the fiar does so, the liferenter must contribute in proportion to his interest; if the liferenter does so, the fiar must compensate him according to his interest, or the fee will be burdened with the capital cost, but not the interest, during the liferent.[80]

If there is danger that the liferenter will dilapidate the estate, he may be required to find caution that he will not do so.[81]

---

[70] *Lamington v. Her Son* (1682) Mor. 8240; *D. Roxburghe v. Duchess*, 19 Jan. 1816, F.C.; *Dickson, supra.*

[71] Ersk. II, 9, 42; Bell, *Prin.* §1048.

[72] Ersk. II, 9, 64; Bell, *Prin.* §1047.

[73] *Trotter v. Cunninghame* (1837) 2 D. 140; *Campbell v. C.* (1849) 11 D. 1426; *Blaikie v. Farquharson* (1849) 11 D. 1456.

[74] Bell, *Prin.* §1049.

[75] *Ewing v. E.* (1872) 10 M. 678; *Gibson v. Caddall's Trs.* (1895) 22 R. 889; contrast *Montgomerie Fleming's Trs. v. M.F.* (1901) 3 F. 591, where held that duplications of feu-duties were to be treated as liferenter's income.

[76] Land Tenure Reform (Sc.) Act, 1974, Ss. 8–10.

[77] Ersk. II, 9, 61; Bell, *Prin.* §1061; *Anstruther v. A's Tutors* (1823) 2 S. 306; *Clark v. C.* (1871) 9 M. 435; *Rodger's Trs. v. R.* (1875) 2 R. 294; *Bayne's Trs. v. B.* (1895) 22 R. 26; *Cathcart's Trs. v. Allardice* (1899) 2 F. 326; *Johnstone v. Mackenzie's Trs.*, 1911 S.C. 321; *Smart's Trs. v. S's Trs.*, 1912 S.C. 87.

[78] Ersk. II, 9, 60; Bell, *Prin.* §1062; *Scott v. Haliburton* (1823) 2 S. 435.

[79] *Laird v. Fenwick* (1807) Mor. Liferenter, Appx. 4.

[80] Ersk. II, 9, 60; Bell, *Prin*, §1063; *Nelson v. Gordon* (1874) 1 R. 1097.

[81] Ersk. II, 9, 59; Bell, *Prin.* §1064; *Ralston v. Leitch* (1803) Hume 293.

A liferenter is not bound to make improvements and if he does so they are presumed made for his own benefit.[82] Expenditure on additions or improvements is a burden on the fiar.[83]

He is not liable for the granter's debts, which attach to the fee, if sufficient to discharge them,[84] but is liable for interest on heritable bonds due from the land during the liferent.[85]

If the fiar has no other means of subsistence, the liferent must aliment the fiar, but this burden does not transmit against his heirs[86] nor is it effectual against his creditors.[87]

Termination of liferent

On the expiry of the liferent, or last liferent, by death, or the event which limits the liferent, the estate falls automatically to the fiar.[88] If he has not already done so, he must complete title as fiar by recording the feu-contract or disposition in his favour, or expeding and recording a notice of title on the will or marriage-contract. A liferent may also be discharged or renounced by the liferenter.[89] It also comes to an end by consolidation with the fee, if liferent and fee come to be vested in the same person.[90]

The liferenter's executors are entitled to any rents or other money which fell due before the liferenter's death, but had not been paid. The executors are entitled to rents due according to the legal terms, notwithstanding the conventional terms,[91] and to any crop sown by the liferenter before his death: *messis sementem sequitur*.[92] The profits of fishings, mines, and similar subjects accrue *de die in diem* and must be apportioned down to the date of death.[93] But natural fruits of the soil, such as woods, belong to the fiar.

Fiar's rights

The fiar has the reversionary right to enter into full possession and enjoyment of the lands on the termination of the liferent, and during its

---

[82] *Wallace* v. *Braid* (1900) 2 F. 754.

[83] *Shaw's Trs.* v. *Bruce*, 1917 S.C. 169.

[84] Bell, *Prin.* §1060; *Stewart* v. *S.* (1792) Bell Oct. Cas. 220.

[85] *Forbes* v. *F.* (1765) 2 Pat. 84; see also *Fraser* v. *Croft* (1898) 25 R. 496; *Wallace* v. *Braid* (1900) 2 F. 754.

[86] Ersk. II, 9, 62–3.

[87] *Blair* v. *Scott's Trs.* (1737) Elch. Aliment 5; Bell, *Prin.* §1065.

[88] Ersk. II, 9, 64; Bell, *Prin.* §1066.

[89] Ersk. II, 9, 68; Bell, *Prin.* §1066; *Pretty* v. *Newbigging* (1854) 16 D. 667; *Foulis* v. *F.* (1857) 19 D. 362; *Smith* v. *Campbell* (1873) 11 M. 639.

[90] *Martin* v. *Bannatyne* (1861) 23 D. 705.

[91] Ersk. II, 9, 64.

[92] Ersk. II, 9, 65; *Macmath* v. *Nisbet* (1621) Mor. 15877; *Guthrie* v. *Mackerston* (1671) Mor. 15891; *Cockburn* v. *Brown* (1748) Mor. 15911; *Keith* v. *Logie's Heirs* (1825) 4 S. 267.

[93] Apportionment Act, 1870, S. 2; see also *Campbell* v. *C.* (1849) 11 D. 1426; *Tennent's Exor.* v. *Lawson* (1897) 35 S.L.R. 72; *Balfour's Exors.* v. *Inland Revenue*, 1909 S.C. 619.

continuance the right to interfere, if necessary, to maintain the integrity of the estate, but not to present possession; hence he cannot remove tenants.[94] He may plant trees during the liferenter's possession and insist on their being protected.[95]

He is entitled to timber which falls or is felled on the estate, to normal thinnings, and to windfalls caused by exceptional storms,[96] but not timber necessary for the comfortable enjoyment of the liferenter's dwelling-house[97] nor is he entitled to denude the estate of timber for ordinary requirements.[98] He may work minerals excepted from the liferent, subject to liability to the liferenter for surface damage, but must leave enough for the liferenter's use. Also he may not hurt the amenity of the liferenter's possession.[99]

---

[94] *Buchanan* v. *Yuille* (1831) 8 S. 843.
[95] *Ewing* v. *E.* (1881) 19 S.L.R. 20.
[96] Craig II, 8, 17; Dirl. & St. 337; Stair II, 3, 74; Bankt. II, 6, 6; Ersk. II, 9, 58; Bell, *Comm.* I, 61; *Prin.* §1046, 1058; *Macalister's Trs.* v. *M.* (1851) 13 D. 1239.
[97] *Fraser* v. *Middleton* (1794) Mor. 7849; *Dickson* v. *D.* (1823) 2 S. 152; *Tait* v. *Maitland* (1825) 4 S. 247.
[98] *Stanfield* v. *Wilson* (1680) Mor. 8244.
[99] Bell, *Prin.* §1070.

CHAPTER 5.10

TEINDS, CHURCH, MANSE AND GLEBE

Teinds or tithes are the proportion of the profit of lands due for the support and maintenance of the church and clergy.[1] In many cases before the Reformation grants of tithes were made to laymen, and they became secularized and temporal rights. At the Reformation church lands and teinds frequently were granted by the Crown as temporal lordships to laymen, sometimes known as titulars of the teinds or Lords of Erection, who presented ministers to charges, sometimes with the right to a stipend.

All former church lands were with certain exceptions annexed to the Crown in 1587[2] and subsequent erections were voided by statute of 1592.[3] In 1625 the Crown revoked all grants of church lands or of teinds made since 1587 and appointed commissions to value teinds and reach a settlement with the titulars. Differences were settled by the King as arbiter and his decrees-arbitral of 1629 were confirmed by statutes of 1663 and 1690.[4]

Teinds are therefore both an interest in land held by a landowner who has a title as titular of teinds, subject to the burden of providing stipend, and a burden on lands due by a heritor to the titular and providing a fund for affording a stipend to the parochial clergy. They were *debita fructuum*, not *debita fundi*, but are now a real burden on the lands.

Teinds might be drawn teinds, valued teinds or redeemed teinds. Drawn teinds, or teinds drawn in kind, were one-tenth of the annual produce of the lands, the balance being known as the stock. They might be parsonage teinds, due to the incumbent of the living, and due from grain raised by cultivation, or vicarage teinds, due to the vicar, deputed to serve the parish, and due from minor and accidental products, such as cattle, fish, fowls and eggs, and regulated by custom. By custom, they were payable in money, not kind. If there were no

---

[1] See generally Stair II, 2, and 8; Ersk. II, 10; Bell, *Prin.* §1146; Buchanan on *Teinds*; Connell on *Tithes* and *Parishes*; and *Galloway* v. *E. Minto*, 1920 S.C. 354, esp. L. Sands at pp. 358–82; affd. 1922 S.C. (H.L.) 24. See also Miller, 32 J.R. 54; 33 J.R. 36, 109.
[2] Ersk. II, 10, 19.
[3] Ersk. II, 10, 23.
[4] Ersk. II, 10, 28.

vicar, they also were due to the parson.[5] The heritor notified the titular to teind the former's crops by a certain day, failing which the heritor himself in presence of witnesses stacked the teind sheaves.

Frequently heritor and titular arranged for delivery by the former annually of a fixed number of bolls of corn. The Act 1633, c. 17, ended the practice of titulars drawing teinds, permitting heritors to lead in their own crop after the teind had been valued and the price paid or secured.

In valued teinds, the teinds were valued judicially by the Teinds Commission or latterly by the Court of Session as Commission of Teinds[6] on the basis of one-fifth of the clear rent.[7] This fixed the value for all time. Valued teind could then be surrendered to the minister in perpetuity, which limited the heritor's liability to the amount of his teinds.[8] Teinds in the hands of titulars or parsons were in 1633 made redeemable by heritors at stated rates of purchase.[9]

Increases in stipend, up to the limit of the free teind of the parish, might be obtained by a minister by a process of augmentation before the Court of Teinds. The minimum stipend was five chalders (80 bolls) of victual or 500 marks.[10] The value of a chalder was later fixed at £100 Scots.[11] An augmentation could not be brought before twenty years from the last augmentation. By the Teinds Act, 1808, stipends were to be awarded in grain or victual, unless where it appeared necessary to provide a money stipend, converted into money, according to the fiars prices of the county; the value of a chalder varied from year to year and county to county.

Standardization of stipend

By the Church of Scotland (Property and Endowments) Act, 1925, stipend is to be payable thereafter only in money at a standard value ascertained in manner fixed by the Act, and fixed at the first term of Martinmas at least six months after the benefice becomes vacant (S. 3), or at the election of a minister then in office (S. 4), or on notification by the General Trustees (S. 5), Standardized stipend is payable half-yearly in arrears to the General Trustees of the Church (S. 8). The minister or General Trustees might down to 1936 apply for augmentation of stipend (S. 10). The Clerk of Teinds has to prepare (S. 11) for every parish in Scotland a teind roll specifying the total teind of the parish,

---

[5] Ersk. II, 10, 13; Bell, *Prin.* §1151; *Scott* v. *Methven* (1851) 13 D. 991. Bishop's teinds were also recognized: *L.A.* v. *E. Galloway* (1873) 11 M. 896.

[6] Court of Session (Sc.) Act, 1825, S. 54.

[7] Acts, 1633, cc. 15 and 17; Bell, *Prin.* §1160.

[8] *McEwan* v. *Watt*, 1922 S.C. 203.

[9] See *Galloway* v. *E. Minto*, 1922 S.C. (H.L.) 24.

[10] £27 : 15 : 6$^{2}/_{3}$ or £27.77 Stg.

[11] £8 : 6 : 8 or £8.33 Stg.

the amount applicable to each heritor, the value of the whole stipend payable to the minister and the proportion payable by each heritor.[12] The standard value of the stipend exigible from teinds, the 'standard charge', is made a real burden on the whole of the lands subject thereto, unless and until intimation of allocation is made by the General Trustees and a disponer of lands to the Clerk of Teinds, when it is allocated on the portions of the lands disponed (Ss. 12–13). Stipend of small amounts is compulsorily redeemed or extinguished (Ss. 14–15),[13] and surplus teinds may be sold (S. 18). Once the teind roll of a parish has been declared final the values entered are binding on titular and heritors.[14]

Church

The expense of maintaining and repairing the parish church formerly lay on the heritors or heritable proprietors of lands within the parish,[15] excluding titulars of teinds,[16] superiors,[17] liferenters,[18] and tenants.[19] Under the Church of Scotland (Property and Endowments) Act, 1925, Ss. 21–32, all property in all churches, with a few exceptions, is transferred to the Church of Scotland General Trustees and heritors are released from duties of maintenance and repair.

Manse

The minister of a landward or burghal-landward parish was entitled to have a manse provided, maintained, and repaired or rebuilt at the expense of the heritors,[20] or to receive an allowance, called manse-maill, from the heritors in lieu[21] but the minister of a burghal parish was not so entitled. He was entitled to have the manse garden walled,[22] to have a water supply[23] and an access road.[24] He may let the manse furnished in the summer.[25] Under the Church of Scotland (Property

---

[12] cf. *Church of Scotland General Trs.* v. *Minto Heritors*, 1933 S.C. 445; *Glasgow University Court* v. *Colmonell Common Agent*, 1933 S.C. 612; *D. Fife's Trs.* v. *Mackessack*, 1934 S.C. 307.

[13] cf. *Ch. of Scotland General Trs.* v. *Dowie*, 1946 S.C. 335.

[14] *Glasgow University Court* v. *Lord Advocate*, 1961 S.C. 246.

[15] Ersk. II, 10, 63; Bell, *Prin.* §1164; *Minister* v. *Heritors of Dunning* (1807) Mor. Kirk. Appx. 4. On the rights of heritors to pews see *Paterson* v. *Brown*, 1913 S.C. 292.

[16] *Reid* v. *Commrs. of Woods* (1850) 12 D. 1215.

[17] *Dundas* v. *Nicolson* (1778) Mor. 8511; *Strathblane Heritors* v. *Glasgow Corpn.* (1899) 2 F. (H.L.) 25.

[18] *Lady Anstruther* v. *A.* (1823) 2 S. 306.

[19] *McLaren* v. *Clyde Trs.* (1868) 6 M. (H.L.) 81.

[20] Ersk. II, 10, 57; Bell, *Prin.* §1165; cf. *Elgin Mags.* v. *Gatherer* (1841) 4 D. 25; *Downie* v. *McLean* (1883) 11 R. 47.

[21] *Church of Scotland General Trs.* v. *D. Fife's Trs.*, 1933 S.C. 102.

[22] *Maxwell* v. *Langholm Presbytery* (1867) 5 S.L.R. 16.

[23] *E. Glasgow* v. *Murray* (1868) 7 M. 6; *Smith* v. *Prestonpans Heritors* (1903) 5 F. 333.

[24] *McPhail* v. *Kilbrandon Heritors*, 1914 S.C. 1015.

[25] *Aberdour Heritors* v. *Roddick* (1871) 10 M. 221; *I.R.C.* v. *Fry* (1895) 22 R. 422.

and Endowments) Act, 1925, Ss. 21–32, the property in manses and the responsibility for the upkeep thereof was transferred to the Church of Scotland General Trustees.[26] Under S. 40 any manse-maill payable in lieu of a manse had to be redeemed by the heritors.[27]

Glebe

The minister of a country parish is entitled to a glebe of four acres of arable land, or sixteen soums of pasture land,[28] picked from church lands in a particular order. The minister may, without the heritors' consent, excamb the glebe lands,[29] and with the consent of the heritors and the Court of Teinds' authority,[30] feu the glebe. He is also entitled to grass for a horse and two cows from church grass lands, failing which to £20 Scots yearly.[31] The minister of a burghal parish is not entitled to a glebe nor to minister's grass.

The rights of ministers to glebe and grass have been preserved by the Church of Scotland (Property and Endowments) Act, 1925, but statutory procedure (S. 30) provides for implement of the heritors' obligations and transfer of the ownership of glebes to the General Trustees of the Church.

[26] cf. *Moffat* v. *Canonbie Kirk Session*, 1936 S.C. 209.

[27] *Church of Scotland General Trs.* v. *D. Fife's Trs.*, 1933 S.C. 102.

[28] Stair II, 3, 40; Ersk. II, 10, 59; Bell, *Prin.* §1172, 1176; *Macmillan* v. *Kintyre Presbytery* (1867) 6 M. 36; cf. *Arbroath Mags.* v. *Presbytery of Arbroath* (1883) 10 R. 767; *Arbroath Heritors* v. *The Minister* (1883) 20 S.L.R. 781; *Alpine* v. *Dumbarton Heritors* (1907) 15 S.L.T. 489.

[29] *Rain* v. *Lady Seafield* (1887) 14 R. 939; *Dalhousie's Tutors* v. *Minister of Lochlee* (1891) 18 R. (H.L.) 72; *Cadell* v. *Allan* (1905) 7 F. 606; *McEwan's Trs.* v. *Ch. of Scotland General Trs.*, 1940 S.L.T. 357.

[30] Glebe Lands (Sc.) Act, 1886, S. 17; *Boyd* (1882) 19 S.L.R. 828; see also *Minister of Carriden* v. *Heritors*, 1910 S.C. 1131; *Minister of Wilton* v. *Heritors*, 1925 S.C. 372.

[31] cf. *Macmillan* v. *Kintyre Presbytery* (1867) 6 M. 36.

CHAPTER 5.11

REAL BURDENS AND GROUND ANNUALS

A person seised of an estate in land may create *jura in re aliena* or interests over his land in favour of other persons, constituting burdens on his rights and limitations on his enjoyment of the lands. The recognized categories of burdens are real burdens and ground annuals, redeemable dispositions in security, servitudes, licences, and leases.

Real Burdens

A real burden is a debt payable from and attaching as a burden to lands themselves and not merely binding the owner personally. It is not a feudal estate in land but a burden qualifying the owner's real rights in the land.[1]

It may be created by reservation, as by disposition of lands to a grantee under burden of a money payment to the granter,[2] or by constitution, as by a disposition or bequest of lands under burden of a payment by the grantee to a third party.[3]

No *voces signatae* are necessary to create a real burden, so long as the intention is clearly to make the payment a real burden payable from the lands.[4] The burden must be clearly, definitely and precisely stated,[5] be included in the dispositive clause of the deed,[6] be declared to affect the lands,[7] and the sum,[8] and the name of the creditor[9] must be clearly specified, and these elements must appear in the disponee's infeftment in the Register of Sasines.[10] A burden cannot be constituted

[1] Ersk. II, 3, 49; Bell, *Prin.* §923.
[2] cf. *Davidson* v. *Dalziel* (1881) 8 R. 990; *Ewing's Trs.* v. *Crum Ewing*, 1923 S.C. 569.
[3] e.g. *Storeys* v. *Paxton* (1878) 6 R. 293.
[4] *Tailors of Aberdeen* v. *Coutts* (1840) 1 Rob. 296; *Arbroath Mags.* v. *Dickson* (1872) 10 M. 630; cf. *Davidson* v. *Dalziel* (1881) 8 R. 990; *Wilson's Trs.* v. *Brown's Exors.* (1907) 15 S.L.T. 747; *Buchanan* v. *Eaton*, 1911 S.C. (H.L.) 40.
[5] *Falconer Stewart* v. *Wilkie* (1892) 19 R. 630; *Ewing's Trs.* v. *Crum Ewing*, 1923 S.C. 569.
[6] Bell, *Prin.* §920; *Williamson* v. *Begg* (1887) 14 R. 720; *Cowie* v. *Muirden* (1893) 20 R. (H.L.) 81; *Scott* v. *S's Trs.* (1898) 6 S.L.T. 119; *Kemp* v. *Largs Mags.*, 1939 S.C. (H.L) 6.
[7] *Tailors of Aberdeen* v. *Coutts* (1840) 1 Rob. App. 296; *Mackenzie* v. *Clark* (1903) 11 S.L.T. 428.
[8] *Tailors of Aberdeen, supra*; *Edmonstone* v. *Seton* (1888) 16 R. 1; *Andertson* v. *Dickie*, 1914 S.C. 706.
[9] *Stenhouse* v. *Innes & Black* (1765) Mor. 10264; *Erskine* v . *Wright* (1846) 8 D. 863.
[10] *Tailors of Aberdeen, supra*; *Mackenzie* v. *Clark* (1903) 11 S.L.T. 428.

by a general disposition of lands,[11] unless by expeding a notice of title on the debtor's lands, specifying the creditor, the burden and the writs imposing it.[12] An obligation *ad factum praestandum* can be made a real burden on lands.[13] A burden originally properly constituted may be continued by reference in later deeds to a recorded deed containing the burden, though reference will not suffice to constitute a burden.[14] An irritancy clause is not necessary nor will it make a burden real, but it may help to indicate the intention to make a burden real, and it provides a sanction against omission of the burden from later deeds. The creditor's title is completed by the disponee's infeftment.[15]

There may be added a personal obligation by the debtor but this will not transmit against any singular successor in the subjects unless he undertakes it,[16] as by agreement in a future disposition signed by the disponee.[17]

In the case of land in an area operational for the purposes of the Land Registration (Sc.) Act, 1979, the creation of a real burden over a registered interest in land is registrable.[18]

Enforcement

The real burden being *debitum fundi,* the creditor may in default of payment bring a personal action for payment, poind the ground, or attach the lands by adjudication, but not bring an action of maills and duties unless preceded by an adjudication, nor enter into possession unless there is an express clause to that effect or a power of sale implying that.[19] A power of sale may be expressly conferred on the creditor in a reserved burden.[20] The disponee is not personally bound by a real burden but a personal bond may be taken by the granter in favour of the creditor in addition. Apart from such personal obligation real burdens do not transmit against heirs who do not take up the subjects.[21] Any personal obligation is enforceable in the same way as a personal bond, and it may be transmitted against singular successors in the lands by an agreement *in gremio* of a subsequent conveyance.[22]

[11] *Morrison's Trs.* v. *Webster* (1878) 5 R. 800; *Cowie's Trs.* v. *Cowie* (1891) 18 R. 706; *Cowie* v. *Muirden* (1893) 20 R. (H.L.) 81; *Scott* v. *S.* (1898) 6 S.L.T. 119.

[12] Conveyancing (Sc.) Act, 1924, S. 4 and Sched. B1.

[13] *Edmonstone, supra*; but see *Beckett* v. *Bisset,* 1921 2 S.L.T. 33.

[14] *Allan* v. *Cameron's Trs.* (1780) 2 Pat. 572; *Wylie* v. *Allan* (1830) 8 S. 337; Titles to Land Consolidation (Sc.) Act, 1868, S. 10; Conveyancing (Sc.) Act, 1874, S. 32.

[15] *Cowie's Trs.* v. *Muirden* (1893) 20 R. (H.L.) 81.

[16] *Gardyne* v. *Royal Bank* (1853) 1 Macq. 358.

[17] Conveyancing (Sc.) Act, 1874, S. 47; *Carrick* v. *Rodger, Watt & Paul* (1881) 9 R. 242; *Ritchie & Sturrock* v. *Dullater Feuing Co.* (1881) 9 R. 358. See also Conveyancing (Sc.) Act, 1924, S. 15.   [18] 1979 Act, S. 2(3) (iii) and 6(1) (e).

[19] Bell, *Comm.* I, 732; *Prin.* §922.

[20] *Wilson* v. *Fraser* (1824) 2 Sh. App. 162.

[21] *Macrae* v. *Mackenzie's Trs.* (1891) 19 R. 138.

[22] 1874 Act, S. 47; *Carrick, supra; Ritchie & Sturrock, supra.*

Succession

Real burdens are now moveable in the creditor's succession.[23] The creditor's executor completes title by recording a notice of title under the Conveyancing (Sc.) Act, 1924.

Assignation

The creditor may assign the benefit of the real burden and the assignee completes his title by recording the assignation in the Register of Sasines.[24] The creditor's heir completes his title to the burdens in the same way as to a bond and disposition in security.[25]

Extinction

The burden is extinguished in the same way as a bond and disposition in security, by executing and recording a discharge in the appropriate Register of Sasines,[26] but a less formal discharge may suffice.[27]

Contract of Ground Annual

A contract of ground annual, whereby a stipulated annual payment is due perpetually from lands and secured as a real burden over them, might be entered into instead of, or in addition to, a feu-contract, but is found particularly where lands could not be sub-feued (as in lands held burgage before 1874,[28] or lands held subject to a valid prohibition, imposed before 1874, against subinfeudation).[29] The right to the payment can be created by direct grant,[30] but normally by reservation, on lands being disponed by the creditor. A proprietor of land cannot create a ground annual in favour of himself.[31]

The contract, which must be probative, may be unilateral, disponing the lands in security of, and under the real burden of, the annual payment of a stated sum by way of ground annual, but is normally bilateral, containing a narrative clause, disposition by the granter of the lands, with description of the lands, reservation of the ground annual and declaration of it to be a real burden in the dispositive clause,[32] other burdens, such as an obligation to build,[33] possibly

---

[23] 1868 Act, S. 117; 1874 Act, S. 30; Succession (Sc.) Act, 1964, Sched. 3; cf. *Hughes' Trs.* v. *Corsane* (1890) 18 R. 299.

[24] Conveyancing Act, 1874, S. 30: formerly the assignation was intimated to the debtor, usually also recorded.   [25] Notice of title; Conveyancing (Sc.) Act, 1924, S. 4.

[26] 1924 Act, Sched. K.

[27] *Cameron* v. *Williamson* (1895) 22 R. 293.

[28] Conveyancing (Sc.) Act, 1874, S. 25; cf. *Arbroath Mags.* v. *Dickson* (1872) 10 M. 630.

[29] cf. Ross, *Lect.* II, 321; *Ch. of Sc. Endowment Cttee.* v. *Provident Assoc. of London*, 1914 S.C. 165, 172.   [30] Bell, *Prin.* §887, 908; *Ch. of Sc., supra.*

[31] *Ch. of Sc., supra.*

[32] Bell, *Prin.* §920; *Cowie* v. *Muirden* (1893) 20 R. (H.L.) 81.

[33] *Marshall's Trs.* v. *McNeill* (1888) 15 R. 762.

provision for its redemption, irritant and resolutive clauses and other clauses appropriate to a disposition, a clause binding the purchaser personally in payment of the ground annual and redisponing the lands in real security thereof to the creditor, a clause of common consent to registration for preservation and execution, and a testing clause. The amount of ground annual must be specific,[34] the creditor clearly ascertainable,[32] it must be clear that the burden is real,[35] and it must enter the Register of Sasines.[36] Registration completes the disponee's title to the lands and also the creditor's real right to the ground annual due from them. The disponee is personally bound independently of registration.[37] The creditor may also become infeft by registration under the disposition in security. In the case of land in an area operational for the purposes of the Land Registration (Sc.) Act, 1979, the grant of an interest in security by way of contract of ground annual is registrable to the extent that the interest has become that of the debtor in the ground annual.[38] The transfer of a ground annual over a registered interest in land is also registrable.[39]

No new ground annuals may be created after 31 July 1974 and existing ground annuals may be redeemed on statutory terms, and are deemed to have been redeemed on a transfer of the lands, or their acquisition by compulsory purchase.[40]

On the analogy of duplicands in feu-contracts contracts of ground annual formerly sometimes stipulated for grassums or duplications periodically.[41] The Feudal Casualties (Sc.) Act, 1914, provides for the redemption of extinction of such payments as in the case of feudal casualties.

Incidence of liability

A contract of ground annual does not create a feudal relation between the granter and the disponee of the lands but merely an obligation to pay or act. The personal obligation of the disponee binds him and his successors in perpetuity, despite transfer of the lands,[42] and does not transmit to a singular successor in the lands.[43] The real burden does, however, transmit to singular successors and ceases to bind the disponee on his parting with the lands. Obligations *ad factum*

---

[34] *Stenhouse* v. *Innes & Black* (1765) Mor. 10264.
[35] *Arbroath Mags.* v. *Dickson* (1872) 10 M. 630.
[36] *McDonald* v. *Place* (1821) Hume 544.
[37] cf. *Inverness Mags.* v. *Bell's Trs.* (1827) 6 S. 160.
[38] 1979 Act, S. 2 (1) (i).
[39] 1979 Act, S. 2 (3) (iii) and (4).
[40] Land Tenure Reform (Sc.) Act, 1974, Ss. 2, 4–6.
[41] e.g. *Murdoch* v. *Caledonian Ry.* (1906) 14 S.L.T. 527; *Murray* v. *Bruce*, 1917 S.C. 623.
[42] *Millar* v. *Small* (1853) 1 Macq. 345; cf. *King's College* v. *Hay* (1854) 1 Macq. 526.
[43] *Gardyne* v. *Royal Bank* (1853) 1 Macq. 358.

praestandum, such as to build, unless made a real burden, do not transmit against singular successors[44] and to be validly made real burdens they must be clear and definite.[45]

A ground annual is postponed to any feu-duty payable for the lands burdened, but is preferable to all charges on the lands created subsequently.

Creditor's remedies

The creditor in a ground annual is entitled to poind the ground,[46] or lead an adjudication; if infeft under the grantee's disposition in security, he may bring an action of maills and duties,[47] or utilize any of the other remedies open to a creditor in a bond and disposition in security. He has no power of sale unless by special stipulation.[48] The personal obligation justifies a personal action for payment against the original disponee or his representatives,[49] but this is discharged by the obligant obtaining his discharge in bankruptcy.[50]

If the contract contains a conventional irritancy, declarator may be sought that it has been incurred. If irritancy be declared it bars any claim for arrears due under the contract.[51] By statute[51] a legal irritancy, comparable to the irritancy *ob non solutum canonem* in feu-rights has been introduced, entitling the creditor to bring an action of adjudication against the proprietor of the lands for forfeiture of the lands and their adjudication to the creditor.

On the bankruptcy of the owners of the lands the creditor in a ground annual may by poinding of the ground recover one year's arrears of annual due and the current half-year's payment, in preference to the claims of the trustees in sequestration.[53]

No interest is due on a ground annual,[54] unless expressly provided for.

Allocation

Where lands subject to a ground annual are divided, each portion remains liable for the whole sum due, unless the creditor consents[55] or

[44] *Marshall's Trs.* v. *Macneill* (1888) 15 R. 762; *Edmonstone* v. *Seton* (1888) 16 R. 1; contrast similar obligations in feu-contract; cf. *Tweeddale's Trs.* v. *E. Haddington* (1880) 7 R. 625.

[45] *Tennant* v. *Napier Smith's Trs.* (1888) 15 R. 671; *Edmonstone* v. *Seton* (1888) 16 R. 1; cf. *Marshall's Trs., supra.*

[46] Bell, *Prin.* §887; cf. *Bell's Trs.* v. *Copland* (1890) 23 R. 651.

[47] *Somerville* v. *Johnstone* (1899) 1 F. 726; see also Conveyancing (Sc.) Act, 1924, S. 23 (4).

[48] *Wilson* v. *Fraser* (1824) 2 Sh. App. 162.

[49] Subject to Conveyancing (Sc.) Act, 1874, S. 12.

[50] Bankruptcy (Sc.) Act, 1913, S. 137.

[51] *Wingate's Trs.* v. *W.* (1892) 29 S.L.R. 406.   [52] 1924 Act, S. 23(5).

[53] Bankruptcy (Sc.) Act, 1913, S. 114; *Bell's Trs.* v. *Copeland* (1896) 23 R. 650.

[54] Bell, *Prin.* §32; *Scott Moncrieff* v. *L. Dundas* (1835) 14 S. 61.

[55] *Thomson* v. *Scott* (1828) 6 S. 526.

has agreed by a clause in the contract to be bound by any allocation made on division.

Compulsory allocation of ground annuals

The provisions of the Conveyancing and Feudal Reform (Sc.) Act 1970, Ss. 3–5, for allocation by notice, or by the Lands Tribunal, apply to ground annuals as they do to feu-duties.[56] It is incompetent by contract to exclude or limit the operation of these provisions.[57]

Redemption

Provision may be made for the debtor redeeming the annual payments for a lump sum.

Succession

Ground annuals were heritable in the creditor's succession till 1964[58] but are moveable since then,[59] and transmit in the debtor's succession with the lands.

Transfer

Right to a ground annual may be transferred by assignation,[60] completed before 1874 by intimation and since then[61] by assignation recorded in the Register of Sasines. Such an assignation has statutorily implied terms.[62]

Restriction

A ground annual may be restricted as regards any portion of the land out of which it is payable by a deed of restriction in statutory form[63] recorded in the appropriate register of Sasines.

Extinction and discharge

If the burden be omitted from the proprietor's title for the prescriptive period, the ground annual will be extinguished.[64] But a failure to repeat or refer to burdening clauses may be rectified by the proprietor granting and recording a deed of acknowledgment.[65] A ground annual is not extinguished *confusione*, by the creditor acquiring the burdened

---

[56] 1970 Act, S. 6.
[57] Ibid., S. 7.
[58] cf. *Campbell's Trs.* v. *L.N.E. Ry.*, 1930 S.C. 182.
[59] 1868 Act, S. 3, 117; 1874 Act, S. 30; Succession (Sc.) Act, 1964, Sched. 3.
[60] For form see Conveyancing (Sc.) Act, 1924, S. 23, and Sched. K.
[61] 1874 Act, S. 30, now 1924 Act, S. 23.
[62] 1924 Act, S. 23.
[63] 1924 Act, S. 23(3), 43, and Sched. K.
[64] Ersk. III, 4, 6; Bell, *Convg.* II, 1156; *King* v. *Johnston*, 1908 S.C. 684, 687.
[65] 1924 Act, S. 9(4) and Sched. E.

lands.[66] It may be renounced and discharged and the land disburdened in whole or in part by a discharge form, recorded in the appropriate Register of Sasines,[67] or discharged on compulsory acquisition of the lands burdened.[68]

Statutory real burdens

The standard value of the stipend exigible from the teinds of any lands, if exceeding £1, is made a statutory real burden (called the standard charge) on the lands in favour of the Church of Scotland General Trustees preferable to all other securities or burdens not incidents of tenure.[69] It may be allocated on part of the lands when these are disponed.[70]

Statutory charging orders

Where an owner of a house has completed in respect of any house or building any works required to be executed by notice of a local authority he may, subject to certain conditions, obtain from the local authority a charging order burdening the house with an annuity to repay the amount at six per cent for thirty years. The charging order must be recorded in the Register of Sasines and has priority over all existing and future estates, interests, and encumbrances, except feu-duties, teinds, ground annuals, stipends, and standard charges in lieu of stipends, and certain statutory charges. Such an annuity is recoverable in the same way as feu-duty.[71]

Statutory charge over land

Where money is payable to an agricultural tenant in respect of compensation by his landlord and the latter has failed to pay it, the Secretary of State may, on the landlord's application, create a charge on the holding by a charging order, burdening the holding with an annuity to pay the sum due, and record it in the Register of Sasines.[72]

---

[66] *Murray* v. *Parlane's Trs.* (1890) 18 R. 287; *Healy and Young's Trs.* v. *Mair's Trs.*, 1914 S.C. 893. See also *King, supra.*
[67] 1924 Act, S. 23(2) and Sched. K.
[68] *Blythswood Friendly Socy.* v. *Glasgow District Council,* 1978 S.L.T. 213.
[69] Church of Scotland (Property and Endowments) Act, 1925, S. 12.
[70] Ibid., S. 13.
[71] Housing (Sc.) Act, 1966, Ss. 28–30.
[72] Agricultural Holdings (Sc.) Act, 1949, S. 70.

SECURITIES OVER HERITAGE

An owner of.lands may use them to support his personal credit by granting redeemable rights in those lands to a lender in security for the repayment of the money borrowed. There are now three main classes of dispositions in security, the bond and disposition in security, which creates a real right qualifying the borrower's rights in the lands, the *ex facie* absolute disposition by which the lender is nominally made owner of the lands, and the standard security which, when recorded, vests the interest in land over which it is granted in the grantee as a security for performance of the contract to which the security relates.

Several modes of creating heritable securities are now obsolete, namely the wadset,[1] infeftment of annualrent,[2] and heritable bond.[3] The first of these has developed into the *ex facie* absolute disposition, and the last into the bond and disposition in security.

Agreement to grant security

The creation of a right in security over heritable property must be effected by agreement solemnly authenticated, holograph or adopted as holograph, followed by disposition of the security subject to the creditor in security, completed by his infeftment thereon. The essentials of the contract are agreement on the amount of the loan, its duration, the rate of interest thereon, the subjects to be conveyed in security, and any special conditions which may be agreed. Statute and common law imply numerous other terms into the contract. If the contract falls through, damages can be claimed for failure to take the loan agreed.[4] *Rei interventus* in the shape of actually lending the money may validate an improbative agreement to borrow and to give security over land. The contract to dispone lands in security by itself confers only a personal right and no real security until the disposition in security has been completed.[5] This must be done while the debtor is

---

[1] Stair II, 10; Ersk. II, 8; Bell, *Prin.* §901–7.
[2] Stair II, 5; Ersk. II, 8, 31; Bell, *Prin.* §908.
[3] Ersk. II, 2, 13; Bell, *Prin.* §909.
[4] *Gilchrist* v. *Whyte*, 1907 S.C. 984.
[5] cf. *Arbroath Mags.* v. *Dickson* (1872) 10 M. 630; *Ch. of Sc. Endowment Cttee.* v. *Provident Assocn.*, 1914 S.C. 165.

solvent, and will be reducible if the disposition is made within sixty days before the debtor's bankruptcy,[6] but not if the creditor has merely delayed formally completing his right till within that time.[7]

The validity of the prospective debtor's title to the lands proposed to be disponed in security requires careful consideration[8] and also his power to borrow and grant a disposition in security.[9] Trustees have power to borrow on the security of heritable trust estate.[10]

BOND AND DISPOSITION IN SECURITY

The commonest form of grant of a right in security was formerly by a bond and disposition in security.[11] The owner of the lands grants a probative deed narrating his having borrowed a stated sum of money from the creditor, which he binds himself and his executors to repay, with a fifth part more of liquidate penalty in case of failure, and interest at a stated rate,[12] and dispones designated lands to the creditor, heritably but redeemably, in security of the personal obligation to repay, reserving power of redemption but granting the creditor power of sale on default in payment.[13] The disposition in security of lands carries also pertinents and fixtures.[14] The creditor must be clearly identified, and the sum repayable definite in amount.[15] Notwithstanding this, it is competent to create a security for an obligation *ad factum praestandum*, certainly if performable by expenditure of money.[16]

The provision for a fifth part more of liquidate penalty covers only the expenses to which the bondholder is put in recovery of his debt[17] or the expenses of defending the creditor's preference against a third party.[18]

[6] Bell, *Comm.* II, 211; *Rose* v. *Falconer* (1868) 6 M. 960; *Stiven* v. *Scott & Simson* (1871) 9 M. 923; *Gourlay* v. *Hodge* (1875) 2 R. 738; *Jones' Trs.* v. *Allan* (1901) 4 F. 374.

[7] *Guild* v. *Young* (1884) 22 S.L.R. 520; *Sc. Provident Instn.* v. *Cohen* (1888) 17 R. 112.

[8] A granter of a bond and disposition in security must be, or become, himself infeft in the lands since his title thereto may not be deduced in the bond itself under the 1924 Act, S. 3.

[9] cf. *Paterson's Trs.* v. *Liqdr. of Caledonian Heritable Security Co.* (1885) 13 R. 369.

[10] Trusts (Sc.) Act, 1921, S. 4(d).

[11] Under the Conveyancing and Feudal Reform (Sc.) Act, 1970, security can now be created in this way in exceptional cases only (see S. 9) without prejudice to existing securities in this form.

[12] Down to this point the deed is in the same form as a personal bond undertaking repayment of debt: see Ch. 4.22, *supra*.

[13] For statutory form see Titles to Land Consolidation (Sc.) Act, 1868, S. 116 and Sched. FF. See also *Cumming* v. *Stewart*, 1928 S.C. 296.

[14] *Yuille* v. *Rushbury* (1888) 15 R. 828; *Howie's Trs.* v. *McLay* (1902) 5 F. 214; *Edinburgh & Leigh Gas Commrs.* v. *Smart*, 1918, 1 S.L.T. 80; *Richardson's Trs.* v. *Ballachulish Slate Quarries Co.*, 1918, 1 S.L.T. 413; see also *Traill's Trs.* v. *Free Church of Scotland*, 1915 S.C. 655.

[15] *Smith Sligo* v. *Dunlop* (1885) 12 R. 907; cf. *Edmonstone* v. *Seton* (1888) 16 R. 1.

[16] *Edmonstone* v. *Seton* (1888) 16 R. 1.

[17] Bell, *Convg.* I, 255; *Allan* v. *Young* (1757) Mor. 10047; *Bruce* v. *Scottish Amicable Life Assce. Socy.*, 1907 S.C. 637; *Mitchell* v. *Allardyce*, 1915, 2 S.L.T. 398.

[18] *Orr* v. *Mackenzie* (1839) 1 D. 1046.

The bond must be precise as to the rate of interest and starting date if there is to be any security for the interest.[19] It is competent to provide that a lower rate of interest will be accepted if interest is paid punctually, but such a provision is strictly applied.[20] The loan must be made at or before the time of delivery of the bond to the creditor or of his taking infeftment on it, because securities for future debts are null so far as contracted after the infeftment,[21] though this does not apply where the lender was under an absolute obligation to make the advance, though it was not in fact made after infeftment,[22] nor where the creditor insisted on having infeftment completed before paying the money lent.[23]

The disposition in security contains a description of the lands and their burdens and conditions, such as is required for an absolute disposition, either particularly or by reference. If the security subjects are capable of being feued, power to feu may be reserved to the granter, but must be exercised subject to any conditions affecting the reservation.[24] It is not necessary to repeat or refer to conditions or irritant or resolutive clauses affecting the lands in a deed creating or transmitting a heritable security.[25]

The clause of assignation of rents imports[26] an assignation to the creditor of the rents and other duties (including feu-duties and casualties in the case of a superiority, and ground annuals and grassums in the case of a ground annual) payable after the date from which interest is to run, power to the creditor to insure buildings against fire and to recover the premiums from the debtor, on default in payment[27] of interest or principal or on the proprietor's notour bankruptcy or his granting a trust deed for creditors to enter into possession and uplift the rents and other duties, to insure against loss by breakage of glass and claims by tenants and third parties and against such other risks as a prudent proprietor would reasonably insure against, and to make all necessary renewals and repairs on the property, subject to accounting to the debtor for any balance of rents or sums received beyond what is necessary for payment of the principal, interest, and penalty and all expenses incurred in reference to possession, including expenses of

---

[19] *Forbes* v. *Welsh and Forbes* (1894) 21 R. 630; *Alston* v. *Nellfield Co.*, 1915 S.C. 912.

[20] *Alston, supra; Gatty* v. *Maclaine*, 1921 S.C. (H.L.) 1; cf. *Don's Trs.* v. *Cameron* (1885) 22 S.L.R. 348.

[21] Bankruptcy Act, 1696, c. 5; *Black* v. *Curror & Cowper* (1885) 12 R. 990; cf. *Bell's Tr.* v. *B.* (1884) 12 R. 85.

[22] *Dempster* v. *Kinloch* (1750) 2 Ross L.C. 632.

[23] *Dunbar* v. *Abercromby* (1789) 2 Ross L.C. 638.

[24] *Cumming* v. *Stewart*, 1928 S.C. 296.

[25] Conveyancing (Sc.) Act, 1924, S. 9.

[26] Conveyancing (Sc.) Act, 1924, S. 25(1) (a).

[27] *McAra* v. *Anderson*, 1913 S.C. 931; *Graham's Tr.* v. *Dow's Tr.*, 1917, 2 S.L.T. 154; *Gibson* v. *Mair*, 1918 S.C. 353.

factorage, management, insurance, renewals, and repair. The assignation of rents is completed by the recording of the bond and there is no need to intimate to the tenants, and it is preferable to a mere assignation or arrestment even though intimated or used before infeftment is taken by recording the bond.[28] Tenants must continue to pay their rents to the proprietor until interpelled by the bondholder.

The clause of assignation of writs imports[29] an assignation of writs and evidents with power to the creditor, in the event of sale, subject to the rights of any person holding prior rights to possession of such writs and evidents, to deliver them to the purchaser and to assign to the purchaser any right to have the writs and evidents made forthcoming.[30]

The warrandice clause in statutory form imports absolute warrandice as regards the lands and the title deeds thereof and warrandice from fact and deed as regards the rents.[31]

The clause reserving right of redemption imports[32] a right to redeem the security in manner prescribed by the Act.

The expenses clause imports that any deed necessarily granted by the creditor on the debtor making payment and the redeeming his lands shall be at the debtor's expense,[33] and that the debtor is to be liable for the whole expenses of preparing, executing and recording the bond, and all reasonable expenses incurred by the creditor in calling it up, realizing or attempting to realize the security subjects, and exercising the other powers conferred on him.[34]

Position of bondholder

The bondholder completes his title to the security subjects by recording the bond in the Register of Sasines or, particularly where the bond is embodied in a deed for other purposes, recording a notice of title to the bond.[35] If the granter is a company it must also effect registration in the Register of Charges kept by the Registrar of Companies.[36] The creditor does not normally take possession of nor man-

---

[28] Bell, *Convg.* I, 641; see also *Stevenson* v. *Dawson* (1896) 23 R. 496.

[29] 1924 Act, S. 25(1) (b).

[30] As to the creditor's right to have delivery of the titles to the property see Bell, *Prin.* §914; *Tawse* v. *Rigg* (1904) 6 F. 544, 546; *Boyd* v. *Turnbull & Findlay*, 1911 S.C. 1006, 1010. The creditor cannot retain the titles against the debtor save in security of the debt, but cannot be compelled to redeliver them until his debt has been repaid: *Boyd* v. *Turnbull & Findlay, supra.* See also 1924 Act, S. 27.

[31] 1868 Act, S. 119.

[32] 1924 Act, S. 25(1) (c).

[33] 1868 Act, S. 119.

[34] 1924 Act, S. 25(2).

[35] 1868 Act, S. 17; 1924 Act, S. 3.

[36] Companies Act, 1948, Ss. 95 and 106A (added by Companies (Floating Charges and Receivers) (Sc.) Act, 1972, S. 6).

age the property. Unless he does so he does not become feudal vassal nor become liable for feu-duty.

He cannot act to the prejudice of the debtor and forfeits the right to recovery of the debt if he renders himself unable to restore the debtor on repayment to his position when the bond was granted.[37] The Court might interfere, at the instance of the debtor or his other creditors, to prevent an unfair use by the bondholder of his power of sale.[38]

He may enter into possession with the debtor's consent, or in pursuance of an action of maills and duties,[39] and may eject summarily a debtor in personal occupation.[40] A creditor in possession may let the security subjects or part of them for not longer than seven years, but may with the sheriff's authority grant leases for up to twenty-one years, or in the case of minerals, thirty-one years.[41] A creditor in possession has power[42] to make all necessary repairs and charge the cost of management, insurance and repairs to the sum due by the debtor. A creditor in possession is liable for feu-duties,[43] and rates,[44] and subject to an occupier's liability to visitors.[45] He has no security over moveables on or in the lands disponed in security unless he executes a poinding of the ground.[46]

Position of debtor

The debtor remains heritable proprietor and while in possession can do all ordinary administration but may not prejudice the creditor's security by contracts outwith ordinary management, without the creditor's consent; such contracts are not enforceable by or against the creditor.[47] Thus the creditor may have set aside leases of unusual length granted by the debtor or granted on unduly favourable terms.[48]

[37] N. Albion Property Inv. Co. v. McBean's C.B. (1893) 21 R. 90; Mackirdy v. Webster's Trs. (1895) 22 R. 340.

[38] Beveridge v. Wilson (1829) 7 S. 279; Bell v. Gordon (1838) 16 S. 657.

[39] e.g. Macrae v. Leith, 1913 S.C. 901.

[40] Heritable Securities (Sc.) Act, 1894, S. 5; altering rules stated in Wylie v. Her. Sec. Inv. Assoc. (1871) 10 M. 253; Sc. Prop. Inv. Co. Bldg. Soc. v. Horne (1881) 8 R. 737; and Smith's Trs. v. Chalmers (1890) 17 R. 1088. See e.g. Hutchison v. Alexander (1904) 6 F. 532. This power does not give the creditor all the powers of a landlord against a tenant, and he may not demand caution for violent profits: Inglis's Trs. v. Macpherson, 1910 S.C. 46. This remedy is incompetent against a liferenter by constitution: Sc. Union and National Ins. Co. v. Smeaton (1904) 7 F. 174.

[41] Heritable Securities (Sc.) Act, 1894, Ss. 6, 7.

[42] 1868 Act, S. 119; Sc. Amicable Herit. Sec. Assocn. v. N. Assce. Co. (1883) 11 R. 287; Glasgow Provident Inv. Soc. v. Westminster Fire Office (1888) 15 R. (H.L.) 89.

[43] City of Glasgow Bank Liqr. v. Nicolson's Trs. (1882) 9 R. 689.

[44] Greenock Police Board v. Greenock Property Inv. Co. Liqr. (1885) 12 R. 832; N.B. Property Inv. Co. v. Paterson (1888) 15 R. 885.

[45] Baillie v. Shearer's J.F. (1894) 21 R. 498.

[46] Royal Bank v. Bain (1877) 4 R. 985; Traill's Trs. v. Free Church, 1915 S.C. 655.

[47] Heron v. Martin (1893) 20 R. 1001; Morier v. Brownlie & Watson (1895) 23 R. 67; Smith v. Soeder (1895) 23 R. 60.

[48] Mitchell v. Little (1820) Hume 661; Reid v. McGill, 1912, 2 S.L.T. 246.

He may sell the lands, but only under burden of the bond, and does not, by so doing, escape liability under his personal obligations to repay. He may, with the creditor's consent, feu parts of the lands.[49] A feu without consent or restriction of the right in security is reducible at the instance of a purchaser from the bondholder if the latter has exercised his power of sale.[50] Until the creditor intimates the assignation of rents to the tenants, they are entitled to pay them to the debtor as landlord.[51]

By the recording of the bond the creditor obtains a right preferable to personal creditors of the debtor,[52] but if the creditor has not taken possession he has no preference over the rents against factors collecting them and given the right by the debtor to retain the rents in satisfaction of their claims.[53]

The debtor may make a personal agreement with the creditor as to repayment which is binding on trust disponees from him who become infeft.[54]

Assignation

A bond may be assigned in whole or in part by the creditor,[55] and when recorded on behalf of the assignee in the Register of Sasines, the assignation constitutes the assignee creditor in the obligation.[56] An unconditional agreement to take an assignation of a bond is binding though the bond be found to be defective.[57] A creditor is not bound to grant an assignation so long as the debtor's objections to the creditor's claim for interest are outstanding.[58] A debtor who has sold the security subjects under burden of the bond is entitled, if the creditor calls on him to pay under the personal obligation, to have the bond assigned to him.[59] A creditor who is being repaid cannot be compelled to grant an assignation if his rights would be in any way prejudiced.[60] An assignation need contain no description of or reference to the property,[61] nor any reference to burdens or conditions of title.[62] An assignation con-

---

[49] *Sones* v. *Mill* (1903) 11 S.L.T. 98.
[50] *Cumming* v. *Stewart*, 1928 S.C. 296; see also *Alston* v. *Nellfield Co.*, 1915 S.C. 912.
[51] *Forsyth* v. *Aird* (1853) 16 D. 197; *Bridge* v. *Brown's Trs.* (1872) 10 M. 958; *Stevenson, Lauder & Gilchrist* v. *Dawson* (1896) 23 R. 496.
[52] *Neils* v. *Lyle* (1863) 2 M. 168.
[53] *Stevenson, Lauder & Gilchrist* v. *Dawson* (1896) 23 R. 496.
[54] *Ashburton* v. *Escombe* (1893) 20 R. 187.
[55] Form in 1924 Act, Sched. K, No. 1, superseding 1868 Act, S. 124 and Sched. GG.
[56] 1924 Act, S. 28.
[57] *Forbes* v. *Welsh & Forbes* (1894) 21 R. 630; cf. *Bennie's Trs.* v. *Couper* (1890) 17 R. 782.
[58] *Bruce* v. *Scottish Amicable Life Assurance Socy.*, 1907 S.C. 637.
[59] *North Albion Property Inv. Co.* v. *MacBean's C.B.* (1893) 21 R. 90; *Mackirdy* v. *Webster's Trs.* (1895) 22 R. 340.
[60] *Guthrie & McConnachy* v. *Smith* (1880) 8 R. 107; *Fleming* v. *Black*, 1913, 1 S.L.T. 386.
[61] 1924 Act, S. 31.
[62] 1924 Act, S. 9.

tains no express warrandice but warrandice *debitum subesse* is implied.[63]

A bond may also be assigned by a general disposition of the creditor's property, title being completed by notice of title.

An assignee may retain a bond in security of other debts due to him by the assignor even though repaid the sum for which he obtained the assignation.[64]

If the holder of a bond assigns it in part under declaration that the debts are to rank *pari passu*, either creditor may cause the security subjects to be sold for payment of his debt without the other's consent, but the other's security remains unaffected.[54]

Creditor's succession to bond

Until 1868 securities over heritage were heritable in the creditor's succession. By S. 117 of the 1868 Act, such securities were to be moveable in succession, unless (a) executors were expressly excluded from the destination,[66] and in relation (b) to claims by the fisc and (c) to legal rights of spouses and of children. Executors might also be excluded by a minute recorded in the Register of Sasines,[67] and the exclusion of executors removed also by minute,[68] or by assigning, bequeathing or conveying the security to himself or any other person without expressing or repeating such exclusion.[69] By the Succession (Sc.) Act, 1964, S. 34, even if executors are excluded bonds are moveable in succession, but remain heritable *quoad fiscum* and as regards a child's claim to legitim.[70]

Completion of title

Persons who come in right of bonds on the creditor's death complete title by recording a notice of title to the bond,[71] but may assign, restrict, discharge, or otherwise deal with the security without completing title thereto, by deducing title in the assignation or other deed from the last recorded title to the bond, specifying the unrecorded writs connecting

---

[63] *Leith Heritages Co.* v. *Edinburgh & Leith Glass Co.* (1876) 3 R. 789; *Reid* v. *Barclay* (1879) 6 R. 1007.

[64] *Colquhoun's Trs.* v. *Diack* (1901) 4 F. 358.

[65] *Nicholson's Trs.* v. *McLaughlin* (1891) 19 R. 49.

[66] Such exclusion had to be maintained by repetition in subsequent assignations if it was to remain effective.

[67] 1868 Act, Sched. DD.

[68] 1868 Act, Sched. EE.

[69] 1868 Act, S. 117.

[70] Legal rights of spouses in heritage were abolished by the 1964 Act.

[71] 1924 Act, S. 4(3). It proceeds on production of the last recorded title to the security, any deeds giving the deceased title thereto, and the deceased's will or confirmation.

them with that title.[72] The methods competent under earlier Acts are still competent.[73]

Debtor's succession

Liability under a bond transmits heritably even if the bond is recorded after the debtor's death. If the heritage disponed in security was insufficient to meet the debt, the debtor's other heritage was liable for the balance.[74] If several properties were subject to one security, the debt was apportioned among the heirs in proportion to the values of their properties, after deduction of preferable burdens.[75] If property subject to a bond was specifically bequeathed, the legatee took it subject to the burden, notwithstanding a direction to the trustees to pay all debts.[76] In no case, however, was an heir liable beyond the value of the heritage to which he succeeded.[77] In a question with the creditor, however, both the deceased's heritable and his moveable estate were liable for payment of the debt, and the creditor could sue his heirs or his executors but if the executor paid he had a right of relief against the heir to the heritage burdened with the bond.

In the case of deaths after 10 September 1964, the deceased's whole estate vests in his executor[78] and the executor is liable to the creditor, save that any rules whereby any particular debt of a deceased fell to be paid out of any particular part of his estate remain unaltered.[79] The executor, as a bare administrator of the estate, is not liable beyond the amount of estate falling under his control.

At common law a successor to the debtor was not personally liable under the personal obligation in the bond, unless he granted a bond of corroboration. By the Conveyancing (Sc.) Act, 1874, S. 47, a heritable security and the personal obligation transmit against any person taking the security subjects[80] by succession, gift or bequest,[81] or by

[72] 1924 Act, S. 3.

[73] Testate succession: bond heritable–notarial instrument: 1868 Act, S. 126, Sched. JJ; bond moveable–writ of acknowledgment, 1868 Act, S. 125, Sched. II; 1874 Act, S. 63; or notarial instrument. Intestate succession: bond heritable–writ of acknowledgment, or notarial instrument: 1868 Act, S. 126, Sched. JJ; or special service; bond moveable–notarial instrument. Writs of acknowledgement have been abolished in the case of creditors' deaths after 10 Sept. 1964: Succession (Sc.) Act, 1964, Sched. 3.

[74] *Douglas' Trs.* v. *D.* (1868) 6 M. 223; *Duncan* (1883) 10 R. 1042; *Bell's Tr.* v. *B.* (1884) 12 R. 85.   [75] *Ferrier* v. *Cowan* (1896) 23 R. 703.

[76] *Brand* v. *Scott's Trs.* (1892) 19 R. 768; *Muir's Trs.* v. *M.*, 1916, 1 S.L.T. 372; *Ballantyne's Trs.* v. *B's Trs.*, 1941 S.C. 35.

[77] 1874 Act, S. 12, repealed by Succession (Sc.) Act, 1964, Sched. 3.

[78] Succession (Sc.) Act, 1964, S. 14.

[79] Hence the principles of the cases of *Douglas, Duncan, Bell, Ferrier, Brand, Muir's Trs.*, and *Ballantyne's Trs.* still apply.

[80] *Lamb* v. *Field* (1889) 27 S.L.R. 242; *Fenton Livingstone* v. *Crichton's Trs.*, 1908 S.C. 1208. Not against the debtor's trustees: *Macrae* v. *Gregory* (1903) 11 S.L.T. 102.

[81] e.g. *Welch's Exors.* v. *Edinburgh Life Assce. Co.* (1896) 23 R. 772, where held legatee's liability limited to the value of the estate inherited.

conveyance where an agreement to this effect appears *in gremio* of the conveyance.[82] By the Conveyancing (Sc.) Act, 1924, S. 15, the personal obligation transmits in terms of the 1874 Act, S. 47, only if the conveyance is signed by the new proprietor and summary diligence is not competent under S. 47 against any obligant taking by succession, gift or bequest unless there is an agreement to the transmission signed by such obligant.[83]

The seller of lands burdened with a bond remains personally liable unless discharged by the creditor, though he may have a right of relief against a purchaser if the latter has undertaken to do so. There may consequently be several successive proprietors all personally bound.[84] Where the seller of bonded lands took the disponee bound to relieve him of the personal obligation, this obligation of relief was held not to transmit against a subsequent disponee under S. 47,[85] but where the seller did so and became bankrupt and his trustee assigned the obligation of relief to the creditor in the bond, the obligation was held to avail the creditor to recover from the purchaser the whole balance due under the bond.[86]

Creditor's remedies

So long as the debtor who granted the bond lives he is personally liable for repayment, and may be sued personally, even if he has disposed of the security subjects. In the normal form of bond he binds himself, his heirs, executors and representatives whomsoever, without the necessity of discussing them in their order, and the creditor may accordingly claim from heirs in moveables[87] or in heritage[88] or both,[89] though *inter heredes* debts heritably secured are payable by heirs in heritage.[90]

If, as is normal, the granter has consented to registration for execution, the creditor may record the bond and do summary diligence; this remedy may be exercised concurrently with notice calling up the bond, as a preliminary to sale.[91] The creditor may, if the proprietor defaults in payment of principal or interest,[92] becomes notour bankrupt, or grants a trust deed for creditors, enter into possession of the security sub-

---

[82] See also *Carrick* v. *Rodger, Watt & Paul* (1881) 9 R. 242; *Ritchie & Sturrock* v. *Dullater Feuing Co.* (1881) 9 R. 358; *Wright's Trs.* v. *McLaren* (1891) 18 R. 841.
[83] Form in 1924 Act, Sched. A, Form 2.
[84] *Glasgow Univ.* v. *Yuill's Tr.* (1882) 9 R. 643.
[85] *Sherry* v. *S's Trs.*, 1918, 1 S.L.T. 31.
[86] *Caledonian Heritable Secy. Co.* v. *Stewart* (1889) 27 S.L.R. 690.
[87] *Carnegie* v. *Knowes* (1627) Mor. 3564.
[88] *B.L. Co.* v. *L. Reay* (1850) 12 D. 949.
[89] Bell, *Convg.* I, 251.
[90] *Bell's Tr.* v. *B.* (1884) 12 R. 85.
[91] *McWhirter* v. *McCulloch's Trs.* (1887) 14 R. 918; *McNab* v. *Clarke* (1889) 16 R. 610.
[92] *McAra* v. *Henderson*, 1913 S.C. 931.

jects,[93] by consent or by bringing an action of maills and duties against the proprietor,[94] and give notice of the raising thereof to the tenants, which notice interpels the tenants from paying rent to the proprietor. Intimation of decree in the action being made to the tenants has the effect of a decree for the rents and a charge thereon, and payment to the creditor is a complete discharge to the tenants. Decree also gives the creditor a title to collect the rents[95] and to use landlord's sequestration if necessary to recover them.[96] Tenants can set off against rents claims against the proprietor arising out of the tenancy only.[97] A creditor who enters into possession becomes liable for feu-duty,[98] rates,[99] and may be liable as occupier to the public.[1] A bondholder who takes possession is entitled to delivery of leases and other estate documents[2] and may grant leases.[3]

Whether or not he has entered into possession, the creditor may, by poinding the ground, attach moveables on the ground belonging to the proprietor,[4] or to tenants but only to the extent of rents due and unpaid.[5] But unless carried through by sale of poinded effects sixty days before the proprietor's sequestration it is not available against his trustee in bankruptcy except to the extent of the current half-year's interest and one year's arrears.[6]

A creditor may, after obtaining decree of poinding the ground, attach the security subjects by adjudication,[7] and, under the debtor's personal obligation in the bond, may also attach the debtor's whole heritable estate by adjudication.[7] But adjudication in the latter case only falls within the Diligence Act, 1661, whereby adjudications in security for debt led within a year and a day of that first made effectual rank *pari passu*, and is postponed to sequestration unless completed for a year and a day.[8]

A creditor may also use inhibition against the debtor.[9]

[93] Conveyancing (Sc.) Act, 1924, S. 25(1).
[94] Heritable Securities Act, 1894, Ss. 3–7; *Inglis's Trs. v. Macpherson*, 1911 2 S.L.T. 176.
[95] *Forsyth v. Aird* (1853) 16 D. 197; *Chamber's J.F. v. Vertue* (1893) 20 R. 257.
[96] *Robertson's Trs. v. Gardner* (1889) 16 R. 705.
[97] *Chamber's J.F. v. Vertue* (1893) 20 R. 257; *Marshall's Trs. v. Banks*, 1934 S.C. 405.
[98] *City of Glasgow Bank Liqdrs. v. Nicholson's Trs.* (1882) 9 R. 689. But he is not a 'singular successor' of a feuar entitled to the latter's rights as to allocation of feu-duty: *Campbell v. Deans* (1890) 17 R. 661.
[99] *Greenock Police Board v. Liqdr. of Greenock Property Inv. Socy.* (1885) 12 R. 832; but see now Valuation and Rating (Sc.) Act, 1956.
[1] *Baillie v. Shearer's J.F.* (1894) 21 R. 498.
[2] *Macrae v. Leith*, 1913 S.C. 901.
[3] *Mackenzie v. Imlay's Trs.*, 1912 S.C. 685.
[4] *N. Albion Property Inv. Co. v. McBean's Curator* (1893) 21 R. 90; *Mackirdy v. Webster's Trs.* (1895) 22 R. 340.
[5] *Brown v. Scott* (1859) 22 D. 273.
[6] Bankruptcy (Sc.) Act, 1913, S. 114.
[7] Ersk. II, 8, 37; Bell, *Comm.* I, 753.
[8] Gloag and Irvine, *Rights in Security*, 109.   [9] *Clarke v. McNab* (1888) 15 R. 569.

Exercise of creditor's power of sale

The statutory form of bond grants the creditor power of sale on the debtor's default in payment. If the debtor fails to pay the sums due under the personal obligation within three months of a demand for payment made to him in statutory form the creditor may without further intimation or process sell the lands by public roup at Edinburgh or Glasgow or the head burgh of the county in which the main part of the lands are situated or the nearest burgh.[10] Or he may sell by private bargain for the best price that can be reasonably obtained.[11] Demand once validly made need not be repeated though sale be delayed,[12] but notice ceases to be effective after five years if no exposure to sale has followed, or five years after the date of the last exposure.[13] The debtor may dispense with the whole or part of the period of notice.[14] On expiry of the notice without payment the creditor must advertise the sale.

Advertisement, specifying the property and stating the time and place of sale and upset price, must be made at least once weekly for not less than three consecutive weeks,[15] and exposure must take place within fourteen days of the day after publication of the third advertisement. In the case of sale by private bargain advertisement must be inserted during not less than two consecutive weeks and an enforceable contract of sale concluded within twenty-eight days after the day following the publication of the second advertisement. Insertion of an advertisement must be (a) in the case of land in Midlothian, in at least one daily newspaper[16] published in Edinburgh; (b) in the case of land in Lanarkshire, in at least one daily newspaper published in Glasgow; (c) in the case of land situated elsewhere in Scotland, in at least one daily newspaper published in Scotland circulating in the district where the land or the main part thereof is situated and in at least one newspaper, if any, circulating there and published in the county in which the land, or any part thereof is situated or in a county in Scotland adjacent to it. A copy of the advertisement with a certificate

[10] 1924 Act, S. 33 and Sched. M. expld. Conveyancing and Feudal Reform (Sc.) Act, 1970, S. 33. See also *Stuart's Tr.* v. *S.* (1904) 12 S.L.T. 356. Intimation to other security holders over the same subjects is also advisable: *Stewart* v. *Brown* (1882) 10 R. 192; *Leach* v. *Johnstone* (1886) 24 S.L.R. 78. As to cases where the debtor is dead and his heir cannot be found, or his address is unknown, or the address of the person entitled to intimation cannot be ascertained, see Heritable Securities Act, 1894, S. 16.

[11] Conveyancing and Feudal Reform (Sc.) Act, 1970, S. 35, modifying 1924 Act.

[12] *Howard & Wyndham* v. *Richmond's Trs.* (1890) 17 R. 990.

[13] 1924 Act, S. 33. S. 34 is amended by 1970 Act, S. 34.

[14] 1924 Act, S. 35.

[15] *Ferguson* v. *Rodger* (1895) 22 R. 643; see also *Glas* v. *Stewart* (1830) 8 S. 843; *Hope* v. *Moncrieff* (1833) 11 S. 324; *Melville and Dundas* (1854) 16 D. 419.

[16] A mere advertising paper suffices: *E. Rosslyn* (1830) 8 S. 964; *Dickson* v. *Dumfries Mags.* (1831) 9 S. 282. See also *Walter's Tr.* v. *O'Mara* (1902) 9 S.L.T. 395.

of publication is sufficient evidence of publication.[17] Similar provisions apply to advertisement of re-exposure.

Exposure to sale may take place in Edinburgh or Glasgow or any burgh in the county where the land lies or nearest to the chief part of it. The sale is invalid if the due time has not elapsed.[18] The lands may be exposed or offered for sale as a whole or in lots, and the creditor may apportion the feu-duty or other burdens but not so as to prejudice the rights of any third party.[19]

Where there is a sale in lots, the creditor may create such rights and impose such duties and conditions as he considers may be reasonably required for the proper management, maintenance and use of any part of the lands to be held in common by the owners for the time being of the lots. For this purpose a creditor has the same right as a proprietor has by virtue of the Conveyancing (Sc.) Act, 1874, to execute and record a deed of declaration of conditions.[20]

The selling creditor and the debtor[21] may not bid, but one of several joint creditors selling may bid[22] and a postponed bondholder may also do so.[23]

In selling the creditor acts in a fiduciary capacity for the owner and any postponed bondholders and he must not do anything prejudicial to a sale at the best obtainable price.[24] The proprietor of part of the security subjects not sold may challenge the validity of the sale of the part sold on the ground of inadequacy of price.[25]

On receipt of the price the creditor must count and reckon therefor with the debtor and any postponed creditors and consign any surplus after deduction of the debt secured, with interest, penalties and expenses, and after paying all previous incumbrances and the expenses of discharging them, in bank in the joint names of the seller and purchaser for behoof of the parties having best rights thereto, the bank being named in the articles of roup.[26] A creditor who sells in lots has no power to allocate the feuduty as between the owners of the lots nor to create real burdens between the portions sold.[27]

The debtor or a postponed bondholder may be barred from challenging irregularities in the procedure if he knew of them and delayed unreasonably to object.[28]

[17] 1924 Act, Ss. 36–8. A new S. 38 is substituted by the 1970 Act, S. 36.
[18] *Ferguson* v. *Rodger* (1895) 22 R. 643; see also *Roscoe* v. *Mackersy* (1905) 7 F. 761.
[19] 1924 Act, S. 40, amd. 1970 Act, S. 37.
[20] 1924 Act, S. 40(2) and (3), added by 1970 Act, S. 37.
[21] *Jamieson* v. *Edinburgh Mutual Inv. & Bldg. Soc.*, 1913, 2 S.L.T. 52.
[22] *Wright* v. *Buchanan*, 1917 S.C. 73.
[23] *Scottish Imperial Ins. Co.* v. *Lamond* (1883) 21 S.L.R. 98.
[24] *Park* v. *Alliance Heritable Secy. Co.* (1880) 7 R. 546; *Scott* v. *Davidson*, 1914 S.C. 791.
[25] *Davidson* v. *Scott*, 1915 S.C. 924.
[26] 1868 Act, S. 122; see also *Tawse* v. *Rigg* (1904) 6 F. 544.
[27] *Johnston* v. *Irons*, 1909 S.C. 305.			[28] *Stewart* v. *Brown* (1882) 10 R. 192.

Protection of purchaser

The bondholder may grant the purchaser a disposition of the lands in the usual form.[29] A sale by a bondholder under the 1924 Act, Ss. 32 to 40, is to be valid and effectual though any person to whom notice requires to be given may be in pupillarity or minority or subject to legal incapacity. Any sale and disposition in implement thereof is to be as valid to the purchaser as if made by a proprietor of land and shall import an assignation to the purchaser of the warrandice contained or implied in the bond and also an obligation by the debtor to ratify, approve, and confirm the sale and disposition.[30]

Where a disposition is duly recorded and bears to be granted in exercise of the power of sale contained in a bond and the exercise of that power was *ex facie* regular, the title of a bona fide purchaser for value is not challengeable on the ground that the debt has ceased to exist, unless that fact appeared on the Register of Sasines or was known to the purchaser prior to payment of the price, or on the ground of any irregularity relating to the sale or in any preliminary procedure thereto, but without prejudice to any claim of damages competent against the person exercising the power.[31]

Where land is sold and no surplus remains,[32] or any surplus has been consigned in bank,[32] a certificate of no surplus or of consignation and the disposition to the purchaser, when recorded in the Register of Sasines, have the effect of completely disencumbering the land sold of the selling creditor's security and of all securities and diligence posterior to that creditor's security, except when the security and diligences are assigned to the purchaser as further or collateral security.[34]

A *pari passu* bondholder who cannot obtain the consent of the other *pari passu* bondholders may apply for warrant to sell to the sheriff, who may authorize either or both creditors or some other person to sell, and may grant a disposition and disencumber the lands of both bonds, the balance of the price after expenses being paid to the creditors according to their rights and preferences.[35] Sale must be by public roup.[36]

A postponed bondholder may sell but cannot disburden the lands of prior bonds unless he can pay them off in full, in which case he can enforce a discharge.[37]

---

[29] 1868 Act, S. 119.   [30] 1924 Act, S. 41(1).

[31] 1868 Act, S. 119; 1924 Act, S. 41(2), substituted by 1970 Act, S. 38, but applicable only to dispositions recorded after commencement of the 1970 Act.

[32] 1874 Act, S. 48.

[33] Titles to Land Consolidation (Sc.) Act, 1868, S. 122.   [34] 1924 Act, S. 42.

[35] Heritable Securities (Sc.) Act, 1894, S. 11, remedying difficulty found in *Nicholson's Trs.* v. *McLaughlin* (1891) 19 R. 49.

[36] Conveyancing and Feudal Reform (Sc.) Act, 1970, S. 35(3).

[37] *Adair's Trs.* v. *Rankine* (1895) 22 R. 975.

Foreclosure

At common law a creditor could not purchase for himself.[38] By the Heritable Securities Act, 1894, S. 8,[39] a creditor who has called for repayment, and advertised and exposed for sale lands held in security[40] at a price not exceeding the amount due under the security and any prior security and any securities ranking *pari passu* with his security, exclusive of expenses, may apply to the sheriff for decree forfeiting the right of redemption and declaring that he has right to the lands described in the bond, at the price at which it was last exposed, which the sheriff may grant, after service on the proprietor and other creditors and such intimation and inquiry as he may think fit. On the extract decree, containing a description of the lands, being recorded in the Register of Sasines, the debtor's right of redemption is extinguished and as from the date of the recording the creditor has right to the lands as if the disposition in security had been an irredeemable disposition as from that date. The recording disencumbers the lands of all securities and diligences posterior to the security of the holder of the decree. Alternatively, the sheriff may order re-exposure at a price fixed by him; the creditor may bid and if he purchases, the sheriff may grant decree to confer title on him, or the creditor may grant a disposition to himself.[41] The decree or disposition must refer to the burdens and conditions of the title.[42]

The surplus price, if any, over the sum due is consigned or a certificate of no surplus executed and recorded,[43] whereupon the creditor's right and title to the lands is absolute and irredeemable and the lands disencumbered of securities and diligences as in the case of sale under the Act. The debtor's personal obligation, so far as not extinguished by the price, remains in force.[44] No purchaser from the creditor or any other successor in title in the lands is under any duty to inquire into the regularity of the proceedings under which such creditor has acquired right to the lands by virtue of the Act, or is affected by any irregularity therein, without prejudice to any competent claim of damages against such creditor.[45]

Pari passu *and postponed bonds*

A proprietor may grant more than one bond and disposition in

---

[38] *Taylor* v. *Watson* (1846) 8 D. 400; *Stirling's Trs.* (1865) 3 M. 851. But another bond-holder may purchase: *Begbie* v. *Boyd* (1837) 16 S. 232.

[39] Amended by Conveyancing and Feudal Reform (Sc.) Act, 1970, S. 39.

[40] The whole lands must be exposed for sale in one lot: *Webb's Exor.* v. *Reid* (1906) 14 S.L.T. 323.

[41] 1894 Act, Ss. 9–10.   [42] 1924 Act, S. 9.

[43] 1874 Act, S. 48.   [44] 1894 Act, S. 9.

[45] 1894 Act, S. 10; *Sutherland* v. *Thomson* (1905) 8 F. (H.L.) 1.

security of the same lands. Such dispositions have priority according to the dates of their recording in the Register of Sasines.[46] But by agreement, stated in a clause in the later bond or a separate deed, signed by the consenting creditors, one bond may be postponed to another, or two or more may be ranked *pari passu*.

A prior bondholder exercising the power of sale may sell at a price leaving nothing for a postponed bondholder,[47] but the court may interdict a sale at an unfavourable time or if the interests of postponed bondholders are being ignored.[48]

A *pari passu* bondholder may take action to sell the security subjects for payment of their own debt without the consent of the other creditors, but their securities are unaffected by the sale.[49] By the Heritable Securities Act, 1894, S. 11, a *pari passu* bondholder desiring to sell, who cannot obtain the consent of another *pari passu* bondholder, may apply to the sheriff for warrant to sell, which the sheriff may order, and on payment or consignation of the price, the sheriff may grant a conveyance and disencumber the lands. The sale must be by public roup.[50] The balance of the price, after payment of expenses, is paid to the creditors according to their just rights and preferences.

A postponed bondholder who shows an interest may pay off a prior bondholder and demand an assignation of the security in favour of his nominee.[51]

Restriction, redemption, and discharge

A bond may be restricted to part only of the lands therein contained by a deed of restriction[52] recorded in the Register of Sasines. Where a superiority has been disponed in security the creditor may consent to the grant of feus and to the restriction of his security to the superiority of the lands feued without prejudice to its subsistence over the fee of the remainder of the lands.[53]

A bond may be renounced and discharged, in whole or in part, and the lands redeemed and disburdened, by a discharge in statutory form recorded in the Register of Sasines.[54] Payment to account may be endorsed on the bond.

[46] 1868 Act, S. 120.
[47] *Wilson* v. *Stirling* (1843) 8 D. 1261.
[48] *Beveridge* v. *Wilson* (1829) 7 S. 279; *Kerr* v. *McArthur's Trs.* (1848) 11 D. 301; *Stewart* v. *Brown* (1882) 10 R. 192, 203.
[49] *Nicholson's Trs.* v. *McLaughlin* (1891) 19 R. 49.
[50] Conveyancing and Feudal Reform (Sc.) Act, 1970, S. 35(3).
[51] *Adair's Trs.* v. *Rankin* (1895) 22 R. 975; *Reis* v. *Mackay* (1899) 6 S.L.T. 331.
[52] 1868 Act, S. 133, Sched. (OO); 1924 Act, S. 30, Sched. K; this may be combined with a partial discharge.
[53] *Sones* v. *Mill* (1903) 11 S.L.T. 98.
[54] 1868 Act, S. 132 and Sched. (NN); 1924 Act, S. 29, Sched. K. An uninfeft creditor may grant a discharge: *Macrae* v. *Gregory* (1903) 11 S.L.T. 102.

The debtor may redeem the lands disponed at the time and place of payment, or at any term of Whitsunday or Martinmas thereafter on three months' warning, on payment of principal, interest, and liquidated expenses and termly failures corresponding thereto, if incurred, or failing acceptance, on consignation in bank.[55] The notice is given in the same way as notice calling up a bond. If the debtor cannot grant a discharge, a certificate of consignation completely disencumbers the land to the extent of the amount consigned.[56] Premonition is necessary even if the creditor is in possession under a decree of maills and duties.[57]

The disposition in security being only an accessory of the personal debt, a bond may be extinguished by payment, proved by writ or oath,[58] a recorded discharge or a narrative of repayment in a recorded deed being necessary only to clear the record,[59] by compensation,[60] or by confusion, as where the creditor succeeds to the lands held by him in security,[61] unless he does so in a different capacity,[62] or by the creditor entering into possession and ingathering the rents, to the extent of his intromissions.[63]

BOND FOR CASH CREDIT AND DISPOSITION IN SECURITY

A disposition of lands in security might be adjected to a bond for cash credit in the same way as to a personal bond, securing repayment of the fluctuating balance on a cash account, up to a stated maximum. This can now[64] be done only by a bond for cash credit and a separate standard security. The bond must state the method whereby the outstanding debt at any given time will be ascertained, normally by a stated account and certificate by a stated official of the lending body. Such an account and certificate suffices for the purpose of summary diligence, but does not bar a challenge of the figures. The clause of consent to registration must expressly be made applicable to the stated

[55] 1868 Act, S. 133, Sched. (OO); 1924 Act, S. 30, Sched. K; this may be combined with a partial discharge.
[56] 1868 Act, S. 119; 1874 Act, S. 49; 1924 Act, S. 32 and Sched. L. See also *Bruce* v. *Scottish Amicable Life Assce. Socy.*, 1907 S.C. 637.
[57] *Bruce, supra.*
[58] *Jackson* v. *Nicoll* (1870) 8 M. 408.
[59] *Cameron* v. *Williamson* (1895) 22 R. 293. As to fraudulent discharge see *Bowie's Trs.* v. *Watson*, 1913 S.C. 326.
[60] *Rankin* v. *Arnot* (1680) Mor. 572; *McDowal* v. *Fullerton* (1714) Mor. 576.
[61] *Hogg* v. *Brack* (1832) 11 S. 198; *Murray* v. *Parlane's Tr.* (1890) 18 R. 287.
[62] *Colvile's Trs.* v. *Marindin*, 1908 S.C. 911; see also *Fleming* v. *Imrie* (1868) 6 M. 363; *Crichton's Trs.* v. *Clarke*, 1909, 1 S.L.T. 467; *Sherry* v. *S's Trs.*, 1918, 1 S.L.T. 31.
[63] *Baillie* v. *Menzies* (1711) 2 Ross L.C. 713.
[64] By reason of the Conveyancing and Feudal Reform (Sc.) Act, 1970, S. 9.

account and certificate. Such a disposition, once recorded, created an effectual security for future as well as past advances, but to do so there must be stated *in gremio* of the bond a statutory clause[65] that the principal and interest which may become due upon such cash accounts or credits shall be limited to a definite sum to be specified in the security, not exceeding the amount of the principal sum[66] and three years' interest thereon at five per cent.[67] If this is done the borrower may draw out and pay in sums as may be agreed, and the infeftment in security is equally valid and effectual as if the whole sums advanced on the cash credit has been paid prior to the date of sasine or infeftment thereon. If the interest limit be overstated in the bond, the security for interest is invalid,[68] and it may be that the whole security is invalid.[69]

In case of default the disposition in security by standard security contains the same powers of realization as any other standard security.

It is thought that a bond for cash credit can be assigned only to the extent of the balance due at the date of assignation, and not transferring the creditor's part of a continuing account so as to permit future dealings with the security.

OTHER BONDS AND DISPOSITIONS IN SECURITY

A disposition of lands in security may also be combined with a bond of corroboration, bond of relief or bond of annuity, or with a bond and assignation in security of moveable rights.

EX FACIE ABSOLUTE DISPOSITION

A proprietor of heritage might also grant a right in security over heritage, particularly for the repayment of a future or fluctuating debt, by an absolute disposition of the heritage to the creditor.[70] Though the disposition is in terms and *ex facie* absolute and not redeemable, the common intention is that the disponee (creditor) should hold the subjects in security only. The terms on which he holds can be proved by writ or oath,[71] and the disponee normally grants a separate writing, a

[65] Debts Securities (Sc.) Act, 1856, S. 7.

[66] Interest accumulated under the agreement as to credit is principal: *Reddie* v. *Williamson* (1863) 1 M. 228.

[67] cf. *Morton* v. *Hunter* (1828) 7 S. 172; 4 W. & S. 379.

[68] *Alston* v. *Nellfield Co.*, 1915 S.C. 912.

[69] *Anderson* v. *Dickie*, 1914 S.C. 706, 717.

[70] Under the Conveyancing and Feudal Reform (Sc.) Act, 1970, security can now be created in this way in exceptional cases only (see S. 9) without prejudice to existing securities in this form.

[71] Trusts Act, 1696 (c. 25); Bell, *Prin.* §1995; *Robertson* v. *Duff* (1840) 2 D. 279; *Seth* v. *Hain* (1855) 17 D. 1117; *Walker* v. *Buchanan, Kennedy & Co.* (1857) 20 D. 259; *Marshall* v. *Lyell*

back-letter or back-bond, setting out the conditions on which the subjects have been conveyed to him, and obliging himself to reconvey on getting repayment of the debt.[72] The back-letter may contain conditions on the use of the subjects as well as relative to repayment.[73] Alternatively, a bilateral minute of agreement states the conditions.[74] Or the disclosure that the disposition was truly in security could be in a personal bond.[75] The disposition is in the same form as a disposition following on sale, save that the consideration is stated as 'for certain onerous causes and considerations'. The creditor completes title by recording the disposition in the Register of Sasines as would a purchaser. A company granting security in this way had to have particulars recorded in the Register of Charges.[76]

If the back-letter is recorded the obligation to denude on repayment is a real limitation on the disponee's right and the security may be limited to sums advanced down to that date.[77] Recording publishes the conditions which qualify the disponee's right.[78] If the back-letter is unrecorded the disponee can sell or burden the subjects and generally act as absolute proprietor, though such action may be in conflict with his undertaking in the back-letter. The disponer has only a personal right to have the hands reconveyed or the proceeds of their sale paid to him, on his repaying the debt secured by the disposition.[79]

An *ex facie* absolute disposition is a valid security for any debt incurred or to be incurred, before or after the date of infeftment thereunder.[80] If, however, the back-letter bears that the disposition was granted in security of a specific debt only, there is no right to retain the subjects in security of other debts.[81]

(1859) 21 D. 514; *Laird* v. *Laird & Rutherford* (1884) 12 R. 294; *Dunn* v. *Pratt* (1898) 25 R. 461. But proof is not thus limited if the holder of the disposition admits that the documents do not give a true account of the agreement between him and the granter; *Burnett* v. *Morrow* (1864) 22 M. 929; *Murray* v. *Wright* (1870) 8 M. 722; *Grant's Trs.* v. *Morrison* (1875) 2 R. 377; *Grant* v. *G.* (1898) 6 S.L.T. 203. And a third party having an interest may prove the trust qualifying the disposition by any evidence: *Wallace* v. *Sharp* (1885) 12 R. 687; *Hastie* v. *Steel* (1886) 13 R. 843. The writ need not be probative; *Paterson* v. *P.* (1897) 25 R. 144, 175.

[72] e.g. *Smith* v. *S.* (1879) 6 R. 794.
[73] e.g. *Macintyre* v. *Cleveland Petroleum Co.*, 1967 S.L.T. 95.
[74] e.g. *Stewart* v. *Brown* (1882) 10 R. 192; *Duncan* v. *Mitchell* (1893) 21 R. 37; *Scottish & Newcastle Breweries* v. *Rathburne Hotel Liqdr.*, 1970 S.C. 215.
[75] *Aberdeen Trades Council* v. *Shipconstructors Asscn.*, 1949 S.C. (H.L.) 45.
[76] Companies (Floating Charges and Receivers) (Sc.) Act, 1972, S. 6; *Scottish & Newcastle, supra.*
[77] Bell, *Prin.* §912; Menzies, 861.
[78] *National Bank* v. *Union Bank* (1885) 13 R. 380, 390; *Edinburgh Entertainments, Ltd.* v. *Stevenson*, 1926 S.L.T. 286.
[79] *Thomson* v. *Douglas, Heron & Co.* (1786) Mor. 10229; *Somervails* v. *Redfearn* (1813) 5 Pat. 707; *Union Bank* v. *National Bank* (1886) 14 R. (H.L.) 1.
[80] *Maitland* v. *Cockerell* (1827) 6 S. 109; *Russell* v. *E. Breadalbane* (1831) 5 W. & S. 256; *Tierney* v. *Court* (1832) 10 S. 664; *James* v. *Downie* (1836) 15 S. 12; *Robertson* v. *Duff* (1840) 2 D. 279, 291.   [81] *Robertson, supra*; cf. *Anderson's Tr.* v. *Somerville* (1899) 36 S.L.R. 833.

Position of creditor (disponee)

If the back-letter is unrecorded the disposition confers on the creditor all the rights of a feudal proprietor[82] so that he can possess and occupy the lands,[83] draw the rents, let on lease,[84] remove tenants, and remove the debtor from possession.[85] He cannot be dispossessed by the trustee in the debtor's sequestration until the sum due has been paid.[86] He may sell the lands without the debtor's consent and give a good title to the purchaser,[87] but if he does so unfairly the debtor, as owner in equity, has an action of damages against him, though he cannot impugn the sale.[88] The purchaser's title is qualified by any trust disclosed in the creditor's title.[89] The debtor may interdict a sale when the balance due by him was neither admitted nor liquidated.[90] The creditor may, however, allow the debtor to remain in possession,[91] in which case he cannot challenge a lease granted by the debtor,[92] nor is he liable as principal for goods bought by the debtor in connection with the lands.[93] He is liable as vassal for feu-duty and implement of all the conditions of the feu due to the superior.[94] If while in possession he makes improvements he is entitled to be reimbursed to the extent that the debtor is *lucratus* thereby.[95]

If the creditor goes bankrupt the trustee in his sequestration stands in his place and takes the property subject to the obligation to the debtor as true owner and with no better title than the creditor had,[95] but the trustee may sell and confer a good title, free of the latent trust, on a purchaser who gives full value and is ignorant of the latent qualification.[96]

As between a bondholder and a creditor infeft under a subsequent *ex facie* absolute disposition, the creditor is not, however, deemed

[82] *Gardyne* v. *Royal Bank* (1853) 1 Macq. 368; *McLelland* v. *Bank of Scotland* (1857) 19 D. 574; *Union Bank* v. *National Bank* (1886) 14 R. (H.L.) 1.

[83] *Sc. Herit. Security Co.* v. *Allan Campbell & Co.* (1876) 3 R. 333.

[84] But not where the lease is a fictitious device: *Heritable Sec. Inv. Assoc.* v. *Wingate's Tr.* (1880) 7 R. 1094.

[85] *Rankin* v. *Russell* (1868) 7 M. 126; *Sc. Property Inv. Co. Bldg. Soc.* v. *Horne* (1881) 8 R. 737.

[86] *Lindsay* v. *Davidson* (1853) 15 D. 583.

[87] Bell, *Prin.* §912; *Edinburgh Entertainments* v. *Stevenson*, 1926 S.C. 363; *Aberdeen Trades Council* v. *Shipconstructors Assocn.*, 1949 S.C. (H.L.) 45.

[88] *Parks* v. *Alliance Her. Sec. Co.* (1880) 7 R. 546; *Baillie* v. *Drew* (1884) 12 R. 199; *Duncan* v. *Mitchell* (1893) 21 R. 37; *Shrubb* v. *Clark* (1897) 5 S.L.T. 125; *Rimmer* v. *Usher*, 1967 S.L.T. 7.

[89] *Livingstone* v. *Allan* (1900) 3 F. 233.

[90] *Lucas* v. *Gardner* (1876) 4 R. 194; contrast *Mackintosh* v. *Leslie* (1907) 15 S.L.T. 2.

[91] *Leckie* v. *L.* (1854) 17 D. 77.

[92] *Abbott* v. *Mitchell* (1870) 8 M. 791; *Edinburgh Entertainments, supra.*

[93] *Newcastle Chemical Co.* v. *Oliphant & Jamieson* (1881) 9 R. 110.

[94] *Clark* v. *City of Glasgow Life Assce. and Reversionary Co.* (1850) 12 D. 1047; *City of Glasgow Bank* v. *Nicolson's Trs.* (1882) 9 R. 689.

[95] *Nelson* v. *Gordon* (1874) 1 R. 1093.

[96] *Heritable Reversionary Co.* v. *Millar* (1892) 19 R. (H.L.) 43.

proprietor and has been held not entitled to reduce a sale by the bondholder[97] but entitled to be relieved of feu-duty by a bondholder who took possession.[98]

Position of debtor (disponer)

The debtor has only a personal right to have the lands reconveyed or the proceeds of their sale paid to him, after satisfying the creditor's claims for principal and interest.[99] A conveyance in security qualified by a back-letter does not cease to be a right in security only by reason of the lapse of time[1] but if the back-letter is unrecorded possession by the creditor for the prescriptive period will confer an absolute right of property and the rights under the back-letter be cut down.[2] The debtor may also confer an indefeasible title by a discharge, or by destroying an unrecorded back-letter.[3] If the back-letter is recorded the debtor's protection is increased and no one deriving title from the creditor can plead ignorance of the fact that his right is in security only, or of any limitation on his rights to deal with the property expressed therein.[4]

The debtor may be left in possession of the lands,[5] in which case he may grant a lease[6] and remove tenants,[7] though an implied mandate from the creditor to grant a lease falls on his bankruptcy.[8] As true owner with the radical right to the lands he may sue for injury to the lands by third parties.[9] If he becomes bankrupt his trusteee in bankruptcy cannot recover the lands without making full payment of the debt.[10]

The debtor's reversionary right is assignable[11] outright or in security, and if assigned and intimated, the security of the creditor is limited to advances made prior to the date of intimation to him of the assignation.[12] The appointment of a judicial factor is equivalent to an

[97] *Stewart* v. *Brown* (1892) 10 R. 192.
[98] *City of Glasgow Bank* v. *Nicolson's Trs.* (1880) 9 R. 689.
[99] *Thomson* v. *Douglas, Heron & Co.* (1786) Mor. 10229; *Somervails* v. *Redfearn* (1813) 5 Pat. 707; *Union Bank* v. *National Bank* (1886) 14 R. (H.L.) 1.
[1] *Smith* v. *S.* (1879) 6 R. 794; cf. *Scott* v. *Stewart* (1779) 3 Ross. L.C. 464; *National Bank* v. *Union Bank* (1885) 13 R. 380, 400.
[2] *Chambers* v. *Law* (1823) 2 S. 366.
[3] *National Bank, supra*, 13 R. 400.
[4] *Aberdeen Trades Council, supra*, 67.
[5] *Leckie* v. *L.* (1854) 17 D. 77.
[6] *Abbott* v. *Mitchell* (1869) 8 M. 268; *Ritchie* v. *Scott* (1899) 1 F. 728; *Edinburgh Entertainments Ltd.* v. *Stevenson*, 1926 S.C. 363.
[7] *Traill* v. *T.* (1873) 1 R. 61.
[8] *Ritchie, supra.*
[9] *McBride* v. *Caledonian Ry.* (1894) 21 R. 620; *Vincent* v. *Wood* (1899) 6 S.L.T. 297; *Scobie* v. *Lind*, 1967 S.L.T. 9.
[10] *Lindsay* v. *Davidson* (1853) 15 D. 583.
[11] *Dundee Calendering Co.* v. *Duff* (1869) 8 M. 289; *Union Bank, supra;* *Ritchie, supra; Aberdeen Trades Council, supra.*
[12] *Union Bank, supra.*

intimated assignation and the disponee can claim interest on the loan to that date only.[13]

Extent of right in security

The creditor is entitled to hold the subjects until satisfaction has been made of all debts due to him by the debtor.[14] The terms of the back-letter may determine whether the security covers debts incurred after the disposition as well as before or at the time thereof. Even if it bear to be granted in security of a specified existing debt, the creditor may retain in respect of later advances.

Creditor—disponee's remedies

The creditor who holds an *ex facie* absolute disposition is *ex facie* proprietor and cannot poind the ground.[15] He may collect rents without an action of maills and duties. He may have the debtor, if in possession, ejected by declarator and removing,[16] but not by summary ejection. If he realizes the security by sale[17] he will be liable to the debtor if he does so excessively and prejudices the latter's reversionary rights[18] or does not have regard to the latter's interest by trying to secure a fair price.[19]

If the creditor possesses under the disposition to him for the prescriptive period, the debtor's right of reversion is cut off.[20]

Similarly, the debtor can vest an unqualified title in the creditor by discharging his right of reversion, or by destroying the back-letter.[21]

Creditor's succession

Land held under a disposition *ex facie* absolute but truly in security is always heritable in succession,[22] and heirs complete title as to any other heritage. But they take the property subject to the debtor's equitable claim to the reversion.

Debtor's succession

The debtor has merely a conditional reversionary claim under the back-letter, which transmits to the debtor's heirs in heritage.

[13] *Campbell's J.F.* v. *National Bank*, 1944 S.C. 495.

[14] *Robertson* v. *Duff* (1840) 2 D. 279; *Nelson* v. *Gordon* (1874) 1 R. 1093.

[15] *Sc. Heritable Security Co.* v. *Allan, Campbell & Co.* (1876) 3 R. 333.

[16] *Rankin* v. *Russell* (1868) 7 M. 126; *Sc. Property Investment Co. Bldg. Soc.* v. *Horne* (1881) 8 R. 737.

[17] The creditor alone can give a good title to the purchaser from him: *Duncan* v. *Mitchell* (1893) 21 R. 37. Unless debarred from doing so the creditor may sell without notice to the debtor: *Aberdeen Trades Council* v. *Shipconstructors Assocn.* 1949 S.C. (H.L.) 45.

[18] *Baillie* v. *Drew* (1885) 12 R. 199; *Nelson* v. *National Bank*, 1936 S.C. 570.

[19] *Rimmer* v. *Usher*, 1967 S.L.T. 7.

[20] *Munro* v. *M.*, 19 May 1812, F.C.; *Paul* v. *Reid*, 8 Feb., 1814, F.C.; *Chambers* v. *Law* (1823) 2 S. 366; cf. *Smith* v. *S.* (1879) 6 R. 794.

[21] *National Bank* v. *Union Bank* (1885) 13 R. 380, 400.

[22] 1868 Act, Ss. 3 and 117; Bell, *Prin.* §1478, 1485; cf. *Stroyan* v. *Murray* (1890) 17 R. 1170.

Redemption and reconveyance

The debtor may discharge his liability by payment without obtaining any deed of discharge, but the only competent mode of recovering the lands is by reconveyance by the creditor.[23] The creditor is entitled, before reconveying, to payment of all debts incurred before or after the back-bond, and reimbursement of outlays made on the subjects by him, which were really of the nature of meliorations.[24] When the creditor has discharged the debt, he is still entitled to require the debtor to take the lands back.[25] A creditor may grant an undertaking to reconvey on conditions, which amounts to a personal obligation and is assignable.[26] It is questionable whether a creditor's recording of a back-letter, execution of a reconveyance to the debtor, and his obtaining of a decree in absence ordaining him to register it, operates as a feudal divestiture in a question with the superior.[27]

Alternatively, a discharge by the creditor in the form of Schedule 9 to the Conveyancing and Feudal Reform (Sc.) Act, 1970, either as a separate deed or as a deed endorsed on the conveyance, as from the date when it is recorded discharges the security, disburdens the land so far as it is the subject of the security, and vests it in the person entitled thereto in the same way as if a conveyance containing a claim of warrandice from fact and deed only and all other usual and necessary clauses had been granted by the creditors to that person and duly recorded.[28]

Competition with prior bondholder

If a proprietor has granted a bond and disposition in security and subsequently grants an *ex facie* absolute disposition the disponee under the latter deed is deemed a mere security-holder in a question with a prior bondholder.[29]

STANDARD SECURITY

By statute[30] a right in security over any interest in land, other than an

---

[23] *National Bank* v. *Union Bank* (1885) 13 R. 380, 400.
[24] *Nelson* v. *Gordon* (1874) 1 R. 1093.
[25] *Clydesdale Bank* v. *McIntyre*, 1909 S.C. 1405.
[26] *McCallum's Trs.* v. *McNab* (1877) 4 R. 520.
[27] *Marshall's Trs.* v. *Macneill* (1888) 15 R. 762.
[28] 1970 Act, S. 40.
[29] *Stewart* v. *Brown* (1882) 10 R. 192; cf. *City of Glasgow Bank* v. *Nicolson's Trs.* (1882) 9 R. 689; *King* v. *Johnston*, 1908 S.C. 684.
[30] Conveyancing and Feudal Reform (Sc.) Act, 1970, Ss. 9–32. Any enactment relating to a bond and disposition in security applies to a standard security, except so far as inconsistent with the 1970 Act, save that the provisions listed in Sch. 8 do not apply.

entailed estate or any interest therein, capable of being owned or held as a separate estate and to which a title may be recorded in the Register of Sasines,[31] may be created by a standard security, expressed in conformity with either Form A or Form B of Schedule 2 of the Act. From the passing of the Act[32] this is the only competent mode of granting a right in security over an interest in land[33] and a deed containing a disposition or assignation of an interest in land, if not in the form of a standard security, is void and, if recorded, the creditor may be required to grant a deed to clear the Register of Sasines of that security.[34] A standard security may be used, if any of the forms is appropriate, for any other purpose for which a heritable security may be used.[35]

A standard security, unlike a bond and disposition in security, gives security for a debt contracted after the recording of the deed, and the sum secured need not be specified in the deed.[36] It may accordingly be a security for a fixed amount or for a fluctuating amount of money, in the latter case advanced before and/or after the deed, and it may or may not be subject to a maximum amount.

A standard security may be granted over an interest in land by a person having right thereto but whose title thereto has not been completed by being recorded if in the deed expressing the security he deduces his title from the person having the last recorded title thereto in the form prescribed in Note 2 or 3 of Schedule 2.[37]

Two forms of standard security are provided in Sched. 2, Form A where the personal obligation is included in the deed, and Form B where the personal obligation is constituted in a separate writing and it creates security only, though in this case the nature of the debt and the writings constituting it must be referred to. The clauses of personal obligation and consent to registration for execution in Form A,[38] and the clauses of warrandice in both forms have statutory import,[39] while

---

[31] Including the creditor's interest in a right of ground annual and a recorded lease (see S. 30 (2)). As to recorded lease see *Trade Development Bank* v. *Warriner & Mason (Sc.) Ltd.,* 1980 S.L.T. 223.

[32] 29 November 1970.

[33] This is without prejudice (S. 31) to the validity of heritable securities recorded prior to the Act, which must be dealt with under the prior law. But (S. 9(7)) it remains competent to constitute a security under the Small Dwellings Ascquisition (Sc.) Acts, 1899 to 1923, by bond and disposition in security, but not by *ex facie* absolute disposition. Security may be granted over entailed estate in any manner (S. 9(8)(b)).

[34] S. 9(1)–(4). The obligation which may be secured thereby is widely defined in S. 9(8)(c) as including obligations to pay, to pay an annuity, and *ad factum praestandum*; see *U.D.T.* v. *Site Preparation*, 1978 S.L.T. (Sh. Ct.) 14.

[35] S. 9(5).

[36] S. 9(6).

[37] 1970 Act, S. 12.

[38] Ibid., S. 10(1) and (3).

[39] Ibid., S. 10(2).

an assignation of writs with statutory import is implied.[40] The personal obligation is to pay the sum on demand in writing at any time but this may be qualified.

The recording of a standard security in the Register of Sasines vests the interest over which it is granted in the grantee as a security for the performance of the contract to which it relates.[41]

In the case of land in an area operational for the purposes of the Land Registration Act, 1979, the creation of a heritable security over a registered interest in land is registrable and creates a registered interest.[42] The Keeper amends the title sheet of the interest in land to which the security relates and issues a charge certificate to the creditor.[43]

Standard conditions

Every standard security is regulated by the standard conditions set out in Schedule 3 to the Act, either as so set out or with such variations as have been agreed by the parties.[44] A creditor may reduce a lease granted in contravention of a condition in Sched. 3 whether it prejudices his security or not.[45] Subject to the Act the parties may vary any of the standard conditions other than Cond. 11 and the provisions of Sched. 3 relating to the powers of sale and foreclosure, but no condition may be varied in any way inconsistent with a non-variable condition and any such purported variation is void and unenforceable.[46] Variation may be effected by a clause in the standard security, or by a separate deed, which does not need to be recorded.[47]

Ranking of standard securities

The ranking of heritable securities, including standard securities, may be defined by a ranking clause in the deed.[48] Apart from that, where the creditor in a recorded standard security has received notice of a subsequent security over the same interest in land or part thereof, or the subsequent assignation or conveyance of that interest in whole or in part, duly recorded, the creditor's preference in ranking is restricted to security for his present advances and future advances which he may be required to make under the contract and interest accrued,

[40] Ibid., S. 10(4).
[41] Ibid., S. 11(1).
[42] 1979 Act, S. 2(3)(i).
[43] 1979 Act, S. 5.
[44] 1970 Act, S. 11(2).
[45] *Trade Development Bank* v. *Lyon*, 1980 S.L.T. 49.
[46] Ibid., S. 11(3) and (4), amd. Redemption of Standard Securities (Sc.) Act, 1971, S. 1(a). Standard Condition 11 is amended by the 1971 Act, S. 1(g).
[47] See also S. 16.
[48] Sched. 2, Note 5.

present and future, thereon, and for expenses reasonably incurred.[49] The creditor is not held to have had notice by reason only of subsequent recording of the other security in the Register of Sasines, but is by any assignation, conveyance or vesting in favour of any other person of the debtor's interest resulting from any judicial decree or otherwise by operation of law. These provisions do not affect any preference in ranking enjoyed by the Crown.[50]

Assignation

A standard security may be transferred in whole or in part by assignation in the form of Form A or B of Schedule 4 which, when duly recorded, vests the security in the assignee and conveys to him all rights competent to the grantor to the writs and vests in him the benefit of all corroborative or substitutional obligations, the right to recover payment from the debtor of all expenses properly incurred by the creditor and entitlement to the benefit of any notices served and all procedure instituted by the creditor in respect of the security.[51] Any transfer of a standard security over a registered interest in land is registrable. The Keeper amends the title sheet of the interest in land to which the standard security relates and amends the charge sheet for the security.[52]

Restriction

The security may be restricted by a deed of restriction in the form of Form C of Schedule 4, which when recorded has the effect of restricting the security to the interest in land other than the part of the interest disburdened, which is released to the extent specified. A partial discharge and deed of restriction may be combined.[53]

Variation

Alterations in the provisions, including standard conditions, of a recorded standard security, may be effected by a variation endorsed thereon in the form of Form E of Schedule 4, or contained in an appropriate separate deed, either being recorded. If the personal obligation or any other provision is in a deed not recorded the variation may be in an appropriate deed which need not be recorded. Variation does not prejudice any other security or right constituted before the variation is recorded or executed.[54]

[49] S. 13(1). cf. *Union Bank* v. *National Bank* (1886) 14 R. (H.L.) 1.
[50] S. 13(2) and (3). By S. 42 S. 13 applies also in relation to the effect on the preference in ranking of any heritable security constituted by *ex facie* absolute disposition or assignation. As to ranking of interests registered in the Land Register see Land Registration (Sc.) Act, 1979, S. 7.
[51] 1970 Act, S. 14.
[52] 1979 Act, S. 2(4) and 5(3).
[53] Ibid., S. 15.   [54] S. 16.

Discharge

Discharge is effected by discharge in the form of Form F of Schedule 4, either separate from or endorsed on the standard security, and duly recorded.[55] In the case of a security over a registered interest in land the discharge is registrable.[56]

Redemption

Subject to any agreement to the contrary, the debtor or proprietor of the security subjects may redeem the security on two months' notice of his intention to do so and in conformity with standard condition 11 and the forms of Schedule 5. If, owing to the death or absence of the creditor or for any other cause the debtor or proprietor of the security subjects (being in either case a person entitled to redeem the security) is unable to obtain a discharge under the foregoing provisions, he may, where the obligation was to pay money, consign in bank the whole amount due to the creditor on redemption other than any unascertained expenses, for the person appearing to have the best right thereto and, in other cases, apply to the court for declarator that the whole obligations under the contract have been performed. On consignation or grant of declarator a certificate to that effect may be expede in the terms of Form D of Schedule 5 which, when recorded, disburdens the interest in land.[57]

A debtor or proprietor of the security subjects may redeem a heritable security executed after 31 July 1974 by giving notice at any time within twenty years if the security subjects are used as or part of a dwelling house but not if the use of the security subjects is in contravention of a conventional condition of or relating to the security unless the creditor approved the use expressly or by actings and it is continuing.[58]

Calling-up of standard security

If the creditor intends to require discharge of the debt secured he must serve a notice calling up the security in conformity with Form A of Schedule 6 on the person last infeft in the security subjects and appearing on the record as the proprietor, or if he be dead, on his representative or the person entitled to the subjects in terms of the last recorded title thereto. If the person last infeft was a company now removed from the Register of Companies or a person deceased who has left no representatives notice is served on the Lord Advocate; if the

[55] S. 17.
[56] Land Registration (Sc.) Act, 1979, S. 2(4).
[57] 1970 Act, S. 18, amd. Redemption of Standard Securities (Sc.) Act, 1971, S. 1(b), (c), and (d).
[58] Land Tenure Reform (Sc.) Act, 1974, S. 11.

person last infeft has been sequestrated notice is served on the trustee in the sequestration, unless discharged, and on the bankrupt. In the case of trustees it is sufficient to serve notice on a majority of trustees. The Act also contains provisions as to the manner of service and evidence thereof. Notice must also be served on any other person against whom the creditor wishes to preserve any right of recourse in respect of the debt. Where the sum and interest due may be subject to adjustment, the creditor must, if requested, furnish the debtor with a statement of the sum finally determined within one month, under penalty of rendering the calling-up notice void. The period of notice may be dispensed with or shortening by the recipient with the consent of any creditors holding securities *pari passu* with or postponed to the security, by minute in conformity with Form C of Schedule 6. A calling-up notice ceases to have effect for the purpose of a sale on the expiry of five years from the date of the notice or, where the subjects have been offered for sale, from the date of the last offer or exposure.[59]

Where debtor defaults to comply with calling-up notice

Where the debtor is in default, in not complying with the calling-up notice, the creditor may exercise such of his rights under the security[60] as he may consider appropriate, in addition to any other remedy arising from the contract, such as personal action and summary diligence, and any right conferred by law on the creditor in a heritable security, such as to use poinding of the ground. He may sell the security subjects under Ss. 25–7 of the Act, obtain lawful possession[61] and let the security subjects for not longer than seven years, or obtain warrant from the court to let them for a longer period, and there are deemed assigned to a creditor in lawful possession[60] all rights and obligations of the proprietor relating to leases, or any permission or right of occupancy, the management and maintenance of the subjects and the effecting of any reconstruction, alteration or improvement reasonably required for maintaining the market value of the subjects.[62]

Notice of default and objection thereto

Where the debtor is in default by failure to comply with any requirement arising out of the security other than a calling-up notice and the

---

[59] S. 19.

[60] i.e., under standard condition 10, without prejudice to other remedies, the following (ii) sale of the security subjects; (iii) entry into possession and recovery of feu-duties, ground-annuals or rents; (iv) entry into possession and letting the security subjects; (v) entry into possession and exercise of rights of letting, occupation and management of the subjects; (vi) power to repair, maintain, reconstruct, alter or improve the subjects; and (vii) application to the court for decree of foreclosure.

[61] Even if standard conditions 10 (iii), (iv), and (v) are excluded a creditor may obtain possession by virtue of decree in an action of mails and duties under the Heritable Securities (Sc.) Act, 1894, S. 3.   [62] S. 20.

default is remediable the creditor may call on the debtor and the proprietor, if different, to purge the default, by serving a notice of default in conformity with Form B of Schedule 6, and which ceases to be authority for the exercise of rights under standard condition 10(2), (6) and (7) on the expiry of five years.[63] The person served with the notice of default may within fourteen days object to the notice by application to the court which may order the notice to be set aside or varied or upheld. The creditor may make a counter-application craving any of the remedies open to him under the Act or under any enactment relating to heritable securities, and lodge a certificate conforming to Schedule 7,[64] which is prima facie evidence of the facts directed to be contained therein.[65] If the notice is not objected to, or it is upheld or varied, the person served must comply with any requirement due to be performed or fulfilled by him contained in the notice. If he fails to comply the creditor may proceed to exercise such of his rights under standard condition 10 (2), (6) and (7) as he may consider appropriate. After the expiry of the period stated in a notice of default but before the conclusion of any enforceable contract to sell the security subjects the debtor or proprietor (being a person entitled to redeem the security) may, subject to any agreement to the contrary, redeem the security without need to observe any requirement of notice.[66]

Application to court for remedies on default

Where the debtor is in default in non-compliance with a requirement arising out of the security other than a calling-up notice, or where the proprietor has become insolvent, the creditor may apply to the sheriff for warrant to exercise any of the remedies which he is entitled to exercise on a default under a calling-up notice, and may, as *prima facie* evidence, lodge a certificate conforming with Schedule 7 of the Act.[67]

Power of sale and its exercise

The creditor's right to sell is conferred by standard condition 10(2), which may not be varied. The sale may be by private bargain or exposure to sale. In either case it is the duty of the creditor to advertise the sale and to take all reasonable steps to ensure that the price at which all or any of the subjects are sold is the best that can be

---

[63] 1970 Act, S. 21; *U.D.T.* v. *Site Preparations*, 1978 S.L.T. (Sh. Ct.) 14 and 21.
[64] Stating, *inter alia*, the nature of the default with full details thereof.
[65] S. 22.
[66] S. 23, amd. Redemption of Standard Securities (Sc.) Act, 1971, S. i(e).
[67] S. 24. The court is bound to grant warrant: *U.D.T.* v. *Site Preparations*, 1978 S.L.T. (Sh. Ct.) 14. Creditors holding warrant to sell may proceed notwithstanding: Companies Act, 1948, S. 227; *U.D.T.*, 1977 S.L.T. (Notes) 56.

reasonably obtained.[68] Where the creditor has effected a sale and granted a disposition in implement of the sale, on its being recorded the subjects are disburdened of the standard security and of all other heritable securities ranking *pari passu* with or postponed to that security. Where on such a sale the security subjects remain subject to a prior security, the recording of the disposition does not affect the rights of the creditor in that security, but the creditor who effected the sale has the same right as the debtor to redeem the security.

Application of proceeds of sale

The money received by the creditor from the sale must be held by him to be applied in payment (a) of expenses connected with the sale, (b) of the amount due under any prior security to which the sale is not subject, (c) of the amount due under the standard security and, in due proportion, of the amount due under a security, if any, ranking *pari passu* therewith and duly recorded, and (d) of any amounts due under any securities with a ranking postponed to that of his own security according to their ranking, and any residue of the money received is to be paid to the person entitled to the security subjects at the time of sale, or to any person authorized to give receipts for the proceeds of sale thereof. If the creditor is unable to obtain a receipt for any payment due he may, without prejudice to his liability to account therefor, consign the amount due in the sheriff court for the person appearing to have the best right thereto and lodge in court a statement of the amount consigned. Such consignation operates as a discharge of the payment of the amount due, and is sufficiently evidenced by a certificate under the hand of the sheriff clerk.[69]

Foreclosure

Where the creditor has exposed the security subjects to sale at a price not exceeding the amount due under the security and any security ranking prior to or *pari passu* with it, and has failed to find a purchaser, or, having so failed, has succeeded in selling only part of the subjects at a lesser price, he may, after two months from the first exposure to sale, apply to the court for decree of foreclosure. He must lodge a statement setting out the amount due and it is sufficient to satisfy the court that the amount stated is not less than the price at which the security subjects have been exposed to sale, or part of them been sold. The application must be served on the debtor, the proprietor, if different, and the creditor in any other heritable security affecting the subjects diclosed by a search in the Register of Sasines for twenty years back. The court may order such intimation and inquiry as

[68] S. 25.   [69] S. 27.

it thinks fit, may allow the debtor or proprietor not more than three months in which to pay the amount due, and may appoint the security subjects or the unsold part to be re-exposed to sale at a price fixed by the court, in which case the creditor may bid and purchase, or grant a decree of foreclosure.[70]

A decree of foreclosure contains a declaration that, on the extract thereof being duly recorded, any right to redeem the security has been extinguished and that the creditor has right to the security subjects or the unsold part thereof, described by a particular description or a description as in the Conveyancing (Sc.) Act, 1924, Sch. D, or the Titles to Land Consolidation (Sc.) Act, 1868, Sch. G, including a reference to any conditions or clauses affecting the subjects, at the price at which the subjects were last exposed under deduction of the price for any part sold, and also contains warrant for recording the extract decree in the Register of Sasines. On extract being duly recorded any right to redeem the security is extinguished, and the creditor has right to and is vested in the subjects as if he had received an irredeemable disposition from the proprietor, the subjects are disburdened of the standard security and of all securities and diligences postponed thereto, and the creditor who has obtained the decree has the same right as the debtor to redeem any security prior to or *pari passu* with his own security. Notwithstanding decree of foreclosure any personal obligation by the debtor remains in force so far as not extinguished by the price at which the security subjects have been acquired and the price for which any part has been sold. Where the security subjects have been acquired by decree of foreclosure, the creditor's title is not challengeable on the ground of any irregularity in the proceedings for foreclosure or on calling-up or default, but this does not affect the competency of any claim for damages in respect of such proceedings against the creditor.[71]

Restriction on effect of reduction of certain discharges

Where the discharge, total or partial, of a security over land is duly recorded, before or after the 1970 Act, and it bears to be granted by a person entitled to do so, the title of a person to any subsequent interest in the land, acquired bona fide and for value is not challengeable after five years from the date of recording the discharge, by reason only of the recording of an extract decree of reduction of the discharge, whether or not decree was before or after the date when the acquisition of the interest was duly recorded. Sec. 46 of the 1924 Act ceases to apply in relation to a decree of reduction of a discharge where the

[70] S. 28(1)–(4).
[71] S. 28 (5)–(8), amd. Redemption of Standard Securities (Sc.) Act, 1971, S. 1(f).

discharge has been recorded for five years or more, though it remains competent to record such a decree of reduction. These provisions do not affect the rights of the creditor in a security as against the debtor.[72] The effect of this, which applies to securities generally, is that a bona fide purchaser need not examine a security deed or its transmissions if a discharge has been recorded for at least five years, because a reduction of the discharge would not affect him.

FLOATING CHARGE OVER HERITAGE

By the Companies (Floating Charges and Receivers) (Sc.) Act, 1972, an incorporated company, or society registered under the Industrial and Provident Societies Acts, 1965 and 1967, may grant security for any present or future debt by creating a floating charge over all or any of the property, heritable and moveable, which may from time to time be comprised in its property and undertaking. It attaches to the property then comprised in the company's property on the commencement of winding up, but is subject to the rights of anyone who has effectually executed diligence, or holds a fixed security ranking in priority to the floating charge, or another floating charge ranking in priority.[73] Whether a charge affects particular heritage depends on the terms of the instrument of charge executed.[74] Subject to the Companies Act, 1948, a floating charge has effect in relation to heritage, notwithstanding that it is not recorded in the Register of Sasines.[75] In relation to land within an area operational for the purposes of the Land Registration (Sc.) Act, 1979, a floating charge is an overriding interest and not registrable, whether or not it has attached to the interest affected. It is implied that a floating charge is assignable,[76] and it is probably heritable in the creditor's succession, if granted over heritage only, but moveable if granted over a mixed aggregate of heritable and moveable property, or over moveable property only.

The charge thereby created can be enforced only by petition for winding-up the company,[77] or by the appointment of a receiver.[78]

---

[72] S. 41.

[73] 1972 Act, S. 1.

[74] 1972 Act, S. 2. As to ranking see also S. 5. 'Fixed security' is defined by S. 31.

[75] S. 3. But a company must record it in its own register of charges and register it with the Registrar of Companies: Companies Act, 1948, Ss. 106A and 106H, added by 1972 Act, Sched. A society must give information to the Assistant Registrar of Friendly Societies for Scotland: 1967 Act, S. 4.

[76] *Libertas-Commerz* v. *Johnson*, 1977 S.C. 191.

[77] 1972 Act, S. 4.

[78] See further Chap. 3.13, *supra*.

LAND HELD ON LEASE AS SECURITY

Ordinary leases

A lease of ordinary duration may, unless assignation is prohibited, be assigned in security, but the creditor obtains no preferential right unless he actually enters into possession of the subjects,[79] which involves liability for the rent,[80] and for performance of the duties of working the subjects, if agricultural or mineral. Even to make the tenant his creditor's manager would not relieve the latter of liability.[81] Even where the creditor would incur no liability for working, as in the case of an urban lease, he must take possession.[82]

Long leases

A lease for not less than thirty-one (now twenty) years, registered under the Registration of Leases Act, 1857, may be assigned in security by bond and assignation in security in the form of Schedule B to that Act. Recording of the assignation completes the right in security, and constitutes it a real security over the lease to the extent assigned.[83] If affecting land within an area operational for the purposes of the Land Registration (Sc.) Act, 1979, an assignation is registrable.[84] Possession need not be surrendered. A bond and assignation in security is transferable, in whole or in part, by translation in the form of Schedule D to the Act, also recorded.[85]

The creditor is entitled under the bond to exercise power of sale on default in payment.[86] Without prejudice thereto, he is entitled, on default of payment of capital, or of a term's interest or annuity for six months after it has fallen due, to obtain warrant from the Sheriff to enter on possession of the lands leased, uplift the rents from any subtenant and to sublet as the tenant might have done. He is not entitled to poind the ground nor to bring an action of maills and duties against subtenants in possession. No such creditor, unless and until he enters into possession, is personally liable to the landlord in any of the obligations of the lease.[87]

---

[79] Bell, *Prin.* §1212; *Inglis* v. *Paul* (1829) 7 S. 469; *Benton* v. *Craig's Tr.* (1864) 2 M. 1365; *Clark* v. *West Calder Oil Co.* (1882) 9 R. 1017; *Mess* v. *Hay* (1898) 25 R. 298; 1 F. (H.L.) 22.

[80] *Ramsay* v. *Commercial Bank* (1842) 4 D. 405; *Moncrieff* v. *Ferguson* (1896) 24 R. 47.

[81] *Macphail* v. *McLean's Tr.* (1887) 15 R. 47; *Mess, supra*

[82] *Wright* v. *Walker* (1839) 1 D. 641; *Roberts* v. *Wallace* (1842) 5 D. 6; *Hardie* v. *Cameron* (1879) 19 S.L.R. 83; *Macphail, supra.*

[83] 1857 Act, S. 4; Bell, *Prin.* §1212A; *Rodger* v. *Crawford* (1867) 6 M. 24; Such a security is moveable in the creditor's succession: *Stroyan* v. *Murray* (1890) 17 R. 1170.

[84] 1979 Act, S. 2(1)(ii).   [85] S. 6.

[86] Sale is carried through under the provisions of the Titles to Land Consolidation Act, 1868, or the Conveyancing Act, 1924, S. 24, as amended.

[87] *Dunbar* v. *Gill*, 1908 S.C. 1054.

On repayment a discharge of the bond and assignation in security is granted in the form of Schedule H to the Act and recorded,[88] which disburdens the lease.

Alternatively security can be granted by standard security, recorded in the Register of Sasines.[89]

A long lease has the disadvantage that, towards its expiry, it is an asset of diminishing value, and would become valueless if it expired while held in security.

CATHOLIC AND SECONDARY SECURITIES

Where one party has a security over two or more subjects of the debtor and another party has a postponed security over only one of these subjects, the parties are termed catholic and secondary creditors and on grounds of equity rules have been developed to minimize prejudice. If the catholic creditor realizes the security subjects over which the secondary creditor's security also extends he must assign to the latter his security over the other subjects,[90] but if the catholic creditor discharges the bond over the other subject, the secondary creditor cannot object.[91] If both subjects are realized, the debtor being bankrupt, the catholic creditor will be deemed to have exhausted first the other subject, thereby giving the secondary creditor the preferable right, in a question with the unsecured creditors, to the balance realized from both subjects.[92] If the catholic creditor himself holds a second bond over the subjects not covered by the secondary creditor's bond he may first exhaust the subjects covered also by the secondary creditor's bond and leave the maximum surplus towards his own second bond over the other subjects.[93] If there are secondary bondholders over both or all subjects, as between them the burden of the catholic bond has to be apportioned rateably according to the value of each estate.[94]

Control of rate of interest on certain heritable securities

Heritable securities created before 8 December 1965 may be either controlled heritable securities or regulated heritable securities.[95]

---

[88] S. 13.

[89] *Trade Development Bank* v. *Warriner & Mason (Sc.)* 1980 S.C. 74.

[90] Kames, *Equity*, I, 125; Bell, *Comm.* II, 417; *Kemp's Trs.* v. *Ure* (1822) 1 S. 235.

[91] *Morton* (1871) 10 M. 292.

[92] *Littlejohn* v. *Black* (1855) 18 D. 207; *Nicol's Trs.* v. *Hill* (1889) 16 R. 416.

[93] *Preston* v. *Erskine* (1715) Mor. 3376.

[94] *Ferrier* v. *Cowan* (1896) 23 R. 703.

[95] Rent (Sc.) Act, 1971, S. 110(1). 'Heritable security' is defined in S. 133(1) as including real burdens, ground annuals and securities over leases, but excluding securities by *ex facie* absolute disposition.

A security is a controlled heritable security if, at any time, if the 1971 Act had not been passed, it would have been a heritable security to which the Rent Act, 1920, would have applied.[96] The interest rate on controlled heritable securities is controlled by the 1971 Act, Sch. 16, Part I, and enforcement of the creditor's rights and remedies is controlled by Sch. 16, Part II. Where the creditor in such a security satisfies the court that greater hardship would be caused if the restrictions continued to apply than if they were removed or modified, the court may by order allow him to exercise such of the rights and remedies as may be specified in the order, on such terms and conditions as may be so specified, and may vary or revoke the order.[97]

The creditor may obtain an apportionment of the money secured between the dwelling-house and other lands to which it applies.[98] Any amount paid by the debtor which is irrecoverable under these provisions, may be recovered from the creditor within two years from the date of payment.[99]

A regulated heritable security is one created before 8 December 1965, not being a controlled heritable security, which exists over land consisting of or including a dwelling-house let on or subject to a regulated tenancy[1] and the regulated tenancy is binding on the creditor in the heritable security, but not if the rateable value on the appropriate day[2] of the house or houses is less than one-tenth of the rateable value of the whole of the land comprised in the heritable security, or if the debtor is in breach of agreement, though for this purpose a breach of the agreement for the repayment of the principal money is to be disregarded unless it provides for repayment by instalments.[3]

If the rate of interest on such a heritable security is increased, or a rent for a dwelling-house comprised in the heritable security is registered under Part IV of the Rent Act, 1971, and is lower than the rent payable immediately before the registration, or the creditor demands payment of the principal money or takes any steps for exercising any foreclosure of sale or for otherewise enforcing his security, and the debtor makes application to the court within twenty-one days and the court is satisfied that by reason of the event and the operation of the Act the debtor would suffer severe financial hardship unless relief were given, the court may by order make such provision as it thinks appropriate limiting the rate of interest, extending the time for repayment of the

---

[96] Ibid., S. 110(2).
[97] Ibid., S. 113; see also Sch. 16, Part II, para 5(1).
[98] Ibid., S. 114.
[99] Ibid., S. 115.
[1] On regulated tenancies see Ch. 5.15, *infra*.
[2] See 1971 Act, S. 6(3).
[3] Ibid., S. 111.

principal or otherwise varying the terms of the security or imposing any limitation or condition on the exercise of any right or remedy. It may apportion the money received between the house let on the regulated tenancy and other land comprised in the security, and vary or revoke its order.[4]

[4] Ibid., S. 112.

CHAPTER 5.13

SERVITUDES

A servitude is a real right conceived in favour of one tenement of land, the dominant tenement, availing against another adjacent tenement, the servient tenement, whereby the owner of the servient tenement is obliged to suffer the other to exercise certain rights over his lands, or is restrained from the unfettered liberty of use of his lands.[1]

Older authorities distinguish personal and praedial servitudes, affecting respectively the rights and the lands of the persons burdened. But the only so-called personal servitude is liferent, which is today better regarded as an interest in land, or a beneficial right under a trust, than as a burden on another's property, and all true servitudes are praedial and affect land.[2]

Servitudes are also classed as natural, legal, and conventional. A natural servitude, or natural burden of land, springs from its natural situation, as where inferior lands are obliged to receive water draining naturally from higher lands. A legal servitude may be created by statute,[3] or by long-standing custom for reasons of public necessity or utlity. Conventional servitudes are created by agreement, express or implied.[4]

Servitudes are also classed as urban or rural according as they affect houses and buildings or open ground, and positive or negative, according as they entitle the dominant tenement to exercise rights of use on or over the servient tenement or merely limit the freedom of the proprietor's use of the servient tenement.[5]

Only restrictions legally recognized can be servitudes

Servitudes being conventional may be of as many kinds as the ways in which one owner of land may agree to have his liberty of use of his lands limited in favour of a neighbour,[6] but not every restriction will be

[1] Generally Craig II, 8, 43; Stair II, 7,; Mack. II, 9; Dirleton, 276; Hope, *Maj. Prac.* III, 24; *Min. Pract.*, 10, 17; Spott., 307; Forbes, II, 4, 1; Bankt. II, 7; Ersk. II, 9; Bell, *Prin.* §979.

[2] Bell, *Prin*, §981; cf. *Patrick* v. *Napier* (1867) 5 M. 683, 699..

[3] e.g. *Caledonian Ry.* v. *Sprot* (1855) 2 Macq. 449; *Caledonian Ry.* v. *Belhaven* (1857) 3 Macq. 56; *McCulloch* v. *Dumfries Water Commrs.* (1863) 1 M. 334.

[4] Bell, *Prin.* §980.

[5] Bell, *Prin.* §982–3.

[6] Stair II, 7, 5, and 9; Ersk. II, 9, 2.

recognized as a servitude. Positive servitudes require sasine or possession, and their existence is usually apparent on inspection though they do not necessarily appear *ex facie* of the title of the servient tenement as recorded. Negative servitudes do not admit of possession, however, and only well-recognized categories are accepted; though they may be created by a writing which is not recorded, that writing must be in terms which clearly indicate the intention to create a permanent right rather than a mere personal licence.[7] they are, in any event, anomalous and a category not to be enlarged.[8] Even among positive servitudes most cases belong to categories with well-known incidents, and a servitude of another category must be specifically created to receive recognition. But the classes of servitudes are not closed, and new kinds may be accepted.[9] It is questionable whether a restriction hedged with unusual qualifications or exceptions falls within the known category of servitude on which it is founded.[10] Questions may arise whether a right is a personal privilege, or to be ascribed to a right of ownership, or to a right of servitude,[11] or whether a burden is a personal prohibition on a disponee or a servitude.[12]

Servitudes real, not personal

A servitude is a burden on one tenement of land for the benefit of an adjacent tenement, which attaches to the lands independently of ownership, and is distinct from a personal privilege which does not benefit the dominant tenement or the owner thereof as such. Thus rights of golfing,[13] or curling and skating,[14] or walking,[15] or fishing,[16] or shooting,[17] are not servitudes; such privileges may subsist only as personal licences.[18]

Transmission of servitudes

A servitude properly constituted transmits for the benefit of successors in the ownership of the dominant tenement, and transmits

---

[7] *Cowan* v. *Stewart* (1872) 10 M. 735.

[8] *Sivwright* v. *Wilson* (1828) 7 S. 210.

[9] *Dyce* v. *Hay* (1852) 1 Macq. 305, 312; *Harvey* v. *Lindsay* (1835) 15 D. 768, 775; *Patrick* v. *Napier* (1867) 5 M. 683, 709.

[10] *Braid Hills Hotel Co.* v. *Manuel*, 1909 S.C. 120.

[11] See *Baird* v. *Feuars of Kilsyth* (1878) 6 R. 116; *Murray* v. *Peddie* (1880) 7 R. 804; *Robertson's Trs.* v. *Bruce* (1905) 7 F. 580.

[12] *Anderson* v. *Dickie*, 1914 S.C. 706.

[13] Distinguish a customary right to play golf: *Kelly* v. *Burntisland Mags.* (1812) in 9 D. 293, note; *Earlsferry Mags.* v. *Malcolm* (1829) 7 S. 755; (1832) 11 S. 74; *Dyce* v. *Hay* (1849) 11 D. 1266, 1279; 1 Macq. 311; *Sanderson* v. *Musselburgh Mags.* (1859) 21 D. 1011; 22 D. 240.

[14] *Harvey* v. *Lindsay* (1853) 15 D. 768.

[15] *Cleghorn* v. *Dempster* (1805) Mor. 16141; *Dyce, supra.*

[16] *Patrick* v. *Napier* (1867) 5 M. 683; *Harper* v. *Flaws*, 1940 S.L.T. 150.

[17] *Huntly* v. *Nicol* (1896) 23 R. 610; cf. *Hemming* v. *D. Athole* (1883) 11 R. 93.

[18] Bell, *Prin.* §979.

against successors in the ownership of the servient tenement, if followed by infeftment or by possession and enjoyment by the owner of the dominant tenement.[19] A grant or reservation of a privilege not constituted a real burden does not transmit against a singular successor[20] A restriction on the use of land, not being a known servitude, even if constituted by agreement registered in the Register of Sasines is not binding on singular successors if it does not form part of the title.[21] Where a servitude is subject to a condition a successor cannot retain the servitude without implementing the condition.[22]

Praedial servitudes generally

Servitudes exist for the benefit of the dominant tenement of land as such and burden the servient tenement. There must therefore be two tenements, reasonably adjacent, and owned by different persons.[23] They are inseparable from the tenements and cannot be alienated separately, or made into rights independently of the title to the lands in question.[24] Hence a servitude cannot be granted in favour of a tenant of land.[25] The right may be exercised only for the benefit of the dominant tenement, not for that of another.[26]

Any land or building may be a dominant tenement, a royal burgh may be,[27] and any lands in private ownership may be a servient tenement, but lands held for statutory purposes cannot be subject to a servitude which would interfere with those purposes.[28] A servitude continues to exist so long as the tenements are capable of identification, even though buildings are altered or rebuilt.[29]

The owner of the servient tenement is not generally bound to do anything, but merely to suffer the invasion of his rights required by the fair exercise of the servitude;[30] thus he need not repair a way over which another has a servitude right of way;[31] still less can he be

[19] Stair II, 7, 1; Bell, *Prin. §979; N.B. Ry. Co. v. Park Yard Co.* (1898) 25 R. (H.L.) 47; *Braid Hills Hotel Co.* v. *Manuel,* 1909 S.C. 120, 126; *Hunter* v. *Fox,* 1964 S.C. (H.L.) 95.

[20] *Allan* v. *MacLachlan* (1900) 2 F. 699.

[21] *Campbell's Trs.* v. *Glasgow Corpn.* (1902) 4 F. 752; *Murray's Trs.* v.*St. Margaret's Convent* (1906) 8 F. 1109, 1120; 1907 S.C. (H.L.) 8. See also *McTavish's Trs.* v. *Anderson* (1900) 8 S.L.T. 80.

[22] *Tennant* v. *Napier Smith's Trs.* (1888) 15 R. 671.

[23] *Donaldson's Trs.* v. *Forbes* (1839) 1 D. 494; *Grierson* v. *Sandsting School Board* (1882) 9 R. 437, 441; *Harper* v. *Flaws,* 1940 S.L.T. 150.

[24] *Patrick* v. *Napier* (1867) 5 M. 683; *Drummond* v. *Milligan* (1867) 17 R. 316.

[25] *Safeway* v. *Wellington Motor Co.,* 1976 S.L.T. 53.

[26] *Murray* v. *Peebles Mags.,* 8 Dec. 1808, F. C.; *Scott* v. *Bogle,* 6 July, 1809, F.C.

[27] *Feuars of Dundee* v. *Hay* (1732) Mor. 1824.

[28] *Ayr Harbour Trs.* v. *Oswald* (1883) 10 R. (H.L.) 85; *Ellice's Trs.* v. *Caledonian Canal Commrs.* (1904) 6 F. 325.

[29] *Irvine Knitters* v. *N. Ayrshire Co-op Socy.,* 1978 S.C. 109.

[30] Stair II, 7, 5; Bankt. II, 7, 7, and 14; Ersk. II, 9, 1; Bell, *Prin.* §984; *Sc. Highland Distillery Co.* v. *Reid* (1877) 4 R. 1118, 1122; *Allan* v. *MacLachlan* (1900) 2 F. 699.

[31] *Allan* v. *MacLachlan* (1900) 2 F. 699.

required to provide any services.[32] Nor is he limited save in so far as the servitude requires.

The servitude must be used for the benefit of the dominant tenement only and not for other persons or lands in lieu, or in addition,[33] nor generally for commercial ends.[34]

The owner of the dominant tenement must exercise his rights *civiliter*, in the way least burdensome to the servient tenement,[35] and the owner of the latter may use his lands as he pleases so long as he permits the continued exercise of the servitude right.[36] The owner of the dominant tenement cannot extend or communicate his servitude right to other grounds or subjects.[37] The burden on the servient tenement may not be increased beyond the right acquired.[38]

A servitude, being a restraint on the free use of property, is strictly construed, in that it may be constituted only in recognized ways, in case of doubt is presumed to be of the degree least burdensome to the servient tenement, and imposes no greater restraint than is necessary for its fair exercise. In particular a negative servitude must be construed strictly.[39]

CREATION OF SERVITUDES

Apart from servitudes created by statute,[40] all have their origin in conventional provisions, though their incidents are determined by law. The constitution may be *in gremio* of a disposition or other deed, in a *mortis causa* settlement, or by separate deed.[41] The deed must be probative, or equivalent thereto.

Questions may arise as to the title of a person to create a servitude; an owner of lands may do so, as may an heir of entail with power of sale,[42] an owner who had disponed the servient tenement in security by

---

[32] *Tailors of Aberdeen* v. *Coutts* (1840) 1 Rob. App. 296, 310.

[33] Bell, *Prin.* §986; *Carstairs* v. *Brown* (1829) 7 S. 607; *Anstruther* v. *Caird* (1861) 24 D. 149; L. *Blantyre* v. *Dumbarton Waterworks Commrs.* (1888) 15 R. (H.L.) 56.

[34] *Agnew* v. *L.A.* (1873) 11 M. 309, 333.

[35] Ersk. II, 9, 34; *Beveridge* v. *Marshall*, 18 Nov. 1808, F.C.; *Rattray* v. *Taayport Patent Slip Co.* (1868) 5 S.L.R. 219; *Sutherland* v. *Thomson* (1876) 3 R. 485; *Orr Ewing* v. *Colquhoun's Trs.* (1877) 4 R. (H.L.) 116, 121; *Crichton* v. *Turnbull*, 1946 S.C. 52.

[36] Ersk. *supra;* Bell, *Prin.* §987; *Oliver* v. *Robertson* (1869) 8 M. 137; *Sutherland* v. *Thomson* (1876) 3 R. 485; *Sc. Highland Distillery Co.* v. *Reid* (1877) 4 R. 1118; *Donaldson* v. *E. Strathmore* (1877) 14 S.L.R. 587.

[37] *Scott* v. *Bogle*, 6 July 1809, F.C.; *Anstruther* v. *Caird* (1862) 24 D. 149; *Carstairs* v. *Spence*, 1924 S.C. 380; *Irvine Knitters* v. *N. Ayrshire Coop Socy.*, 1978 S.C. 109.

[38] Ersk. II, 9, 4; Bell, *Prin.* §988; *Dunbar Mags.* v. *Sawers* (1829) 7 S. 672; *Young* v. *Cuddie* (1831) 9 S. 500; *White* v. *W.* (1906) 8 F. (H.L.) 41.

[39] *Hunter* v. *Fox*, 1964 S.C. (H.L.) 95.

[40] e.g. *Caledonian Ry.* v. *Sprot* (1855) 2 Macq. 449; *Caledonian Ry.* v. *Belhaven* (1857) 3 Macq. 56; *McCulloch* v. *Dumfries Water Commrs.* (1863) 1 M. 334.

[41] e.g *Smith* v. *Stewart* (1884) 11 R. 921; *Cronin* v. *Sutherland* (1889) 2 F. 217.

[42] *Bowman Ballantine* (1883) 10 R. 1061.

ex facie absolute disposition,[43] but an estate factor may not[44] nor may one of several *pro indiviso* proprietors.[45]

A servitude may be created in return for a periodical payment,[46] or without payment expressly therefor.

Express grant

Both positive and negative servitudes may be created by express grant[47] from a person who is, or at least comes later to be,[48] owner of the servient tenement, contained in the titles of the tenements, or in a separate probative writ,[50] or by oral or improbative agreement followed by *rei interventus*,[51] but it need not be recorded in the Register of Sasines.[52] If, however, a positive servitude be not so recorded it is not valid against singular successors of the granter unless it has been followed by possession so as to be discoverable by inspection or reasonable inquiry.[53] A negative servitude, however, is incapable of possession and, if the grant is not recorded, may not come to the notice of a singular successor of the granter. This is the only way in which a negative servitude can be created[54] and the grant must be in terms clearly indicating the intention to create a permanent right.[55] In relation to land within an area operational for the purposes of the Land Registration (Sc.) Act, 1979, a servitude is an overriding interest and not registrable.

The intention to grant,[56] and the nature and extent of the right granted,[57] must be clear.

Implied grant

A positive servitude may be held granted by implication only exceptionally, where lands are disponed and certain servitude rights over the

---

[43] *Union Heritable Securities Co. v. Co. v. Mathie* (1886) 13 R. 670.

[44] *Macgregor v. Balfour* (1899) 2 F. 345.

[45] *Grant v. Heriot's Trust* (1906) 8 F. 647.   [46] *Stewart v. Steuart* (1877) 4 R. 981.

[47] Ersk. II, 9, 35; Bell, *Prin.* §994; *Dundas v. Blair* (1886) 13 R. 759; *Inglis v. Clark* (1901) 4 F. 288; *Metcalfe v. Purdon* (1902) 4 F. 507. As to power to grant, see also *Bowman Ballantine* (1883) 10 R. 1061; *Macgregor v. Balfour* (1899) 2 F. 345; *Grant v. Heriot's Trust* (1906) 8 F. 647.   [48] *Stephen v. Brown's Trs.*, 1922 S.C. 136.

[49] *Gray v. Fergusson* (1792) Mor. 14513, and see 7 S. 212, note, *Argyllshire Commrs. v. Campbell* (1885) 12 R. 1255.

[50] *Macgregor v. Balfour* (1899) 2 F. 345; *Campbell's Trs. v. Glasgow Corpn.* (1902) 4 F. 752, 757; *Murray's Trs. v. St. Margaret's Convent* (1906) 8 F. 1109, 1120.

[51] *Stirling v. Haldane* (1829) 8 S. 131; *Macgregor, supra.*

[52] Bell, *Prin.* §994; *Cowan v. Stewart* (1872) 10 M. 735; *Banks v. Walker* (1874) 1 R. 981. See also *Alexander v. Butchart* (1875) 3 R. 156.

[53] Bell, *Prin.* §990; *N.B. Ry. Co. v. Park Yard Co.* (1898) 25 R. (H.L.) 47; *Campbell's Trs. v. Glasgow Corpn.* (1902) 4 F. 752.

[54] *Dundas v. Blair* (1886) 13 R. 759.   [55] *Cowan v. Stewart* (1872) 10 M. 735.

[56] *Sivwright v. Wilson* (1828) 7 S. 210; *Cowan v. Stewart* (1872) 10 M. 735; *Russell v. Cowper* (1882) 9 R. 660; *King v. Barnetson* (1896) 24 R. 81.

[57] *Ross v. Cuthbertson* (1854) 16 D. 732.

granter's other lands are necessary for the use of the disponed lands, as for access to them,[58] not merely where they were used in connection with and are required for the convenient and comfortable enjoyment of the lands retained.[59] Statute may create a servitude by implication.[60] An implied grant may be established by possession short of that required for prescription.[61] Negative servitudes, such as of light, cannot be constituted by implied grant.[62]

Express or implied reservation

If the disponer of a tenement wishes to retain any positive right over lands disponed he may and should reserve it expressly,[63] and the constitution of a servitude by implied reservation is possible but is seldom upheld. Both tenements must have been in the ownership of the same person and later separated.[64]

Reservations may be implied where after separation some right over one tenement is absolutely necessary for the use of the other tenement[65] but not where some use was being made of one part for the benefit of the other and was necessary for the comfortable or convenient enjoyment of the other,[66] as such would be a derogation from the disponer's own grant.[67]

Prescription

A positive servitude may be held created by actual use of a right for an uninterrupted period of twenty years.[68] The claimant must be infeft in the tenement claiming the servitude right.[69] The possession or use of the right claimed must be uninterrupted,[70] open and such as to amount

[58] Stair II, 7, 6, 10; Ersk. II, 6, 9; *Balds* v. *Alloa Coal Co.* (1854) 16 D. 870; *Caledonian Ry.* v. *Sprot* (1856) 2 Macq. 449; *McGavin* v. *McIntyre* (1874) 1 R. 1016; *Walton Bros.* v. *Glasgow Mags.* (1876) 3 R. 1130; *McLaren* v. *City of Glasgow Union Ry. Co.* (1878) 5 R. 1042; *Rome* v. *Hope Johnstone* (1884) 11 R. 653; *Union Herit. Secy. Co.* v. *Mathie* (1886) 13 R. 670; *Fraser* v. *Cox*, 1938 S.C. 506.

[59] *Ewart & Cochrane* (1861) 4 Macq. 117; *Gow's Trs.* v. *Mealls* (1875) 2 R. 729; *Alexander* v. *Butchart* (1875) 3 R. 156; *Campbell* v. *Halkett* (1890) 27 S.L.R. 1000; *Cullens* v. *Cambusbarron Soc.* (1895) 23 R. 209. See also *Argyllshire Commrs. of Supply* v. *Campbell* (1885) 12 R. 1255; *Boyd* v. *Hamilton*, 1907 S.C. 912.

[60] *Central Regional Council* v. *Ferns*, 1980 S.L.T. 126.

[61] *Cochrane* v. *Ewart* (1861) 4 Macq. 117; *Carstairs* v. *Spence*, 1924 S.C. 380.

[62] *Inglis* v. *Clark* (1901) 4 F. 288; *Metcalfe* v. *Purdon* (1902) 4 F. 507.

[63] *Shearer* v. *Peddie* (1899) 1 F. 1201.

[64] *Menzies* v. *M. Breadalbane* (1901) 4 F. 59.

[65] Bell, *Prin.* §992: *Ferguson* v. *Campbell*, 1913, 1 S.L.T. 241.

[66] *Edwart* v. *Cochrane* (1861) 4 Macq. 117; See also *Gow's Trs.* v. *Mealls* (1875) 2 R. 729; *McLaren* v. *City of Glasgow Union Ry. Co* (1878) 5 R. 1048.

[67] Bell, *Prin.* §992; *Shearer* v. *Peddie* (1899) 1 F. 1201.

[68] Conveyancing (Sc.) Act, 1924, S. 16 (2); *Scotland* v. *Wallace*, 1964 S.L.T. (Sh. Ct.) 9; Prescription and Limitation (Sc.) Act, 1973, S. 3.

[69] Stair II, 3, 73; II, 7, 2; Ersk. II, 9, 3; Bell, *Prin.* §993; *Beaumont* v. *Lord Glenlyon* (1843) 5 D. 1337; *McDonald* v. *Dempster* (1871) 10 M. 94.

[70] *Macnab* v. *Ferguson* (1890) 17 R. 397; *McInroy* v. *D. Atholl* (1891) 18 R. (H.L.) 46.

to a clear assertion of the kind of servitude right claimed, must not
have been in reliance on any permission or licence, must have been
exercised peaceably rather than in face of opposition, and known, or
such as reasonably should have been known, to the owner of the
servient tenement or his agents on the spot.[71] If acquired in this way,
the kind and extent of servitude right acquired is determined by the
prescriptive possession proved, *tantum praescriptum quantum
posessum*, though it may be extended to include such a development of
the use as could reasonably be held involved in the possession,[72] but it
may not be increased.[73]

Acquiescence

A servitude may be held established by acquiescence in the exercise
of a servitude right, yielding an inference of a grant and personally
barring challenge thereof. The right acquiesced in must be obvious and
such as to preclude the inference that it was a mere licence.[74]

POSITIVE SERVITUDES

Positive servitudes are those rights which the owner of the dominant
tenement of land is entitled to exercise over the servient tenement and
which are capable of possession in the form of active exercise. They
consist *in patiendo*. An obligation consisting *in faciendo* is not a
servitude.[75] Some are urban, appropriate to tenements in towns, other
rural, appropriate to country district.

POSITIVE URBAN SERVITUDES

Support

Two servitudes of support are recognized;[76] the servitude *tigni
immittendi*[77] is the right to insert into the wall of the servient tenement
a beam or other structural member of the dominant tenement, main-

[71] McInroy v. D. Atholl (1891) 18 R. (H.L.) 46; McGregor v. Crieff Co-operative Socy. 1915
S.C. (H.L.) 93; Kerr v. Brown, 1939 S.C. 140.
[72] Ersk. II, 9, 4; Bell, Prin. §993; L.A. v. Wemyss (1900) 2 F. (H.L.) 1; Carstairs v. Spence,
1924 S.C. 380, 385; Kerr v. Brown, 1939 S.C. 140; See also E. Kintore v. Pirie (1906) 8 F. (H.L.)
16; White v. W. (1906) 8F. (H.L.) 41.
[73] Dunbar Mags. v. Sawers (1829) 7 S. 672; Kerr v. Brown, 1939 S. C. 140.
[74] Bell, Prin. §946; Muirhead v. Glasgow Highland Socy.(1864) 2 M. 420; Macgregor v.
Balfour (1899) 2 F. 345, 351; Robson v. Chalmers Property Inv. Co., 1965 S.L. 381; More v.
Boyle, 1967 S.L.T. (SL. Ct.) 38.
[75] Nicolson v. Melvill (1708) Mor. 14516.
[76] Stair II, 7, 6; Mack. II, 9, 6, 7; Forbes II, 4, 3, 2; Bankt. II, 7, 7; Ersk. II, 9, 7; Bell, Prin.
§1003.
[77] Inst. II, 1, 29; Dig. 50, 16, 62.

tain it there, and renew it when necessary. The servitude *oneris ferendi*[78] is the right to rest the beams of the dominant on the wall of the servient tenement and latterly to have whole rooms resting on another's tenement. In this case alone the servitude implies a duty on the servient owner to maintain the servient tenement.[79]

Stillicide

The servitude of stillicide or eavesdrop[80] entitles the dominant tenement to dischare rainwater from a roof on to the servient tenement.[81] Apart from this servitude there is no right to do so though there is a right to discharge surface water by natural drainage on to the inferior lands.[82]

POSITIVE RURAL SERVITUDES

Way, Access, or Passage

A servitude right of way differs from a public right of way in that the rights of use, and the title to vindicate it, are in the owner of the dominant tenement only, not in the public or any members thereof.[83] The place to which, and the ground over which the right exists must be defined by the grant or possession. Access 'along' a boundary is not necessarily in immediate proximity to it.[84] The kind of right of way granted, whether for foot passage, horse road, drove road, or carriage road,[85] depends on the grant or the possession exercised. A grant of wider use implies grant of narrower uses.[86] The right may be limited to use for particular purposes[87] in which case the dominant owner may be restricted to that use, and the right lapses if that use is no longer necessary.[88] The dominant owner cannot communicate the benefit of a

[78] Dig. 8, 5; *Robertson* v. *Sc. Union and National Ins. Co.*, 1943 S.C. 427.

[79] Stair II, 7, 6; Ersk. II, 9, 8; Bell, *Prin.* §1003; *Murray* v. *Brownhill* (1715) Mor. 14521

[80] Stair II, 7, 7; Mack. II, 9, 8; Forbes II, 4, 3, 2; Bankt. II, 7, 12; Ersk. II, 9, 9; Bell, *Prin.* §1004.

[81] *Stirling* v. *Finlayson* (1752) Mor. 14526; *Scouller* v. *Pollock* (1832) 10 S. 241; *Mathieson* v. *Gibson* (1874) 12 S.L.R. 124.

[82] Bell, *Prin.* §968; *Campbell* v. *Bryson* (1864) 3 M. 254; *Anderson* v. *Robertson*, 1958 S.C. 367.

[83] *Thomson* v. *Murdoch* (1862) 24 D. 975; cf. also *Paterson* v. *Airdrie Water Co.* (1893) 20 R. 370; *Ayr Burgh Council* v. *B.T.C.*, 1955 S.L.T. 219.

[84] *Millar* v. *Christie*, 1961 S.C. 1.

[85] Including motor cars: *Smith* v. *Saxton*, 1928 S.N. 59; but see *Crawford* v. *Lumsden*, 1951 S.L.T. (Notes) 62.

[86] *Swan* v. *Buist* (1834) 12 S. 316 : *Malcolm* v. *Lloyd* (1886) 13 R. 512; *Carstairs* v. *Spence*, 1924 S.C. 380. See also *Reid* v. *Haldane's Trs.* (1891) 18 R. 744, 746; *Millar* v. *Christie*, 1961 S.C. 1.

[87] *Bruce* v. *Wardlaw* (1748) Mor. 14525; *Porteous* v. *Allan* (1773) Mor. 14512; *Winans* v. *L. Tweedmouth* (1888) 15 R. 540; *Carstairs* v. *Spence*, 1924 S.C. 380, 385.

[88] *Winans, supra; Cronin* v. *Sutherland* (1899) 2 F. 217.

servitude to other subjects, as by using a right of way as access to other lands occupied under a separate title.[89]

The servient owner may erect gates but may not lock them[90] and, with the consent of the dominant owner or the authority of the court, may substitute an alternative way equally convenient.[91] The court cannot sanction alteration if the right is clearly defined by grant or possession.[92] The owner of the servient tenement cannot allow a dangerous animal access to land over which persons have a right of way.[93]

Aqueduct

The servitude of aqueduct[94] is the right to lead water from the servient into the dominant tenement, and implies a right of access to the lade or pipes at reasonable times for repair[95] and a right to prevent buildings interfering with the line of supply.[96] The water may be for natural uses or for water power.[97] The dominant owner must maintain the works.[98] Neither dominant nor servient owner may pollute the water any more than he may pollute a stream.[99] Similar to this is the servitude of dam or dam-head, the right of gathering water on the neighbour's land and of building dykes or dams for containing the water.[1]

Aquaehaustus

This is the right of drawing water at a stream, well or pond on the servient tenement, particularly for cattle but possibly for other purposes also.[2] The servient owner may still take water so long as he does not prejudice the dominant owner's requirements.[3]

---

[89] *Anstruther v. Caird* (1862) 24 D. 149; *Irvine Knitters v. N. Ayrshire Co.-op. Socy.* 1978 S.C. 109.

[90] *Oliver v. Robertson* (1869) 8 M. 137; *Sutherland v. Thomson* (1876) 3 R. 485.

[91] *Bain v. Smith* (1871) 8 S.L.R. 539; *Moyes v. McDiarmid* (1900) 2 F. 918.

[92] *Hill v. McLaren* (1879) 6 R. 1363; *Moyes, supra.*

[93] *Lanarkshire Water Board v. Gilchrist,* 1973 S.L.T. (Sh. Ct.) 58.

[94] Stair II, 7, 8; Mack. II, 9, 4; Forbes II, 4, 3; Bankt. II, 7, 28; Ersk. II, 9, 13, and 35; Bell, *Prin.* §1012.

[95] *Weir v. Glenny* (1833) 7 W. & S. 244.

[96] *Tennant's Trs. v. Dennistoun* (1894) 2 S.L.T. 78.

[97] *Prestoun v. Erskine* (1714) Mor. 10919; *L. Blantyre v. Dunn* (1848) 10 D. 509; See also *McIntyre v. Orr* (1868) 6 S.L.R. 152

[98] *Scottish Highland Distillery v. Reid* (1877) 4 R. 1118; *Smith v. Denny Police Commrs.* (1880) 7 R. (H.L.) 28; *Strachan v. Aberdeen* (1905) 12 S.L.T. 725.

[99] *Ewen v. Turnbull's Trs.* (1857) 19 D. 513; *Mackay v. Greenhill* (1858) 20 D. 1251; *Caledonian Ry. v. Baird* (1876) 3 R. 839.

[1] *Sc. Highland Distillery, supra;* see also *Robson v. Chalmers Property Co.,* 1965 S.L.T. 381.

[2] Stair II, 7, 11; Ersk. II, 9, 12; Bell, *Prin.* §1011: *Macnab v. Munro Ferguson* (1890) 17 R. 397; as to underground water, see *Harper v. Stuart* (1907) 15 S.L.T. 550; *Crichton v. Turnbull,* 1946 S.C. 52.

[3] *Donaldson v. E. Strathmore* (1877) 14 S.L.R. 587; *Crichton v. Turnbull* 1946 S.C. 52.

Pasturage

The grant is normally of a right of pasturage of stock in common with others of a community.[4] If indefinite in extent the grant is measured by the amount of stock that can be pastured on the servient tenement.[5] Tree planting on servient land is permissible so long as sufficient pasturage is left to satisfy the servitude,[6] but cutting peat on a commercial scale is an interference with pasturage right over the land in question.[7]

Fuel, feal, and divot

In these servitudes[8] the right is to dig peat for fuel,[9] or take clods for fencing and roofing. There is implied a right of access to the locality and liberty to stack and dry peats.[10]

Discharge of drainage

A servitude right to discharge waste water has been recognized, but not closet sewage.[11]

Other rural servitudes

Other recognized rural servitudes include taking sea-ware,[12] stone, slate,[13] sand or gravel,[14] for the benefit of the dominant tenement, and of bleaching linen.[15]

NEGATIVE SERVITUDES

Negative servitudes consist *in non faciendo,* in rights in the owner of the dominant tenement to prevent or restrain some action by the

[4] Stair II, 7, 14; Ersk. II, 9, 15; Bell, *Prin.* §1013; see e.g. *Cunninghame* v. *Dunlop* (1836) 15 S. 295; *Dundee Mags.* v. *Hunter* (1843) 6 D. 18; (1858) 20 D. 1067; *Campbell* v. *McKinnon* (1867) 5 M. 636.

[5] *L. Breadalbane* v. *Menzies* (1741) 5 B.S. 710.

[6] *Fraser* v. *Secy. of State for Scotland,* 1959 S.L.T. (Notes) 36.

[7] *Ferguson* v. *Tennant,* 1978 S.C. (H.L.) 19.

[8] Stair II, 7,31; Mack. II, 9, 32; Bankt. II, 7, 31; Ersk. II, 9, 17; Bell, *Prin.* §986, 1014.

[9] cf. *Watson* v. *Sinclair,* 1966 S.L.T. (Sh. Ct.) 77; as to coal, see *Harvie* v. *Stewart* (1870) 9 M. 129.

[10] *Dingwall* v. *Farquharson* (1797) 3 Pat. 564; *Dinwiddie* v. *Corrie·*(1821) 1 S. 164; *Grierson* v. *Sandsting School Board* (1882) 9 R. 437.

[11] *Kerr* v. *Brown,* 1939 S.C. 140.

[12] *E. Morton* v. *Covingtree* (1760) Mor. 13528; *Baird* v. *Fortune* (1800) 4 Macq. 127; *Agnew* v. *L.A.* (1873) 11 M. 309, 333; *McTaggart* v. *McDouall* (1867) 5 M. 534, 547.

[13] Bell, *Prin.* §1015; *Murray* v. *Peebles Mags.,* 8 Dec. 1808, F.C.; *Keith* v. *Stonehaven Harbour Commrs.* (1830) 5 W. & S. 234.

[14] *Sharp* v. *D. Hamilton* (1829) 7 S. 679; *Aikman* v. *D. Hamilton* (1830) 8 S. 943; 6 W. & S. 64.

[15] *Sinclair* v. *Dysart Mags.* (1779) Mor. 14159; 2 Pat. 554; *Rattray* v. *Tayport Patent Slip Co.* (1868) 5 S.L.R. 219.

owner of the servient tenement but which are not capable of possession in the sense of being exercised, and which therefore require
constitution by express grant.[16] Any probative writing will suffice and
it need not enter the title.[17] Words purporting to create a negative
servitude must be construed strictly, there being a presumption for
freedom.[18] Meaningless words must be ignored.[18]

The only recognized negative servitudes are of light and air and of
prospect;[19] based on the servitudes *ne luminibus officiatur, non
aedificandi,* and *altius non tollendi.*

In each case the servitude is a restriction on the liberty of the owner
of the servitude tenement to use his property. He may be taken bound
not to build,[20] or to plant trees or bushes,[21] so as to cut off the
dominant tenement's light or view,[22] or not to build higher than a
stated height,[23] or not to open a window in his wall which would
overlook the dominant tenement.[24] Servitudes of light cannot be constituted by implied grant.[25] There is no recognized servitude of prospect in favour of an upper proprietor against a lower proprietor in
flatted premises.[26] The servitude is enforced by interdict against a
threatened or an actual contravention.

A restriction not of the nature of a recognized servitude but rather of
the nature of a restriction on the ordinary uses of property must appear
in the Register of Sasines to be effectual against singular successors.[27]

EXTINCTION OF SERVITUDES

A servitude may be extinguished (1) by express discharge or renuncia-

---

[16] *Dundas* v. *Blair* (1886) 13 R. 759; *King* v. *Barnetson* (1896) 24 R. 81; *Inglis* v. *Clark* (1901)
4 F. 288; *Metcalfe* v. *Purdon* (1902) 4 F. 507.
[17] *Cowan* v. *Stewart* (1872) 10 M. 735; *Banks* v. *Walker* (1874) 1 R. 981; *Campbell's Trs.* v.
Glasgow Corpn. (1902) 4 F. 752; *Proprs. of Royal Exchange, Glasgow* v. *Cotton,* 1912 S.C.
1151; *Stephen* v. *Brown's Trs.,* 1922 S.C. 136.
[18] *Hunter* v. *Fox,* 1964 S.C. (H.L.) 95.
[19] Stair II, 7, 9; Mack. II, 9, 9; Forbes II, 4, 3, 2; Bankt. II, 7, 5; Ersk. II, 9, 10; Bell, *Prin.* §1005;
Largs Hydropathic v. *Largs Town Council,* 1967 S.C. 1.
[20] *Proprs. of Royal Exchange, Glasgow, supra; Sharp* v. *Haddington Assessor,* 1923 S.C. 703.
[21] *Hunter* v. *Fox,* 1964 S.C. (H.L.) 95.
[22] *McNeill* v. *Mackenzie* (1870) 8 M. 520; *Malloch* v. *Gray* (1872) 10 M. 774; *Argyllshire
Commrs.* v. *Campbell* (1885) 12 R. 1255; *Johnson* v. *MacRitchie* (1893) 20 R. 539; *Taylor's
Trs.* v. *McGavigan* (1896) 23 R. 945. *Clark* v. *Perth School Board* (1898) 25 R. 919; *Hunter* v.
Fox, 1964 S.C. (H.L.) 95.
[23] Bell, *Prin.* §1007; *Edinburgh Mags.* v. *Brown* (1833) 11 S. 255; *Edinburgh Mags.* v. *Paton
& Ritchie* (1858) 20 D. 731; *Malloch* v. *Gray* (1872) 10 M. 774; but see *Banks* v. *Walker* (1874)
1 R. 980.
[24] Bell, *Prin.* §1006; *Forbes* v. *Wilson* (1724) Mor. 14505.
[25] *Inglis* v. *Clark* (1901) 4 F. 288; *Metcalfe* v. *Purdon* (1902) 4 F. 507; cf. *King* v. *Barnetson*
(1896) 24 R. 81.
[26] *Birrell* v. *Lumley* (1905) 12 S.L.T. 719.					[27] *Banks* v. *Walker, supra.*

tion in probative writing by the owner of the dominant tenement.[28] (2)
It may be lost by conduct on the part of the owner of the dominant
tenement evidencing an intention to relinquish it or barring him
personally from seeking to enforce it.[29] (3) It may be extinguished, as
by acquisition of the servient tenement under compulsory powers free
of servitudes.[30] (4) It is extinguished if either dominant or servient
tenement be destroyed, though only suspended if either tenement be
merely temporarily incapacitated, as by requisition.[31] (5) It is extinguished *confusione* if both tenements come into the ownership of the
same person.[32] If the tenements are subsequently separated again, the
servitude does not revive but must be reconstituted.[33] This does not,
however, happen if though the same person comes to own both
tenements he does so on different titles and a subsequent separation of
the tenements is to be anticipated independently of his volition.[34] (6) It
may be extinguished by the running of the negative prescription. A
positive servitude will be lost by the complete non-exercise of the rights
conferred for twenty years, from the last occasion on which the right
was exercised.[35] If there is interruption of user by the servient
tenement, it must be, and can be intended as, an assertion of adverse
right.[36] A negative servitude will be lost by the failure to challenge
conduct by the servient owner infringing the servitude restriction for
twenty years from the date of the first contravention.[37] The negative
prescription may apply even though the servitude appears in the titles
of the servient tenement.[38] (7) Statutory powers may interfere with or
extinguish servitudes.[39]

[28] Stair II, 7, 4; Ersk. II, 9, 37; Bell, *Prin.* §998; see also *Macdonald* v. *Inverness Mags.*, 1918
S.C. 141; *Macdonald* v. *M.* (1959) 48 L.C. 22.
[29] Bell, *Prin.* §999; Rankine, *L.O.* 441; *Murihead* v. *Glasgow Highland Socy.* (1864) 2 M.
420; *Bridges* v. *L. Saltoun* (1873) 11 M. 588; *Campbell Douglas* v. *Hozier* (1878) 16 S.L.R. 14;
Mags. of Rutherglen v. *Bainbridge* (1886) 13 R. 745; *Davidson* v. *Thomson* (1890) 17 R. 287;
cf. *Stevenson* v. *Donaldson,* 1935 S.C. 551. Acquiescence in a limitation of a right does not
extinguish it: *Millar* v. *Christie*, 1961 S.C. 1.
[30] *Oban Mags.* v. *Callander and Oban Ry. Co.* (1892) 19 R. 912; *Largs Hydropathic, Ltd.* v.
Largs Town Council, 1967 S.C. 1.
[31] Ersk. II, 9, 37; Bell, *Prin.* §995; *Forbes's Trs.* v. *Davidson* (1892) 19 R. 1022; *Porteous* v.
Haig (1901) 3 F. 347; *Gordon's Trs.* v. *Thompson*, 1910 S.C. 22; cf. *Winans* v. *L. Tweedmouth*
(1888) 15 R. 540, 568.
[32] Mack. II, 9, 32; Ersk. II, 9, 16, and 37; Bell, *Prin.* §997; *Donaldson's Trs.* v. *Forbes* (1839) 1
D. 449.   [33] Ersk. II, 9, 37; *Union Bank* v. *Daily Record* (1902) 10 S.L.T. 71.
[34] Bell, *Prin.* §997; *Carnegie* v. *MacTier* (1844) 6 D. 1381, 1407; *Union Bank* v. *Daily Record*
(1902) 10 S.L.T. 71.
[35] Conveyancing (Sc.) Act, 1924, S. 17(2); Ersk. II, 9, 37; *Beaton* v. *Ogilvie* (1670) Mor.
10912; *Graham* v. *Douglas* (1735) Mor. 10745; Prescription and Limitation (Sc.) Act, 1973, S.
8; cf. *Brown* v. *Carron Co.*, 1909 S.C. 452.   [36] *Stevenson* v. *Donaldson*, 1935 S.C. 551.
[37] Ersk. II, 9, 37; Bell, *Prin.* §999; *Wilkie* v. *Scott* (1688) Mor. 11189; Conveyancing (Sc.) Act,
1924 S. 17(2); Prescription Act, 1973, S. 8.   [38] *Graham* v. *Douglas* (1735) Mor. 10745.
[39] E.g. Lands Clauses Consolidation (Sc.) Act, 1845, Ss. 93–8; Public Parks (Sc.) Act, 1878, S.
12; Housing (Sc.) Act, 1966, S. 51; New Towns (Sc.) Act, 1968, S. 19. See *Largs Hydropathic*,
supra.

THIRLAGE

Thirlage is frequently classed with servitudes, though it really depends on other principles. Thirlage is the restriction of lands and their inhabitants to particular mills for the grinding of corn with the burden of paying such duties and services as are expressed or implied in the constitution of the right. Multures are the proportion of grain paid to the miller for the grinding of the rest.[40]

WAYLEAVES AND PIPELINES

A modern development is the wayleave, or right to run a pipeline through land,[41] or an electricity or telephone line over it. This differs from a servitude in there being no dominant tenement. A party having a right of wayleave for pipes has a right of occupation of the land thereby.[42]

The Pipelines Act, 1962, enables the Minister of Power to control the development of cross-country pipelines, and enables bodies wishing to construct such lines to obtain compulsorily the rights needed therefor.

[40] Ersk. II, 9, 18 et seq.; Bell, Prin. §1016 et seq.; see also Stobbs v. Caven (1873) 11 M. 530; Sutherland v. Reid's Trs. (1881) 8 R. 514; Forbes' Trs. v. Davidson (1892) 19 R. 1022; L.A. v. E. Home (1895) 2 S.L.T. 435; Porteous v. Haig (1901) 3 F. 347; Sempill v. Leith-Hay (1903) 5 F. 868; Edinburgh Mags. v. Edinburgh United Breweries (1903) 5 F. 1048; Brown v. Livingstone-Learmonth's Trs. (1906) 14 S.L.T. 142; Brown v. Carron Co., 1909 S.C. 452; Gordon's Trs. v. Thompson, 1910 S.C. 22.

[41] cf. Hay v. Edinburgh Water Co. (1850) 12 D. 1240; 1 Macq. 682; Mackenzie v. Gillanders (1870) 7 S.L.R. 333; Bridges v. Fraserburgh Police Commrs. (1889) 25 S.L.R. 151; Strathblane Heritors v. Glasgow Corpn. (1899) 1 F. 523. See also Macdonald, 1918 S. C. 141; Independent TV Authority, 1968 S.C. 249.

[42] Hay, supra; Strathblane Heritors, supra.

CHAPTER 5.14

LICENCES

A licence is an express or implied permission by a landowner or tenant to enter on to do on or in relation to land what would otherwise be a trespass or other wrong, such as to transverse anthor's land save in the exercise of a right of way, or enter on, or occupy, or lodge in premises[1] or camp on land, or site a caravan on it, or shoot over it,[2] or fish a stream through lands,[3] or post bills on a wall,[4] or graze sheep on a hill,[5] or plough and crop fields,[6] or grow potatoes in another's field,[7] or park vehicles on land. A licence to enter is frequently implied, as by the exhibition of goods for sale,[8] or by the opening of a place as a public park.[9] It is only by licence that persons other than travellers may enter such premises as stations.[10] The exhibition of a notice may be necessary to counter the inference that licence is implied. It may be a gratuitous grant, or onerous, granted in pursuance of contract,[11] such as the contract to take in as a lodger, or to admit to a theatre to see a show, and, in either case, conditional[12] or unconditional.

A licence confers no real right in the land, but is a personal right only, revocable at any time, unless the grant or contract provides to the

[1] *Johnston* v. *J.* (1904) 6 F. 665; cf. *Clark* v. *C.* (1871) 9 M. 430; *Rodger's Trs.* v. *R.* (1875) 2 R. 294; *Gibson* v. *Stewart* (1894) 21 R. 437; *Bayne's Trs.* v. *B.* (1894) 22 R. 26; *Cathcart's Trs.* v. *Allardice* (1899) 2 F. 326; *Wallace* v. *Simmers*, 1960 S.C. 255.

[2] cf. Night Poaching Act, 1828, S. 1; Game (Sc.) Act, 1832 (Day Trespass Act), S. 1; *Calder* v. *Robertson* (1878) 6 R. (J.) 3; *Jack* v. *Nairne* (1887) 14 R. (J.) 20; *Richardson* v. *Maitland* (1897) 24 R. (J.) 32; *Thurlow* v. *Tait* (1893) 1 S.L.T. 62; *Morrison* v. *Anderson* 1913 S.C. (J.) 114; *I.R.* v. *Anderson*, 1922 S.C. 284.

[3] *Copland* v. *Maxwell* (1871) 9 M. (H.L.) 1.

[4] *U.K. Advertising Co.* v. *Glasgow Bag Wash Co.*, 1926 S.C. 303; cf. *Popular Amusements, Ltd.* v. *Edinburgh Assessor*, 1909 S.C. 645; see also *Wilson* v. *Kincardineshire Assessor*, 1913 S.C. 704; *Allen* v. *Clydebank Assessor*, 1936 S.C. 318; *L.N.E.Ry.* v. *Glasgow Assessor*, 1937 S.C. 309; *Perth Mags.* v. *Perth Assessor*, 1937 S.C. 549, 558.

[5] *E. Ancaster* v. *Doig*, 1960 S.C. 203.

[6] *Stirrat* v. *Whyte*, 1967 S.C. 265.

[7] *Paton's Trs.* v. *Finlayson*, 1923 S.C. 872, 879.

[8] The distinction formerly drawn between invitees (persons expressly or impliedly invited to enter) and licensees (persons expressly or implicitly permitted to enter) which was relevant to the question of the occupier's liability for harm, is not relevant for the purposes of this chapter.

[9] cf. *Taylor* v. *Glasgow Corpn.*, 1922 S.C. (H.L.) 1; *Plank* v. *Stirling Mags.*, 1956 S.C. 92.

[10] *Perth General Stn. Office* v. *Ross* (1897) 24 R. (H.L.) 44.

[11] *Johnston, supra*; see also *Inland Revenue* v. *Anderson*, 1922 S.C. 284; *Glasgow Tramway Co.* v. *Glasgow Corpn.* (1898) 25 R. (H.L.) 77.

[12] Thus children may be allowed to enter certain premises only if accompanied.

contrary,[13] and is invalid against singular successors of the landlord. It cannot be recorded in the General Register of Sasines nor registered in the Land Register. It is not assignable by the licensee. If revoked before the due termination, expressly or by sale of the land or use inconsistently with the licence, the licensee has only a personal claim against the licensor for breach of contract. Thus an employee permitted to occupy a house in connection with his employment is not entitled to stay after dismissal and, if he does, may be ejected as a trespasser.[15]

The occupier of premises owes to a person invited or licensed to enter the duty of reasonable care in the circumstances, owed by an occupier to a legitimate visitor.[16]

A person expressly or impliedly licensed to come on premises becomes a trespasser if he stays there after the purpose on which he came has been fulfilled, and may be ejected, if necessary by reasonable force.[17] But a person prima facie a trespasser may be deemed a licensee if trespass in such circumstances has been so repeatedly tolerated as to imply acquiescence by the occupier in his presence.[18]

Time-sharing

In 'time-sharing' schemes different persons have rights of occupancy of particular premises, particularly holiday lodges, for particular periods of time in each year. The premises are owned by a developer, or a custodian trustee for behoof of all the members of the club formed by individuals who become members by buying outright or for a period of years entitlement to a licence or right of occupancy of designated premises for a stated period in each year. Each entitled person receives a certificate evidencing his entitlement to occupy but this confers a personal right only and it is not recorded in the Land Register or any other public register, and each contributes to the common expenses. The club is responsible for maintenance and repairs, usually through a management contractor. Entitled persons may, subject to the rules of the club, sell, gift, bequeath or assign their entitlement, or sub-license other parties to occupy.

Mobile homes

The Caravan Sites and Control of Development Act, 1960, provides for the licensing of caravan sites. The Caravan Sites Act, 1968, pro-

[13] *Johnston, supra;* see also *Inland Revenue* v. *Anderson,* 1922 S.C. 284; *Glasgow Tramway Co.* v. *Glasgow Corpn.* (1898) 25 R. (H.L.) 77.
[14] *Morier* v. *Brownlie & Watson* (1895) 23 R. 67; *Mann* v. *Houston,* 1957 S.L.T. 89; *Wallace* v. *Simmers,* 1960 S.C. 255; cf. *Stirrat* v. *Whyte,* 1967 S.C. 265, 268.
[15] *Sinclair* v. *Tod,* 1907 S.C. 1038.
[16] Occupiers Liability (Sc.) Act, 1960, Ss. 1–2. See also Safety of Sports Grounds Act, 1975.
[17] *Wood* v. *N.B. Ry.* (1899) 2 F. 1.
[18] *Dumbreck* v. *Addie's Collieries,* 1929 S.C. (H.L.) 51; *Breslin* v. *L.N.E. Ry.,* 1936 S.C. 816.

vides for a four-week minimum period for a notice to remove, and gives protection against eviction and harassment. The Mobile Homes Act, 1975, applies these provisions to Scotland and provides that in certain cases the owner of the site must offer into a written agreement with the person intending to occupy the mobile home as his only or main residence. The agreement must generally be for not less than five years and contain specified particulars. Such an agreement binds the successors in title of the owner of the site.

Licensing by public authorities

Many kinds of businesses can be conducted in premises only if the person is licensed to do so by a public authority. The commonest is licensing to retail alcoholic liquors.[19]

---

[19] Licensing (Sc.) Act, 1976.

CHAPTER 5.15

LEASES

A lease or tack is the letting on hire of lands or buildings for a
determinate period on conditions including a pecuniary return known
as rent,[1] or in mineral leases lordship. The return may be in goods
rather than money. The grant of occupancy of a house to a servant, if
his occupancy is ancillary and necessary to the performance of his
duties, is treated as an incident of a service contract rather than a
lease,[2] unless there are exceptional provisions.[3] While the same
principles are generally applicable modern statutory modifications
have made the rules applicable to urban leases for habitation or
business and to agricultural leases for farming diverge so that they
require separate treatment, while special legislation deals with
crofters' holdings. The conveyance of lands for minerals to be mined or
quarried therefrom, though in reality a sale of part of the lands, is
normally known as a mineral lease and the incidents of such a transaction are treated as within the law of leases,[4] save that a power to grant
leases does not, generally, unless minerals have previously been let,
import a power to grant mineral leases.[5] The lease of land for a long
term for the erection of buildings, and the letting of sporting rights
over land are also exceptional classes of leases.

It may sometimes be a narrow question whether an agreement is a
lease or, on the other hand, a licence,[6] or a sale,[7] or a disposition in

[1] Stair II, 9, 1; Mack. II, 6, 5; Bankt. II, 9, 1; Ersk. II, 6, 20; Ross. *Lect.* II, 456; Bell, *Prin.*
§1177; Hunter, *Landlord and Tenant*; Rankine, *Leases*; Paton and Cameron, *Landlord and
Tenant*.
[2] *Sinclair* v. *Tod*, 1907 S.C. 1038; *M. Bute* v. *Prenderleith*, 1921 S.C. 281; *Pollock* v. *Inverness
Assessor*, 1923 S.C. 693; *Cairns* v. *Innes*, 1942 S.C. 164; *MacGregor* v. *Dunnett*, 1949 S.C. 510;
Cargill v. *Phillips*, 1951 S.C. 67.
[3] *Dunbar's Trs.* v. *Bruce* (1900) 3 F. 137; *Carron Co.* v. *Francis*, 1915 S.C. 872.
[4] *Campbell* v. *Grant* (1827) 6 S. 188; *Gowans* v. *Christie* (1873) 11 M. (H.L.) 1, 12; *Mungall*
v. *Bowhill Coal Co.* (1900) 2 F. 1073.
[5] *Campbell* v. *Wardlaw* (1883) 10 R. (H.L.) 65; *Nugent's Trs.* v. *N.* (1898) 25 R. 475.
[6] *Brand* v. *Bell's Trs.* (1872) 11 M. 42; *Glasgow Tramway Co.* v. *Glasgow Corpn.* (1897) 24
R. 628; *Bo'ness Mags.* v. *Linlithgowshire Assessor*, 1907 S.C. 774; *Popular Amusements, Ltd.* v.
Edinburgh Assessor, 1909 S.C. 645; *Wilson* v. *Kincardineshire Assessor*, 1913 S.C. 704; *I.R.C.*
v. *Anderson*, 1922 S.C. 284; *U.K. Advertising Co.* v. *Glasgow Bagwash Co.*, 1926 S.C. 303;
Broomhill Motor Co. v. *Glasgow Assessor*, 1927 S.C. 447; *Perth Mags.* v. *Perth Assessor*, 1937
S.C. 549; *L.M.S. Ry.* v. *Assessor of Public Undertakings*, 1937 S.C. 773; *Chaplin* v. *Perth
Assessor*, 1947 S.C. 373; *Mann* v. *Houston*, 1957 S.L.T. 89.
[7] *Ferguson* v. *Fyffe* (1868) 6 S.L.R. 68; *Brand* v. *Bell's Trs.* (1872) 11 M. 42; *McCosh* v.
Ayrshire Assessor, 1945 S.C. 260; *Collective Securities Co.* v. *Ayrshire Assessor*, 1946 S.C. 244.

security,[8] or a joint adventure,[9] or an incident of a contract of employment.[10]

Contract for a lease

The parties to a contract to let and to take lands on lease must respectively have capacity to grant[11] and to take[12] lands on lease. They must have reached agreement[13] on at least the salient elements of the contract, namely the parties, the subjects, the duration of the lease, and the rent. Some other terms, if not expressed, will be supplied by legal implication, such as that entry, if not stated, is to be immediate.[14]

Their agreement, if the lease is intended to endure for more than a year, must be constituted by writing, probative or holograph or adopted as holograph of both parties, failing which either has *locus poenitentiae*,[15] unless resiling has been barred by actings on the faith of oral or improbative agreement, established by writ or oath, and held to amount to homologation or *rei interventus*.[16] The actings relied on may be proved by parole.[17] An inference of grant of a lease may be drawn from a unilateral obligation to grant followed by *rei interventus* and possession by the tenant.[18]

But a contract to let heritage for not more than a year may be constituted orally and proved *prout de jure*.[19] A verbal lease for more than a year, if followed by possession, is obligatory for a year. A personal obligation to grant a lease is not binding on a singular successor such as an heir of entail.[20]

---

[8] *Heritable Securities Inv. Assoc.* v. *Wingate* (1880) 7 R. 1094; c. *Paterson's Tr.* v. *P's Trs.* (1891) 19 R. 91.

[9] *Beresford's Tr.* v. *Argyllshire Assessor* (1884) 11 R. 818.

[10] *Cairns* v. *Innes,* 1942 S.C. 164.

[11] Only an infeft proprietor can grant a valid lease: Bell, *Prin.* §1181. A liferenter cannot grant a lease for longer than his liferent: *Thomson* v. *Merston* (1628) Mor. 8252. As to trustees' powers, see Trusts (Sc.) Act, 1921, Ss. 4–5. As to bondholder in possession, see Heritable Securities Act, 1894, Ss. 6–7: *Mackenzie* v. *Imlay's Trs.,* 1912 S.C. 685; as to *ex facie* absolute disponee, see *Abbott* v. *Mitchell* (1870) 8 M. 791; *Ritchie* v. *Scott* (1899) 1 F. 728; as to agent for landlord see *Danish Dairy Co.* v. *Gillespie,* 1922 S.C. 656.

[12] As to trustees' powers, see Trusts (Sc.) Act, 1921, S. 10.

[13] *Dallas* v. *Fraser* (1840) 11 D. 1058; *Erskine* v. *Glendinning* (1871) 9 M. 656; *Buchanan* v. *D. Hamilton* (1878) 5 R. (H.L.) 69; *Christie* v. *Fife Coal Co.* (1899) 2 F. 192; *Wight* v. *Newton,* 1911 S.C. 762; *Gray* v. *Edinburgh University,* 1962 S.C. 157.

[14] *Christie, supra.* cf. *Watters* v. *Hunter,* 1927 S.C. 310.

[15] *Walker* v. *Flint* (1863) 1 M. 417; *Fowlie* v. *McLean* (1868) 6 M. 254; *Gibson* v. *Adams* (1875) 3 R. 144; *Sinclair* v. *Caithness Flagstone Co.* (1880) 7 R. 1117.

[16] *Sellar* v. *Aiton* (1875) 2 R. 381; *Gibson* v. *Adams* (1875) 3 R. 144; *Wilson* v. *Mann* (1876) 3 R. 527; *Wight, supra; Station Hotel, Nairn* v. *Macpherson* (1905) 13 S.L.T. 456; *Danish Dairy Co., supra.*

[17] *Gowan's Trs.* v. *Carstairs* (1862) 24 D. 1382; *Walker* v. *Flint* (1863) 1 M. 417; *Allan* v. *Gilchrist* (1875) 2 R. 587.

[18] *Campbeltown Coal Co.* v. *D. Argyll,* 1926 S.C. 126.

[19] Bell, *Prin.* §1187; *Monteith* v. *Tenants* (1582) Mor. 8397; *Fraser* v. *Leslie* (1581) Mor. 12405; *Gibson* v. *Adams* (1875) 3 R. 144.

[20] *Kerr* v. *Redhead* (1794) 3 Pat. 309; *Campbeltown Coal Co., supra.*

Duration

A lease may be for any duration, even renewable for ever.[21] If no duration be expressed the lease is treated as one for a year only, renewable by tacit relocation,[22] provided that possession is taken.[23]

The lease in implement of the contract

A contract to let heritage should be implemented by a written lease, which should, if for over a year, be probative or holograph of both parties. If not holograph or probative of both, it is equally binding if followed by possession or other actings implying homologation or *rei interventus*.[24] But written agreement to let on stated terms for more than a year may equally be completed by possession or other actings unequivocally referable thereto and implying homologation or *rei interventus*.[25] An oral agreement to let for more than one year, if followed by possession thereunder, is binding on both parties for one year, or till the end of any year thereof.[26] If it is later followed by a written lease the obligations thereof run from the date of entry under the oral lease.[27]

An agreement for a lease for not more than a year does not require to be completed by a written lease. A presumption of the relationship of lease arises from mere occupation of lettable subjects.[28]

Failure to grant a lease in implement of a prior contract justifies an action of damages for breach of contract.[29]

A lease is liable to reduction on such a ground as that it was obtained by fraudulent misrepresentation.[30]

A formal lease normally contains a clause of warrandice undertaking to indemnify the lessee if he is evicted from the subjects of let.[31]

---

[21] *Campbell* v. *McLean* (1870) 8 M. (H.L.) 40; cf. *L.A.* v. *Fraser* (1762) 2 Pat. 66 (1140 years); *Carron Co.* v. *Henderson's Trs.* (1896) 23 R. 1042 (171 years); *Crawford* v. *Livingstone's Trs.*, 1938 S.C. 609 (354 years). Building leases are commonly for 99 or 999 years.

[22] *Dunlop* v. *Steel Co. of Scotland* (1879) 7 R. 283.

[23] *Gray* v. *Edinburgh Univ.*, 1962 S.C. 157.

[24] *Carlyle* v. *Baxter* (1869) 6 S.L.R. 425; *Bathie* v. *L. Wharncliffe* (1873) 11 M. 490; *Ballantine* v. *Stevenson* (1881) 8 R. 959; *Wight* v. *Newton*, 1911 S.C. 762; *Wares* v. *Duff-Dunbar's Trs.*, 1920 S.C. 5; *Pollok* v. *Whiteford*, 1936 S.C. 402.

[25] *Campbell* v. *McLean* (1870) 8 M. (H.L.) 40; *Forbes* v. *Wilson* (1873) 11 M. 454; *Sellar* v. *Aiton* (1875) 2 R. 381; *Gardner* v. *Beresford's Trs.* (1878) 5 R. 638; 5 R. (H.L.) 105; *Bell* v. *Goodall* (1883) 10 R. 905; *Sutherland's Tr.* v. *Miller's Tr.* (1888) 16 R. 10; *Buchanan* v. *Harris & Sheldon* (1900) 2 F. 935; *Watters* v. *Hunter*, 1927 S.C. 310; *Skene* v. *Cameron*, 1942 S.C. 393.

[26] *Neill* v. *E. Cassilis*, 22 Nov. 1810, F.C.

[27] *Ramsay* v. *Howison*, 1908 S.C. 697.

[28] *Glen* v. *Roy* (1882) 10 R. 239.

[29] *Danish Dairy Co.* v. *Gillespie*, 1922 S.C. 656.

[30] *Beresford's Tr.* v. *Gardner* (1877) 4 R. 363.

[31] *Menzies* v. *Whyte* (1888) 15 R. 470; *D. Bedford* v. *E. Galloway's Tr.* (1904) 6 F. 971; *Dougall* v. *Dunfermline Mags.*, 1908 S.C. 151; *Wolfson* v. *Forrester*, 1910 S.C. 675.

A lease does not, in general, require any registration to complete the title of the tenant.

Interpretation

The ordinary principles of construction fall to be applied to a lease. If it relates to lands in Scotland, it prima facie falls to be interpreted by Scots law, even if drawn in English form.[32] If the terms are ambiguous, the lease may be construed by the possession which has followed on it,[33] but not by the circumstances in which it was granted.[34] Where certain terms are uncertain, as by describing lands as formerly tenanted by another, extrinsic evidence is admissible to clarify the doubt.[35]

Modification of lease

The usual principle applies that a written lease cannot be qualified or modified save by other probative writing.[36] Alleged collateral agreements made prior to the execution of the lease may be proved by writ or oath.[37] Alleged agreements made subsequent to the lease and modifying it similarly require proof by writ or oath followed by *rei interventus*,[38] or parole evidence of an oral agreement followed by actings in pursuance thereof and implying acquiescence.[39] Apart from agreement, consent to actings in contravention of a lease may be implied from knowledge and acquiescence, which may be proved by parole,[40] and a lease may be altered *rebus ipsis et factis* by acts of the parties necessarily and unequivocally importing an agreement to alter the lease, which acts may be proved by parole.[40]

Real rights under lease

At common law leases were purely contractual and conferred only personal rights on the tenants, binding the landlord and his representatives but not binding on the landlord's singular successors such as purchasers of the lands from him. The Leases Act, 1449, as interpreted, in certain circumstances confers on tenants real rights in the

[32] *Mackintosh* v. *May* (1895) 22 R. 345.
[33] *Mackay* v. *Maclachlan* (1899) 7 S.L.T. 48; *Watters* v. *Hunter*, 1927 S.C. 310.
[34] *Shawrigg Fireclay Co.* v. *Larkhall Collieries* (1903) 5 F. 1131.
[35] *E. Ancaster* v. *Doig*, 1960 S.C. 203.
[36] *Carmichael* v. *Penny* (1874) 11 S.L.R. 634; *Downie* v. *Laird* (1902) 10 S.L.T. 28; *Norval* v. *Abbey*, 1939 S.C. 724; *Korner* v. *Shennan*, 1950 S.C. 285.
[37] *Philip* v. *Gordon Cumming's Exors.* (1869) 7 M. 859; *Stewart* v. *Clark* (1871) 9 M. 616; *Perdikou* v. *Pattison*, 1958 S.L.T. 153; see also *Pollok* v. *Whiteford*, 1936 S.C. 402.
[38] *Kirkpatrick* v. *Allanshaw Coal Co.* (1880) 8 R. 327; *Skinner* v. *L. Saltoun* (1886) 13 R. 823; *Turnbull* v. *Oliver* (1891) 19 R. 154; *Page* v. *Strains* (1892) 30 S.L.R. 69; *Garden* v. *E. Aberdeen* (1893) 20 R. 896; *Dickson* v. *Bell* (1899) 36 S.L.R. 343; *Campbeltown Coal Co.* v. *D. Argyll*, 1926 S.C. 126.
[39] *Ballie* v. *Fraser* (1853) 15 D. 747; *Bargaddie Coal Co.* v. *Wark* (1858) 3 Macq. 467; *Kirkpatrick, supra; Carron Co.* v. *Henderson's Trs.* (1896) 23 R. 1042.
[40] *Bargaddie Coal Co., supra; Carron Co., supra*, 1049.

lands leased. It has been held applicable to all heritable rights capable of being the subjects of separate lease, farms, houses, minerals, salmon-fishings, and shootings.[41] The Act avails against the landlord's singular successors, such as purchasers and adjudging creditors, succeeding heirs of entail, superiors taking the lands by liferent escheat of the vassal, and the Crown.[42]

As interpreted, the Act requires five elements for its application, viz.: (1) that the lease, if for longer than a year, be in writing;[43] (2) that it applies to lands and other heritable subjects, such as houses, minerals or salmon-fishings;[44] (3) that the tenant has taken possession under the lease;[45] This is most important as for long possession under a lease has been held the equivalent of sasine in feudal property;[46] that there is a defined duration of the lease, and hence a definite ish or expiry.[47] This may not be defined in years but, e.g. for a lifetime;[48] and (5) that there is a specified rent, not necessarily substantial, but at least not illusory.[49] It is immaterial whether or not a grassum or capital payment has been payable at the commencement of the lease as well as an annual rent.[50]

Registration of leases

The Registration of Leases Act, 1857,[51] provides that probative leases for twenty years or more, or with an obligation of renewal so as to endure for that period, of land not exceeding fifty acres (save in mining leases) may be recorded in the Register of Sasines. When recorded, such leases are valid against singular successors though there be no rent, no definite ish, and the lessee has not entered into possession. A lease so recorded may be assigned, absolutely or in security[52] the

[41] *Farquharson*, (1870) 9 M. 66.

[42] Stair II, 4, 66; II, 9, 25; Bankt. II, 9, 45; Ersk. II, 5, 79.

[43] Stair II, 9, 4,; Mack. II, 6, 5; Bankt. II, 9, 5; Ersk. II, 9, 24; Bell, *Prin.* §1190; Bell, *Leases*, I, 34.

[44] Bankt. II, 9, 1; Ersk. II, 6, 27; Bell, *Comm.* I, 65; *Campbell* v. *McKinnon* (1867) 5 M. 651; also a lease for sporting purposes, and probably even a lease of shootings without the land: *Farquharson* (1870) 9 M. 66; but not game or fishing leases: *Birkbeck* v. *Ross* (1865) 4 M. 272; *E. Galloway* v. *D. Bedord* (1902) 4 F. 851. As to fishing leases see now Freshwater and Salmon Fisheries (Sc.) Act, 1976, S. 4.

[45] Stair II, 9, 7; Mack. II, 6, 5; Bankt. II, 9, 3; Ersk. II, 6, 25; Bell, *Prin.* §1209–11. The possession must be by the tenant, and after the date of entry fixed by the lease: *Johnston* v. *Cullen* (1676) Mor. 15231. Limited acts of occupation before the date of entry will not suffice: *Millar* v. *McRobbie*, 1949 S.C. 1.   [46] *Millar, supra.*

[47] Stair II, 9, 16; Mack. II, 6, 5; Bankt. II, 9, 5; Ersk. II, 6, 24; Bell, *Prin.* §1194; Bell, *Leases*, I, 38, 215; Bell, *Convg.* II, 1210; cf. *Wilson* v. *Mann* (1876) 3 R. 527; *Barbour* v. *Chalmers* (1891) 18 R. 610; *Bisset* v. *Aberdeen Mags.* (1898) 1 F. 87.

[48] *Thomson* v. *T.* (1896) 24 R. 269; see also *Campbell* v. *McLean* (1870) 8 M. (H.L.) 40.

[49] Stair II, 9, 29; Mack. II, 6, 5; Bankt. II, 9, 5; Ersk. II, 6, 24; Bell, *Prin.* §1197–1202; Bell, *Convg.* II, 1114; *Keith* v. *Ogilvie* (1629) Mor. 15238; *Mann* v. *Houston*, 1957 S.L.T. 89.

[50] Bell, *Prin.* §1201; *Mann, supra.*

[51] Amended by Conveyancing (Sc.) Act, 1924, S. 24; Long Leases (Sc.) Act, 1954, Ss. 26–7 and Land Tenure Reform (Sc.) Act, 1974, Sch. 6.

[52] *Crawford* v. *Campbell*, 1937 S.C. 596.

assignee's right being completed by recording. In the case of land in an area operational for the purposes of the Land Registration (Sc.) Act, 1979, the grant of an interest by way of long lease in registrable but only to the extent that the interest has become that of the lessee and this creates a real right even without possession,[53] and the assignation of the interest is also registrable.[54] Save in these cases a lease cannot be recorded in the Register of Sasines nor registered in the Land Register; it is an overriding interest only.

Death of or sale by landlord

When a landlord dies, or sells lands or buildings leased, if the leases come within the Acts of 1449 or 1857, the heirs or purchasers take the lands subject to the burden of all the natural incidents of the leases, but free of any purely personal incidents or conditions which transmit against the landlord's executors only.[55]

Personal conditions in leases

Notwithstanding the Leases Act, 1449, and the Registration of Leases Act, 1857, there may be terms and conditions in a lease deemed purely personal to the parties and not real or among the normal incidents of the relationship of landlord and tenant, and such will not bind a singular successor of the landlord. Among such have been a provision whereby rent is to be attributed towards a prior debt;[56] that an abatement from rent is to be made for services to be rendered by the tenant;[57] that, in a lease for 999 years, the landlord would grant a feu on demand;[58] that, on expiry of the lease, the landlord would grant a renewal for four years;[59] that a tenant could cut peats from another part of the landlord's estate.[60]

But a right of pasturage on commonty has been held an incident of a lease and so to be enforceable against a singular successor of the landlord,[61] and possibly also an obligation to repay tenants' improvement expenditure.[62]

---

[53] 1979 Act, S. 2(1)(a)(i).
[54] 1979 Act, S. 2(4).
[55] *Arbuthnot* v. *Colquhoun* (1772) Mor. 10424; *Walker* v. *Masson* (1857) 19 D. 1099; *Gardiner* v. *Stewart's Trs.*, 1908 S.C. 985; *Riddell's Exors.* v. *Milligan's Exors.*, 1909 S.C. 1137.
[56] Bell, *Prin.* §1202.
[57] *Ross* v. *Duchess of Sutherland* (1838) 16 S. 1179; cf. *Montgomery* v. *Carrick* (1848) 10 D. 1387; *Page* v. *Strains* (1892) 30 S.L.R. 69.
[58] *Bissett* v. *Aberdeen Mags.* (1898) 1 F. 87.
[59] *Jacobs* v. *Anderson* (1898) 6 S.L.T. 234.
[60] *Duncan* v. *Brooks* (1894) 21 R. 760.
[61] *Findlay* v. *Stuart* (1890) 29 S.L.R. 15.
[62] *Swan* v. *Fairholme* (1894) 2 S.L.T. 74.

Assignation and subletting

Assignation imports transferring the lessee's rights to another who will stand in his place as tenant of the landlord, assuming his rights and liabilities. Subletting imports the letting by the tenant of the whole or part of the subjects let to him to another, himself continuing as tenant of his landlord but becoming landlord of his subtenant.[63]

Leases are contracts involving *delectus personae* so that assignation and subletting are incompetent, unless permitted expressly by the lease, or by a recognized exception to this rule.[64] There is no power, unless expressly conferred, to assign or sublet agricultural subjects, or shootings or fishings.[65] This rule does not impliedly exclude a tenant's heir, or the trustee in his sequestration.[66] Express power to assign or sublet is, however, conferred if the destination in the lease is to the tenant, his assignees and subtenants.

Implied power to assign and sublet is recognized, as common law exceptions to the general rule, in the cases of (1) liferent leases;[67] (2) leases for the duration of the tenant's tenure of an office;[68] (3) farm leases of extraordinary endurance;[69] (4) urban leases,[70] though this implied power may be expressly excluded and the exception probably does not extend to furnished lettings;[71] and (5) leases of mines and minerals, unless expressly excluded.

An express exclusion of power may be fenced by a conventional irritancy, which, if incurred, cannot be purged before decree.[72] Where there is an express exclusion, and exclusion of subtenants does not import exclusion of assignees also, and conversely.[73]

Where assignation or subletting is excluded by law, or expressly, the

[63] Stair II, 9, 22; Bankt. II, 9, 17; Ersk. II, 6, 34; *Skene* v. *Greenhill* (1825) 4 S. 25; *Burns* v. *Martin* (1887) 14 R. (H.L.) 20.
[64] Stair II, 9, 22, III, 1, 16; Mack. II, 6, 7–8; Bankt. II, 9, 11; Ersk. II, 6, 31; Bell, *Comm.* I, 76; *Prin.* §1215; Bell, *Leases* I, 175; *D. Porland* v. *Baird* (1865) 4 M. 10, 22.
[65] Bell, *Prin.* §1214; *Fife* v. *Wilson* (1864) 3 M. 323; *Mackintosh* v. *May* (1895) 22 R. 345; *Jardine-Patterson* v. *Fraser,* 1974 S.L.T. 93.
[66] *Alison* v. *Proudfoot* (1788) Mor. 15290.
[67] Stair II, 9, 26; Mack. II, 6, 7; Bankt. II, 9, 11, and 46; Ersk. II, 6, 32; Bell, *Comm.* I, 77; Bell, *Leases,* I, 186.
[68] *Pringle* v. *McLagan* (1802) Hume 808.
[69] Ersk. II, 6, 32; Bell, *Prin.* §1215; Interpreted to mean leases of 37 or more years: Bell, *Leases,* I, 186; *Pringle, supra;* but possibly covering any lease of over 21 years; cf. *Bain* v. *Mackenzie* (1896) 23 R. 528, 533.
[70] Bankt. II, 9, 12; Ersk. II, 6, 31; Bell, *Comm.* I, 76; II, 32; *Prin.* §1274; Bell, *Leases* I, 184; *Hatton* v. *Clay & McLuckie* (1865) 4 M. 263; *Robb* v. *Brearton* (1895) 22 R. 885.
[71] Rankine, *Leases,* 175. Failure expressly to exclude does not amount to implied consent to sublet: *Dalrymple's Trs.* v. *Brown,* 1945 S.C. 190.
[72] *Porter* v. *Paterson* (1813) Hume 862; *Lyon* v. *Irvine* (1874) 1 R. 512; *Penman* v. *Mackay,* 1922 S.C. 385.
[73] Bell, *Comm.* I, 77; *Crawford* v. *Maxwell* (1758) Mor. 15307; *Trotter* v. *Dennis* (1770) Mor. 15282.

court will set aside transactions or devices designed to evade the prohibition.[74]

The lease frequently expressly excludes from the destination assignees and/or subtenants, sometimes qualifying this by providing an exception for such as may be approved by the landlord,[75] or if the landlord consents in writing.[76] Where consent is required the landlord is not bound to give any reason for withholding consent.[77] The fact that a landlord does not object to assignees taking possession does not automatically imply his recognition of them as tenants.[78]

Difficult issues may arise, as to whether a trustee for creditors is in substance as assignee or merely a manager.[79] In many older cases a tenant was held to have forfeited his lease if he left the country permanently and committed the management of the farm to another.[80] An heir-at-law claiming to succeed on death is not excluded by an exclusion of assignees.[81]

Assignation, as between tenant and assignee

The agreement to assign and the terms thereof are a separate contract, liable to reduction for fraud like any other,[82] and normally to be constituted and proved by formal writings.[83] An intending assignee must be presumed to have seen the lease and to be aware of limitations therein on subletting.[84] If the assignee cannot implement his part of the bargain the assignation falls.[85]

Completion of assignation

Where assignation is competent it is effected by a probative deed of assignation, delivered to the assignee[86] and intimated to the landlord, assignations having priority in competition by date of intimation.[87] Intimation may be formal, evidenced by an instrument of intimation signed by a notary and witnesses,[88] or under the Transmission of

[74] *Porter, supra; Hamilton v. Somerville* (1855) 17 D. 344; *Hatton, supra; Lyon v. Irvine* (1874) 1 R. 512.   [75] *Dewar v. Ainslie* (1892) 20 R. 203.
[76] *M. Breadalbane v. Whitehead* (1893) 21 R. 138.
[77] *Muir v. Wilson*, 20 Jan. 1820, F.C.; *Wight v. E. Hopetoun* (1855) 17 D. 364.
[78] *Elphinstone v. Monkland Iron Co.* (1886) 13 R. (H.L.) 98; contrast *Aglionby v. Watson* (1809) Hume 845.
[79] *Young's Trs. v. Anderson* (1809) Hume 843; *Dewar, supra;* cf. *M. Breadalbane, supra.*
[80] *E. Dalhousie v. Wilson* (1802) Mor. 15311; *Arnot & Bell* (1805) Hume 576; *Monro v. Miller*, 11 Dec. 1811, F.C.; *Watson v. Douglas*, 13 Dec. 1811, F.C.; *Stirling v. Miller*, 29 June 1813, F.C.; *Sydserf v. Todd*, 8 Mar. 1814, F.C.
[81] *Murdoch v. M's Trs.* (1863) 1 M. 330.
[82] *Duncan v. Cowie* (1841) 4 D. 47; *Hay v. Rafferty* (1899) 2 F. 302.
[83] *Smith v. Riddell* (1886) 14 R. 95. But see *Kinnimont v. Paxton* (1892) 20 R. 128.
[84] *Leechman v. Sievwright* (1826) 4 S. 683.   [85] *Smith, supra.*
[86] Ersk. III, 5, 3; *Grant v. Gray* (1828) 6 S. 489.
[87] *Inglis v. Paul* (1829) 7 S. 469.
[88] Stair II, 10, 17; III, 3, 7; Mack. II, 5, 3; Bankt. III, 1, 6; Ersk. III, 5, 3; Bell, *Prin.* §1463; Bell, *Convg.* I, 307.

Moveable Property (Sc.) Act, 1862, S. 2,[89] or conduct may be held equivalent thereto.[90] In a question with third parties the assignation must be completed by transfer of possession to the assignee.[91]

Where assignation is competent it may be made absolutely or in security, but in the latter case the creditor must take possession, and he becomes liable to the landlord for all the prestations due under the lease.[92]

Under the Registration of Leases (Sc.) Act, 1857, probative leases for twenty years or more, or containing an obligation to renew so as to endure for that period, and assignations thereof, in the form of Schedule A to the Act, may be recorded in the Register of Sasines to the effect (S. 3) of making the lease effectual to the assignee against any singular successor of the landlord infeft after the recording. Assignations in security in the form of Schedule B when recorded complete the right thereunder and constitute a real security over the lease to the extent assigned (S. 4).[93] The creditor under an assignation in security may (S. 6), on default, apply to the sheriff for warrant to enter on possession, which warrant, if granted, is a title to the creditor to enter into possession, uplift rents and sublet as freely as the tenant might have done, subject to becoming personally liable to the landlord for the obligations of the lease.

Obligations arising out of assignations

A completed and intimated or recorded assignation substitutes the assignee in place of the cedent as tenant. Unless continuing liability be stipulated for,[94] the cedent ceases to be liable and the assignee becomes liable for the rent for the future.[95] The assignee becomes liable, and the cedent continues to be liable, for arrears of rent.[96] In the event of the tenant's bankruptcy an assignation, though completed and intimated, does not give the assignee a complete right against the tenant's trustee in bankruptcy unless the assignee has taken possession,[97] or the lease is one registered under the Registration of Leases Act, 1857, when the assignation is completed by registration under that Act.

[89] Strictly speaking this Act is inapplicable to a heritable right.
[90] Stair I, 7, 9, and 45; Mack. II, 5, 5; Bankt. III, 1, 12; Ersk. III, 5, 4; Bell, *Comm.* II, 17; *Prin.* §1465; *Tod's Trs.* v. *Wilson* (1869) 7 M. 1100.
[91] Stair II, 1, 6; Bankt. II, 9, 4; Ersk. II, 6, 25; Bell, *Comm.* I, 66, 755; Bell, *Prin.* §1209–12; Bell, *Leases* I, 451; *Brock* v. *Cabbell* (1830) 5 W. & S. 476; *Ramsay* v. *Commercial Bank* (1842) 4 D. 405; *Clark* v. *West Calder Oil Co.* (1882) 9 R. 1017, 1024.
[92] *Brock, supra; Inglis* v. *Paul* (1829) 7 S. 469.
[93] *Crawford* v. *Campbell*, 1937 S.C. 596.
[94] *Gray's Trs.* v. *Benhar Coal Co.* (1881) 9 R. 225.
[95] *Skene* v. *Greenhill* (1825) 4 S. 25; *Burns* v. *Martin* (1887) 14 R. (H.L.) 20, 25.
[96] *Bannatine* v. *Scot* (1632) Mor. 15274; *Gemmell* v. *Low* (1823) 2 S. 486; *Ramsay* v. *Commercial Bank* (1842) 4 D. 405.
[97] *Ramsay, supra.*

Sublease

If competent, a sublease must be constituted and proved in the same way as the main lease. If it satisfies the requirements of the Acts of 1449 or 1857 it confers a real right against the main tenant. If he can competently sublet in whole in in part the tenant cannot confer on his subtenant any greater rights in the lands than he himself enjoys under his lease.

The duration of a sublease cannot be greater than that of the main lease and, if silent as to duration, it must expire then. If expressed to endure so long, a claim for damages lies if the main lease be reduced before its due ish.[98] If the main lease be terminated at a break, the subtenant has no claim on being then evicted.[99]

If the sublease were competent, the subtenant's right is valid against the landlord, and if entitled to protection under the Acts of1449 or 1857, valid also against the landlord's singular successors so that the subtenant cannot be evicted if the tenant deserts his lease or renounces it in favour of the landlord.[1]

If, however, the sublease were incompetent, the subtenant may be removed by the landlord as possessing without title,[2] or the landlord may consent to or ratify the sublease or may bar himself from objecting by conduct inferring acquiescence in the sublease.[3]

Obligations arising from subleases

All obligations due under the main lease continue in force.[4] As between landlord and subtenant, no obligations arise *ex contractu*[5] but may arise *ex delicto*.[6] The landlord, if the sublease were competent or acquiesced in, may not eject the subtenant as possessing without title, but only at the termination of the main lease.[7] He may enforce his claim for rent against the tenant by arresting the subrents due by the subtenant to the tenant and, if otherwise competent, under his right of

---

[98] *Middleton* v. *Yorstoun* (1826) 5 S. 162; *Middleton* v. *Megget* (1828) 7 S. 76; contrast *Laidlaw* v. *Wilson* (1830) 8 S. 440.

[99] *Logan* v. *Weir* (1872) 9 S.L.R. 268.

[1] Stair II, 9, 22; Bankt. II, 9, 17; Ersk. II, 6, 34; Bell, *Leases* I, 470; *E. Morton* v. *Tenants* (1625) Mor. 15228.

[2] In this case the subtenant has a claim of damages against the tenant.

[3] e.g. *Hay* v. *McTier* (1806) Hume 836; *Maule* v. *Robb* (1807) Hume 835; see also *Fraser* v. *F.* (1833) 11 S. 565; *Elgin's Trs.* v. *Walls* (1833) 11 S. 585.

[4] Bankt. II, 9, 17; Ersk. II, 6, 34; Bell, *Comm.* I, 76.

[5] *Maxwell* v. *Queensberry's Exors.* (1830) 5 W. & S. 771; cf. *Dick* v. *Taylor's Trs.* (1831) 10 S. 19.

[6] *Duffy* v. *Mungle* (1871) 8 S.L.R. 537; Occupiers Liability (Sc.) Act, 1960, S. 3.

[7] *Robb* v. *Menzies* (1859) 21 D. 277; including termination at a break in the main lease: *Logan* v. *Weir* (1872) 9 S.L.R. 268.

hypothec sequestrate the subtenant's *invecta et illata,* at least so far as the subrents have not been paid to the tenant.[8]

A sublease, in the absence of contrary stipulation, contains an implied warrandice against eviction which gives the subtenant a claim if prematurely evicted as by the landlord's resumption of part of the lands.[9]

Even if the main tenant's possession has come to an end, a subtenant cannot be summarily ejected without warning.[10]

As between tenant and subtenant, the obligations depend on their contract together with such terms as may be implied from the general relaitonship of landlord and tenant. If the subtenant is in breach of contract the tenant may recover damages.[11] A subtenant may have an option to renew if the tenant himself obtains an extension of the lease from the landlord; this does not transmit further unless expressly assigned.[12] Conditions binding on the tenant under the main lease do not bind the subtenant unless incorporated in the sublease.[13] A subtenant is not a servant of the tenant for the purposes of vicarious liability for his fault.[14]

Succession

A lease is an incorporeal heritable right passing at common law on the tenant's death intestate to his heir.[15] The heir might take up the lease, assuming liability for all future obligations, and liberating the tenant's estate for the future, though not for arrears of rent.[16] If the heir renounced the lease he was liable to the landlord in damages for obligations unfulfilled.[17] The heir might be held by his conduct to have abandoned the lease.[18]

Under the Succession (Sc.) Act, 1964, S. 16, the lease now vests in the tenant's executor,[19] who may assign it to any one of the persons entitled to succeed to the estate, irrespective of prohibitions on assignation, or if unable to dispose of the lease may terminate it.

---

[8] *Edinburgh Mags.* v. *Provan's Creditors* (1665) Mor. 6235; *Blane* v. *Morrison* (1785) Mor. 6232; *Williamson* v. *Forbes* (1830) 8 S. 405.

[9] *Downie* v. *Laird* (1902) 10 S.L.T. 28.

[10] *Robb* v. *Brearton* (1895) 22 R. 885.

[11] *Ebbw Vale Steel Co.* v. *Wood's Tr.* (1898) 25 R. 439.

[12] *Robertson* v. *Player* (1876) 4 R. 218.

[13] *Fergusson* v. *Brown* (1902) 9 S.L.T. 341.

[14] *Phillips* v. *Hunter* (1904) 6 F. 814.

[15] Ersk. II, 2, 6; II, 6, 3; *Comm.* I, 76; *Prin.* §1219; Bell, *Leases* I, 146, 508; *Bain* v. *Mackenzie* (1896) 23 R. 528; the heir takes also improvements made by the tenant: *Reid's Exors.* v. *R.* (1890) 17 R. 519.

[16] *Burns* v. *Martin* (1887) 14 R. (H.L.) 20; *Bain* v. *Mackenzie* (1896) R. 528.

[17] *Bethune* v. *Morgan* (1874) 2 R. 186; cf. *Scott's Exors.* v. *Hepburn* (1876) 3 R. 816.

[18] *Watt* v. *Duff* (1852) 14 D. 879; *Gray* v. *Low* (1859) 21 D. 293.

[19] *Garvie's Trs.* v. *Garvie's Tutors,* 1975 S.L.T. 94.

The tenant cannot bequeath a lease unless it is assignable, or he is empowered to name an heir[20] or bequeath the lease.[21] By the 1964 Act, S. 29, provided there is no express prohibition, a tenant may validly bequeath a lease to any one of the persons who would have been entitled to succeed to it as his intestate heirs. It may be a question of construction whether a bequest includes a lease.[22]

If an heir refuses to take up a lease which has not reached its natural termination, he is liable in damages to the landlord for any obligations undertaken by the tenant remaining unfulfilled at his death.[23]

Tenant's bankruptcy

Whether a lease be assignable voluntarily or not, it will, in the absence of express contrary provision, pass on the tenant's bankruptcy to the trustee in his sequestration.[24] The latter may adopt the lease, in which case he incurs personal liability for arrears[25] and for future rent, or disclaim the lease without incurring any liability. He must elect within a reasonable time and ultimate disclaimer will not be prejudiced by temporary intromissions with the subjects in connection with realization of the bankrupt's effects.[26] The express exclusion of assignees does not prevent the lease vesting in the trustee in bankruptcy if the landlord accepts him to enable him to terminate the lease, but it cannot be founded on by the bankrupt.[27]

Unless there is an express provision to that effect the tenant's bankruptcy does not by itself terminate the lease.[28]

Company tenant going into liquidation

Where a company holding a lease goes into liquidation the liquidator must unequivocally indicate adoption of the lease within a reasonable time or be held to have abandoned it and to become liable in damages.[29]

Landlord's duties—to give possession

The landlord must cede to the tenant full possession of the subjects let,[30] and the tenant is entitled to call on the landlord to remove or eject

---

[20] Bell, *Prin.* §1219; *Irvine* v. *Fiddes* (1827) 5 S. 534.
[21] *Stewart* v. *Pirie* (1832) 11 S. 139; statutory powers under Agricultural Holdings (Sc.) Act, 1949, S. 20; Crofters (Sc.) Act, 1955, S. 10.
[22] e.g. *Hardy's Trs.* v. *H.* (1871) 9 M. 736; *Edmond* v. *E.* (1873) 11 M. 347; *Grant* v. *Morren* (1893) 20 R. 404; *Maclagan's Trs.* v. *L.A.* (1903) 11 S.L.T. 227.
[23] *Bethune* v. *Morgan* (1874) 2 R. 186.
[24] Bell, *Prin.* §1216. See also *McKinley* v. *Hutchison's Tr.*, 1935 S.L.T. 62.
[25] *Dundas* v. *Morrison* (1857) 20 D. 225.
[26] *McGavin* v. *Sturrock's Tr.* (1891) 18 R. 576.
[27] *Dobie* v. *M. Lothian* (1864) 2 M. 788.
[28] *Dobie, supra*, 800.
[29] *Crown Estate Commrs.* v. *Highland Engineering Liqdrs.*, 1975 S.L.T. 58.
[30] *Tennent's Trs.* v. *Maxwell* (1880) 17 S.L.R. 463.

possessors,[31] or to authorize him to do so. Possession must be given timeously, failing which the tenant may rescind the cotnract.[32] Unless any portion of the subjects is reserved, possession must be given of the whole subjects let.[33] But in the lease of agricutlural land minerals,[34] woods,[35] and game and wild animals are reserved by law, and other rights may be reserved by the lease.

Maintenance of tenant's possession

The landlord must also do nothing and, so far as within his power, permit to be done nothing to evict the tenant from the subjects let or any material part of them during the lease, on pain of an action on the warrandice expressed or implied in the lease.[36] The warrandice, if not expressed, always implied in a lease, is absolute warrandice[37] as to title and not as to causes independent of title. In the lease of subjects for a particular purpose, there is implied warrandice also that they are fit for that purpose.[38]

Claim under warrandice

A claim under warrandice is competent only when eviction has taken place, or is certain to take place in consequence of the landlord's fault, or is threatened when liability is disputed,[39] or is avoided by the expiry of the lease, leaving a liability for violent profits.[40] A claim lies where the tenant is deprived of the whole or part of the subjects let or loses the full use of the subjects.[41]

Recourse under warrandice against eviction does not lie where the eviction results from change in the law,[42] compulsory purchase or requisition under statute,[43] the actings of a third party for whom the landlord is not liable,[44] the actings of a third party, the risk of which both landlord and tenant had taken,[45] or the prohibition of the tenant's business as a nuisance.[46]

[31] Stair I, 15, 6; Bankt. II, 9, 21; Ersk. II, 6, 28.

[32] Drummond v. Hunter (1869) 7 M. 347.

[33] But cf. Webster v. Lyell (1860) 22 D. 1423: when letting a house furnished the landlord may lock certain cupboards and wardrobes: Miller v. Wilson, 1919, 1 S.L.T. 223.

[34] Bell, Prin. §1226.   [35] Bell, Prin. §1226.

[36] Ersk. II, 6, 25, and 39; Bell, Comm. I, 644; Prin. §894, 1208, 1253; Bell, Convg. I, 200.

[37] Middletons v. Yorstoun (1826) 5 S. 162; Middleton v. Meggat (1828) 7 S. 76; Kinloch v. Fraser (1829) 7 S. 819.

[38] Mackeson v. Boyd, 1942 S.C. 56, 61.

[39] Ersk. II, 3, 30; Ross, Lect. II, 493; Bell, Comm. I, 645; Lyell v. Shepherd (1894) 2 S.L.T. 440.

[40] Hyslop v. Queensberry's Exors. (1823) 2 Sh. App. 63; Bell v. Queensberry's Exors. (1824) 3 S. 416; Kelloch v. Queensberry's Exors. (1824) 3 S. 418.

[41] Guthrie v. Shearer (1873) 1 R. 181; Christie v. Wilson, 1915 S.C. 645.

[42] Holliday v. Scott (1830) 8 S. 831; Kirkcaldy Cinema v. Kirkcaldy Mags., 1915, 2 S.L.T. 42.

[43] cf. Tay Salmon Fisheries v. Speedie, 1929 S.C. 592; Mackeson v. Boyd, 1924 S.C. 56.

[44] Gardner v. Walker (1862) 24 D. 1430.

[45] Piers v. Black (1680) Mor. 16605; Reid v. Shaw (1822) 1 S. 334.

[46] Murray v. Buchanan (1776) Mor. 10636.

Where the eviction is partial and temporary, the appropriate compensation is by way of claim of damages,[47] including indemnification for loss and inconvenience caused and any expenses reasonably incurred by the tenant in seeking to preserve the property;[48] where it is partial but permanent, compensation is normally by way of deduction from the rent.[49]

Where the eviction is total, as where the lease is reduced, a claim for damages lies against the landlord.[50]

Eviction by damnum fatale *or accident*

Where the tenant is evicted in whole or in part by *damnum fatale*, or unforeseeable accident for which neither party was to blame, such as fire, neither party is, in the absence of express or necessarily implied stipulation to the contrary, bound to restore the damaged subjects;[51] and the tenant may abandon the lease and treat the contract as at an end if the eviction is total,[52] or have an abatement of rent if it be partial.[53] If the premises are destroyed the contract is dissolved *rei interitu*.[54] Hence tenants have been held entitled to abandon where agricultural lands have been overwhelmed by sand[55] or swept away by water[56] or houses or shops rendered uninhabitable and unusable by fire[57] or by reason of requisition.[58] An obligation to renew and replace when necessary does not require rebuilding after fire.[59] An obligation to insure does not entitle the tenant to demand that the insurance money be expended in reinstating the property.[60]

In mineral leases abandonment is competent if the mineral seam is exhausted[61] or is unworkably thin,[62] but probably not because of physical difficulties of mining.[63]

---

[47] *Bisset* v. *Whitson* (1842) 5 D. 5; *Menmuir* v. *Airth* (1863) 1 M. 929.

[48] *Robertson* v. *Menzies* (1828) 6 S. 452; *Huber* v. *Ross*, 1912 S.C. 898.

[49] *Craig* v. *Miller* (1888) 15 R. 1005; *Duncan* v. *Brooks* (1894) 21 R. 760; *Dougall* v. *Dunfermline Mags.*, 1908 S.C. 151.

[50] *Hyslop* v. *Queensberry's Exors.* (1823) 2 Sh. App. 63; cf. *Eliott's Trs.* v. *E.* (1894) 21 R. 858.

[51] *Walker* v. *Bayne* (1815) 6 Pat. 217; see also *Duff* v. *Fleming* (1870) 8 M. 769; *D. Hamilton's Trs.* v. *Fleming* (1870) 9 M. 329.

[52] Stair I, 15, 2; *Duff, supra; Gowans* v. *Christie* (1873) 11 M. (H.L.) 1.

[53] Stair, *supra*; Mack. III, 3, 5; Bankt. II, 9, 24; Ersk. II, 6, 41; *Muir* v. *McIntyre* (1887) 14 R. 470; *Sharp* v. *Thomson*, 1930 S.C. 1092.   [54] *Duff, supra.*

[55] *Lindsay* v. *Home* (1612) Mor. 10120.

[56] *Futt* v. *Ruthven* (1671) 2 B.S. 504.

[57] *Drummond* v. *Hunter* (1869) 7 M. 347; *Duff* v. *Fleming* (1870) 8 M. 769; *Allan* v. *Markland* (1882) 10 R. 383; *Cantors* v. *Swears & Wells*, 1978 S.C. 310.

[58] *Mackeson* v. *Boyd*, 1942 S.C. 58.

[59] *Cantors, supra.*

[60] *D. Hamilton's Trs., supra; Clark* v. *Hume* (1903) 5 F. 252; *Cantors, supra.*

[61] *Wilson* v. *Mader* (1699) Mor. 10125; *Murdoch* v. *Fullerton* (1829) 7 S. 404; *Fleming* v. *Baird* (1871) 9 M. 730; cf. *Gowans, supra.*

[62] *Gray* v. *Hog* (1706) 4 B.S. 635.

[63] *Edmiston* v. *Preston* (1675) Mor. 15172, on which see *Gowans, supra,* 5.

Tenants have been held entitled to abatement of rent where premises were damaged by fire, but not beyond repair.[64]

If, however, the tenant be evicted by foreseeable accident for which either party was to blame, that party is liable to restore the subjects and compensate the other for loss caused by the calamity.[65]

A tenant is not, however, entitled to abandon or to abatement of rent merely because the enterprise carried on in the premises let proves unprofitable, or less profitable than expected,[66] or is made less profitable by some event for which the landlord is not to blame.[67] Nor is the landlord responsible for deterioration of the soil, the effects of wind and weather, nor the condemnation of a farm's water supply.[68]

Tenant's duty to take possession

A tenant is under a duty to take possession at the due date of entry, failing which he is liable in damages.[69] He must further retain possession unless he has lawfully assigned or sublet the premises or has justification for abandoning possession. If he does not, the landlord may claim damages,[70] or rescind the lease.[71] Unless personal possession be expressly stipulated for[72] a tenant may possess by his family or employees.[73]

Tenant's duty not to invert possession

A tenant inverts possession when he uses premises let in a way inconsistent with the purposes of the lease and of any particular qualifications on use imposed by the lease, but not necessarily by isolated illegalities or conduct unconnected with his character as tenant. In every case it is a question of interpretation of the lease, and of circumstances and degree of conduct. Thus it has been held inversion to turn a market garden into an amusement park,[74] to establish an alehouse on a farm,[75] to convert a shop into an exhibition,[76] to use a farm building as a posting station,[77] to use back premises as a stable,[78] to use stables and offices for

---

[64] *Allan v. Markland* (1882) 10 R. 383; *Critchley v. Campbell* (1884) 11 R. 475.

[65] *Sutherland v. Robertson* (1737) Mor. 13979; *Hardie v. Black* (1768) Mor. 10133; *Maclellan v. Kerr* (1797) Mor. 10134.

[66] *Dixon v. Campbell* (1824) 2 Sh. App. 175.

[67] e.g. road diversion diminishing trade of restaurant.

[68] *Wilkie v. Gibson* (1902) 9 S.L.T. 431.

[69] Stair II, 9, 31; Bankt. II, 9, 21; Ersk. II, 6, 39; Bell, *Prin.* §1222; *Mathieson v. Nicolson* (1819) 2 Mur. 141.

[70] *Graham v. Stevenson* (1792) Hume 781; *Smith v. Henderson* (1897) 24 R. 1102.

[71] *Watson v. Douglas*, 13 Dec. 1811, F.C.

[72] *Edmund v. Reid* (1871) 9 M. 782.

[73] *Gibson v. Clark* (1895) 23 R. 295.

[74] *Heriot's Hospital v. Heriot's Gardener* (1751) Elch., *Pactum Illicitum*, 20.

[75] *Miln v. Mitchell* (1787) Mor. 15254.

[76] *Leechman v. Sievwright* (1826) 4 S. 683.

[77] *Bailie v. Mackay* (1842) 4 D. 1520.

[78] *Hood v. Miller* (1855) 17 D. 411.

stage-coach horses,[79] to sublet land to a railway company for use as a siding,[80] or even to turn a grist mill into a flour mill,[81] or into a grist and yarn mill,[82] though it is not inversion to hold auction sales in premises let as a shop.[83]

Inversion is even more wrongful if involving unauthorized building[84] or structural alterations[85] on the subjects let, including even attaching a show-case to the front of a shop,[86] or nuisance.[87]

Inversion is a fundamental breach of contract which entitles the landlord to interdict the offending use, or to declare the lease at an end and to eject the tenant. One the other hand the landlord may expressly ratify the conduct, or act in such a way as to imply acquiescence.[88]

Tenant's duty to pay rent

The tenant is bound to pay the agreed rent at the terms agreed upon, failing which he is liable to various sanctions.[89]

Tenant's duty of care

The tenant is bound to make reasonable use and take reasonable care of the premises and will be liable in damages if by misuse or overloading[90] he causes damage or destruction. The general and recognized practice of tenants and of any trade in question is the criterion of reasonable use.[90]

Tacit relocation

If the stipulated duration of a lease expires without either party having given notice to the other of intent to terminate the lease, the parties are held, by the principle of tacit relocation, to have renewed their lease for one further year.[91] This applies only if there has been nothing in the conduct of parties to rebut their presumed intention to renew. Where tacit relocation applies the lease is continued on the same

---

[79] D. Argyll v. McArthur (1861) 23 D. 1236.

[80] Mercer v. Esk Valley Ry. (1867) 5 M. 1024; cf. Leck v. Merryflats Brick Co. (1868) 5 S.L.R. 619.

[81] Bayley v. Addison (1901) 8 S.L.T. 379.

[82] Ford v. Hillocks (1808) Mor. Appx. Tack, 17.

[83] Reid v. Keith (1870) 8 M. (H.L.) 110.

[84] Inglis v. Balfour (1778) Mor. Appx. Tack, 34; Armstrong v. Bryceson (1807) Hume 837; cf. Kehoe v. M. Lansdowne [1893] A.C. 451.

[85] Muir v. Wilson (1822) 1 S. 406; Leck v. Fulton (1854) 17 D. 408.

[86] B.L. Co. v. Purdie (1905) 7 F. 923; cf. Morrison v. Forsyth, 1909 S.C. 329.

[87] Mowbray v. Ewbank (1833) 11 S. 714; cf. D'Eresby's Trs. v. Strathearn Hydropathic Co. (1873) 1 R. 35.

[88] Young v. Ramsay (1825) 1 W. & S. 560; Ferguson v. Methven (1857) 19 D. 794; cf. D. Portland v. Samson (1847) 5 D. 476.

[89] See further Tenant's duties, infra.

[90] Glebe Sugar Refining Co. v. Paterson (1900) 2 F. 615.

[91] Stair II, 9, 23; Ersk. II, 6, 35; Bell, Prin. §1265; Rankine, Leases, 602.

terms and conditions as before but for one further year only and so on from year to year. It may be terminated by due notice before the expiry of any year. If the duration was initially less than a year the extention is for the same short term again. Tacit relocation is based on implied contract and is inapplicable where there is no basis for implying a new contract. It is accordingly inapplicable to seasonal lets of grazing, furnished houses, shootings and fishings.[92]

Where tacit relocation applies conditions in the lease relative to duration, such as an option to renew for a lengthy period, which are inconsistent with a holding by tacit relocation, fall.[93]

The implication that parties intended to continue their relationship is excluded by an arrangement, even improbative, for a new lease,[94] or by a notice of increase of rent.[95] An ineffectual notice to quit[96] or a notice not followed by steps to evict the tenant,[97] may be held not to exclude tacit relocation.

URBAN LEASES

An urban lease is a lease of buildings, with or without land, for residential or business purposes.

Control of letting agencies

By the Accommodation Agencies Act, 1953, it is an offence to demand or take money for registering the requirements of a person seeking the tenancy of a house, for giving particulars of a house to let, or for advertising a house as to let without authority. This does not strike at bona fide advertising or acting as agent for letting.

Constitution and proof of contract

The general principles as to constitution and proof of leases apply. In the case of small dwelling-houses regulated by the House Letting and Rating Act, 1911, no agreement, verbal or written, for the let of a small dwelling-house is binding if made more than two months before the commencement of the let.[98] In accordance with the general rule, the landlord is bound to give the tenant possession of the whole subjects let at the due date of entry, failing which the tenant may abandon the lease.[99]

[92] *Macharg* (1805) Mor. Removing. Appx. 4.
[93] *Neilson* v. *Mossend Iron Co.* (1886) 13 R. (H.L.) 50; *Commercial Union Assce. Co.* v. *Watt & Cumine*, 1964 S.C. 84.   [94] *Buchanan* v. *Harris & Sheldon* (1900) 2 F. 935.
[95] *Macfarlane* v. *Mitchell* (1900) 2 F. 901.   [96] *Gates* v. *Blair*, 1923 S.C. 430.
[97] *Taylor* v. *E. Moray* (1892) 19 R. 399.   [98] 1911 Act, S. 2.
[99] *Drummond* v. *Hunter* (1869) 7 M. 347; cf. *Winans* v. *Mackenzie* (1883) 10 R. 941. But in the case of a furnished let the owner may probably lock cupboards, etc.: *Miller* v. *Wilson*, 1919, 1 S.L.T. 223. Similarly the tenant may abandon if the premises are requisitioned for an uncertain period: *Mackeson* v. *Boyd*, 1942 S.C. 56.

Fitness for habitation or other use

The landlord impliedly warrants that the subjects let are reasonably fit for the purpose of the let.[1] If they are not so, he must put them into tenantable condition at entry.[2] Whether a house is habitable or not is a question of fact.[3] There is, however, no warranty that no defects exist, nor that none will arise during the tenancy. If the landlord has failed to make the premises tenantable, the tenant should refuse to enter and may claim damages;[4] if he does he may be held barred from resiling[5] unless he entered in reliance on promises to repair.[6] Similarly the tenant may resile if the premises are alleged to possess advantages which they do not.[7]

Maintenance during lease

During the let the landlord must maintain the premises in wind- and water-tight condition, habitable and tenantable against the ordinary attacks of the elements.[8] This imports tightness against ordinary attacks of the elements, not against exceptional encroachments.[9] He is bound to take due care to put them into wind and watertight condition if by accident they become not so, but this is not a warranty, and he is not in breach of contract till a defect is brought to his notice and he fails to remedy it,[10] nor unless defect arises from the inconsiderate or culpable act of the landlord.[11]

But the landlord is not liable for deterioration or destruction caused by the fault of the tenant[12] or a third party,[13] nor for the consequences of accident or *damnum fatale*,[14] nor does he contract that due care will be taken by independent contractors whom he employs.[15]

[1] Ersk. II, 6, 39; Bell, *Prin.* §1253; *Glebe Sugar Refining Co.* v. *Paterson* (1900) 2 F. 615.
[2] Bankt. I, 20, 15; II, 9, 20; Ersk. II, 6, 43; *Dickie* v. *Amicable Property Investment Co.*, 1911 S.C. 1079.   [3] *Mechan* v. *Watson*, 1907 S.C. 25.
[4] *Kippen* v. *Oppenheim* (1847) 10 D. 242; *Critchley* v. *Campbell* (1884) 11 R. 475; *Anderson* v. *Watson* (1894) 2 S.L.T. 293.
[5] *Whitelaw* v. *Fulton* (1871) 10 M. 27; *Webster* v. *Brown* (1892) 19 R. 765; *Scottish Heritable Security Co.* v. *Granger* (1881) 8 R. 459; *Baikie* v. *Wordie's Trs.* (1897) 24 R. 1098; *McManus* v. *Armour* (1901) 3 F. 1078.
[6] *Hall* v. *Hubner* (1897) 24 R. 875; *Caldwell* v. *McCallum* (1901) 4 F. 371; *Dickie, supra.*
[7] *Brodie* v. *McLachlan* (1900) 8 S.L.T. 145.
[8] Ersk. II, 6, 43; this does not extend to damp rising from the foundations: *McGonigal* v. *Pickard*, 1954 S.L.T. (Notes) 62.   [9] *Reid* v. *Baird* (1876) 4 R. 234.
[10] *Wolfson* v. *Forrester*, 1910 S.C. 675; see also *Baikie* v. *Wordie's Trs.* (1897) 24 R. 1098; *Irvine* v. *Caledonian Ry.* (1902) 10 S.L.T. 363.
[11] *Golden Casket* v. *B.R.S. (Pickfords)*, 1972 S.L.T. 146.
[12] *Smith* v. *Henderson* (1897) 24 R. 1102; *Mickel* v. *McCoard*, 1913 S.C. 896; cf. *Corrie, Mackie & Co.* v. *Stewart* (1885) 22 S.L.R. 350.
[13] *Allan* v. *Robertson's Trs.* (1891) 18 R. 932; *Sandeman* v. *Duncan's Trs.* (1897) 5 S.L.T. 21; *Hampton* v. *Galloway & Sykes* (1899) 1 F. 501; *N.B. Storage Co.* v. *Steele's Trs.*, 1920 S.C. 194.
[14] *Allan* v. *Robertson's Trs.* (1891) 18 R. 932; *Sandeman* v. *Duncan's Trs.* (1897) 5 S.L.T. 21; *Hampton* v. *Galloway & Sykes* (1899) 1 F. 501; *N.B. Storage Co.* v. *Steele's Trs.*, 1920 S.C. 194.
[15] *Wolfson, supra; Dickie, supra.*

If the premises become unfit the tenant may suspend possession for a time,[16] or if the defect is material, renounce it and give up the lease[17] but may be held barred if he delays substantially, even in reliance on promises of repairs.[18] The tenant may retain or withhold the rent, or claim damages for loss sustained.[19] The landlord can be held liable in damages only if the defects are his fault.[20] If the tenant fails to claim damages timeously, the court may infer abandonment of the claim in return for acceptance of abandonment of the lease.[21]

If the tenant or his family sustain personal injuries by reason of the state of the premises the landlord may be liable in damages under principles of delictual liability.[22]

Statutory conditions of fitness for habitation

By the Housing (Sc.) Act, 1966, S. 6, in any contract to which the section applies[23] there shall, notwithstanding any stipulation to the contrary, be implied a condition that the house is, at the commencement of the tenancy, and an undertaking that it will be kept by the landlord during the tenancy, in all respects reasonably fit for human habitation,[24] but not when a house is let for not less than three years on the terms that will be put by the lessee into a condition in all respects reasonably fit for human habitation, and the lease is not determinable at the option of either party before the expiration of three years. The landlord, or any person authorized by him may at reasonable times on notice given in writing enter premises affected to view the state and condition thereof. S. 5 lists factors to be considered in determining whether a house is unfit for human habitation if and only if it is so far defective in one or more of the said matters that it is not reasonably suitable for occupation in that condition.[25]

---

[16] *Burns* v. *McNeil* (1898) 5 S.L.T. 289; *Souter* v. *Mulhern*, 1907 S.C. 723.

[17] *McKimmie's Trs.* v. *Armour* (1899) 2 F. 156.

[18] *Forbes* v. *Ferguson* (1899) 7 S.L.T. 293; *Dickie* v. *Amicable Property Inv. Co.*, 1911 S.C. 1079; *Mullen* v. *Dunbarton C.C.*, 1933 S.L.T. 185; *Proctor* v. *Cowlairs Co-op. Socy.*, 1961 S.L.T. 434.

[19] *Reid* v. *Baird* (1876) 4 R. 234.

[20] *Hampton* v. *Galloway & Sykes* (1899) 1 F. 501; *Irvine* v. *Caledonian Ry.* (1902) 10 S.L.T. 363; *N.B. Storage Co.* v. *Steele's Trs.*, 1920 S.C. 194.

[21] *Lyons* v. *Anderson* (1886) 13 R. 1020.

[22] *Miller* v. *Addie's Collieries*, 1934 S.C. 150; *McLaughlan* v. *Craig*, 1948 S.C. 599; Occupier's Liability (Sc.) Act, 1960, S. 3. See also *McCormick* v. *Fife Coal Co.*, 1931 S.C. 19.

[23] i.e. to contracts before 31 July 1923 for letting a house at not over £16, or contract thereafter for letting a house at not over £26, but not to contracts for the letting by a local authority of any house purchased or retained by it for housing under Ss. 20 or 40 of the Act.

[24] This implies a duty to report defects to the landlord: *Morgan* v. *Liverpool Corpn.* [1927] 2 K.B. 131. There may be a duty under this section to prevent flood water entering a house: *Duff* v. *Glasgow Corpn.*, 1968 S.L.T. (Sh. Ct.) 6.

[25] cf. *Haggarty* v. *Glasgow Corpn.*, 1964 S.L.T. (Notes) 95.

Statutory obligation to repair

In any lease of a house granted on or after 3 July 1962 for less than seven years[26] there is implied a provision that the lessor will (a) keep in repair the structure and exterior of the house (including drains, gutters, and external pipes) and (b) keep in repair and proper working order the installations for the supply of water, gas, and electricity and for sanitation (including basins, sinks, baths and sanitary conveniences) and for the space heating or heating water, and any provision that the lessee will repair the premises shall be of no effect in respect of these matters.[27] This implied repairs provision does not reqire the lessor (a) to carry out any works or repairs for which the lessee is liable by virtue of his duty to use the premises in a proper manner, or would be so liable apart from any express undertaking on his part; (b) to rebuild or reinstate the premises in the case of destruction or damage by fire, or by tempest, flood, or other inevitable accident; or (c) to keep in repair or maintain anything which the lessee is entitled to remove from the house; subsection (1) does not avoid the part of any provision which imposes on the lessee any of the requirements of (a) or (c).[28] In determining the standard of repair required by the implied repairs provision regard must be had to the age, character, and prospective life of the house and the locality in which it is situated. The lessor has implied power, on written notice, to enter the premises to view their condition.[29]

Section 8 may be excluded or modified by provisions in a lease, authorized by the sheriff on the application of either party with the other's consent, if it is reasonable to do so. Beyond that, contracting-out is void, as is provision for irritancy or penalty on the lessee if he relies on S. 8.[30]

Landlord's duty of care for visitor's safety

The landlord owes *ex contractu* a duty of reasonable care to his tenant to have regard for the latter's safety, but owes no such duty *ex contractu* to the tenant's family or visitors.[31] Under the Occupiers' Liability (Sc.) Act, 1960, S. 3, where premises are occupied or used by virtue of a tenancy[32] under which the landlord is responsible for the

[26] Housing (Sc.) Act, 1966, S. 9.
[27] Ibid., S. 8(1).
[28] Ibid., S. 8(2).
[29] Ibid., S. 8(3) and (4).
[30] Ibid., S. 10.
[31] *McMartin* v. *Hannay* (1872) 10 M. 411; *Grant* v. *McClafferty*, 1907 S.C. 201; *Cameron* v. *Young*, 1908 S.C. (H.L.) 7; *Mellon* v. *Henderson*, 1917, 1 S.L.T. 257; *Grant* v. *Fleming*, 1914 S.C. 228.
[32] Defined as including a subtenancy, a statutory tenancy, and any contract conferring a right of occupation, e.g. a service contract with a right to occupy premises.

maintenance or repair of the premises, he must show towards any persons who or whose property may from time to time be on the premises[33] the same reasonable care in respect of dangers arising from any failure on his part in carrying out his responsibility as is required under S. 2 of the Act to be shown by an occupier of premises to persons entering on them. The standard of reasonable care may be extended, restricted, modified or excluded by agreement,[34] and no obligation is imposed in respect of risks which the visitor has willingly accepted as his,[35] i.e. as to which *volenti non fit injuria* applies.[36] A tenant may be *volens* if he has not complained of a danger or stayed long after it has arisen or not been remedied.

Tenant's remedies

Where the landlord has been in breach of his obligation to maintain the premises in tenantable condition the tenant may have a claim of damages, or may withhold the rent, or may relinquish possession of the premises. Damages are appropriate where inconvenience and loss have been caused,[37] but not for destruction by *damnum fatale*,[38] nor for damage not attributable to any fault on the landlord's part.[39] A tenant who remains in occupation after becoming aware of a defect is not entitled to damages unless he remained in reliance on an assurance that the defect would be cured: *volenti non fit injuria*. If the landlord does not remove the defect the tenant should leave and claim damages for the expense of so doing.[40] Tenants have been held entitled to throw up the lease,[41] or at least to suspend possession,[42] where the landlord's failure has been material and is not readily remediable. The materiality of the defect and the time necessary to make the premises tenantable are questions of fact.[43] Where the landlord has unreasonably delayed or refused to perform some of his duties, the tenant may retain rent for

---

[33] i.e. tenants, their family, guests, and casual visitors.

[34] S. 2(1); but such agreement could affect only a party to it: if contained in the lease it binds the tenant only.

[35] S. 2(3); cf. *Birrell* v. *Anstruther* (1866) 5 M. 20.

[36] cf. *Grant* v. *McClafferty,* 1907 S.C. 201.

[37] *Hamilton* (1667) Mor. 10121; *Deans* v. *Abercrombie* (1681) Mor. 10122; *Bissett* v. *Whitson* (1842) 5 D. 5; *Reid* v. *Baird* (1876) 4 R. 234; *Tennent's Trs.* v. *Maxwell* (1880) 17 S.L.R. 463; *Scott, Croall & Sons* v. *Moir* (1895) 3 S.L.T. 70; *Irvine* v. *Caledonian Ry.* (1902) 10 S.L.T. 363.

[38] *Sandeman* v. *Duncan's Trs.* (1897) 5 S.L.T. 21.

[39] *Allan* v. *Robertson's Trs.* (1891) 18 R. 932.

[40] *Proctor* v. *Cowlairs Co-operative Socy.,* 1961 S.L.T. 434.

[41] *Kippen* v. *Oppenheim* (1847) 10 D. 242; *Anderson* v. *Watson* (1894) 2 S.L.T. 293; *Souter* v. *Mulhern,* 1907 S.C. 723. Contrast *Lowndes* v. *Buchanan* (1854) 17 D. 63.

[42] *Burns* v. *McNeil* (1898) 5 S.L.T. 289; cf. *Sc. Heritable Secy. Co.* v. *Granger* (1881) 8 R. 459.

[43] *McKimmie's Trs.* v. *Armour* (1899) 2 F. 156.

the period of non-implement,[44] unless he has, in the lease, waived the right to do so.[45]

Tenant's duties

Within a reasonable time of the date of entry the tenant must enter into possession.[46] Failure or refusal, unless justifiable, infers liability in damages.[47] Thereafter, he is bound to occupy the subjects without unreasonable intermission until the end of the lease. Possession may normally be taken and retained by the tenant's family or others on his behalf, but prolonged absence may justify termination of the contract for breach of a material condition.[48]

The tenant must take reasonable care of the premises let;[49] thus a shop tenant must furnish the premises, keep them heated and aired, but need not open nor carry on a business there.[50] It is relevant matter for damages that a tenant has left a house unoccupied, unheated and uncleaned, whereby damage resulted.[51] A tenant is liable if, by not having turned off the water, damage resulted from burst pipes.[52] He will also be liable for damage caused by overloading floors.[53] He must plenish urban subjects, so as to provide security for rent, and may be ordered by the court to do so or to find caution for rent.[54] He must not invert the possession as by carrying on a trade in premises let as a house.

Rates

The tenant as occupier is normally liable for local rates, but the owner is liable for occupier's rates in small houses subject to the House Letting and Rating Act, 1911.[55]

Secure tenancies—public sector housing

A tenancy is a secure tenancy if the house is let as a separate dwelling, the tenant is an individual and the dwelling-house is his only

---

[44] *Buchan* v. *Leith* (1708) 4 B.S. 716; *Gordon* v. *Suttie* (1826) 4 Mur. 86; *Kilmarnock Gas Co.* v. *Smith* (1872) 11 M. 58; *Corrie* v. *Stewart* (1882) 22 S.L.R. 350.

[45] *Skene* v. *Cameron*, 1942 S.C. 393; *Glasgow Corpn.* v. *Seniuk*, 1968 S.L.T. (Sh. Ct.) 47.

[46] Stair II, 9, 31; Bankt. II, 9, 21; Ersk. II, 6, 39; Bell, *Prin.* §1222; *Robertson* v. *Cockburn* (1875) 3 R. 21.

[47] *Mathieson* v. *Nicolson* (1819) 2 Mur. 141; cf. *Bethune* v. *Morgan* (1874) 2 R. 186; *Scott's Exors.* v. *Bethune* (1876) 3 R. 816.

[48] *Blair Trust* v. *Gilbert*, 1941 S.N. 2 (tenant imprisoned).

[49] Ersk. II, 6, 43.

[50] *Whitelaw* v. *Fulton* (1871) 10 M. 27.

[51] *Smith* v. *Henderson* (1897) 24 R. 1102.

[52] *Mickel* v. *McCoard*, 1913 S.C. 896.

[53] *Caledonian Ry.* v. *Greenock Sacking Co.* (1875) 2 R. 671; *Corrie, Mackie & Co.* v. *Stewart* (1885) 22 S.L.R. 350; *Glebe Sugar Refining Co.* v. *Paterson* (1900) 2 F. 615.

[54] *Wright* v. *Wightman* (1875) 3 R. 68; *McLelland* v. *Garson* (1883) 10 R. 445.

[55] S. 7; the application of the Act is amended by the Rent Restriction Act, 1920, S. 16(1).

or principal home, and the landlord is a local authority, a development corporation for a new town, the S.S.H.A., the Housing Corporation, a housing association, cooperative or trust, but not if it is a long lease, premises occupied under a contract of employment, a temporary letting to a person seeking accommodation or pending development or during works, accommodation for a homeless person, or consists of or includes land exceeding two acres or business premises.[56]

A secure tenancy must be constituted by writing probative or holograph of the parties and a copy given to the tenant. The sheriff may adjust the terms of lease so that they fairly reflect the terms and, if the tenant will not execute it, make it effective as if it had been duly executed.[57] The terms may be varied by agreement or under statutory powers.[58] There are statutory terms prohibiting assignation, subletting or taking in lodgers without consent[59] and as to rent if assignation, subletting or lodging is allowed[60], and prohibiting work on the house, other than decoration or repairs.[61]

A secure tenancy may be ended only (a) by the tenant's death; (b) by S. 13 of the Act; (c) by written agreement; (d) by S. 19 of the Act; (e) by an order for possession under S. 15; (f) by four weeks' notice by tenant to landlord; if the house is not available for occupation, and the tenant is temporaily accommodated, the landlord may not end the temporary occupation before the normal house is available unless the secure tenancy has been terminated.[62]

On the death of the tenant under a secure tenancy, it passes by law to a qualified person, i.e. the spouse, the survivor of joint tenants, or any member of the tenant's family over sixteen where the house had been his only or principal home for at least twelve months. A qualified person may by notice decline the tenancy. A secure tenancy transmits once only and on a second transmission a qualified person may continue as tenant for six months only.[63]

RENT

The rent is fixed contractually and is payable at such intervals as may be agreed. If the rent is not fixed nor otherwise ascertainable, a reasonable rent, *quantum valeat,* is implied.[64]

[56] Tenants' Rights (Sc.) Act, 1980, Ss. 10–11 and Sched. 1.
[57] Ibid., S. 16.
[58] Ibid., S. 17.
[59] Ibid., S. 21.
[60] Ibid., S. 22.
[61] Ibid., S. 23.
[62] Ibid., S. 12.
[63] Ibid., S. 13.
[64] *Ogilvie* v. *Booth* (1868) 5 S.L.R. 231.

Statutory control and regulation of rents

Since 1915 the rents of certain categories of unfurnished dwellings have been statutorily controlled or regulated by a series of statutes mostly consolidated by the Rent (Sc.) Act, 1971, later amended.[65]

Protected tenancies

For the purposes of the 1971 Act a tenancy[66] under which a dwelling-house[67] (which may be a house or part of a house) is let as a separate dwelling[68] is a protected tenancy unless (a) the rateable value[69] on the appropriate day exceeds £200;[70] or (b) under the tenancy no rent is payable, or the rent payable is less than two-thirds of the rateable value of the house on the appropriate day,[71] or it is bona fide let at a rent which includes payments in respect of board, attendance,[72] or (bb) is granted by an educational institution to a student,[73] or (bbb) it is let as a holiday home,[73] or it is let together with land;[74] or (c) the tenancy is for the time being precluded from being a protected tenancy by reason of the body or entity in whom the landlord's interest is vested.[75] A tenancy was not protected if the immediate landlord is the Crown,[76] a government department, a trustee for the Crown for a government department, a local authority, development corporation, the Housing Corporation, the S.S.H.A., certain housing trusts, or, subject to conditions, a housing association under the Housing (Sc.) Act, 1966,[77] nor did a statutory tenancy arise in any of these cases;[78] or (d) by virtue of

---

[65] Certain other statutes have incidental effect on matters of rent control or regulation. This body of legislation is complicated and extremely difficult to state clearly or concisely. The case-law is voluminous. See generally, Megarry, *The Rent Acts*; Paton and Cameron, *Landlord and Tenant*.

[66] Defined, S. 133, as including a subtenancy. A mere licensee, such as a lodger, is not protected.

[67] *Langford Property Co.* v. *Goldrick* [1949] 1 K.B. 511.

[68] *Neale* v. *Del Soto* [1945] K.B. 144; *Cole* v. *Harris* [1945] K.B. 474; *Cowan* v. *Acton*, 1952 S.C. 73; *Goodrich* v. *Paisner* [1957] A.C. 65.

[69] Except where the Act otherwise provides, ascertained in accordance with S. 6. This applies to regulated tenancies, not to controlled tenancies.

[70] Amended: Housing (Financial Provisions) (Sc.) Act, 1972, S. 77 and Tenants' Rights (Sc.) Act, 1980, S. 43. In case of doubt a house is deemed to be within the limits of rateable value: S. 1(3); *Harrison* v. *Hopkins* [1950] 1 K.B. 124.

[71] cf. *Thomson* v. *Lann*, 1967 S.L.T. (Sh. Ct.) 76; *Fennel* v. *Cameron*, 1968 S.L.T. (Sh. Ct.) 30.

[72] The amount of rent attributable to attendance must form a substantial part of the whole rent: S. 2(3); *Palser* v. *Grinling* [1948] A.C. 291.

[73] Cases added by Rent Act, 1974, S. 2.

[74] Land, unless consisting of agricultural land exceeding two acres in extent, is treated as part of the dwelling-house: S. 1(2).   [75] Ss. 1, 2.

[76] cf. *T.A. & A.F.A. of London* v. *Nichols* [1949] 1 K.B. 35. Altered by Tenants' Rights (Sc.) Act, 1980, S. 40.

[77] Ss. 4, 5. For the purposes of ascertaining recoverable rent a subtenancy under a tenancy excepted from protection by S. 5 is treated as if protected. S. 5 is amended by 1980 Act, S. 41.

[78] Ss. 4(2), 5(1).

S. 5A, the tenancy has at all times since it was granted been precluded from being a protected tenancy.[79]

A tenant is protected though he shares the use of some accommodation with another tenant.[80] Certain sublettings do not exclude the sublessor's premises from protection under the Act.[81] There is no protected tenancy where the landlord is also resident in the building.[82]

Where under a protected or statutory tenancy rent is payable weekly the landlord must provide a rent book.[83]

Short tenancies

A protected tenancy is a short tenancy if let, subject to certain conditions, for from one to five years. On its expiry the landlord may, subject to conditions, recover possession of the house.[84]

Controlled tenancies and regulated tenancies

The 1971 Act, being a consolidating one, retains the distinctions developed in superseded legislation, between 'controlled tenancies', themselves divided into 'old control' tenancies and 'new control' tenancies, and 'regulated tenancies'. All three categories come within the scope of 'protected tenancies'.

A 'controlled tenancy' is a tenancy which prior to the Rent Act 1965 was protected by the Rent Acts, 1920–39, covering generally tenancies of houses built or converted before 29 August 1954 whose 1956 rateable value did not exceed £40 and which were let before 6 July 1957 to a sitting tenant or a tenant whose successor occupies as statutory tenant.[85] A tenancy is also a controlled tenancy if, though the rent is less than two-thirds of the rateable value, certain conditions are satisfied.[86]

The fact that part of the premises comprised in a dwelling-house is used as a shop or office or for business, trade or professional purposes does not prevent it being subject to controlled tenancy, but premises including a public house may not be a protected or statutory tenancy, nor may a tenancy to which the Tenancy of Shops (Sc.) Acts, 1949, and 1964, apply be a regulated tenancy.[87]

All controlled tenancies were converted to regulated tenancies by the Tenants' Rights (Sc.) Act, 1980, S. 46.

[79] Rent Act, 1974, S. 2(3), adding new S. 5A, amended 1980 Act, S. 44.
[80] S. 119.
[81] Ss. 120–1. S. 121A is added by 1980 Act. S. 60.
[82] Rent Act, 1974, Sched. 2(2) adding S. 5A to 1971 Act, amended 1980 Act, S. 44.
[83] S. 132.
[84] Tenants' Rights (Sc.) Act, 1980, Ss. 34–6, Short Tenancies (Prescribed Information) (Sc.) Order, 1980 (S.I. 1666, 1980).
[85] S. 7(1) and Sch. 2, Part I.
[86] S. 7(3).   [87] S. 9.

A 'regulated tenancy' is a protected or statutory tenancy which is not a controlled tenancy.[88] Where a regulated tenancy is followed by a statutory tenancy of the same dwelling-house, the two are treated as a single regulated tenancy.[89]

The Secretary of State may release regulated tenancies from regulation.[90]

Rent agreements with tenants having security

A rent agreement with a tenant having security of tenure increasing the rent payable under a regulated tenancy, or granting a fresh regulated tenancy at a higher rent, if taking effect after 1 January 1973, and when no rent is registered under the 1971 Act, Part IV, must be in writing signed by landlord and tenant and contain a statement at the head thereof that the tenant's security under the 1971 Act will not be affected if he refuses to enter into the agreement and that entry will not deprive either party of the right to apply to the rent officer for registration of a fair rent.[91] Special provisions apply following conversion or where grant-aided improvements are carried out.[92] Failure on the landlord's part to observe any of the requirements of Ss. 42–4 renders the extra rent irrecoverable.[93]

Release from rent regulation

The Secretary of State has power on conditions to release dwelling-houses subject to regulated tenancies from protection.[94]

Security of tenure—statutory tenancy

After the termination of a 'protected tenancy' under the 1971 Act, the person who, immediately before that termination, was the protected tenant, so long as he retains possession of the dwelling-house,[95] without being entitled to do so under a contractual tenancy, is the statutory tenant. After the death of a tenant who was a protected tenant or a statutory tenant Schedule 1, as amended, determines what person is the statutory tenant by succession.[96] A statutory tenancy may be transmitted twice under Sch. 1, and the second transmission

[88] S. 7(2).
[89] S. 7(4).
[90] S. 117.
[91] 1972 Act, S. 42.
[92] Ibid., Ss. 43–4.
[93] Ibid., S. 45.
[94] S. 117.
[95] Loss of possession to a substantial extent involves loss of protection: *Skinner* v. *Geary* [1931] 2 K.B. 546; *Menzies* v. *Mackay*, 1938 S.C. 74; *Stewart* v. *Mackay*, 1947 S.C. 287. Occupation by a deserted wife is not equivalent to possession by the tenant: *Temple* v. *Mitchell*, 1956 S.C. 267.
[96] S. 3. Sched. 1 is amended by 1980 Act, S. 56.

converts it into a regulated tenancy. A statutory tenancy is a personal right to retain possession and in general cannot be assigned or bequeathed.[97] So long as he retains possession a statutory tenant is bound by the terms and conditions of the original tenancy, so far as consistent with the 1971 Act.[98] It is an offence for a statutory tenant to ask or receive any money from any person other than the landlord as a condition of giving up possession.[99] With the consent of the landlord a statutory tenant may assign the statutory tenancy by agreement in writing; the assignee obtains no better title than enjoyed by the assignor.[1]

Premiums

It is, subject to qualifications, an offence to require or receive any premium or loan as a condition of the grant, renewal, continuance or assignation of a protected tenancy.[2]

Rents under regulated tenancies

The rent payable during any contractual period may not exceed the contractual rent limit, which, if rent has been registered under Part IV[3] of the Act is the contractual rent limit.[4] The rent payable for any statutory period may not exceed the rent payable for the last contractual period save that, where the rent is registered under Part IV of the Act,[4] it may be the registered rent, failing which the rent determined under Ss. 22 to 24.[5] Notices of increases must be in the prescribed form.[6] Sums paid in excess of recoverable rent may be recovered, or deducted from rent payable, within two years from the date of payment.[7]

In the case of regulated tenancies rent officers and rent assessment committees must be appointed and constituted in registration areas.[8] The rent officer maintains a register and landlord or tenant may apply for the registration of a rent. Once registered an application for review may only exceptionally be made within three years.[9] The rent officer may grant a certificate of fair rent to a person proposing to let a dwelling-house.[10] In determining a fair rent under a regulated tenancy

---

[97] *Lovibond* v. *Vincent* [1929] 1 K.B. 687.
[98] S. 12.
[99] S. 13.
[1] Ss. 14–15.
[2] Ss. 101–3; see also Ss. 106–7.
[3] Ss. 37–47.
[4] S. 19. Ss. 19(3) and 20 are repealed by 1972 Act, S. 41.
[5] S. 21, amd. 1980 Act, S. 61.
[6] S. 25.   [7] S. 31.
[8] Ss. 37–8 and Sch. 5.
[9] Ss. 39–40 and Sch. 6; see also 1972 Act, S. 38.
[10] S. 41 and Sch. 7.

regard must be had to all the circumstances (other than personal circumstances) and in particular to the age, character, locality and state of repair of the dwelling-house and, if furniture is provided, to its quantity, quality and condition, it being assumed that the number of persons seeking to become tenants of similar dwelling-houses in the locality on the terms (other than those relating to rent) of the regulated tenancy is not substantially greater than the number of such dwelling-houses in the locality which are available for letting on such terms, and disregarding (a) any disrepair or other defect attributable to failure by the tenant, (b) any improvement including improvement to furniture, or the replacement of any fixture or fitting, carried out by the tenant otherwise than under the lease,[11] (c) any deterioration in the condition of any furniture provided due to ill-treatment by the tenant or sub-tenant. The amount to be registered as rent must include the amount payable for furniture or services provided, and is exclusive of local rates.[12] If the rent registered exceeds the rent contractually payable the difference cannot be recovered without a notice of increase; if it falls below the contractual rent the excess may be recovered.[13]

It is, subject to qualifications, an offence to require or receive any premium or loan as a condition of the grant renewal, continuance or assignation of a protected tenancy.[14] A requirement that rent be paid in advance is void and irrecoverable from the tenant, and if paid may be recovered by the tenant within two years from the date of payment.[15]

Public sector housing

Much housing is provided by local authorities and other public sector bodies. Statutory guidance is given on the allocation of houses to applicants.[16]

Rents of local authority houses

A local authority may make such reasonable charges as it may determine for the tenancy or occupation of houses provided by it. It

[11] S. 42 amd. 1974 Act, Sch. 1 and 1980 Act, S. 47; see *Stewart's J.F.* v. *Gallagher,* 1967 S.C. 59; *Crofton Inv. Tr.* v. *Greater London Rent Cttee.* [1967] 2 Q.B. 955; *Anglo Italian Properties* v. *London Rent Panel* [1969] 1 W.L.R. 730; *Tormes Property Co.* v. *Landau* [1970] 3 All E.R. 653; *Skilling* v. *Arcari's Exrx.,* 1974 S.C. (H.L.) 42; *Western Heritable Investment Co.* v. *Inglis,* 1978 S.C. 304. A Rent Assessment Committee must observe the rules of natural justice: *Learmonth Property Investment Co.* v. *Aitken,* 1970 S.C. 223. On a Rent Assessment Committee's duty to give reasons for its decision see *Albyn Properties Ltd.* v. *Knox,* 1977 S.C. 108 reversed by 1980 Act.
[12] S. 43; see also 1972 Act, S. 40.
[13] S. 44, substituted by 1980 Act, S. 48. See also S. 44A added by 1972 Act, S. 39 and S. 44B added by 1980 Act, S. 50.
[14] Ss. 101–3; see also Ss. 106–7.
[15] Ss. 108–9 amd. 1980 Act, S. 57.
[16] Tenants' Rights (Sc.) Act, 1980, Ss. 26–7.

must from time to time review rents and make such changes of rents and rebates as circumstances may require.[17]

Rents of subsidised private houses

The rent of houses provided under certain enactments are limited to the rent which might properly be charged by virtue of a condition mentioned in any of the said enactments together with any sum recoverable by way of repairs increase or S. 50 increase.[18]

Rents of houses let by housing associations and the Housing Corporation

Where a house belongs to a housing association or the Housing Corporation and the tenancy would be a protected tenancy but for the 1971 Act, S. 5 rents are to be registrable under the 1971 Act, Part IV, with effect from 1 January 1973, and the rent registered is the rent limit, with certain qualifications. Provision is made for phased progression to a registered rent.[19]

Rent rebates and rent allowances

Every local authority must have a scheme for granting to occupants of local authority houses rebates from rent calculated in accordance with the scheme by reference to their needs and resources. This applies also to development corporation and S.S.H.A. houses.[20] Every local authority must have a scheme for granting to private tenants (protected tenants or statutory tenants and certain others) in their district allowances towards the rent payable under their tenancies.[21] Rebate schemes and allowances schemes must conform with the 1972 Act.[22] Private landlords must inform tenants about the allowance scheme.

Payment of rent

The general rules as to discharge of an obligation by payment apply to payments of rent. Discharge may be made expressly or by implication, by the presumption from the production of three discharges for consecutive termly payments that all preceding payments have been made.[23] Furthermore actions for rent prescribe in five years.[24]

---

[17] Housing Rents and Subsidies (Sc.) Act, 1975, S. 1.
[18] Rent Act, 1971, S. 128.
[19] Housing (Financial Provisions) (Sc.) Act, 1972, Ss. 60–8.
[20] Housing (Financial Provisions) (Sc.) Act, 1972, S. 15.
[21] Ibid., S. 16, amd. Furnished Lettings (Rent Allowances) Act, 1973, Sch. 2, and Rent Act, 1974, S. 12.
[22] Ibid., S. 17 and Sch. 2 and 3.
[23] i.e. The *apocha trium annorum*; Stair I, 18, 2; Bankt. I, 24, 13; Ersk. III, 4, 10; Bell, *Prin.* §567, 585.
[24] Prescription and Limitation (Sc.) Act, 1973, S. 6.

A claim for rent may be extinguished by compensation,[25] as where the tenant has a liquid counter-claim for goods sold to the landlord, but not where the tenant's claim is illiquid, as for damages,[26] unless that claim can be liquidated at once.[27]

Retention of rent

The tenant[28] may retain, and withhold payment of the whole or part of the rent admittedly due if the landlord has failed substantially to perform obligations incumbent on him under the lease, such as failing to put the tenant or maintain him in possession of a material part of the subjects let,[29] or withholding an accessory of the subjects let,[30] or failure to erect buildings promised,[31] or failure to put buildings into tenantable state,[32] or failure to execute necessary repairs, whereby the tenant suffered damage,[33] but not for failure in minor respects, such as temporary failure of water supply to a farm[34] or temporary defects in drainage.[35]

Retention of rent is an equitable remedy and, apart from express provision, not an implied term of a lease. It may be excluded by the terms of the lease.[36]

Whether to allow retention or not is in the discretion of the court, and it is rarely allowed where the landlord's failure is in a respect collateral to the giving and maintenance of possession or the main purpose of the lease, or the damage alleged is insubstantial.[37] If retention is refused the tenant must resort to a claim of damages, but a valid claim of retention does not preclude a claim of damages as well.[38]

A tenant who has obtained damages against the landlord cannot

[25] Compensation Act, 1592; Stair I, 18, 6; Bankt. I, 24, 23; Ersk. III, 4, 11; Bell, *Comm.* II, 553; *Prin.* §572.

[26] *Humphrey* v. *Mackay* (1883) 10 R. 647; *Sheppherd* v. *McNab* (1896) 3 S.L.T. 240; *Christie* v. *Birrell,* 1910 S.C. 986.

[27] *Johnstone* v. *Cleghorn* (1824) 2 S. 688; *Johnston* v. *Inglis* (1832) 10 S. 260; *Davie* v. *Stark* (1876) 3 R. 1114; *Inch* v. *Lee* (1903) 11 S.L.T. 874.

[28] Excluding a statutory tenant holding under the Rent Acts: *Stobbs* v. *Hislop,* 1948 S.C. 216.

[29] *Duncan* v. *Brooks* (1894) 21 R. 760.

[30] *Kilmarnock Gas Light Co.* v. *Smith* (1872) 11 M. 58.

[31] *Campbell* v. *Mundell* (1896) 3 S.L.T. 287.

[32] *Munro* v. *McGeochs* (1888) 16 R. 93; *McDonald* v. *Kydd* (1901) 3 F. 923; *E. Galloway* v. *McConnell,* 1911 S.C. 846; *Haig* v. *Boswall-Preston,* 1915 S.C. 339; contrast *Stewart* v. *Campbell* (1889) 16 R. 346.

[33] *Fingland & Mitchell* v. *Howie,* 1926 S.C. 319.

[34] *Russell* v. *Sime,* 1912, 2 S.L.T. 344.

[35] *Burns* v. *McNeil* (1898) 5 S.L.T. 289; *Brown* v. *Simpson,* 1910, 1 S.L.T. 183.

[36] *Skene* v. *Cameron,* 1942 S.C. 393.

[37] *Johnston* v. *Inglis* (1832) 10 S. 260; *McRae* v. *Macpherson* (1843) 6 D. 302; *Dods* v. *Fortune* (1854) 16 D. 478.

[38] *Fingland & Mitchell* v. *Howie,* 1926 S.C. 319.

also retain his rent,[39] but he may retain in respect of an unsatisfied decree for damages for fundamental breach of the lease.[40]

A wider right of retention may be exercised in the event of the landlord's bankruptcy, on the principle of balancing accounts in bankruptcy,[41] of arrears due at the date of the first deliverance in the landlord's sequestration.[42]

Where a right of retention is properly exercised the rent may be consigned till the conditions are satisfied which will make it payable.[43]

Abatement of rent

By agreement rent fixed may be abated. A tenant is entitled to an abatement of rent if part of the subjects let have been rendered unusable by *damnum fatale,* as where houses have been burned.[44]

Landlord's remedies for rent

On non-payment of rent the landlord may bring a personal action for payment of the sum due and do any form of diligence thereon. An alleged agreement to allow an abatement from the rent stated in a written lease must be proved by writ or oath.[45]

At common law a legal right of irritancy existed when two years' rent was unpaid.[46] The Act of Sederunt of 14 December 1756 which regulated this remedy applies only to agricultural leases, so that in relation to urban leases irritancy can be enforced only by an extraordinary removing in the Court of Session.

The lease may contain provision for a conventional irritancy for non-payment of rent, which is non-purgeable and enforceable according to its terms.[47] Enforcement of an irritancy bars a claim of damages for premature termination of the lease.[48]

Under the House Letting and Rating Act, 1911, S. 5, if the tenant of a small dwelling-house under that Act is in arrears with rent for not less than seven days, forty-eight hours' notice of termination of let may be given, and (S. 6) if the tenant fails to remove a summary application for removing may be brought in the Sheriff or Burgh Police Court. The

---

[39] *Christie* v. *Wilson,* 1915 S.C. 645.

[40] *Marshall's Trs.* v. *Banks,* 1934 S.C. 405.

[41] Bell, *Comm.* II, 124.

[42] Bankruptcy (Sc.) Act, 1913, Ss. 41, 97.

[43] *McDonald* v. *Kydd* (1901) 3 F. 923.

[44] *Duff* v. *Fleming* (1870) 8 M. 769; *Allan* v. *Markland* (1882) 10 R. 383; *Critchley* v. *Campbell* (1884) 11 R. 475; *Sharp* v. *Thomson,* 1930 S.C. 1092.

[45] *Turnbull* v. *Oliver* (1891) 19 R. 154.

[46] Stair II, 9, 32; Bankt. II, 9, 23; Ersk.II, , 44; cf. *M. Breadalbane* v. *Stewart* (1904) 6 F. (H.L.) 23.

[47] *Stewart* v. *Watson* (1864) 2 M. 1414; *McDouall's Tr.* v. *Macleod,* 1949 S.C. 593; *Lucas's Exors.* v. *Demarco,* 1968 S.L.T. 89; *Dorchester Studios Ltd.* v. *Stone,* 1975 S.C. (H.L.) 56.

[48] *Buttercase* v *Geddie* (1897) 24 R. 1128.

court may grant not more than forty-eight hours delay unless on cause shown, or on caution for, or consignation of, the rent due being found or made.

Hypothec

The landlord also has at common law a right of hypothec[49] in the case of houses, shops, market gardens, and mines,[50] but not now available over subjects let for agriculture or pasture and exceeding two acres in extent,[51] which confers a right in security, without the need to take possession, over *invecta et illata* in the subjects, such as furniture and plenishing, stock in trade, and equipment, and moveables generally,[52] but not over money, bonds, bills, the tenant's clothes[53] and, probably, his tools of trade.[54] It covers also goods on the premises, held on hire[55] or hire-purchase, or sold but not removed,[56] but not goods, not hired, belonging to a third party such as a member of the family or lodger,[57] nor single articles, hired or not hired, in premises let furnished, where the remainder of the furnishing does not fall within the hypothec.[58] The true owner's remedy in these cases is to appear before the sheriff and claim to have them withdrawn from the sequestration.[59] Hypothec covers a subtenant's goods in respect of his subrent, and also of the principal rent.[60]

In the case of lets of small dwellings covered by the House Letting and Rating Act, 1911, it does not (S. 10) cover bedding material, all tools and implements of trade, used or to be used by the occupier or any member of his family as his means of livelihood, which are in the house, and also such further furniture and plenishing as the occupier may select to the value of £10, according to the sheriff-officer's valuation.

The landlord may interdict the tenant from removing the *invecta et*

---

[49] Stair I, 13, 14; Bankt. I, 18, 7; Ersk. II, 6, 56; Bell, *Prin.* §1234.

[50] *Linlithgow Oil Co. v. E. Rosebery* (1903) 6 F. 90.

[51] Hypothec Abolition Act, 1880; as to houses and fields let separately see *Clark v. Keirs* (1888) 15 R. 458.

[52] Including animals: *Lamb v. Grant* (1874) 11 S.L.R. 672 (cow and calf); hired goods: *Dundee Corpn. v. Marr*, 1971 S.C. 96; beer kegs left by brewers: *Scottish & Newcastle Breweries v. Edinburgh District Council*, 1979 S.L.T. (Notes) 11.

[53] Bell, *Prin.* §1276.

[54] *Macpherson v. M's Tr.* (1905) 8 F. 191.

[55] *Penson v. Robertson*, 6 June 1820, F.C.; *Nelmes v. Ewing* (1883) 11 R. 193; *McIntosh v. Potts* (1905) 7 F. 765.

[56] *Ryan v. Little*, 1910 S.C. 219; but see *Lippe v. Colville* (1894) 1 S.L.T. 616.

[57] *Bell v. Andrews* (1885) 12 R. 961; *Pulsometer Engineering Co. v. Gracie* (1887) 14 R. 316 (agent's samples).

[58] *Edinburgh Albert Bldgs. Co. v. General Guarantee Corpn.*, 1917 S.C. 239; *Dundee Corpn.*, *supra*. As to goods under 'sale or return' contract see *Macdonald v. Westren* (1888) 15 R. 988.

[59] *Lindsay v. E. Wemyss* (1872) 10 M. 708.

[60] *Steuart v. Stables* (1878) 5 R. 1024.

illata and, if they have been removed, may after intimation to the tenant, which may for exceptional reasons stated be dispensed with,[61] obtain judicial warrant to have them brought back,[62] but these are exceptional measures importing liability in damages if obtained by statements not justified[63] or if there is genuine dispute as to rent and such extreme measures are unnecessary in the circumstances.[64]

If no application is made to enforce the hypothec by landlord's sequestration the *invecta et illata* may be removed or sold, but if sequestration is granted it attaches goods not removed even though sold and the landlord's claim is superior to that of the purchaser.[65]

Extent of security conferred by hypothec

The right of hypothec gives security for one year's rent, but not for prior arrears.[66] If not sought to be enforced within three months of the last term of payment, the right falls.[67]

Sequestration for rent

The landlord enforces his right of hypothec by petition for land-lord's sequestration in the Sheriff Court.[68] It is usual to sequestrate for rent due and in security of that falling due at the next term.[69] Warrant to sequestrate is normally obtained on an *ex parte* statement by the landlord, and under this a sheriff officer inventories and values the *invecta et illata*.[70] They are then deemed *in manibus curiae* and any person removing them, if acting in good faith, must account for their value, or, if in bad faith, incurs liability for the rent.[71] The order for sequestration will be recalled on payment or consignation of the rent.[72] Failing payment, the landlord then obtains warrant from the court to have the sequestrated goods sold by auction. The owner of property hired by the tenant should apply to the sheriff or judge of the roup to

---

[61] *Johnston . Young* (1890) 18 R. (J.) 6; *McLaughlan* v. *Reilly* (1892) 20 R. 41; *Jack* v. *Black*, 1911 S.C. 691.

[62] *Nelmes* v. *Ewing* (1883) 11 R. 193; *Donald* v. *Leitch* (1886) 13 R. 790.

[63] *Jack, supra; Shearer* v. *Nicoll*, 1935 S.L.T. 313.

[64] *Gray* v. *Weir* (1891) 19 R. 25.

[65] *Ryan* v. *Little*, 1910 S.C. 219.

[66] *Young* v. *Welsh* (1833) 12 S. 233.

[67] *Thomson* v. *Barclay* (1883) 10 R. 694; *Donald* v. *Leitch* (1886) 13 R. 790.

[68] *Duncan* v. *Lodijinsky* (1904) 6 F. 408. A landlord has been held disentitled to sequestrate where he was himself materially in breach of contract; *Guthrie* v. *Shearer* (1873) 1 R. 181; *Tennent's Trs.* v. *Maxwell* (1880) 17 S.L.R. 463. But it is no defence that the tenant merely has an illiquid claim against the landlord: *Hoggs* v. *Caldwell* (1882) 19 S.L.R. 452.

[69] *Donald* v. *Leitch* (1886) 13 R. 790.

[70] Including effects belonging to unauthorized subtenant: *Lippe* v. *Colville* (1894) 1 S.L.T. 616. As to procedure see *Taylor* v. *MacKnight* (1882) 9 R. 857.

[71] Bell, *Prin.* §1244; *Stewart* v. *Peddie* (1874) 2 R. 94; *Jack* v. *McCaig* (1880) 7 R. 465.

[72] *Tennant's Trs.* v. *Maxwell* (1880) 17 S.L.R. 463.

have the property reserved and the tenant's own property sold first, failing which he has no claim against the landlord.[73]

Sequestration for rent does not prevent an ordinary creditor providing the sequestrated effects to attach any reversion left after the landlord's debt is satisfied.[74]

The landlord is liable in damages if he has used sequestration unjustifiably[75] but not merely because the tenant propounded a counter-claim which is well founded.[76]

The landlord's right to sequestrate for rent is unaffected by the mercantile sequestration of the tenant[77] but claims having preferential ranking in bankruptcy have priority over the landlord's claim for rent out of the proceeds of sale.

Regulation of use of subjects let

Apart from not inverting the possession, common law does not impose restrictions on the use made of subjects let. Express conditions frequently prohibit use of the premises for business,[78] for particular trades,[79] or for any trade likely to be a nuisance.[80]

Extension or renewal of lease

A lease may be extended for a further period on the same terms and conditions, or be renewed on different terms, in any of the modes in which an original lease can be constituted and proved. Neither party is bound by negotiations or proposals not accepted but the continuance of negotiations excludes any inference of agreement, such as extends the lease under the principle of tacit relocation.[81] Hence if the tenant remains in possession after the expiry of the old lease, this may raise an inference of acceptance of the new terms offered.

Termination of lease before ish

An urban lease may be terminated before the date of expiry by renunciation, or where an irritancy has been incurred.

---

[73] *Lindsay* v. *E. Wemyss* (1872) 10 M. 708; *McIntosh* v. *Potts* (1905) 7 F. 765.

[74] *Wyllie* v. *Fisher*, 1907 S.C. 686.

[75] *Riddle* v. *Mitchell* (1870) 8 S.L.R. 140; *Turnbull* v. *Oliver* (1891) 19 R. 154; *Pollock* v. *Goodwin's Trs.* (1898) 25 R. 1051; *Alexander* v. *Campbell's Trs.* (1903) 5 F. 634; *Gilmour* v. *Graig* (1908) 15 S.L.T. 797; *Gray* v. *Smart* (1892) 19 R. 692; *Jack* v. *Black*, 1911 S.C. 691; *Shearer* v. *Nicoll*, 1935 S.L.T. 313.

[76] *Craig* v. *Harkness* (1894) 2 S.L.T. 307.

[77] Bankruptcy (Sc.) Act, 1913, S. 115.

[78] e.g. *Ewing* v. *Hastie* (1878) 5 R. 439 (school); cf. *Colville* v. *Carrick* (1883) 10 R. 1241; *Graham* v. *Shiels* (1901) 8 S.L.T. 368 (nursing home).

[79] e.g. *Macdonald* v. *Campbell* (1889) 16 R. 540.

[80] *Frame* v. *Cameron* (1864) 3 M. 290.

[81] *Macfarlane* v. *Mitchell* (1900) 2 F. 901; *Buchanan* v. *Harris & Sheldon* (1900) 2 F. 935. On tacit relocation, see *infra*.

Renunciation

A tenant may renounce his lease where the landlord has been in fundamental breach of contract.

Extraordinary removing

A declarator that an irritancy has been incurred and that a tenant must remove, under pain of ejection, may be brought in the Court of Session, or Sheriff Court.[82] The irritancy may be legal, arising on default in payment of rent for two successive years,[83] or conventional, contained in the lease, to cover such cases as the tenant's bankruptcy[84] or non-payment of rent for a stated period.[85] The declaratory conclusion is not always essential.[85] A legal irritancy may be purged by payment before decree passes, but a conventional irritancy cannot be so purged unless it merely expresses a legal irritancy.[86] A landlord may found on an irritancy provision though on a previous default he has waived his option to terminate the lease.[87]

Restriction on diligence and expenses

No diligence may be done in respect of the rent of any dwelling-house let on a protected tenancy or subject to a statutory tenancy except with the leave of the sheriff, and on any such application the sheriff has powers to adjourn, sist, suspend or postpone, just as he has under S. 11 in relation to possession.[88] In certain circumstances the court may not award expenses to the landlord unless it considers it reasonable to do so.[89]

TERMINATION OF LEASE

Termination of lease at ish

The expiry of the contractual duration of a lease terminates it only if either party has given due notice to the other of his intention to terminate it. Failing such notice tacit relocation applies.

---

[82] Sheriff Courts (Sc.) Act, 1907, Ss. 5(3), (4), 7.
[83] Stair II, 9, 32; Bankt. II, 9, 23; Ersk. II, 6, 44; In the case of urban subjects (not affected by the Act of Sederunt, 14 Dec. 1756) the extraordinary removing must be in the Court of Session: *Cormack* v. *Copland* (1754) 5 B.S. 820; *Nisbet* v. *Aikman* (1866) 4 M. 284.
[84] *Bidoulac* v. *Sinclair's Tr.* (1889) 17 R. 144.
[85] *D. Argyll* v. *Campbeltown Coal Co.*, 1924 S.C. 844.
[86] *Duncanson* v. *Giffen* (1878) 15 S.L.R. 356; *McDouall's Trs.* v. *Macleod*, 1949 S.C. 593.
[87] *Lurie* v. *Demarco*, 1967 S.L.T. (Notes) 110.
[88] Rent Act, 1971, S. 129(1).
[89] Ibid., S. 129(2).

Tacit relocation

Where there has been no express agreement for a renewal or extension of a lease, but neither party has given due notice of intention to terminate the lease at the expiry of its term, an extension of the lease is implied by law for the same period as the expiring lease, if for less than a year, and, if for a term of years, for a further year, on the same terms and conditions.[90] It may continue thereafter for further periods in the same way. Tacit relocation may be inferred also where a landlord has given notice to quit but has taken no further action and allowed the tenant to remain in possession.[91] It is founded on the implied consent of all parties to the lease; accordingly notice by one of joint tenants is enough to exclude tacit relocation.[92] Tacit relocation is excluded by agreement for a new lease, even if improbative, but on which possession had continued,[93] or by the tenant's continuance in circumstances implying his acquiescence in new conditions intimated,[94] or by even verbal notice of intention to terminate,[95] but not by an ineffectual notice to quit.[96] If a tenant has given notice but then refuses to leave he cannot rely on tacit relocation, and is liable to be ejected as a squatter and liable for violent profits, i.e. for the greatest sum for which the subjects could have been let.[97]

The principle of tacit relocation is probably inapplicable to leases which are, by common understanding, seasonal only, such as of furnished houses, grass parks, fishings and shootings.[98] It does not apply to rights of occupancy of a house as an incident of a contract of service.[99] An option to renew a lease is not a term continued by tacit relocation after its expiry.[1]

Ordinary removings

A lease accordingly terminates at the ish only if either party has given to the other, before the date of expiry of the lease, due notice of termination.

Where houses, with or without land attached not exceeding two

---

[90] Stair II, 9, 23; Bankt. II, 9, 32; Ersk. II, 6, 35; Bell, *Prin.* §1265; cf. *Neilson* v. *Mossend Iron Co.* (1887) 13 R. (H.L.) 50, 54; *Douglas* v. *Cassillis & Culzean Estates*, 1944 S.C. 355.

[91] *Taylor* v. *E. Moray* (1892) 19 R. 399; *Milner's C.B.* v. *Mason*, 1965 S.L.T. (Sh. Ct.) 56.

[92] *Smith* v. *Grayton Estates, Ltd.*, 1960 S.C. 349.

[93] *Buchanan* v. *Harris & Sheldon* (1900) 2 F. 935.

[94] *Macfarlane* v. *Mitchell* (1900) 2 F. 901.

[95] *Craighall Cast-Stone Co.* v. *Wood*, 1931 S.C. 66.

[96] *Gates* v. *Blair*, 1923 S.C. 430.

[97] *Tod* v. *Fraser* (1889) 17 R. 226.

[98] *Macharg* (1805) Mor. Removing, Appx. 4.

[99] *Dunbar's Trs.* v. *Bruce* (1900) 3 F. 137; *Sinclair* v. *Tod*, 1907 S.C. 1038; *Cairns* v. *Innes*, 1942 S.C. 164.

[1] *Commercial Union Assce. Co.* v. *Watt*, 1964 S.C. 85.

acres, lands not exceeding two acres let without houses, mills, fishings and shootings, and other heritable subjects (except land exceedings two acres in extent) are let for a year or more, notice of termination must be given in writing by or on behalf of one party to the other at least forty days before the termination of the tenancy (Whitsunday or Martinmas as the case may be).[2]

The normal term dates are Whitsunday (15 May) and Martinmas (11 November) but, in the absence of express stipulation, a tenant shall enter or remove from a house at noon on 28 May or 28 November, as the case may be, or if that date be a Sunday, on the next day.[3] Despite this, where warning to remove is given forty days before, it must be forty days before 15 May or 11 November.[4] Notice does not warrant summary ejection from the subjects let, but entitles the proprietor to apply to the sheriff for a warrant for summary ejection[5] in common form against the tenant and everyone deriving right from him.[6] Informal notice by the tenant of intention to quit suffices, the requirement of written notice applying only where the procedure for summary ejection is being followed out.[7]

Summary application for removing

Where houses or other heritable subjects are let for less than a year, any authorized person may present to the sheriff a summary application for removing, decree in which has the effect of a decree of removing and warrant of ejection. In the absence of express stipulation notice to remove[8] must be, in the case of a let for not more than four months, one third of the period of let,[9] and where the let exceeds four months, at least forty days.[10]

---

[2] Sheriff Courts (Sc.) Act, 1907, S. 37; see also Sched. I, Rules 110–14, and Form V. The notice must specify the subjects: *Scott* v. *Livingstone,* 1919 S.C. I. Where two premises are let for a *cumulo* rent a notice to quit applicable to one only is ineffectual to exclude tacit relocation in respect of both: *Gates, supra.* The common law form of action applies also to controlled tenancies: *Purves* v. *Graham,* 1924 S.C. 477. The requirement of written notice applies only when procedure for summary ejection is being followed and informal notice, at least by the tenant, suffices for an ordinary removing.

[3] Removal Terms (Sc.) Act, 1886, S. 4. Notice to remove 'at Whitsunday' is good: *Campbell's Trs.* v. *O'Neill,* 1911 S.C. 188.

[4] 1907 Act, S. 37; cf. *Dunlop* v. *Meiklem* (1876) 4 R. 11; *Fraser's Trs.* v. *Maule* (1904) 6 F. 819. Contrast case of service tenancy: *Stewart* v. *Robertson,* 1937 S.C. 801.

[5] This is a misnomer for 'summary removing': *Campbell's Trs.* v. *O'Neill,* 1911 S.C. 188.

[6] 1907 Act, S. 37; cf. *Robb* v. *Brearton* (1895) 22 R. 885.

[7] *Craighall Cast Stone Co.* v. *Wood Bros.,* 1931 S.C. 66.

[8] Sheriff Courts (Sc.) Act, 1907, S. 38, and Sched. Form K.

[9] Subject to a minimum of 28 days: Rent Act, 1971, S. 131.

[10] Sheriff Courts (Sc.) Act, 1907, S. 38, and Sheriff Court Rules, 115–22, Actions for summary removing are dealt with summarily as under the Small Debt Acts, and are not subject to review: Rule 119; but the decree may be suspended if the proceedings are fundamentally null: *Robertson* v. *Thorburn,* 1927 S.L.T. 562; see also *Mackay* v. *Menzies,* 1937 S.C. 691. No appeal lies to the High Court of Justiciary: *Lovell* v. *Macfarlane,* 1949 J.C. 123.

Summary removing from small dwelling-houses

In small dwellings, regulated by the House Letting and Rating Act, 1911, lets, except for a shorter period than a month, terminate and are terminable only at noon on the 28th of a month or, if that date be a Sunday, on the next Monday, and lets for a shorter period than a month terminate and are terminable at noon on a Monday.[11] Notice of termination on the day on which the next payment of rent falls due may be given by either party in accordance with the provisions of the 1907 Act but expire only at noon on the day on which a payment of rent falls due or, if that is not a lawful date for the termination of a let under the Act, at noon on the next lawful day. If the let is for more than three months, forty days' notice must be given; if for less, the notice is one-third of the period of let[12] with a minimum of twenty-eight days.[13] If, however, the occupier of a small dwelling-house is in arrear with the rent for not less than seven days, the landlord may give notice to terminate the let twenty-eight days later.[14]

If the occupier fails to remove, the owner may make to the sheriff a summary application for removing, decree in which has the effect of a decree of removing and warrant of ejection. The sheriff or magistrate may not grant a delay of more than forty-eight hours unless on cause shown, or on caution found for or consignation of the rent due.[15]

Extraordinary removing

An extraordinary removing is brought to give effect to an irritancy incurred. Caution for violent profits can be required only after the incurring of the irritancy has been established.[16]

Statutory powers to terminate leases

If an executor in whom a deceased intestate's interest under a lease has vested, is satisfied that the interest cannot be disposed of according to law and so informs the landlord, or the interest is not so disposed of within a year or such longer period as may be agreed or fixed by the sheriff, either party may, on giving six months' notice, terminate the lease.[17]

Where premises, in respect of which a closing order, demolition order, clearance order or resolution declaring a building an obstruction has become operative, is the subject of a lease or sublease, either

---

[11] 1911 Act, S. 3.
[12] S. 4, as amd. by Rent Act, 1957, Sched. 6, para. 30.
[13] Rent Act, 1957, S. 16, and Sched. 6, para. 30.
[14] S. 5, as amd. by Rent Act, 1957, ched. 6, para. 30.
[15] 1911 Act, S. 6.
[16] *Simpson* v. *Goswami,* 1976 S.L.T. (Sh. Ct.) 94.
[17] Succession (Sc.) Act, 1964, S. 16(3); see also S. 16(7).

party may apply to the sheriff for an order determining the lease which he may order, conditionally or unconditionally.[18]

Ejection

An action of ejection,[19] craving warrant summarily to eject the defender from certain premises, is appropriate where the occupier has never had legal title to occupy the premises,[20] such as a squatter, or intruder encroaching on property, or a tenant whose tenancy has been terminated by notice but who, though not entitled to remain as a statutory tenant, refuses to remove,[21] or a person whose title to occupy has terminated, such as a servant entitled to occupy a house as part of his remuneration and now dismissed.[22] The pursuer must show that the possession was *vi, clam, aut precario*.[23] It is incompetent where the person in possession founds on a title to possess,[24] or had a title which is said to have terminated.[25]

An owner is not entitled at his own hand to eject a person in possession on an *ex facie* valid title, even on allegation that the person obtained the let by fraud.[26]

Caution for violent profits

A defender may be required to find caution for violent profits resulting from his delay or refusal to remove. This should normally be by bond of caution and is confined to cases falling under the Sheriff Courts (Sc.) Act, 1907, Sched. I, rules 110 (removing after forty days' notice) or 121 (summary removing).[27]

Statutory restrictions on removing tenants

In houses protected by the Rent Act, 1971, the landlord may, save by

[18] Housing (Sc.) Act, 1966, S. 187.

[19] A warrant of ejection is the executory part of the decree in an action for removing or summary removing. As to the substantive action of ejection see *Price* v. *Watson,* 1951 S.C. 359. An ejection is not incompetent merely because a question of law is involved: *Whyte* v. *Haddington Sch. Bd.* (1874) 1 R. 1124; *Cairns* v. *Innes,* 1942 S.C. 164; *Asher* v. *Macleod,* 1948 S.C. 55. As to appeal see *Mackay* v. *Menzies,* 1937 S.C. 691.

[20] *Colquhoun's Trs.* v. *Purdie,* 1946 S.N. 3; cf. *Paterson* v. *Robertson,* 1944 J.C. 166. As to ejection of spouse see *McLure* v. *McL.,* 1911 S.C. 200; *Millar* v. *M.,* 1940 S.C. 56; *Labno* v. *L.,* 1949 S.L.T. (Notes) 18.

[21] e.g. *Cowan* v. *Acton,* 1952 S.C. 73; *N.C.B.* v. *McInnes,* 1968 S.C. 321.

[22] cf. *Dunbar's Trs.* v. *Bruce* (1900) 3 F. 137; *Sinclair* v. *Tod,* 1907 S.C. 1038; *Cairns, supra;* contrast *MacGregor* v. *Dunnet,* 1949 S.C. 510.

[23] *Hally* v. *Lang* (1867) 5 M. 951; *Sc. Prop. Inv. Co.* v. *Horne* (1881) 8 R. 737; *Lowe* v. *Gardiner,* 1921 S.C. 211; *Cairns, supra.*

[24] *Wallace* v. *Kerr,* 1917 S.C. 102; *Lowe* v. *Gardiner,* 1921 S.C. 211; *Scottish Supply Assocn.* v. *Mackie,* 1921 S.C. 882.

[25] *Hally* v. *Lang* (1867) 5 M. 951; *Scottish Property Inv. Co. Bldg. Soc.* v. *Horne* (1881) 8 R. 737; *Lowe, supra;* *Cook* v. *Wylie,* 1963 S.L.T. (Sh. Ct.) 29.

[26] *Brash* v. *Munro & Hall* (1903) 5 F. 1102.

[27] *Mackays* v. *Deas,* 1977 S.L.T. (Sh. Ct.) 10.

agreement, recover possession of the controlled house only under a decree of court.

Statutory tenancy

After the termination of a protected tenancy of a dwelling-house the person who, immediately before the termination was the protected tenant is the statutory tenant so long as he retains possession of the dwelling-house[28] without being entitled to do so under a contractual tenancy.[29]

After the death of a person who, immediately before his death, was either a protected tenant or the statutory tenant under S. 3(1)(a), Sched. 1 of the 1971 Act determines what person, if any, is the statutory tenant.[30] That person is the tenant's widow, or a member of the original tenant's family residing with him at the time of and for six months before his death, or, if more than one such person, such one of them as may be decided by agreement or, failing agreement, by the sheriff. Such a person is the first successor.[31]

If immediately before his death the first successor was still a statutory tenant his widow, or a member of his family residing with him is to be statutory tenant.[32]

These provisions override any prohibition of assignation in the lease and apply whether the tenant died testate or intestate. If a protected tenant dies and the lease is not thereby terminated it may pass under his will or to his heirs on intestacy. The rights of the heir are deemed suspended while the statutory successor, or successors, occupy the house.[33] If the heir and the statutory successor are the same person, he is presumed to occupy as successor under the Act.[34]

A statutory tenancy is not assignable nor inheritable nor capable of bequest nor does it pass to an executor.[35]

Recovery of possession of house under protected or statutory tenancy

A court may not make an order for possession of a dwelling-house let on a protected tenancy or subject to a statutory tenancy unless the court considers it reasonable to do so[36] and (a) the court is satisfied that suitable alternative accommodation is available for the tenant or will

[28] cf. *Stewart* v. *Mackay,* 1947 S.C. 287.
[29] S. 3(1)(a).
[30] S. 3(1)(b).
[31] Sch. I, paras. 1–4.
[32] Ibid., paras. 5–8. The second transmission converts the controlled tenancy into a regulated tenancy: Sched. 2, para. 15. These paragraphs do not apply where the statutory tenancy of the original tenant arose by virtue of the Rent Act, 1965, S. 20.
[33] *Moodie* v. *Hosegood* [1952] A.C. 61.
[34] *Grant's Trs.* v. *Arrol,* 1954 S.C. 306.
[35] *Lovibond* v. *Vincent* [1929] 1 K.B. 687.
[36] cf. *Barclay* v. *Hannah,* 1947 S.C. 245.

be available for him when the order takes effect,[37] or (b) the circumstances are as specified in any of the Cases in Sched. 3, Part I of the Act.[38] These Cases, stated shortly, are where (1) rent due has not been paid,[39] or any other obligation of the tenancy[40] has been broken or not performed; (2) the tenant or subtenant or lodger has been guilty of a nuisance or annoyance to adjoining occupiers or convicted of using the house, or allowing it to be used for immoral or illegal purposes;[41] (3) the tenant has by neglect or default caused deterioration of the dwelling-house; (3A)[42] where furniture has deteriorated by ill-treatment; (4) the tenant has given notice to quit and in consequence the landlord contracted to sell or let the house or has taken other steps whereby he would be prejudiced if he could not obtain possession;[43] (5) the tenant has without consent assigned or sublet the house;[44] (6) the premises consist of or include off-licensed premises and the tenant has committed an offence as licence-holder or the renewal of the licence has been refused; (7) the house is reasonably required by the landlord for a full-time employee;[45] (8) the house is reasonably required by the landlord for occupation by himself or certain close relatives;[46] (9) the rent charged by the tenant (a) for any sublet part of the house exceeded the maximum rent recoverable for that part under Parts III or V of the Act[47] or (b) exceeded the maximum which the lessor could recover under Part VII; (10) the house is so overcrowded as to be dangerous or injurious to the health of the inmates and the tenant has not removed any person causing the overcrowding.

The court in any such case may adjourn proceedings for possession, sist execution of the order, or postpone the date of possession for such period and subject to such conditions as it thinks fit.[48]

If an order is made under S. 10(1)(a) or (b) an authorized subtenant is protected from eviction and is thereafter deemed the tenant.[49]

---

[37] Sch. 3, Part IV, determines whether suitable alternative accommodation is or will be available: cf. *Burgh of Paisley* v. *Bamford*, 1950 S.L.T. 200; *Turner* v. *Keiller*, 1950 S.C. 43.

[38] S. 10(1). See Notices to Quit (Prescribed Information) (Protected Tenancies and Part VII contracts) (Sc.) Regulations, 1980 (S.I. No. 1667, 1980).

[39] cf. *Bird* v. *Hildage* [1948] 1 K.B. 91; *Dallanty* v. *Pellow* [1951] 2 K.B. 858.

[40] cf. *M. Bute* v. *Prenderleith*, 1921 S.C. 281; *Chapman* v. *Hughes* (1923) 129 L.T. 223.

[41] cf. *Schneiders* v. *Abrahams* [1925] 1 K.B. 301; *Hodson* v. *Jones* [1951] W.N. 127.

[42] Added by 1974 Act, Sched. 1.

[43] cf. *Craighall Cast-Stone Co.* v. *Wood*, 1931, S.C. 66.

[44] cf. *Dalrymple's Trs.* v. *Brown*, 1945 S.C. 190; *Baker* v. *Turner* [1905] A.C. 401; *Regional Properties Ltd.* v. *Frankenschwerth* [1951] 1 All E.R. 178; *Hyde* v. *Pimley* [1952] 2 Q.B. 506.

[45] cf. *M. Bute, supra; Barclay* v. *Hannah*, 1947 S.C. 245; *Grimond* v. *Duncan*, 1949 S.C. 195; as to obtaining order by misrepresentation, see S. 18.

[46] In relation to this case Sch. 3, Part III, applies. cf. *Kerrigan* v. *Nelson*, 1946 S.C. 388. As to obtaining order by misrepresentation, see S. 18.

[47] Amended by 1974 Act, Sched. 1. See also S. 64.

[48] S. 11.

[49] S. 17, amd. Rent Act, 1974, S. 13.

Where court must order possession of house let under regulated tenancy

If the landlord is otherwise entitled to possession of a house let on a regulated tenancy the court must make an order for possession if the circumstances fall under any of the Cases in Sched. 3, Part II.[50] These are, briefly, where (11) the house is required by the owner for occupation personally, or by a member of his family;[51] (11A) the owner bought it for retirement; (11B) it was let for a holiday; (11C) it was let for not more than twelve months;[52] (12) the house is held, and is now required, for occupation by a minister or full-time lay missionary; (13) the house is required for occupation by a person employed or to be employed in agriculture;[53] (14) the house is required for a person employed in agriculture where an amalgamation has been effected under the Agriculture Act, 1967; (15) the house is required for occupation by a person responsible for the control of farming in certain other circumstances; (16) the house was designed for a person with special needs and there is no longer such a person and the landlord requires it for a person with special needs;[54] (17) the house was let by member of the armed forces and is required by him.[54]

Other conditions of lease

A lease may contain other conditions such as an option to the tenant to buy, if the landlord should decide to sell,[55] or an option to purchase on notice given,[56] or permitting the erection and removal of greenhouses or temporary buildings.[57]

Recovery of possession of premises let under secure tenancy

The landlord may seek to recover possession of a house held under secure tenancy only after notice given in statutory form, specifying the ground which must be one of: (1) non-payment of rent, or breach of another obligation of the tenancy; (2) conviction for using the house for immoral or illegal purposes; (3) deterioration by the waste, neglect or default of the tenant, subtenant or lodger; (4) damage to furniture;

---

[50] S. 10(2). As regards the relevant dates for these Cases see Sch. 3, Part III.

[51] cf. *Maxwell* v. *Mulhern*, 1968 S.L.T. (Sh. Ct.) 43. Case 11 is amended by 1980 Act, S. 63.

[52] Cases added by 1974 Act, S. 3.

[53] cf. *Kemp* v. *Ballachulish Estate Co.*, 1933 S.C. 478; *Barclay* v. *Hannah*, 1947 S.C. 245.

[54] Cases (16) and (17) added by Tenants' Rights (Sc.) Act, 1980, S. 63, amd. Tenants' Rights (Sc.) Amdt. Act, 1980, S. 2.

[55] *Pickett* v. *Lindsay's Trs.* (1905) 13 S.L.T. 440; cf. *Fraser* v. *Denny, Mott & Dickson*, 1944 S.C. (H.L.) 35.

[56] *Penman* v. *Mackay*, 1922 S.C. 385.

[57] *Murray* v. *Campbell* (1879) 6 R. 1163; *Ferguson* v. *Paul* (1885) 12 R. 1222; see also *Burns* v. *Fleming* (1880) 8 R. 226.

(5) absence without reasonable cause for at least six months or non-occupation; (6) wish to transfer the secure tenancy to the spouse, former spouse or cohabitant of the tenant; (7) causing a nuisance or annoyance; (8) causing a nuisance or annoyance so that the tenant should be moved elswhere; (9) the house is overcrowded; (10) the house is to be demolished or reconstructed; (11) it has been designed or adapted for a person with special needs, there is no longer such a person and it is required for another such person; (12) it has been provided with or located near facilities for persons in need of special social support, there is no longer a person with such a need, and it is required for another such person; (13) the landlord is a housing association providing for special categories of persons, the accommodation is no longer suitable and it is required for a person in a special category; (14) the landlord's interest is that of lessee and his lease has terminated or will terminate within six months.[58] The notice must also give the date, at least four weeks from the notice or the date on which the tenancy could otherwise have been ended, on or after which the landlord may raise proceedings for recovery of possession. Such a notice is in force for six months unless withdrawn.[59]

In proceedings for possession the court may adjourn the proceedings on grounds (1) to (6), with or without conditions. The court must make an order for possession if the landlord has a ground within (1) to (7) and specified in the notice, and it is reasonable to make the order, or a ground within (8) to (14) is specified and it appears that other suitable accommodation will be available for the tenant when the order takes effect.[60]

On termination of a secure tenancy the landlord may make payments in respect of works carried out by the tenant which have added to the value of the house.[61]

Abandonment of secure tenancy

Where a landlord under a secure tenancy has reasonable grounds for believing that the house is unoccupied and that the tenant does not intend to occupy it, he may enter to secure it against vandalism, and may take possession under S. 19.[62]

A landlord wishing repossession must serve on the tenant a notice stating that he has reason to believe that the house is unoccupied and that the tenant does not intend to occupy, requiring the tenant to

---

[58] Ibid., S. 14 and Sched. 2.
[59] Ibid., S. 14. For form of notice see Secure Tenancies (Proceedings for Possession) (Sc.) Order, 1980 (S.I. 1389, 1980).
[60] Ibid., S. 15.
[61] Ibid., S. 24.
[62] Ibid., S. 18.

inform him within four weeks if he intends to occupy it, and warning that if he does not, the secure tenancy will be terminated forthwith. After inquiries and after the four weeks he may serve a further notice ending the tenancy forthwith. The landlord may take posession without any further proceedings. Provision may be made for securing any tenant's property or disposing of it.[63] A tenant aggrieved by termination of the tenancy under S. 19 may apply to the sheriff who in certain cases may order that the secure tenancy continues or in any other case may direct the landlord to make other suitable accommodation available to the tenant.[64]

Right of public sector tenants to purchase houses

The tenant of a house owned by one of a large range of public authorities may purchase the house on statutory terms.[65]

LEASES OF FURNISHED HOUSES

The lease of a house, or part thereof, furnished, is governed by the same principles as unfurnished houses. In the absence of express stipulation the landlord must relieve the tenant of the liability for occupier's rates.[66]

The landlord may lock cupboards and other receptacles.[67] The tenant may remove pictures and store them in one of the rooms, even against the landlord's wishes.[68]

Furnished premises

The Rent of Furnished Houses Control (Sc.) Act, 1943[69] created in areas to which the Act was applied tribunals to which the lessor or lessee of houses or parts of houses within the same limits of rateable value as the Rent Acts let with furniture or services, or the local authority for the area, might refer the contract. The tribunal may after inquiry approve the rent payable or reduce it to such sum as they thought reasonable. Particulars of the contract and the rent have to be registered by the tribunal.

[63] Ibid., S. 19.
[64] Ibid., S. 20 and Sched. 2, Part II.
[65] Tenants' Rights (Sc.) Act, 1980, Ss. 1–9, amended by Tenants' Rights (Sc.) Amdt. Act, 1980.
[66] *Macome* v. *Dickson* (1868) 6 M. 898; *Sturrock* v. *Murray*, 1952 S.C. 454.
[67] *Miller* v. *Wilson*, 1919, 1 S.L.T. 223.
[68] *Miller* v. *Stewart* (1899) 2 F. 309.
[69] Amended, Landlord and Tenant (Rent Control) Act, 1949, S. 17 and Sched. 2, and 1965 Act, S. 39(1) and (12).

Furnished lettings—Part VII contracts

Part VII of the 1971 Act (Ss. 83–100) applies to a contract[70] whereby one person grants to another in consideration of a rent which includes payment for furniture or services the right to occupy as a residence a dwelling-house, or part of a dwelling-house, whether or not the lessee is entitled, in addition to exclusive possession of that part, to the use in common with anyone else of other accommodation in the house,[71] but not to a contract for the letting of a dwelling-house at a rent which includes payment for board if that forms a substantial proportion of the whole rent, nor to a contract which creates a regulated tenancy, nor to a contract which creates a controlled tenancy if that subsequently becomes a converted tenancy, within the 1972 Act, nor to the letting of a dwelling-house for a holiday.[72] Part VII applies to any dwelling-house the rateable value of which on the appropriate day did not exceed £200.[73] Where rent is payable weekly a rent book must be provided.[74]

Lessor, lessee or the local authority may refer a Part VII contract to a rent assessment committee[75] which may approve the rent, reduce or increase it to what they deem reasonable, or dismiss the reference.[76] They must keep a register of rents[77] and may reconsider a rent so registered on the ground of change of circumstances, and on a reconsideration may increase the rent payable.[78] Once rent has been registered it is not lawful to require or receive a greater sum as rent for that house and any excess paid is recoverable by the payer.[79] A notice to quit served after a reference to a rent assessment committee is ineffective till six months after the decision or, if the rent assessment committee directs, a shorter period thereafter, or if the reference is withdrawn, till seven days after the withdrawal.[80] If a notice to quit has been served and the contract has been referred to a rent assessment committee, the lessee may apply to the committee for a grant or an extension of security of tenure.[81] The committee may reduce the period

[70] cf. R. v. *London Rent Tribunal, ex parte Honig* [1951] 1 K.B. 641.
[71] cf. *Helman* v. *Horsham and Worthing Assessment Cttee.* [1949] 2 K.B. 335.
[72] S. 85, amd. 1972 Act, Sch. 9 and 1980 Act S. 53.
[73] S. 86 amended 1972 Act, S. 77 and 1980 Act, S. 54.
[74] S. 98
[75] S. 87, amended 1980 Act, S. 52.
[76] S. 88, a rent cannot be reconsidered for 3 years: 1974 Act, S. 9; the tribunal may also apportion rateable value: S. 96.
[77] S. 89.
[78] S. 90, amd. Local Government (Sc.) Act, 1973, Sch. 13.
[79] S. 91. The rent is fixed for that house and not merely as between the parties to the contract: R. v. *Fulham Rent Tribunal, ex p. Marks* [1951] 2 K.B. 694. S. 91A is added by 1980 Act, S. 51.
[80] S. 92.
[81] S. 93; cf. *Preston Rent Tribunal* v. *Pickavance* [1953] A.C. 562.

of security of tenure if the tenant has beeen in breach of the terms of the lease[82] and the sheriff may reduce the period of notice to quit.[83] An owner who previously occupied the house as a residence himself may, however, exclude in advance Ss. 92–3.[84]

It is an offence to require the payment of a premium for the grant, renewal, continuance or assignation of rights under a Part VII contract.[85]

Part VII also applies where a tenant shares some accommodation with the landlord or with him and other persons and the accommodation is for that reason not let on a protected tenancy.[86]

By the Furnished Lettings (Rent Allowances) Act, 1973, S. 2, persons occupying houses to which Part VII applies and certain tenants under furnished lettings of housing authority houses come within the scope of rent allowances schemes operated by local authorities under the Housing (Financial Provisions) (Sc.) Act, 1972.

LEASES FOR BUSINESS PURPOSES

The principles applicable to urban leases apply generally also to leases for business premises. Thus the implied undertaking of fitness for the purpose of let applies,[87] the right to abandon if the premises are destroyed,[88] the obligation to keep the premises wind- and watertight,[89] and the landlord's liability for damage caused by fault.[90]

The lease is not terminated by failure of the purpose for which the premises were let, such as the loss of a licence,[91] nor does it imply any obligation on the landlord not to establish a rival business.[92]

The tenant is liable for harm caused by overloading the premises.[93]

The tenant has been held bound to furnish and air premises, but not to open and carry on business therein.[94] The tenant of a shop, unless expressly prohibited, may use it for auction sales.[95] A tenant's loss of

---

[82] S. 95, amd. 1974 Act, S. 10.
[83] S. 95A, added by 1974 Act, S. 14. S. 95B added by 1980 Act, S. 55.
[84] S. 94.
[85] Ss. 104–5.
[86] Ss. 118–19. As to tenancies where the landlord is resident see S. 119A added by 1974 Act, Sch. 2.   [87] *Sandeman* v. *Duncan's Trs.* (1897) 5 S.L.T. 21.
[88] *Drummond* v. *Hunter* (1869) 7 M. 347; *Duff* v. *Fleming* (1870) 8 M. 769.
[89] *Wolfson* v. *Forrester*, 1910 S.C. 675.
[90] *Hampton* v. *Galloway & Sykes* (1899) 1 F. 501; *N.B. Storage Co.* v. *Steele's Trs.*, 1920 S.C. 194.
[91] *Donald* v. *Leitch* (1886) 13 R. 790; *Hart's Trs.* v. *Arrol* (1903) 6 F. 36.
[92] *Craig* v. *Millar* (1888) 15 R. 1005; see also *Randall* v. *Summers*, 1919 S.C. 396..
[93] *Caledonian Ry. Co.* v. *Greenock Sacking Co.* (1875) 2 R. 671; *Corrie, Mackie & Co.* v. *Stewart* (1885) 22 S.L.R. 350; *Glebe Sugar Refining Co.* v. *Paterson* (1900) 2 F. 615.
[94] *Whitelaw* v. *Fulton* (1871) 10 M. 27.
[95] *Keith* v. *Reid* (1870) 8 M. (H.L.) 110.

his licence does not entitle the landlord to damages.[96] In the absence of general custom, the tenant may not attach showcases outside the shop,[97] but this does not prevent temporary signs on special occasions.[98]

The landlord is liable for detriment of the tenant's business by operations *in suo* only so far as they amount to derogation from his grant.[99]

The landlord may object to a tenant converting part of the premises for living, but may be barred by delay from objection.[1]

Shops—prolongation of tenancies

The Tenancy of Shops (Sc.) Act, 1949,[2] entitles the tenant of a shop, as defined by the Shops Act, 1950, whose lease has ended and who is unable to obtain a renewal on terms satisfactory to him, to apply to the sheriff within twenty-one days of the notice and before it takes effect for a renewal of his tenancy. The sheriff, whose decision is final, may determine that the tenancy be renewed for not longer than a year at such rent and terms as he thinks reasonable, or may dismiss the application, and shall not determine that the tenancy be renewed, if satisfied of one of stated conditions.[3] Further renewals may be made.[4] If renewal is granted a new lease is deemed to arise.[5] This Act does not protect subtenants,[6] and a tenant protected by this Act cannot claim protection under the Rent Acts as a regulated tenant.[7]

BUILDING LEASE

The grant of plots of ground at an annual rental on long leases, of 99 or 999 years, on which the tenant is obliged to build a house of specified size and value, is uncommon in Scotland, but competent as an alternative to granting a feu,[8] and indeed necessary where the vassal was prohibited from granting feus, as he would be if holding under an entail. Conditions are commonly imposed as to the use of premises to be built.[9] Where such a lease is granted it is assignable by the tenant, *inter vivos* or by will, and passes as heritage on his death intestate. On the expiry of the lease the land and buildings revert to the landlord.

[96] *Hart's Trs.* v. *Arrol* (1903) 10 S.L.T. 733. [97] *B.L. Co.* v. *Purdie* (1905) 7 F. 923.
[98] *Morrison* v. *Forsyth*, 1909 S.C. 329. [99] *Huber* v. *Ross*, 1912 S.C. 898.
[1] *Moore* v. *Munro* (1896) 4 S.L.T. 172.
[2] Made permanent by the Tenancy of Shops (Sc.) Act, 1964.
[3] S. 1(1)–(3) and (7); cf. *Craig* v. *Saunders & Connor*, 1962 S.L.T. (Sh. Ct.) 85.
[4] S. 1(4).
[5] *Scottish Gas Board* v. *Kerr's Trs.*, 1956 S.L.T. (Sh. Ct.) 69.
[6] *Ashley Wallpaper Co.* v. *Morrisons Assoc. Cos.*, 1952 S.L.T. (Sh. Ct.) 25.
[7] 1965 Act, S. 1(3).
[8] e.g. *Bisset* v. *Aberdeen Mags.* (1898) 1 F. 87.
[9] e.g. *Gold* v. *Houldsworth* (1870) 8 M. 1006; *L. Macdonald* v. *Campbell* (1889) 16 R. 540; *Ferguson* v. *Brown* (1902) 9 S.L.T. 341.

Such leases, formerly if for over thirty-one years and not exceeding fifty acres, and now if exceeding twenty years,[10] are registrable in the Register of Sasines under the Registration of Leases Act, 1857. If registered the lease is a real right valid against singular successors of the landlord even without possession. The lease is assignable under the Act, absolutely or in security.[11] In the case of land in an area operational for the purposes of the Land Registration (Sc.) Act, 1979, the grant of an interest of long leasehold is registrable, but only to the extent that the interest has become that of the lessee,[12] and a transfer is also registrable.[13]

In long leases which could extend to more than twenty years executed after 31 July 1974 no part of the property is to be used as or part of a private dwelling-house, on pain of being removed.[14]

No casualties may be imposed in any future lease.[15]

The Long Leases (Scotland) Act, 1954[16] enabled certain lessees and sublessees of property let under a lease for not less than fifty years granted before 10 August 1914 and occupied as a private dwelling-house forming his usual residence, to require the landlord before 1959 and subject to certain conditions to grant a feu right of the property (S. 1). An occupying lessee who acquired his interest otherwise than by inheritance, on or after 10 May 1951, is not so entitled (S. 3). A grant of a feu might be refused in certain cases on the ground of public interest (S. 4). Leases and subleases expiring within five years of the Act may be continued to Whitsunday, 1960 (Ss. 15–16).

AGRICULTURAL LEASES

Common law principles regulate the capacity of parties, and the modes of constitution and proof of leases of land for agricultural purposes.[17] The Leases Act, 1449, and the Registration of Leases Act, 1857, as amended, apply to agricultural leases. A lease is 'a letting of land for a term of years, or for lives, or for lives and years, or from year to year'.[18]

---

[10] Land Tenure Reform (Sc.) Act, 1974, Sched. 6.
[11] *Crawford* v. *Campbell*, 1937 S.C. 596.
[12] 1979 Act, S. 2(1)(a)(i).
[13] 1979 Act, S. 2(4)(a).
[14] Land Tenure Reform (Sc.) Act, 1974, Ss. 8–10.
[15] 1974 Act, S. 16.
[16] Superseding Leasehold Property (Temporary Provisions) Act, 1951, and Long Leases (Temporary Provisions) (Sc.) Act, 1951, extended by Leasehold Property Act and Long Leases (Sc.) Act Extension Act, 1953.
[17] cf. *Gray* v. *Edinburgh University*, 1962 S.C. 157.
[18] Agricultural Holdings (Sc.) Act, 1949, S. 93. As to an arrangement which was not a lease: see *Stirrat* v. *Whyte*, 1967 S.C. 265.

Numerous statutory provisions, however, apply to agricultural holdings.[19] Save as expressly provided in the Agricultural Holdings (Sc.) Act, 1949, any question or difference of any kind whatsoever between the landlord and the tenant of an agricultural holding arising out of the tenancy or in connection with the holding (not being a question or difference as to liability for rent) is to be determined by arbitration[20] or by the Land Court.[21] The arbiter may, and shall if so directed by the sheriff, state a case for the opinion of the sheriff, whose opinion is final unless within a limited time either party appeals to the Court of Session.[22]

Minimum duration

Unless a letting for less than a year was approved by the Secretary of State before the lease was entered into, a lease of land for use as agricultural land for a shorter period than from year to year takes effect as a lease from year to year, unless leased only for grazing or mowing during some specified period of the year,[23] or leased by a tenant under a lease for less than from year to year.[24]

Written leases, and terms therin

Where there is not in force a lease in writing[25] embodying the terms of the tenancy, or, there is such a lease (i) entered into on or after 1 November 1948, or (ii) entered into before then, the period of which has expired and is being continued in force by tacit relocation, and the lease contains no provision for one or more of the matters specified in Schedule V to the 1949 Act, or a provision inconsistent therewith or with S. 5, of the Act, either party may call on the other to enter into such a lease; if no lease has been concluded within six months, the terms of the tenancy stand referred to arbitration.[26] The arbiter may

---

[19] 'Agricultural holding' means the aggregate of land comprised in a lease, not being land let during the tenant's continuance in any office, appointment or employment held under the landlord, which is used for agriculture (including horticulture, fruit growing, seed growing, meadow land, osier land, market gardens, dairy farming and livestock breeding and keeping, grazing land and nursery grounds, and the use of land for woodlands when that is ancillary to the farming of land) for the purpose of a trade or business: Agricultural Holdings (Sc.) Act, 1949, Ss. 1, 93(1). No extent is prescribed. Land may be designated as agricultural land by the Secretary of State: Agriculture (Sc.) Act, 1948, S. 86(1). The only lands apparently excluded are lands let e.g. for a rifle range, or for grazing and exercising racehorses, or for a golf course. cf. *Stirrat* v. *Whyte*, 1967 S.C. 265.

[20] 1949 Act, S. 74; *Houison-Crawford's Trs.* v. *Davies*, 1951 S.C. 1; *Brodie* v. *Ker*, 1952 S.C. 216. See also *Roger* v. *Hutcheson*, 1922 S.C. (H.L.) 140.

[21] 1949 Act, S 78; as to Crown land, see Ss 86–7.

[22] 1949 Act, S. 75; *MacNab* v. *Wilson*, 1960 S.C. 83; *Forsyth Grant* v. *Salmon*, 1961 S.C. 54.

[23] *Mackenzie* v. *Laird*, 1959 S.C. 266; *Gairneybridge Farm and King*, 1974 S.L.T. (Land Ct.) 8.

[24] Agricultural Holdings (Sc.) Act, 1949, S. 2; cf. *Mackenzie* v. *Laird*, 1959 S.C. 266.

[25] Not limited to probative leases: *Grieve* v. *Barr*, 1954 S.C. 414.

[26] 1949 Act, S. 4(1).

make provision for Schedule V matters not covered by the lease, and further provisions which may be agreed.[27] Where liability for the maintenance or repair of any fixed equipment is transferred from one party to the other thereunder consequential adjustments may be made.[28]

Record of holding

Where a lease has been entered into, a record of the condition of the fixed equipment on the holding must be made forthwith, and is then deemed to form part of the lease.[29]

Landlord's duties

The landlord must yield vacant possession of the subjects let.[30] If it is not given timeously, or not at all, the tenant may rescind the lease and claim damages.[31]

If there is material discrepancy between the subjects let and the subjects to which entry is given, the tenant may reduce the lease and claim damages,[32] or claim a deduction from the rent for the past period of possession,[33] or withhold rent till the deficiency is remedied.[34]

The landlord must also allow the use of such roads on his estate or adjoining farms as are reasonably incidental to the lands let.[35]

Reservations

In agricultural leases there are impliedly reserved to the landlord the minerals, with liberty to prospect for them, of access thereto and working them, on payment of damages for surface damage,[36] woods, with liberty of access thereto,[37] and game, and wild animals.[38]

Conventional reservations may be included to any effect agreed on, but common reservations include power to resume parts of the subjects let for mining, roads, planting, feuing or excambing.[39] The extent

---

[27] S. 4(2) and (3).

[28] S. 6.

[29] 1949 Act, S. 5(1).

[30] cf. *Winans* v. *Mackenzie* (1883) 10 R. 941.

[31] *Smith* v. *Robertson* (1832) 10 S. 829; *Tennant's Trs.* v. *Maxwell* (1880) 17 S.L.R. 463.

[32] *Oliver* v. *Suttie* (1840) 2 D. 514.

[33] *Riddell* v. *Grosset* (1791) 3 Pat. 203; *Yeaman* v. *Gilruth* (1792) Hume 783.

[34] *Kilmarnock Gas Co.* v. *Smith* (1872) 11 M. 58; *Guthrie* v. *Shearer* (1873) 1 R. 181.

[35] *Duncan* v. *Scott* (1876) 3 R. (H.L.) 69; *Galloway* v. *Cowden* (1885) 12 R. 578; *Addison* v. *Brown* (1907) 15 S.L.T. 674.

[36] Stair II, 9, 31; Bankt. II, 9, 21; Ersk. II, 6, 22; Bell, *Prin.* §1226; *Colquhoun* v. *Watson* (1668) Mor. 15233.

[37] Bankt. II, 9, 21; Ersk. II, 6, 22; Bell, *Prin.* §1226.

[38] *Maxwell* v. *Copland* (1870) 9 M. (H.L.) 1; cf. *Wemyss* v. *Gulland* (1847) 10 D. 204.

[39] *Menmuir* v. *Airth* (1863) 1 M. 929; *Caledonian Ry.* v. *Smith* (1877) 14 S.L.R. 510; *Crichton Stuart* v. *Ogilvie*, 1914 S.C. 888; *Thomas* v. *Gair*, 1949 S.C. 425; *Sykes and Edgar*, 1974 S.L.T. (Land Ct.) 4; *Edmonstone* v. *Lamont*, 1975 S.L.T. (Sh. Ct.) 57.

of resumption permitted depends on the fair interpretation of the reserved power.[40] Whether the purpose for which resumption is intended falls within the power is again a matter of interpretation.[41] Power of resumption implies liability to compensate the tenant, normally by reduction of rent,[42] but sometimes in other ways.[43] The claim to compensation may be held departed from by express or implied renunciation.[44]

Power to enter on holding

The landlord or anyone authorized by him may at all reasonable times enter on the holding to view the state of the holding, to fulfil the landlord's responsibilities to manage the holding in accordance with the rules of good estate management,[45] or to provide, improve, replace or renew fixed equipment otherwise than in fulfilment of these responsibilities.[46]

Implied duties

The landlord is impliedly bound at common law to furnish the buildings necessary to enable the tenant to cultivate the land in the mode contemplated,[47] and to put the houses, offices, water supply,[48] and fences, but not drains,[49] on a farm into tenantable repair at the time of entry,[50] such as to render them capable of lasting, with ordinary care, to the ish.[51] If the tenant sustains loss by reason of the insufficiency of any of these items, he may claim damages, but must make timeous intimation of the defect and of his claim.[52] If the landlord fails to give possession of buildings in tenantable order, the tenant is entitled to an abatement of rent,[53] or to retain the rent.[54]

---

[40] *Stewart* v. *Lead* (1825) 1 W. & S. 68; *Trotter* v. *Torrance* (1891) 18 R. 848.

[41] *Admiralty* v. *Burns*, 1910 S.C. 531; *Turner* v. *Wilson*, 1954 S.C. 296; *Pigott* v. *Robson*, 1958 S.L.T. 49; *Secy. of State for Scotland* v. *Campbell* (1959) 47 L.C. 49.

[42] *Menmuir*, *supra*; claim lies against the landlord only: *Lanark Middle Ward Dist. Ctee.* v. *Marshall* (1896) 24 R. 139.

[43] *Bertram* v. *Guild* (1880) 7 R. 1122; see also *Kininmonth* v. *British Aluminium Co.*, 1915 S.C. 271.

[44] *Belshes* v. *Fraser* (1839) 1 D. 1071.

[45] See Agriculture (Sc.) Act, 1948, Sched. V.

[46] 1949 Act, S. 18.

[47] *Barclay* v. *Neilson* (1878) 5 R. 909.

[48] *Christie* v. *Wilson*, 1915 S.C. 645.

[49] *Wight* v. *Newton*, 1911 S.C. 762.

[50] Bankt. I, 20, 10; II, 11, 21; Ersk. II, 6, 39; Bell, *Prin.* §1253.

[51] *Davidson* v. *Logan*, 1908 S.C. 350; cf. *Mossman* v. *Brocket* (1810) Hume 850.

[52] *Ferrier* v. *Readman* (1898) 6 S.L.T. 109; *Hamilton* v. *D. Montrose* (1906) 8 F. 1026; *Christie* v. *Wilson*, 1915 S.C. 645.

[53] *Munro* v. *McGeoghs* (1888) 16 R. 93; *Stewart* v. *Campbell* (1889) 16 R. 346.

[54] *McDonald* v. *Kydd* (1901) 4 F. 923; *E. Galloway* v. *McConnell*, 1911 S.C. 846; *Haig* v. *Boswall-Preston*, 1915 S.C. 339.

Statutorily implied terms

There is deemed incorporated in every lease of an agricultural holding (a) an undertaking by the landlord that, at the commencement of the tenancy or as soon as is reasonably possible thereafter, he will put the fixed equipment on the holding into a thorough state of repair, and will provide such buildings and other fixed equipment as will enable an occupier reasonably skilled in husbandry to maintain efficient production as respects both the kind of produce specified in the lease, or in use to be produced on the holding, and the quality and quantity thereof, and will during the tenancy effect such replacement or renewal of the buildings or other fixed equipment as may be rendered necessary by natural decay or by fair wear and tear; and (b) a provision that the liability of the tenant in relation to the maintenance of fixed equipment shall extend only to a liability to maintain the fixed equipment on the holding in as good a state of repair (natural decay and fair wear and tear excepted) as it was in immediately after it was put in repair or, in the case of equipment provided, improved, replaced or renewed during the tenancy, as it was in immediately after it was so provided, improved, replaced or renewed. Nevertheless, either party may by agreement undertake work legally incumbent on the other. The tenant cannot be required to pay the whole or part of the premium due under a fire insurance policy over any fixed equipment.[55] The landlord cannot contract out of his statutory liability to put the fixed equipment into order and to provide buildings.[56]

Tenant's rights and duties

The tenant is entitled to be given vacant possession of the subjects let at the date of entry.

The tenant must maintain the buildings, fences, and gates on the farm, unless they have decayed to the extent where renewal is necessary.[57] He is not liable for damage caused by *damnum fatale*[58] or by sheer accident. Damages may be recovered for the loss of use of premises by reason of decay.[59]

If the tenant is bound to reside on the subjects let, he is in breach if he does not, even by reason of imprisonment.[60]

A lease is deemed to include a provision that the liability of the tenant in relation to fixed equipment extends only to a liability to

[55] 1949 Act, S. 5(2)–(4).
[56] *Secretary of State for Scotland* v. *Sinclair* (1959) 48 L.C. 10.
[57] Bell, *Prin.* §1254: *Johnstone* v. *Hughan* (1894) 21 R. 777. See also *Halliday* v. *Ferguson*, 1961 S.C. 24.
[58] *York Building Co.* v. *Adams* (1741) Mor. 10127; *Clerk* v. *Baird* (1741) Mor. 10128.
[59] *Johnstone, supra; Hamilton* v. *D. Montrose* (1906) 8 F. 1026.
[60] *Blair Trust Co.* v. *Gilbert*, 1940 S.L.T. 322.

maintain the fixed equipment in as good a state of repair (natural decay and fair wear and tear excepted) as it was in immediately after it was put in repair as aforesaid or, in the case of equipment provided, improved, replaced or renewed during the tenancy, as it was in immediately after it was so provided.[61]

Good husbandry

The lease frequently contains an express, and always an implied, obligation on the tenant to conform to the rules of good husbandry.[62] These depend in part on the practice of the district and deviation, if alleged, must be determined by the opinion of men of experience in the district.[63]

Permanent pasture

Either party may demand a reference to arbitration of whether the amount of land required by the lease to be maintained as permanent pasture should be reduced.[64]

Compensation to outgoing tenants

Certain agreements by incoming tenants to compensate outgoing tenants or refund compensation to the landlord are declared void.[65]

Freedom of cropping and of disposal of produce

Notwithstanding any custom or the terms of the lease or of any agreement, a tenant is entitled, subject to certain provisos, without incurring any penalty, forfeiture or liability, to dispose of the produce of the holding other than manure produced thereon and to practise any system of cropping of the arable land.[66] But if the tenant exercises his rights in such a manner as to injure or deteriorate the holding, or to be likely to do so, the landlord may interdict him or recover damages for deterioration, on his quitting the holding.[67]

Record of condition of holding

Either party may at any time during the tenancy require the making of a record of the condition of the fixed equipment on, and of the

[61] 1949 Act, S. 5(2)(b).
[62] Maxwell v. McMurray (1776) 5 B.S. 515; Thomson's Reps. v. Oliphant (1824) 3 S. 275; Hunter v. Miller (1863) 1 M. (H.L.) 49; cf. Hendry v. Marshall (1878) 5 R. 687; Countess of Stair v. Willison (1883) 20 S.L.R. 315.
[63] M. Tweeddale v. Brown (1821) 2 Mur. 563.
[64] 1949 Act, S. 9, as amd. by Agriculture Act, 1958, Sched. I.
[65] S. 11.
[66] cf. Carron Co. v. Donaldson (1858) 20 D. 681; Hunter v. Miller (1862) 24 D. 1011.
[67] 1949 Act, S. 12. See Mackenzie's Trs. v. Somerville (1900) 2 F. 1278; Taylor v. Steel-Maitland, 1913 S.C. 502. Damages are measured by the diminution in rent obtainable on reletting: Williams v. Lewis [1915] 3 K.B. 493.

cultivation of, the holding and the tenant may require the making of a record of existing improvements carried out by him or in respect of which he has, with the landlord's consent, paid compensation to an outgoing tenant, and of any fixtures or buildings which under the Act he is entitled to remove.[68]

Compensation for game damage[69]

Where the tenant of an agricultural holding has sustained damage to his crops from game,[70] the right to kill and take which is vested neither in him nor in anyone claiming under him other than the landlord and which the tenant has not permission in writing to kill, he is entitled to compensation from his landlord for the damage if it exceeds in amount one shilling per acre of the area over which it extends.[71] Notice must be given when the damage is first observed and a reasonable opportunity given to inspect the damage, and written notice of the claim must be given within a month after the end of the calendar year, or other period of twelve months agreed upon, in respect of which it is made.[72] The amount of compensation, in default of agreement, is to be determined by arbitration. Where the right to kill and take game is vested in some person other than the landlord, the landlord is entitled to be indemnified by him against claims for compenstion.[73] Where a tenant had permission to kill deer, it was held that the permission excluded a claim for compensation for damage caused by that kind of game.[74] The statutory right to kill deer[75] does not take away the right to compensation where the tenant had no written permission to kill deer.[76]

Rent

The amount of rent, and the terms for payment thereof, are determined by the lease. As between landlord's executor and his heir-at-law, and between landlord and purchaser from him, however, a difference may arise between the terms when the rent is legally due and those when it is due according to the lease. In principle rent is not due legally, though it may be conventionally, until the tenant has had the

---

[68] 1949 Act, S. 17.

[69] 1949 Act, S. 15.

[70] Defined, S. 15(4) as deer, pheasant, partridges, grouse, and black game. Ground game is excluded, because a tenant can protect himself against ground game at common law and under the Ground Game Acts.

[71] Even if damage is done partly by game coming from an adjacent estate: *Thomson* v. *E. Galloway,* 1919 S.C. 611.

[72] See *E. Morton's Trs.* v. *MacDougall,* 1944 S.C. 410.

[73] cf. *Kidd* v. *Byrne* (1875) 3 R. 255. The agricultural tenant cannot claim direct against the sporting tenant: *Inglis* v. *Moir's Tutors* (1871) 10 M. 204.

[74] *Ross* v. *Watson,* 1943 S.C. 406.

[75] Agriculture (Sc.) Act, 1948, S. 43.

[76] *L. Auckland* v. *Dowie,* 1965 S.C. 37.

benefit of the crop. Hence in arable farms, with entry at Martinmas, the legal terms are the following Whitsunday and Martinmas. In pastoral farms, with entry at Whitsunday, the legal terms are the Whitsunday of entry, and the following Martinmas. Rents payable conventionally before the legal terms are designated forehand rents; if payable later, backhand rents. As between landlord's executor and his heir-at-law, the legal terms apply, except in the case of forehand rents, when the conventional terms apply.[77]

As between selling landlord and purchasing landlord, the purchaser is entitled to the rents falling due for possession following his term of entry according to the legal terms, but in the case of forehand rents he is entitled to rents payable at the conventional terms following the term of his entry.[78]

Abatement of rent

If the tenant is deprived of the beneficial use of a substantial part of the subjects let more than temporarily he is entitled to an abatement of rent.[79]

Variation of rent

Either party may demand a reference to arbitration of what rent should be payable as from the next date when the tenancy could have been terminated by notice to quit.[80]

Where the landlord has carried out one or more stated improvements to the holding he may increase the rent to the extent of the increase in rateable value.[81]

Restriction of penal rent or liquidated damages

Notwithstanding anything in the lease making the tenant of an agricultural holding liable to pay a high rent or other liquidated damages in the event of breach or non-fulfilment of any of the terms or conditions of the lease, the landlord is not entitled to recover any sum in such cases in excess of the damage actually suffered by him in consequence of the breach or non-fulfilment.[82]

---

[77] Stair III, 8, 57; Bankt. II, 6, 35; Ersk. II, 9, 64; Bell, *Comm.* II, 8; *Prin.* §1501; Bell, *Conv.* I, 639; Menzies, 618; Rankine, *L.O.*, 737; *Baillie* v. *Fletcher*, 1915 S.C. 677.

[78] Titles to Land Consolidation (Sc.) Act, 1868, S. 8; *Baillie* v. *Fletcher*, 1915 S.C. 677.

[79] *Sharp* v. *Thomson*, 1930 S.C. 1092.

[80] 1949 Act, S. 7, as amd. Agriculture Act, 1958, S. 2; *Guthe* v. *Broatch*, 1956 S.C. 132; *Secy. of State* v. *Young* (1960) 48 L.C. 31; *Secy. of State* v. *Sinclair* (1961) 50 L.C. 6; *Anderson* v. *Bennie* (1962) 50 L.C. 38; *Graham* v. *Gardner*, 1966 S.L.T. (Land Ct.) 12.

[81] 1949 Act, S. 8.

[82] 1949 Act, S. 16.

Remedies for non-payment of rent

If rent is not duly paid, the landlord may bring a personal action for payment and do diligence thereon.[83] A formal lease frequently contains a clause of consent to registration on which summary diligence may proceed.

The landlord's hypothec over *invecta et illata* has been abolished in the case of land exceeding two acres in extent let for agriculture or pasture.[84]

The legal irritancy *ob non solutum canonem* exists in case of non-payment of rent for two successive years.[85] The Act of Sederunt of 14 December 1756 authorizes caution to be required on one year's rent being in arrear, and a declarator of irritancy and summary removing to be brought in the sheriff court on the rent being two years in arrears.

A conventional irritancy to any effect, including non-payment of rent, may be inserted in the lease, and is enforceable according to its terms.[86]

When six months' rent is due and unpaid, the landlord may raise an action for removing in the Sheriff Court against the tenant, concluding for his removal at the next term of Whitsunday or Martinmas, and, unless the arrears are paid or caution found for them and for one year's rent further, the sheriff may decern the tenant to remove and eject him at the term.[87] Removal in this way does not prejudice the tenant's outgoing claims.[88]

Retention of rent

The right to retain rent on the landlord's breach exists in agricultural leases.[89] A tenant may not retain on account of temporary failure of the water supply[90] or defect in the drains,[91] nor in addition to an award of damages.[92] But he may retain until the amount of compensation due to him for improvements is paid or accounted for.[93]

---

[83] A tenant's claim for damages is not a relevant defence: *Christie* v. *Birrell*, 1910 S.C. 986.

[84] Hypothec Abolition (Sc.) Act, 1880, S. 1; but see *Clark* v. *Keirs* (1888) 15 R. 458.

[85] Stair II, 9, 32; Bankt. II, 9, 23; Ersk. II, 6, 44.

[86] *Stewart* v. *Watson* (1864) 2 M. 1414; *McDouall's Trs.* v. *Macleod*, 1949 S.C. 593; *Dorchester Studios* v. *Stone*, 1975 S.C. (H.L.) 56.

[87] 1949 Act, S. 19; cf. *Ballantyne* v. *Brechin* (1893) 1 S.L.T. 306; *Fletcher* v. *F.*, 1932 S.L.T. (Sh. Ct.) 10. If there is a dispute as to liability for rent it is for the court though other disputes have to be determined by arbitration: S. 74; *Brodie* v. *Ker*, 1952 S.C. 216.

[88] S. 19(2).

[89] e.g. *Ramsay* v. *Howison*, 1908 S.C. 697; *E. Galloway* v. *McConnell*, 1911 S.C. 846; *Haig* v. *Boswall-Preston*, 1915 S.C. 339.

[90] *Russell* v. *Sime*, 1912, 2 S.L.T. 344.

[91] *Brown* v. *Simpson*, 1910, 1 S.L.T. 183.

[92] *Christie* v. *Wilson*, 1915 S.C. 645.

[93] *D. Argyll* (1935) 23 L.C. 58.

The right to retain rent may be excluded by the lease.[94] A claim to retain is not necessarily departed from because rent is paid in full for several years.[95]

Assignation

At common law agricultural leases of ordinary duration, and also leases of shootings and fishings, are not assignable without express power to do so[96] or the landlord's consent.

Tenant's death testate—Bequest of lease

The tenant[97] may, unless his legatee is expressly excluded,[98] by will or other testamentary writing, bequeath his lease to his son-in-law or daughter-in-law or anyone of the persons who would be, or would in any circumstances have been, entitled to succeed to his estate on intestacy.[99] The landlord cannot by the lease deprive the tenant of his right of bequest.[1] A legatee accepting must give notice within twenty-one days, or as soon as possible;[2] the landlord may give a counter-notice objecting to the legatee as tenant, whereupon the legatee may apply to the Land Court to be declared tenant.[3] If any reasonable ground of objection by the landlord is established the Land Court shall declare the bequest null.[4] If the legatee does not accept, or the bequest is declared null, the lease devolves as intestate estate.[5] The acquirer of the lease must give notice to he landlord and unless the landlord gives a counter-notice, the lease binds the landlord and the acquirer from the date of acquisition. The landlord may object before the Land Court to the person thus acquiring the lease.[6] The Land Court must declare the acquirer tenant unless the landlord establishes a reasonable ground of objection.[7] A testator's trustees, if authorized by the will to carry on the farm, may claim to be accepted as tenants.[8] The fact that, on the

---

[94] *Skene* v. *Cameron,* 1942 S.C. 393.

[95] *Ramsay, supra.*

[96] Bell, *Prin.* §1214; Hunter, *L. & T.,* I, 236; *Mackintosh* v. *May* (1895) 22 R. 345.

[97] Defined, 1949 Act, S. 93.

[98] *Kennedy* v. *Johnstone,* 1956 S.C. 39.

[99] Succession (Sc.) Act, 1964, Sched. 2, para. 19, replacing 1949 Act, S. 20(1); *Reid's Trs.* v. *Macpherson,* 1975 S.L.T. (Notes) 18.

[1] *Kennedy, supra,* disapproving *Howie* v. *Lowe* (1952) 40 L.C. 14.

[2] cf. *Wight* v. *M. Lothian's Trs.* (1952) 40 L.C. 25.

[3] cf. *Kennedy, supra.*

[4] See *Sloss* v. *Agnew,* 1923 S.L.T. (Sh. Ct.) 33; *Service* v. *D. Argyll,* 1951 S.L.T. (Sh. Ct.) 2; *Howie* v. *Lowe,* 1952 S.L.C.R. 14; *Fraser* v. *Murray's Trs.,* 1954 S.L.C.R. 10; *Reid* v. *Duffus Estate, Ltd.,* 1955 S.L.C.R. 13. The validity of the bequest falls to be determined by an ordinary court: *Mackenzie* v. *Cameron* (1894) 21 R. 427.

[5] Succession (Sc.) Act, 1964, Sched. 2, para, 21, replacing 1949 Act, S. 20(7).

[6] Ibid., para. 22, replacing 1949 Act, S. 21.

[7] 1949 Act, S. 20(4); *Reid* v. *Duffus Estate, Ltd.,* 1955 S.L.C.R. 13.

[8] *Dalgety's Trs.* v. *Drummond,* 1938 S.C. 709.

tenant's death, his interest vests in his executor[9] does not prevent the operation, in relation to the legatee, of the Crofters Holdings (Sc.) Act, 1886, S. 16(a) to (h), or the 1949 Act, S. 20(2) to (7).[10]

Tenant's death intestate

On a tenant's death intestate his interest in the lease vests, formerly in his heir,[11] and now in his executor,[12] unless it was subject to a special destination in favour of any person which had not been evacuated, in which case it passes to the person named in the special destination.[13] The executor acquires a vested right only when he obtains confirmation as executor.[14]

If the tenant's interest is not the subject of bequest[15] or is the subject of bequest but it has not been accepted, or has been rendered void by the Crofters Holdings (Sc.) Act, 1886, S. 16 or the Agricultural Holdings (Sc.) Act, 1949, S. 20, and a condition of the lease prohibits assignation, the executor may nevertheless transfer the interest to any one of the persons entitled to succeed to the deceased's intestate estate, or to claim legal rights or the prior rights of a surviving spouse, in or towards satisfaction of that person's claim. But he may not transfer the interest to any other person without the landlord's consent.[16]

If the executor is satisfied that the interest cannot be disposed of according to law and so informs the landlord, or if it has not been disposed of within a year or such longer period as, failing agreement, may be fixed by the sheriff, landlord or executor may, on giving notice of such length as may be agreed, failing which, notice of not less than one year nor more than two years ending with such term of Whitsunday of Martinmas as may be specified, terminate the lease, notwithstanding any contrary rule of law or provision therein, without prejudice to any claim for compensation or damages in respect of the termination of the lease.[17]

Further protection of tenants who are near relatives of a deceased tenant and who have acquired right on his death is conferred by the Agriculture (Misc. Prov.) Act, 1968, S. 18.

Tenant's insolvency

At common law neither the tenant's insolvency, nor granting a trust

[9] Succession (Sc.) Act, 1964, S. 14.
[10] Ibid., S. 16(8).
[11] Bell on *Leases* I, 146; *Kennedy* v. *Johnstone*, 1946 S.C. 39.
[12] Ibid., S. 14; *Garvie's Trs.* v. *Garvie's Tutors*, 1975 S.L.T. 94.
[13] Ibid., S. 36(2); *Reid's Trs.* v. *Macpherson*, 1975 S.L.T. 101; *Cormack* v. *McIldowie's Exors.* 1975 S.C. 161.
[14] *Rotherwick's Trs.* v. *Hope*, 1975 S.L.T. 187.
[15] As in the case of intestacy *quoad* the lease, whether or not there is total intestacy.
[16] S. 16(1) and (2). See also *Garvie's Trs.* v. *Still*, 1972 S.L.T. 9.
[17] 1964 Act, S. 16(3)–(5); see also S. 16(6).

deed, nor notour bankruptcy, nor sequestration, annuls the lease but it is customary to provide for a conventional irritancy arising in such cases.[18]

Partnership tenant—change in partners

Where land is let to a partnership and the partners change the effect depends on whether the lease was to a firm as then constituted or to the firm however it might be constituted, and in the former case the lease comes to an end when there is change in the partnership.[19]

Tacit relocation

Notwithstanding any agreement or contrary provision in the lease, the tenancy of an agricultural holding, instead of terminating at the stipulated date, continues by tacit relocation and then from year to year unless and until notice of termination is given.[20] Tacit relocation is based on implied consent of all parties and a notice of removing by one of joint tenants excludes it and ends the lease.[21]

Termination of lease for breach of condition

A landlord may give notice to quit if the tenant is in breach of a condition of the lease.[22]

Termination of lease at break

Agricultural leases commonly contain provision for either party to terminate the lease at a break, or term short of the full duration of the lease, on due notice given.[23]

Termination of lease of agricultural holding

Notwithstanding the expiry of the stipulated endurance of a lease of an agricultural holding, the tenancy, including tenancies continued by tacit relocation, does not terminate unless either party[24] has given the other written notice, not less than one nor more than two years before the termination, of intention to end the tenancy.[25] Notice has to be given in the manner of notice of removal under the Removal Terms

---

[18] *Lindsay* v. *Hogg* (1855) 17 D. 788; *Chalmers's Tr.* v. *Dick's Tr.*, 1909 S.C. 761.

[19] *Jardine-Paterson* v. *Fraser*, 1974 S.L.T. 93.

[20] 1949 Act, S. 3; cf. *Macfarlane* v. *Mitchell* (1900) 2 F. 901; *Mackie* v. *Gardner*, 1973 S.L.T. (Land Ct.) 11.

[21] *Smith* v. *Grayton Estates*, 1960 S.C. 349.

[22] *Halliday* v. *Ferguson*, 1961 S.C. 24.

[23] On notice, see *Strachan* v. *Hunter*, 1916 S.C. 901.

[24] As to joint tenants see *Graham* v. *Stirling*, 1922 S.C. 90; *Smith* v. *Grayton Estates, Ltd.*, 1960 S.C. 349.

[25] 1949 Act, S. 24(1) and (2). The notice must be clear and explicit: Bell, *Prin.* §1271; *Strachan* v. *Hunter*, 1922 S.C. 901; *Gilmour* v. *Cook*, 1975 S.L.T. (Land Ct.) 10. It is incompetent to contract out of this provision: *Duguid* v. *Muirhead*, 1926 S.C. 1078.

(Sc.) Act, 1886, S. 6,[26] or in the manner prescribed by the Sheriff
Courts (Sc.) Act, 1907,[27] and such notice comes in place of that
required by the 1907 Act.[28] The provisions as to notice do not affect
the right to remove a tenant whose estate has been sequestrated under
the Bankruptcy (Sc.) Act, 1913, or who has incurred an irritancy or
other liability to remove, nor to a notice in performance of a stipulation entitling the landlord to resume land for building or other non-
agricultural purposes.[29] Notice to quit is not precluded by the fact that
the lease contains a clause empowering the landlord to remedy the
breach at the tenant's expense.[30] A question whether the ground stated
for the removal is justified falls to be decided by arbitration.[31]

Consent of Land Court

Where notice to quit is given to the tenant of an agricultural holding
and within one month the tenant serves a counter-notice, the notice to
quit is not effective unless the Land Court consents to the operation
thereof. Certain cases are excepted from this restriction; if one is relied
on the notice to quit must state that it is given by reason of one of the
excepted ground.[32] The Land Court may consent to the operation of a
notice to quit only if satisfied as to one or more of specified matters,
stated by the landlord in his application for their consent,[33] and even if
satisfied, the Land Court may withhold consent if in all the circumstances it appears that a fair and reasonable landlord would not insist

[26] The 1886 Act, S. 6, deals only with the manner of sending the notice: the form of notice must conform to the 1907 Act, Sched. I and relative forms: *Dept. of Agriculture* v. *Goodfellow*, 1931 S.C. 556; *Rae* v. *Davidson*, 1954 S.C. 361.

[27] Ss. 34–6; See *Scott* v. *Livingstone*, 1919 S.C. 1; *Watters* v. *Hunter*, 1927 S.C. 310.

[28] S. 24(4). By S. 24(3) the provision of the 1907 Act relative to removings have effect subject, in the case of agricultural holdings, to S. 24. See also *Austin* v. *Gibson*, 1979 S.L.T. (Land Ct.) 12; *Milne* v. *E. Seafield*, 1981 S.L.T. (Sh. Ct.) 37.

[29] S. 24(6).

[30] *Halliday, supra.*

[31] *Houison-Craufurd's Trs.* v. *Davies*, 1951 S.C. 1; see also *McCallum* v. *Macnair*, 1952 S.C. 216.

[32] S. 25; and see also S. 28, amd. Agriculture Act, 1958, Sched. I, pra. 38; Agriculture (Misc. Prov.) Act, 1968, S. 18; cf. *McCallum* v. *Buchanan-Smith*, 1951 S.C. 73; *Edinburgh University* v. *Craik*, 1954 S.C. 190; *Macnabb* v. *Anderson*, 1957 S.C. 213; *Halliday* v. *Fergusson*, 1961 S.C. 24; *Carnegie* v. *Davidson*, 1966 S.L.T. (Land Ct.) 3; *Glencruitten Trs.* v. *Love*, 1966 S.L.T. (Land Ct.) 5; *Pentland* v. *Hart*, 1967 S.L.T. (Land Ct.) 2; *Murray* v. *Nisbet*, 1967 S.L.T. (Land Ct.) 14; *Austin* v. *Gibson*, 1979 S.L.T. (Land Ct.) 12; *E. Seafield* v. *Currie*, 1980 S.L.T. (Land Ct.) 10; *Somerville* v. *Watson*, 1980 S.L.T. (Land Ct.) 14; *Hutchison* v. *Buchanan*, 1980 S.L.T. (Land Ct.) 17.

[33] Ss. 26–7, amd. by Agriculture Act, 1958, Sched. 2, Part II. See *Grant* v. *Murray*, 1950 S.L.C.R. 3; *Burnett* v. *Gordon*, 1950 S.L.C.R. 9; *Cooper* v. *Muirden*, 1950 S.L.C.R. 45; *Mackenzie* v. *Tait*, 1951 S.L.C.R. 3; *Macnabb* v. *Anderson*, 1955 S.C. 38; *McCallum* v. *Arthur*, 1955 S.C. 188; *Shaw Mackenzie* v. *Forbes* (1957) 45 L.C. 34; *E. Angus Properties, Ltd.* v. *Chivers*, 1960 S.L.C.R. 1. The Land Court may, by S. 30, as amd. by Agriculture Act, 1958, Sched. 1, Part II, impose a penalty on the landlord for breach of such a condition. The landlord has no title to apply for consent after selling the lands: *Gordon* v. *Rankin*, 1972 S.L.T. (Land Ct.) 7.

on possession.[34] If the Land Court consents it may impose such conditions as appear requisite for securing that the land will be used for the purpose for which the landlord proposes to terminate the tenancy, and may vary or revoke any such conditions.[33]

Removings from other lands over two acres

Where lands exceeding two acres are held under a probative lease specifying a term of endurance, and written notice to remove is given (a) when the lease is for three years and upwards not less than one nor more than two years before the termination of the lease, and (b) when the lease is from year to year (including lands occupied by tacit relocation) or for any other period less than three years, not less than six months before the termination, the lease or an extract thereof has the same effect as an extract decree of removing and, along with written authority from the lessor of his agent, is sufficient warrant to eject the party in possession. Ejection under this provision is not competent after six weeks from the ish.[35]

Letter of removal—lands over two acres

Where a tenant in possession of lands exceeding two acres, with or without a written lease, has granted a letter of removal, holograph or attested by one witness, it has the same force and effect as an extract decree of removing and is a sufficient warrant for ejection after the same notice as is required under S. 34, unless the letter is dated and signed within twelve months before the date of removal or first ish, in which case no notice of any kind is necessary.[36]

Removal—lands over two acres held without written lease

Where lands exceeding two acres in extent are occupied by a tenant without a written lease and the tenant has given no letter of removal the lease terminates on written notice to either party by or on behalf of the other, not less than six months before the termination of the tenancy; if the tenant fails to remove the notice entitles the landlord to apply for and obtain a summary warrant of ejection against the tenant and everyone deriving right from him.[37]

Extraordinary removing

Where an irritancy has been incurred, the landlord may bring a declarator and removing, seeking warrant to eject the tenant.[38]

[34] *Altyre Estate Trs.* v. *McLay,* 1975 S.L.T. (Land Ct.) 12.
[35] Sheriff Courts (Sc.) Act, 1907, S. 34, and Sched. I, rules 110–14.
[36] Sheriff Courts (Sc.) Act, 1907, S. 35, and Sched. I, rules 110–14.
[37] Sheriff Courts (Sc.) Act, 1907, S. 36, and Sched. I, rules 110–14; see e.g. *Scott* v. *Livingstone,* 1919 S.C. 1; *Watters* v. *Hunter,* 1927 S.C. 310.
[38] e.g. *Macnab* v. *Nelson,* 1909 S.C. 1102.

A declaratory conclusion is unnecessary if the fact on which the irritancy depends is admitted or instantly verifiable,[39] or if the lease provides that declarator is unnecessary,[40] or if there is provision for nullity at the landlord's option.[41] A dispute whether rent is being not paid, so as to incur an irritancy, or retained, falls to be determined by arbitration.[42]

Other provisions as to notices to quit

Special provisions are made for notices to quit where the holding has been agreed to be sold.[43] Notices to quit part of holdings are not to be invalid in certain special cases.[44] A tenant may treat a notice to quit part as a notice to quit the entire holding.[45] Where a tenant is dispossessed of part of the holding, the tenant is entitled to a reduction of rent.[46]

Ejection

Ejection is competent where a person without title is in possession and declines to remove.[47]

Removal of manure

After notice to terminate the tenancy has been given by either party the tenant may not, subject to any contrary agreement, sell or remove from the holding manure or compost, or hay or straw or roots grown in the last year of the tenancy, unless he has given the landlord or incoming tenant a reasonable opportunity of purchasing any of these at their fair market value or value provided by the lease.[48]

Removal of fixtures and buildings

A tenant may, during his tenancy or within six months, or longer if agreed, from the end thereof, remove any engine, machinery, fencing or other fixture[49] affixed to an agricultural holding by the tenant, and any building erected by him on the holding, other than one for which he is entitled to compensation under the Act or otherwise, not being affixed or built in pursuance of some obligation or instead of some-

---

[39] e.g. *Lyon* v. *Irvine* (1874) 1 R. 512.
[40] As in *Waugh* v. *More Nisbett* (1882) 19 S.L.R. 427.
[41] As in *Stewart* v. *Warnocks* (1883) 20 S.L.R. 863; see also *Bidoulac* v. *Sinclair's Tr.* (1889) 17 R. 144; *Buttercase & Geddie's Trs.* v. *Geddie* (1897) 24 R. 1128.
[42] *Brodie* v. *Ker*, 1952 S.C. 216.
[43] 1949 Act, S. 31.
[44] 1949 Act, S. 32.
[45] 1949 Act, S. 33.
[46] 1949 Act, S. 34.
[47] *Walker* v. *Kerr*, 1917 S.C. 102; *Colquhoun's Trs.* v. *Purdie*, 1946 S.N. 3.
[48] 1949 Act, S. 13.
[49] The common law principles determine whether a thing is or is not a fixture.

thing belonging to the landlord, provided he has paid all rent owed by him and performed or satisfied all his other obligations to the landlord in respect of the holding and given written notice of his intention to remove them. The landlord may give a counter-notice electing to purchase a fixture or building.[50]

Compensation to tenant for disturbance

Where the tenancy of an agricultural holding terminates by reason of a notice to quit or counter-notice under S. 33,[51] but not where a tenant's counter-notice under S. 25 is excluded, the landlord must compensate the tenant for disturbance to the extent of the loss or expense directly attributable to the quitting of the holding[52] which is unavoidably incurred by the tenant,[53] to the amount of at least one year's and not more than two years' rent[54] of the holding.[55] Even where the minimum statutory compensation is claimed the tenant must have sustained some loss or expense and particulars of the claim must be furnished.[56]

Compensation to tenant for improvements

Tenants are entitled also, on quitting the holding at the termination of the tenancy, to compensation for certain old improvements made under the Agricultural Holdings Acts of 1923 and 1931, subject in some cases to conditions,[57] and to compensation for new improvements begun after 1 November 1948.[58]

Compensation for special standard of farming

If the value of the holding to an incoming tenant has been increased during the tenancy by the continuous adoption of a special standard of farming, the tenant is entitled on notice given to compensation from the landlord in respect of the value thereof to an incoming tenant.[59]

---

[50] 1949 Act, S. 14.

[51] cf. *Johnston* v. *Malcolm,* 1923 S.L.T. (Sh. Ct.) 81; *Hendry* v. *Walker,* 1927 S.L.T. 333.

[52] cf. *Keswick* v. *Wright,* 1924 S.C. 766; *Macgregor* v. *Board of Agriculture,* 1925 S.C. 613.

[53] *Barbour* v. *McDouall,* 1914 S.C. 844.

[54] As to what is 'rent' see *Bennie* v. *Mack* (1832) 10 S. 255; *D. Hamilton's Trs.* v. *Fleming* (1870) 9 M. 329; *Callander* v. *Smith* (1900) 8 S.L.T. 109; *Clark* v. *Hume* (1902) 5 F. 252; *M. Breadalbane* v. *Robertson,* 1914 S.C. 215.

[55] 1949 Act, S. 35; cf. *McHarg* v. *Speirs,* 1924 S.C. 272.

[56] *McLaren* v. *Turnbull,* 1942 S.C. 179; see also *Simpson* v. *Henderson,* 1944 S.C. 365; *Edinburgh Corpn.* v. *Gray,* 1948 S.C. 538.

[57] Ss. 37–46; as to pre-1909 improvements, see S. 96; see also *Mackenzie* v. *Macgillivray,* 1921 S.C. 722; *Gibson* v. *Sherret,* 1928 S.C. 493; *Turnbull* v. *Millar,* 1942 A.C. 521.

[58] Ss. 47–55; see also *E. Galloway* v. *McClelland,* 1915 S.C. 1062; *Findlay* v. *Munro,* 1917 S.C. 419; *Waddell* v. *Howat,* 1925 S.C. 484.

[59] S. 56.

Payment to assist in reorganization of tenant's affairs

In cases where compensation for disturbance is payable, a landlord must also in certain cases pay the tenant a sum to assist in the re-organization of the tenant's affairs, amounting to four times the annual rent of the holding.[60] Where land is acquired compulsorily these provisions apply as if the acquiring authority were the landlord.[61]

Compensation to landlord for deterioration of holding

The landlord may, on the tenant quitting the holding on the termination of the tenancy, claim compensation for any dilapidation or deterioration of or damage to any part of the holding by non-fulfilment by the tenant of his responsibilities to farm in accordance with the rules of good husbandry,[62] and also for the diminished value of the holding generally.[63]

Contracts as to compensation

Save as provided in the Act, either party is entitled to compensation in accordance with the 1949 Act and not otherwise, and is so entitled notwithstanding any agreement to the contrary.[64]

Settlement of claims between landlord and tenant

Any claim of whatever nature by the tenant or the landlord of an agricultural holding against the other arising under the Act or any custom or agreement, and on or out of the termination of the tenancy, falls to be determined by arbitration.[65] An award or agreement under the Act as to compensation, expenses or otherwise, may, if not paid within a month, be recorded for execution in the Books of Council and Session or Sheriff Court books and is enforceable like a recorded decree arbitral.[66] A sum payable to a tenant as compensation may be created by the Secretary of State a charge on the holding by a charging order, burdening the holding with an annuity to pay the sum due, recorded in the Register of Sasines.[67]

The Act also[68] refers to arbitration any question or difference of any

---

[60] Agriculture (Misc. Prov.) Act, 1968, Ss. 9 and 11; *Barns-Graham* v. *Lamont*, 1971 S.C. 170.

[61] Ibid., Ss. 12 and 14—15.

[62] Ss. 57, 59—64. See also *Westwood* v. *Barnett*, 1925 S.C. 624; *Dougla* v. *Cassillis and Culzean Estates*, 1944 S.C. 355.

[63] Ss. 58, 59—64. As to claim see *D. Montrose* v. *Hart*, 1925 S.C. 160; *Adam* v. *Smyth*, 1948 S.C. 455.

[64] cf. *Young* v. *Oswald*, 1949 S.C. 412.

[65] S. 68; see also Ss. 74—8; *Chalmers Property Inv. Co.* v. *McColl*, 1951 S.C. 24.

[66] S. 69.

[67] S. 70; as to charge in favour of a landlord not himself absolute owner of the holding, see S. 82.

[68] S. 74; *Brodie* v. *Ker*, 1952 S.C. 216.

kind between the parties, except a question or difference as to liability for rent. An arbiter acting under the Act may at any stage in the arbitration *ex proprio motu* state a case on a question of law for the opinion of the sheriff, and either party may apply to the sheriff to direct the arbiter to do so. The sheriff's opinion is final and binding on the arbiter,[69] unless either party appeals to the Court of Session whose decision is final.[70]

Settlement of differences

Any question or difference which by the 1949 Act or under the lease is required to be determined by arbitration may be determined by the Land Court on joint application.[71]

SMALL LANDHOLDERS AND CROFTERS

The Crofters Holdings (Sc.) Acts, 1886 to 1908, made special provision for the holding of lands in the crofting counties[72] and established the Crofters Commission. The Small Landholders Act, 1911, substituted the expression 'landholder', extended the special provisions to holdings throughout the whole country,[73] and established the Scottish Land Court, which superseded the Crofters Commission.[74] The Crofters (Scotland) Acts, 1955, 1961 and 1976 recreated the category of crofters in the crofting counties only, applied portions of the earlier legislation as amended thereto, and established a new Crofters Commission for administration purposes, leaving the Land Court with its judicial functions.

SMALL LANDHOLDERS

The Small Landholders (Scotland) Acts 1886 to 1931[75] made the Crofters Acts 1886 to 1908, applicable throughout Scotland[76] to then

---

[69] *Mitchell-Gill* v. *Buchan*, 1921 S.C. 390.

[70] 1949 Act, Sched. 6, paras. 19–20.

[71] 1949 Act, S. 78; *Rattray and Kennedy* (1950) 40 L.C. 36.

[72] Argyll, Caithness, Inverness, Orkney, Ross and Cromarty, Sutherland and Zetland.

[73] This was amended by the Land Settlement Act, 1919, and the Small Landholders and Agricultural Holdings (Sc.) Act, 1931.

[74] 1911 Act, Ss. 3, 25. As to the relation of the Land Court of the Court of Session see *Kennedy* v. *Johnstone*, 1956 S.L.T. 73.

[75] I.e. the Crofters Holdings (Scotland) Acts, 1886 and 1887; the Crofters Common Grazings Regulation Acts, 1891 and 1908; and the Small Landholders (Scotland) Acts, 1911, 1919, and 1931. Parts of these Acts do not now, under the Crofters Act, 1955, Sched. 6, apply in the crofting counties.

[76] 1911 Act, S. 1.

existing crofter holdings under the 1886 Act,[77] to holdings held by a tenant from year to year who resides on or within two miles from the holding and cultivates it by himself or his family, and, with effect from the end of the lease, to every holding held on lease at the date of the Act for longer than a year by such a tenant, subject to certain provisos, and to holdings constituted by the registration of an applicant under the 1912 Act.[78] Separate subjects worked as one may be a single 'holding'.[79] There were excluded land rented at more than £50 per annum, unless not exceeding fifty acres, garden ground or any land to which the Land Court determined the Acts should not apply, land within burghs, market gardens,[80] glebes, small holdings, allotments, woodlands, permanent grass parks, land held and used for public recreation, or land acquired for any public undertaking.[81]

Conditions of tenure

Such a landholder may be removed only for breach of one or more of the statutory conditions[82] or for non-payment of rent.[83] Holdings may be resumed by the landlord for reasonable purposes,[84] or acquired compulsorily under statute.[85]

The rent may be altered by agreement or fixed by the Land Court,[86] which may also cancel arrears.[87] The tenancy may be renounced,[88] but not assigned[89] but if the landholder is by age or infirmity unable to work the holding he may obtain power from the Land Court to assign it to his son-in-law or to any person who would succeed him on intestacy.[90] Without the landlord's consent the landholder has no power to subdivide the holding, or sublet, except to holiday visitors, or for less than a year.[91] He may not erect a new house on the holding,

[77] *Yool v. Shepherd*, 1914 S.C. 689; *Stormonth-Darling v. Young*, 1915 S.C. 44; *Taylor v. Fordyce*, 1918 S.C. 824.
[78] 1911 Act, S. 2. See also *Kidd v. Morison*, 1916 S.C. 759; *Rogerson v. Chilston*, 1917 S.C. 453; *Sinclair v. Campbell*, 1919 S.C. 341.
[79] *Fullarton v. D. Hamilton's Trs.*, 1918 S.C. 292.
[80] *Grewar v. Moncur's C.B.*, 1916 S.C. 764.
[81] 1911 Act, S. 26(3); see also *McNeill v. D. Hamilton's Trs.*, 1918 S.C. 221.
[82] 1886 Act, S. 1, amd. 1911 Act, S. 10. This includes bankruptcy: *Secy. of State for Scotland v. Black*, 1965 S.L.T. (Land Ct.) 2.
[83] Ibid., S. 3.
[84] Ibid., S. 2, amd. 1911 Act, S. 19; *Whyte v. Stewart*, 1914 S.C. 675.
[85] *McLean v. Inverness C.C.*, 1949 S.C. 69; *McMillan v. Inverness C.C.*, 1949 S.C. 77.
[86] Ibid., Ss. 5–6; see also 1911 Act, S. 13; *McNeill v. D. Hamilton's Trs.*, 1918 S.C. 221; *McKelvie v. D. Hamilton's Trs.*, 1918 S.C. 301; *Dept. of Agriculture v. Burnett*, 1937 S.L.T. 292.
[87] Ibid., S. 6.
[88] Ibid., S. 7, amd. 1911 Act, S. 18.
[89] Ibid., S. 1, amd. 1911 Act, S. 21.
[90] 1911 Act, S. 21 amd. Succession (Sc.) Act, 1964, Sched. 2, para. 15; Land Settlement Act, 1919, S. 13; *McGregor v. Garrow*, 1973 S.L.T. (Land Ct.) 3.
[91] 1886 Act, S. 1; 1911 Act, S. 10; *McNeill, supra; Little v. McEwan*, 1965 S.L.T. (Land Ct.) 3.

except in substitution for one already there, unless he is a new holder established by the Department of Agriculture when he may do so with the consent of the Department and the landlord.[92] There is provision for compensation for improvements[93] and holdings may be enlarged.[94] A holding may be bequeathed,[95] new holdings may be created,[96] and there is provision for vacant holdings,[97] the regulation of common grazings[98] and the making by the Land Court of a record of the holding.[99]

COTTARS

A cottar is the occupier of a dwelling-house with or without land who pays no rent, or the tenant from year to year of a dwelling-house situated in a crofting parish who resides therein and who pays an annual rent, not exceeding £6 in money, with or without garden ground, but without arable or pasture land.[1] Cottars, if removed, or if paying rent and renouncing their tenancy or being removed, are entitled to compensation for permanent improvements, and may receive loans or assistance from the Secretary of State like crofters.[2] A cottar may, by agreement or order of the Land Court, acquire the site of the dwelling-house on or pertaining to his subject.[3]

STATUTORY SMALL TENANTS

The Small Landholders Acts apply also, only so far as expressly applied, to statutory small tenants, who are tenants from year to year, or leaseholders, not otherwise disqualified in terms of the 1911 Act, in regard to whom the 1911 Act, S. 2, provides that they shall not be held existing yearly tenants or qualified leaseholders, and the successors of such tenants or leaseholders, being their heirs, legatees, or assignees.[4] Certain other provisions apply only to statutory small tenants.[5] They

[92] 1886 Act, S. 1; 1911 Act, S. 10(2).
[93] 1886 Act, Ss. 11–15, amd. 1911 Act, S. 16.
[94] Ibid., Ss. 8–10; see also Agriculture (Misc. Prov.) Act, 1968, S. 16.
[95] Ibid., S. 16, amd. 1911 Act, Ss. 20, 22 and Succession (Sc.) Act, 1964, Sched. 2, paras. 9, 15.
[96] 1911 Act, S. 7.
[97] 1911 Act, S. 17.
[98] 1911 Act, S. 24.
[99] Small Landholders Act, 1931, S. 10.
[1] 1886 Act, S. 34; Crofters (Sc.) Act, 1955, S. 28(4).
[2] 1955 Act, S. 28(1); 1961 Act, Sched. 1, para. 7; White v. Cameron, 1966 S.L.T. (Land Ct.) 7.
[3] Crofting Reform (Sc.) Act, 1976, Ss. 1–8.
[4] 1911 Act, Ss. 2(iii)(b), 32(1) and (2). See also Irvine v. Fordyce, 1927 S.C. 72.
[5] 1911 Act, S. 32(3) to (15). See Clelland v. Baird, 1923 S.C. 370.

may, notwithstanding contrary agreement, obtain from the Land Court renewal of tenancies at the expiry of leases, unless the landlord can satisfy the Land Court of a reasonable objection.[6] The Agricultural Holdings (Scotland) Acts apply as if the tenancy were a lease.[7] Either party may apply to the Land Court to fix an equitable rent, or the period for which the tenancy is to be renewed.[8] Such a tenant has no power to assign his lease[9] but may bequeath it, and it transmits on intestacy.[10] A statutory small tenant has the option, on giving notice to the landlord, to convert his tenure into that of a landholder and acquire the privileges thereof.[11]

CROFTERS' HOLDINGS

Special provision is now made for the tenure of lands by crofters by parts of the Crofters Holdings (Scotland) Acts, 1886, parts of the Small Landholders (Scotland) Acts 1911, 1919, and 1931,[12] and the Crofters (Scotland) Acts, 1955, 1961 and 1976. A new Crofters Commission was established in 1955.[13] The Land Court has power, with stated exceptions, to determine any question of fact or law arising under the Acts of 1955 or 1961.[14]

A croft is a holding situated in the crofting counties[15] to which before the 1955 Act, any of the provisions of the Landholders Acts 1886 to 1931 relating to landholders, or to statutory small tenants, applied,[16] or a holding in the crofting counties constituted a croft by the registration of the tenant thereof as a crofter under S. 4 of that Act,[17] or a holding which the Secretary of State has directed that it be a croft.[18] Any right in pastoral or grazing land held by the tenant of a croft, alone or in common, is deemed part of the croft.[19]

The Crofters Commission maintains a Register of Crofts containing specified particulars.[20]

[6] Ibid., S. 32(4); *Wilkie* v. *Hill,* 1916 S.C. 892; *Cheyne* v. *Paterson,* 1929 S.C. 119.
[7] Ibid., S. 32(5); and see *Cheyne, supra,* 124.
[8] Ibid., S. 32(6) to (8); *Stormonth-Darling* v. *Young,* 1915 S.C. 44; *Fullarton* v. *D. Hamilton's Trs.,* 1918 S.C. 292.   [9] Ibid., S. 32(1).   [10] Ibid., S. 32(1).
[11] Ibid., S. 32(11); Small Landholders (Sc.) Act, 1931, S. 14.
[12] Parts of these Acts have, by the 1955 Act, Sched. 6, ceased to have effect in the crofting counties, and parts of the 1911 Act are modified in their application to the crofting counties.
[13] 1955 Act, s. 1, and Sched. 1. The Commission may (S. 15) obtain information about crofts.
[14] 1961 Act, S. 4.
[15] Argyll, Caithness, Inverness, Orkney, Ross and Cromarty, Sutherland, and Zetland.
[16] See 1886 Act, Ss. 34; 1911 Act, S. 1; *Laird,* 1973 S.L.T. (Land Ct.) 4.
[17] 1955 Act, S. 3, amd. 1961 Act, Sched. I, para. 9, 1976 Act, S. 14. *Fea Mortification Trs.* v. *Cursiter,* 1967 S.L.T. (Land Ct.) 10; *Macdonald's Exor.* v. *North Uist Estates Trs.,* 1977 S.L.T. (Land Ct.) 10.   [18] 1961 Act, S. 2.
[19] 1955 Act, S. 3(5). But see *Campbell* v. *Secretary of State for Scotland* (1960) 48 L.C. 41; *Ross* v. *Graesser,* 1962 S.C. 66.   [20] 1961 Act, S. 3.

Enlargement of holdings

Crofters may apply to the Land Court for enlargement of their holdings and that court, if satisfied that there is land available may subject to certain limitations order the lease of the land or part thereof by the landlord to the applicants at a fair rent and on such terms and conditions as the court considers just.[21]

Security of tenure

A crofter is not subject to be removed from his croft except where one year's rent is unpaid, or in consequence of a breach of one or more of the statutory conditions of tenure[22] other than payment of rent, or in pursuance of any statute.[23] Contracts to the contrary are void unless approved by the Land Court.

Rent

The rent is that payable in 1955 or at the date of first letting, if thereafter, unless and until altered under the 1955 Act.[24] It may be altered by agreement in writing.[25] The Land Court may, on the application of either party, determine a fair rent, which is not, save by agreement, alterable for seven years.[26]

Record of croft

The Land Court must, on the application of either party make a record of the condition of the cultivation of a croft and of the buildings and other permanent improvements thereon, and by whom they have been executed and paid for. In the absence of contrary agreement a crofter is entirely responsible for the maintenance of buildings whether provided by himself or by his landlord.[27]

Renunciation; assignation; subdivision; subletting

A crofter may renounce his tenancy at any term of Whitsunday or Martinmas on one year's written notice to the landlord.[28] He may not, save with the written consent of the Crofters' Commission, assign his croft[29] nor, save with written consent of the landlord and the Commission, subdivide his croft.[30]

---

[21] 1886 Act, Ss. 11–15 and 21, as amd. 1911 Act, S. 16.

[22] 1955 Act, Sched. 2. These include prohibitions on purporting to assign the tenancy, dilapidation, subletting, or subdividing the croft. See, e.g., *Culfargie Estates* v. *Leslie* (1957) 45 L.C. 38.

[23] 1955 Act, S. 3.

[24] 1955 Act, S. 5(1).   [25] 1955 Act, S. 5(2).   [26] 1955 Act, s. 5(3).

[27] *Holman* v. *Henderson,* 1965 S.L.T. (Land Ct.) 13.

[28] 1955 Act, S. 7, amended 1961 Act, Sched. I, para. 1; *Sutherland* v. *Fletcher,* 1977 S.L.T. (Land Ct.) 5.

[29] 1955 Act, S. 8, amd. 1976 Act, S. 15; *Vestey* v. *Holmes,* 1967 S.L.T. (Land Ct.) 7.

[30] 1955 Act, S. 9.

After 1961 a crofter may sublet his croft without the landlord's consent,[31] but requires the written consent of the Commission.[32] Subleases existing in 1961 are validated by intimation to the Commission.[33] The Commission may require crofts inadequately used to be sublet.[34] A subtenant, save exceptionally, is not a crofter nor the tenant of an agricultural holding.[35]

Succession

A crofter may, by testamentary writing,[36] bequeath his tenancy to any one person, but a bequest to a person not one of the crofter's family is void unless the Commission determines otherwise. The landlord may object, and if the Commission upholds the objection, the right to the croft devolves on the deceased crofter's heir-at-law.[37] If the right devolves on the heir-at-law the landlord shall, subject to the determination of any dispute by the Commission, accept as successor any heir who would be entitled to succeed failing nearer heirs and who applies within three months.[38] If thereafter no person has been accepted as successor the Commission must nominate the person who appears to be the nearer heir and who has intimated a desire to succeed to the tenancy, failing which it must declare the croft vacant.[39]

Resumption of croft

The Land Court may authorize the resumption of a croft or part thereof by the landlord, for some reasonable purpose[40] having relation to the good of the croft or of the estate or to the public interest, on terms and on the landlord making adequate compensation in money or

[31] 1961 Act, S. 11(2).
[32] 1961 Act, S. 11(3)–(6).
[33] 1961 Act, S. 11(1).
[34] 1961 Act, S. 12.
[35] 1961 Act, S. 13.
[36] Cf. *Cameron* v. *Holman* (1951) 39 L.C. 14; *McKillop* v. *Secretary of State for Scotland* (1951) 39 L.C. 17.
[37] 1886 Act, S. 16; 1955 Act, S. 10; *Kennedy* v. *McInnes*, 1977 S.L.T. (Land Ct.) 3. Questions as to the validity or effect of the bequest fall to be determined by any court having jurisdiction to determine the validity and effect of the deceased's whole testamentary writings. The Land Court has no power to determine questions arising in connection with distributing the deceased's estate, other than succession to the tenancy: *MacLennan's Exrx.* v. *M.* 1974 S.L.T. (Land Ct.) 3.
[38] cf. *MacDonald* v. *Doxford Estates Co.* (1952) 40 L.C. 39.
[39] 1955 Act, S. 11, 1961 Act, Sched. I, para. 2. The provisions of the Succession (Sc.) Act, 1964, did not apply to crofts: 1964 Act, S. 37(1)(b), until made applicable by the Law Reform (Misc. Prov.) (Sc.) Act, 1968, S. 8.
[40] Defined, S. 12(2); See *Andrew* v. *Mackay* (1938) 47 L.C. 30; *Mackay's Trs.* v. *Colthart* (1958) 47 L.C. 43; *Murray's Trs.* v. *Ross*, 1964 S.L.T. (Land Ct.) 9; *Lochiel Estates* v. *Campbell*, 1968 S.L.T. (Land Ct.) 2; *Martin* v. *Luib*, 1973 S.L.T. (Land Ct.) 9; *Libberton Proprs.* v. *Mackay*, 1973 S.L.T. (Land Ct.) 13; *Grimersta Estate* v. *MacLeod*, 1972 S.L.C.R. 96, 128; *Beardsell* v. *Bell*, 1975 S.L.T. (Land Ct.) 2; *Galston Estate* v. *Fivepenny Borve Crofters*, 1975 S.L.T. (Land Ct.) 4; *Simburgh Co.* v. *Mail*, 1975 S.L.T. (Land Ct.) 9. A subtenant cannot object to proposed resumption: *Carnach Crofts* v. *Robertson*, 1973 S.L.T. (Land Ct.) 8.

by letting other land of equivalent value in the neighbourhood or otherwise.[41]

Removal of crofter

The Land Court may make an order for the removal of a crofter when one year's rent of a croft is unpaid, or a crofter has broken one or more of the statutory conditions, other than that as to payment of rent.[42] That Court may on the application of the Secretary of State make an order for the removal of a crofter whose right to compensation for permanent improvements has been transferred to the Secretary of State[43] if the crofter has abandoned his croft, or broken any of the other statutory conditions or broken any of the conditions of repayment of a loan contained in the agreement therefor.[44]

Compensation for improvements and for deterioration

If a crofter renounces his tenancy or is removed, he is entitled to compensation for permanent improvements made on the croft[45] if suitable thereto, executed and paid for by him or any of his predecessors and executed otherwise than in pursuance of a specific agreement or, if so executed, not recompensed.[46] The landlord is entitled to compensation for any deterioration of, or damage to, fixed equipment.[47] The amount of compensation is fixed, failing agreement, by the Land Court.[48]

Vacant crofts

When a croft becomes vacant the landlord must notify the Crofters' Commission and may not let the croft save with the consent of the Commission or of the Secretary of State. The Commission may require the landlord to submit his proposals for reletting the croft, failing which the Commission may themselves let the croft, in which case the landlord may apply to the Land Court for variation of the terms and conditions of letting.[49]

[41] 1955 Act, S. 12, amd. 1961 Act, Sched. I; *M. Bute* v. *Baxter,* 1966 S.L.T. (Land Ct.) 6; *Foljambe* v. *McInnes Crofters,* 1979 S.L.T. (Land Ct.) 9; *MacLean* v. *Secretary of State for Scotland,* 1980 S.L.T. (Land Ct.) 18.

[42] 1955 Act, S. 13(1); *Culfargie Estates* v. *Leslie* (1957) 45 L.C. 38; *Bray* v. *Morrison,* 1973 S.L.T. (Land Ct.) 6. This includes bankruptcy: *Secy. of State for Scotland* v. *Black,* 1965 S.L.T. (Land Ct.) 2.

[43] Under S. 23(3), where the Secretary of State has given financial assistance to the crofter by way of loan under S. 22.   [44] 1955 Act, S. 13(2).

[45] *Mackenzie* v. *Roger,* 1964 S.L.T. (Land Ct.) 8.

[46] 1955 Act, S. 14(1)–(3), and (10); see also 1961 Act, S. 6; *Church of Scotland General Trs.* v. *Thomson* (1958) 47 L.C. 17; *Davidson's Exrx.* v. *Stewart,* 1964 S.L.T. (Land Ct.) 6.

[47] 1955 Act, S. 14(6)–(7) amended 1961 Act, Sched. 1, para. 4.

[48] 1955 Act, S. 14(8)–(9).

[49] 1955 Act, S. 16 amd. 1961 Act, Sched. 1, para. 5 and 1976 Act, S. 13; *Gray* v. *Crofters' Commission,* 1980 S.L.T. (Land Ct.) 2.

Absentee crofters

If a crofter is not ordinarily resident on, or within ten miles of, the croft, and it is in the general interest of the crofting community in the district that the tenancy be terminated and the croft let to some other person, the Commission may terminate the tenancy and require the crofter to relinquish occupation.[50] In certain circumstances the crofter may obtain a feu of the dwelling-house and garden ground.[51]

Aged crofters

If a crofter is unable through illness or old age or infirmity properly to work his croft and is willing to renounce the tenancy on retaining the dwelling-house, and it is in the general interest of the crofting community that he be authorized to do so, the Commission may authorize him to renounce his tenancy. In such a case the crofter may obtain a feu of the dwelling-house and garden.[52]

Improvements

Crofters may erect buildings or other structures or execute works on the croft reasonably required to enable them to make use of the croft for any subsidiary or auxiliary occupation which will not interfere substantially with the use of the croft as an agricultural subject, and such are permanent improvements of the croft.[53]

Reorganization schemes

The Commission may promote schemes for the reorganization of crofting townships, providing, subject to safeguards, for the reallocation of the land in such amounts as is most conducive to the efficient use of that land and the general benefit of the township.[54]

Financial assistance

The Secretary of State may make schemes for providing grants and loans to crofters.[55]

New crofts

The landlord and tenant of certain kinds of holdings, not being crofts, may apply jointly to the Secretary of State to have such holding

[50] 1955 Act, S. 17(1)–(3), amd. 1961 Act, S. 7.
[51] 1955 Act, S. 17(4)–(10), amd. 1961 Act, S. 7 and Sched. 1, para. 6; *Anderson* v. *MacLeod's Trs.,* 1973 S.L.T. (Land Ct.) 2.
[52] 1955 Act, S. 18; *McLean* v. *Roger,* 1964 S.L.T. (Land Ct.) 11; *MacKenzie* v *Crofters' Commission,* 1966 S.L.T. (Land Ct.) 13.
[53] 1961 Act, S. 5.
[54] 1961 Act, Ss. 8–9, replacing 1955 Act, Ss. 19–20.
[55] 1955 Act, Ss. 22–3; 1961 Act, S. 14.

declared a croft. Provision is made for enlarging crofts, and land may be added to common grazings.[56]

Right to acquire crofts

A crofter may, by agreement or order of the Land Court, acquire croft land tenanted by him, or the site of the dwelling-house on or pertaining to the croft with its building and garden, on terms agreed or fixed by the Land Court. Where part of the land is conveyed an adjustment of the rent for the remainder must be made.[57] The crofter has right to share in the value of land resumed by the landlord, or taken compulsorily.[58]

Common grazings

Crofters sharing in a common grazing may appoint a grazings committee whose duty is to maintain the common grazings and fixed equipment, to carry out works for their improvement and to make and administer common grazings regulations, which require the Commission's confirmation, for management and use of the common grazings.[59] Common grazings may be enlarged.[60] Rights in a common grazing imply rights to water thereon for stock.[61] The common grazings committee may be made responsible for the dyke or fence separating the grazings from the individual holdings,[62] but has no power in relation to a township access road.[63] The Commission may apportion part of common grazing for the exclusive use of a crofter who applies.[64]

SPORTING LEASE

A sporting lease, or lease of shooting, is normally the grant for a term of years of the personal privilege of entering on lands and there

[56] 1961 Act, S. 2; see also 1911 Act, S. 7.
[57] 1976 Act, Ss. 1–8; *Ferguson* v. *Ross Estates Co.*, 1977 S.L.T. (Land Ct.) 19; *Gilmour* v. *Lorat*, 1979 S.L.T. (Land Ct.) 2; *Mackintosh* v. *Seafield's Trs.* 1979 S.L.T. (Land Ct.) 6; *Cameron* v. *Argyll's Trs.*, 1981 S.L.T. (Land Ct.) 2. The conveyance may be by feu-charter incorporating feuing conditions: *Campbell* v. *Argyll's Trs.*, 1977 S.L.T. (Land Ct.) 22.
[58] 1976 Act, Ss. 9–10.
[59] 1955 Act, Ss. 24–7, amd. 1961 Act, S. 15 and 1976 Act, S. 16; *Neish* v. *North Talisker Grazing Cttee.*, 1968 S.L.T. (Land Ct.) 4.
[60] 1961 Act, S. 2
[61] *MacColl* v. *Downie's Trs.* (1961) 50 L.C. 28.
[62] *Crofters Commission* v. *Cameron of Garth*, 1964 S.C. 229.
[63] *MacDonald* v. *Greig*, 1964 S.L.T. (Land Ct.) 5.
[64] *Crofters Commission* v. *South Scorrybreck Grazings Cttee.*, 1968 S.L.T. (Land Ct.) 8.

shooting certain kinds of game, and removing them thence.[65] Assignation or subletting is incompetent.[66] The terms of the lease may exclude the right of the landlord and his agricultural tenants.[67] Such is a proper lease binding on singular successors.[68] It is an implied condition that the game tenant shall not allow the stock of game to be increased to an extravagant extent;[69] if he does allow the game to increase to an excessive and unreasonable extent, whereby injury is done to the estate, he is liable in damages. The landlord commonly makes the game tenant bound to free and relieve him of any claims made on him by agricultural tenants for game damage to his crops, and to keep the game population down to a reasonable extent,[70] with liberty, if this be not done, himself to enter and protect himself by reducing the number of game.

A landlord who believes his estate is being detrimentally affected by an unreasonable stock of game, and wishes to claim damages therefor, must give notice thereof timeously, so that the shooting tenant may rectify his default or at least obtain evidence that the game is not excessive, failing which he may be barred by delay.[71]

An agricultural tenant may claim damages from his landlord if the latter has increased the game on the farm beyond a fair average stock.[72] The agricultural tenant has no direct right of action against the game tenant, unless there be some contractual relation between them.[73]

A lease of fishings is of the same general character.[74] An onerous contract for not less than a year whereby a landowner having a right to fish for freshwater fish in inland waters, or the occupier of such a right, authorizes another to fish in deemed a lease within the Leases Act, 1449, and the right to fish authorized is deemed a heritable right.[75]

---

[65] cf. *Middleton* v. *L.A.* (1876) 3 R. 599; *Fraser* v. *Patrick* (1879) 6 R. 581; *Stewart* v. *Bulloch* (1881) 8 R. 381; *Critchley* v. *Campbell* (1884) 11 R. 475; *Eliott's Trs.* v. *E.* (1894) 21 R. 858, 863; *Butter* v. *Foster*, 1912 S.C. 1218 S.C. 1218. The lease may take the form of a lease of the lands, the anticipated use being only the harbouring of game, which the tenant has liberty to shoot: e.g. *Farquharson* (1870) 9 M. 66; cf. *Patrick* v. *Harris's Trs.* (1904) 6 F. 985. The contract may, however, not be a lease but merely a personal licence to shoot: *I.R.* v. *Anderson*, 1922 S.C. 284.

[66] *E. Fife* v. *Wilson* (1864) 3 M. 323; *Mackintosh* v. *May* (1895) 22 R. 345.

[67] *North* v. *Cumming* (1864) 3 M. 173. By the Ground Game Act, 1880, S. 1, the occupier of lands has an inalienable right to kill and take ground game thereon so that a landlord cannot now by a game lease exclude the agricultural tenant's rights to kill ground game.

[68] *Farquharson* (1870) 9 M. 66. As to damages for not getting full possession see *Critchley* v. *Campbell* (1884) 11 R. 475.

[69] *Kidd* v. *Byrne* (1875) 3 R. 255; *Eliott's Trs., supra.*

[70] *Kidd, supra*; see also *Inglis* v. *Moir's Tutors* (1871) 10 M. 204.

[71] *Eliott's Trs., supra.*

[72] *Drysdale* v. *Jamieson* (1832) 11 S. 147; *Wemyss* v. *Wilson* (1847) 10 D. 194; *Morton* v. *Graham* (1876) 6 M. 71; cf. *Broadwood* v. *Hunter* (1855) 17 D. 340. As to interdicting landlord see *Wemyss* v. *Gulland* (1847) 10 D. 204.

[73] *Inglis* v. *Moir's Tutors* (1871) 10 M. 204; *Kidd, supra.*

[74] *Gemmill* v. *Riddell* (1847) 9 D. 727.

[75] Freshwater and Salmon Fisheries (Sc.) Act, 1976, S. 4.

MINERAL LEASES

A so-called mineral lease is truly a sale of the minerals coupled with a licence for a period to enter on the lands and extract and remove the minerals, on payment of a lordship or royalty.[76] The word 'mineral' is elastic and requires to be construed in the particular circumstances in which it is used. In its widest sense it includes every substance which can be got from beneath the surface of the earth for profit by means of mining, quarrying or excavation, including not merely coal and ironstone but also clay and other strata.[77] The rights of parties are almost always regulated by a written lease[78] and most of the cases concern the interpretation of particular deeds. A tenant is not, unless the lease provides therefor,[79] entitled to have the lease reduced merely on the grond that the minerals cannot be worked at a profit, even if no rent be payable,[80] but only if there proves to be none of the mineral sought, or it becomes exhausted, or the working of it becomes impracticable.[81]

Landlord's duties

The landlord is bound to cede possession to the tenant of so much of the surface of his lands as is necessary for working the minerals, to permit access thereto, and to cede possession of the mineral field or strata comprised in the lease, with liberty to make the necessary shafts and access roads.[82]

Assignation is normally excluded.[83]

Landlord's rights—rent or royalty

The payment due by the tenant may be an annual rent and/or a lordship or royalty based on the quantity or value of the minerals extracted.[84] The landlord has the usual remedies for the recovery of his

---

[76] *Gowans v. Christie* (1873) 11 M. (H.L.) 1, 12; *Campbell v. Wardlaw* (1883) 10 R. (H.L.) 65, 68; *McCosh v. Ayrshire Assessor*, 1945 S.C. 260; *Secy. of State v. Inverness Assessor*, 1948 S.C. 334; *Moray Estates Dev. Co. v. I.R.C.*, 1951 S.C. 754.

[77] *Portobello Assessor v. Mitchell* (1896) 23 R. 686; *Secretary of State v. Inverness Assessor*, *supra*.

[78] The common law regulates constitution and proof of such a lease.

[79] *Wylie & Hill v. Belch* (1867) 4 S.L.R. 29; *Fleming v. Baird* (1871) 9 M. 730.

[80] *Gowans, supra*.

[81] Stair I, 15, 2; Bankt. I, 2, 14; Bell, *Prin.* §1208; *Gowans, supra*; cf. *Murdoch v. Fullerton* (1829) 7 S. 404; *Dixon v. Campbell* (1829) 8 S. 970; *Sinclair v. Mossend Iron Co.* (1854) 17 D. 258; *Bargaddie Coal Co. v. Wark* (1860) 23 D. 44; *Thomson v. Gordon* (1869) 7 M. 687.

[82] See *Harrowar's Trs. v. Erskine* (1827) 5 S. 307; *Galbraith's Tr. v. Eglinton Iron Co.* (1868) 7 M. 167.

[83] *M. Breadalbane v. Whitehead* (1893) 21 R. 138; see also, *Elphinstone v. Monkland Iron Co.* (1886) 13 R. (H.L.) 98; *Ebbw Vale Steel Co. v. Wood's Tr.* (1898) 25 R. 439.

[84] cf. *Adam v. Napier* (1843) 5 D. 736; *Guthrie v. Cochran* (1846) 19 S. Jur. 69; *Waugh v. Russel* (1870) 7 S.L.R. 222; *Dalgleish v. Fife Coal Co.* (1892) 30 S.L.R. 58.

lordship or royalties; landlord's hypothec extends to royalties.[85] He is not prevented from claiming arrears by having for years accepted a fixed rent by reason of the tenant's inaccurate returns of output.[86]

Tenant's rights

The tenant is entitled to be given possession of the mineral strata.

Assignation and subletting are not competent at common law unless expressly permitted.[87]

Tenant's duties and liabilities

The mode of working is normally provided for by the lease, and the tenant may incur liability in damages for contravention of those provisions.[88]

The tenant is normally taken bound to fence the ground occupied and all workings and access roads[89] and as occupier of the lands leased he must take reasonable care for the safety of persons coming in the vicinity of the premises.[90]

He may incur liability to adjacent mineral tenants if by abnormal operations he causes flooding or other damage to their workings.[91]

Duty to support superincumbent land

Unless permitted by his lease to do so, with or without provision for compensation, a mineral tenant is not entitled to work the minerals in such a way as to bring down the surface or damage buildings thereon. If he does so the mineral tenant may accordingly incur liability to his landlord, or to the latter's feuars[92] or surface tenants.[93]

The mineral tenant is frequently taken bound to relieve his landlord of all claims made against the latter for damage by subsidence.[94]

A clause binding the tenant to pay for damage to the surface has been held not to cover damage done by smoke or vapour emitted in the process.[95]

---

[85] *Linlithgow Oil Co.* v. *E. Rosebery* (1903) 6 F. 90.

[86] *Simpson's Trs.* v. *Gower* (1874) 11 S.L.R. 309.

[87] cf. *D. Portland* v. *Baird* (1865) 4 M. 10; *Clark* v. *West Calder Oil Co.* (1882) 9 R. 1017.

[88] *Carron Co.* v. *Henderson's Trs.* (1896) 23 R. 1042; *Jackson's Tr.* v. *Dixon* (1901) 3 F. 782; *Shawsrigg Fireclay Co.* v. *Larkhall Collieries* (1903) 5 F. 1131.

[89] *Ferrier* v. *Readman* (1898) 6 S.L.T. 109; cf. *Hislop* v. *Durham* (1842) 4 D. 1168; *McFeat* v. *Rankin's Trs.* (1879) 6 R. 1043; *McLean* v. *Warnock* (1883) 10 R. 1052; *Gavin* v. *Arrol* (1889) 16 R. 509; *Prentice* v. *Assets Co.* (1890) 17 R. 484.

[90] Occupiers Liability (Scotland) Act, 1960, Ss. 1, 2.

[91] *Durham* v. *Hood* (1871) 9 M. 474; contrast *Wilson* v. *Waddell* (1876) 4 R. (H.L.) 29; cf. *Rankin* v. *Dixon* (1847) 9 D. 1048.

[92] *Dryburgh* v. *Fife Coal Co.* (1905) 7 F. 1083; cf. *Highgate* v. *Paisley Mags.* (1896) 23 R. 992.

[93] cf. *Hamilton* v. *Turner* (1867) 5 M. 1086; *Stewart's Hospital* v. *Waddell* (1890) 17 R. 1077.

[94] e.g *Mid & E. Calder Gas Light Co.* v. *Oakbank Oil Co.* (1891) 18 R. 788.

[95] *Galbraith's Tr.* v. *Eglinton Iron Co.* (1868) 7 M. 167.

Obligation not to encroach beyond boundary

The tenant must confine his operations to the parts of underground strata underlying the landlord's land. If he goes beyond the boundary he encroaches on another's minerals and becomes liable in damages for wrongful abstraction of minerals.[96] Nor may he discharge water which accumulates in the workings into another's workings.[97] An inferior mineowner may carry out operations to prevent the influx of water from the upper mine,[98] but the upper mineral tenant is not obliged to leave a barrier of unworked mineral as a protection to neighbouring workings against being inundated with water.[99] An encroaching mineral tenant may also incur liability for surface damage.[1]

Termination

On the termination of the lease the tenant is bound to leave the workings in good order and may be liable in damages for breach of an express condition of the lease on that matter.[2] He is normally taken bound to restore the surface when mining or quarrying is completed. If he fails to remove in terms of his lease the tenant is liable for damages for breach of contract.[3] A customary provision allows the tenant to remove buildings an machinery erected by him, if they are not taken over by the landlord at valuation.[4]

SMALL HOLDINGS

The Small Holdings Act 1892, empowers county councils to acquire land for the provision of small holdings, i.e. holdings exceeding one acre and not exceeding fifty acres or with an annual value for income tax purposes not exceeding £50, which they may sell or let to persons desiring themselves to cultivate the holdings.[5] Such a holding is to be held subject to statutory conditions.[6] Such holdings are not small landholdings under the Small Landholders (Sc.) Act, 1911.[7]

---

[96] cf. *Houldsworth* v. *Brand's Trs.* (1877) 3 R. 304; (1877) 4 R. 369; *Livingstone* v. *Rawyards Coal Co.* (1880) 7 R. (H.L.) 1; *Davidson's Trs.* v. *Caledonian Ry.* (1895) 23 R. 45.

[97] *Baird* v. *Monklands Iron Co.* (1862) 24 D. 1418; cf. *Irving* v. *Leadhills Mining Co.* (1856) 18 D. 833.   [98] *Wauchope* v. *E. Abercorn* (1780) 2 Pat. 519.

[99] *Harvey* v. *Wardrop* (1824) 3 S. 322.

[1] *Allan* v. *Robertson's Trs.* (1891) 18 R. 932.

[2] *Elphinstone* v. *Monkland Iron Co.* (1886) 13 R. (H.L.) 98; *Duke of Portland* v. *Wood's Trs.*, 1927 S.C. (H.L.) 1.

[3] *Houldsworth* v. *Brand's Trs.* (1876) 3 R. 304.

[4] *Wilson* v. *Douglas* (1868) 7 M. 112.

[5] 1892 Act, Ss. 1–4.

[6] Ibid., S. 9.   [7] 1911 Act, S. 26(3)(e).

ALLOTMENTS

The Allotments (Sc.) Act, 1892, empowers local authorities to acquire land for letting in allotments to persons resident in their areas. An allotment may not exceed one acre, and no building other than a shed or greenhouse may be erected. Such holdings are not small landholdings under the Small Landholders (Sc.) Act, 1911.[7]

VOLUNTARY TRANSFER OF LAND

Voluntary transfer of land may be effected in pursuance of an intention to gift or of an enforceable contract of sale or of excambion. Transfer of possession does not transfer title, which is effected only, formerly by the purchaser taking sasine under a precept of sasine granted by the disponer and recording an instrument of sasine, and now by the seller granting a disposition in the purchaser's favour and the purchaser becoming infeft by recording the disposition in the Register of Sasines.

DONATION

An intention to donate land is enforceable only if there is a promise or unilateral undertaking to give, embodied in writing, probative or privileged, and delivered, or otherwise constituted but followed by actings amounting to *rei interventus* or homologation.[1] The gift may be conditional, in which case the donor retains the right to demand a reconveyance on failure of the condition, which right is an incorporeal heritable right transmissible by will or on intestacy.[2]

A disposition of land in pursuance of an intention to gift is effected in the same form as a disposition on sale,[3] save that the consideration is stated as for love, favour and affection, or words to the same effect. The donee completes title in the same way as an onerous disponee.[3] Questions may arise whether taking the title of heritage in the names of particular persons, who had not given the consideration for the heritage, amounts to gift of the heritage to them.[4] Prima facie it does,[5] though as between husband and wife, such a donation was revocable prior to the Married Women's Property (Sc.) Act, 1920, S. 5.[6] A

---

[1] Stair I, 10, 3; Ersk. III, 3, 88; Bell, *Prin.* §889; *Barron* v. *Rose* (1794) Mor. 8444; *Goldston* v. *Young* (1868) 7 M. 188; See also *Malcolm* v. *Campbell* (1891) 19 R. 278; *Banff Mags.* v. *Ruthin Castle*, 1944 S.C. 36; *Mowat* v. *Thain*, 1947 S.N. 180; *McGregor* v. *Hepburn*, 1979 S.L.T. 87.

[2] *Connell's J.F.* v. *McWatt*, 1961 S.L.T. 203.

[3] See further latter parts of this Chapter.

[4] cf. *Newton* v. *N.*, 1923 S.C. 15; 1925 S.C. 715; *Galloway* v. *G.*, 1929 S.C. 160.

[5] *Gilpin* v. *Martin* (1869) 7 M. 807. cf. *Ballantyne's Trs.* v. *B's Trs.*, 1941 S.C. 35; *Linton* v. *I.R.*, 1928 S.C. 209.

[6] *Johnstone's Trs.* v. *J.* (1896) 23 R. 538.

husband has been held entitled to prove that the price of heritage taken in the wife's name had been paid by him, though the disposition bore that it had been paid by her.[7]

If subjects gifted are burdened with a security, the gift is taken under that burden so that the donee is bound to discharge the debt[8] but the donee is liable for the donor's debts *quantum lucratus* only.[9]

SALE OF HERITAGE

The contract of sale of heritage[10] is regulated by common law;[11] the parties must respectively have power to sell and to buy, and the contract must be constituted in writing probative, or holograph,[12] or adopted as holograph,[13] of both parties,[14] or their agents,[15] or by informal agreement proved by writ or oath and perfected by *rei interventus* or homologation.[16] It must evidence *consensus in idem*.[17] The writings are usually known as missives of sale, but the contract is sometimes contained in a minute of sale,[18] or where land is sold by public auction, in Articles of Roup containing the conditions of sale, to which a document is appended narrating the offers and the preference of the highest offer.[19] Such must be executed by or on behalf of both parties.[19] The creation in favour of another of an option to purchase

---

[7] *Smith* v. *S.*, 1917 2 S.L.T. 219.

[8] *Johnstone's Trs., supra; Ballantyne's Trs., supra.*

[9] Bell, *Prin.* §910, 1922; More, Notes, cccxxxii; Menzies, 868; *Welch's Exors.* v. *Edinburgh Life Assce. Co.* (1896) 23 R. 772; *Ballantyne's Trs., supra.*

[10] Including land and buildings, whether held feudally or on leasehold, and other rights heritable by nature, such as feu-duties and ground annuals.

[11] If moveables, e.g. furniture or stock-in-trade, are sold by the same contract, the Sale of Goods Act, 1979, applies to the contract *quoad* the moveables: see e.g. *Allan* v. *Gilchrist* (1875) 2 R. 857; see also *Allan* v. *Millar*, 1932 S.C. 620.

[12] *Scottish Lands and Buildings Co.* v. *Shaw* (1880) 7 R. 756; *Caithness Flagstone Co.* v. *Sinclair* (1880) 7 R. 1117. See also *Weir* v. *Robertson* (1872) 10 M. 438; *Littlejohn* v. *Hadwen* (1882) 20 S.L.R. 5; *McGinn* v. *Shearer*, 1947 S.C. 334.

[13] *Gavine's Trs.* v. *Lee* (1883) 10 R. 448; *Harvey* v. *Smith* (1904) 6 F. 511; *Brown's Trs.* v. *McDonald*, 1922 S.L.T. 7.

[14] Stair I, 10, 9; Ersk. III, 2, 2; *Goldston* v. *Young* (1868) 7 M. 188; *McLaren* v. *Law* (1871) 44 S. Jur. 17; *Littlejohn* v. *Hadwen* (1882) 20 S.L.R. 5; *Gavine's Trs.* v. *Lee* (1883) 10 R. 448; *Malcolm* v. *Campbell* (1891) 19 R. 278; *McGinn* v. *Shearer*, 1947 S.C. 334.

[15] *Whyte* v. *Lee* (1879) 6 R. 699; *Scottish Land Co.* v. *Shaw* (1880) 7 R. 756; cf. *Caithness Flagstone Co.* v. *Sinclair* (1880) 7 R. 1117; see also *Mitchell* v. *Scott's Trs.* (1874) 2 R. 162 and, on authentication by partnership, *Littlejohn* v. *Mackay*, 1974 S.L.T. (Sh. Ct.) 82.

[16] *Gowan's Trs.* v. *Carstairs* (1862) 24 D. 1382, 1388; *Stewart* v. *Burns* (1877) 4 R. 427; *Heiton* v. *Waverley Hydropathic Co.* (1877) 4 R. 830; *Mowat* v. *Caledonian Bank* (1895) 23 R. 270; *McLean* v. *Scott* (1902) 10 S.L.T. 447; *Kinnear* v. *Young*, 1936 S.L.T. 574; But see *Errol* v. *Walker*, 1966 S.C. 93 which is unsound: with it contrast *Law* v. *Thomson*, 1978 S.C. 343.

[17] *Harvey, supra; East Kilbride Development Corpn.* v. *Pollock*, 1953 S.C. 370.

[18] Bell, *Lect.* II, 698; Menzies, 889.

[19] *Shiell* v. *Guthrie's Trs.* (1874) 1 R. 1083; *Moncrieff* v. *Lawrie* (1896) 23 R. 577.

heritage must be similarly constituted[20] but the exercise of an option does not require probative writing.[21] A contract to build and to sell the site and building must doubtless be similarly constituted, but a contract to build for a person on his land does not require formal constitution. Agreements collateral to the sale of land need not be constituted formerly.[22] A unilateral undertaking to sell land at a price is possible, but it is a question whether the writing is a unilateral undertaking or one side of a bilateral contract.[23]

Power of sale or purchase

Parties must have contractual capacity and the requisite legal power of sale or purchase; if the authority of the court is necessary it should be obtained first,[24] rather than a contract be concluded conditional on the power being obtained.[25] A sale is void if vitiated by illegality.[26]

Advertisements

Statements in advertisements about the property are not normally held obligatory[27] but may be, as where an offer referred to the property 'as advertised' and thereby imported into the offer the advertisement and the conditions of the title deeds therein referred to.[28]

Consensus in idem

It may be a narrow question in some cases whether *consensus* has been reached, where in the negotiations new conditions and qualifications are introduced.[29] In many cases the question has arisen whether *consensus* was precluded by error, as to the seller's title,[30] or the

---

[20] cf. *Hamilton v. Lochrane* (1899) 1 F. 478; *Burns v. Garscadden* (1901) 8 S.L.T. 321. See also *Anderson v. A.*, 1961 S.C. 59.

[21] *Sichi v. Biagi*, 1946 S.N. 66; *Stone v. Macdonald*, 1979 S.C. 363, 369; *Scott v. Morrison*, 1979 S.L.T. (Notes) 65.

[22] *Masson v. Scottish Breweries Ltd.*, 1966 S.C. 9.

[23] *Malcolm v. Campbell* (1891) 19 R. 278; *Haldane v. Watson*, 1972 S.L.T. (Sh. Ct.) 8.

[24] cf. *Clyne, Petr.* (1894) 21 R. 849; *Hodge, Petr.* (1904) 11 S.L.T. 709; *Campbell Wyndham Long's Trs.*, 1951 S.C. 685; 1962 S.C. 132.

[25] cf. *Dow's Trs.*, 1947 S.C. 524; *Horne's Trs.* 1952 S.C. 70.

[26] *McPherson's Trs. v. Watt* (1877) 5 R. (H.L.) 9; contrast *Noble v. Campbell* (1876) 4 R. 77; *Shiell v. Guthrie's Trs.* (1874) 1 R. 1083.

[27] *Hamilton v. Western Bank* (1861) 23 D. 1033.

[28] *Nisbet v. Smith* (1876) 3 R. 781 explained in *Bremner v. Dick*, 1911 S.C. 887; see also *Mossend Theatre Co. v. Livingstone*, 1930 S.C. 90.

[29] e.g. *Consensus: Colquhoun v. Wilson's Trs.* (1860) 22 D. 1035; *Westren v. Millar* (1879) 7 R. 173; *Charles v. Shearer* (1900) 8 S.L.T. 273; *Freeman v. Maxwell*, 1928 S.C. 682. No consensus: *Milne v. Marjoribank's Trs.* (1836) 14 S. 533; *Johnston v. Clark* (1855) 18 D. 70; *Bate v. Corstorphine* (1869) 6 S.L.R. 401; *Dickson v. Blair* (1871) 10 M. 41; *Heiton v. Waverley Hydro Co.* (1877) 4 R. 830; *Westren v. Millar* (1879) 7 R. 173; *Nelson v. Assets Co.* (1889) 16 R. 898; *Hay v. Aberdeen Mags.*, 1909 S.C. 554; *Harvey v. Smith* (1904) 6 F 511; *E. Kilbride Development Corpn. v. Pollok*, 1953 S.C. 370.

[30] *McConnell v. Chassels* (1903) 10 S.L.T. 790.

holding,[31] the identification[32] or extent of the subjects,[33] or the ground burdens,[34] or by misrepresentation.[35] *Consensus* may be deemed suspended by conditions in offer or acceptance[36] or may be subject to a resolutive condition.[37] The missives embody the contract until a disposition in implement is signed and delivered, and till then *dissensus* may be found.[38] *Rei interventus* cannot supply lack of *consensus*.[39]

Essentials of contract

The essentials of the contract, apart from formalities of constitution and *consensus*, are the parties, identification of the property and agreement on the price or on means of fixing a price; the term of entry is not essential.[40] Identification depends largely on the description employed, which may be in any form which adequately designates the lands.[41] An error in extent, if substantial, may justify rescission of the contract.[42] The price may be fixed by the contract, or means for fixing it, such as valuation or arbitration,[43] be settled thereby. Interest runs on the price from the date of settlement.

Any qualifications on the prima facie rule that a selling proprietor has right to the whole subjects *a caelo usque ad centrum*, other than those imposed by general law or actually known to the other party, should be made the subject of express statement in the contract. Thus the absence of any provision that the minerals, if reserved to the superior, are so reserved entitles the other party to resile.[44]

---

[31] e.g. *McConnell* v. *Chassels* (1903) 10 S.L.T. 790.

[32] e.g. *Macdonald* v. *Newall* (1898) 1 F. 68; *Houldsworth* v. *Gordon Cumming*, 1910 S.C. (H.L.) 49.

[33] e.g. *Hamilton* v. *Western Bank* (1861) 23 D. 1033; *Morton* v. *Smith* (1877) 5 R. 83; *Woods* v. *Tulloch* (1893) 20 R. 477; and see Ch. 4.7, *supra*; cf. *Anderson* v. *Lambie*, 1954 S.C. (H.L.) 43.

[34] e.g. *Clason* v. *Steuart* (1844) 6 D. 1201; *Johnston* v. *Clark* (1855) 18 D. 70; *Steuart's Trs.* v. *Hart* (1875) 3 R. 192; *Welsh* v. *Russell* (1894) 21 R. 769; *Bremner* v. *Dick*, 1911 S.C. 887.

[35] *Brownlie* v. *Miller* (1880) 7 R. (H.L.) 66.

[36] *Stobo* v. *Morrisons (Gowns), Ltd.*, 1949 S.C. 184; *Effold Properties* v. *Sprot*, 1979 S.L.T. (Notes) 84; *Secy. of State for Scotland* v. *Ravenstone Securities Ltd.*, 1976 S.C. 171. Contrast *Erskine* v. *Glendinning* (1871) 9 M. 656. See also *Campbell* v. *Douglas* (1676) Mor. 8470; *Broomfield* v. *Young* (1757) Mor. 9446; *Fulton* v. *Johnston* (1761) Mor. 8446.

[37] *Hardy* v. *Sime*, 1938 S.L.T. 18; *Gilchrist* v. *Payton*, 1979 S.L.T. 135.

[38] *Morrison* v. *Gray*, 1932 S.C. 712.

[39] *E. Kilbride Development Corpn.* v. *Pollok*, 1953 S.C. 370.

[40] *Smith* v. *Marshall* (1860) 22 D. 1158; *Secy. of State* v. *Ravenstone Securities Ltd.* 1976 S.C. 171, 189, 196; see also *Freeman* v. *Maxwell*, 1928 S.C. 682; *Stobo*, *supra*. Normally there must be an agreed date of entry: *Law* v. *Thomson*, 1978 S.C. 343; this is criticised: *Stone* v. *Macdonald*, 1979 S.C. 363, 370. In *Sloan's Dairies* v. *Glasgow Corpn.* 1977 S.C. 223 it was conceded that an agreed date of entry was not of the essence.

[41] For cases of error on this account see *Macdonald* v. *Newall* (1898) 1 F. 68; *Houldsworth* v. *Gordon Cumming*, 1910 S.C. (H.L.) 49; cf. *Anderson* v. *Lambie*, 1954 S.C. (H.L.) 43.

[42] *Hamilton* v. *Western Bank* (1861) 23 D. 1033; *Morton* v. *Smith* (1877) 5 R. 83; *Woods* v. *Tulloch* (1893) 20 R. 477.

[43] e.g. *E. Selkirk* v. *Nasmyth* (1778) Mor. 627; *McLaren* v. *Aikman*, 1939 S.C. 222.

[44] *Whyte* v. *Lee* (1879) 6 R. 699; *Crofts* v. *Stewart's Trs.*, 1927 S.C. (H.L.) 65; *Mossend Theatre Co.* v. *Livingstone*, 1930 S.C. 90; *Campbell* v. *McCutcheon*, 1963 S.C. 505.

It is implied, and normally expressed, that a sale carries fixtures and fittings on and in the subjects sold,[45] but not moveables readily separable from the lands. It is also implied, unless expressly excluded by the contract, that the lands are free from encumbrances in the form of security rights affecting them, or that any encumbrances will be discharged before the sale is completed.[46]

Conditions

The contract may be conditional on e.g. obtaining planning permission for a contemplated development.[47] The party entitled to insist on satisfaction may waive the condition, expressly or by implication, but one party can withdraw the condition and treat the contract as unconditional only if the condition exists for that party's benefit only, but not if it is, or even can be interpreted as, for the benefit of the other party also.[48] If an express condition is not satisfied the party protected by the condition may resile.[49]

The contract may impose restrictions on the buyer's use of the land, which may be made real burdens on the land. Such are prima facie enforceable by the sellers, but the buyer may establish that the seller has no legal interest to enforce the restriction.[50]

Other usual provisions

Other usual provisions of the contract include the date of entry, the date for payment of the price, an undertaking to give vacant possession, provisions as to fittings and fixtures, the amount of any feu-duty, ground annual, or stipend payable, the incidence of liability for common parts of properties, such as a roof, the apportionment of local rates and rents, and arrangements as to any existing securities. A stipulation for immediate entry means only to give entry as early as is practicable.[51] If a date for entry be specified and the seller cannot meet it, the purchaser may resile.[52] If no date of entry be specified, entry at the date of settlement[53] is implied.[54] Until the date of entry the sellers have beneficial right and interest in the subjects sold and are entitled to remain in beneficial possession and to exercise all the rights of

---

[45] *Christie* v. *Smith*, 1949 S.C. 572.

[46] *Christie* v. *Cameron* (1898) 25 R. 824.

[47] e.g. *Gorrie & Banks Ltd.* v. *Musselburgh*, 1973 S.C. 33.

[48] *Dewar and Finlay Ltd.* v. *Blackwood*, 1968 S.L.T. 196; *Ellis* v. *Pringle*, 1975 S.L.T. 10; *Gilchrist* v. *Payton*, 1979 S.C. 380; *Imry Property Holdings* v. *Glasgow Y.M.C.A.*, 1979 S.L.T. 261.

[49] *Kelly* v. *Clark*, 1968 S.L.T. 141.

[50] *S.C.W.S.* v. *Finnie*, 1937 S.C. 835.

[51] *Heys* v. *Kimball & Morton* (1890) 17 R. 381.

[52] *Kelman* v. *Barr's Tr.* (1878) 5 R. 816.

[53] i.e. exchange of the price against executed disposition.

[54] As to disposition see Conveyancing (Sc.) Act, 1874, S. 28.

owners.[55] If entry depends on a third party's certificate that something has been done it must be a certificate granted for that purpose, and not for another one unless it is clear that parties were to be bound by such a certificate.[56] The contract may be rescinded if the feu-duty is materially different from that stated in the contract.[57] Nor is a purchaser bound to accept a title subject to liability for a *cumulo* unallocated feu-duty. Many stipulations are, however, implied into such contracts by long standing custom. Thus it is implied that the title is feudal.[58]

The purchaser is not affected by any agreement between the seller and another relative to the lands if it is not, or is not capable of being made, a real burden or condition affecting the lands.[59] Such creates a personal right against the seller only. If it is capable of being made real then the purchaser is put on inquiry.[60] A restriction on use which has the effect of securing a commercial monopoly may be unenforceable.[61]

The contract may include collateral conditions, such as to complete the erection of the premises with proper materials and skill.[62]

Risk

The contract being a common law sale, the risk passes to the purchaser immediately on conclusion of the contract: *periculum rei venditae nondum traditae est emptoris*;[63] the purchaser should accordingly insure at once.

Conditional sale—regulated agreements

A conditional sale is an agreement for the sale of land under which the price or part of it is payable by instalments and the property in the land is to remain in the seller, although the buyer is to have possession of the land, until the conditions as to payment of instalments or otherwise specified in the agreement are fulfilled.[64] If the price, or part of it, for which credit is given does not exceed £5,000 it is a regulated consumer credit agreement for restricted-use credit and subject to all

---

[55] *Caledonian Stores* v. *Allard Hewson*, 1970 S.C. 168.

[56] *Sworn Securities Ltd.* v. *Chilcott*, 1977 S.C. 53.

[57] *Clason* v. *Steuart* (1844) 6 D. 1201; *Steuart's Trs.* v. *Hart* (1875) 3 R. 192; *Welsh* v. *Russell* (1894) 21 R. 769; *Bremner* v. *Dick*, 1911 S.C. 887; As to the phrase 'nominal feu-duty' see *Johnston* v. *Clark* (1855) 18 D. 70. As to allocation of feuduty see *Robertson* v. *Douglas* (1886) 13 R. 1133.

[58] cf. *McConnell* v. *Chassels* (1903) 10 S.L.T. 790.

[59] *Morier* v. *Brownlie & Watson* (1896) 23 R. 67; *Mann* v. *Houston*, 1957 S.L.T. 89; *Wallace* v. *Simmers*, 1960 S.C. 255.

[60] *Stodart* v. *Dalzell* (1876) 4 R. 236.

[61] *Aberdeen Varieties* v. *Donald*, 1940 S.C. (H.L.) 52; *Phillips* v. *Muir*, 1962 S.L.T. (Sh. Ct.) 57.

[62] *McKillop* v. *Mutual Securities Ltd.*, 1945 S.C. 166.

[63] Ersk. III, 3, 7; Bankt. I, 19, 35; Bell, *Comm.* I, 472; R. Brown, *Sale*, 355; *Sloan's Dairies* v. *Glasgow Corpn.*, 1977 S.C. 223.

[64] Consumer Credit Act, 1974, S. 189.

the regulations of the Consumer Credit Act applicable to money lending,[65] unless the agreement is an exempt agreement under S. 16 thereof.

Effect of contract

A contract validly concluded gives the purchaser a *jus ad rem*, or rather a *jus in personam ad rem specificam*, or personal right to have the subjects of sale conveyed to him, but not a *jus in re* or real right, which requires the execution, delivery and registration of a disposition.[66] It gives the seller a right to demand payment of the price and acceptance of a disposition of the lands.

SELLER'S OBLIGATIONS

The seller's main obligations are to execute a disposition conveying the property sold, to give a good marketable title, vacant possession of the property, clear searches, and warrandice. The seller is entitled to a reasonable time to produce a good title or to clear defects from it.

Good title

A purchaser is entitled to a good or at least marketable title, such as to protect him from eviction or even the risk of reasonable challenge, and to make the land an acceptable subject of future sale or disposition in security.[67] This may be waived by a contract whereby the seller has undertaken only to put the buyer in his place,[68] but not by a condition that the seller will give no search,[69] nor by an offer of absolute warrandice.[70] In articles of roup there is commonly a clause that the buyer will take the title as it stands. If the title tendered is not good the purchaser may resile, or, even after settlement, have the disposition reduced and the price repaid.[71]

What is good title

A good title is constituted by an *ex facie* valid charter of the lands now sold in favour of the seller, or one from whom the seller has derived title, recorded in the appropriate Register of Sasines and

---

[65] Ss. 8, 9, 11; Ch. 4.12, *supra*.

[66] *Gibson and Hunter Home Designs Ltd.*, 1976 SC. 23; *Sloan's Dairies Ltd.* v. *Glasgow Corpn.* 1977 S.C. 223; *McManus's Tr.* v. *McManus* 1978 S.L.T. 255.

[67] *Christie* v. *Cameron* (1898) 25 R. 824; *Liqdr. of Style & Mantle, Ltd.* v. *Prices Tailors, Ltd.*, 1934 S.C. 548.

[68] *Leith Heritage Co.* v. *Edinburgh & Leith Glass Co.* (1876) 3 R. 789.

[69] *Mackenzie* v. *Clark* (1895) 3 S.L.T. 128.

[70] *Nairne* v. *Scrymgeour* (1676) Mor. 14169.

[71] *Crofts* v. *Stewart's Trs.*, 1927 S.C. (H.L.) 65.

followed by possession thereon, peaceably and without interruption for at least ten years continuously.[72] If the estate now sold was created less than ten years ago the title of the creator of the fee must be examined to ensure that he had capacity and power to create the fee. If created substantially more than ten years ago the latest *ex facie* valid irredeemable title to the estate in land more than ten years old will suffice as the basis for prescription[72] but reference will almost certainly be made therein back to the founding charter, and possibly to other deeds outwith the prescriptive period, as containing burdens and conditions.

The running of the positive prescription fortifies any challengeable title but the buyer must inquire whether within the prescriptive period there is any intrinsic defect, such as a conveyance *a non domino*. Examination of the titles will not, however, disclose any extrinsic defect, such as that an earlier proprietor conveying the lands by will was not of sound disposing mind. But the obligation to transfer a good title is not concerned with such extrinsic objections.[73]

Where the title contains a number of transfers or transmissions within the prescriptive period, each link must validly connect the new with the previous proprietor. Each deed constituting a link must have been granted by a person having legal capacity and power to grant it; it must have been properly executed and stamped; the destination must connect with the next proprietor; the description of the property must be such as can support the possession enjoyed in reliance thereon;[74] there must be no burdens or qualifications other than those known and agreed to be assumed by the purchaser; and there must be no claims for death duties outstanding exigible from the property. A notarial instrument or notice of title is now a valid link in title without the warrants, e.g. trust disposition, on which it proceeds.[75] A decree of service of an heir is reducible within the prescriptive period,[76] but is a valid link in title. [77] An extract decree of reduction of a deed, decree or instrument recorded or forming a link in a title recorded in the Register of Sasines must be recorded in the Register of Sasines[78] but this provision protects only persons acquiring rights in the lands between the obtaining and the recording of the decree of reduction.[79]

A title tendered is good notwithstanding the existence of a reason-

---

[72] Conveyancing and Feudal Reform (Sc.) Act, 1970, S. 8.
[73] *Sutherland* v. *Garrity*, 1941 S.C. 196, 201.
[74] *Auld* v. *Hay* (1880) 7 R. 663; *Troup* v. *Aberdeen Heritable Securities Co.*, 1916 S.C. 918.
[75] Prescription and Limitation (Sc.) Act, 1973, S. 5(1), altering *Sutherland* v. *Garrity*, 1941 S.C. 196.
[76] *Stobie* v. *Smith*, 1921 S.C. 894.
[77] *Mackay's Exrx.* v. *Schonbach*, 1933 S.C. 747; *Sibbald's Heirs* v. *Harris*, 1947 S.C. 601.
[78] Conveyancing (Sc.) Act, 1924, S. 46.
[79] *Mulhearn* v. *Dunlop*, 1929 S.L.T. 59.

able feu-duty, which is a natural element of a feu, or servitudes of an ordinary character,[80] or leases usual in such a property,[81] or a description of the land by reference to a prior disposition incorrectly referred to,[82] or that the seller was only a heritable creditor when he sold with the consent of the party entitled to the reversion,[83] or there are restrictions not shown to preclude contemplated redevelopment,[84] or that one link in the title is a decree of general service,[85] or is the confirmation of an executor.[86] It is not good if the title tendered is that of long leaseholder not feudal proprietor,[87] if the title tendered imposes liability for an unallocated feu-duty,[88] or the superior has a right of redemption of the feu,[89] or there are restrictions[90] or a prohibition[91] on building, or prohibitions on use,[92] or the subjacent minerals are reserved to the superior, particularly if with power to work them[93] (unless parties knew that the minerals were reserved to a third party), or the title is to a long lease only and not a feu,[94] or the lands were possibly still affected by a creditor's debts,[95] or the titles include a declarator of irritancy under a contract of ground annual, pronounced in absence,[96] or the only description of the lands was by reference to a missing plan,[97] or the titles included an excambion, the parties to which had no power to excamb,[98] or the feu-duty was only a part of an unallocated feu-duty,[99] or the seller proposed not to convey lands, but only his right and interest in the lands.[1]

[80] *Gordonston v. Paton* (1682) Mor. 16606; *Welsh v. Russell* (1894) 21 R. 769.
[81] cf. *Lothian and Border Farmers v. McCutchion*, 1952 S.L.T. 450.
[82] *Matheson v. Gemmell* (1903) 5 F. 448 (mere *falsa demonstratio*).
[83] *Dundee Calendering Co. v. Duff* (1869) 8 M. 289.
[84] *Armia v. Daejean Developments Ltd.*, 1978 S.C. 152.
[85] *Mackay's Exrx. v. Schonbach*, 1933 S.C. 747; *Sibbald's Heirs v. Harris*, 1947 S.C. 601.
[86] Succession (Sc.) Act, 1964, S. 17 (where the death occurred after 9 Sept. 1964 only).
[87] *McConnell v. Chassels* (1903) 10 S.L.T. 790.
[88] *Morrison v. Gray*, 1932 S.C. 712.
[89] *McElroy v. D. Argyll* (1901) 4 F. 885.
[90] *Louttit's Trs. v. Highland Ry.* (1892) 19 R. 791; *Smith v. Soeder* (1895) 23 R. 60.
[91] *Urquhart v. Halden* (1835) 13 S. 844; *Robertson v. Rutherford* (1841) 4 D. 121.
[92] *Ewing v. Hastie* (1878) 5 R. 439; *Graham v. Shiels* (1901) 8 S.L.T. 368; *McConnell v. Chassels* (1903) 10 S.L.T. 790.
[93] *Whyte v. Lee* (1879) 6 R. 699; *Todd v. McCarroll* (1917) 55 S.L.R. 17; *Crofts v. Stewart's Trs.*, 1927 S.C. (H.L.) 65; *Mossend Theatre Co. v. Livingstone*, 1930 S.C. 90; *Campbell v. McCutcheon*, 1963 S.C. 505. See also *Macdonald v. Newall* (1898) 1 F. 68; *Bremner v. Dick*, 1911 S.C. 887.
[94] *Carter v. Lornie* (1890) 18 R. 353.
[95] *D. Devonshire v. Fletcher* (1874) 1 R. 1056.
[96] *Bruce v. Stewart* (1900) 2 F. 948.
[97] *Maclachlan v. Bowie* (1887) 25 S.L.R. 734.
[98] *Bruce v. Stewart* (1900) 2 F. 948.
[99] *Morrison v. Gray*, 1932 S.C. 712.
[1] *Hay v. Aberdeen Mags.*, 1909 S.C. 554.

Time for furnishing title

The seller must furnish a satisfactory title within a reasonable time,[2] though not necessarily by the date of entry. If he cannot or will not do so the purchaser may resile.[3] Timeous furnishing of title may be expressly stipulated for,[4] or the purchaser may call on the seller to furnish a title within a specified but reasonable time.[5] If the purchaser has objections to the title tendered he must make them within a reasonable time.[6] The seller is entitled to a reasonable time, on any objection being made, in which to furnish a good title, and for this purpose a date may be fixed. The buyer must either accept the title offered, or rescind the contract; he is not entitled to accept but insist on a deduction from the price.[7] It may be expressly agreed that the buyer take the title as it stands, or that he be held to have examined the titles and satisfied himself, in which case, unless the seller has absolutely no title to the lands or is wholly unable to give a title, warrandice only can be asked unless there be an actual challenge. If a buyer is saddled with a defective title by his solicitor's neglect he may recover in damages from the solicitor the diminished value of the land on resale.[8]

Curing defective title

When a seller tenders a defective title but asserts his ability and willingness to cure the defect, he must be given a reasonable opportunity to do so, especially where possession is immediately given or does not fall to be given till a later date.[9]

A seller is not entitled to tender a valid title after the purchaser has rescinded the contract on the ground of the tender of an admittedly unmarketable title,[10] or has rescinded for delay in tendering a title,[11] but may do so after the court has held that a title previously tendered was not acceptable.[12] Conversely a buyer has been held barred from taking an objection to the title after the seller had remedied the only defect and the buyer had taken possession and paid the price.[13]

[2] *Raeburn* v. *Baird* (1832) 10 S. 761.
[3] Allowed in *Fleming* v. *Harley's Trs.* (1823) 2 S. 373 (3 yrs.); *Hutchinson* v. *Scott* (1830) 8 S. 377 (14 mos.); *Kelman* v. *Barr's Trs.* (1878) 5 R. 816 (6 mos.). Refused in *Dick* v. *Cuthbertson* (1831) 5 W. & S. 712 (11 years); *Raeburn* v. *Baird* (1832) 10 S. 761 (6 mos.); *Carter* v. *Lornie* (1890) 18 R. 353 (18 mos.).
[4] *Kelman, supra; Gilfillan* v. *Caddell & Grant* (1893) 21 R. 269.
[5] cf. *Burns* v. *Garscadden* (1901) 8 S.L.T. 321; *Stickney* v. *Keeble* [1915] A.C. 386.
[6] *Macdonald* v. *Newall* (1898) 1 F. 68.
[7] *Earl of Morton* (1738) Mor. 14176; *Aikman* (1772) Mor. 14179; 2 Paton 326.
[8] *Haberstich* v. *McCormick & Nicholson*, 1975 S.C. 1.
[9] *Kinnear* v. *Young*, 1936 S.L.T. 574.
[10] *Gilfillan* v. *Cadell & Grant* (1893) 21 R. 269.
[11] *McNeill* v. *Cameron* (1830) 8 S. 362.
[12] *Carter* v. *Lornie* (1890) 18 R. 353.
[13] *Macdonald* v. *Newall* (1898) 1 F. 68.

In many cases a defect in title will be cured if possession is taken and runs without challenge for the period of the positive prescription.[14]

Undertaking to 'take the title as it stands'

A provision to this effect is common in articles of roup.[15] Such a provision will not avail the seller if there is mistake as to the identity or extent of the property professedly sold,[16] unless the discrepancy is really insubstantial,[17] or the title is radically bad, or at least very questionable,[18] but avails where there is curable defect in the title[19] or doubt as to a burden.[20] If there is curable defect the purchaser must implement the contract and cure the defect in title at his own expense.[19]

Extent of subjects sold

The seller is bound to yield possession of and convey title to the whole subjects sold, everything included in but to nothing excluded from the description. If he cannot do so, e.g. where the minerals had not been excepted from the sale but were in fact reserved to the superior, the buyer may resile.[21] The seller is not entitled to time in which to try to acquire the part of the subjects sold to which he had no title.[21] A buyer has been held barred from resiling when articles of roup stated that the buyer should be held to have satisfied himself as to the extent of the subjects and he had not done so, but complained subsequently.[22] A buyer has also been held barred from founding on his completed title to lands as excluding a personal right in another to part of the lands when he was fully aware that that other had long been in occupation with some sort of right.[23]

Identity of subjects sold

The seller must convey, and the buyer is bound to take, only the precise subjects sold, and not any equivalent or adjacent land.[24]

---

[14] Prescription and Limitation (Sc.) Act, 1973, S. 1.
[15] See generally *Morton* v. *Smith* (1877) 5 R. 83.
[16] *Waddell* v. *Pollock* (1828) 6 S. 999; *Wood* v. *Edinburgh Mags.* (1886) 13 R. 1006; *Young* v. *McKellar*, 1909 S.C. 1340.
[17] *Morton* v. *Smith* (1877) 5 R. 83.
[18] *Carter* v. *Lornie* (1890) 18 R. 353.
[19] *Sorley's Trs.* v. *Grahame* (1832) 10 S. 319; *Carter* v. *Lornie* (1890) 18 R. 353.
[20] *Davidson* v. *Dalziel* (1881) 8 R. 990.
[21] *Campbell* v. *McCutcheon*, 1963 S.C. 505.
[22] *Wood* v. *Edinburgh Mags.* (1886) 13 R. 1006; *Young* v. *McKellar*, 1909 S.C. 1340.
[23] *Stodart* v. *Dalzell* (1877) 4 R. 236.
[24] *E. Moray* v. *Pearson* (1842) 4 D. 1411; cf. *Scottish Temperance Assce. Co.* v. *Law Union and Rock Assce. Co.*, 1917 S.C. 175.

Vacant possession

The seller must give the purchaser entry and, unless excluded, entitlement to actual possession and occupation of the whole subjects of sale.[25] The seller cannot enforce the contract if the time of entry is material and he is unable to give entry or possession at the time specified.[26] *De facto* possession or a claim to a right of occupation by a third party, if substantial and affecting a substantial part of the subjects of sale, is an impediment to the giving of actual possession.[27] But if the time of giving of entry is not essential the seller is not in breach merely because his title is not complete so long as he can complete it within a reasonable time.[28] The purchaser is not bound by any merely personal agreement between the seller and a third party to allow the latter to occupy any part of the lands.[29]

Clearing burdens

The seller is bound, unless there be contrary agreement, to discharge all burdens secured over the lands, and the buyer is entitled to the lands free of conditions, reservations or burdens not stipulated for, or at least, not reasonable in the circumstances or known to the purchaser.[30] But a servitude is not a burden required to be cleared,[31] nor an ordinary lease, normal for that kind of property.[32] A condition that nothing in the titles prevents demolition and redevelopment has been interpreted to mean burdens preventing meaningful, worthwhile, practical or profitable commercial development and the burdens which existed were held not to do so.[33]

Exhibition and delivery of titles

The seller must exhibit for the buyer's examination and, so far as possible, deliver with the disposition of the lands sold, a progress of titles for at least the prescriptive period evidencing a clear title to the buyer.[34] So far as the titles relate also to other subjects he cannot

[25] *Heys* v. *Kimball and Morton* (1890) 17 R. 381.
[26] *Hunter* v. *Carsewell* (1822) 1 S. 248; *Kelman* v. *Barr's Tr.* (1878) 5 R. 816; *Stuart* v. *Lort-Phillips*, 1977 S.C. 244.
[27] *Stuart, supra.*
[28] *Kelman, supra.*
[29] *Mann* v. *Houston*, 1957 S.L.T. 89; *Wallace* v. *Simmers*, 1960 S.C. 255.
[30] *Robertson* v. *Rutherford* (1841) 4 D. 121; *Whyte* v. *Lee* (1879) 6 R. 699; *Robertson* v. *Douglas* (1886) 13 R. 1133. As to redemption of instalments of stipend see *Church of Scotland Trustees* v. *Dowie*, 1946 S.C. 335.
[31] Bell, *Prin.* §895: see also *Gordonston* v. *Paton* (1682) Mor. 16606; *Welsh* v. *Russell* (1894) 21 R. 769.
[32] Bell, *Convg.* I, 644.
[33] *Armia Ltd.* v. *Daejean Developments Ltd.* 1978 S.C. 152.
[34] cf. *Porteous* v. *Henderson* (1898) 25 R. 563.

deliver them but binds himself to make them available to the buyer on necessary occasions.[35]

Clear search

The seller must also obtain, and normally deliver with the titles, a search, i.e. a record, made by a professional searcher, of all entries in relevant public Registers relating to the property sold or to the seller within certain time limits. If any encumbrances or diligences are revealed thereby the seller is bound to clear them.[36]

Search must be made in the appropriate division of the General Register of Sasines[37] for any writs transferring title to, or burdening the title to, or otherwise affecting, the land in question, for not less than ten years back[38] from the close of the transaction now effected, to ensure that the seller has a good title and that there are no unextinguished bonds or burdens affecting the land.

The obligation to produce clear searches is not satisfied if the search discloses inhibitions against the seller, even if they are alleged to be invalid.[39]

Searches do not reveal liability for feu-duty,[40] real burdens,[40] building conditions or restrictions,[40] servitudes, leases,[41] whether a conveyance was in favour of a conjunct or confident person under the Bankruptcy Act, 1621, heritable securities created before the period of search but still valid, rights of terce or courtesy arising from a death before the Succession (Sc.) Act, 1964,[42] estate duty liabilities, floating charges granted by a company,[43] and certain other unimportant burdens. Nor do searches disclose local authority planning proposals, demolition and closing orders, and notices requiring repairs to be done.

Search must also be made in the Register of Inhibitions and Adjudications for any legal bars to voluntary transactions in heritage affecting the seller, or any of his predecessors in title within the ten years of

---

[35] cf. *Bald* v. *Scott* (1841) 3 D. 564.

[36] *Dryburgh* v. *Gordon* (1896) 24 R. 1; *Christie* v. *Cameron* (1898) 25 R. 824.

[37] And also in the Burgh Register of Sasines in the case of land in burghs whose burgh register has been discontinued within the period of search.

[38] From the Prescription Act, 1617, to the Conveyancing (Sc.) Act, 1874, the period for prescription fortifying title, and hence for search, was 40 years, thereafter 20, in certain cases, 30 years, thereafter until the Conveyancing (Sc.) Act, 1924, S. 16, 20 years until the Conveyancing and Feudal Reform (Sc.) Act, 1970, and 10 years thereafter.

[39] *Dryburgh* v. *Gordon* (1896) 24 R. 1.

[40] These burdens are disclosed by the deeds, but not by the mere entry in the Register.

[41] Except leases recorded under the Registration of Leases Act, 1857.

[42] See *Macnaughton* v. *M.*, 1940 S.C. 441.

[43] Companies (Floating Charges and Receivers) (Sc.) Act, 1972, Ss. 3, 6.

the positive prescription, for not less than five years back[44] from the close of the transaction now effected.

If the seller is a registered company it is necessary also to show a clear search in the Register of Charges to disclose any floating charges affecting the land.

The onus is on the seller to instruct the requisite searches and to deliver, or at least exhibit, at settlement of the transaction, a search showing the records clear of encumbrances and diligences, other than any known to and accepted by the parties.[45]

If the purchaser dispenses with the seller's producing a search, that does not bar him from objecting if a clear marketable title is not disclosed,[46] nor does it absolve the seller from his obligations to clear the record of encumbrances.[47]

Warrandice

Warrandice is the undertaking by the granter of the conveyance that the right granted shall be good and effectual to the grantee, and that if the grantee is evicted by reason of defect in the granter's title, or any fact or deed on his part, the granter will make reparation to him for the loss.[48]

Warrandice may be simple, which gives recourse only against loss resulting from the granter's subsequent deeds, or from fact and deed, which infers recourse against loss arising from the granter's acts, past or future, but not against eviction following on reduction of the granter's title on grounds not personal to himself,[49] or absolute warrandice, which infers recourse on eviction due to any lack of right or default of title of the granter to convey the subjects, whether due to his own act or deed or to defect in his own title, though not against burdens inherent in the grant[50] nor against eviction by supervening legislation.[50]

Warrandice may be expressed in any terms agreed by the parties.

---

[44] Prior to the Titles to Land Consolidation (Sc.) Act, 1868, Ss. 155, 157 and 159, inhibitions, interdictions, adjudications and sequestrations prescribed only after 40 years, and search had accordingly to be carried back 40 years from the close of the present transaction against each proprietor within that period so long as he was proprietor. See now Conveyancing (Sc.) Acts, 1874, Ss. 34, 42, and 1924, S. 44.

[45] *Graham* v. *Hunter's Trs.* (1831) 9 S. 543; *Campbell* v. *Clason* (1838) 1 D. 270; *Fea* v. *Macfarlane* (1887) 24 S.L.R. 628; *Christie* v. *Cameron* (1898) 25 R. 824. As to liability of solicitor for loss arising from burdens which a search would have revealed, see *Fea, supra; Fearn* v. *Gordon & Craig* (1893) 20 R. 352.

[46] *Mackenzie* v. *Clark* (1895) 3 S.L.T. 128.

[47] *D. Devonshire* v. *Fletcher* (1874) 1 R. 1056.

[48] Bell, *Convg.* I, 214. Real warrandice was also formerly recognised: see Ersk. II, 3, 28: but cannot be created, save in the case of securities, since 1924: Conveyancing (Sc.) Act, 1924, S. 14.

[49] *MacRitchie's Trs.* v. *Hope* (1836) 14 S. 578.

[50] Bell, *Prin.* §915; *Tay Salmon Fisheries* v. *Speedie*, 1929 S.C. 593.

Failing that, simple warrandice is implied in donations, warrandice from fact and deed in assignations of debt,[51] and absolute warrandice in sales, leases and other onerous transactions.

Warrandice may, however, be expressly granted in any terms the parties may agree.[52] Warrandice in limited terms excludes any wider warrandice which the law might otherwise imply,[53] and even a grant of absolute warrandice may be limited by the terms of the disposition, as where it conveyed only whatever title the seller could claim to certain subjects.[54]

A purchaser has been held entitled to insist on absolute warrandice from sellers who were, *ex facie* of the records, absolute proprietors, though they alleged that they were only trustees.[55]

The obligation constituted by granting warrandice affects the granter and his heirs until the possibility of adverse claims is extinguished by the long prescription.[56]

Effects of warrandice

If a grantee is evicted from possession on a ground covered by the warrandice he is entitled by virtue thereof to full compensation for loss caused thereby.[57] The claim also arises where the grantee's title is found to be burdened with a liability which diminishes the value of his right.[58]

No claim is competent till eviction, unless the ground for eviction arises from the act of the granter[59] or the granter disputes his liability to relieve.[60] Hence the grantee is not entitled to recover the expenses of a successful defence of his title, but may normally recover the expenses of an unsuccessful defence.[61]

The claim is only for indemnification against eviction and gives no right to recover the price on offering a reconveyance.[62] If the eviction is total, the claim is for the whole value of the subjects lost, if partial, as where another is held to have a right of servitude over the lands, the

[51] There is also implied in this case warrandice *debitum subesse*, i.e. that the debt is valid and subsisting, but not that the debtor is solvent: see also *Reid* v. *Barclay* (1879) 6 R. 1007.

[52] e.g. *Coventry* v. *C.* (1834) 12 S. 895; *Strang* v. *S.* (1851) 13 D. 548.

[53] *Craig* v. *Hopkins* (1732) Mor. 16623; cf. *Hay* v. *Aberdeen Mags.*, 1909 S.C. 554.

[54] *Leith Heritages Co.* v. *Edinburgh & Leith Glass Co.* (1876) 3 R. 789.

[55] *Mackenzie* v. *Neill* (1899) 37 S.L.R. 666.

[56] *Welsh* v. *Russell* (1894) 21 R. 769, 773.

[57] Ersk. II, 3, 30; *Cairns* v. *Howden* (1870) 9 M. 284; *Welsh* v. *Russell* (1894) 21 R. 769; cf. *Middleton* v. *Meggett* (1828) 7 S. 76.

[58] *Dewar* v. *Aitken* (1780) Mor. 16637; *Briggs's Trs.* v. *Dalyell* (1851) 14 D. 173.

[59] Bell, *Prin.* §895.

[60] *L. Melville* v. *Wemyss* (1842) 4 D. 385; *Leith Heritages Co.* v. *Edinburgh & Leith Glass Co.* (1876) 3 R. 789.

[61] *Dougall* v. *Dunfermline Mags.*, 1908 S.C. 151.

[62] *Welsh* v. *Russell* (1894) 21 R. 769.

claim is for compensation for the loss. The existence of a lease in ordinary terms is not a breach of warrandice.[63]

BUYER'S OBLIGATIONS

The buyer's primary obligation is to pay the price on the date fixed or at the term of entry, in exchange for the disposition of the land to him. If there is express provision voiding the sale for non-payment by a fixed date, the seller may, if payment be not then made, rescind the contract.[64] Failing such provision, failure to pay by a stipulated date is not generally a ground for rescission[65] and only an unnecessary or unjustifiable delay will justify the imposition of a time for payment and, failing payment, rescission.[65]

If entry has been given the seller has a personal action for the price and, even though he has signed but not delivered a disposition, the seller has a preference for the price over other creditors.[66] The seller is not entitled to the price if he is still litigating to clear the title, or possibly in some cases so long as it remains subject to appeal.[67]

If settlement, i.e. exchange of price and disposition, is delayed after the purchaser has been given entry, interest runs *ex lege* on the unpaid price[68] until or unless it is consigned on deposit receipt in joint names, the seller receiving the deposit receipt interest at settlement.[69] If a disposition has been granted but the price has not been fixed or paid and the parties cannot agree, the sale is void and the purchaser must relinquish possession.[70]

If the buyer delays unreasonably to pay the price the seller may rescind the contract, but premature rescission is a breach of contract.[71]

Buyer's duty to become infeft

The buyer is probably also bound to become, or to secure that another becomes, infeft within a reasonable time, so as to relieve the

---

[63] *Lothian & Border Farmers* v. *McCutchion*, 1952 S.L.T. 450.
[64] *Young* v. *Dunn* (1785) Mor. 14191.
[65] *Rodger (Builders) Ltd.* v. *Fawdry*, 1950 S.C. 483.
[66] *Baird* v. *Jap* (1758) Mor. 14156.
[67] *Traill* v. *Connon* (1877) 5 R. 25.
[68] *Speirs* v. *Ardrossan Canal Co.* (1827) 5 S. 764; *Grandison's Trs.* v. *Jardine* (1895) 22 R. 925; *Aitken* v. *Hyslop*, 1977 S.L.T. (Notes) 50. As to rate of interest see *Traill* v. *Connon* (1877) 5 R. 25; *Greenock Harbour* v. *G.S.W. Ry.*, 1909 S.C. (H.L.) 49.
[69] *Prestwick Cinema Co.* v. *Gardiner*, 1951 S.C. 98. As to partial consignation see *Dickson* v. *Munro* (1855) 17 D. 524. A purchaser is not bound to accede to an extra-contractual term proposed by the vendor as to entry on terms of paying interest on the price: *Bowie* v. *Semple's Exors.*, 1978 S.L.T. (Sh. Ct.) 9.
[70] *Stirling* v. *Honyman* (1824) 2 S. 765.
[71] *Burns* v. *Garscadden* (1901) 8 S.L.T. 321.

seller of his liabilities to the superior for feu-duty and any other obligations incumbent on him.

BREACH OF CONTRACT AND REMEDIES

Either party may be in breach of contract or the contract may be discharged by supervening impossibility of fact or law.[72] If it is subject to suspensive condition the parties are not to be held bound beyond a reasonable time, unless the contract indicates that intention, where the condition is subject to a third party and cannot be purified by the parties alone.[73]

Seller's default

If the seller is able to, but refuses or delays unreasonably to convey the property sold, or refuses or delays unreasonably to produce a title, so that it is uncertain whether he can or cannot give a good title, the remedies appropriate are specific implement with a conclusion for adjudication in implement[74] or, alternatively, damages, if the buyer does not wish to insist on the purchase, or the court deems it highly inconvenient or unjust to enforce performance.[75] If the seller is no longer able to convey the property, e.g. having sold and conveyed it to another in circumstances where that sale cannot be impugned,[76] only damages are competent. If the seller produces a title which is not a valid and marketable title to the subjects sold the buyer is probably not entitled to take or retain the subjects purchased subject to an abatement from the price (the *actio quanti minoris*), but must rescind the entire contract and claim damages for loss of the bargain.[77] But where the sale has been induced by fraud damages may be recovered without rescission of the contract.[78] Damages may be recovered without rescission in case of breach of a collateral bargain, such as to fit the premises

---

[72] *Packman v. Dunbar's Trs.*, 1977 S.L.T. 140.

[73] *Boland v. Dundas's Trs.*, 1975 S.L.T. (Notes) 80.

[74] *McKellar v. Dallas's, Ltd.*, 1928 S.C. 503. It is competent to seek implement in relation to heritage only of a composite contract for the sale of heritage and moveables: *Mackay v. Campbell*, 1966 S.C. 237.

[75] *Moore v. Paterson* (1881) 9 R. 337; *Stewart v. Kennedy* (1890) 17 R. (H.L.) 1, 10; *Harvey v. Smith* (1904) 6 F. 511; *Plato v. Newman*, 1950 S.L.T. (Notes) 30; *Mackay v. Campbell*, 1967 S.C. (H.L.). 53.

[76] cf. *Burns v. Garscadden* (1901) 8 S.L.T. 321; *Rodger (Builders), Ltd. v. Fawdry*, 1950 S.C. 483; *Boland v. Dundas's Trs.*, 1975 S.L.T. (Notes) 80.

[77] *Bald v. Scott & Globe Ins. Co.* (1847) 10 D. 289; *Louttit's Trs. v. Highland Ry.* (1892) 19 R. 791; *Wood v. Edinburgh Mags.* (1886) 13 R. 1006; *Brownlie v. Miller* (1880) 7 R. (H.L.) 66; *McKillop v. Mutual Securities, Ltd.*, 1954 S.C. 166.

[78] *Dobbie v. Duncanson* (1872) 10 M. 810; *Smith v. Sim*, 1954 S.C. 357.

or lay out the grounds.[79] It is incompetent for the court to reform a contract; it can only reduce it, but may do so on conditions.[80]

Buyer's default

If the buyer has refused or delayed unreasonably to pay the price the seller may sue him therefor, with interest, offering to deliver a valid disposition,[81] or, if the missives so provide, claim under a provision therein for liquidate damages.[82]

If the buyer has absolutely refused or is manifestly unable to complete his purchase, the seller may rescind the contract and claim damages for the loss of the bargain, or, if the contract so provides, claim forfeiture of any deposit paid[83] or payment under a provision for liquidate damages. Failure to pay the price on the date fixed for settlement, unless that is expressed to be an essential condition of the contract, is not a repudiation *per se*; the buyer should be given a reasonable time within which to pay; only after that has elapsed is rescission justified.[84] The claim of damages is subject to the obligation to mitigate loss, by finding another purchaser.[85]

If the buyer justifiably objects to the title tendered and, no other being tendered, repudiates the contract, he is not liable for breach,[86] even though the seller later tenders a valid title,[87] nor is he if the seller has not been able to give entry or a good title at the stipulated date.[88] He is, however, in breach if he takes an objection to the title tendered which is held unjustifiable and has sought to repudiate in reliance thereon.

If the buyer has taken possession under the contract but failed to pay the price he is liable to an action of removing, but is not a precarious possessor or liable to ejection.[89]

DISPOSITION

An enforceable contract for the sale of lands is given effect to, and title to the lands transferred, by a disposition. It transmits a fee already

---

[79] *McKillop v. Mutual Securities Ltd.*, 1945 S.C. 166; *Hoey v. Butler*, 1975 S.C. 87.
[80] *Steuart's Trs. v. Hart*(1875) 3 R. 192.
[81] *B.R. Board v. Birrell*, 1971 S.L.T. (Notes) 17.
[82] *Commercial Bank v. Beal* (1890) 18 R. 80.
[83] *Reid v. Campbell*, 1958 S.L.T. (Sh. Ct.) 45.
[84] *Rodger v. Fawdry*, 1950 S.C. 483; *Johnstone v. Harris*, 1977 S.C. 365.
[85] *Johnstone, supra.*
[86] *Morrison v. Gray*, 1932 S.C. 712; *Campbell v. McCutcheon*, 1963 S.C. 505.
[87] *Gilfillan v. Caddell & Grant* (1893) 21 R. 269.
[88] *Kelman v. Barr's Tr.* (1878) 5 R. 816.
[89] *Lowe v. Gardiner*, 1921 S.C. 211.

constituted to a singular successor of the vassal disponing to be held in his place of the same superior.[90] Prior to 1874 the participation of the superior was essential, and a disposition required infeftment followed by charter or writ of confirmation by the superior, or infeftment following on a charter or writ of resignation by the superior. A disposition is not reducible because of dispute between the purchaser and another in whose name the purchaser had undertaken to take the title; this is *res inter alios* to the disponer.[91]

Effect of disposition

A disposition in implement of a sale, once delivered to and accepted by the purchaser, becomes the sole measure of the contracting parties' rights, and supersedes all previous communings and contracts, however formal.[92] Until delivered, the disposition cannot be founded on and the missives rule.[93] The parties may agree to exclude this rule,[94] or the disposition may bear to be, or be shown to be, in only part performance of the contract,[95] and a collateral obligation contained in the same contract is not discharged by acceptance of a disposition and taking possession thereon.[96] Where a disposition follows on a decree arbitral it may be permissible to refer to the decree.[97]

A disposition does not, however, exclude reference to the missives where it is averred that it does not in a material respect truly express the agreement contained in the missives.[98]

A disponee is not bound by any merely personal claim against the disponer even if he were aware of it, such as a third party's reserved right of occupancy of part of the premises.[99]

Modern form of disposition

The modern form of disposition[1] is in the main regulated by the Titles to Land Consolidation (Sc.) Act, 1868, as amended, and contains the following clauses.

[90] It is a disposition of the lands, not of the seller's right, title, and interest therein: *Hay* v. *Aberdeen Corpn.*, 1909 S.C. 554.   [91] *Hartdegen* v. *Fanner*, 1980 S.L.T. (Notes) 23.

[92] *Lee* v. *Alexander* (1883) 10 R. (H.L.) 91; *Orr* v. *Mitchell* (1893) 20 R. (H.L.) 27; *Butter* v. *Foster*, 1912 S.C. 1218; cf. *Norval* v. *Abbey*, 1939 S.C. 724; *Secretary of State* v. *Portkil Estates*, 1957 S.C. 1; but see *E. Glasgow's Trs.* v. *Clark* (1889) 16 R. 545; *Baird* v. *Alexander* (1898) 25 R. (H.L.) 35; *Wigan* v. *Cripps*, 1908 S.C. 394; *Winston* v. *Patrick*, 1981 S.L.T. 41.

[93] *Morrison* v. *Gray*, 1932 S.C. 712.

[94] *Young* v. *McKellar*, 1909 S.C. 1340; *Fraser* v. *Cox*, 1938 S.C. 506.

[95] *Jamieson* v. *Welsh* (1900) 3 F. 176.

[96] *McKillop* v. *Mutual Securities Ltd.*, 1945 S.C. 166; *Bradley* v. *Scott*, 1966 S.L.T. (Sh. Ct.) 55.

[97] *G.N.S. Ry.* v. *D. Fife* (1901) 3 F. (H.L.) 2; cf. *Young* v. *McKellar*, 1909 S.C. 1340.

[98] *Anderson* v. *Lambie*, 1954 S.C. (H.L.) 43.

[99] *Wallace* v. *Simmers*, 1960 S.C. 255.

[1] Titles to Land Consolidation (Sc.) Act, 1868, Sched. B, No. 1, modified by Conveyancing (Sc.) Act, 1874.

Narrative clause

This clause names and designs the granter of the deed, who must have power to sell and convey the lands, normally as heritable proprietor of the subjects hereinafter disponed, and states the price or other consideration for the grant of the lands and acknowledges receipt thereof. If the granter of the disposition had at the time no right to the subjects he purports to convey but acquires right by subsequent title, the disposition is validated by accretion.[2] If the seller is not himself infeft but has right to land by a title, e.g. as trustee or judicial factor[3] or executor,[4] a clause is inserted after the clause of entry naming and designing the person last infeft, specifying his infeftment, and deducing the seller's title from him by specifying the writs between the last infeftment and the present seller.[5] Failure to deduce title is a defect which renders the subjects less valuable than they would otherwise be.[6] When an interest in land has been registered and is transferred by an uninfeft proprietor there is no need to incorporate a clause of deduction of title because the Keeper when registering can satisfy himself of the validity and sufficiency of the midcouples or links connecting the title of the person last infeft with the now uninfeft proprietor.[7]

Dispositive clause

No particular words of conveyance are essential so long as present intention to transfer title to the lands is clear.[8] The dispositive clause cannot be denied effect on the ground that other parts of the deed show a different intention, unless its terms are ambiguous, when other parts of the deed may be referred to in aid of its construction.[9]

The dispositive clause contains the destination, i.e. the identification of the person or persons in whose favour the title is being taken. Reference to the disponee's 'heirs and assignees whomsoever', or now to his 'successors or assignees', is usual but is implied. This clause may be, and formerly commonly was, complicated by references to survivorship, conjunct fee and liferent, or other special destination,[10] which may raise questions such as of the survivor's power to alter the

---

[2] *Swans v. Western Bank* (1866) 4 M. 663.
[3] Conveyancing Act, 1938, S. 1.
[4] Succession (Sc.) Act, 1964, Ss. 14, 15 and 17.
[5] Conveyancing Act, 1924, S. 3.
[6] *Haberstich v. McCormick & Nicholson*, 1975 S.C. 1.
[7] Land Registration (Sc.) Act, 1979, S. 15(3).
[8] 1874 Act, S. 27. Formerly the word 'dispone' was essential.
[9] *Orr v. Mitchell* (1893) 20 R. (H.L.) 27.
[10] cf. *Brown's Tr. v. B.*, 1943 S.C. 488; *Hay's Tr. v. Hay's Trs.*, 1951 S.C. 329.

destination.[11] The seller may be requested to dispone to another than the buyer from him, e.g. to a subpurchaser or donee, in which case the buyer's request is narrated and his consent taken and evidenced by his signature to the disposition.[11]

The lands are described, and the description may be in any way competent in the case of a feu-charter.[12] Once an interest in land has been registered in the land Register all that is necessary for its description is a reference to the number of the title sheet.[13] The subjects conveyed include pertinents such as trout-fishing, but not salmon-fishing which right is a separate interest requiring express conveyance.[14] Any exceptions from the property conveyed must be mentioned. The dispositive clause must also contain all reservations, burdens, conditions, limitations and qualifications of the grant, new or old, expressed *ad longum*, or, if old, incorporated by reference to the deed creating them.[15] A deed of declaration of conditions executed after the commencement of the Land Registration (Sc.) Act, 1979, is a real obligation if recorded in the Register of Sasines or registered in the Land Register.[16] Once a real burden, condition or provision affecting a registered interest in land has been entered on the title sheet for that interest it is unnecessary to insert or refer to it in any deed relating to that interest; the deed is deemed to import for all purposes a full insertion of the real burden or other matter.[17]

The dispositive clause may also contain any allocation of feu-duty or other common burdens agreed upon, as where the proprietor of a tenement is selling one of the flats therein.

Term of Entry

The term of the purchaser's entry and actual occupation is normally expressed, but, if not, it is deemed to be the first term of Whitsunday or Martinmas after the last date of the disposition, unless it appears that another date was intended.[18] Postponed entry does not prevent or postpone infeftment.[19]

---

[11] cf. *Anderson* v. *Dick* (1901) 8 S.L.T. 482; *McDougal's Trs.* v. *L.A.*, 1952 S.C. 260. The clause of warrandice is also modified in the case of a disposition direct to a sub-purchaser: cf. *Mackenzie* v. *Neill* (1899) 37 S.L.R. 666.

[12] cf. *Murray's Tr.* v. *Wood* (1887) 14 R. 856; *Matheson* v. *Gemmell* (1903) 5 F. 448; *Johnston's Trs.* v. *Kinloch*, 1925 S.L.T. 124. As to agreement on common boundary see Land Registration (Sc.) Act, 1979, S. 19.

[13] Land Registration (Sc.) Act, 1979, S. 15(1).

[14] *McKendrick* v. *L.A.*, 1970 S.L.T. (Sh. Ct.) 39.

[15] 1874 Act, S. 32.

[16] Ibid., S. 17.

[17] Ibid., S. 15(2).

[18] 1874 Act, S. 28.

[19] *Burgh-Smeaton* v. *Whitson* (1907) 14 S.L.T. 839; *Anderson* v. *Dickie*, 1913 S.L.T. 198.

Obligation to infeft and manner of holding

Originally a vassal might subfeu, but might not substitute another as vassal in his stead without the superior's consent. Hence the practice arose of a disponer granting two deeds, one bearing that the lands were to be held *de me*, of and under the disponer, the other that the lands were to be held *a me (de superiore meo)*. The buyer expede and recorded an instrument of sasine referable either to the holding *de me* or that *a me*, and infeftment thereon completed his real right to the lands, and being ascribed to the *de me* holding constituted him a vassal of the disponer and a subvassal of the superior. When confirmed by the superior the disposition divested the seller and infeftment thereon was ascribed to the *a me* holding, the seller then dropping out as mid-superior. Subsequently the two charters, *de me* and *a me*, were superseded by a disposition with an alternative holding, *a me vel de me*, and a precept of sasine applicable to either holding.[20] Till confirmed this infeftment gave the disponee a title as vassal of the disponer but when confirmed, it substituted him as vassal in place of the disponer. After confirmation the disponee could not impute his infeftment to the *de me* holding.[21] The 1868 Act, repeating earlier provisions, made it unnecessary to insert an obligation to infeft and gave the statutory clause, 'to be holden the said lands *a me* (or *a me vel de me*),' with stated effect.[22] Since 1874 no holding need be mentioned in a disposition, a holding *a me* being implied.[23] The 1868 Act rendered the precept of sasine unnecessary, direct recording of the disposition coming in place of infeftment and the instrument of sasine recording that fact. This clause accordingly does not appear in modern dispositions.

Procuratory or clause of resignation in favorem

The procuratory (later clause) of resignation *in favorem*[24] was a mandate by the disponer authorizing the relinquishment of the lands to the superior for new infeftment, that he might reconvey them to the disponee to be held under the superior as the disponer had himself held them. The 1868 Act, S. 81, replacing earlier legislation, provided a statutory form of clause, 'And I resign the said lands and others for new infeftment or investiture', but the clause was impliedly abolished by the 1874 Act which rendered incompetent the granting of charters

---

[20] An alternative holding was not intended to create a permanent base fee and was not deemed a contravention of a prohibition against subinfeudation: *Colquhoun* v. *Walker* (1867) 5 M. 773; *Inglis* v. *Wilson*, 1909 S.C. 1393.
[21] *Chancellor* v. *Brown* (1688) Mor. 3012.
[22] 1868 Act, S. 6.
[23] 1874 Act, S. 2.
[24] A procuratory of resignation *ad remanentiam* authorized the surrender of the feu by the vassal to the superior.

or writs of resignation. Under the 1874 Act, the procuratory became unnecessary and, even if inserted, could not be used. It does not appear in modern dispositions.

Assignation of writs

The statutory clause 'And I assign the writs' imports, in the absence of qualification, an absolute and unconditional assignation to such writs and evidents, and to all open procuratories, clauses and precepts, if any, and, as the case may be, therein contained, and to all unrecorded conveyances to which the disponer has right.[25] But the seller, if he needs to retain the writs in respect of other subjects, may bind himself only to make the writs forthcoming on necessary occasions, or if he does not himself possess all the writs, he may assign to his disponee the writs in his possession and any right he has to make the others forthcoming. The obligation to assign does not cover security writs, the creditor being entitled to hold them.[26] In deeds executed after the passing of the Land Registration (Sc.) Act, 1979, this clause is unnecessary and any such deed unless specially qualified, imports an assignation to the grantee of the title deeds and searches and all deeds not duly recorded, and imposes on the parties obligations to deliver or make forthcoming deeds and searches relevant to the interest conveyed.[27]

Assignation of rents

The statutory form of clause, 'And I assign the rents', unless modified, imports an assignation of the rents to become due for the possession following the term of entry according to the legal and not the conventional terms, unless in the case of forehand rents, in which case it imports an assignation to the rents payable at the conventional terms subsequent to the date of entry.[28] The possession in question is that of the purchaser, not of the tenant under his lease.[29] In deeds executed after the passing of the Land Registration (Sc.) Act, 1979, this clause is unnecessary and any such deed unless specially qualified, imports an assignation of the rents payable (i) in the case of backhand rents, at the legal terms following the date of entry, and (ii) in the case of forehand rents, at the conventional terms following that date.[30]

Obligation of relief

The statutory form of clause, 'And I bind myself to free and relieve my said disponee and his foresaids of all feu-duties, and public

[25] 1868 Act, S. 8; cf. *Porteous* v. *Henderson* (1898) 25 R. 563.
[26] *Bowie's Trs.* v. *Watson*, 1913 S.C. 326.
[27] 1979 Act, S. 16(1).
[28] 1868 Act, S. 8; cf. *Butter* v. *Foster*, 1912 S.C. 1218; *Baillie* v. *Fletcher*, 1915 S.C. 677.
[29] *Baillie, supra*, 677, 715.   [30] 1979 Act, S. 16(3).

burdens', imports an obligation to relieve of all feu-duties and other duties, or casualties or services due to the superior, and all public, parochial or local burdens due from or on account of the lands conveyed prior to the date of the disponee's entry.[31] Even if unqualified this clause does not preclude apportionment of feu-duty, ground annual and public burdens between the parties by reference to their respective periods of possession.[32] An obligation in wider terms may saddle the disponer with liability even for rates imposed by subsequent legislation.[33] Liability for work done, e.g. on roads, by local authorities, arises only when the authority has allocated the cost to proprietors and requested payment.[34] In the case of deeds executed after the passing of the Land Registration (Sc.) Act, 1979, it is not necessary to insert this clause and any such deed unless specially qualified, imports an obligation on the granter to release the grantee of all feu-duties, ground annuals, annuities and public, parochial and local burdens exigible in respect of the interest conveyed prior to the date of entry and, in the case of a grant of land in feu, of all feu-duties payable by the granter to his superiors from and after the date of entry.[35]

Certain obligations or rights of relief do not automatically transmit with land on its being conveyed and require to be specially assigned to the grantee if he is to have the benefit of them. A statutory form for doing so is in the 1874 Act; S. 50 and Sched. M. Once the obligation or right has been entered in the title sheet of a registered interest in land it is not necessary expressly to assign the obligation or right in a conveyance of the registered interest and such a deed imports a valid and complete assignation of that obligation or right.[36]

Clause of warrandice

The statutory clause, 'And I grant warrandice', imports absolute warrandice as regards the lands and writs and evidents, and warrandice from fact and deed as regards the rents.[37] In dispositions by trustees or judicial factors the granters customarily grant warrandice from their own facts and deeds only, and bind the estate under their charge in absolute warrandice. Even if the disponee knows of it any right excepted from warrandice, such as a bond, should be excepted expressly.[38] A grant of warrandice in statutory form has been held to

---

[31] 1868 Act, S. 8.
[32] cf. E. Glasgow's Trs. v. Clark (1889) 16 R. 545.
[33] Dunbar Mags. v. Mackersy, 1931 S.C. 180.
[34] McIntosh v. Mitchell Thomson (1900) 8 S.L.T. 48.
[35] 1979 Act, S. 16(3).
[36] Ibid., S. 15(4).
[37] 1868 Act, S. 8.
[38] Horsburgh's Trs. v. Welsh (1886) 14 R. 67.

warrant only what was conveyed by the dispositive clause, and warranted the assignation of writs only for the purpose for which they
were assigned, and not that any writ should have any specific effect in
law or be valid beyond challenge.[39] The existence of an ordinary urban
lease is not a breach of warrandice.[40]

Clause of consent to registration

A disposition can be recorded for preservation in the Books of
Council and Session or any other competent record and the granter
normally expressly consents thereto. It is not customary to record a
disposition for execution, unless the disponee undertakes liability
therein for some future payment, in which case, if the disposition
contains the disponee's consent to registration and is signed by him, it
may be recorded for execution and the disponee may subsequently be
charged for payment thereunder.

Precept of Sasine

The precept of sasine was a mandate by the disponer to his bailie,
and later, to any notary public, to give his disponee sasine of the lands.
Since 1858 it has been unnecessary (though competent) to expede and
record any instrument of sasine, but necessary only to record the
conveyance itself, with a warrant of registration, in the Register of
Sasines, and it is accordingly now unnecessary to insert a precept of
sasine in any conveyance.[41]

Clause of direction

It is competent to insert a clause of direction specifying which parts
of the disposition the granter desires to be recorded in the Register of
Sasines. If the warrant of registration bears reference to the clause of
direction the disponee may have the disposition recorded in part only,
but even though there is such a clause in the disposition the disponee
may record the whole deed, or a notarial instrument thereon.

Testing clause

The disposition is attested in customary form. It is only when the
disposition is executed that the disponee becomes proprietor with the
rights and obligations attaching to feudal ownership, and the disposition is effective from that date.[42] If a granter, such as one joint
proprietor, cannot be found or refuses to sign, the parties may, on

[39] *Brownlie* v. *Miller* (1880) 7 R. (H.L.) 66.
[40] *Lothian and Border Farmers* v. *McCutchion*, 1952 S.L.T. 450.
[41] 1868 Act, S. 15.
[42] *Secretary of State* v. *Portkil Estates*, 1957 S.C. 1.

petition to the *nobile officium*, have the deputy clerk of session authorized to sign the disposition in place of the recalcitrant proprietor.[43]

Effect of execution and delivery of disposition

Until a duly executed disposition is delivered the seller is undivested and the purchaser has no right of property, even if he has paid the price and taken actual occupation. On delivery of the disposition he becomes vested in a personal right to the subjects in question.[44] Hence payment of the price and delivery of a duly executed disposition should be contemporaneous counterpart performances of the parties' respective duties under the contract.

Disposition vitiated by error

If a disposition contains an inaccurate description of the subjects sold, so that it does not correctly give effect to the parties' contract, even though it has been delivered and recorded in the Register of Sasines, it may be reduced and the seller ordained to execute a disposition in the correct terms.[45]

COMPLETION OF TITLE

Completion of disponee's title

Completion of title makes the disponee infeft in the lands or vests the disponee with a real right to the lands to which he acquired only a personal right by the contract and the disposition in implement thereof. Formerly he became infeft by taking sasine and recording the instrument of sasine in the Register of Sasines.[46] Since 1847 registration has had the effect of taking sasine.[47] But in some cases, such as real burdens,[48] registration completes the creditor's right though there is no infeftment. If there is no infeftment the disponer is not divested and the disponee not invested.[49] It is essential for fortification of title by positive prescription.

---

[43] *Lennox*, 1950 S.C. 546; *Boag*, 1967 S.C. 322; *Mackay v. Campbell*, 1966 S.C. 237; cf. *Wallace's C.B. v. W.*, 1924 S.C. 212; *Pennell's Tr.*, 1928 S.C. 605.

[44] *Dowie v. Tennant* (1891) 18 R. 986; *Embassy Picture House v. Cammo Developments Ltd.*, 1970 S.L.T. (Notes) 85; *Gibson and Hunter Home Designs Ltd.*, 1976 S.C. 23.

[45] *Anderson v. Lambie*, 1954 S.C. (H.L.) 43; *Equitable Loan Co. v. Storie*, 1972 S.L.T. (Notes) 20.

[46] An unrecorded sasine was null: *Young v. Gordon's Trs.* (1847) 9 D. 932.

[47] Now 1868 Act, S. 15.

[48] 1874 Act, S. 30.

[49] Bell, *Prin.* §802.

*Completion of disponee's title—older form, by resignation
or confirmation*

Prior to 1874 the disponee required the superior's intervention to complete his title and establish him as a vassal. By virtue of the disponer's mandate, the procuratory of resignation in the disposition, the disponer resigned the lands to the superior for new infeftment, and the superior granted a charter of resignation in favour of the disponee, similar to an original charter but narrating the deduction of the disponee's title from the disponer and describing the ceremony of resignation (which, latterly, was in most cases imaginary). This contained a precept of sasine on which the disponee could expede an instrument of sasine and complete title by recording it in the Register of Sasines.

Alternatively the disponee under a disposition with a holding *a me vel de me* might take sasine under the *de me* holding and apply to the superior for a charter of confirmation. When granted the disponee's sasine was attributed to the *a me* holding and the holding *de me* (under the disponer as mid-superior) dropped out of the titles.

A combined charter of resignation and confirmation was necessary in certain cases.

The 1868 Act, Ss. 97 and 99, re-enacting provisions from 1847 onwards, permitted direct recording of the disposition, with writ of resignation or of confirmation endorsed thereon, in the Register of Sasines.

The 1874 Act, S. 4, provided that infeftment should imply entry with the superior, so that resignation for new infeftment and confirmation were both unnecessary.

Completion of title in modern practices

The disponee now completes his feudal title to the subjects, if the subjects are described generally, or particularly, or by statutory reference, or by general name under the 1868 Act, S. 13, by endorsing on the disposition a warrant of registration in his favour and recording the deed in the appropriate division of the General Register of Sasines,[50] or by expeding a notarial instrument or notice of title and recording it with a warrant of registration.[51] If the granter has granted a general disposition of his lands the disponee completes title by notice of title with warrant of registration, recorded in the Register of Sasines.[52]

A disposition once recorded may still be reduced if the purchaser

---

[50] 1868 Act, S. 15.
[51] 1868 Act, S. 17; 1924 Act, S. 6.
[52] 1868 Act, S. 19; 1924 Act, S. 6.

when he accepted the disposition was aware of a prior contract between seller and a third party and did not inquire whether that contract was still binding or not,[53] or if the disposition contains an inaccurate description of the lands sold, so that it has not correctly given effect to the parties' intentions.[54]

In the case of lands in an area operational for land registration the purchaser makes application for registration of his interest under the Land Registration (Sc.) Act, 1979, and receives a title certificate evidencing his interest.[55]

Notice of change of ownership

To free the seller from liability for feu-duty the disponee must not only become infeft but the seller must give notice to the superior of change of ownership of the lands.[56]

Continuing personal obligations

Where a seller was liable to the superior in a personal obligation, he does not get rid of it by selling the lands, unless the superior consents, not even if the buyer subjects himself to the same obligation by recording the disposition in his favour while the obligation is still unperformed.[57]

Assignation of unrecorded dispositions

The disponee under a disposition, delivered but not recorded, or any person in right thereof, may assign the disposition to an assignee by assignation endorsed on the disposition, or separately. The assignee may further assign the disposition. The assignee must deduce his title from the latest prior endorsed assignation. The last assignee may complete his title by recording the disposition and the assignation, or the disposition with a notarial instrument or notice of title, or a notarial instrument or notice of title narrating the transmissions since the last infeftment.[58]

Assignation of personal right to land

A personal right to an estate in land descendible to heirs vested formerly in the heir by survivance and was transmissible in the same manner as an unfeudalized conveyance.[59] Heritage now vests in the

[53] *Rodger (Builders), Ltd.* v. *Fawdry*, 1950 S.C. 483.
[54] *Anderson* v. *Lambie*, 1954 S.C. (H.L.) 43.
[55] 1979 Act, Ss. 2–6.
[56] *Hyslop* v. *Shaw* (1863) 1 M. 535.
[57] *Marshall* v. *Callander Hydro Co.* (1875) 22 R. 954; *Rankine* v. *Logie Den Land Co.* (1902) 4 F. 1074.
[58] 1868 Act, S. 22; Conveyancing (Sc.) Act, 1924, S. 7.
[59] 1874 Act, S. 9.

deceased's executor, by virtue of his confirmation, for the purposes of administration,[60] and a personal right vests in a person entitled to the land under the deceased's will or intestacy to have the land transferred to him by the executor.[61] This personal right is probably assignable and if intimation is made to the executor, the assignee will be entitled to transfer of the land to him.

Assignation of jus crediti to land

A person has a *jus crediti* to land where it is vested in another who is under an obligation, by trust or contract, to convey it to him. Such *jura crediti* are transferable by assignation intimated to the person subject to the obligation, but such an assignation does not confer a feudal title but only entitles the assignee to obtain a conveyance or to lead an adjudication of the lands.

DISPOSITION OF SUPERIORITY

A superior may gift or sell his interest of superiority in lands. The superiority of lands can be conveyed only if a vassal's estate has already been separated from the superiority by charter and infeftment. It is incompetent to seek in one deed to convey the superiority to one disponee and the fee to another, or to dispone lands reserving the superiority.[62] Nor can a superior, unless he reserved liberty to do so, without his vassal's consent, divide a superiority,[63] though he may dispone it to two or more persons jointly[64] and may dispone separately the superiorities of two parcels of land held by the one vassal.[65] The right to object may be waived, or a division acquiesced in. Similarly a superior cannot, unless by reserved right or with the vassal's consent, interpose a mid-superior between himself and his vassal.[66]

Form of deed

The form of a disposition of the superiority of lands is the same as that of the fee of the lands, save that the disponer assigns the feu-rents,

[60] Succession (Sc.) Act, 1964, S. 14.

[61] Under S. 15.

[62] *Norton* v. *Anderson*, 6 July 1813, F.C.; *Williams and James* v. *Maclaine's Trs.* (1872) 10 M. 362.

[63] D. *Montrose* v. *Colquhoun* (1780) 6 Pat. 805; *Graham* v. *Westenra* (1826) 4 S. 615. The vassal's right to object may be lost by consent or acquiescence or the lapse of the long prescriptive period; Bell, *Convg.* II, 754.

[64] *Cargill* v. *Muir* (1837) 15 S. 408.

[65] *Dreghorn* v. *Hamilton* (1774) Mor. 15015.

[66] *Douglas of Kelhead* v. *Torthorall* (1670) Mor. 15012; *Archbishop of St. Andrews* v. M. *Huntly* (1682) Mor. 15015; *Hotchkis* v. *Walker's Trs.* (1822) 2 S. 70.

duties and casualties instead of the rents, and that the feu-rights of the lands are excepted from the warrandice clauses.[67] The superiority can be disponed without conveyance of the lands themselves.[68] Disposition of the superiority carries right to the minerals, if reserved to the superior, unless they are excluded.[69] There transmits with the superiority all obligations of the superior which are inherent conditions of the relationship, such as to free and relieve vassals of over-feuduty but not any conditions purely personal to the disponing superior.[70]

If the disposition of the superiority is to the vassal, its grant implies a discharge of past unpaid feu-duties,[71] and the destination in the disposition of the superiority will regulate the succession to the united fee, if superiority and fee are later consolidated.

CONTRACT OF EXCAMBION

The contract of excambion is that for the barter or mutual exchange of lands by heritable proprietors, possibly with a monetary payment to equalize the considerations. The contract to excamb is subject to the same requirements of formalities as the contract to sell.[72] A power to sell heritage does not imply a power to excamb.[73]

EXCAMBION

A contract to excamb lands is given effect by a deed of excambion, which narrates the agreement to excamb and any consideration which was passed to equalize the counterpart transactions, contains clauses dispositive of the one's lands to the other and of the other's lands to the one, as in a disposition, clauses of entry, of assignation by each respectively of writs and of rents, of obligations of relief, of the grant of warrandice, and of consents to registration, and a testing clause. Prior to 1925[74] mutual grants of real warrandice were expressed or implied in excambions. The deed is recorded with two warrants of registration, one on behalf of each party, for preservation and for publication. Alternatively, excambion can be effected by separate dispositions. Title is completed as under a disposition.

[67] Ceres School Board v. Macfarlane (1893) 23 R. 279.
[68] Gardner v. Leith Trinity House (1841) 3 D. 534; Williams and James v. Maclaine's Trs. (1872) 10 M. 362.   [69] Orr v. Moir's Trs. (1893) 20 R. (H.L.) 27.
[70] Jolly's Exrx. v. V. Stonehaven, 1958 S.C. 635.
[71] E. Argyle v. L. McDonald (1676) Mor. 6323.
[72] Melville v. Wilson (1829) 7 S. 889; (1830) 8 S. 841.
[73] Bruce v. Stewart (1900) 2 F. 948. See also Trusts (Sc.) Act, 1921, S. 4(e).
[74] Conveyancing (Sc.) Act, 1924, S. 14.

INVOLUNTARY TRANSFER OF LAND

Involuntary transfer of land takes place on compulsory purchase of the land, by judicial sale, on the owner's death, or his sequestration, or by operation of legal diligence.

COMPULSORY PURCHASE

Powers to acquire lands compulsorily from the owners thereof is conferred by many statutes, both public-general and local statutes. Statutory codes have been provided to regulate the modes of acquisition, and to provide for compensation.

The main code of procedure is contained in the Lands Clauses Consolidation (Sc.) Act, 1845, amended in 1860, which (S. 1) applies to every undertaking authorized by a subsequent Act which authorized the taking of lands, and is incorporated with that Act, but a subsequent Act may incorporate only parts of the 1845 Act. Other 'Clauses Acts' must also be considered in the case of acquisition for the specific purposes regulated by the relevant Clauses Act, e.g. for waterworks.

Compulsory powers are strictly construed,[1] especially in the case of á trading body.[2] They must be exercised bona fide[3] and within the prescribed time or, if none be specified, within three years of the authorizing Act (S. 116).

Purchases by agreement

The undertaking empowered to utilize the 1845 Act may (S. 6) purchase the lands desired by agreement for a lump sum, or for a feu-duty or ground annual secured on the revenues of the undertaking (S. 10). This power is confined to lands authorized by the Special Act to

[1] *Moncreiffe* v. *Perth Harbour Commrs.* (1843) 5 D. 879.
[2] *Galloway* v. *London Corpn.* (1866) L.R. 1 H.L. 34.
[3] *Michael* v. *Edinburgh Corpn.* (1895) 3 S.L.T. 109; *Sydney Corpn.* v. *Campbell* [1925] A.C. 338; cf. *Boswell* v. *G.S.W. Ry.* (1851) 13 D. 1157.

be taken,[4] though it may also give power to purchase other lands for extraordinary purposes.[5] If exercised this power creates a common law relationship with the superior. It is a question of interpretation whether an agreement to acquire lands is conditional on the carrying out of the undertaking, or absolute, rendering the undertaking liable to damages if they abandon the undertaking without having completed the purchase.[6]

Purchase otherwise than by agreement—notice to treat

The promoters of the authorized undertaking must first (S. 17) give notice to all parties interested in the lands they propose to take of their intention to do so, that they are willing to treat, and as to the compensation to be made.[7] If parties fail to treat or do not agree on the compensation, it may be determined by the sheriff (S. 21), or referred to arbitration (Ss. 19–34).[8] If the matter is not referred to arbitration, or an award is not made within the time set by the Act, the party claiming compensation may require a jury to be summoned by the sheriff (Ss. 35–9).[9] Thirteen jurors are to be empanelled, with the sheriff presiding, and they have to assess separately sums payable for the purchase of the land and for damage for injury to it (Ss. 40–8).[10] A tenant is entitled to full compensation for all loss resulting from dispossession.[11] Compensation to absent parties is to be determined by a valuator appointed by the sheriff (Ss. 56–60). Provision is made for the application of the compensation money (Ss. 61–73). On deposit in bank of the purchase money or compensation awarded, the owners of the lands are to convey the lands to the promoters of the undertaking, failing which the promotors may expede a notarial instrument narrating the compulsory purchase, whereupon the interest of the owners vests absolutely in the promoters of the undertaking who became entitled to immediate possession (Ss. 74–6).[12] Feus and conveyances of lands may be in the form of Schedules A and B to the Act and if

[4] N.B. Ry. Co. v. Tod (1846) 5 Bell, 184; Maule v. Moncrieffe (1846) 5 Bell, 333; Edinburgh Tramways v. Black (1873) 11 M. (H.L.) 57.
[5] Ss. 12, 13; City of Glasgow Union Ry. Co. v. Caledonian Ry. (1871) 9 M. (H.L.) 115.
[6] Edinburgh, etc. Ry. Co. v. Philip (1857) 2 Macq. 514; Scottish N.E. Ry. Co. v. Stewart (1859) 3 Macq. 382; N.B. Ry. Co. v. Benhar Coal Co. (1886) 14 R. 141.
[7] Notice once given cannot be withdrawn without the owners' consent, and compensation is due; Lockerby v. City of Glasgow Improvement Trs. (1872) 10 M. 971.
[8] cf. Smith v. Lanarkshire and Ayrshire Ry. (1905) 12 S.L.T. 783.
[9] Where a special Act incorporates the 1845 Act, it may permit alternative procedure; Davie v. Edinburgh Mags., 1951 S.C. 720; cf. Alexander v. N. of Sc. Hydro-Electric Board, 1952 S.C. 367 where 1845 Act procedure held inapplicable as there was no acquisition of land, but only entry for other purposes but causing damage.
[10] cf. City of Glasgow Union Ry. v. Hunter (1870) 8 M. (H.L.) 156.
[11] Venables v. Dept. of Agriculture, 1932 S.C. 573.
[12] Alexander v. Bridge of Allan Water Co. (1868) 6 M. 324.

recorded in the General Register of Sasines within sixty days constitute a good and undoubted right and complete and valid feudal title to the promoters for all time (S. 80).[13] The statutory conveyance duly recorded appears to create a statutory tenure and to extinguish the superior–vassal relationship.[14] The promoters may not, in general, without liability to penalty, enter on the lands until the price has been paid, or consigned in bank (Ss. 83–9).[15] Provision is made for intersected land and common land (Ss. 90–8)[16] lands subject to security-rights (Ss. 99–106) or feu-duty or ground annual (Ss. 107–111)[17] or to leases (Ss. 112–116),[18] interests omitted to be purchased (Ss. 117–119),[19] and the sale of superfluous land (Ss. 120–7).[20]

The Acquisition of Land (Authorization Procedure) (Sc.) Act, 1947, regulates the compulsory purchase of land by local authorities, where authorized by any Act prior to that Act, with certain exceptions, by certain ministries under certain powers, and in future cases where the 1947 Act is incorporated.[21] The procedure is embodied in Schedule 1 of the Act. There must be a compulsory purchase order by the acquiring authority, advertised, and copies served on owners, lessees and occupiers.[22] The acquiring authority may enter and take possession before depositing the price and without the consent of the owners.[23] If no objection is made, the confirming authority may confirm it; if objections are made the confirming authority must cause a public inquiry to be held, in accordance with Schedule IV,[24] or afford any objector an opportunity of appearing before and being heard by a

---

[13] cf. *Campbell* v. *Ayr C.C.* (1904) 11 S.L.T. 587; *Heriot's Trust* v. *Caledonian Ry.*, 1915 S.C. (H.L.) 52; *D. Argyll* v. *L.M.S. Ry.*, 1931 S.C. 309. In the case of land in an area operational for the purposes of the Land Registration (Sc.) Act, 1979, the conveyance must be registered in the Land Register.

[14] *Macfarlane* v. *Monklands Ry. Co.* (1864) 2 M. 519, 529; *Elgin Mags.* v. *Highland Ry.* (1884) 11 R. 950; *Inverness Mags.* v. *Highland Ry.* (1893) 20 R. 551; *Inverness Mags.* v. *Highland Ry.*, 1909 S.C. 943; *Fraser* v. *Caledonian Ry.*, 1911 S.C. 145; *Heriot's Trust, supra; D. Argyll, supra; Barr* v. *Glasgow Corpn.*, 1972 S.L.T. (Sh. Ct.) 63.

[15] *Glasgow District Subway Co.* v. *Johnstone* (1892) 20 R. (J.) 28.

[16] cf. *Glasgow City and District Ry. Co.* v. *Mackenzie* (1883) 10 R. 894; *Glasgow Coal Exchange Co.* v. *Glasgow City and District Ry. Co.* (1883) 10 R. 1283; *Glasgow, Yoker & Clydebank Ry. Co.* v. *Moore* (1894) 1 S.L.T. 498; *Bryson & McIntosh* v. *Caledonian Ry.* (1894) 2 S.L.T. 90; *Caledonian Ry.* v. *Turcan* (1898) 25 R. (H.L.) 7.

[17] cf. *Campbell's Trs.* v. *L.N.E. Ry.*, 1930 S.C. 182.

[18] cf. *Hunter* v. *N.B. Ry.* (1849) 12 D. 37.

[19] *Davidson's Trs.* v. *Caledonian Ry.* (1894) 21 R. 1060.

[20] cf. *Glover's Trs.* v. *City of Glasgow Union Ry.* (1869) 7 M. 338; *Caledonian Ry.* v. *City of Glasgow Union Ry.* (1871) 9 M. (H.L.) 115; *N.B. Ry.* v. *Moon's Trs.* (1879) 6 R. 640; *Stewart* v. *Highland Ry.* (1889) 16 R. 580; *Macfie* v. *Callander and Oban Ry.* (1898) 25 R. (H.L.) 19; *Brown* v. *N.B. Ry.* (1906) 8 F. 534; *N.B. Ry.* v. *Birrell's Trs.*, 1918 S.C. (H.L.) 33.

[21] e.g. Housing (Sc.) Act, 1966, Ss. 14, 20, 23, 81, 135, 143, 175, 176; cf. *Scottish Aviation* v. *Lord Advocate*, 1951 S.C. 33; *Peter Holmes & Son* v. *Secretary of State for Scotland*, 1965 S.C. 1.

[22] cf. *McMillan* v. *Inverness C.C.*, 1949 S.C. 77.

[23] *Glasgow Corpn.* v. *Friendly Bar*, 1971 S.C. 71.

[24] On procedure see *Hamilton* v. *Secretary of State for Scotland*, 1972 S.C. 73.

person appointed by the confirming authority for the purpose, and the acquiring authority an opportunity of being heard also.[25] The confirming authority may then consider the objections and the report of the person who held the inquiry and confirm the order with or without modifications. In confirming the Secretary of State exercises a quasi-judicial, not an administrative, function, and must observe the requirement of natural justice.[26] After confirmation, the acquiring authority must publish the fact of confirmation and serve a notice thereof on owners, lessees and occupiers. Similar provision is made for compulsory purchase by Ministers (Sched. I, Part II). Special provision is made for certain descriptions of land (Sched. I, Part III). A person aggrieved by a compulsory purchase order may appeal to the Court of Session within six weeks from the notice of confirmation on specified and limited grounds only (Sched. I, Part IV).[27] Where land is acquired compulsorily certain public rights of way over the land may be extinguished. The Lands Clauses Acts are deemed incorporated with the enactment under which compulsory purchase under Schedule I is authorized, with certain modifications (Sched. II).

Compensation is governed by the Land Compensation (Sc.) Acts, 1963 and 1973.[28] Under that Act any question of disputed compensation falls to be determined by one of a panel of official arbiters (1963 Act, S. 2) or in certain cases by the Lands Tribunal for Scotland (1963 Act, S. 8). Rules are provided for the assessment of compensation (1963 Act, Ss. 12–24).[29] Compensation should be fixed at the date of the award, not of the original notice to treat.[30] It should be a fair equivalent for what the acquiring authority takes and for what the proprietor has to give up.[31]

Feu-duties and ground annuals are deemed to be redeemed on land being acquired compulsorily.[32]

The Offshore Petroleum Development (Sc.) Act, 1975, authorizes the acquisition of land by the Secretary of State for purposes connected with offshore petroleum.

---

[25] On the effect of failure to serve on an owner, and his inability to object see *McCowan* v. *Secy. of State for Scotland*, 1972 S.C. 93.

[26] *Hamilton* v. *Secy. of State for Scotland*, 1972 S.C. 73.

[27] e.g. *Watson* v. *Lord Advocate*, 1956 S.C. 302; *Hamilton* v. *Secy. of State for Scotland*, 1972 S.C. 73.

[28] Superseding the Acquisition of Land (Assessment of Compensation) Act, 1919, and certain other enactments.

[29] cf. *Venables* v. *Dept. of Agriculture*, 1932 S.C. 573; *McEwing* v. *Renfrewshire C.C.*, 1960 S.C. 53; *Robertson's Trs.* v. *Glasgow Corpn.*, 1967 S.C. 124; *Menzies* v. *Stirling D.C.*, 1977 S.C. 33; *Woolfson* v. *Strathclyde Regional Council*, 1978 S.C. (H.L.) 90; *Cupar Trading Estate* v. *Fife Regional Council*, 1979 S.L.T. (Lands Tr.) 2.

[30] *Miller* v. *Edinburgh Corpn.*, 1978 S.C. 1.

[31] *I.R.C.* v. *G.S.W. Ry.* (1887) 14 R. (H.L.) 33; *Miller, supra.*

[32] Land Tenure Reform (Sc.) Act, 1974, S. 6.

JUDICIAL SALE OR FORECLOSURE

Involuntary transfer also takes place where land is sold in the creditor's exercise of his power of sale under a standard security, or if he forecloses under such a security.[33]

DEATH

On the death of an owner of lands his interest in the lands vests, if he died intestate *quoad* the land, in his executor, to be held and disposed of in accordance with the law of intestate succession,[34] and if he died testate *quoad* the land, in the executor or trustee appointed by his will, whom failing in the person deemed entitled to the office of executor, to be held and disposed of in accordance with the directions of the deceased's will. This subject is more appropriately considered in the context of succession.[35]

SEQUESTRATION

If an owner of land is sequestrated, the Act and Warrant of the trustee transfers to and vests in him, as at the date of the first deliverance, the whole heritable estate belonging to the bankrupt in Scotland, subject always to such preferable securities as existed over the land at that date and are not reducible.[36] This is more fully considered in relation to sequestration.[37]

DILIGENCE

Inhibition

Inhibition is a form of diligence which strikes against the voluntary debts or deeds of the person inhibited, preventing dealing with land unless the person inhibited had been obliged, prior to the inhibition, to grant the deed.[38] It does not transfer possession or property of the debtor's lands to the creditor. An inhibition of the debtor in a bond

---

[33] Ch. 5.12, *supra.*
[34] Succession (Sc.) Act, 1964, Ss. 1(1), 14(1).
[35] Chs. 7.1–7.4, *infra.*
[36] Bankruptcy (Sc.) Act, 1913, S. 97(2).
[37] Ch. 10.1, *infra.*
[38] Ersk. III, 11, 11: *Scottish Waggon Co.* v. *Hamilton's Tr.* (1906) 13 S.L.T. 779; *McGowan* v. *Middlemas*, 1977 S.L.T. (Sh. Ct.) 141; *Wilson* v. *W.* 1981 S.L.T. 101.

and disposition in security gives the inhibiting creditor a preference over other creditors who had taken no steps to secure their debts to the free proceeds of the sale of the land by the creditor in the bond.[39] An inhibition of the creditor in a bond does not prevent him demanding payment of the debt or, on being paid, assigning the bond to the debtor's nominee.[40]

Adjudication

Adjudication is the mode of attaching land in security of or in satisfaction of debt, and also the mode whereby the creditor in an obligation to convey lands may judicially obtain title thereto.

Adjudication for debt

Adjudication proceeds by an action in the Court of Session.[41] Adjudgeable subjects include heritage and heritable rights, liferents, reversions, leases, mines, fishings, heritable securities,[42] a personal right to a conveyance of land,[43] and beneficial rights in heritage generally,[44] but not titles of honour, a hereditary office,[45] arrears of rent or interest,[46] lands taken by a railway and being used for their undertaking,[47] moveables and moveable rights, and some other classes of rights. It is available against the debtor's estate whether he be alive or dead, but in the latter case the heir must be called as defender. It proceeds only on a liquid document of debt, or a debt constituted by decree; the debt must be subsisting and not contingent or prescribed, due and payable, and vested in the adjudger. If the debt is not liquid, or there is no written document of debt, or it is conditional the action must be constitution of the debt and for adjudication. Constitution is not necessary if the debt has been made real by real burden or heritable bond, but in such a case the adjudication must be preceded by an action of poinding the ground, which makes the arrears of interest a real debt and the accumulated principal and interest itself bear interest and become a real burden.[48]

Litigiosity

A notice of signeted summons of adjudication or of constitution and adjudication may be registered in the Register of Inhibitions and

[39] *Bank of Scotland* v. *L.A.*, 1977 S.L.T. 24.
[40] *Mackintosh's Trs.* v. *Davidson & Garden* (1898) 25 R. 554.
[41] Adjudications Act, 1672 (c. 45), and Titles to Land (Consolidation) (Sc.) Act, 1868. S. 59.
[42] 1868 Act, S. 117; *Hare* (1889) 17 R. 105.
[43] *Watson* v. *Wilson* (1868) 6 M. 258.
[44] *Stewart* v. *Forbes* (1888) 15 R. 383.
[45] *E. Lauderdale* v. *Scrymgeour Wedderburn*, 1910 S.C. (H.L.) 35.
[46] *Broughton* v. *Fraser* (1832) 10 D. 418.
[47] *Glover's Trs.* v. *Glasgow Union Ry. Co.* (1869) 7 M. 328.
[48] Mackay, *Manual*, 518.

Adjudications, whereby the lands concerned are rendered litigious,[49] so that the debtor cannot alienate the lands to the prejudice of the creditor, but neither action nor decree has this effect unless the decree of adjudication is recorded in the appropriate Register of Sasines.[50] Notices of litigiosity prescribe in five years[51] and it cannot be founded on after six months from the final decree in the action creating it.[52] Even when completed litigiosity strikes only at voluntary deeds and does not affect those granted in implement of prior obligations.

Competition among adjudgers

All adjudications prior to that first made effectual, and all led subsequently, within a year and a day, rank *pari passu*.[52] Sequestration is statutorily equivalent to a decree of adjudication as at the date of the first deliverance, and consequently other adjudications not made effectual within a year and a day before that date confer no preferential right.[53]

Completion of title

Heritable property not requiring sasine is vested in the adjudger by the decree alone. Where the property is feudal, a decree of adjudication is, except in the case of heritable securities, equivalent to a disposition of the lands in favour of the adjudger, and he may complete title by recording the decree, or expeding a notarial instrument or notice of title thereon, and recording it in the Register of Sasines.[54] Title to heritable securities adjudged is completed by recording the abbreviate of adjudication or the extract decree in the Register of Sasines,[55] and title to long leases by recording the extract decree.[56]

Redemption; expiry of the legal

The right acquired by an adjudger is a judicial security, not a right of property[57] and the debtor retains a right of redemption for ten years, called 'the legal' (i.e. legal period of redemption).[58] On the expiry of the legal the adjudging creditor may foreclose by obtaining decree in an action of declarator of expiry of the legal, decree in which excludes redemption by the debtor.[59] Decree of expiry of the legal may be

---

[49] Titles to Land Consolidation (Sc.) Act, 1868, S. 159, and Sched. RR.
[50] Conveyancing (Sc.) Act, 1924, S. 44(2).
[51] 1924 Act, S. 44(3).
[52] Bankruptcy Act, 1661, (c. 62); Bell, *Comm.* I, 721.
[53] Bankruptcy (Sc.) Act, 1913, S. 103.
[54] Conveyancing (Sc.) Acts, 1874, S. 62; 1924, S. 4.
[55] 1874 Act, S. 65; 1924 Act, S. 4(3).
[56] Registration of Leases (Sc.) Act, 1857, S. 10, amd. 1924 Act, S. 27.
[57] *Hill* v. *Hill* (1871) 10 M. 3.
[58] *Grindley* v. *Drysdale* (1833) 11 S. 896; *Cochrane* v. *Bogle* (1850) 7 Bell, 65.
[59] *Govan* v. *G.* (1758) 2 Paton 27.

reopened, e.g. if the debtor has been a minor during part of the legal and was abroad,[60] or reduced.[61] If no such action be raised the lands remain redeemable though the legal has expired.[62] Alternatively decree of adjudication followed by charter and sasine, or their modern equivalent, recording in the Register of Sasines, and possession thereunder for ten years after expiry of the legal excludes redemption.[63] But a decree of adjudication, infeftment thereon, charter of confirmation and decree of expiry of the legal do not constitute as '*ex facie* valid irredeemable title to an estate in land' sufficient to found a title by twenty years' prescription.[64]

Payment and Extinction

If the debtor pays off all sums due to the creditor, the adjudication may be extinguished automatically and the debtor's infeftment revive,[65] but he may obtain decree of declarator of extinction and payment, or of reduction and extinction.

Adjudication in security

Adjudication in security is competent if the term of payment of a debt constituted by writing has not arrived,[66] or where the debt is future or contingent.[67] In this form of adjudication there is no legal limit of time for redemption.

Adjudication on debita fundi

Adjudication is competent on such *debita fundi* as heritable bonds, ground annuals, feu-duties, and debts constituted real burdens on land, but attaches only to the lands affected by the burden. Such adjudications need not be intimated,[68] nor do they rank *pari passu* under the Bankruptcy Act, 1661. In a competition of adjudgers adjudications on *debita fundi* are preferable to all adjudications on personal debts; *inter se* they have preference according to priority of infeftment. An adjudger may secure preference for arrears of interest by obtaining decree in an action of poinding of the ground, subsequently accumulating principal and interest and adjudging for the total, with interest.

[60] *Aitken* v. *Aitken* (1809) Bell, *Comm.* I, 744.
[61] *Paul* v. *Reid*, 8 Feb. 1814, F.C.
[62] *Govan, supra.*
[63] *Spence* v. *Bruce*, 21 Jan. 1807, F.C. Prescription Act, 1973, S. 1(3).
[64] *Hinton* v. *Connell's Trs.* (1883) 10 R. 1110.
[65] Ersk. II, 12, 37.
[66] Ersk. II, 12, 42.
[67] *Queensberry's Exors.* v. *Tait*, 11 June 1817, F.C.
[68] *Young* v. *Scott* (1893) 1 S.L.T. 15.

Adjudication in implement

This form of diligence is appropriate where a party has contracted to sell or dispone land in security but refuses voluntarily to convey the lands.[69] The procedure is by action of adjudication in implement. Decree declares the lands to belong to the purchaser, or to be conveyed as security for a loan, as the case may be.[70] This action also lay against the heir of the obligee, the appropriate form being by action of constitution and adjudication,[71] but these provisions have been repealed[72] without making any special provision for such an action being brought against the executor of a deceased obligee. It is also appropriate where no person can be traced who could give a title.[73] This has been held to be the proper way of making up the title of a general disponee to the purchaser of a house where the disponer had died and his heirs could not be found and the disponee had died.[74] The effect of decree is equivalent to a conveyance in ordinary form of the lands contained therein granted in favour of the adjudger. The adjudger completes his title by infeftment on the decree as on a conveyance.[75] In this form of action there is no question of ranking of adjudgers, nor of redemption, the transference effected by decree being absolute and irredeemable.

[69] Bell, *Comm.* I, 783; Menzies, 778.
[70] *Macgregor* v. *Macdonald* (1843) 5 D. 888.
[71] Titles to Land Consolidation (Sc.) Act, 1868, S. 60.
[72] Succession (Sc.) Act, 1964, Sched. 3.
[73] e.g. *Stewart* v. *Tennant* (1868) 5 S.L.R. 684.
[74] *Cunningham's Exor.* v. *Millar's Heirs* (1902) 10 S.L.T. 109.
[75] 1868 Act, S. 62, as amd. 1869, S. 4, replaced by Conveyancing (Sc.) Acts, 1874, S. 62; 1924 Act, S. 4.

CHAPTER 5.18

EXTINCTION OF INTERESTS IN LAND

Consolidation

A superiority of lands is extinguished by sale to or inheritance by the over-superior and consolidation with the over-superiority. The vassal's estate is extinguished if the superior purchases or inherits the fee, or the vassal purchases or inherits the superiority. The purchaser or successor in each case completes his title to each feudal estate in the usual way and records a minute of consolidation in the Register of Sasines,[1] or appends a minute of consolidation to the disposition to him of the interest later acquired and records it with that disposition.[2] In an appropriate case the transfer of a registered interest is registered in the Land Register.[3] Consolidation is not effected *ipso jure* when both estates come to be vested in one person, and they can again be separated,[4] nor can two estates not in immediate proximity in the chain of tenure be consolidated, e.g. over-superiority and fee. Consolidation does not extinguish the fee of the property, but merely unites superiority and fee.[5] The destination of the superiority rules the fee also.[6]

Consolidation is also effected by prescription, if the superiority contains the lands in question and it and the lands are possessed on infeftment for the prescriptive period.[7]

---

[1] Conveyancing Act, 1874, S. 6. Methods of consolidation competent prior to that Act are still competent, viz. resignation *ad remanentiam* and possession of both estates for the prescriptive period: see Bell, *Prin.* §787–91, 821; Bell, *Convg.* II, 781; Menzies, 619; *Walker* v. *Grieve* (1827) 5 S. 469; *Wilson* v. *Pollok* (1839) 2 D. 159.

[2] Conveyancing (Sc.) Act, 1924, S. 11, and Sched. G.

[3] Land Registration (Sc.) Act, S. 2(4)(b).

[4] *Morton* (1668) Mor. 6917; *Bald* v. *Buchanan* (1786) Mor. 15084, 15089; 2 Ross L.C. 210, 230; see also *Park's Curator* v. *Black* (1870) 8 M. 671; *E. Zetland* v. *Glover Incorpn. of Perth* (1870) 8 M. (H.L.) 144; *Motherwell* v. *Maxwell* (1903) 5 F. 619.

[5] *E. Zetland* v. *Glover Incorporation of Perth* (1870) 8 M. (H.L.) 144.

[6] *Pattison* v. *Dunn's Trs.* (1868) 6 M. (H.L.) 147; *Park's Curator* v. *Black* (1870) 8 M. 671.

[7] *L. Elibank* v. *Campbell* (1833) 12 S. 74; 3 Ross L.C. 534; *Bontine* v. *Graham* (1840) 1 Rob. 347; *Wilson* v. *Pollock* (1839) 2 D. 159; *Gordon's Trs.* (1849) 21 S. Jur. 174; *Hay* v. *Paterson*, 1910 S.C. 509.

Forfeiture of superiority

Prior to 1847 heirs of a vassal desiring entry could charge a superior who had not completed his own title to the *dominium directum* to do so under penalty of forfeiture of casualties. If the superior did not make up a title, the vassal's heir could obtain decree of tinsel of the superiority, and then charge the over-superior to enter him, and so up to the Crown, who would always enter him.[8] The Titles to Land Consolidation (Sc.) Act, 1868, S. 104, re-enacting an Act of 1847, provides that where a superior had not completed his feudal title, it is competent for a party entitled to obtain an entry to the lands to petition the court to have the superior ordained to complete his title and grant an entry and if he will not, to obtain decree declaring that the superior has forfeited all right to the superiority. The Conveyancing Act, 1874, S. 4, superseded these provisions by making infeftment imply entry with the superior whether the latter's title had been completed or not. Such implied entry extinguishes a mid-superiority.[9]

Relinquishment of superiority

A superior may also relinquish his right of superiority in favour of his immediate vassal by a deed of relinquishment which, when accepted by the vassal, recorded in the Register of Sasines, and followed by a writ of investiture by the over-superior, extinguishes the superiority and brings the vassal into an immediate relation of tenure with the next over-superior, subject to no greater duties and casualties than if the superior had remained vassal of the over-superior.[10]

Irritancy or tinsel of the feu

The feu may be forfeited to the superior if the latter is entitled to and does invoke the statutory irritancy *ob non solutum canonem* or a conventional irritancy contained in the feu-charter.[11] Decree of declarator of irritancy annuls the vassal's rights and all that has followed thereon, including the rights of sub-vassals.[12] Statute may also provide for obtaining declarator of irritancy of a feu.[13]

Statutory expropriation

An expropriating statute may acquire not only the *dominium utile* of land but any rights of superiority therein other than of the Crown,

---

[8] Bell, *Convg.* II, 788; Menzies, 834; *Dickson* v. *L. Elphinstone* (1802) Mor. 15024; *Rossmore's Trs.* v. *Brownlie* (1877) 5 R. 201.

[9] *Ferrier's Trs.* v. *Bayley* (1877) 4 R. 738; *Rossmore's Trs., supra.*

[10] Titles to Land Consolidation (Sc.) Act, 1868, Ss. 110–12.

[11] Ch. 5.4, *supra.*

[12] *Cassels* v. *Lamb* (1885) 12 R. 722; *Sandeman* v. *Scottish Property Investment Co.* (1885) 12 R. (H.L.) 67.   [13] e.g. *Neill's Trs.* v. *Macfarlane's Trs.*, 1952 S.C. 356.

and accordingly extinguish all other feudal interests in that land.[14] But in an acquisition under the Lands Clauses Consolidation (Sc.) Act, 1845, the titles granted, unless specially provided for, do not affect the right of superiority.[15] If the title granted is by way of schedule conveyance it extinguishes the superiority.[16]

Prescription

An interest in land is not extinguished by mere non-use for any period of time, but a personal right to heritage not completed by infeftment is subject to the long negative prescription[17] and rights to exact a particular term's payment of feu-duty or rent also prescribe.[18]

---

[14] Coal Industry Nationalization Act, 1946, Ss. 5, 64(3), and Sched. I: *Wauchope Settlement Trs. v. N.C.B.*, 1947 S.N. 185.

[15] *Elgin Mags. v. Highland Ry.* (1884) 11 R. 950; *Inverness Mags. v. Highland Ry.* (1893) 20 R. 551; *Heriot's Trs. v. Caledonian Ry.*, 1915 S.C. (H.L.) 52; *Argyll, supra.*

[16] 1845 Act, S. 126; *D. Argyll v. L.M.S. Ry.*, 1931 S.C. 309.

[17] Hume, *Lect.* IV, 535; *Paul v. Reid*, 8 Feb. 1814, F.C.; *Pettigrew v. Harton*, 1956 S.C. 67; Prescription and Limitation (Sc.) Act, 1973, S. 7.

[18] Prescription and Limitation (Sc.) Act, 1973, Sch. 1.

PART 3

RIGHTS IN INCORPOREAL HERITABLE OBJECTS OF PROPERTY

CHAPTER 5.19

RIGHTS IN INCORPOREAL HERITABLE OBJECTS

Incorporeal heritable objects of property rights comprise those bodies of rights which have no corporeal existence in themselves, though frequently they can be exercised only in relation to corporeal objects, and which are deemed heritable by reason, in most cases, of their actual or supposed connection with land. They may in many cases be exercised by actual occupation or possession and use, and be asserted and in case of dispute vindicated by action. Among such incorporeal heritable objects which are necessarily connected with particular parcels of corporeal land are rights of superiority of land, of the *dominium utile* of land, of the interest of an heir of entail in possession, of the interest of a proper liferenter in possession, of rights to teinds, to servitudes, to leases, the rights of creditors in some rights in security over land, reversionary rights and *jura crediti* to heritage, and claims to feu-duties, ground annuals and rents, though the arrears of these are moveables. Among those not necessarily so connected are annuities and similar rights having a tract of future time, carrying an annual profit to the creditor unrelated to any capital sum or stock, some cases of commercial goodwill, heritable offices, titles of honour and armorial bearings.[1] The right to challenge deeds relating to heritage is heritable.[2] A decree of cognition of a Dean of Guild Court whereby one party was declared a real creditor on certain heritable subjects has been held a right heritable in character, though made moveable in succession by the Titles to Land Consolidation (Sc.) Act, 1868.[3]

In some cases such as the fee of land, servitudes and leases, the concepts in question have a double aspect. They may be considered as

[1] Ersk. II, 2, 5–6; Bell, *Comm.* II, 3; *Prin.* §1476–505.
[2] Bell, *Prin.* §1485.
[3] *Peterkin* v. *Harvey* (1902) 9 S.L.T. 434.

giving various rights in and over certain physical pieces of land and consequently as rights in corporeal heritable objects,[4] but they may also be considered collectively as items of the assets of a person in right of them and consequently as items of incorporeal heritable property.[5] In the former aspect one is concerned with the individual rights in and over land exercisable by virtue of the kinds of proprietary rights in question, particularly as against other persons; in the latter one is concerned rather with the aggregate of rights regarded as a collective asset. The nature of the right is clearer in the cases of such rights as annuities which are unrelated to any particular piece of land or capital stock.

Rights in incorporeal heritable objects

Such *corpora* of rights may be owned and, subject to certain qualifications in particular cases, be made the subject of security for debt, be sold, gifted, bequeathed and otherwise dealt with. They may be asserted and vindicated by action. They may also be possessed, by the exercise of some or all of the individual rights which collectively make up the whole right. Thus a superior may exercise possession of his superiority by exacting feuduties, a vassal possess his fee by occupying his lands, a tenant possess his lease by using the subjects let to him, an annuitant his annuity by exacting payment of his due, and so on. By the Land Registration (Sc.) Act, 1979, S. 2(3) the creation of an incorporeal heritable right, except by S. 28(1), a right to salmon-fishings, over a registered interest in land is itself registrable and on registration becomes a registered interest in land conferring on the person registered as entitled a real right in and to the object of the right.

Rights of superiority

A right of superiority, comprising the aggregate of the rights which a person has as the *dominium directum* of a piece of land held under feudal tenure, is a heritable right.[6] It amounts to the totality of the rights which the superior has by law and by reservation from his grant of feus, in and to the lands and against the vassals who hold portions thereof.[7] It is the radical right and the vassal's rights revert to it if they should be suspended or fail.

Right of ownership of land in fee

The right of ownership of the fee of land held by feudal tenure comprises the aggregate of all the rights a person has by virtue of

[4] Ch. 5.2–5.15, *supra*.
[5] Ch. 5.20–5.24, *infra*.
[6] Ersk. II, 5, 1; Bell, *Prin.* §676–77, 855, 1478; Ch. 5.5, *supra*.
[7] As to these see Ch. 5.4, *supra*.

holding the *dominium utile* of land, including rights to occupy, cultivate, cut timber, extract minerals, let to tenants, shoot over it, and so
on.[8] The right of ownership is heritable. Also heritable are all the
individual rights which are incidents of ownership, such as to cultivate,
fish, shoot and so on. The right of salmon-fishing is not an incident of
ownership but a distinct interest which may or may not be granted
along with lands.

Rights of heir of entail in possession

An heir of entail in possession has all the rights a person has by virtue
of ownership in fee, save that he is subject to the fetters of the entail
and has only the powers conferred on the heir in possession by the
general law and the Entail Acts.[9] His right is heritable in terms of the
destination in the deed of entail. Money disbursed by an heir of entail
in possession on improvements is heritable.[10]

Right of liferent of lands

A proper liferent of lands is an *interim dominium* and the liferenter
may exercise all the rights of an owner except any prejudicial to the
concurrent reversionary interest of the fiar. Superiority or fee may be
enjoyed by a liferenter. His rights do not include the rights of alienation *inter vivos* or *Mortis causa* nor, unless the destination is expressly
to him and his heir in liferent, does his interest pass by succession. His
right is heritable but not inheritable. Save with the consent of the fiar
he may not grant a lease for longer than his lifetime.[11]

Rights of titular of teinds

Heritors have heritable right to surplus teinds left after provision has
been made therefrom for payment to the minister of the parish of a due
stipend.[12]

Right of servitude

A person has a right of a servitude over land only by virtue of his
ownership or possession of some other land, which has the advantage
of a servitude right as dominant tenement over the land burdened by
the servitude as, and so long as, owner or possessor of the dominant
tenement of land. It is not a, nor like a, personal privilege.[13]

---

[8] Ersk. II, 6, 1; Bell, *Prin.* §1478; Ch. 5.5, *supra.*
[9] Ch. 5.8, *supra.*
[10] *E. Kintore* v. *Ctss. Kintore* (1885) 12 R. 1213.
[11] Ersk. II, 9, 57; Bell, *Prin.* §1057.
[12] Bell, *Prin.* §837, 1148.
[13] Bell, *Prin.* §979.

Right of wayleave

A wayleave is a permission to pass over a heritable subject for a particular purpose subsidiary to other uses of the subject.[14]

Real burden

A real burden over lands in favour of a named person for the payment of money to him[15] is a heritable right, though not a proper feudal estate in the lands. The creditor's right is completed by the infeftment of the disponee in the lands burdened. The creditor has no title to possess, or sell the lands. Prior to 1874 a real money burden passed to the heir of the creditor but the Conveyancing Act, 1874, S. 30, provided that the Titles to Land Consolidation (Sc.) Act, 1868, S. 117,[16] should apply to real burdens on land. Real burdens are accordingly now moveable except *quoad fiscum*, and as regards the legal rights of *jus relicti, jus relictae* and legitim.

Ground annual

A ground annual or perpetual rent charge secured over land as a real burden thereon is not an estate in the land but only a burden thereon. It is a heritable right, and is expressly excepted from the provisions making real burdens moveable in succession.[17]

Personal rights to land

A right though not yet completed as a real right but connected with or affecting land, which the creditor has power to complete, is heritable.[18]

Leaseholder

The rights of leaseholding comprise the aggregate of the rights enjoyed by a person having a valid lease of heritage from a landlord, including the rights to occupy and use the premises let for any purpose, within the terms of the lease, for which they are appropriate, in any way which does not contravene any express or implied term of the lease. Leases are real rights in land and heritable, and pass with a bequest of heritage.[19]

---

[14] *I.T.A.* v. *Lanarkshire Assessor,* 1968 S.C. 249.
[15] Ch. 5.11, *supra.*
[16] Now amended by Succession (Sc.) Act, 1964, Sched. 3.
[17] Conveyancing Act, 1874, S. 30, applying Titles to Land Consolidation Act, 1868, S. 117.
[18] Ersk. II, 2, 5; Bell, *Comm.* II, 4: *Fisher* v. *Pringle* (1718) Mor. 5516. See also *Allan's Factor* v. *Allan* (1893) 1 S.L.T. 59; *L.A.* v. *Macfarlane's Trs.* (1893) 1 S.L.T. 385.
[19] Stair II, 9, 43; Ersk. II, 2, 6; II, 6, 31; Bell, *Comm.* I, 76; McLaren, *Wills,* I, 92; Rankine, *Leases,* 157; *Moncrieff* v. *Seivwright* (1896) 3 S.L.T. 262.

Right in security over land

A creditor who holds a bond and disposition in security of lands completed by registration of the bond in the appropriate division of the General Register of Sasines holds thereby an estate in the lands which at common law formed part of the creditor's heritable estate for all purposes. But since the Titles to Land Consolidation (Sc.) Act, 1868, S. 117,[20] such bonds are moveable estate in his succession except as regards *jus relicti, jus relictae* and legitim, and *quoad fiscum*. But S. 117 made no change except in relation to the creditor's succession, intestate, or testate, in relation to the interpretation of the terms 'heritable' and 'moveable'.[21]

A creditor who holds a disposition of lands *ex facie* absolute completed by registration in the Register of Sasines qualified by a back-letter narrating that the disposition is truly in security, is clearly holder of an estate in the lands. In regard to third parties he is absolute owner of the *dominium directum* or *dominium utile* as the case may be. His right is accordingly one heritable for all purposes. This form of security is unaffected by the Titles to Land Consolidation Act, 1868, S. 117, as amended.[22]

A creditor in a standard security over land[23] holds a heritable right over the lands but the right is moveable in the creditor's succession in the same cases as in a bond and disposition in security.[24]

Reversionary rights

The reversionary right of a heritable proprietor in his lands while they are subject to a security right or lease in favour of another is heritable. A right of redemption or of reversion of land created in a deed executed after 31 July 1974, if exercisable on the happening of an event bound to occur or the occurrence of which is within the control of a person entitled to exercise the right, is exercisable only within twenty years of the date of creation.[25]

Jus crediti

A *jus crediti* is the personal right of one who has a claim against another for payment or delivery of something, including a claim that the latter grant him a title to heritage. It need not be presently exigible

---

[20] Amended by Succession (Sc.) Act, 1964, Sched. 3.
[21] *Hare* (1889) 17 R. 105; *Hughes' Trs.* v. *Corsane* (1890) 18 R. 299; *Gilligan* v. *G.* (1891) 18 R. 387; see also *Hodge* v. *H.* (1879) 7 R. 259; *Guthrie* (1880) 8 R. 34.
[22] 1868 Act, S. 3, definition of 'heritable security'.
[23] Conveyancing and Feudal Reform (Sc.) Act, 1970, Part II.
[24] 1970 Act, S. 32.
[25] Land Tenure Reform (Sc.) Act, 1974, S. 12.

but must be effectual in competition with the granter's creditors. It may be heritable or moveable according to the nature and quality of the thing or fund against which the claim lies.[26] It will be heritable if it is right to transfer of a heritable object. It includes such cases as a feuar who has made a contract for a feu and accordingly has a *jus crediti* to obtain a feu-charter, a purchaser of heritage, who has a *jus crediti* to obtain a disposition from the seller, and a trust beneficiary entitled by the terms of the trust to have a conveyance of heritage, who has a *jus crediti* to obtain a disposition from the trustees,[27] an obligation to infeft an heir at a determinate date or age,[28] a claim to improvement expenditure not charged on the estate by the maker but bequeathed by him[29] and a claim by a debtor who had granted an *ex facie* absolute disposition to demand a conveyance from the creditor on paying the sums due.[30] All such *jura crediti* are heritable. The right of the assignee of a *spes successionis* to heritage, though merely a *jus crediti*, is a heritable right.[31] But a right to a share of the proceeds of heritage is moveable.[32]

Party in rights of feu-duties or ground annual

The person in right to exact payment of feu-duties by vassals holding land under feudal tenure, whether he be the superior or one to whom the superior has assigned his right to uplift feu-duties, or to exact payments under a contract of ground annual, has a heritable right.

Claims to rents

The rent due by the tenant of a particular holding or tenement of land is payable to the owner thereof but may by the terms of the lease, or by separate assignation, be made payable to another party.[33] If so, it is a heritable right.[34]

Interest on heritable bonds

Claims to interest on heritable bonds are heritable.[35]

---

[26] Bell, *Comm.* I, 36; II, 4; *Prin.* §1482; *Buchanan v. Angus* (1862) 4 Macq. 374; *Young v. Martin* (1868) 6 S.L.R. 230.
[27] *Durie v. Coutts* (1791) Mor. 4624; *Thain v. Thain* (1891) 18 R. 1196; contrast *Wardlaw's Trs. v. W.* (1880) 7 R. 1070; *Borland's Trs. v. B.,* 1917 S.C. 704.
[28] *Douglas v. Douglas and Drummond* (1724) Mor. 12910.
[29] *E. Kintore v. Ctss. of Kintore* (1885) 12 R. 1213.
[30] *Ritchie v. Scott* (1899) 1 F. 728.
[31] *Thain, supra.*
[32] *Gilligan v. G.* (1891) 18 R. 387.
[33] *Stewart v. Cameron* (1827) 5 S. 557.
[34] *Justice v. Ross* (1829) 8 S. 108.
[35] Bell, *Prin.* §1484.

Arrears

Arrears of annual payments of feu-duty, ground annual, rents, of interest of heritable bonds and of annual returns of debts and funds themselves heritable are, however, moveable.[36]

Rights having a tract of future time

Such a right, though of a personal nature and unconnected with land, is heritable, being periodical, future and the payments being unrelated to any particular capital or principal debt.[37] The chief instance is an annuity.

Annuities

An annuity is a right continuing for a period of time, carrying a stated yearly profit to the creditor unrelated to any capital sum or stock.[38] It may be payable for any period, according to the gift or contract creating it, but commonly for the granter's, or grantee's, or a third party's life. An annuity may be unsecured, or secured over heritage (by bond of annuity and standard security), or made a real burden by reservation.[39] Annuities are by nature heritable in the creditor's succession,[40] but if secured over heritage or by real burden they are moveable in the cases affected by the Titles to Land Consolidation (Sc.) Act, 1868, S. 117, as amended. As they become due the termly payments are always moveable.[41] They burden the debtor's heritable succession[42] and, though payable primarily out of income, must in case of deficiency be paid from capital.[43]

An annuity may be declared alimentary, in which case there must be a continuing trust,[44] in which case it cannot be attached except for alimentary debts[45] unless in so far as it exceeds a reasonable sum[46] and as regards arrears.[47]

[36] Ersk. II, 9, 64; Bell, *Prin.* §1479; *Reid* v. *McWalter* (1878) 5 R. 630.
[37] Ersk. II, 2, 6; Bell, *Comm.* II, 4, *Prin.* §1480.
[38] Ersk. II, 2, 6; Bell, *Comm.* II, 4; *Prin.* §1480.
[39] *Buchanan* v. *Eaton*, 1911 S.C. (H.L.) 40.
[40] Bell, *Prin.* §1480; *Reid* v. *McWalter* (1878) 5 R. 630.
[41] *Hill* v. *H.* (1872) 11 M. 247; *M. Breadalbane's Trs.* v. *Jamieson* (1873) 11 M. 912; *Reid, supra.*
[42] *Wallace* v. *Ritchie's Trs.* (1846) 8 D. 1038; *Crawford's Trs.* v. *C.* (1867) 5 M. 275; *Mackintosh* v. *M's Trs.* (1873) 11 M. (H.L.) 28; *Breadalbane's Trs., supra; Moon's Trs.* v. *M.* (1899) 2 F. 201.
[43] *Knox's Trs.* v. *K.* (1869) 7 M. 873; *Kinmond's Trs.* v. *K.* (1873) 11 M. 381; *Adamson's Trs.* v. *A's Exors.* (1891) 18 R. 1133; *Colquhoun's Trs.* v. *C.*, 1922 S.C. 32.
[44] *Murray* v. *Macfarlane's Trs.* (1895) 22 R. 927; *Kennedy's Trs.* v. *Warren* (1901) 3 F. 1087; *Turner's Trs.* v. *Fernie*, 1908 S.C. 883; *Brown's Trs.* v. *Thom*, 1916 S.C. 32; *Dempster's Trs.* v. *D.*, 1921 S.C. 332; *Forbes' Trs.* v. *Tennant*, 1926 S.C. 264.
[45] *Monypenny* v. *E. Buchan* (1835) 13 S. 1112; *Harvey* v. *Calder* (1840) 2 D. 1095; *Lewis* v. *Anstruther* (1853) 15 D. 263.
[46] *Livingstone* v. *L.* (1886) 14 R. 43.   [47] Bell, *Comm.* I, 127.

Personal bond with clause of interest

A personal bond with a stipulation for interest was at common law moveable until the term of payment, but deemed heritable thereafter[48] or if the date of payment were distant or uncertain. Statute,[49] however, made such bonds moveable in succession, but to remain heritable, if including an express obligation to infeft, or expressed in favour of heirs and assignees excluding executors, *quoad fiscum* in questions of forfeiture,[50] and formerly also[51] so far as regarded the legal rights of husband and wife.[52]

Commercial goodwill

The goodwill of a business comprises its reputation, connections, trade name, and the advantages it enjoys from being established with these elements over other businesses in the same trade.[53] It is a distinct object of property, having value, and susceptible of transfer. It may be local, associated with the locality and the premises in which the business has been carried on,[54] or personal, or pertaining partly to both.[55] Whether the goodwill of a public house is heritable or moveable depends on the circumstances of each case.[56] If, or in so far as, it attaches to the locality or the premises it is heritable, like the premises, and inseparable therefrom, and passes with the premises as a pertinent thereof.[57] Goodwill may be bequeathed but, if local, will pass with the heritage to which it attaches notwithstanding the will.[58]

Heritable offices

Certain of the great Offices of State of Scotland are heritable, being held *jure sanguinis*, and the right thereto is not personal but an

---

[48] Ersk. II, 2, 10–13; Bell, *Comm.* II, 7; Menzies, 220; *Gray* v. *Walker* (1859) 21 D. 709; *Downie* (1866) 4 M. 1067.

[49] Bonds Act, 1661 (c. 244); Ersk. II, 2, 9–10.

[50] Until Statute Law Revision (Sc.) Act, 1964, Sch. 1.

[51] *Downie* v. *D's Trs.* (1866) 4 M. 1067; *Dawson's Trs.* v. *D.* (1896) 23 R. 1006; *Bennett's Extrx.* v. *B's Exors.*, 1907 S.C. 598; *Heath* v. *Grant's Trs.*, 1913 S.C. 78; *Stewart's Trs.* v. *Battcock*, 1914 S.C. 179. See also *Stark* v. *S.*, 1910 S.C. 397; *Robertson's Trs.* v. *Maxwell*, 1922 S.C. 267; *McWiggan's Trs.* v. *McW.*, 1922 S.C. 276.

[52] Bell, *supra; Monro* v. *M.* (1735) Elchies, Her. and Mov. 2; *Kennedy* v. *K.* (1747) Elchies, Her. & Mov. 13.

[53] cf. generally *Churton* v. *Douglas* (1859) John 164; *Trego* v. *Hunt* [1896] A.C. 7.

[54] cf. *Drummond* v. *Leith Assessor* (1886) 13 R. 540; *Philip's Exor.* v. *P's Exor.* (1894) 21 R. 482.

[55] *Murray's Tr.* v. *McIntyre* (1904) 6 F. 588.

[56] *Graham* v. *G.* (1898) 5 S.L.T. 319; *Leishman* v. *Glen & Henderson* (1899) 6 S.L.T. 328; *Ross* v. *R's Trs.* (1901) 9 S.L.T. 340; *Town and County Bank* v. *McBain* (1902) 9 S.L.T. 485; *Graham* v. *G's Trs.* (1904) 6 F. 1015; *Muirhead's Trs.* v. *M.* (1905) 7 F. 496; see also *Hughes* v. *Stirling Assessor* (1892) 19 R. 840; *Barr* v. *Lions, Ltd.*, 1956 S.C. 59.

[57] *Bain* v. *Munro* (1878) 5 R. 416; *Bell's Tr.* v. *B.* (1884) 12 R. 85; *Brown* v. *Robertson* (1896) 34 S.L.R. 570.

[58] cf. *Robertson* v. *Quiddington* (1860) 28 Beav. 529.

incorporeal heritable right.[59] Though heritable, such an office is not, in general, alienable or adjudgeable, or otherwise *in commercio*.[60]

Titles of honour

The dignities of grades of peerage are created by the Crown and are heritable,[61] being presumed destined to the grantee and the heirs male of his body,[62] though a special destination may be provided in the patent of ennoblement,[63] and peeragee may now be created for the grantee's lifetime only,[64] or a hereditary peerage renounced for the lifetime of the renouncing heir.[65] Hereditary peerages descend *jure sanguinis* according to the destination in the grant, and vest without service or possession.[66] The dignity of peerage is indivisible and incapable of sale or assignation.

The dignity of baronet is similarly heritable, normally destined to the heir male of the first grantee, and vests without service, though service has been the normal mode of establishing a right of succession.

Knighthood is the lowest dignity or title of honour but is personal and not heritable.

Armorial bearings

The grant of arms is part of the royal prerogative[67] but the grant, differencing and registration of arms has long been exercised by the Lord Lyon King of Arms.[68] Arms are a recognized form of incorporeal heritable property held of the Crown and legally protected against infringement.[69] The Public Register of All Arms and Bearings in Scot-

[59] e.g. High Constable of Scotland: Earl of Erroll; Hereditary Standard Bearer for Scotland: Earl of Dundee; see also *E. Lauderdale* v. *Scrymgeour Wedderburn*, 1910 S.C. (H.L.) 35; Hereditary Keeper of Palace of Holyroodhouse: Duke of Hamilton; of Falkland: Major Michael Crichton-Stuart; of Dunstaffnage: Duke of Argyll; of Stirling: Earl of Mar and Kellie; Hereditary Master of the Queen's Household in Scotland: Duke of Argyll; Principle Usher to the Crown in Scotland: see *Walker Trs.* v. *Lord Advocate*, 1912 S.C. (H.L.) 12; Earl Marshal: see *Bower* v. *Earl Mareschal* (1682) 2 B.S. 18; 3 B.S. 420; Lord Clerk Register: Duke of Buccleuch and Queensberry; see also Act of Union, 1707, S. 20. Other great Offices of State (Keeper of the Great Seal, Keeper of the Privy Seal, Lord Justice General, Lord Advocate, Lord Justice Clerk, Solicitor General) are personal and not heritable. See Ferguson (1911) 23 J.R. 152.

[60] See further *Walker Trs., supra; E. Lauderdale, supra.*

[61] Ersk. II, 2, 6; Bell, *Comm.* I, 120; *Prin.* §1481.

[62] *Kennedy* v. *E. of Ruglen and March* (1762) 2 Pat. 55; *Glencairn Peerage* (1797) 1 Macq. 444; *Lady Ruthven of Freeland*, 1971 S.L.T. (Lyon Ct.) 2.

[63] *Herries Peerage Claim* (1858) 3 Macq. 588.

[64] Life Peerages Act, 1958.

[65] Peerage Act, 1963.

[66] Ersk. III, 8, 77; as to legitimation see *Viscount Drumlanrig's Tutor*, 1977 S.L.T. (Lyon Ct.) 16.

[67] *McDonnell* v. *Macdonald* (1846) 4 Sh. App. 371.

[68] Lyon King of Arms Acts, 1592 (c. 29), 1669 (c. 95), 1672 (c. 47). See also *Cuninghame* v. *Cunyngham* (1849) 11 D. 1139; *Stewart-Mackenzie* v. *Fraser-Mackenzie*, 1922 S.C. (H.L.) 39.

[69] *Cuninghame, supra.*

land is to armorial bearings what the Register of Sasines is to corporeal heritable property. A grant of arms confers on the grantee a right to bear the full undifferenced arms of the grant, and a similar right in perpetuity to the person who is at the time the heir of the grantee according to the grant.

A grant is deemed to be destined to the grantee and his male heirs-at-law.[70] Grants are normally to the grantee and his descendants, or to a series of heirs of entail. Arms, once granted and registered, vest in the heir *jure sanguinis* and without service or sasine, though service or rematriculation may be the best evidence that it has vested.

Clauses are sometimes included in settlements requiring the heir under the deed to assume the name and arms of the granter. In such a case the grantee must constructively resign the arms to the Crown for new grant, by petitioning Lyon, who may give effect to the settler's desires in such mode as he deems right. The extent and manner of implementing the conditions of the deed depend on its terms.[71] An heir is deemed to have satisfied an arms condition if he has made an unsuccesful application to Lyon for authority to bear the prescribed arms.[72]

Armorial bearings cannot be sold, assigned or transferred *inter vivos*.

Succession

Formerly all incorporeal heritable rights passed to the heir-at-law on the holder's death, but they now pass to his executor for purposes of administration,[73] except for titles, coats of arms, honours or dignities transmissible on the death of the holder, which still devolve on the heir-at-law.[74]

[70] Stevenson, *Heraldry in Scotland*, 335.
[71] *Hunter* v. *Weston* (1882) 9 R. 492; *Munro's Trs.* v. *Spencer*, 1912 S.C. 933; *Munro-Lucas-Tooth*, 1965 S.L.T. (Lyon Ct.) 2; Munro's Trs. v. *Monson*, 1962 S.C. 414; 1965 S.C. 84.
[72] cf. *Moir of Leckie* (1794) Mor. 15537.
[73] Succession (Sc.) Act, 1964, S. 14.
[74] Ibid., S. 37(1).

ACQUISITION OF RIGHTS IN INCORPOREAL HERITABLE OBJECTS

Most rights in incorporeal heritable objects may be acquired by gift or grant, by contract, or disposition *mortis causa*. Some, particularly those involving titles of honour and dignities, are conferred by Crown grant only.

Superiority and dominium utile

A superiority is created and acquired only by the grant by a land-owner, whether the Crown or a vassal of the Crown, of an estate of fee to be held of and under the granter, not by attempting to distinguish estates of superiority and of *dominium utile* by words or description, nor by an attempt to convey a *dominium directum* to one disponee and a *dominium utile* to another.[1] The creation of a fee implies also the creation of a superiority. The grant must be recorded in the Register of Sasines or, in appropriate cases, in the Land Register,[2]

Entailed interest

An entailed interest in lands cannot now be created.[3]

Liferent

A proper liferent interest in the superiority or the *dominium utile* of lands may be created by constitution, including a grant by disposition, testamentary settlement, or marriage contract, in each case requiring infeftment to make the grantee's right real, or by reservation, by conveyance of the fee to another under reservation of the granter's liferent.[4] The right of a liferenter by reservation has been looked upon as greater than that of a liferenter by constitution and more akin to one of fee. The creation of a liferent over a registered interest in land is registrable in the Land Register and thereby becomes a registered interest in land.[5]

[1] Bell, *Prin.* §675, 687; Menzies, 666; *Norton* v. *Anderson*, 6 July 1813, F.C.
[2] Land Registration (Sc.) Act, 1979, S. 2(1)(a)(i).
[3] Entail Act, 1914, S. 2.
[4] Bell, *Prin.* §1040–1.
[5] 1979 Act, S. 2(3)(ii).

Real burdens and ground annuals

These may be created by constitution, or by reservation on a transfer of lands, or by statute.[6] A grant in security by contract of ground annual is, in appropriate cases, registrable in the Land Register.

Lease

The right of lease is created only by express grant in pursuance of contract.[7] In the case of a long lease it is, in appropriate cases, registrable in the Land Register.[8]

Rights in security

A right in security is similarly created in pursuance of express contract, by deed containing a disposition of land in security. A right in security over a registered interest in land is registrable in the Land Register.[9]

Reversions

A right of reversion is created by legal implication in every case of lease or disposition of lands in security.

Jura crediti

Jura crediti are created by contract, testamentary settlement, marriage-contract or trust.[10] If in relation to a registered interest in land it is registrable in the Land Register.[11]

Annuities

An annuity is created by contract (gratuitous or onerous), the provisions of a *mortis causa* settlement or marriage-contract.[12]

Goodwill

Goodwill, in so far as heritable, arises from social conditions, from the proximity of persons to a particular establishment and their practice of habitually resorting there for business. In some cases it is the product of monopoly or quasi-monopoly situations.

---

[6] Ch. 5.11, *supra*.
[7] Ch. 5.15, *supra*.
[8] 1979 Act, S. 2(1)(a)(i).
[9] 1979 Act, S. 2(3)(i).
[10] Bell, *Prin.* §1482; *Macdonald* v. *Scott*, 1981 S.L.T. 128.
[11] 1979 Act, S. 2(3)(iii).
[12] As to power of heir of entail in possession to infeft his wife in an annuity see Entail Provisions Act, 1824; Entail Amendment (Sc.) Act, 1868; *Paul* v. *Anstruther* (1864) 2 M. (H.L.) 1; *Lamont Campbell* v. *Carter Campbell* (1895) 22 R. 260; *Somervell's Tr.* v. *S.*, 1909 S.C. 1125.

Honours and dignities

All honours and dignities are conferred by the Crown. The dignity of a peerage may be hereditary[13] or for life.[14] Baronetcies are hereditary, and knighthoods and lesser honours are for life only.

Armorial bearings

The right to bear arms is granted by Lord Lyon exercising power delegated by the Crown.

---

[13] At common law.
[14] Life Peerages Act, 1958.

TRANSFER IN SECURITY OF RIGHTS IN INCORPOREAL HERITABLE OBJECTS

Some rights in incorporeal heritable objects are incapable of being assigned to another in security. Thus hereditary offices, titles of honour and armorial bearings cannot be so assigned. Some others are rarely, if ever, utilized as subjects of security because of their uncertain value and difficulty of realisation. The general rule is that securities constituted over heritable rights are themselves heritable.[1]

Superiorities and rights of dominium utile

Each of these kinds of interest in land may be conveyed in security, now only by standard security.[2] If the security is over a registered interest in land it is registrable in the Land Register.[3] It is competent to grant security over the superiority, reserving power to feu, and to restrict the security to the *dominium directum* of parts of the lands feued, leaving it applicable to the *dominium utile* of the rest.[4]

Entailed interests

Under the Entail Act, 1685, lands held under entail could not be disponed in security of debt, and the interest of an heir in possession could not validly be burdened but statutes,[5] have permitted heirs in possession to charge the estate of heirs-substitute in their order with the whole or part of the outlays expended in certain kinds of improvements on the estate. An heir of entail in possession may grant bonds over the entailed lands affecting his life interest only.[6]

Liferent

A proper liferenter of heritage cannot dispone his interest in security, because it terminates with his death. He can at most assign the

---

[1] *Stroyan* v. *Murray* (1890) 17 R. 1170, 1173.

[2] Ch. 5.12, *supra*.

[3] Land Registration (Sc.) Act, 1979, S. 2(3)(i).

[4] *Morier* v. *Brownlie & Watson* (1895) 23 R. 67; *Sones* v. *Mill* (1903) 11 S.L.T. 98. See also *Arnott's Trs.* v. *Forbes* (1881) 9 R. 89; *Mackirdy* v. *Webster's Trs.* (1895) 22 R. 340.

[5] Entail Improvement Act, 1770; Entail Amendment Acts, 1848, 1853, and 1868, S. 11; Entail Amendment Acts, 1875 and 1878; Entail (Sc.) Act, 1882.

[6] *Somervell's Tr.* v. *Somervell* (1904) 6 F. 926. See also *E. Lindsay* v. *Cuninghame's Trs.* (1898) 6 S.L.T. 101; *Colvile's Trs.* v. *Marindin*, 1908 S.C. 911.

rents and rights of possession for the duration of the liferent.[7] In such a case the liferenter is not liable to be summarily ejected by the creditor under the Heritable Securities (Sc.) Act, 1894, S. 5, not being the proprietor.[8] The fiar may with the consent of the liferenter grant a bond over lands.[9]

Servitude

A right to a servitude being inseparable from the dominant tenement cannot be separately transferred in security.

Lease as security

A lease which is not assignable, or assignable only with consent and consent is not obtained, cannot be conveyed in security.

If a lease is assignable it may be assigned in security as well as absolutely, and by the same means, but the assignation must be intimated to the landlord and actual possession must be ceded to the assignee to give the latter a real right and to make the transfer a matter of public knowledge.[10] An assignation without possession gives the assignee a personal right only and no security.[11] Or it may be assigned *ex facie* absolutely, with a separate back-letter or obligation from the assignee undertaking to reconvey on payment of the debt.[12] In this case also actual possession must be ceded. The assignee becomes liable for the rent.[13] The device of assigning the lease to an assignee, who then grants a sublease to the assignor, and thereby avoids the necessity of his surrendering possession, has never been approved, because it prevents publicity of the transfer.[14] If the tenant is constituted manager for the security-holder, the latter has been held personally liable for goods furnished for the subjects let.[15]

Leases over twenty years within the Registration of Leases (Sc.) Act, 1857, may be assigned in security,[16] the real right being completed by recording in the General Register of Sasines or, in appropriate cases,

---

[7] Stair II, 6, 7; Bankt. II, 6, 33; Ersk. II, 9, 41. See also *Fraser* v. *Carruthers* (1875) 2 R. 595.

[8] *Scottish Union and National Ins. Co.* v. *Smeaton* (1904) 7 F. 174.

[9] *Crichton's Trs.* v. *Clarke*, 1909, 1 S.L.T. 467.

[10] Stair III, 1, 6; Bankt. II, 9, 4; Ersk. II, 6, 25; Bell, *Comm.* I, 66, 755; *Prin.* §1209–12; Bell, *Leases*, I, 451; Rankine, *Leases*, 184; *Wallace* v. *Campbell* (1750) Mor. 2805; *Kennedy* v. *Forsyth* (1829) 7 S. 435; *Inglis* v. *Paul* (1829) 7 S. 469; *Hamilton's Tr.* v. *Stewart* (1830) 8 S. 799; *Roberts* v. *Wallace* (1842) 5 D. 6; *Hardie* v. *Cameron* (1879) 19 S.L.R. 83; *Clarke* v. *West Calder Oil Co.* (1882) 9 R. 1017, 1024; *Mess* v. *Hay* (1899) 1 F. (H.L.) 22.

[11] *Clarke, supra*, 1024.

[12] e.g. *Stroyan* v. *Murray* (1890) 17 R. 1170.

[13] *Ramsay* v. *Commercial Bank* (1842) 4 D. 405; *Moncrieffe* v. *Ferguson* (1896) 24 R. 47.

[14] *Brock* v. *Cabbell* (1831) 5 W. & S. 476; *Ramsay* v. *Commercial Bank* (1842) 4 D. 405; *Bett* v. *Murray* (1845) 7 D. 447.

[15] *Macphail* v. *McLean's Tr.* (1887) 15 R. 47; *Mess, supra*.

[16] S. 4. Form in 1857 Act, Sched. B; Bell, *Prin.* §1212A.

registration in the Land Register of Scotland.[17] It is also competent to constitute a security by assignation *ex facie* absolute, with a separate deed from the creditor acknowledging that the assignation is truly in security.[18] An assignation may be further translated,[19] and discharged.[20] Registration completes the security holder's right and establishes a preference by virtue thereof as effectively as actual possession.[21] Priority between competing assignees depends on the date of registration.[22] It has been held[23] that an assignee who had completed title by registration was preferable to a prior assignee whose title was intimated to the landlord but not recorded. But an assignation completed by actual possession might be preferable to one subsequently registered.[24] Registration of an assignation does not import any liability for the rent.[25] Actual entry into possession, however, subjects to liability for all the obligations incumbent on the tenant.

The assignee in security of a registered lease has powers similar to those belonging to the holder of a bond and disposition in security. The assignee has a real right in the lease but is not the holder of a *debitum fundi* and therefore cannot poind the ground.[26] The power of sale given in the assignation in security of a lease may be exercised by utilizing the forms applicable to a bond and disposition in security.[27] By the Registration of Leases Act, 1857, S. 6, the party in right of a translation of an assignation,[28] on default in payment of the capital sum secured, or of a term's interest, for six months after such sum of interest is due, may apply to the sheriff for warrant to enter into possession of the lands and heritages leased, which warrant entitles the creditor to enter into possession, uplift the rents from subtenants and to sublet as the lessee might have done.

Money secured by an assignation in security of a lease has been held moveable in the creditor's succession[29] but the decision is questionable.[30]

---

[17] 1979 Act, S. 2(4)(a).
[18] *Ramsay, supra; Rodger* v. *Crawfords* (1867) 6 M. 24; *Stroyan* v. *Murray* (1890) 17 R. 1170.
[19] S. 6 and Sched. D.
[20] S. 13 and Sched. 4.
[21] S. 16. As to case where long lease not recorded, see *Russell* v. *Campbell* (1888) 26 S.L.R. 209.
[22] S. 12.
[23] *Rodger, supra.*
[24] Gloag & Irvine, 184.
[25] S. 6.
[26] *Luke* v. *Wallace* (1896) 23 R. 634.
[27] Conveyancing (Sc.) Act, 1924, S. 24.
[28] Despite the words the procedure has been invoked by the holder of an assignation, not a translation of an assignation: *Fleming* v. *Burgess' Tr.* (1867) 5 M. 856.
[29] *Stroyan, supra.*
[30] The 1857 Act makes provision for the 'heir' making up title: Ss. 7–8.

If a sublease is assignable it similarly may be assigned in security.

The tenant under a long lease has been held entitled to assign the lease to his creditor and this, when intimated to the landlord gave the creditor an effectual right and that he was entitled to sell it for his own behoof.[31]

Since the coming into force of the Conveyancing and Feudal Reform (Sc.) Act, 1970, the creation of a right of security over a registered lease is effected by means of a standard security in terms of Form A or B of Schedule 2 of that Act, and the assignation thereof must be in terms of Form A or B of Schedule 4 thereof.[31a]

Rights in security

A right in security held over particular lands may itself be assigned in security for repayment of an advance made by the assignee to the assignor (the creditor in the original bond). The assignation must be intimated to the original debtor.[32] In appropriate cases this transfer must be registered in the Land Register.[33]

Radical or reversionary right

The debtor's reversionary right in lands conveyed in security may itself be conveyed in security by assignation in security, which must be intimated to the creditor in the primary disposition in security, whose security-right is limited to loans made before the date when the assignation was intimated.[34]

Annuities

An annuity, unless declared alimentary, may be assigned by the annuitant in security of an advance. If declared alimentary it cannot be so assigned but each term's payment, when paid, may be assigned.[35]

Goodwill

Where premises to which goodwill of a heritable character is a pertinent are conveyed in security, the goodwill passes with the premises to the security-holder.[36]

Honours and dignities

These are not assignable in security.

---

[31] *Yeoman v. Elliot and Foster*, 2 February 1813, F.C.
[31a] *Trade Dev. Bank v. Warriner & Mason*, 1980 S.C. 74.
[32] *McCutcheon v. McWilliam* (1876) 3 R. 565.
[33] 1979 Act, S. 2(4)(c).
[34] *Union Bank v. National Bank* (1886) 14 R. (H.L.) 1.
[35] *Hewats v. Roberton* (1881) 9 R. 175.
[36] *Re Pile, ex parte Lambton* (1876) 3 Ch. D. 36; *Bain v. Munro* (1878) 5 R. 416; *Selkirk v. Coupland* (1886) 23 S.L.R. 456.

OUTRIGHT TRANSFER OF RIGHTS IN INCORPOREAL HERITABLE OBJECTS

Rights in some kinds of incorporeal heritable objects are alienable by gift, exchange or sale, but others inalienable. Where alienable the mode of transfer is normally assignation, completed by intimation to the holder of the property or the debtor in the obligation.

Rights of superiority or dominium utile

A right of superiority may be gifted or sold, but, unless the superior in granting feus has reserved power to divide the superiority without the vassal's consent, it is indivisible and cannot be split into parts without such consent.[1] It can be disponed without conveyance of the lands themselves.[2] It may be conveyed to two or more persons jointly.[3] Similarly a superior cannot, without the vassal's consent, feu the superiority to the effect of interjecting a new mid-superior between him and the vassal.[4] The form of disposition is generally the same as that of a fee save that it assigns feu-duties not rents, and feu rights are excepted from the warrandice clause.[5] Such a disposition will carry all rights, such as reserved rights to minerals, not previously conveyed in fee to a vassal.

A right of *dominium utile* can only be gifted or sold with and comprising the actual rights of possession and use of the lands.

If the land concerned is in an operational area transfer of either of these kinds of rights must be registered in the Land Register.[6]

Feu-duties

The right to feu-duties may be sold or bequeathed, the superiority being in other respects reserved. The transfer is effected by assignation and it must be intimated to each vassal so that he may know to whom

---

[1] Ersk. II, 3, 12; *Graham* v. *Westenra* (1826) 4 S. 615.

[2] *Mackenzie* v. *M.*, 14 December 1822, F.C.; *Hill* v. *D. Montrose* (1828) 6 S. 1133; *Gardiner* v. *Trinity House of Leith* (1841) 3 D. 534; *Williams and James* v. *Maclaine's Trs.* (1872) 10 M. 362; *Stewart's Trs.* v. *S.*, 1931 S.C. 691.

[3] *Cargill* v. Muir (1837) 15 S. 408.

[4] Bell, *Lect.* II, 753; *Abp. of St. Andrews* v. *Huntly* (1682) Mor. 15015.

[5] Ch. 5.16, *supra*.

[6] Land Registration (Sc.) Act, 1979, S. 2(4)(a).

to pay and who is entitled to exact payment.[7] Similarly a superior may dispone his lands in security, reserving power to feu and assigning the prospective feu-duties.[8]

Rents

Without gift or sale of the fee of land an owner may assign the right to receive the rents of lands let.[9] Such assignation must be intimated to the tenants so that they may know to whom to pay.[10]

Real burdens

Real burdens are conveyed by assignation intimated to the debtor and recorded in the appropriate Register of Sasines,[11] or in appropriate cases in the Land Register of Scotland.[12]

Entail

The rights of an heir of entail in possession cannot be alienated any more than can the entailed lands themselves.

Liferent

A proper liferent of heritage cannot be alienated[13] but a liferenter may assign the rents and profits accruing from the liferent but for the duration of his liferent only. The assignee has a personal claim only against his liferenter and cannot acquire any real right in the lands.[14]

Assignation of leases

Prima facie a lease is not assignable[15] but express power to assign may be conferred, or power be held to have been conferred by implication from the terms of the destination in the lease, and, exceptionally, power is implied unless power to assign is expressly excluded, in certain kinds of leases, namely, liferent leases,[16] leases for the duration of a person's tenure of an office,[17] farm leases of extraordinary en-

---

[7] Stair II, 4, 10; Bell, *Prin.* §688, 703; *Douglas* v. *Vassals* (1671) Mor. 9306.

[8] *Arnott's Trs.* v. *Forbes* (1881) 9 R. 89.

[9] *Wilson* v. *W.* (1859) 21 D. 309; *Mackenzie's Tr.* v. *M.* (1899) 2 F. 330; *Sim* v. *Duncan* (1900) 2 F. 434.

[10] *Forsyth* v. *Aird* (1853) 16 D. 197.

[11] Conveyancing (Sc.) Act, 1874, S. 30.

[12] 1979 Act, S. 2(3)(iii).

[13] cf. *Ferguson* v. *F.* (1875) 2 R. 627; *Chaplin's Trs.* v. *Hoile* (1890) 18 R. 26; *Devlin* v. *Lowrie*, 1922 S.C. 255; *Carruthers* v. *Crawford*, 1945 S.C. 82.

[14] Stair II, 6, 7; Ersk. II, 9, 41; *Ker's Trs.* v. *Justice* (1868) 6 M. 627; 63; cf. *Chaplin's Trs., supra; Scottish Union and National Ins. Co.* v. *Smeaton* (1904) 7 F. 174.

[15] Stair II, 9, 22; III, 1, 16; Ersk. II, 6, 31; Bell, *Comm.* I, 76; *Prin.* §1215; Rankine, *Leases*, 172.

[16] Stair II, 9, 6; Ersk. II, 6, 32; Bell, *Comm.* I, I, 77; Rankine, *Leases*, 173.

[17] *Pringle* v. *McLagan* (1802) Hume 808.

durance[18] and leases of unfurnished urban tenements.[19] Where a lease is assignable assignation is effected by written assignation to the assignee of the granter's interest in and to the lease during its whole currency. No set form is essential,[20] so long as it be constituted and proved in the same mode as the lease itself.[21] It is completed by delivery and, so far as concerns the landlord, by intimation to him, either formally, by notarial intimation,[22] or now, by a notary-public delivering a copy of the assignation to the landlord, or by the assignee transmitting a copy to him by post.[23] Various facts have been treated as equivalents of intimation, but not mere private knowledge, nor registration for preservation in the Books of Council and Session or other court books,[24] nor parole evidence of a promise to recognize the assignee, nor parole evidence of notice, nor a reference to the landlord's oath.[25] To complete the assignee's real right in the tenancy valid against third parties he must obtain physical possession of the subjects leased.[26]

A lease registrable under the Registration of Leases Act, 1857, if assignable, may be assigned outright.[27] In appropriate cases this must be registered in the Land Register.[28]

An assignation may be translated or further assigned, or retrocessed to the original tenant.[29]

If a sublease be assignable, it may similarly be assigned, the assignee's right being completed by possession, not merely by intimation to the lessee.[30]

Rights in security

A right in security over heritage may be transferred outright, in whole or in part, in the case of bond and disposition in security by

---

[18] Ersk. II, 6, 32–3; Bell, *Comm.* I, 76; Rankine, *Leases*, 173. Extraordinary duration is duration exceeding 21 years.

[19] Ersk. II, 6, 31–3; Bell, *Comm.* I, 76; *Prin.* §1274; Rankine, *Leases*, 174; *Robb v. Brearton* (1895) 22 R. 885.

[20] *Carter* v. *McIntosh* (1862) 24 D. 925.

[21] *Irvine* v. *McHardy* (1892) 19 R. 458; *Moncrieff* v. *Sievwright* (1896) 3 S.L.T. 262.

[22] Stair II, 10, 17; III, 3, 7; Bankt. III, 1, 6; Ersk. III, 5, 3; Bell, *Comm.* II, 17; *Prin.* §1463–4; Bell, *Convg.* 307; Rankine, *Leases*, 181.

[23] Transmission of Moveable Property (Sc.) Act, 1861, S. 2, a provision said by Rankine (*Leases* 182) not to be confined to moveable rights; see also *Skinner* v. *Beveridge* (1872) 10 S.L.R. 12; *Clarke* v. *West Calder Oil Co.* (1882) 9 R. 1017.

[24] *Tod's Trs.* v. *Wilson* (1869) 7 M. 1100.

[25] Bell, *Comm.* II, 17–18.

[26] *Brock* v. *Cabell* (1822) 2 S. 52; (1830) 8 S. 647; (1831) 5 W. & S. 476; *Inglis* v. *Paul* (1829) 7 S. 469; *Clarke* v. *West Calder Oil Co.* (1882) 9 R. 1017.

[27] e.g. *Rodger* v. *Crawfords* (1867) 6 M. 24.

[28] 1979 Act, S. 2(4)(a).

[29] *Ramsay* v. *Commercial Bank* (1842) 4 D. 405.

[30] Bell, *Comm.* I, 67; cf. *Robertson* v. *Boyd and Winans* (1885) 12 R. 419.

assignation in the form provided by the 1868 Act, S. 124 and Sched.,[31] in the case of an *ex facie* absolute disposition by further disposition, and in the case of a standard security by assignation in the form of the Conveyancing and Feudal Reform (Sc.) Act, 1970, S. 14 and Sched. 4, Form A or B, in all cases duly recorded in the Register of Sasines or in appropriate cases in the Land Register of Scotland.[32]

Such a right may also be conveyed outright by a general disposition by the creditor in the right.

The assignation of the beneficial interest in a bond does not affect the title of the original grantee to use inhibition against the debtor in the bond.[33]

Radical or reversionary rights

The radical or reversionary right of the debtor in and to lands conveyed in security to another may be conveyed outright but only under burden of the security right affecting the lands, and without prejudice to the debtor's continuing personal obligation under security right.[34] In appropriate cases the transfer must be registered in the Land Register.[35]

Contingent interest or spes successionis

Such a right relative to heritage may be assigned by the person in expectancy, but until or unless the interest becomes vested the assignation carries only the expectancy.[36]

Annuities

If declared alimentary an annuity is not assignable outright, save *quoad excessum*[37] though each term's payment, when received, may be assigned.[38] If not so declared it may be assigned by assignation intimated to the payer. If an annuity be non-alimentary and be given with power to dispone of it, the party in right can claim its capitalized value at the outset,[39] or subsequently dispose of it.

Assignation of jus crediti to lands

A trust beneficiary, or purchaser of lands, or person otherwise

---

[31] cf. *McCutcheon* v. *McWilliam* (1876) 3 R. 565; *Forbes* v. *Welsh & Forbes* (1894) 21 R. 630.
[32] 1979 Act, S, 2(4)(c).
[33] *Clarke* v. *McNab* (1888) 15 R. 569.
[34] *McWhirter* v. *McCulloch's Trs.* (1887) 14 R. 918; *McNab* v. *Clarke* (1889) 16 R. 610.
[35] 1979 Act, S. 2(4)(c).
[36] *Reid* v. *Morrison* (1893) 20 R. 510. cf. *Trappes* v. *Meredith* (1871) 10 M. 38; *Salaman* v. *Todd*, 1911 S.C. 1214; *Coats* v. *Bannochie's Trs.*, 1912 S.C. 329.
[37] *Claremont's Trs.* v. *C.* (1896) 4 S.L.T. 144; *Cuthbert* v. *C's Trs.*, 1908 S.C. 967.
[38] *Cosens* v. *Stevenson* (1873) 11 M. 761; *Hewats* v. *Robertson* (1881) 9 R. 175.
[39] *Tod* v. *T's Trs.* (1871) 9 M. 728; *Kippen* v. *K's Trs.* (1871) 10 M. 134; *Dow* v. *Kilgour's Trs.* (1877) 4 R. 403. Contrast *Branford's Trs.* v. *Powell*, 1924 S.C. 439.

entitled to a conveyance of lands from another, may effectually transfer his *jus crediti* to the land by an assignation purporting to transfer
his right and duly intimated to the persons liable to implement the
obligations in question.[40] The assignation does not, however, by itself
confer on the assignee a right capable of being completed by infeftment, and he still requires to obtain a disposition from the person who
holds the lands subject to the obligation to dispone them, or alternatively, if the latter cannot or will not grant such a conveyance, adjudge
them.[41] When the assignation is intimated the cedent is divested of the
jus crediti and the assignee will have preference over creditors adjudging subsequently,[42] and if the cedent becomes bankrupt the lands do
not pass to his trustee.[43] In appropriate cases the transfer is registrable
in the Land Register.[44]

Personal right of succession to land

Until 1964 a personal right to every estate in land descendible to
heirs vested in the heir entitled to succeed by his survivance of the
person whom he was entitled to succeed.[45] This right could be transferred by disposition or disposition and assignation. Under the Succession (Sc.) Act, 1964, a title to heritable estate vests for the purposes of
administration in the deceased's executor, and he may probably assign
it,[46] the assignee using the assignation as a link in title.

Assignation of unrecorded conveyances

Where a disposition of lands has been granted and delivered to, but
not recorded in the appropriate Division of the General Register of
Sasines by, the disponee, he had thereby a personal right only to the
lands which he might transfer to another by assignation. The assignation might be total or partial, but if partial could not be engrossed on
the disposition, as it might otherwise be.[47] A disposition assigned
might be further assigned. An assignee might convert the personal
right under the disposition into a real right and complete his title by

---

[40] Bell, *Convg.* II, 771; McLaren, *Wills*, II, 843; Craigie, *Her.*, 462; *Paul* v. *Boyd's Trs.* (1835)
13 S. 818.

[41] McLaren, II, 846.

[42] *Russell* v. *McDowall*, 6 Feb. 1824, F.C. On intimation see also *Paul, supra; Tod's Trs.* v.
Wilson (1869) 7 M. 1100; *Campbell's Trs.* v. *Whyte* (1894) 11 R. 1078; *Jameson* v. *Sharp*
(1887) 14 R. 643.

[43] *Edmond* v. *Aberdeen Mags.* (1855) 18 D. 47; (1858) 3 Macq. 116; cf. *Macgregor* v.
Macdonald (1843) 5 D. 888; *Watson* v. *Wilson* (1868) 6 M. 258.

[44] 1979 Act, S. 2(4)(c).

[45] Conveyancing (Sc.) Act, 1874, S. 9.

[46] 1964 Act, S. 15(2) *ad fin.* Transfer by endorsing a docket on the confirmation or certificate of
confirmation is applicable by S. 15(2) to persons acquiring the heritage as prior rights, legal rights
or on intestacy or under a testamentary disposition.

[47] Conveyancing (Sc.) Act, 1924, S. 7, repealed by Conveyancing and Feudal Reform (Sc.) Act,
1970, Sch. 11, Part II.

endorsing a warrant of registration on the disposition and recording it in the General Register of Sasines, or, where the assignations were separate, recording disposition and assignations, or the disposition and a notice of title without assignations, or last recorded title. By the Conveyancing and Feudal Reform (Sc.) Act, 1970, S. 48, an unrecorded conveyance must be recorded along with a notice of title, with one warrant of registration on the notice of title.[48]

Commercial goodwill

If, or in so far as, commercial goodwill is heritable it may be, and may only be, sold or otherwise transferred along with the heritable property in question. The contract of sale should deal expressly with the goodwill of the business carried on in the premises being sold, and provide for the sale of the trade name and whole assets of the business as well as for the sale of the premises. No separate assignation or deed of transfer of the goodwill is necessary. An agreement to sell goodwill mainly or entirely attached to premises in enforceable by specific implement.[49]

Honours and dignities

These are not assignable outright.

---

[48] 1924 Act, S. 10(4), amd. 1970 Act, Sch. 11, Part II.
[49] *Darbey* v. *Whitaker* (1857) 4 Drew. 134.

CHAPTER 5.23

COMPULSORY TRANSFER OF RIGHTS IN INCORPOREAL HERITABLE OBJECTS

A person's right in incorporeal heritable objects may be taken from him by adjudication or under mercantile sequestration.

Adjudication for payment

Some rights in incorporeal heritable objects may be attached by action of adjudication for payment.[1] Not only feudal estates in land but all rights or interests connected with land, entailed estates,[2] liferents,[3] real burdens, heritable securities,[4] leases,[5] rights of reversion,[6] *jura crediti*,[7] and heritable rights unconnected with land such as annuities,[8] unless declared alimentary, and bonds heritable *destinatione* may be so attached.[1] Servitudes cannot be adjudged separately from the dominant tenement.[9] An hereditary office cannot be adjudged[10] nor can heritable titles of honour. Moveable rights are not subject to adjudication.

Adjudication for payment is founded on a debt constituted by decree, or on a document of debt such as a bill or bond.[11] If there is no written document of debt, or it is ambiguous, conditional, or has been lost, a decree of constitution is necessary. At least in the case of an unentered heir the actions for constitution and adjudication may be combined. Any question of the amount of debt must be determined in the action of constitution.

The summons may be restricted to particular debts, or to particular portions of the debtor's lands.

After decree a state of the debt, interest, and expenses is prepared,

---

[1] Stair III, 2, 16; Bankt. III, 2, 38; Ersk. II, 12, 6; Bell, *Comm.* I, 693; Graham Stewart, 600.
[2] *Graham* v. *Hunter* (1828) 7 S. 13; *Graham* v. *Alison* (1830) 6 W. & S. 518.
[3] *Hay* v. *Littlejohn* (1666) Mor. 13974.
[4] *Stuart* v. *S.* (1705) Mor. 140; Ersk., *supra.*
[5] Unless the lease expressly excludes assignees; Ersk., *supra*; Bell, *Comm.* I, 73; *Prin.* §1216–18.
[6] *Herries, Farquhar & Co.* v. *Burnett* (1846) 9 D. 111; cf. *McKidd* (1890) 17 R. 547.
[7] *Watson* v. *Wilson* (1868) 6 M. 258.
[8] *Macleod's Trs.* v. *Murray* (1891) 18 R. 830.
[9] Ersk. II, 9, 5.
[10] *Lauderdale* v. *Scrymgeour Wedderburn*, 1910 S.C. (H.L.) 35.
[11] Stair III, 2, 15; Bankt. III, 2, 37; Ersk. II, 12, 19; Bell, *Comm.* I, 775.

setting out the total accumulated sum down to the date of decree, which is inserted in the extract decree.

A creditor adjudging heritage by the debtor under a latent trust is in no better situation *vis-à-vis* the beneficiary thereunder than if he had obtained a gratuitous conveyance from his debtor.[12]

Completion of title

An adjudger completes title, except in the case of heritable securities, under the Conveyancing (Sc.) Act, 1874, S. 62, by recording the decree or expeding and recording a notice of title thereon. An abbreviate of adjudication is made out at the same time as the extract decree and recorded within sixty days in the Register of Inhibitions and Adjudications.[13]

In the case of heritable securities completion of title is effected by the adjudger recording the abbreviate of adjudication or an extract of the decree in the Register of Sasines.[14] In the case of long leases the recording of the abbreviate of adjudication in the register in which the lease is recorded completes the right of the adjudger.[15]

In the case of lands in an operational area an adjudger must record his decree in the Land Register.[16]

Pari passu *ranking*

All creditors who adjudge within a year and a day after the decree in the first effectual adjudication may be ranked *pari passu* with it and with any conjoined with it.[17]

Reversionary right of debtor

The right acquired by an adjudger is not a right of property but a judicial security only and the debtor retains a reversionary right,[18] which he may exercise by paying off the debt within ten years, known as 'the legal', i.e. legal term of redemption. After the lapse of the ten years, the creditor may exclude the right of redemption by obtaining decree in an action of declarator of expiry of the legal. The debtor's right is redeemable until decree of declarator of expiry is pronounced.[19] The expiry of the legal by itself does not vest the estate in

---

[12] *Heritable Reversionary Co.* v. *Millar* (1892) 19 R. (H.L.) 43.
[13] Conveyancing (Sc.) Act, 1924, S. 44.
[14] 1874 Act, S. 65, replacing Titles to Land Consolidation (Sc.) Act, 1868, S. 129.
[15] Registration of Leases (Sc.) Act, S. 10, amd. Conveyancing Act, 1924, S. 24.
[16] Land Registration (Sc.) Act, 1979, S. 2(1)(b) and 2(4)(c).
[17] Diligence Act, 1661; Bell, *Comm.* I, 721.
[18] *Grindlay* v. *Drysdale* (1833) 11 S. 896; *Cochrane* v. *Boyle* (1850) 7 Bell 65.
[19] *Govan* v. *G.* (1758) 2 Pat. 27.

the creditor, unless it is followed by possession on recorded title for the prescriptive period of ten years.[20]

Decree of declarator of the expiry of the legal is reducible within the period of the long negative prescription.[21]

Extinction of adjudication

An adjudication may be extinguished by payment in full by the debtor, or the creditor's intromission with the rents of the lands adjudged, within the legal, and this may be evidenced by an action of declarator of extinction and payment.[22] Similarly a postponed adjudger may extinguish an adjudication prior to his own by paying off the prior creditor.

Adjudication contra haereditatem jacentem

After a debtor's death a creditor can adjudge his heritable estate by proceedings against the heir or, if the latter renounces the succession, against the debtor's *haereditas jacens*. The Adjudication Act, 1621, provides in such a case for a legal period of redemption of seven years.

The right of the heir's creditors to adjudge his ancestor's lands were postponed by the Act, 1661, c. 88, to that of the ancestor's creditors who did diligence within three years of the ancestor's death.

In this case it is competent to bring a combined action of constitution and adjudication.

Adjudication on debita fundi

Adjudication may proceed not only on a personal obligation but on such *debita fundi* as heritable bonds, real burdens and ground annuals,[23] but in such a case is confined to the heritable subjects which are security for the obligation in question. They are preferable to adjudications on personal debts and rank *inter se* according to priority of infeftment.

Adjudication in security

Adjudication in security may be used in debts which are not yet payable or contingent,[24] or where the debtor is *vergens ad inopiam*. There is no legal term of redemption, the debtor being entitled to redeem at any time.

---

[20] Bell, *Prin.* §831; *Spence* v. *Bruce* (1807) Bell, *Comm.* I, 745n; *Robertson* v. *D. Atholl* (1815) 3 Dow. 108; *Hinton* v. *Connell's Tr.* (1883) 10 R. 1110.

[21] *Aitken* v. *A.* (1809) Bell, *Comm.* I, 744, n.; *Paul* v. *Reid*, 8 February 1814, F.C.

[22] Ersk. II, 12, 37–8.

[23] See Conveyancing (Sc.) Act, 1924, S. 23(5) and (6) and Sched. K, Form 8, making this a competent remedy where a ground annual is two years in arrears.

[24] Ersk. II, 12, 42; see also *Queensberry's Exors.* v. *Tait*, 11 June 1817, F.C.

Mercantile sequestration

The Act and Warrant of a trustee in sequestration transfers to and vests in him, absolutely and irredeemably, *inter alia*, the whole heritable estate belonging to the bankrupt in Scotland to the same effect as if a decree of adjudication in implement of sale, as well as a decree of adjudication for payment and in security of debt, subject to no legal reversion, had been pronounced in favour of the trustee and recorded at the date of the sequestration.[25]

[25] Bankruptcy (Sc.) Act, 1913, S. 97(2).

EXTINCTION OF INTERESTS IN INCORPOREAL HERITABLE OBJECTS

Consolidation of superiority and fee

The superiority and the fee of lands as distinct estates may be extinguished if either superior or vassal acquires the right of the other. Consolidation is effected by endorsing a minute on the disposition in the form of Sch. G to the Conveyancing (Sc.) Act, 1924 and recording it with the disposition.[1] Where a superior has acquired the fee and the disposition contains a clause *ad perpetuam remanentiam*, the recording of the disposition has the effect of consolidating the superiority and fee.[1] Consolidation can also be effected by prescription.[2] In a case of consolidation the destination of the superiority regulates the succession of the united fee.[3] A disposition of the superiority to a vassal implies a discharge of any past unpaid feu-duty.[4] After consolidation the united fee is subject to all the burdens imposed on the property prior thereto and has all the rights thereof.[5]

If either superior or vassal succeeds to the estate of the other he must make up title as successor and record a minute of consolidation under the Conveyancing (Sc.) Act, 1874, S. 6, recorded in the Register of Sasines or in appropriate cases registered in the Land Register.[6]

Relinquishment of superiority

A superior may relinquish his superiority in favour of his immediate vassal by a deed of relinquishment which, accepted by the vassal and recorded in the Register of Sasines, and followed by a writ of investiture by the over-superior, extinguishes the superiority.[7] In appropriate cases this must be registered in the Land Register.[6]

---

[1] Conveyancing (Sc.) Act, 1924, S. 11.
[2] *Bontine* v. *Graham* (1837) 15 S. 711; affd. (1840) 1 Rob. 347; *Wilson* v. *Pollock* (1839) 2 D. 159; *Gordon's Trs.* (1849) 21 Sc. Jur. 174.
[3] *Pattison* v. *Dunn's Trs.* (1868) 6 M. (H.L.) 147; *Park's Curator* v. *Black* (1870) 8 M. 671.
[4] *E. Argyle* v. *Lord Macdonald* (1676) Mor. 842.
[5] Ersk. II, 7, 21; Bell, *Conv.* II, 784; Menzies, 621; *Wilson* v. *Fraser* (1824) 2 Sh. App. 164; *E. Zetland* v. *Perth Glovers Incorpn.* (1870) 8 M. (H.L.) 144.
[6] Land Registration (Sc.) Act, 1979, S. 2(4)(c).
[7] Titles to Land Consolidation (Sc.) Act, 1868, Ss. 110–12.

Forfeiture of superiority

It may also be extinguished if a superior has not completed his title thereto and cannot grant a vassal entry, by the vassal petitioning the court for decree that the superior has forfeited his right to the superiority, enabling the petitioning vassal to apply to the over-superior for an entry,[8] or to petition the court for interim decree that the superior had forfeited all rights to the feu-duties and casualties, in which case the superior might relinquish the superiority to the petitioner who could then apply to the over-superior for an entry.[9] These provisions have been superseded and even virtually repealed by the Conveyancing Act, 1874, S. 4, making infeftment imply entry with the superior.

Extinction by compulsory purchase

Procedures for acquisition of land under compulsory powers may have the effect of extinguishing the right of superiority over that land.[10]

Forfeiture of fee

A fee is forfeited and extinguished if a superior obtains decree or irritancy of the feu. In appropriate cases the decree must be registered in the Land Register.[11]

Extinction of liferent

A proper liferent may be renounced or surrendered by the liferenter[12] and in any event is extinguished by his death, when the estate automatically falls to the fiar.[13] The fiar, if he has not already done so, must complete title by recording the feu-contract or disposition in his favour, or recording a notice of title on the will or marriage-contract. Liferent is also extinguished if liferent and fee come to be vested in the same person.[14] As regards apportionment between the liferenter's executors and the fiar the principle is that the executor may claim whatever part of the rents and profits had accrued before the liferenter's death.[15]

---

[8] Titles to Land Consolidation (Sc.) Act, 1868, S. 104.
[9] Ibid., Ss. 105–6.
[10] e.g. *Wauchope Settlement Trs.* v. *N.C.B.*, 1947 S.N. 185.
[11] 1979 Act, S. 2(4)(c).
[12] Ersk. II, 9, 68; Bell, *Prin.* §1066; *Pretty* v. *Newbigging* (1854) 16 D. 667; *Foulis* v. *F.* (1857) 19 D. 362; *Smith* v. *Campbell* (1873) 11 M. 639.
[13] Ersk. II, 9, 64; Bell, *Prin.* §1066.
[14] *Martin* v. *Bannatyne* (1861) 23 D. 705.
[15] Apportionment Act, 1870; Ersk. II, 9, 64–6; Bell, *Prin.* §1047; see also *Campbell* v. *C.* (1849) 11 D. 1426; *Tennent's Exor.* v. *Lawson* (1897) 35 S.L.R. 72; *Macpherson's Trs.* v. *M.*, 1907 S.C. 1067; *Balfour's Exors.* v. *Inland Revenue*, 1909 S.C. 619.

Extinction of servitude

Servitude rights may be extinguished by express discharge by the dominant owner,[16] *confusione* when dominant and servient tenements come to be vested in the same ownership,[17] by non-exercise of a positive servitude for the period of the long negative prescription,[18] or in the case of a negative servitude by contravention not checked for the same period,[18] or by abandonment evidencing intention to renounce the right.[19]

A servitude may be extinguished by the exercise of compulsory powers under statute,[20] or discharged by the Lands Tribunal.[21] It may be suspended or extinguished by change of circumstances, as by the extinction of either tenement, or the abandonment of premises to which access was had, but in this case the servitude revives if the premises are restored.[22]

Real burdens

Real burdens are discharged in the same way as heritable securities[23] though there are dicta to the effect that a less formal discharge will suffice.[24]

Variation and discharge of land obligations by Lands Tribunal

Under the Conveyancing and Feudal Reform (Sc.) Act, 1970, Ss. 1–2, a land obligation is an obligation relating to land which is enforceable by a proprietor of an interest in land,[25] by virtue of his being such proprietor and which is binding upon a proprietor of another interest in the land, or in other land, by virtue of his being such proprietor, including a future or contingent obligation, an obligation to defray or contribute to some cost, an obligation to refrain from doing something, and an obligation to permit or suffer something to be done or maintained, but not an obligation to pay feu-duty, ground annual, rent or other similar payment, or certain other stated obligations.[26] The Lands Tribunal for Scotland, on the application of any

---

[16] Stair II, 7, 4; Ersk. II, 9, 37; Bell, *Prin.* §998; Rankine, *L.O.*440. See also *Macdonald v. Inverness Mags.*, 1918 S.C. 141.

[17] Ersk. II, 9, 37; Bell, *Prin.* §997; *Donaldson's Trs. v. Forbes* (1839) 1 D. 449.

[18] Ersk., *supra*; Bell, *Prin.* §999; *Brown v. Carron Co.*, 1909 S.C. 452. The period is now twenty years: Prescription and Limitation (Sc.) Act, 1973, S. 8.

[19] Bell, *Prin.* §999; *Hill v. Ramsay* (1810) 5 Pat. 299; *Campbell Douglas v. Hozier* (1878) 16 S.L.R. 14.

[20] e.g. *Oban Town Council v. Callander & Oban Ry.* (1892) 19 R. 912.

[21] Conveyancing and Feudal Reform (Sc.) Act, 1970, Ss. 1–2.

[22] Bell, *Prin.* §995–6; *Winans v. L. Tweedmouth* (1888) 15 R. 540.

[23] Conveyancing (Sc.) Act, 1924, S. 29.

[24] *Cameron v. Williamson* (1895) 22 R. 293.

[25] Defined, 1970Act, S. 2(6).   [26] 1970 Act, S. 1(2) and Sched. 1.

person who, in relation to a land obligation, is a burdened proprietor, may from time to time by order vary or discharge the obligation wholly or partially in relation to the interest in land in respect of which the application is made,[27] on being satisfied in all the circumstances (a) by reason of changes in the character of the land affected or of the neighbourhood thereof or other circumstances which the Tribunal may deem material, the obligation is or has become unreasonable or inappropriate;[28] or (b) the obligation is unduly burdensome compared with any benefit resulting or which would result from its performance,[29] or (c) the existence of the obligation impedes some reasonable use of the land.[30]

An order by the Lands Tribunal varying or discharging a land obligation may direct the applicant to pay such sum as the Lands Tribunal thinks just, either (i) to compensate for any substantial loss or disadvantage suffered by the benefited proprietor in consequence of the variation or discharge, or (ii) to make up for any effect which the obligation produced, at the time when it was imposed, in reducing the consideration then paid for the interest in land affected by it. The Tribunal may refuse to vary or discharge a land obligation on ground (c) if of opinion that, due to exceptional circumstances related to amenity or otherwise, money would not be an adequate compensation for any loss or disadvantage which a benefited proprietor would suffer from the variation or discharge.[31] The power to vary or discharge includes power to add or substitute such provision as appears reasonable as a result of the variation or discharge.[32] When such an order takes effect, any irritant or resolutive clause or other condition relating to the enforcement of the obligation is to be effective only in so far as it would if the obligation had to that extent been varied or discharged by the person entitled to enforce the obligation.[33]

Leases

A lease is extinguished if the tenant surrenders the lease, or removes or is removed at the expiry of the lease or earlier, in the case of an

---

[27] S. 1(3).

[28] e.g. *Devlin* v. *Conn*, 1972 S.L.T. (Lands Tr.) 11 (servitude); *Murrayfield Ice Rink* v. *S.R.U.*, 1973 S.C. 21; *Bolton* v. *Aberdeen Corpn.*, 1972 S.L.T. (Lands Tr.) 26; *Crombie* v. *Heriot's Tr.*, 1972 S.L.T. (Lands Tr.) 40; *Morris* v. *Waverley Park Feuars*, 1973 S.L.T. (Lands Tr.) 6.

[29] e.g. *West Lothian Coop. Socy.* v. *Ashdale Land Co.*, 1972 S.L.T. (Lands Tr.) 30; *Smith* v. *Taylor*, 1972 S.L.T. (Lands Tr.) 34; *McQuiban* v. *Eagle Star Ins. Co.*, 1972 S.L.T. (Lands Tr.) 39; *Manz* v. *Butter's Trs.*, 1973 S.L.T. (Lands Tr.) 2.

[30] e.g. *Main* v. *Lord Doune*, 1972 S.L.T. (Lands Tr.) 14; *McVey* v. *Glasgow Corpn.*, 1973 S.L.T. (Lands Tr.) 15.

[31] S. 1(4). See e.g. *West Lothian Coop. Socy.* v. *Ashdale Land Co.*, 1972 S.L.T. (Lands Tr.) 30; *Smith* v. *Taylor*, 1972 S.L.T. (Lands Tr.) 34.

[32] S. 1(5).

[33] S. 1(6).

extraordinary removing. In the case of a long lease of land in an operational area the extinction must be registered in the Land Register.[34]

Rights in security

A right in security is extinguished if the obligation secured is paid or otherwise performed,[35] but in questions with third parties a discharge must be recorded in the Register of Sasines.

It may be extinguished by compensation, where each party is indebted to the other, and even though one debt is secured and the other unsecured.[36]

It is also extinguished *confusione* if the interests of debtor and creditor come to be united in one person.[37]

In appropriate cases the extinction must be recorded in the Land Register.[34]

Jura crediti

A *jus crediti* is extinguished by satisfaction of the creditor's claim.

The long negative prescription extinguishes a *jus crediti* in land rights such as an obligation to create a real burden over land[38] or, formerly, to lay out funds in purchasing and entailing lands.[39]

Annuities

If an annuity is validly declared alimentary it cannot be, but if not so declared it can be, renounced.[40] A wife cannot, *stante matrimonio*, renounce an annuity provided under her marriage contract, if protected by a trust.[41]

Extinction by prescription

Among rights in incorporeal heritable objects which cannot be extinguished by the lapse of any period of time are (a) any real right of ownership in land;[42] (b) the right in land of the lessee under a recorded lease; (c) any right exercisable as a *res merae facultatis*; (d) any right to recover property *extra commercium*; and (h) any right to be served as

---

[34] Land Registration (Sc.) Act, 1979, S. 2(4)(c).

[35] Stair II, 3, 48; *Wylie* v. *Duncan* (1803) 3 Ross, L.C., 136.

[36] *Hay* v. *Crawford* (1712) Mor. 2571.

[37] *Love* v. *Storie* (1863) 2 M. 22; *Murray* v. *Parlane's Tr.* (1890) 18 R. 287; contrast *Fleming* v. *Imrie* (1868) 6 M. 363; *King* v. *Johnston*, 1908 S.C. 684.

[38] *Pearson* v. *Malachi* (1892) 20 R. 167.

[39] *Barns* v. *B's Trs.* (1857) 19 D. 626; *Paterson* v. *Wilson* (1859) 21 D. 322; *E. Eglinton* v. *E. Eglinton* (1861) 23 D. 1369.

[40] *Standard Property Inv. Co.* v. *Cowe* (1877) 4 R. 695; *Christie's Factor* v. *Hardie* (1899) 1 F. 703.

[41] *Ker's Trs.* v. *K.* (1895) 23 R. 317.

[42] This includes all rights of superiority, fee, liferent and of heir of entail in possession.

heir to an ancestor or to take any steps necessary for making up or completing title to any interest in land.[43] Rights to periodical payments due by way of annuity, feu-duty, ground annual, rent, payment in respect of the occupancy or use of land, or in respect of a land obligation, prescribe in five years, unless a relevant claim is made in relation to the obligation or its subsistence is relevantly acknowledged within that time.[44] Other rights in incorporeal heritable property prescribe after twenty years, unless relevantly claimed or acknowledged within that time.[45]

Forfeiture and extinction of titles of honour

Titles of honour and dignities which are heritable and not merely personal may be extinguished by failure of the heirs named in the destination of the grant, or be extinguished by statute. The presumption is that a dignity is limited to heirs-male only.[46] In the case of English, but not Scottish,[47] peerages, a peerage may fall into abeyance. A peeress may resign her dignity in favour of her eldest son.[48] A hereditary peerage may now be disclaimed for life[49] but this does not affect any right to or in any estates or other property limited or settled to devolve with the peerage.

Non-heritable titles and life peerages lapse on the holder's death.

---

[43] Prescription and Limitation (Sc.) Act, 1973, Sch. 3.
[44] Ibid., S. 6 and Sch. 1.
[45] Ibid., S. 7, Schs. 1 and 3; *Macdonald* v. *Scott*, 1981 S.L.T. 128 (right to claim disposition under agreement to convey land).
[46] *Glencairn Peerage Case* (1791) 1 Macq. 444; *Herries Peerage Case* (1858) 3 Macq. 585.
[47] *Herries, supra.*
[48] *Herries, supra.*
[49] Peerage Act, 1963, Ss. 1–3.

PART 4

RIGHTS IN CORPOREAL MOVEABLE OBJECTS OF PROPERTY

CHAPTER 5.25

RIGHTS IN CORPOREAL MOVEABLE OBJECTS

Corporeal moveable objects of property comprise all things having a physical corpus capable of actual possession and which alone, unlike land, formerly transmitted to the executor on death.[1] They include animals, clothing, books, pictures, furniture, implements, raw materials, manufactured goods, ships, vehicles and aircraft, banknotes and coin, and in general all tangible things which are physically moveable.[2] Some things initially heritable may become moveable, e.g. trees, on being felled, or conversely things moveable may cease to be moveable, e.g. by things being attached to heritage as fixtures.[3]

Two legal interests are recognized in corporeal moveables, property or ownership, and possession.

OWNERSHIP

As contrasted with land, where several proprietary estates and interests such as those of the Crown, superior, vassal and liferenter, may co-exist at one time in the one piece of land, there is only one interest of a proprietary nature in moveables, viz. dominion or absolute ownership, which implies, at least at common law, absolute and exclusive liberty of dealing with the object in any way possible, using, consuming, enjoying, letting, selling, bequeathing, giving away or otherwise dealing with it.[4] Ownership is the totality of powers of use

---

[1] Since the Succession (Sc) Act, 1964, all property, both heritable, with limited exceptions, and moveable, now vests in the owner's executor on the owner's death.

[2] Bell, *Comm.* I, 100, 176; cf. Sale of Goods Act, 1979, S. 62(1) defining 'goods' as 'all corporeal moveables except money'.

[3] cf. Bell, *Prin.* §1283, 1285, 1470.

[4] Bell, *Comm.* I, 177; *Prin.* §1284.

and disposal allowed by law. The owner may relinquish for a time some of the bundle of rights which collectively amount to ownership without sacrificing ownership altogether, as by lending or letting the goods on hire to another, retaining the radical right.

The acquisition of ownership may be original, by first appropriation of something hitherto unowned, or by creation of a new subject of property,[5] or derivative, by acquisition or transference from another of something hitherto owned by him.[6] Ownership may be lost by transfer to another, by consumption or use, or by dereliction.[7]

Title to corporeal moveables

In general a person's title to the ownership of corporeal moveables is not evidenced by any kind of written title.[8] To this there are certain exceptions.

Every British ship,[9] except river boats or coasters not exceeding fifteen tons burthen, must be registered with the Registrar of Shipping and the register is the evidence of title to the ship;[10] possession does not prove title to it.[11] The register discloses the ownership of the sixty-four shares into which the property in a ship may be divided.[12] The register does not record trusts.[13] A registered owner of a ship or share thereof has an absolute power of disposal of his share, but interests arising under contract or other equitable interests may be enforced against owners or mortgagees of ships in respect of their interest therein in the same way as in respect of other moveable property.[14]

Aircraft must be registered with the Department of Trade, the register showing the person or persons appearing to the Minister owners for the time being of that aircraft, who must be persons qualified to be owners of an aircraft so registered.[15]

Motor vehicles must, on being first licensed, be registered with the local authority for the area in which the vehicle is ordinarily kept, and

---

[5] Bell, *Prin.* §1286; Ch. 5.26, *infra.*
[6] Bell, *Prin.* §1286; Ch. 5.31, *infra.*
[7] Ch. 5.36, *infra.*
[8] Some evidence of ownership may, however, be provided by, e.g., a receipt for purchase of goods, if identified with the goods in dispute and good evidence is provided by, e.g., a name or library stamp on a book, or a medallion on a dog's collar. Farm animals frequently bear a mark of ownership.
[9] Defined, Merchant Shipping Act, 1894, S. 1.
[10] 1894 Act, S. 5.
[11] *Hooper* v. *Gumm* (1867) L.R. 2 Ch. 282.
[12] A corporate body, or not more than five persons jointly, may be registered as owning a share: S. 5. Under the Sea Fishing Boats (Sc.) Act, 1886, sea fishing boats are owned in 16 shares by not more than 16 individuals.
[13] 1894 Act, S. 56.
[14] 1894 Act, S. 57.
[15] Air Navigation Order, 1970, Art. 4.

a registration book is issued to the registered owner.[16] The registration book is issued to the person by whom the vehicle is kept and used and the name appearing therein may not be the legal owner of the vehicle. The registration book is not a document of title,[17] but it is evidence of title[18] and the provision of a registration book is ordinarily a suspensive condition of a contract for the hire-purchase of a car.[19]

Documents of title to goods

In the case of goods which are the subjects of commercial dealings, documents of title thereto, such as bills of lading under which they are shipped, dock warrants or warehouse warrants under which goods are stored, or delivery orders on a warehouse keeper, are customarily treated as equivalent to the goods themselves, and may be pledged or transferred on sale as if they were the goods themselves.[20] But such are not permanent title-deeds of moveable property in the way the title deeds of heritage are.

Joint and common property in moveables

Moveable property is vested in parties jointly if not only is it possessed *pro indiviso* but they have one title to the whole property which on the death of one joint owner accresces to the survivors.[21] The ownership of trustees is joint. It is vested in parties in common if, though enjoyed in common, each has a separate title to a determinate share, which transmits separately, and if each can call on the others to divide the property, or sell their shares, or sell the property and divide the proceeds.[22] Where persons have collaborated in producing a new thing by each contributing labour or materials or both, the thing belongs to them as common property in shares proportional to the value of their respective contributions.[23] Whether moveable property belongs to persons jointly or in common may depend on the means of acquisition of the property, or on the terms of any gift or bequest of it to them. A gift or bequest to several persons is joint, but if there are words of severance such as 'equally' or 'in equal shares' the donees are owners in common.

---

[16] Road Vehicles (Registration and Licensing) Regulations, 1955.

[17] i.e. within the Factors Act, 1889, S. 1(4), applied to Scotland by Factors Act, 1890; see *Joblin* v. *Watkins and Roseveare (Motors), Ltd.* [1949] 1 All E.R. 47.

[18] *Central Newburn Car Auctions, Ltd.* v. *Unity Finance, Ltd.* [1957] 1 Q.B. 371.

[19] *Bentworth Finance* v. *Lubert* [1968] 1 Q.B. 680.

[20] Ch. 5.41, *infra.* 'Documents of title' are statutorily defined in the Factors Act, 1889, S. 1(4), applied to Scotland by Factors (Sc.) Act, 1890.

[21] e.g. *Edinburgh Veterinary Medical Socy.* v. *Dick's Trs.* (1874) 1 R. 1072; *Murray* v. *Johnstone* (1896) 23 R. 981.

[22] e.g. if a farmer leaves his pedigree herd 'to my sons equally'.

[23] *Wylie & Lochhead* v. *Mitchell* (1870) 8 M. 552. In this and some other cases no proper distinction is drawn between joint and common property.

Ownership by husband and wife

While husband and wife may each own moveables individually, other moveables may belong to them jointly, or in common, depending on the source and mode of acquisition of the property.[24]

The Married Women's Property Act, 1964, provides that money derived from any housekeeping allowance or similar provision made by the husband and any property acquired out of such money shall, in the absence of contrary agreement, be treated as belonging to the spouses in equal shares.[25] It is uncertain whether the right in any property acquired is joint or in common.

Ownership of moveables in liferent and fee

It is competent to grant a proper liferent of moveables, such as those in a house conveyed in liferent;[26] but a proper liferent cannot be constituted over fungibles, which perish by use, but only over such moveables as wear out only so gradually that they will normally continue fit for use beyond the normal duration of a liferent.[27] A liferent of moveables is normally achieved through the intervention of a trust, in which case the liferenter's obligation is to maintain the stock of moveables and replace it as it becomes worn out[28] though the liferenter may consume fungibles.[29]

POSSESSION

Possession is a factual relationship between a person and a corporeal moveable, the holding of the object as against other persons. It is distinguishable into natural possession, or actual possession by the owner himself, and civil possession, which is possession through an intermediary such as an employee.[30] Two elements are relevant to possession, *animus possidendi*, or the mental claim to hold the thing as against others or to retrieve it from them, and *corpus possessionis*, or the actual control of the thing.[31] To acquire legal possession of moveables requires both elements; once possession has been acquired it may

[24] See *Re Roger's Question* [1948] 1 All E.R. 328; *Rimmer v. R.* [1953] 1 Q.B. 63.
[25] cf. *Pyatt v. P.*, 1966 S.L.T. (Notes) 73.
[26] cf. *McMillan v. Price* (1837) 15 S. 916; *Fraser v. Croft* (1898) 25 R. 496; but see Lord Dunedin's dictum in *Miller v. Inland Revenue*, 1930 S.C. (H.L.) 49, 56.
[27] Ersk. II, 9, 40; *Rogers v. Scott* (1867) 5 M. 1078; *Miller's Trs. v. M.*, 1907 S.C. 833.
[28] *Rogers, supra.*
[29] *Miller's Trs., supra.*
[30] Ersk. II, 1, 22; Bell, *Prin.* §1312; *Union Bank v. Mackenzie* (1865) 3 M. 765; *Moore v. Gledden* (1869) 7 M. 1016; *Mitchell's Trs. v. Gladstone* (1894) 21 R. 586.
[31] Stair II, 1, 17; Bankt. II, 1, 26; Ersk. II, 1, 20.

be retained though either element be lacking, at least temporarily;[32] and possession can be lost only when both elements are permanently withdrawn, as where one, having 'lost' a thing, gives up the attempt to find it, or puts it out with intent to get rid of it.[33] More than one person can possess concurrently on different rights which do not mutually conflict; thus an owner of moveables and a pledgee thereof both simultaneously possess, the owner civilly, the pledgee actually, for their respective rights and interests.[34]

Distinct from possession is mere custody; the custodier has physical control but his *animus* is only to hold it for the lawful possessor; thus an employee normally has control only for behoof of his employer (who has civil possession through him) and not full possession.[35]

Possession is of great importance; it is to moveables what sasine is to heritage, the badge of real right.[36] It raises some presumption that the possessor is owner, or an acquirer under hire-purchase, and is generally an essential for the existence of a right in security over moveables.

Lawful possession, possession held vi, clam, aut precario

Possession may also be distinguished into that obtained lawfully, and that obtained *vi, clam, aut precario*.[37] A lawful possessor such as a hirer, may vindicate possession against even the owner. One who possesses *vi*, such as a thief, acquires possession good against all except the true owner, but his possession is not lawful and can never ripen into legal ownership.[38] A possessor *clam*, such as one to whom goods are sent by mistake, acquires possession defeasible by a claim to possession by the true owner or anyone having a title from the owner to possess.[39] A possessor *precario*, such as a gratuitous borrower, may have his right of possession withdrawn at any time at the will of the true owner.

Temporary transfer of possession

Possession of moveable property may be transferred for temporary purposes under the contracts of *commodatum*, deposit, pledge and *locatio* (other than *locatio operarum*). In each case possession only is

[32] e.g. a person absent from home possesses goods therein *animo* but not *facto*; a forgetful person possesses his goods e.g. the books in his study, *facto* but not *animo*.

[33] cf. *Fraser* v. *Glasgow Corpn.*, 1972 S.C. 162, where an owner abandoned a car.

[34] Ersk. II, 1, 22–3.

[35] Stair, Bankt, Ersk., *supra*, Bell, *Prin.* §1311; *Dickson* v. *Nicholson* (1855) 17 D. 1011; *Gladstone* v. *McCallum* (1896) 23 R. 782; *Barnton Hotel Co.* v. *Cook* (1899) 1 F. 1190; with which contrast *Meikle & Wilson* v. *Pollard* (1880) 8 R. 69; and *Robertson* v. *Ross* (1887) 15 R. 67; cf. *Sim* v. *Grant* (1862) 24 D. 1033; *O'Brien* v. *Strathern*, 1922 J.C. 55.

[36] *Moore* v. *Gledden* (1869) 7 M. 1076, 1022.

[37] Ersk. II, 1, 23.

[38] cf. *Henderson* v. *Gibson*, 17 June 1806, F.C.

[39] cf. *Louson* v. *Craik* (1842) 4 D. 1452.

transferred, for the purposes and subject to the limitations of the contract in question, and not ownership.[40]

Possession in different characters

Persons may have possession of corporeal moveables in many different characters, their rights against the owners and third parties varying somewhat according to the character in which possession is held. Thus goods may be possessed as owner, as seller who has not delivered,[41] as seller or buyer in possession after sale,[42] as buyer on sale or return,[43] as pledgee, hirer, hire-purchaser, borrower, depositary, in the exercise of a lien, as carrier, poinding creditor, or finder.

Possession presumes ownership

Older authorities lay down that, in a question with a wrongdoer, or a person asserting an adverse title, a possessor of corporeal moveables is presumed to be owner thereof and that one claiming moveables against a possessor must prove not only that he had once been owner, but how he came to lose possession.[44] This is a mere prima facie presumption and is today of lesser weight in view of the common practices of holding goods on hire or hire-purchase,[45] but it still applies to the extent that a possessor is entitled to have his possession protected, and to have it restored, if he has been forcibly dispossessed,[46] and he may be required to surrender possession only by proof that the claimant has a continuing title of ownership. Even a thief is entitled to have his possession protected against everyone except the true owner.

Reputed ownership

The doctrine of reputed ownership was to the effect that a person in possession of moveables was reputed their owner and thus deemed entitled to dispose of the moveables and confer a good title. The object of the doctrine was to protect creditors who were misled by the credit acquired by the debtor, by his having been permitted to possess as apparent owner moveables truly belonging to another. Its effect was to bar the true owner from asserting his right of ownership against the

[40] Chs. 5.27–5.29, infra.
[41] Sale of Goods Act, 1979, S. 17.
[42] Ibid., S. 25.
[43] Ibid., S. 18, R. 4.
[44] Stair II, 1, 42; III, 2, 7; IV, 30, 9; Ersk. II, 1, 20, 24; Bell, Prin. §1313; Scot v. Elliot (1672) Mor. 12727; Sharpe v. Smyth (1832) 11 S. 38; Macdougall v. Whitelaw (1840) 2 D. 500; Anderson v. Buchanan (1848) 11 D. 270; Orr's Tr. v. Tullis (1870) 8 M. 936.
[45] Hopkinson v. Napier, 1953 S.C. 139.
[46] Spoliatus ante omnia restituendus.

creditors.[47] Hence the plea requires some fraud or gross fault on the true owner's part whereby false credit has been given.[48] In modern practice the doctrine is not important because ownership and possession are now so frequently separated that persons dealing with a possessor of goods are not warranted merely by his possession in believing that he is the owner thereof,[49] and there must be other factors present before the owner will be held barred from vindicating his property from a creditor of the possessor.[50] Mere possession does not confer even apparent authority to dispose of the property, and does not preclude the owner from vindicating his property from one who has dealt with the possessor.[51]

Recovery of possession when lost

An owner who loses possession may follow and recover his property without judicial authority so long as he does so *ex incontinenti*, but not *ex intervallo*.[52] He may by action seek redelivery or restitution of his property, or damages in lieu if it be not returned.[53] In the case of illegal possession he may seek recovery by action, proving his ownership, and how he lost possession, as by fraud, theft, or deposit, to counter the presumption of property arising from possession. The action lies against the possessor or one who has fraudulently put away the goods to avoid action.[54] It lies against one who, even in good faith, acquired *in bona fide* from one obtaining the goods by fraud,[55] and against anyone who has bought goods stolen,[56] but not against the innocent

[47] Ersk. II, 1, 24; III, 5, 5; Bell, *Comm.* I, 269; *Prin.* §1315; *Cargill v. Somerville* (1820) Hume 223; *Shearer v. Christie* (1842) 5 D. 132, 141; *Anderson v. Buchanan* (1848) 11 D. 270; *Edmond v. Mowat* (1868) 7 M. 59; *Orr's Tr. v. Tullis* (1870) 8 M. 936; *Marston v. Kerr's Tr.* (1879) 6 R. 898, 901; *Hewat's Tr. v. Smith* (1892) 19 R. 403; *Mitchell's Trs. v. Gladstone* (1894) 21 R. 586.

[48] *McBain v. Wallace* (1881) 8 R. (H.L.) 106; *Bell, Rannie & Co. v. Smith* (1885) 22 S.L.R. 597; *Liqdr. of Brechin Auction Co. v. Reid* (1895) 22 R. 711; *Glen v. Cameron* (1896) 3 S.L.T. 231.

[49] *Bryce v. Ehrmann* (1904) 7 F. 5.

[50] *Hopkinson v. Napier*, 1953 S.C. 139; cf. *Marston, supra*; *Ducanson v. Jefferis' Tr.* (1881) 8 R. 563; *Thomson v. Scoular* (1882) 9 R. 430; *Robertson v. McIntyre* (1882) 9 R. 772; *Hogarth v. Smart's Tr.* (1882) 9 R. 964; *Scott v. S's Tr.* (1889) 16 R. 504.

[51] *Robertson v. McIntyre* (1882) 9 R. 772; *Mitchell v. Heys* (1894) 21 R. 600; *Lamonby v. Foulds*, 1928 S.C. 89.

[52] Ersk. II, 1, 23; Bell, *Prin.* §1319.

[53] Bell, *prin.* §1318; *Henderson v. Gibson*, 17 June 1806, F.C.; *Gorebridge Co-operative Socy. v. Turnbull*, 1952 S.L.T. (Sh. Ct.) 91; *Dalhanna Knitwear Co. v. Mohammed Ali*, 1967 S.L.T. (Sh. Ct.) 74. As to recovery of possession of goods let on hire purchase, see Consumer Credit Act, Ss. 90–2.   [54] Bell, *Prin.* §1320–1.

[55] *Morrisson v. Robertson*, 1908 S.C. 322, where intermediate party's title void: *Secus* if intermediate party's title voidable only: *Macleod v. Kerr*, 1965 S.C. 253.

[56] Bell, *Comm.*, I. 307; Bell, *Prin.* §1320; *Bp. of Caithness v. Edinburgh Fleshers* (1629) Mor. 4145; *Forsyth v. Kilpatrick* (1680) Mor. 9120; *Mackay v. Forsyth* (1758) Mor. 4944; *Henderson v. Gibson* (1806) Mor. Moveables, Appx. 1; *E. Fife's Trs. v. Snare* (1849) 11 D. 1119; cf. *Todd v. Armour* (1882) 9 R. 901.

transferee from a thief of money or negotiable instruments.[57] Failing restitution a claim lies against the possessor for the value of the thing.[58] But once the possessor has lost possession to a third party his liability to make restitution or pay the value disappears, save in so far as he was *lucratus* by handling the thing.[59]

Possession cannot ripen into ownership

No lapse of time converts mere possession of moveables into ownership. But if possession has been lawfully transferred initially, as by loan, the owner's claim to recovery will be extinguished by the lapse of the long negative prescription.[60]

---

[57] *Walker & Watson* v. *Sturrock* (1897) 35 S.L.R. 26; *Gorebridge Co-operative Socy.* v. *Turnbull*, 1952 S.L.T. (Sh. Ct.) 91.

[58] *International Banking Corpn.* v. *Ferguson Shaw & Sons*, 1910 S.C. 182.

[59] *Faulds* v. *Townsend* (1861) 23 D. 437; *North West Securities* v. *Barrhead Coachworks Ltd.*, 1976 S.C. 68.

[60] *Parishioners of Aberscherder* v. *Parishioners of Gemrie* (1633) Mor. 10972.

ORIGINAL ACQUISITION OF RIGHTS IN CORPOREAL MOVEABLE OBJECTS

Original acquisition is acquisition of rights of property in a moveable object not previously owned by another, as distinct from derivative acquisition from a previous owner. It may be effected in many ways, depending to some extent on the nature of the thing in question.

Occupation

Occupation is the taking possession of a thing not hitherto owned with the intention of acquiring ownership of it.[1] The rule is: *quod nullius est, fit occupantis.* This mode covers taking shells, pearls, pebbles or precious stones on the seashore, wild birds, animals or fish,[2] even though the taking may be penalized or involve trespass on lands or some other contravention of law.[3] Appropriation confers a right of property only when complete, or proceeding towards full accomplishment, as when pursuing a wounded animal.[4] Once appropriated a wild creature cannot be appropriated by another so long as the first holder's possession continues. If a wild creature, reduced to possession, escapes, the owner loses his ownership as soon as he ceases to pursue and the creature reverts to its ownerless state, and it may be validly acquired by any other person who subsequently reduces it to possession.[5]

Creatures which have been domesticated, including all farm animals and birds, or carry a mark of ownership, or are confined in a cage or pen or fishpond, or which, though allowed to roam freely, have a homing instinct (*animus revertendi*) such as cats or pigeons or bees, cannot be acquired by anyone who seizes them.[6]

Finding

Things found in a public place, having been lost, forgotten or

[1] Stair II, 1, 33; Ersk. II, 1, 10; Bell, *Prin.* §1287–94.
[2] *Wilson* v. *Dykes* (1872) 10 M. 444. Royal fish, however, belong to the Crown: Stair, Ersk., *supra.*
[3] *Scott* v. *Everitt* (1853) 15 D. 288; cf. *Livingstone* v. *E. Breadalbane* (1791) 3 Paton 221; *Leith* v. *L.* (1862) 24 D. 1059, 1062.
[4] Stair, *supra*; Bell, *Prin.* §1289. As to whale-fishing, see also *Hutcheson* v. *Dundee Whale-fishing Co.* (1830) 5 Mur. 164; *Sutter* v. *Aberdeen Arctic Co.* (1862) 4 Macq. 355.
[5] Stair, *supra*, Bell, *Prin.* §1290.
[6] Ersk., *supra*; Bell, *Prin.* §1290.

dropped, are still deemed constructively in the possession of the true owner, so long as he retains *animus possidendi*, and the finder should make restitution to him, if he knows or can reasonably find the true owner. If he cannot do so, the rule is: *quod nullius est, fit domini regis.*[7] The finder acquires no title by finding and commits theft if he appropriates the thing found.[8] But the finder is entitled to possession against anyone other than the true owner.[9]

Under the Winter Herding Act, 1686, cattle which stray may be detained by the finder until the statutory penalty is paid but the owner retains his right of property.

Under the Burgh Police (Sc.) Act, 1892, S. 412, goods,[10] articles or money found in burghs must under penalty be deposited with the police within forty-eight hours. If not claimed within six months they may be awarded to the finder; if claimed by the owner they fall to be returned to him under deduction of expenses and a reward to the finder. Under the Lost Property (Sc.) Act, 1965, the same provision is applied to landward areas of counties. These provisions are probably wide enough to cover also things found in public vehicles within burghs or counties.

Things found in other moveables, as in a vehicle or in the drawer of a desk which has been bought, continue to belong constructively to the former owner thereof and property in them is not acquired with the container.[11]

Things found in or on the heritage of another are constructively still the property of the former owner and the finder acquires no right of property, but has a possessory right good against all but the true owner,[12] unless the latter has abandoned *animus possidendi*, in which case the finder has a possessory right good against all but the heritable proprietor.[13]

Things found buried in or attached to the lands of another belong not to the finder nor to the owner of the lands but to the Crown: *quod nullius est, fit domini regis.*[14]

[7] Stair II, 1, 33; Ersk. II, 1, 10; Bell, *Prin.* §1291; cf. *Sands* v. *Bell & Balfour*, 22 May 1810, F.C.
[8] *Lawson* v. *Heatly*, 1962 S.L.T. 53.
[9] cf. *Bridges* v. *Hawkesworth* (1851) 21 L.J.Q.B. 75.
[10] Including lost animals: *R.* v. *Slade* (1888) 21 Q.B.D. 433; *Mirams* v. *Our Dogs Co.* [1901] 2 K.B. 564; cf. Dogs Act, 1906, S. 4 and Dogs (Amdt.) Act, 1928, S. 2.
[11] cf. *Cartwright* v. *Green* (1803) 8 Ves. 405; *Merry* v. *Green* (1841) 7 M. & W. 623; *Speaker's Exor.* v. *Spicker*, 1969 S.L.T. (Notes) 7.
[12] *Cleghorn and Bryce* v. *Baird* (1696) Mor. 13523.
[13] cf. *South Staffs Water Co.* v. *Sharman* [1896] 2 Q.B. 44 (rings found in pond); *Hannah* v. *Peel* [1945] K.B. 509 (brooch found in requisitioned house); *Hibbert* v. *McKiernan* [1948] 2 K.B. 142 (golf balls found in rough); *Re Cohen* [1953] Ch. 88 (money found in house); *London Corpn.* v. *Appleyard* [1963] 2 All E.R. 834.
[14] *Lord Advocate* v. *Aberdeen University*, 1963 S.C. 533; cf. *Elwes* v. *Brigg Gas Co.* (1886) 33 Ch. D. 562.

Treasure Trove

Treasure consists of precious articles, found concealed in the ground or in the fabric of a building,[15] there being no proof of their property or reasonable presumption of their former ownership.[16] Such are among the *regalia minora* and fall to the Crown under the rule: *quod nullius est, fit domini regis*.[17] Treasure concealed in the earth or a secret place of hiding is presumed hidden, and a claimant must overcome this presumption.[18]

Goods not reclaimed

Goods lent or deposited, forgotten and not reclaimed probably continued recoverable for forty years at common law.[19] Right to property unexercised or unenforced for twenty years continuously and without any relevant claim having been made for that time are extinguished.[20]

Stray animals

Stray animals belong to the Crown if not claimed by the true owner.[21] Under the Dogs Act, 1906, the police may seize and detain a dog believed to be a stray. Notice is served on the owner, if known, and after seven days, if he has not claimed it and paid all expenses, the dog may be destroyed.[22] A person taking possession of a stray dog must return it to the owner or take the dog to the police. If the finder desires to keep the dog he may, after taking it to the police station, remove it on giving his name and address, and must keep it for one month, whereupon ownership vests in the finder.[23]

Wrecks

Maritime wreck is governed by statute.[24] If the owner of wreck takes possession of it he must notify the receiver of wreck, and if not the possessor must deliver it to the receiver.[25] The Crown is entitled to all

---

[15] *Cleghorn* v. *Bryce & Baird* (1696) Mor. 13522.

[16] *Lord Advocate* v. *Aberdeen University*, 1963 S.C. 533, 548.

[17] Craig, *J.F.* I, 16, 40; Stair II, 1, 5; III, 3, 27; Bankt. I, 3, 14–16; I, 8, 9; II, 1, 8; Ersk. II, 1, 11–12; II, 6, 13; Bell, *Prin.* §1293; *Lord Advocate, supra.*

[18] *A.G.* v. *British Museum* [1903] 2 Ch. 598.

[19] *Sands* v. *Bell & Balfour*, 22 May 1810, F.C.

[20] Prescription and Limitation (Sc.) Act, 1973, S. 8.

[21] Ersk. II, 1, 12; Bell, *Prin.* §1294.

[22] Dogs Act, 1906, S. 3.

[23] Ibid., S. 4; Dogs (Amdt.) Act, 1928, S. 2.

[24] Merchant Shipping Act, 1894, Ss. 510–37; for older law see Stair III, 3, 27; Ersk. II, 1, 13; Bell, *Prin.* §1292.

[25] 1894 Act, S. 518.

unclaimed wreck, except where the Crown has granted the right to wreck to anyone else.[26]

Creation

A person who makes a thing from materials which he owns owns the completed thing.[27]

Severance

Trees and crops while growing and minerals while in the ground are heritable but become moveable when felled or gathered or extracted and ownership is acquired by the severance, so long as lawful. If the severance is not lawful, the party severing acquires no title of ownership thereby, nor even lawful possession.

Accessio

On the principle *accessorium sequitur principale* a person who owns a principal subject becomes owner of what is necessarily accessory thereto; thus the owner of an animal thereby owns its young from their birth.[28] Similarly the owner of money owns the interest produced by that money.[29] By artificial or industrial accession, where a new thing is produced or the value of an old one augmented by the application of skill or art, the owner of the principal subject owns the new form of it or the enhanced value of it, but it is frequently difficult to decide to whom the property in the finished article should belong.[30]

Adjunction

Adjunction takes place where one thing is added to another so as to form a new thing or to alter the character of each, as where embroidery is applied to cloth, or paint to canvas, or accessories to a vehicle. The property belongs to the owner of the major element, subject to liability to compensate the other for the value of his materials or skill.[31] Bell lays down[32] that, for determining which is principal, that of two substances, one of which can exist separately, the other not, the former is the principal; where both can exist separately, the principal is that which the other is taken to adorn or complete: in the absence of these

[26] 1894 Act, S. 523. cf. *M. Breadalbane* v. *Smith* (1850) 12 D. 602; *L.A.* v. *Hebden* (1868) 6 M. 489.

[27] Bell, *Prin.* §1296.

[28] Ersk. II, 1, 14–15; Bell, *Prin.* §1297; *Lamb* v. *Grant* (1874) 11 S.L.R. 672; cf. *Tucker* v. *Farm and General Investment Trust* [1966] 2 All E.R. 508.

[29] *Brown* v. *Inland Revenue*, 1964 S.C. (H.L.) 180.

[30] Bell, *Prin.* §1297–8.

[31] Inst. II, 1, 33; Dig. 41, 1, 9, 1; Stair II, 1, 39; Bankt. II, 1, 18; Ersk. II, 1, 15; *Cochrane* v. *Stevenson* (1891) 18 R. 1208.

[32] *Prin.* §1298.

indications, bulk prevails; next value. And in all such cases where there can be no separation, the property is with the owner of the principal, leaving to the other a claim for indemnification.

Specificatio

Where a person *in bona fide*, as by mistake, makes a new thing from materials wholly belonging to another, if the materials are thereby wholly destroyed, the property in the new thing is with the maker, subject to a claim by the owner of the materials for return of an equivalent quantity and quality or for the value of the materials used, but if the materials can be restored to their original state the property in the new thing is in the owner thereof, subject to a claim by the workman for the work done, measured *quantum lucratus*.[33] If the new thing be made from materials belonging partly to two or more persons, it belongs to them in common in proportion to the value of the contribution of each.[34]

Where, however, the new thing is made *in mala fide*, as where the whole or part of the materials have been stolen, no title to the new thing vests in the maker, the doctrine of *specificatio* being an equitable one and applicable only where there is complete good faith on the part of the manufacturer.[35]

Confusion of liquids: commixtion of solids

In the cases of solids and liquids, if the things mixed are of the same kind and the result is inseparable, e.g. salt and sugar, the owners of the quantities mixed have common property in the mixture, sharing it in proportion to the quantity and value each has contributed. If the mixture is again separable into its constituents, e.g. a mixed collection of books, each owner continues to own his elements of the mixture. If the things mixed are of different kinds so that the resultant mixture is *tertium quid* the property is with the manufacturer if the mixture be inseparable, and with the owners of the materials inmixed if separable, as in the case of *specificatio*.[36]

---

[33] Stair II, 1, 41; Ersk. II, 1, 16; Bell, *Prin.* §1298; *International Banking Corpn.* v. *Ferguson Shaw & Son*, 1910 S.C. 182; cf. *Inst.* II, 1, 25.

[34] *Wylie & Lochhead* v. *Mitchell* (1870) 8 M. 552.

[35] *McDonald* v. *Provan (of Scotland St.), Ltd.*, 1960 S.L.T. 231.

[36] Stair II, 1, 34, 36, 41; Ersk. II, 1, 14–17; Bell, *Comm.* I, 276; Bell, *Prin.* §1298(2).

TEMPORARY TRANSFER OF MOVEABLES—
LOAN AND MONEYLENDING

One purpose of the temporary transfer of moveables is for the temporary convenience of another, effected by the contract of loan. In Scots law, following Roman law, loan is a real contract effected not merely by agreement but only by the actual transfer of the thing lent,[1] and a distinction is drawn between loan for use, when the thing lent has to be returned, and loan for consumption when the thing lent may be used up but its equivalent must be returned.

COMMODATUM—LOAN FOR USE

Commodatum[2] or proper loan is the contract whereby the lender gratuitously transfers to the borrower some moveable object, such as a book or a car, to be used and restored specifically at the end of the agreed time, or when the purpose of the loan has been served, in as good condition as when lent, fair wear and tear excepted. The contract is not completely constituted till the thing is transferred, though the terms on which delivery is made may be proved by parole evidence. The right of property in the thing remains with the lender, the borrower acquiring only possession and a right of use; the lender has a claim for restitution when the period of loan has expired or the contemplated purpose has been served or after a reasonable time has elapsed.[3]

The risk of the thing perishing or deteriorating during the loan accordingly remains with the lender, unless it were attributable to the borrower's lack of care. The borrower must take all reasonable care of the thing borrowed and if it is returned damaged the onus is on the borrower to show that he exercised all reasonable care and that the damage did not arise through his fault.[4] He is excused by proof of

---

[1] Stair I, 10, 11; Bankt. I, 11, 1; Ersk. III, 1, 17.
[2] D. 13, 6, 8; Stair I, 11, 8; Ersk. III, 1, 20; Bell, *Prin.* §195; More, *Lect.* I, 160.
[3] Ersk. III, 1, 20, 24; *Duncan* v. *Fea* (1824) 2 S. 636.
[4] *Bain* v. *Strong* (1888) 16 R. 186; cf. *Pyper* v. *Thomson* (1843) 5 D. 498; *Pullars* v. *Walker* (1858) 20 D. 1238; *Wilson* v. *Orr* (1879) 7 R. 266; *Bullen* v. *Swan Electric Co.* (1906) 22 T.L.R. 276; *Wiehe* v. *Dennis Bros.* (1913) 24 T.L.R. 250.

purely accidental loss or injury, or damage by *damnum fatale*. Failing such proof he is liable for the diminution in value of the thing lent. If he fails to restore the thing when he ought to, or puts it to another use than that for which it was lent and it then perishes, even by mere accident, the borrower must pay the value, as being in fault.[5]

The thing borrowed may be used only for the express purpose for which it was lent, or for any purpose for which it was suitable, and its use therefor contemplated, and the borrower will be liable for any damage or loss arising from use in excess thereof.[6] The lender is liable to the borrower for injury caused by any known defect in the thing lent,[7] or for loss caused by taking back the thing wrongfully, before the use could be made for which it was lent.[8] The borrower is bound to defray expenses necessarily incurred while he has the use of the subject, as for food or fuel, but the owner is liable for, and must reimburse the borrower for, expenditure on extraordinary or exceptional expenditures, such as for repairs.[9]

If documents are borrowed and to be returned on demand they cannot be retained by the borrower even on the plea that they are his own property.[10]

Precarium

Precarium[11] is a kind of *commodatum* where the thing is lent to be recalled at the lender's pleasure, or to be used by the borrower without any determinate term or use specified; in either case it may be recalled when the owner thinks fit. The borrower is liable only for gross lack of care, but if he retains the subject after its return has been demanded, he is accountable for the slightest omission, even for accidental loss or damage. It is personal and terminable on the borrower's death, his heir being obliged to return the subject and to account for its fruits during the borrower's possession. If the lender dies, his heir may redemand the subject but, till then, his consent to the continuance of the contract is presumed.

MUTUUM—LOAN FOR CONSUMPTION

Mutuum[12] or improper loan is the contract whereby the lender

[5] Ersk. III, 1, 22.
[6] *Bain, supra; Douglas* v. *Colvill* (1905) 13 S.L.T. 665; cf. *Seton* v. *Paterson* (1880) 8 R. 236; *Wilson* v. *Shepherd*, 1913 S.C. 300.
[7] *Coughlin* v. *Gillison* [1899] 1 Q.B. 145; *Oliver* v. *Saddler*, 1928 S.C. 608, 615.
[8] Ersk. III, 1, 23.   [9] Ibid.
[10] *McLay, McAllister & McGibbon* v. *Hampton* (1898) 25 R. 1198.
[11] Stair I, 11, 10; Ersk. III, 1, 25; Bell, *Prin.* §195.
[12] Stair I, 11, 1; Ersk. III, 1, 18; Bell, *Comm.* I, 274; *Prin.* §200; More, *Lect.* I, 160.

transfers a fungible, such as bread or coal, to another, gratuitously, to be consumed, on an express or implied undertaking to restore as much of the same kind and quality on request, or on the expiry of the agreed time, or after a reasonable time, without regard to variation of market value. The contract is constituted by agreement followed by actual transfer, but the terms on which delivery was made may be proved by parole evidence. The right of property in the subject lent passes to the borrower; hence the risk of destruction or deterioration is with him,[13] and the lender has only a personal right to demand the transfer of the equivalent, or its value, at the due time for restoration.[14] The lender is liable neither for risk nor for expense.

Loan of money

The loan of money is a particular instance of *mutuum*,[15] but differs in that, unless expressly excluded, interest runs *ex lege* on the principal sum until repayment,[16] save in exceptional cases.[17] The loan, if exceeding £100 Scots,[18] unless admitted without qualification[19] can be proved to have been made and to be resting-owing[20] only by the debtor's writ[21] or his admission on oath.[22] The requisite writ may be a formal personal bond, a holograph I.O.U.,[23] a letter,[24] entries in the debtor's business books[25] or similar acknowledgment. It may be the writ of an authorized agent.[26] A bill of exchange, although it has prescribed, is admissible in evidence in proof by oath.[27] A cheque in the

[13] cf. *Anderson* v. *Crompton* (1870) 9 M. 122.

[14] Bell, *Prin.* §1315.

[15] Hume, *Lect.* II, 125; More, *Lect.* I, 161.

[16] *Cuninghame* v. *Boswell* (1868) 6 M. 890; *Hope Johnstone* v. *Cornwall* (1895) 22 R. 314.

[17] *Forbes* v. *F.* (1869) 8 M. 85; *Christie* v. *Matheson* (1871) 10 M. 9; *Thiem's Trs.* v. *Collie* (1899) 1 F. 764; *Smellie's Exrx.* v. *S.*, 1933 S.C. 725.

[18] *Annand's Trs.* v. *A.* (1869) 7 M. 526; cf. *Macfarquhar* v. *MacKay* (1869) 7 M. 766.

[19] *McKie* v. *Wilson*, 1951 S.C. 15.

[20] *Walker* v. *Garlick*, 1940 S.L.T. 208.

[21] *Williamson* v. *Allan* (1882) 9 R. 859; *McAdie* v. *McA's Exrx.* (1883) 10 R. 741; *Penman* v. *White*, 1957 S.C. 338; it need not be tested or holograph: *Bryan* v. *Butters* (1892) 19 R. 490; *Paterson* v. *P.* (1897) 25 R. 144.

[22] *Wright's Trs.* (1870) 8 M. 708; *Grant's Exrx.* v. *G.*, 1922 S.L.T. 156; *McKinney* v. *Allan*, 1975 S.C. 79. cf. *Stuart* v. *S.* (1869) 7 M. 366; contrast *Hendry* v. *Cowie* (1904) 12 S.L.T. 31, 261.

[23] *Woodrow* v. *Wright* (1861) 24 D. 31; *Bowe & Christie* v. *Hutchison* (1868) 6 M. 642; *Paterson* v. *Wilson* (1883) 21 S.L.R. 272; *Nicholson* v. *Stuart's Exor.* (1896) 3 S.L.T. 233; *Black* v. *Gibb*, 1940 S.C. 24; *Winestone* v. *Wolifson*, 1954 S.C. 77.

[24] *Christie's Trs.* v. *Muirhead* (1870) 8 M. 461; *Balfour-Melville's Factor* v. *B.M.* (1901) 8 S.L.T. 454; contrast *Duncan's Trs.* v. *Shand* (1873) 11 M. 254; *Patrick* v. *P's Trs.* (1904) 6 F. 836. A writing failing to repudiate does not imply admission of loan: *MacBain* v. *MacB.*, 1930 S.C. (H.L.) 72.

[25] *Muir* v. *Goldie's Trs.* (1898) 6 S.L.T. 188; *Hope* v. *Derwent Rolling Mills* (1905) 7 F. 837; contrast *Wink* v. *Speirs* (1868) 8 M. 657; *McRae* v. *Williamson* (1877) 14 S.L.R. 562.

[26] *Laidlaw* v. *Shaw* (1886) 13 R. 724; *Bryan* v. *Butters Bros.* (1892) 19 R. 490; *Dryburgh* v. *Macpherson*, 1944 S.L.T. 116.

[27] *McKinney* v. *Allan*, 1975 S.C. 79. cf. *Nisbet* v. *Neil's Trs.* (1869) 7 M. 1097.

debtor's favour, endorsed by him, does not by itself instruct loan and the creditor may not prove by parole the circumstances in which the cheque was granted,[28] but an endorsed cheque may prove advances in a continuing account.[29] A writing admitting receipt of money does not prove present indebtedness to repay.[30] Proof by writ or oath has been held applicable only where the loan is an isolated transaction and if the loan is alleged to be one incident in a series of transactions between parties any evidence which is natural proof in the circumstances may be admitted.[31] A receipt for money in unqualified terms is presumed to be for money lent and casts the onus on the granter to explain it otherwise.[32] The granter of an I.O.U. may be allowed to prove that the money was received not on loan but on some other basis.[33] If it is alleged, as it may be, in defence to a claim for repayment that the money was a gift the mode of proof may not be restricted but the onus is on the defender.[34] Payments may be neither loans nor donations but explicable in another way.[35] In bankruptcy writ dated after the commencement of sequestration[36] and reference to the bankrupt's oath[37] are both incompetent, though an acknowledgment granted when the debtor was insolvent or within sixty days of notour bankruptcy may suffice.[38]

Proof that a loan has been repaid must normally be by writ or oath, but exceptionally facts and circumstances have been allowed to be proved from which an inference of repayment has been drawn.[39]

What is in substance a loan may be constituted by a shop allowing personal credit.[40]

It is criminal to send circulars to a pupil or minor inviting him to borrow money, or retain goods on credit or hire and knowledge of

---

[28] *Haldane* v. *Speirs* (1872) 10 M. 537; *Scotland* v. *S.* 1909 S.C. 505; contrast *Robb* v. *R's Trs.* (1884) 11 R. 881; *Dunn's Trs.* v. *Hardy* (1896) 23 R. 621.

[29] *Robb, supra.*

[30] *Patrick* v. *P's Trs.* (1904) 6 F. 836.

[31] *Smith's Tr.* v. *S.*, 1911 S.C. 653, 659; *Boyd* v. *Millar*, 1934 S.N. 7; *McKie* v. *Wilson*, 1951 S.C. 15.

[32] *Thomson* v. *Geikie* (1861) 23 D. 693; *Christie's Exors.* v. *Muirhead* (1870) 8 M. 461; *Haldane* v. *Speirs* (1872) 10 M. 537; *Todd* v. *Wood* (1897) 24 R. 1104; *Gill* v. *G.*, 1907 S.C. 532. See also *Duncan's Trs.* v. *Shand* (1873) 11 M. 254.

[33] *Thomson, supra; Neilson's Trs.* v. *N.* (1883) 11 R. 119; *Welsh's Trs.* v. *Forbes* (1885) 12 R. 851.

[34] *Penney* v. *Aitken*, 1927 S.C. 673; *Penman* v. *White*, 1957 S.C. 338.

[35] *Forbes* v. *F.* (1869) 8 M. 85; *Wright's Trs.* (1870) 8 M. 708; cf. *Balfour Melville's Factor* v. *B.M.* (1901) 8 S.L.T. 454; *Hendry* v. *Cowie* (1904) 12 S.L.T. 261.

[36] *Carmichael's Tr.* v. *C.*, 1929 S.C. 265.

[37] *Adam* v. *Maclachlan* (1847) 9 D. 560.

[38] *Matthew's Tr.* v. *M.* (1867) 5 M. 957; *Williamson* v. *Allan* (1882) 9 R. 859.

[39] *Bishop* v. *Bryce*, 1910 S.C. 426; *Clark's Exor.* v. *Brown*, 1935 S.C. 110; *Simpson's Trs.* v. *S.*, 1933 S.N. 22; *Jackson* v. *Ogilvie's Exor.*, 1935 S.C. 154.

[40] *Napier* v. *Crosbie*, 1964 S.C. 129.

pupillarity or minority is presumed in certain cases. Ratification after attaining full age is void.[41]

Security for repayment

The debtor's personal undertaking to repay may be secured by the giving in security of objects of property heritable,[42] moveable[43] or incorporeal,[44] in the manner appropriate for each. It is doubtful if a promissory note is a 'security'.[45] A note, bill, bond or security for repaying money lent for gaming or betting is deemed made for an illegal consideration.[46]

Moneylending—unregulated agreements

A person carrying on the business of moneylending[47] must be licensed by the Director General of Fair Trading to carry on a consumer credit business[48] but personal credit agreements in excess of £5000[49] are not regulated by that Act but by common law principles. But the powers of the court to reopen extortionate credit bargains apply to unregulated agreements as if they were regulated.[50]

Moneylending—regulated agreements

A personal credit agreement, if the creditor provides the debtor with credit, including a cash loan and any other form of personal accommodation, is a consumer credit agreement if the credit does not exceed £5000 and regulated by the Consumer Credit Act, 1974, unless it is an exempt agreement under S. 16 thereof.[51] A person carrying on such a business must be licensed.[52] S. 16 exempts agreements where the creditor is a local authority, building society, or other body specified by order and the agreement is secured by a security charged on land. Personal credit agreements may be for running-account credit or fixed-sum credit,[53] and be restricted-use credit agreement or unrestricted-use credit agreements.[54] A debtor—creditor agreement is a regulated consumer credit agreement to finance a transaction between debtors and

---

[41] Consumer Credit Act, 1974, S. 50.
[42] Chs. 5.12, 5.21, *supra.*
[43] Chs. 5.30, 5.40, *infra.*
[44] Chs. 5.21, 5.40, *infra.*
[45] cf. *Shaw* v. *Duffy*, 1943 S.C. 350, 356.
[46] Gaming Act, 1710, S. 1; Gaming Act, 1835, S. 1; *Cumming* v. *Mackie*, 1973 S.C. 278.
[47] Until the relevant provisions of the Consumer Credit Act, 1974, were brought into force moneylending was controlled in some cases by the Moneylenders Acts, 1900–27. The repeal of these Acts by the Consumer Credit Act leaves unregulated agreements controlled by common law, not by the Moneylenders Acts.
[48] Consumer Credit Act, 1974, Ss. 21–42. Persons requiring to be licensed include moneylenders, banks and shops which allow credit to customers.
[49] Ss. 8–9.　　[50] S. 142.　　[51] Ss. 8–9.
[52] Ss. 21–42.　　[53] S. 10.　　[54] S. 11.

a supplier other than the creditor, not made under pre-existing arrangements or in contemplation of future agreements between creditor and supplier, or to finance any existing indebtedness of the debtor's or being an unrestricted-use credit agreement other than one made under pre-existing arrangements.[55]

A debtor–creditor–supplier agreement is a regulated consumer credit agreement to finance a purchase by the debtor from the creditor or any other transaction between them, or to finance a transaction between the debtor and a supplier made under pre-existing arrangements or in contemplation of future arrangements between creditor and supplier or an unrestricted-use credit agreement by the creditor with the supplier to be used to finance a transaction between the debtor and the supplier.[56] Restrictions are imposed on advertisements and canvassing.[57] Regulations require specified information to be disclosed before a regulated agreement is made, and the form and content of agreements and the signing of them is regulated.[58] A copy of the unexecuted agreement must be given to the debtor, and a copy of the executed agreement given him when he executes it.[59] Notice of the debtor's right to cancel must be included therein and sent him within seven days.[60] An improperly executed agreement is enforceable only on a court order.[61]

A regulated agreement may be cancelled if the antecedent negotiations included oral representations made by one acting as or for the negotiator, unless the agreement is concerned with land or is signed at the creditor's business premises.[62] Notice of cancellation may be served until the fifth day following the day the debtor received the statutory copy of the agreement or notice of the right to cancel, or the fourteenth day following the day the debtor signed the agreement.[63] On cancellation money paid is repayable, credit is repayable, and goods returnable.[64] Part V (Ss. 55–74) does not, except for S. 56, apply to non-commercial agreements, agreements to allow overdrawing, nor, except for Ss. 55–6, to small agreements[65] for restricted-use credit.[66]

The creditor must give the debtor at least seven days' notice of intention to enforce a regulated agreement and on request give the debtor information about the state of his debt.[67] Provision is made for appropriation of payments.[68] Notice must be given of variation of an agreement.[69] Limits are placed on the creditor's liberties in the event of the debtor's death.[70]

---

[55] S. 12.   [56] S. 13.   [57] Ss. 43–54.   [58] Ss. 55–61.
[59] Ss. 62–3.   [60] S. 64.   [61] S. 65.   [62] S. 67.
[63] Ss. 68–9.   [64] Ss. 70–3.   [65] Not over £30: S. 17.   [66] S. 74.
[67] Ss. 76–8.   [68] S. 81.   [69] S. 82.   [70] S. 86.

The creditor may not, on the debtor's breach, without serving a default notice on the debtor, terminate the agreement, demand earlier payment of any sum, recover possession of land or goods, treat the right of the debtor or hirer as terminated or enforce any security.[71] Interest may not be increased on default.[72] The debtor may pay off his debt ahead of time, and he may be entitled to a rebate for early settlement.[73] In non-default cases the creditor may not terminate save after at least seven days' notice.[74]

There are restrictions on taking and negotiating negotiable instruments in discharge of sums due.[75] A security over land securing a regulated agreement is enforceable on the order of the court only.[76]

If the court finds a credit bargain extortionate it may reopen the agreement so as to do justice between the parties.[77] These provisions are not confined to regulated agreements.[78]

It is forbidden to contract out of the Act.[79]

Cheque cards

A cheque card issued by a bank to a customer *inter alia* guaranteeing cheques drawn by him to a stated amount is a consumer credit agreement within the Consumer Credit Act, 1974, and an unrestricted-use debtor–creditor agreement.[80]

Credit token agreements

A credit token agreement is made by a person carrying on a consumer credit business who undertakes that on production of a card, check, voucher, coupon or other document given to an individual, he will supply cash, goods or services on credit, or will pay a third party who so supplies in return for payment to him by the individual. It is a regulated agreement within the Consumer Credit Act, 1974[81] and a person carrying on such a business must be licensed under that Act.[82] Advertising and canvassing are regulated.[83] It is an offence to give a credit

[71] Ss. 87–9.
[72] S. 93. cf. *Malcolm Muir Ltd.* v. *Jamieson*, 1947 S.C. 314.
[73] Ss. 94–6.
[74] S. 99.
[75] Ss. 124–6.
[76] S. 127.
[77] Ss. 139–41; *Ketley* v. *Scott* [1981] I.C.R. 241. cf. *Midland Discount Co.* v. *Macdonald*, 1909 S.C. 477.
[78] S. 142.
[79] S. 174.
[80] Ss. 8, 9, 11, 12.
[81] S. 14. This category covers Barclaycard, Access, and other credit cards, and check-trading, e.g. with the Provident Clothing Co.
[82] Ss. 21–42.
[83] Ss. 43–54.

token unasked.[84] The requirements of the 1974 Act as to negotiations, making of agreement, cancellation, and rights during the currency of the agreement applicable to regulated consumer credit business[85] apply.[86]

The debtor is not liable for use made of the credit token by any person unless he had accepted it,[87] but may be liable for misuse of the credit token.[88]

Giving credit

For a trader to give credit, i.e. to sell goods, payment being post-poned in whole or in part, is in substance to lend money, but if such lending is incidental to trading, and done in the course of and for the purposes of other business, it is not moneylending within the Acts.[89] Such a sale may be regulated by the Sale of Goods Act, 1979, or, if it is a hire-purchase or credit sale transaction as defined therein, by the Consumer Credit Act, 1974. It is an offence for an undischarged bankrupt to obtain credit to the extent of £50 or upwards without disclosing that he is an undischarged bankrupt.[90]

Ancillary credit businesses

Ancillary credit businesses[91] must be licensed and many of the provisions of the Consumer Credit Act, 1974, are applicable to such businesses.[92]

[84] S. 51.
[85] *Supra.*
[86] Ss. 55–99.
[87] S. 66.
[88] Ss. 83–4.
[89] e.g. *MacDonald* v. *Napier*, 1960 J.C. 123.
[90] Bankruptcy (Sc.) Act, 1913, S. 182. *Maclean* v. *McCord*, 1965 S.L.T. (Sh. Ct.) 69, seems wrong.
[91] Defined, Ss. 147–8.
[92] Ss. 149–61.

TEMPORARY TRANSFER OF MOVEABLES— DEPOSIT AND CUSTODY

Another purpose of the temporary transfer of moveables is to leave them in the care of another. This care may be gratuitous, in which case it is governed by the real contract of deposit, or onerous, in which case it is governed by the consensual contract of the hiring of care and custody, *locatio custodiae*.[1]

DEPOSIT

Deposit[2] is the contract whereby the owner of corporeal moveables delivers them to another for custody on his account, the depositary undertaking gratuitously to keep them safe and restore them on demand. The contract is perfected by delivery of the subject deposited and may be proved by parole evidence.[3]

Proper and improper deposit

In proper deposit a specific thing is deposited, to be specifically returned; in improper deposit a fungible, such as money with a banker, is deposited on an undertaking to return an equal quantity. In the former the depositer retains the right of property and may sue for return of the thing; the risk of loss remains with him, the depositary being liable only for gross lack of care, though after redelivery is demanded he is liable for exact diligence and liable for the value of the thing even if it perish by mere misfortune, unless he shows it would have perished, or been as likely to perish, even if redelivered to the owner when called for. In the latter the property and risk pass, and the depositor is merely a creditor with a personal action for payment or delivery.

---

[1] Deposit for reward, as in a garage or left-luggage office, is *locatio custodiae: Central Motors* v. *Cessnock Garage Co.*, 1925 S.C. 796. Allowing vehicles to park e.g. on a vacant site, may be licence rather than deposit: *Ashby* v. *Tolhurst* [1937] 2 K.B. 242; *Tinsley* v. *Dudley* [1951] 2 K.B. 18; *Halbauer* v. *Brighton Corpn.* [1954] 2 All E.R. 707. Similarly to hang one's coat on a peg in a restaurant may be mere licence; to give it to a waiter may be deposit.

[2] D. 16, 3, 1; Stair I, 13, 1; Ersk. III, 1, 26; Bell, *Comm.* I, 257; *Prin.* §210.

[3] *Taylor* v. *Nisbet* (1901) 4 F. 79.

Duty of care

The duty of the depositary is to take reasonable care of the thing deposited, such as a man of reasonable prudence generally exercises about his own property,[4] not to use it, save by permission, and not to penetrate any secret, as by opening a box. He performs his trust if he restore the box or package in as good condition as he received it and undamaged, even though the contents have perished. A deposit for safe-keeping, which may be expressly undertaken, or implied from the circumstances or the nature of the deposit, demands a higher standard of care.[5] The depositary will not be liable for accidental loss or destruction, as by fire,[6] or if the goods are stolen, if all proper precautions were taken.[7] A depositary may also be liable if by negligence he causes loss to the person for whose benefit the goods were deposited.[8]

Duty to restore

The depositary must restore the thing on demand, or as otherwise agreed, with any fruits or accessories; he has no claim for reward but may claim reimbursement for all loss or necessary outlays incurred. The depositary has a lien over the subject for his damage or expenses disbursed. He is not entitled to refuse to deliver the subject deposited on the ground that it is not the depositor's property,[9] or because of any claim against the depositor for expense in ascertaining the claim to meet which a fund had been deposited with him.[10] If the depositary's heir, believing himself owner of the subject, sell it, he must account to the depositor for the price received, not for the value, and may discharge himself by assigning the right to the price to the depositor.[11] The onus of proving restoration is on the depositary.[12]

Special cases—liability under praetorian edict

Under the praetorian edict *nautae, caupones, stabularii,*[13] incorporated by custom in Scots law,[14] a higher standard of care than is

---

[4] *Laing* v. *Darling* (1850) 12 D. 1279; *Allan & Poynter* v. *Williamson* (1870) 7 S.L.R. 214; cf. *Wilson* v. *Orr* (1879) 7 R. 266; *Walker* v. *Scottish & Newcastle Breweries*, 1970 S.L.T. (Sh. Ct.) 21; *Kyle* v. *East Kilbride*, 1970 S.L.T. (Sh. Ct.) 37.

[5] Bell, *Prin.* §212; *Giblin* v. *McMullen* (1868) L.R. 2 P.C. 317; *Taylor* v. *Nisbet* (1901) 4 F. 79.

[6] *Grierson* v. *Muir* (1802) Hume 329; cf. *Sinclair* v. *Juner*, 1952 S.C. 35, 43.

[7] D, 18, 1, 35; 18, 6, 14; Inst. 3, 14, 3. See also *Bullen* v. *Swan Electric Co.* (1906) 22 T.L.R. 275; 23 T.L.R. 258.

[8] *Stiven* v. *Watson* (1874) 1 R. 412.

[9] *Gelot* v. *Stewart* (1871) 9 M. 957.

[10] *McGregor* v. *Alley & McLellan* (1887) 14 R. 535.

[11] Ersk. III, 1, 27.

[12] *Taylor* v. *Nisbet* (1901) 4 F. 79. [13] Dig. IV, 9, 1.

[14] Stair I, 9, 5; I, 13, 3; Bankt. I, 17, 1; Ersk. III, 1, 28; Ersk. *Prin.* III, 1, 11 Bell, *Comm.* I, 498; *Prin.* §236. On its incorporation see *Mustard* v. *Paterson*, 1923 S.C. 142, 154. In Roman law this liability was quasi-delictual, not contractual at all.

due by other depositaries is incurred in some cases by innkeepers and livery-stable keepers.[15] 'Innkeeper' at common law covers the proprietors of inns[16] and hotels,[17] who make a continuing offer of accommodation to travellers, but probably not lodging houses[18] or boarding houses,[19] and not the keeper of a restaurant,[20] nor a small land-holder holding a licence to sell ale,[21] nor a public house,[22] whose liability is only for failure to take reasonable care for the safety of their guests' property. 'Stable keepers' include all livery-stable keepers, whether or not attached to an inn,[23] but probably not keepers of a motor garage.[24]

Strict liability

At common law, under the Edict, an innkeeper or livery-stable keeper is strictly liable, without proof of fault, for the loss of, but probably not for mere damage to, property brought to the stable or inn,[25] unless he can prove that it arose from the negligence of the owner,[26] or is attributable to act of the Queen's enemies, or act of God,[27] or *damnum fatale*, i.e. an accident due to natural causes, directly and exclusively, without human intervention, which could not have been prevented by any amount of foresight or pains or care reasonably to be expected.[28] Accidental fire is an exception to strict liability,[29] as is loss by housebreaking.[30] The innkeeper or stable keeper may discharge the onus by proving the purely accidental nature of the fire, or that he had taken every usual and necessary precaution so that

[15] For strict liability of carriers see Chs. 4.17–4.19.

[16] *White* v. *Crocket* (1661) Mor. 9233; *Gooden* v. *Murray* (1700) Mor. 9237; *McPherson* v. *Christie* (1841) 3 D. 930. The definition of an 'inn' or 'hotel' for the purposes of edictal liability has been limited by the Hotel Proprietors Act, 1956, S. 1.

[17] *Rothfield* v. *N.B. Ry.*, 1920 S.C. 805.

[18] *Scott* v. *Yates* (1800) Hume 207; *Watling* v. *McDowall* (1825) 4 S. 83; contrast *May* v. *Wingate* (1694) Mor. 9236.

[19] *Caldecutt* v. *Piesse* (1932) 49 T.L.R. 26.

[20] *Ultzen* v. *Nichols* [1894] 1 Q.B. 92.

[21] *Taylor* v. *Fordyce*, 1918 S.C. 824.

[22] Liability extended in old cases to vintners in burghs: *Forbes* v. *Steil* (1687) Mor. 9233, and householders who took in lodgers: *May* v. *Wingate* (1694) Mor. 9236.

[23] *Chisholm* v. *Fenton* (1714) Mor. 9241; *Hay* v. *Wordsworth*, 13 Feb. 1801, F.C.; *McDonell* v. *Ettles*, 15 Dec. 1809, F.C.; *Mustard, supra*.

[24] *Central Motors, supra; Sinclair* v. *Juner*, 1952 S.C. 35.

[25] Stair I, 9, 5; Ersk. III, 1, 28; Bell, *Prin.* §235–42A.

[26] *Mustard, supra*. 156; see also *Filipowski* v. *Merryweather* (1860) 2 F. & F. 285; *Cashill* v. *Wright* (1856) 6 E. & B. 891; *Oppenheim* v. *White Lion Hotel Co.* (1871) L.R. 6 C.P. 515; *Carpenter* v. *Haymarket Hotel Ltd.* [1931] 1 K.B. 364; *Shacklock* v. *Ethorpe* [1939] 3 All E.R. 372; *Brewster* v. *Drennan* [1945] 2 All E.R. 705; *Gresham* v. *Lyn* [1954] 2 All E.R. 786.

[27] *Mustard, supra*, 148, 153, 156.

[28] *Mustard, supra*, 153, quoting *Nugent* v. *Smith* (1876) 1 C.P.D. 423, 444.

[29] *McDonell* v. *Ettles*, 15 Dec. 1809, F.C., explained *Sinclair* v. *Juner*, 1952 S.C. 35. Fire is not always or necessarily an excepted peril; only accidental fire is.

[30] *Watling* v. *McDowall* (1825) 4 S. 83.

it must have arisen from inevitable accident.[31] Thus an innkeeper has been held liable for the loss of a parcel containing money,[32] theft by a servant from a guest's coat,[33] and the loss of a car by fire,[34] and a stable keeper for fright to a horse by explosion[35] or for its death.[36]

Innkeepers

The strict liability attaches only where the property is within the inn buildings or their precincts,[37] including yards,[38] car parks[39] and garages,[40] where the innkeeper has placed or invited his guest to put his property there. At common law the liability extended to the goods of travellers even stopping temporarily,[41] but the statutory liability of the hotel proprietor[42] is now only towards guests for whom sleeping accommodation has been booked. At common law edictal liability could not be limited by notice[43] nor by warning.

Hotel Proprietors Act

The strict liability of innkeepers has been limited in certain cases by the Hotel Proprietors Act, 1956.[44] Under the Act only a hotel[45] is an inn, and the duties, liabilities and rights formerly attaching to an innkeeper now attach to the proprietor of a hotel and not to any other person.[46] The proprietor is, as an innkeeper, under the like liability, if any, to make good to any guest any damage to property as he would be under to make good loss thereof.[47] Without prejudice to any other liability incurred by him with respect to property brought to the hotel,[48] the proprietor is not liable as an innkeeper to make good any loss of or damage to such property except where (a) sleeping accom-

---

[31] *Burns* v. *Royal Hotel (St. Andrews)*, 1956 S.C. 463; 1958 S.C. 354.
[32] *Williamson* v. *White*, 21 June 1810, F.C.; *Meikle* v. *Skelly*, 16 Feb. 1813, F.C.
[33] *McPherson* v. *Christie* (1841) 3 D. 930.
[34] *Burns* v. *Royal Hotel (St. Andrews)*, 1958 S.C. 354.
[35] *Laing* v. *Darling* (1850) 12 D. 1279.
[36] *Hay* v. *Wordsworth*, 13 Feb. 1801, F.C.; *Hagart* v. *Inglis* (1832) 10 S. 506; *Mustard, supra.*
[37] *White* v. *Crocket* (1661) Mor. 9233; *Williams* v. *Linnitt* [1951] 1 K.B. 565; *Burns* v. *Royal Hotel (St. Andrews)*, 1958 S.C. 354.
[38] *Davies* v. *Clarke* (1953) 103 L.J. 141.
[39] *Gee, Walker & Slater, Ltd.* v. *Friary Hotel* (1949) 66 T.L.R. (Pr. 1) 59; *Williams, supra*; *Watson* v. *People's Refreshment House Assocn.* [1952] 1 K.B. 318.
[40] *Burns, supra.*
[41] *Williams, supra.*
[42] Hotel Proprietors Act, 1956, *infra.*
[43] *Burns* v. *Royal Hotel (St. Andrews)*, 1956 S.C. 463, 466.
[44] Replacing Innkeepers Liability Act, 1863.
[45] Defined, S. 1(3).
[46] S. 1(1); i.e. the Edict now applies only to keepers of 'hotels', as defined in S. 1(3), and not to public houses, restaurants, boarding-houses, etc., the keepers of which are liable only for negligence.
[47] S. 1(2).
[48] e.g. under contract, or for negligence.

modation had been engaged; and (b) loss or damage occurred between the midnight before and the midnight after the traveller was a guest.[49] The proprietor is not as innkeeper liable to make good to any guest any loss of or damage to, or have any lien on, any vehicle or property therein, or any horse or other live animal or its harness or other equipment.[50]

Where the proprietor is liable as an innkeeper for loss or damage, his liability to any one guest is not to exceed £50 in respect of any one article, or £100 in aggregate,[51] except where (a) the property was lost, stolen or damaged through the default, neglect or wilful act of the proprietor or some servant of his;[52] or (b) it was deposited expressly for safe custody[53] and, if so required, in a container fastened or sealed by the depositor;[54] or (c) either the property was offered for deposit and refused, or the guest wished to offer it but through the proprietor's fault was unable to do so.[55] The proprietor is entitled to the protection of S. 2(3) only if, when the property was brought to the hotel, a copy of the notice set out in the Schedule to the Act was conspicuously displayed where it could conveniently be read by his guests at or near the reception office or desk, failing which, at or near the main entrance to the hotel.[56] A notice exhibited only in a bedroom and not seen till after the guest was accepted is not part of the contract.[57] The limitations of Ss. 2(1) and (2) leave open the possibility of the innkeeper's liability for deliberate or negligent loss or injury. If the notice provided for in S. 2(3) is not exhibited or exhibited misprinted,[58] the hotel proprietor is liable as an innkeeper under the Edict without financial limit. A notice in a bedroom that valuables should be deposited at the office is not evidence of a special contract.[59] A notice wholly disclaiming liability is probably ineffective.[60]

[49] S. 2(1); hence, there is no edictal liability to guests stopping for a meal only.
[50] S. 2(2). This alters such cases as *Williams* v. *Linnitt* [1951] 1 K.B. 318. On lien see *Bermans & Nathans* v. *Weibye* 1981 S.L.T. 181.
[51] There is no limit in the case of proprietors of premises not 'hotels' under the Act, and therefore not 'inns'.
[52] S. 2(3)(a). The onus of proof is on the guest; see *Whitehouse, infra; Behrens* v. *Grenville Hotels (Bude) Ltd.* (1925) 69 Sol. Jo. 346; see also *Medawar* v. *Grand Hotel Co.* [1891] 2 Q.B. 11; *Bonham Carter* v. *Hyde Park Hotel Ltd.* (1948) 64 T.L.R. 177; *Olley* v. *Marlborough Court* [1949] 1 K.B. 532; *Kott and Kott* v. *Gordon Hotels* [1968] 2 Lloyd's Rep. 228.
[53] In *Whitehouse* v. *Pickett*, 1908 S.C. (H.L.) 31, it was held that mere deposit of a bag in the office was not a deposit expressly for safe custody. See also *Moss* v. *Russell* (1884) 1 T.L.R. 13; *O'Connor* v. *Grand International Hotel Co.* [1898] 2 I.R. 92.
[54] S. 2(3)(b).
[55] S. 2(3)(c).
[56] S. 2(3), proviso; see *Shacklock* v. *Ethorpe* [1937] 4 All E.R. 672.
[57] *Olley, supra.*
[58] *Spice* v. *Bacon* (1877) 2 Ex. D. 463.
[59] *Huntly* v. *Bedford Hotel Co., Ltd.* (1891) 56 J.P. 53.
[60] *Williams* v. *Linnitt* [1951] 1 K.B. 318.

Stable keepers

Strict liability under the Edict continues to apply to stable keepers.[61]

Other categories of deposit

Sequestration of moveables is a kind of deposit whereby a subject claimed by two or more persons is deposited with a neutral person pending a decision on who has best right to it. It may be voluntary, or judicial, under order of a court. Such sequestration is not gratuitous, especially if judicial, the depositary being entitled to a fee for his trouble and being liable for reasonable care only.[62]

Consignation of money is the species of deposit by which money in dispute is deposited in the hands of a neutral person to be delivered to the claimant to whom it is ultimately adjudged.[63] It may be voluntary,[64] or judicial,[65] and is commonly done by lodging money in bank on deposit receipt. The consignee must keep the sum consigned in safety and is not liable for interest, but banks pay interest on money consigned on deposit receipt.

The institutional writers treat trust also as a species of deposit but it is more a relation *sui generis*.[66]

CUSTODY—*LOCATIO CUSTODIAE*

By this contract, which is a special instance of *locatio operis faciendi*, one party lets to another the task, for a fee, of taking care and custody of moveable property for a time.[67] It covers not only contracts expressly for warehousing or storage,[68] and probably for parking a car in a garage or parking place for which a charge is made, but every contract of *locatio operis faciendi*, such as of repair, which entails that the subject has to be left in the contractor's possession and care, is presumed to include as an inherent element a contract of *locatio custodiae*,[69] and other contracts such as for accommodation at premises not being a hotel or inn, may include a *locatio custodiae*.[70] The

[61] *Mustard* v. *Paterson*, 1923 S.C. 142.
[62] Ersk. III, 1, 30, Bell, *Prin.* §214. Sequestration in bankruptcy is dealt with in Ch. 10.1.
[63] Ersk. III, 1, 31; Bell, *Prin.* §215.
[64] e.g. *Calder* v. *Stevens* (1871) 9 M. 1074.
[65] It may be ordered as a condition of suspending diligence.
[66] Ersk. III, 1, 32. See Chs. 6.1–6.5.
[67] Dig. XIX, 2; 40; Stair I, 13, 1–2; Ersk. III, 1, 26; Bell, *Comm.* I, 488; *Prin.* §155.
[68] Including left-luggage offices.
[69] *Sinclair* v. *Juner*, 1952 S.C. 35; *Forbes* v. *Aberdeen Motors Ltd.*, 1965 S.C. 193; *Verrico* v. *Hughes*, 1980 S.L.T. 175; cf. *Cochran* v. *Leckie's Tr.* (1906) 8 F. 975; *Uprichard* v. *Dickson*, 1981 S.L.T. (Sh. Ct.) 5.
[70] cf. *Martin* v. *L.C.C.* [1947] K.B. 628.

contract differs from deposit in being onerous, not gratuitous, and consequently the duty of care incumbent on the custodier is higher than on the gratuitous depositary. In some cases it is not clear whether the contract was deposit or *locatio custodiae*.[71]

The contract may be made orally and proved *prout de jure*, but is frequently embodied in a document which seeks to limit or exclude liability for loss or damage.[72]

The property in the goods remains with the owner, and he entrusts only possession to the custodier. The risk of damage or accident is with the owner; the custodier is liable for neglect or any actionable fault, but not for pure accident without fault.[73]

Duty of owner (hirer of custody of goods)

The duty of the owner is to deliver possession of the agreed goods at the custodier's place of custody or other receiving point. He probably warrants that the goods deposited are not, to his knowledge, dangerous or harmful to the custodier, his servants, or other goods in the latter's store, and will be liable if his goods do injury or damage.[74] He is bound to pay the agreed charge for custody.[75] He must also uplift the goods deposited before or at the end of the agreed period of deposit, or on reasonable request.

Duty of custodier (lessor of custody)

The custodier is bound to take the goods into his custody and store them in a place reasonably safe, secure and suitable for goods of that kind.[76] He must take reasonable care of the goods, such as a careful man would take of his own property,[77] and must show greater diligence than is demanded of the gratuitous depositary; his engagement is for safe-keeping of the goods;[78] he must inspect periodically for signs of damage,[79] and he will be liable for deterioration brought about by improper method of storing,[80] or for damage caused by exposing the goods to risk.[81] The liability extends to articles contained in the goods

[71] e.g. in *Ballingall* v. *Dundee Ice Co.*, 1924 S.C. 238, 243, Lord Anderson says the case is one of deposit, but the defenders were entitled to charge for storage.
[72] *Ballingall, supra.*
[73] *Sutherland* v. *Hutton* (1896) 23 R. 718, 722; *Forbes* v. *Aberdeen Motors*, 1965 S.C. 193.
[74] cf. *Cramb* v. *Caledonian Ry.* (1892) 19 R. 1054.
[75] As to liability see *Wilson's Tr.* v. *Fraser's Tr.* (1887) 14 R. 504.
[76] cf. *Glebe Sugar Co.* v. *Paterson* (1900) 2 F. 615.
[77] *Handon* v. *Caledonian Ry.* (1880) 7 R. 966, 971; *Lyons* v. *Caledonian Ry.*, 1909 S.C. 1185, 1193; *Copland* v. *Brogan*, 1916 S.C. 277; *Ballingall, supra: Sinclair* v. *Juner*, 1952 S.C. 35, 43.
[78] Bell, *Prin.* §155; *Searle* v. *Laverick* (1874) L.R. 9 Q.B. 122; *Brabant* v. *The King* [1895] A.C. 632; *Forbes* v. *Aberdeen Motors*, 1965 S.C. 193.
[79] *Allan & Poynter* v. *Williamson* (1870) 7 S.L.R. 214.
[80] *Snodgrass* v. *Ritchie & Lamberton* (1890) 17 R. 712.
[81] *Laing* v. *Darling* (1850) 12 D. 1279; *Robertson* v. *Connolly* (1851) 13 D. 779; (1852) 14 D. 315; *McLean* v. *Warnock* (1883) 10 R. 1052; *Sutherland* v. *Hutton* (1896) 23 R. 718.

stored, such as the contents of a van.[82] His liability is for fault only, which may be inferred from the circumstances and the absence of adequate explanation by the custodier. He is not liable for theft by a third party, nor for loss by purely accidental fire, or other *damnum fatale*.[83] Fire unexplained is not *damnum fatale*.[84] The contract implies the personal care of the custodier and his servants to prevent injuries to the property;[85] the custodier is liable for damage done by his servant, if the latter were acting in the course of his employment, or had been entrusted with the responsibility of custody.[86] He may insure the goods in which case if they are lost by a risk insured against, the owner has a *jus quaesitum tertio* to the insurance money.[87] It is probably, in at least some cases, a breach of contract to transfer or delegate the custody to a third party.[88] It is certainly a breach of contract to allow a third party to remove the goods deposited, or articles from those goods, without the owner's authority.[89]

He must redeliver the goods on request, without unreasonable delay,[90] or when the period of custody has elapsed. If there is no stipulation as to the duration of the custody, the custodier is not entitled to insist on their being removed at his pleasure without showing reasonable cause therefor.[91] If the custodier cannot redeliver the goods he must compensate for their loss unless he can adduce an explanation relieving him from liability, such as theft from outside, or accidental fire.[92] If he has misdelivered the goods to the wrong person, or a person not authorized by the owner, the custodier is liable for the value.[93]

Exemptions from liability

The contract frequently contains terms exempting the custodier from liability for loss or damage in stated, or in all, circumstances. Such a term, if incorporated in the contract, may be effective,[94] but

---

[82] *Tognini Bros.* v. *Dick Bros., Ltd.*, 1968 S.L.T. (Sh. Ct.) 87.
[83] *Sinclair* v. *Juner*, 1952 S.C. 35; contrast *Macrae* v. *K. & I. Ltd.*, 1962 S.L.T. (Notes) 90.
[84] *Sinclair, supra.*
[85] Bell, *supra; Central Motors* v. *Cessnock Garage Co.*, 1925 S.C. 796.
[86] *Coupé Co.* v. *Maddick* [1891] 2 Q.B. 413; *Central Motors, supra.*
[87] *Cochrane* v. *Leckie's Tr.* (1906) 8 F. 975.
[88] *Edwards* v. *Newland* [1950] 1 All E.R. 1072; cf. *Central Motors, supra.*
[89] *Alexander* v. *Ry. Executive* [1951] 2 K.B. 882.
[90] *Stallard* v. *G.W. Ry.* (1862) 2 B. & S. 419; *Shaw* v. *Symmons* [1917] 1 K.B. 799. See also *Craig* v. *Thomson* (1847) 9 D. 409.
[91] *Whyte* v. *Millar & Young* (1881) 8 R. 432.
[92] *Copland* v. *Brogan*, 1916 S.C. 277; *Sinclair* v. *Juner*, 1952 S.C. 35, 47.
[93] cf. *Smith* v. *Allan and Poynter* (1859) 22 D. 208.
[94] e.g. *Van Toll* v. *S.E. Ry.* (1862) 12 C.B. (N.S.) 75; *Harris* v. *G.W. Ry.* (1876) 1 Q.B.D. 513; *Pratt* v. *S.E. Ry.* [1897] 1 Q.B. 718; *Lyons* v. *Caledonian Ry.*, 1909 S.C. 1185; *Gibaud* v. *G.E. Ry.* [1921] 2 K.B. 426; *Rutter* v. *Palmer* [1922] 2 K.B. 87; *Ballingall* v. *Dundee Ice Co.*, 1924 S.C. 238; *Alderslade* v. *Hendon Laundry* [1945] 1 K.B. 189.

may be ineffective, as where the custodier has delegated his function without authority,[95] or the loss might have occurred in a way not excepted,[96] or the custodier has acted in breach of contract.[97]

Liability under praetorian edict

The more stringent liability of the praetorian edict *nautae, caupones, stabularii* applies to cases of onerous deposit of goods, within the classes of cases to which the edictal provisions applied in Scots law,[98] such as lodging horses with a livery-stable keeper,[99] and formerly to leaving vehicles in a hotel garage[1] (but not vehicles in a non-hotel garage),[2] but it apparently does not now apply to hotel garages or car parks by reason of the Hotel Proprietors Act, 1956, Ss. 1(1) and 2(2). The ordinary defences to edictal strict liability, act of the Queen's enemies, Act of God, and inevitable accident apply.[3]

---

[95] *Davies* v. *Collins* [1945] 1 All E.R. 247.

[96] *Woolmer* v. *Delmer Price, Ltd.* [1955] 1 Q.B. 291.

[97] *Handon* v. *Caledonian Ry.* (1880) 7 R. 966; *L.N.W. Ry.* v. *Neilson* [1922] 2 A.C. 263; *Bontex* v. *St. John's Garage* [1944] 1 All E.R. 381; *Alexander* v. *Ry. Executive* [1951] 2 K.B. 882. See also Unfair Contract Terms Act, 1977.

[98] Stair I, 9, 5; I, 13, 2; Bankt. I, 17, 1; Ersk. III, 1, 28; *Prin.* III, 1, 11; Bell, *Comm.* I, 498; *Prin.* §236.

[99] *Mustard* v. *Paterson*, 1923 S.C. 142.

[1] *Burns* v. *Royal Hotel (St. Andrews) Ltd.*, 1956 S.C. 463; 1958 S.C. 354.

[2] *Central Motors* v. *Cessnock Garage Co.*, 1925 S.C. 796; *Sinclair* v. *Juner*, 1952 S.C. 35.

[3] *Mustard, supra*, 148; cf. *McDonell* v. *Ettles*, 15 Dec. 1809, F.C.

CHAPTER 5.29

TEMPORARY TRANSFER OF MOVEABLES— LETTING ON HIRE OF MOVEABLES—*LOCATIO REI*

Hiring or location is the mutual consensual contract whereby one person, the lesser or *locator*, lets out to another, the hirer or *conductor*, for a certain time or a certain purpose, a moveable object, or his services, or a piece of work to be done, or the task of keeping custody of a thing, or of transporting it, for a monetary consideration variously called the hire or rent, the wages or salary, or the fee, price or freight, in these different contexts. The principles of the Scots law are based on the contract of *locatio conductio* of the Roman law.[1] Hiring is distinguishable into various branches, namely, hiring of moveables (*locatio rei*),[2] hiring of service (*locatio operarum*),[3] hiring of some services or the performance of work and labour (*locatio operis faciendi*),[4] hiring of care and custody (*locatio custodiae*)[5] and hiring of carriage (*locatio operis mercium vehendarum*).[6] The hiring of heritage falls under the head of lease.[7]

HIRING OF MOVEABLES—*LOCATIO REI*

The essentials are the object, the rate of hire, and the time or occasion for which the subject is let and hired.

The contract may be constituted in any form and proved *prout de jure*.[8] The terms will be such as may be agreed; failing express agreement they will be supplied by legal implication, including terms of which adequate notice had regularly been given in previous contracts between the parties.[9]

[1] Stair I, 15, 1; Bankt. I, 20, 1; Ersk. III, 3, 14; Bell, *Comm.* I, 275; I, 481; *Prin.* §133–93.
[2] Ch. 5.29.
[3] Ch. 4.15.
[4] Ch. 4.16.
[5] Ch. 5.28.
[6] Chs. 4.17–4.19. The last two heads are sometimes regarded as special cases of the third and are certainly analogous thereto.
[7] Ch. 5.15.
[8] Bell, *Prin.* §136; *Grayston Plant* v. *Plean Precast*, 1976 S.C. 206.
[9] *Grayston, supra.*

Object of hiring

The object may be any corporeal moveable, not being a fungible, either a specific thing, or a thing of a particular kind or class. If a specific thing is to be let and perishes without the fault of either party before the date of the hiring, the contract is frustrated;[10] but not so if a thing of a class be let: *genus nunquam perit*.

Purpose of hiring

The purpose of hiring is the grant to the hirer of a temporary right of possession and use of a thing for purposes defined in the contract, or for the obvious purposes for which that kind of thing would normally be used. To hire a thing for an unusual purpose not disclosed to the lessor, particularly if it involves extra stress or danger, is a material breach of contract.

The hire

The hire or sum charged must be fixed by the contract or ascertainable by a standard there fixed.

Duration of hiring

The duration may be fixed by the contract, or be indefinite, subject to termination by reasonable notice by either party.

Obligations of lessor

The lessor undertakes to give the hirer possession and full use of the thing let to him, and, if he fails to do so, at the due date, is liable for non-delivery. He must maintain the hirer in possession for the agreed time, or a reasonable time, and is liable if the hirer is deprived of, or cannot obtain, possession by an act or omission attributable to the lessor.[11] If let by description there is probably an implied term that the thing supplied corresponds with the description.[12] The lessor warrants the fitness of the thing let for the purpose for which it was let,[13] and is liable if harm is caused by a known fault or one which reasonable care and examination would have diclosed,[14] or if it is caused by a danger of which he knew but did not give warning.[15] He does not, in general, give

[10] Ersk. III, 3, 15.
[11] Ersk. III, 3, 15; Bell, *Prin.* §135, 141.
[12] cf. *Astley Industrial Trust* v. *Grimley* [1963] 2 All E.R. 33.
[13] Ersk. III, 3, 15; Bell, *Prin.* §141; *Wilson* v. *Norris*, 10 Mar. 1810, F.C.; cf. *Oliver* v. *Saddler*, 1928 S.C. 608, 615; *Hadley* v. *Droitwich Construction Co.* [1967] 3 All E.R. 911.
[14] *Lyon* v. *Lamb* (1838) 16 S. 1188; *Wilson* v. *Wordie* (1905) 7 F. 927. cf. *Fowler* v. *Lock* (1872) L.R. 7 C.P. 272; *Hyman* v. *Nye* (1881) 6 Q.B.D. 685; *Chapleton* v. *Barry U.D.C.* [1940] 1 K.B. 532; *Read* v. *Dean* [1949] 1 K.B. 188; *White* v. *Warwick* [1953] 2 All E.R. 1021.
[15] *Coughlin* v. *Gillison* [1899] 1 Q.B. 145.

any warranty against latent defects.[16] Liability for defects may be excluded by an appropriately phrased clause in the contract.[17]

Property and risk

The property remains in the lessor and the risk is with him, unless the thing should perish or be damaged by the fault of the hirer.[18] He is liable for all major repairs and maintenance, and for any exceptional outlays incurred thereon by the hirer, provided they were necessary, not due to the fault of the hirer, and notice is given by the hirer as soon as reasonably possible.[19] But by contract or custom the hirer may be liable for ordinary running costs. Both parties are discharged if the thing let perishes by accident, the loss falling on the lessor. Things hired by a tenant fall under the landlord's hypothec,[20] unless the landlord has been informed that they are excluded,[21] but do not pass to the trustee on the hirer's bankruptcy.

Obligations of hirer

The hirer must take possession of the thing let, or will be liable in damages for non-acceptance. He may not use the thing hired save for the purpose disclosed, or for the normal purpose of the hire of a thing of that kind.[22] He must take reasonable care of the thing, such as a diligent and prudent man takes of his own property,[23] and if it is damaged or perishes while in his possession he must produce at least prima facie evidence that the cause was one for which he was not responsible, failing which he will be liable for the diminution in value of the thing.[24] Thus hirers have been held liable for loss or damage caused by excessive use and neglect,[25] overloading the thing hired,[26] using it in a way involving additional risk and forbidden by the contract,[27] failing to take precautions against injury[28] and failing to

[16] Bell, *Prin.* §141.
[17] *Chapelton, supra.*
[18] *Jacksons v. Constructors John Brown, Ltd.,* 1965 S.L.T. 37.
[19] Bell, *Comm.* I, 482; *Prin.* §145; *Johnston v. Rankin* (1687) Mor. 10080.
[20] *Penson v. Robertson,* 6 June 1820, F.C.; *Nelmes v. Ewing* (1884) 11 R. 193; *Bell v. Andrews* (1885) 12 R. 961; *McIntosh v. Potts* (1905) 7 F. 765; *Edinburgh Albert Buildings Co. v. General Guarantee Corpn.,* 1917 S.C. 239; *Dundee Corpn. v. Marr,* 1971 S.C. 96.
[21] *Jaffray v. Carrick* (1836) 15 S. 43; *Dundee Corpn., supra.*
[22] Bell, *Prin.* §143.
[23] Bell, *Prin.* §145; cf. *Campbell v. Kennedy* (1828) 6 S. 806.
[24] *Binny v. Veaux* (1679) Mor. 10079; *Robertson v. Ogle,* 23 June 1809, F.C.; *Marquis v. Ritchie* (1823) 2 S. 386; *Pyper v. Thomson* (1843) 5 D. 498; *Smith v. Melvin* (1845) 8 D. 264; *Pullars v. Walker* (1858) 20 D. 1238; *Hinshaw v. Adam* (1870) 8 M. 933; *Wilson v. Orr* (1879) 7 R. 266; *Seton v. Paterson* (1880) 8 R. 236; *McLean v. Warnock* (1883) 10 R. 1052. cf. *Grayston Plant Ltd. v. Plean Precast Ltd.* 1976 S.C. 206.
[25] *Campbell, supra.*
[26] *Pullars, supra.*
[27] *Seton, supra.*
[28] *Davidson* (1749) Mor. 10081; *McLean v. Warnock* (1883) 10 R. 1052.

take steps, after theft, to have the stolen property traced.[29] The hirer
must also see to everyday maintenance and repair,[30] with a right of
recourse against the lessor for the expense of extraordinary repairs.

The hirer is not responsible for the fault of persons, others than his
own servants, to whom he properly entrusts the thing,[31] nor for loss
due to natural causes, *damnum fatale*, pure accident, theft,[32] or other
cause for which he is not responsible, nor for ordinary depreciation or
fair wear and tear. He is not obliged to examine the thing hired for
latent defects, though he should look for obvious defects.[33]

He must also pay the hire agreed, or, at all events, a reasonable sum
by way of hire. If he fails, he may be sued and if the failure be continued
the lessor may rescind the contract and claim redelivery of the thing let.

At the end of the period of hire or, if no time be fixed, on demand,
the hirer must restore the thing hired, and if he cannot or will not, is
liable to pay the value thereof.[34] If the thing is accidentally destroyed or
perishes during the hire the contract is terminated; if it is accidentally
damaged without his fault the hirer may terminate the contract, or
claim an abatement from the hire.[35]

The hirer has no ostensible authority to sell or pledge the thing
hired,[36] and he can confer no better title than he himself has by
purported sale or pledge,[37] nor may he, unless contractually permitted
sub-let the thing hired or assign the hiring or subject it to a third party's
claim of lien for the cost of repairs.[38] But things hired by a tenant fall
under the landlord's hypothec for rent.[39]

Liability to third parties

Harm done to a third party by the hirer or his servants using the
thing negligently prima facie imposes liability on the hirer only,[40] but if
an employee of the lessor is hired along with a thing and harm is done,
the lessor is liable unless he can show that control has been so transferred to the hirer as to make the lessor's employee *pro hac vice* employee

[29] cf. *Coldman* v. *Hill* [1919] 1 K.B. 443.
[30] *Tappenden* v. *Artus* [1963] 3 All E.R. 213.
[31] *Smith* v. *Melvin* (1845) 8 D. 264.
[32] *Trotter* v. *Buchanan* (1688) Mor. 10080.
[33] *Sullivan* v. *Gallagher & Craig*, 1959 S.C. 243.
[34] Bell, *Prin.* §135; *Trotter* v. *Buchanan* (1688) Mor. 10080; *McPherson* v. *Sutherland* (1791)
Hume 296; *Shaw* v. *Donaldson* (1792) Hume 297; *Gardners* v. *McDonald* (1792) Hume 299;
Shaw v. *Symmons* [1917] 1 K.B. 799.
[35] Bell, *Prin.* §141; *Muir* v. *McIntyre* (1887) 14 R. 470.
[36] *Jaffray* v. *Carrick* (1836) 15 S. 43. Such conduct is a spuilzie.
[37] *Mitchell* v. *Heys* (1894) 21 R. 600, 610.
[38] *Lamonby* v. *Foulds*, 1928 S.C. 89, 95; see also *Albermarle Supply Co.* v. *Hind* [1928] 1 K.B.
307.
[39] *Dundee Corpn.* v. *Marr*, 1971 S.C. 96.
[40] *Smith* v. *Bailey* [1891] 2 Q.B. 403; see also Employer's Liability (Defecticve Equipment)
Act, 1969.

of the hirer.[41] The lessor, moreover, is liable if the harm to the third party has arisen from a defect in the thing let when reasonable inspection and maintenance by him would have revealed and remedied the defect.[42] The contract of hiring may provide for recourse against the lessor if the hirer incurs liability in stated circumstances.

Letting on hire—regulated agreements

An agreement for the letting of goods on hire to a hirer is a consumer hire agreement and regulated by the Consumer Credit Act, 1974, if it (a) is not a hire-purchase agreement, and (b) is capable of subsisting for more than three months, and (c) provides for payments capable in total of not exceeding £5000, unless it is an exempt agreement under S. 16.[43] A person carrying on a consumer hire business must be licensed by the Director-General of Fair Trading.[44] Restrictions are imposed on advertising and canvassing.[45] Specified information may have to be disclosed and the form and contents of documents are regulated.[46] The agreement must be signed in the prescribed manner and a copy given to the hirer and a copy given him when it becomes an executed agreement, together with a notice of cancellation rights.[47] An improperly executed agreement is enforceable only on order of the court.[48] Agreements may be cancelled if the antecedent negotiations included oral representations, unless the agreement was signed by the hirer at business premises,[49] by notice, in which case money is repayable and goods returnable.[50] Part V (Ss. 55–74) does not, except S. 56, apply to a non-commercial agreement.[51]

The owner may not enforce an agreement in stated ways except after giving the hirer at least seven days' notice.[52] If requested he must give the hirer information showing the sum unpaid, and the hirer must give the owner information where the goods are.[53] Provision is made for appropriation of payments.[54] An agreement may not be varied without notice.[55] The owner may not treat the hirer's death as a default.[56]

The owner may not take action on default without serving a default notice,[57] nor enter premises to take possession of goods, save by order of a court.[58]

---

[41] *Anderson v. Glasgow Tramways Co.* (1893) 21 R. 318; *Cairns v. C.N.T.* (1898) 25 R. 1021; *Malley v. L.M.S. Ry.*, 1944 S.C. 129; *Mersey Docks v. Coggins & Griffiths* [1947] A.C. 1.
[42] *Sullivan v. Gallagher & Craig*, 1959 S.C.243; *Hadley v. Droitwich Construction Co.* [1967] 3 All E.R. 911.
[43] Consumer Credit Act, 1974, S. 15. See also Ch. 4.12, *supra*.
[44] Ss. 21–42.   [45] Ss. 43–54.   [46] Ss. 55–60.
[47] Ss. 61–4.   [48] S. 65.   [49] Ss. 67–9.
[50] Ss. 70–3.   [51] S. 74.   [52] S. 76.
[53] Ss. 79–80.   [54] S. 81.   [55] S. 82.
[56] Ss. 86–7.   [57] Ss. 87–9.   [58] S. 92.

In non-default cases the owner may terminate only after giving the hirer at least seven days' notice.[59] The hirer may in certain cases terminate at the end of at least eighteen months by giving notice, usually of three months.[60]

There are restrictions on taking or negotiating negotiable instruments in discharge of sums payable.[61]

It is forbidden to contract out of the Act.[62]

Linked transactions

Linked transactions[63] are transactions by a hirer with a third party connected with the consumer hire agreement. Withdrawal from a prospective regulated agreement operates as withdrawal from a linked transaction;[64] cancellation has a similar effect,[65] and makes money repayable or cease to be due.[66]

Leasing

Increasingly expensive equipment, plant and machinery, aircraft, vehicles, computers and office equipment, and other expensive things which depreciate rapidly are hired from leasing companies rather than bought or acquired on hire-purchase.[67] Certain companies specialize in this kind of supply and complicated forms of contracts have been devised to regulate the relations of parties.[68] The contract usually runs for several years and may confer an option to purchase at the end of the lease, being then hardly distinguishable from hire-purchase. Equipment leasing contracts will normally be outside the financial limits of regulated consumer hire and the right to terminate is excluded from most such cases by S. 101(7).

---

[59] S. 99.
[60] Ss. 100–3.
[61] Ss. 124–6.
[62] S. 174.
[63] Defined, S. 19.
[64] Ss. 57, 69.
[65] S. 69.
[66] S. 70.
[67] There are tax advantages in leasing rather than acquiring outright.
[68] There are leasing brokers who engage in putting lessors in touch with lessees.

TRANSFER OF CORPOREAL MOVEABLE OBJECTS IN SECURITY

One person may acquire rights over corporeal moveable property belonging to another in security of the performance by that other of some obligation, such as payment of money, either by express contract or by operation of law.

The general principle of Scots law is that no security right conferring any real right over the moveables themselves can be created without transfer to the security-holder of possession, actual, constructive or symbolical, of the property over which the right exists,[1] but there are important exceptions where a right in security may exist without possession.

SECURITY RIGHTS REQUIRING POSSESSION

PLEDGE

Pledge[2] is the real contract whereby the possessor[3] of corporeal moveables transfers them to another to be held in security for payment or performance of some obligation due, and redelivery thereafter. The contract is constituted by actual delivery following on agreement (which by itself creates only a personal obligation to deliver in security) and the terms and conditions of the contract may be proved by parole evidence. The contract is applicable only to corporeal moveables and delivery to the pledgee is essential, bare agreement conferring only a

---

[1] e.g. *MacKinnon* v. *Nanson* (1868) 6 M. 974; *Stiven* v. *Scott* (1871) 9 M. 923; *Watson's Tr.* v. *Cowan* (1878) 15 S.L.R. 422; *Heritable Securities Investment Assocn.* v. *Wingate's Tr.* (1880) 7 R. 1094; *Robertson* v. *McIntyre* (1882) 9 R. 772; *Clark* v. *West Calder Oil Co.* (1882) 9 R. 1017; *Ewart* v. *Hogg* (1893) 1 S.L.T. 63; *Jones & Co.'s Tr.* v. *Allan* (1901) 4 F. 374; See also *Newbigging* v. *Ritchie's Tr.*, 1930 S.C. 273.

[2] D. 20, 1; Stair I, 13, 11; Ersk. III, 1, 33; *Prin.* III, 1, 13; Bell, *Comm.* I, 258; II, 19; *Prin.* §§203, 1363.

[3] A person in lawful possession of goods with the owner's consent may pledge them: *Brown* v. *Marr* (1880) 7 R. 427; *Martinez y Gomez* v. *Allison* (1890) 17 R. 332; *Bryce* v. *Ehrmann* (1904) 7 F. 5. A mercantile agent in possession of goods, or of the documents of title to goods may pledge them to the same effect as if he were expressly authorized to do so: Factors Act, 1889, S. 2, applied by Factors (Sc.) Act, 1890.

personal right ineffectual against the pledgor's other creditors.[4] Fictitious transactions designed to create security without delivery of possession are ineffectual,[5] though the same result can sometimes be achieved by other means.[6]

The requisite delivery may be actual, symbolical or constructive.[7] Actual delivery is effected by physical transfer of the thing pledged or a complete transfer of the control of possession, as by handing over the keys of a store containing the articles pledged.[8] It is doubtful if any security can be created by setting aside goods within premises under the pledgor's control.[9] It is not delivery to mark or label goods with the pledgee's name.[10]

Symbolical delivery is effected by endorsing and transferring a document of title to goods, such as a bill of lading, as representing the goods shipped, but it is questionable whether this is effective where the goods are not ascertained or distinguished from other similar goods in the cargo.[11] The holder in security of a bill of lading loses his security if he permits actual delivery of the goods to a third party without payment or an undertaking to pay the security-holder.[12] In other cases symbolical delivery is ineffectual.[13]

Constructive delivery is effected by endorsing in favour of the pledgee a storekeeper's receipt or warehouse delivery order and intimating the transfer to the store or warehouse keeper[14] so that he henceforth holds the goods for the pledgee.[15] For the right to be

---

[4] cf. *Dublin City Distillery* v. *Doherty* [1914] A.C. 823.

[5] *Paul* v. *Cuthbertson* (1840) 2 D. 1286; *Roberts* v. *Wallace* (1842) 5 D. 6; *Benton* v. *Craig* (1864) 2 M. 1365; *Mackinnon* v. *Max Nanson & Co.* (1868) 6 M. 974; *Orr's Tr.* v. *Tullis* (1870) 8 M. 936; *Stiven* v. *Scott & Simson* (1871) 9 M. 923; *Watson's Tr.* v. *Cowan* (1878) 15 S.L.R. 422; *Heritable Securities Investment Assocn.* v. *Wingate's Tr.* (1880) 7 R. 1094; *Clark* v. *West Calder Oil Co.* (1882) 9 R. 1017; *Ewart* v. *Hogg* (1893) 1 S.L.T. 63; *Jones's Tr.* v. *Allan* (1901) 4 F. 374; *Newbigging* v. *Ritchie's Tr.,* 1930 S.C. 273; *Scottish Transit Trust* v. *Scottish Land Cultivators,* 1955 S.C. 254; *G. and C. Finance Corpn.* v. *Brown,* 1961 S.L.T. 408. But see *Duncanson* v. *Jefferis' Tr.* (1881) 8 R. 563; *Miller* v. *Muirhead* (1894) 21 R. 658.

[6] *Union Bank* v. *Mackenzie* (1865) 3 M. 765; *Duncanson, supra; Darling* v. *Wilson's Tr.* (1887) 15 R. 180.

[7] *Moore* v. *Gledden* (1869) 7 M. 1016.

[8] *West Lothian Oil Co.* v. *Mair* (1892) 20 R. 64; contrast *Pattison's Trs.* v. *Liston* (1893) 20 R. 806.

[9] *Gibson* v. *Forbes* (1833) 11 S. 916; *Boak* v. *Megget* (1844) 6 D. 662; but see *Mathison* v. *Alison* (1854) 17 D. 274.

[10] *Smith* v. *Allan & Poynter* (1859) 22 D. 208; *Orr* v. *Tullis* (1870) 8 M. 936.

[11] *Hayman* v. *McLintock,* 1907 S.C. 936, 952.

[12] *Tod* v. *Merchant Banking Co. of London* (1883) 10 R. 1009.

[13] *Fraser* v. *Frisby* (1830) 8 S. 982; *Roberts, supra.*

[14] Bell, *Comm.* I, 198; *Connal* v. *Loder|*(1868) 6 M.|1095; *Pochin* v. *Robinow* (1869) 7 M. 622; *Vickers* v. *Hertz* (1871) 9 M. (H.L.) 65; *Distillers Co.* v. *Russell's Tr.* (1889) 16 R. 479; *Price & Pierce* v. *Bank of Scotland,* 1912 S.C. (H.L.) 19. It is not enough merely to intimate to such a person as an excise officer: *Rhind's Tr.* v. *Robertson & Baxter* (1891) 18 R. 623; and see *Dobell* v. *Neilson* (1904) 7 F. 281.

[15] *Inglis* v. *Robertson & Baxter* (1898) 25 R. (H.L.) 70.

effectual the custodier must be wholly independent of the owner.[16] The goods must also be ascertained and distinguished in the store from others,[17] though if subsequently ascertained by separation, they are held constructively delivered from the time when they are ascertained.[18]

The property in the goods pledged, and the risk, remain with the pledgor.[19] But where documents of title are taken in security the contract is not strictly one of pledge and the right of property passes, subject to an obligation to restore on performance of the obligation due.[20] During his possession the creditor has no right to use the pledged goods, but must take reasonable care of them.[21] If he surrenders possession unless for a specific and limited purpose, such as for repair,[22] his right in security disappears.

Pledge constitutes a security for the whole debt or any part thereof, and is unaffected by payments to account.[23] If deemed of adequate value it is good security for advances made subsequently to the original pledging.[24]

When performance has been made of the obligation to secure which the pledge was made, such as repayment, the pledgee must return the property pledged, in the condition it was in when pledged, apart from natural deterioration, with all natural fruits thereof.

Pledge confers no implied power to sell but it implies a mandate, on failure to fulfil the obligation due at the stipulated time, or on demand, to seek judicial authority, by way of summary application to the sheriff, to sell.[25] The pledgee must account for any surplus on sale after fulfilling the obligations due him and his necessary expenses. The agreement for pledge may include an express power of sale.[26]

Pawnbroking—unregulated agreements

A person carrying on the business of pawnbroking i.e. of making advances of money on the security of moveables pledged with the

[16] *Melrose* v. *Hastie* (1851) 13 D. 880; *Mathison* v. *Alison* (1854) 17 D. 274; *Lindsay* v. *Shield* (1862) 24 D. 821; *Anderson* v. *McCall* (1866) 4 M. 765; *Pochin, supra; Rhind's Tr., supra; Dobell, supra;* cf. *Roy's Tr.* v. *Colvill & Drysdale* (1903) 5 F. 769; but see *Browne* v. *Ainslie* (1893) 21 R. 173.

[17] *Hayman, supra.*

[18] *Black* v. *Incorporation of Bakers* (1867) 6 M. 136; *Pochin, supra.*

[19] Bell, *Prin.* §206.

[20] *Hayman, supra,* 952.

[21] Hume, *Lect.* IV, 8; Bell, *Prin.* §206; *Wolifson* v. *Harrison,* 1977 S.C. 384. Use is not *per se* a material breach of the contract justifying rescission.

[22] Bell, *Comm.* II, 22.

[23] Ersk. II, 12, 67.

[24] *Hamilton* v. *Western Bank* (1856) 19 D. 152; *National Bank* v. *Forbes* (1858) 21 D. 79.

[25] Stair, Ersk., *supra;* Bell, *Prin.* §207; see also *Industrial and General Trust* (1890) 27 S.L.R. 991.

[26] *North-Western Bank* v. *Poynter, Son & Macdonalds* (1894) 22 R. (H.L.) 1.

pawnbroker,[27] must be licensed by the Director-General of Fair Trading.[28] An agreement for loan in excess of £5000 is not regulated by the Consumer Credit Act, 1974.[29]

Pawnbroking—regulated agreements

A transaction with a pawnbroker is a personal credit agreement for unrestricted use credit and if the loan does not exceed £5000 is regulated by the credit provisions of the Consumer Credit Act, 1974.[30] A pawnbroker must be licensed by the Director-General of Fair Trading.[31] Advertisements and canvassing for business are regulated.[32] Regulations may require specified information to be disclosed to the debtor, and govern the form and content of agreements.[33] The agreement must be signed in the prescribed form and copies given, and notices of cancellation rights.[34] Certain agreements may be cancelled within stated periods.[35] The creditor must give at least seven days' notice before enforcing the agreement,[36] and give the debtor information as to the state of debt.[37] Provision is made for appropriation of payments.[38] Notice must be given of variation of the agreement.[39] The creditor may not treat the debtor's death as a default.[40] The creditor may not act on the debtor's breach without serving a default notice.[41]

A person taking an article in pawn under a regulated agreement must give a pawn-receipt in the prescribed form. It is an offence to take an article in pawn from a person known to be, or appearing to be and being, a minor.[42] A pawn is redeemable at any time within six months, and subject thereto for the period fixed by the parties for the duration of the credit secured by the pledge or such longer period as they may agree.[43] The pawn is redeliverable to the bearer of the pawn-ticket on surrender thereof and payment of any amount owing, unless the pawnee knows or has reasonable cause to suspect that the bearer is neither owner of the pawn nor authorized to redeem it. The pawnee is not delictually liable for redelivery to the holder of the ticket, nor for refusing to do so where he knows or suspects that the bearer is not owner or authorized to redeem.[44] A claimant not in possession of the pawn-ticket may redeem on making a statutory declaration or, where the sum advanced did not exceed £15, a statement in writing.[45]

If at the end of the redemption period the pawn has not been redeemed the property passes to the pawnee if the redemption period

---

[27] Until replaced by the Consumer Credit Act, 1974, pawnbroking was regulated in some cases by the Pawnbrokers Acts, 1872–1960. When the repeal is effective cases not regulated by the Consumer Credit Act are regulated by common law, not by the Pawnbrokers Acts.

[28] Consumer Credit Act, 1974, Ss. 21–42. [29] Ss. 8, 9, 11.
[30] Ss. 8, 9, 11. [31] Ss. 21–42. [32] Ss. 43–54.
[33] Ss. 55–60. See Ch. 5.27, supra. [34] Ss. 61–5; see also S. 116.
[35] Ss. 67–74. [36] S. 76. [37] S. 77. [38] S. 81.
[39] S. 82. [40] S. 86. [41] Ss. 87–8. [42] S. 115.
[43] S. 117. [44] S. 118. [45] S. 119.

is six months and the sum secured does not exceed £15, and in other cases is realizable by the pawnee.[46] In the latter case the pawnee may sell it after giving the pawnor, save in cases of sale by auction, notice of intention to sell, the price and any offer so far received. After selling the pawnee must give the pawnor written information as to the sale, its proceeds and expenses. If the sale produces not less than the sum payable for redemption the debt is discharged and the surplus payable to the pawnor; in other cases the debt is reduced to the sum still due.[47] If a pawn is stolen property or obtained by fraud and a person is convicted, or a person refuses without reasonable cause to allow a pawn to be redeemed, the court may order delivery of the pawn to the owner or person entitled thereto.[48]

It is forbidden to contract out of the Act.[49]

Security by use of sale or hire-purchase transactions

The Sale of Goods Act, 1979, by S. 61(4) does not apply to any transaction in the form of a contract of sale which is intended to operate by way of pledge, charge or other security. A sale with such an object is regulated by common law and must be completed by *traditio*. The rule that no security can be created over moveables without delivery of possession cannot be defeated by such a simulate transaction as a sale of property to another party who immediately lets the property back to the sellers on hire or hire-purchase terms, reserving the right to retake possession if there is default in payments of hire.[50] In each case the form is not conclusive but the reality of the transaction must be examined,[51] and a genuine outright sale, followed by hire or hire-purchase back, seems unobjectionable.[52]

Any bona fide hire-purchase contract does, however, in substance provide for security over moveables without possession in that ownership does not pass to the hirer until all payments of rental have been made and the option to purchase exercised and during that time the owner can on default, subject to the Consumer Credit Act, 1974, repossess the goods. The owner in substance has lent the hirer the unpaid balance of the purchase price at interest,[53] as provided in the hire-purchase agreement.

[46] S. 120.
[47] S. 121.
[48] S. 122.
[49] S. 174.
[50] *Rennet* v. *Mathieson* (1903) 5 F. 591; *Hepburn* v. *Law*, 1914 S.C. 918; *Gavin's Tr.* v. *Fraser*, 1920 S.C. 674; *Newbigging* v. *Ritchie's Tr.*, 1930 S.C. 273; *Scottish Transit Trust* v. *Scottish Land Cultivators*, 1955 S.C. 254; *G. & C. Finance Corpn., Ltd.* v. *Brown*, 1961 S.L.T. 408.
[51] *Robertson* v. *Hall's Tr.* (1897) 24 R. 120; *Newbigging, supra; Scottish Transit Trust, supra*.
[52] Bell, *Prin.* §1317; *Newbigging, supra,* 291.
[53] The decision in *Maclean* v. *McCord*, 1965 S.L.T. (Sh. Ct.) 69 is unsupportable.

RETENTION OF PROPERTY

(a) RETENTION OR LIENS

A lien[54] is the right of a creditor to retain moveable property, belonging to the debtor but entrusted to the creditor's possession for some purpose, until the creditor's claims against the debtor are satisfied. It may be created by express contract, in any form, in which case it is hardly distinguishable from pledge, or by implication of law, as an implied term of various kinds of contracts of employment.

A lien may be general or special. A general lien is the right of the creditor to withhold the debtor's goods until the balance due to him under a course of dealing is discharged; a special lien is the right of the creditor to withhold the debtor's goods until the balance due to him under the transaction in the course of which he obtained possession of those goods is discharged.[55] Only exceptionally is a general right of lien recognized in Scots law, and normally only a special lien is admitted.[56]

Requisite possession

Actual possession, not merely constructive or fictional, is essential for lien.[57] The possession must be lawful, not acquired by fraud, under a void contract, by informal diligence, nor by mere accident or mistake.[58] Mere custody, as by an employee, will not suffice to confer a lien.[59] Nor can lien be claimed if there is possession but with a specific appropriation inconsistent with the claims of lien.[60]

The right of lien terminates with the loss of possession, unless possession has been surrendered by error, or lost by fraud,[61] or has

---

[54] The terms retention and lien are confused. Properly speaking the Scottish term is retention (of which there are three varieties: (a) special and general retention (or lien), (b) retention on a property title, and (c) retention of debt), but the English term lien is commonly now used for the right of withholding property and the term retention for the right of withholding money payable to the other party in security of a claim against him. In *Gladstone* v. *McCallum* (1896) 23 R. 783, Lord McLaren distinguishes retention (b) from lien (or retention (a)).

[55] Stair I, 18, 7; Ersk. III, 4, 20; Bell, *Comm.* II, 91; *Prin.* §1411.

[56] *Harper* v. *Faulds* (1791) Bell's Oct. Cas. 440; *Anderson's Tr.* v. *Fleming* (1871) 9 M. 718.

[57] Bell, *Prin.* §1412; *Young* v. *Stein's Trs.* (1789) Mor. 14218; *Paton's Tr.* v. *Finlayson*, 1923 S.C. 872.

[58] Bell, *Prin.* §1413; *Glendoning's Crs.* v. *Montgomery* (1745) Elch. Arrest. 24; *MacKenzie* v. *Newall* (1824) 3 S. 206; *Lawson* v. *Craik* (1842) 4 D. 1452; *Dickson* v. *Nicholson* (1855) 17 D. 1011; *Martinez y Gomez* v. *Allison* (1890) 17 R. 332; *Mitchell* v. *Heys* (1894) 21 R. 600; *Shepherd's Trs.* v. *Macdonald, Fraser & Co.* (1898) 5 S.L.T. 296.

[59] *Dickson, supra; Gladstone* v. *McCallum* (1896) 23 R. 783; *Barnton Hotel Co.* v. *Cook* (1899) 1 F. 1190; contrast *Meikle & Wilson* v. *Pollard* (1880) 8 R. 69; *Robertson* v. *Ross* (1887) 15 R. 67; *Findlay* v. *Waddell*, 1910 S.C. 670; where parties had possession, not merely custody.

[60] Bell, *Prin.* §1414; *Brown* v. *Somerville* (1844) 6 D. 1267; *Laurie* v. *Denny's Tr.* (1853) 15 D. 404; *Gray's Tr.* v. *Royal Bank* (1895) 23 R. 199.

[61] Bell, *Prin.* §1415.

been relinquished under reservation of the creditor's claim.[62] To avoid depreciation the court may order sale of the subject of lien under reservation of the holder's preference.[63]

If it has once terminated, it does not revive on possession being recovered.[64]

Special lien

A special lien is a right, implied in contracts under which the owner of goods entrusts possession of the goods to another that he may do some work on or in relation to the goods, to retain possession of those goods until his claim for remuneration for the work done on those goods under the contract is satisfied.[65] It is essential that the person claiming the lien have possession of the goods;[66] bare custody, as an employee, will not suffice.[67] The right of lien is lost if possession be surrendered, though part of the goods may be surrendered without prejudicing the lien over the remainder.[68] The right may also be refused if the apparent owner of the goods had only a limited title thereto which excluded the right to create any lien over the goods.[69]

Lien over ship for repairs

A lien is competent for repairs to a ship, but not for the furnishing of necessaries.[70]

Lien for freight

In carriage by land, and by sea, a carrier under a contract *locatio operis mercium vehendarum* has a lien on goods carried for the freight but, in the case of carriage by sea, not for dead freight or wharfage dues.[71] It extends over the whole of the goods carried under that contract;[72] if cargo is loaded by a sub-freighter it extends over it to the extent of the sub-freight.[73]

---

[62] *Reid* v. *Galbraith* (1893) 1 S.L.T. 273.
[63] *Parker* v. *Brown* (1878) 5 R. 979.
[64] Bell, *Prin.* §1416.
[65] Bell, *Comm.* II, 92; *Prin.* §1419; *Harper* v. *Faulds* (1791) Mor. 2666; Bell's Oct. Cas. 432; *Miller* v. *Hutcheson* (1881) 8 R. 489; *Robertson* v. *Ross* (1887) 15 R. 67.
[66] *Paton's Tr.* v. *Finlayson*, 1923 S.C. 872.
[67] *Barnton Hotel Co.* v. *Cook* (1899) 1 F. 1190; contrast *Findlay* v. *Waddell*, 1910 S.C. 670.
[68] *Gray* v. *Graham* (1855) 2 Macq. 435.
[69] *Lamonby* v. *Foulds*, 1928 S.C. 89.
[70] Bell, *Prin.* §1420; *Barr & Shearer* v. *Cooper* (1875) 2 R. (H.L.) 14; *Ross & Duncan* v. *Baxter* (1885) 13 R. 186; *Garscadden* v. *Ardrosan Dry Dock Co.*, 1910 S.C. 178.
[71] Bell, *Prin.* §1423; *Malcolm* v. *Bannatyne*, 15 Nov. 1814, F.C.; *Maclean & Hope* v. *Fleming* (1871) 9 M. (H.L.) 38; As to carriage by rail see *Sc. Central Ry. Co.* v. *Ferguson* (1864) 2 M. 781; *N.B. Ry.* v. *Carter* (1870) 8 M. 998; *Peebles* v. *Caledonian Ry.* (1875) 2 R. 346.
[72] *Lamb* v. *Kaselack, Alsen & Co.* (1882) 9 R. 482.
[73] *Youle* v. *Cochrane* (1868) 6 M. 427.

Lien for average loss

In carriage by sea the shipowners have a lien over the cargo for contributions due in respect of general average losses.[74]

Lien for salvage reward

Salvors who have taken possession of a ship or cargo as salvage, have a lien over the salved property for their salvage reward.[75]

Innkeeper's lien

An innkeeper or hotel proprietor has a lien over the guest's property, such as clothing and luggage, brought to the inn, for the expenses of his keep.[76] It is not lost by the guest's temporary absences *animo revertendi*, nor by allowing the guest to depart if his luggage remains at the hotel. By the Innkeepers Act, 1878, the innkeeper has power, subject to certain conditions, to sell goods left at his inn.[77]

Lien of person bestowing skill and labour

In general any person having possession of goods that he may bestow skill and labour on them, has a lien on the goods for the price of his work thereon.[78] A trustee under a trust deed for creditors has been held entitled to a lien over the trust estate in respect of his possession of the trust deed.[79]

Seller's lien

An unpaid seller of goods has, *inter alia*, a lien or right to retain the goods for the price while he is in possession of them, notwithstanding that the property therein may have passed to the buyer.[80] He may exercise this right until payment or tender of the price in cases where (a) the goods have been sold without any stipulation as to credit; (b) where the goods have been sold on credit, but the term of credit has expired; and (c) where the buyer becomes insolvent.[81] The seller may exercise his right of lien notwithstanding that he is in possession of the

---

[74] Bell, *Prin.* §1426.

[75] Bell, *Prin.* §1427.

[76] It includes articles held by the guest on hire: *Bermans & Nathans* v. *Weibye* 1981 S.L.T. 181. But see Hotel Proprietors Act, 1956, S. 2(2) which excludes hotel proprietors' lien on any vehicle or property therein, or any horse or animal or its harness or equipment.

[77] Bell, *Prin.* §1428.

[78] Bell, *Prin.* §1430; *Meikle & Wilson* v. *Pollard* (1880) 8 R. 69; *Robertson* v. *Ross* (1887) 15 R. 67; *Morrison* v. *Fulwell's Tr.* (1901) 9 S.L.T. 34; *Garscadden* v. *Ardrossan Dry Dock Co.*, 1910 S.C. 178; *Findlay* v. *Waddell*, 1910 S.C. 670; *Train & McIntyre Ltd.* v. *Wm. Forbes Ltd.*, 1925 S.L.T. 286; *Lamonby* v. *Foulds*, 1928 S.C. 89.

[79] *Miln's J.F.* v. *Spence's Trs.*, 1927 S.L.T. 425.

[80] Sale of Goods Act, 1979, S. 39(1).

[81] Ibid., S. 41(1).

goods as agent or custodier for the buyer.[82] It may be exercised even after partial delivery has been made.[83] The unpaid seller loses his lien (a) when he delivers the goods to a carrier or other custodier for transmission to the buyer without reserving the right of disposal of the goods; (b) when the buyer or his agent lawfully obtains possession of the goods; and (c) by waiver thereof,[84] but not by reason only that he has obtained decree for the price of the goods.[85] Exercise of the right of lien does not automatically effect rescission of the contract of sale.[86] Where by the contract the seller expressly reserves the right of disposal of the goods until he has been paid in full and makes the buyer his agent to resell the goods the seller may have a claim against the buyer preferable to the buyer's other trade creditors.[87]

General lien

Exceptionally, by agreement express or implied in certain relationships, by the custom of particular professions and trades, a general right of lien is recognized whereby a person, given possession of goods under a contract to do work on or in relation to those goods is entitled to withhold redelivery of them in security of the whole balance due to him under the employment.[88] It may be created by notice imported into a contract to do work, but must be construed consistently with the usages of the trade in question.[89] If founded on usage of trade, the usage must be general, well-known and accepted as the rule. The precise range of the general lien depends in such a case on the usage of the particular profession or trade in question.[90]

Lien of mercantile agent or similar agent

A mercantile agent or factor has a general lien over all goods, documents, bills or money belonging to his principal which have come into his possession in the course of the employment as such agent.[91] It covers the factor's claim for salary or commission,[92] any advances

---

[82] Ibid., S. 41(2).

[83] Ibid., S. 42.

[84] Ibid., S. 43(1); cf. *Paton's Trs.* v. *Finlayson*, 1923 S.C. 872.

[85] Ibid., S. 43(2).

[86] Ibid., S. 48(1).

[87] *Aluminium Industrie Vaassen* v. *Romalpa Aluminium Co.* [1976] 2 All E.R. 552; *Re Bond Worth* [1979] 3 All E.R. 919; *Borden* v. *Scottish Timber Products* [1979] 3 All E.R. 961.

[88] Bell, *Comm.* II, 101; *Prin.* §1431–2; *Harper* v. *Faulds* (1791) Bell's Oct. Cas. 440; *Sibbald* v. *Gibson* (1852) 15 D. 217; *Hamilton* v. *Western Bank* (1856) 19 D. 152; *Borthwick* v. *Scottish Widows Fund* (1864) 2 M. 595; *Paul and Thain* v. *Royal Bank* (1869) 7 M. 361.

[89] *Anderson's Trs.* v. *Fleming* (1871) 9 M. 718.

[90] See e.g. *Strong* v. *Phillips* (1878) 5 R. 770.

[91] Bell, *Comm.* II, 87; *Prin.* §1445: not for debts arising from other transactions: *Brown* v. *Smith* (1893) 1 S.L.T. 158.

[92] *Mackenzie* v. *Cormack*, 1950 S.C. 183.

made to the principal, and any liabilities incurred on behalf of the principal[93] but not sums due to the factor arising on a separate account.[94]

A lien similar in extent to that of the mercantile agent has been held to attach in the cases of an auctioneer[95] and a stockbroker,[96] and it extends over the unpaid price of the things sold, entitling him to sue the buyer for the price in his own name.[97]

Solicitor's lien

A solicitor has by custom a general right of lien over all deeds, documents and papers entrusted to him by a client,[98] including title-deeds, share certificates and the client's will,[99] but not the register of shareholders of a company,[1] nor papers entrusted for a special purpose, inconsistent with the lien,[2] nor the papers in a case which he has been employed to conduct,[3] nor the money received in such a process,[4] nor papers obtained after the client's notour bankruptcy,[5] nor papers acquired while acting for third parties,[6] nor money put in his hands for a specific purpose,[7] nor to money, whether advances or cash balances.[7] The right is to retain the papers only, not to dispose of them.[8]

It covers his business account with the client, and also outlays made in the ordinary course of that business such as counsel's fees or the expenses of witnesses,[9] but not a salary as agent[10] nor cash advanced to the client[11] nor the account of the solicitor's Edinburgh agent in Court of Session business,[12] nor the account of the solicitor's English correspondent, at least unless that account has been paid or the Scottish

[93] Sibbald v. Gibson (1852) 15 D. 217; Glendinning v. Hope, 1911 S.C. (H.L.) 73.
[94] Miller v. McNair (1852) 14 D. 955.
[95] Miller v. Hutcheson & Dixon (1881) 8 R. 489; Crockart's Trs. v. Hay, 1913 S.C. 509; Mackenzie, supra.
[96] Glendinning, supra.
[97] Mackenzie, supra.
[98] Bell, Prin. §1438.
[99] Paul v. Meikle (1868) 7 M. 235; Drummond v. Muirhead & Guthrie Smith (1900) 2 F. 585; cf. McIntosh v. Chalmers (1883) 11 R. 8; Tawse v. Rigg (1904) 6 F. 544.
[1] cf. Gaepel Haematite Co. v. Andrew (1866) 4 M. 617; cf. Companies Act, 1948, S. 110.
[2] Chisholm v. Fraser (1825) 3 S. 442.
[3] Callman v. Bell (1793) Mor. 6255.
[4] Cullen v. Smith (1845) 8 D. 77.
[5] Jackson v. Fenwick's Tr. (1899) 6 S.L.T. 319.
[6] National Bank v. Thomas White & Park, 1909 S.C. 1308.
[7] Middlemas v. Gibson, 1910 S.C. 577.
[8] Ferguson v. Grant (1856) 18 D. 536, 538.
[9] Ersk. III, 4, 21; Murdoch (1841) 4 D. 257; Richardson v. Merry (1863) 1 M. 940, 946; Palmer v. Lee (1880) 7 R. 651.
[10] Christie v. Ruxton (1862) 24 D. 1182.
[11] Christie v. Ruxton (1862) 24 D. 1182; Wylie's Exor. v. McJannet (1901) 4 F. 195.
[12] Largue v. Urquhart (1883) 10 R. 1229.

solicitor has accepted liability therefor.[13] The existence of a lien does not prevent the running of prescription of the account.[14]

The lien cannot be claimed against a trustee in bankruptcy, or the liquidator of a company, either of whom can require the surrender of all papers in the solicitor's charge relating to the estate being administered.[15] Such a surrender, made under reservation of the lien, entitles the solicitor to rank as a preferred creditor for his account,[16] but not to claim against the trustee or liquidator personally.[17] The lien need not be expressly reserved since it is automatically preserved by statute.[18]

In some cases a solicitor may exercise his right of lien not only against the client but against a third party deriving right from the client, such as a purchaser of heritage from, or a lender on heritable security to, the client.[19] No lien can now be acquired as against a heritable creditor by obtaining possession of title deeds after the heritable security has been recorded.[20] Nor can the right be claimed if the solicitor is acting for both parties in connection with the sale or loan, unless he has intimated to the purchaser or lender that he holds the title-deeds and claims a lien over them.[21]

It expires with the loss of possession, but that does not cover lodging the papers in process[22] nor transmitting them to his town agent.[23] Its exercise is subject to the equitable control of the court.[24] It may be waived but not merely by taking a bill at short date for the money due.[25]

Lien of banker

A banker has a general lien over all bills, notes and negotiable securities in his hands in security of any balance due him by his customer,[26] but not over non-negotiable securities, nor non-negotiable

[13] *Grand Empire Theatre Liqr.* v. *Snodgrass*, 1932 S.C. (H.L.) 73.

[14] Bell, *Prin.* §1441; *Foggs* v. *McAdam* (1780) Mor. 6252.

[15] Bankruptcy (Sc.) Act, 1913, Ss. 76 and 97; Companies Act, 1948, S. 243; *Liqdr. of Weir & Wilson* v. *Turnbull & Findlay*, 1911 S.C. 1006; *Rorie* v. *Stevenson*, 1908 S.C. 559; *Train* v. *McIntyre's J.F.*, 1925 S.L.T. 286; *Garden, Haig-Scott & Wallace, infra.*

[16] *Skinner* v. *Henderson* (1865) 3 M. 867; *Liqdr. of Donaldsons & Co.* v. *White & Park*, 1908 S.C. 309; see also *Miln's J.F.* v. *Spence's Trs.*, 1927 S.C. 425.

[17] *Adam* v. *Winchester* v. *White's Tr.* (1884) 11 R. 863; *Lochee Sawmills Co.* v. *Stevenson*, 1908 S.C. 559; see also *Garden, Haig-Scott & Wallace, infra.*

[18] *Garden, Haig-Scott & Wallace* v. *White*, 1962 S.C. 51.

[19] Bell, *Prin.* §1442.

[20] Conveyancing (Sc.) Act, 1924, S. 27, overruling *Provenhall's Crs.* (1781) Mor. 6253.

[21] *Gray* v. *Graham* (1855) 2 Macq. 435; *Drummond* v. *Muirhead & Guthrie Smith* (1900) 2 F. 585.   [22] Bell, *Prin.* §1440.

[23] Bell, *Comm.* II, 112.

[24] *Ferguson & Stuart* v. *Grant* (1856) 18 D. 536.

[25] *Palmer* v. *Lee* (1880) 7 R. 651.

[26] Bell, *Prin.* §1451; *Paul & Thain* v. *Royal Bank* (1869) 7 M. 361; *Alston's Tr.* v. *Royal Bank* (1893) 20 R. 887; *Clydesdale Bank* v. *Allan's Liqdr.*, 1926 S.C. 235.

securities deposited solely for safe-keeping,[27] unless in special circumstances where the banker had made an advance in reliance on a right of lien,[28] nor securities known to belong to the customer's principal.[29] His right is to retain the securities only, not to realize them,[30] and the right may be excluded by agreement, express or implied.[30]

If a stockbroker lodges negotiable securities with a banker, the latter is entitled to assume that they are the stockbroker's own property, and to claim a lien over them, in the stockbroker's bankruptcy, as against the real owners. But if the banker has notice, either actual, or implied by his knowledge of the usual course of business, that the securities belong to the stockbroker's client, he is not entitled to assume that the stockbroker had any authority to subject his client's securities to a lien for his own general debit balance with the banker, though if the securities are expressly pledged for a specific advance he is entitled to assume that the stockbroker had his client's authority to pledge them, and may accordingly retain them in security of an advance made.[31]

Other cases

A general lien has also been recognized in the cases of bleachers[32] and of calenderers and packers.[33] The factor on a landed estate has no right to retain the leases or estate papers in security of a debt to him.[34]

Enforcement of lien

A claim of lien merely deprives the owner of his moveables until the claimant's claim be satisfied or the counterpart of the contract be performed. The holder is not entitled to sell unless the court authorizes it which it can do possibly only in the case of marketable commodities.

(b) RETENTION ON PROPERTY TITLE

Where one party has a title of property to some subject, heritable or moveable, but is under a personal obligation to transfer or convey it to another, he is entitled to retain it in security of the payment of any debt, or the performance of any obligation, due to him by the party to whom

---

[27] *Brandao v. Barnett* (1846) 12 Cl. & F. 787.
[28] *Robertson's Tr. v. Royal Bank* (1890) 18 R. 12.
[29] *National Bank v. Dickie's Tr.* (1895) 22 R. 740; cf. *Gray's Tr. v. Royal Bank* (1895) 23 R. 199.
[30] *Robertson's Tr., supra.*
[31] *National Bank v. Dickie's Tr.* (1895) 22 R. 740.
[32] *Anderson's Trs. v. Fleming* (1871) 9 M. 718.
[33] *Strong v. Phillips* (1878) 5 R. 770.
[34] *Macrae v. Leith*, 1913 S.C. 901.

he is bound to convey.[35] This right depends on property rather than on possession, and may be exercised over a subject to which the claimant has a title of property, though it be not in his actual possession,[46] and even against the good faith of the contract between the parties.[37]

This right was recognized in cases of sale of goods at common law, when goods sold remained the seller's property till delivered.[38] By the Sale of Goods Act, 1979, the seller's right of retention was in most cases abrogated by the provisions for the passing of the property independently of delivery (Ss. 17, 18) though the unpaid seller was given (S. 39) a lien on the goods, or right to retain them, if still in possession of them, but in security only for the price. The right still exists, however, where the passing of the property in the goods is postponed, and is ratified by S. 39(2).

The principle also applies where property is transferred *ex facie* outright but truly in security only and subject to an obligation to reconvey, as in cases of heritage conveyed in security by *ex facie* absolute disposition qualified by back bond, or of an incorporeal right assigned without qualification,[39] or of corporeal moveables transferred in security by giving the creditor a delivery order for the goods in the hands of a warehouse-keeper, completed by intimation of the order to and alteration of the custodier's books,[40] or transferred by outright sale subject to an obligation to sell back.[41] In such cases, if there is no back bond, or if it does not limit the right of retention, the creditor having *ex facie* a title of property, may retain the subjects untill all debts due to him by the granter are paid.[42]

The creditor cannot, however, retain against parties deriving right from the debtor, such as the latter's trustee in bankruptcy,[43] or an

[35] Bell, *Comm.* I, 724; Gloag, *Contract*, 639–44; *Mein v. Bogle* (1828) 6 S. 360; *Robertson v. Duff* (1840) 2 D. 279; *Melrose v. Hastie* (1850) 12 D. 655; (1851) 13 D. 880; *Hamilton v. Western Bank* (1856) 19 D. 152; *National Bank v. Forbes* (1858) 21 D. 79; *Nelson v. Gordon* (1874) 1 R. 1093; *Distillers Co. v. Russell's Tr.* (1889) 16 R. 479; *Colquhoun's Tr. v. Diack* (1901) 4 F. 358.

[436] *Nelson, supra,* 1099.

[37] *Hamilton, supra,* 162.

[38] *Mein, supra; McEwan v. Smith* (1847) 9 D. 434; (1849) 6 Bell 340; *Melrose, supra; Robertson's Tr. v. Baird* (1852) 14 D. 1010; *Wyper v. Harveys* (1861) 23 D. 606; *Black v. Incorpn. of Bakers* (1867) 6 M. 136; *Distillers Co., supra; Robertson & Baxter v. McPherson* (1893) 1 S.L.T. 159.

[39] *Russell v. E. Breadalbane* (1831) 5 W. & S. 256; *Colquhoun's Tr. v. Diack* (1901) 4 F. 358; *Robertson's Tr. v. Riddell,* 1911 S.C. 14.

[40] *Hamilton v. Western Bank* (1856) 19 D. 152; see also *Hayman v. McLintock,* 1907 S.C. 936.

[41] *McBain v. Wallace* (1881) 8 R. (H.L.) 106; *Darling v. Wilson's Tr.* (1887) 15 R. 180; *Robertson v. Hall's Tr.* (1896) 24 R. 120; *Gavin's Tr. v. Fraser,* 1920 S.C. 674.

[42] *Hamilton, supra; Nelson v. Gordon* (1874) 1 R. 1093; *National Bank v. Union Bank* (1886) 14 R. (H.L.) 1 (heritage).

[43] *Callum v. Goldie* (1885) 12 R. 1137; *Morton's Tr. v. Kirkhope* (1907) 15 S.L.T. 203.

assignee of the debtor's reversionary right[44] in respect of advances made after the date of the sequestration or intimation of the assignation.

The principle applies also to other cases of absolute right qualified by contract such as a mandate to buy lands in the mandatary's own name,[45] a trust constituted by *ex facie* absolute conveyance,[46] a lease of premises to which were attached trade fixtures removeable by the tenant,[47] and ownership of a heritable security.[48]

The party having the right of property may not, however, in exercising his right of retention, disregard the express conditions of the contract under which he held that title so as to make the subjects a security for any debt owed to him by the other contracting party.[49]

(c) RETENTION OF DEBT

In the exercise of a right of retention a party to a mutual contract may withhold payment due to the other in security of performance by the other of the obligations due by him.[50] The mutual obligations must arise out of one and the same contract[51] and the right of retention may be asserted in respect both of a demand for a specific thing and of a claim of damages. Thus a buyer may retain the price in security of his claim of damages for failure to deliver within the specified time,[52] or a reasonable time,[53] a consignee for damage in transit,[54] an owner for damage to goods stored,[55] an employer for non-performance of duty,[56] and a tenant may withhold payment of rent if the landlord has failed to a material extent to execute repairs.[57]

The claim to retain may not apply to a building contract with provision for instalment payment where the employer has unliquidated claims against the builder.[58]

[44] *National Bank, supra.*
[45] *Brough's Crs. v. Jollie* (1793) Mor. 2385.
[46] *Robertson v. Duff* (1840) 2 D. 279.
[47] *Smith v. Harrison & Co's Tr.* (1893) 21 R. 330; *Jaffrey's Trs. v. Milne* (1897) 24 R. 602.
[48] *Colquhoun's Tr. v. Diack* (1901) 4 F. 358.
[49] *Stewart v. Bisset* (1770) Mor. Compensation, Appx. 2; *Anderson's Tr. v. Somerville* (1899) 36 S.L.R. 833.
[50] Bell, *Comm.* II, 118; Gloag, *Contract*, 626; *Johnston v. Robertson* (1861) 23 D. 646, 652, 656.   [51] *Fulton Clyde, Ltd. v. McCallum*, 1960 S.L.T. 253.
[52] *Johnston, supra; MacBride v. Hamilton* (1875) 2 R. 775.
[53] *British Motor Body Co. v. Shaw*, 1914 S.C. 922.
[54] *Taylor v. Forbes* (1830) 9 S. 113.
[55] *Gibson & Stewart v. Brown* (1876) 3 R. 328.
[56] *Tait v. McIntosh* (1841) 13 S. Jur. 280; *Scottish N.E. Ry. v. Napier* (1859) 21 D. 700; *Gibson v. McNaughton* (1861) 23 D. 358; *Sharp v. Rettie* (1884) 11 R. 745; *Moore's Carving Machine Co. v. Austin* (1896) 4 S.L.T. 38.
[57] *Macdonald v. Kydd* (1901) 3 F. 923; *E. Galloway v. McConnell*, 1911 S.C. 846; *Haig v. Boswall-Preston*, 1915 S.C. 339; *Fingland & Mitchell v. Howie*, 1926 S.C. 319.
[58] *Field & Allan v. Gordon* (1872) 11 M. 132.

In all cases the claim to retain is not an absolute right but a plea to which the court may refuse effect where the result would be inequitable, or if it is being used merely to delay,[59] or where money has been deposited specifically appropriated to some purpose.[60]

But a right of retention of a sum of money or thing due to the other cannot be exercised by virtue of an illiquid and unascertained claim against the other party not arising out of the mutual obligations of one and the same contract.[61]

Extended right of retention

On equitable grounds, however, an extended right of retention may be recognised in cases where an illiquid claim not arising out of the same contract can be readily verified and quantified,[62] where in the view of the court it would be inequitable to reject the plea of retention,[63] and where the creditor in the liquid claim (against whom the illiquid claim is made) is bankrupt, as that would require the debtor to pay in full and obtain only a ranking in bankruptcy for his illiquid claim if ultimately constituted.[64] In such a case, on the principle of balancing accounts in bankruptcy, a sum admittedly payable may be retained by virtue of an illiquid or disputed or contingent claim, unless the contingency is so remote that it cannot be evaluated.[65]

Operation of retention

Where retention is justifiably exercised the party retaining must quantify his claim as quickly as practicable, whereupon compensation will operate between the parties to the effect of extinguishing the lesser claim and diminishing the greater *pro tanto*.[66]

SECURITY RIGHTS WITHOUT POSSESSION

In certain limited circumstances rights in security over moveables

[59] *Graham* v. *Gordon* (1843) 5 D. 1207; *Ferguson & Stewart* v. *Grant* (1865) 18 D. 536; *Garscadden* v. *Ardrossan Dry Dock Co.*, 1910 S.C. 178; *E. Galloway, supra*.

[60] *Field, supra*; *McGregor* v. *Alley & McLellan* (1887) 14 R. 535; *Middlemas* v. *Gibson*, 1910 S.C. 577.

[61] Ersk. III, 4, 15; Bell, *Prin.* §573; *National Exchange Co.* v. *Drew* (1855) 2 Macq. 103, 122; *Smith* v. *S.* (1866) 4 M. 279; *Mackie* v. *Riddell* (1874) 2 R. 115; *Sutherland* v. *Urquhart* (1895) 23 R. 284; *Asphaltic Limestone Co.* v. *Glasgow Corpn.*, 1907 S.C. 463; *Christie* v. *Birrells*, 1910 S.C. 986; *Smart* v. *Wilkinson*, 1928 S.C. 383.

[62] *Ross* v. *R.* (1895) 22 R. 461.

[63] *Munro* v. *Macdonald's Exors.* (1866) 4 M. 87; *Ross, supra*; *Lovie* v. *Baird's trs.* (1895) 23 R. 1 (expld. *Sutherland* v. *Urquhart* (1895) 23 R. 284).

[64] Bell, *Comm.* II, 122; *Ross, supra*.

[65] *Mill* v. *Paul* (1825) 4 S. 219; *Borthwick* v. *Scottish Widows Fund* (1864) 2 M. 595; *Hannay & Son's Trs.* v. *Armstrong Bros.* (1877) 4 R. (H.L.) 43; *Scott's Trs.* v. *S.* (1887) 14 R. 1043; *Taylor's Tr.* v. *Paul* (1888) 15 R. 313.   [66] Compensation Act, 1592.

are recognized though the creditor has not been given possession of the security subjects.[67] These are truly hypothecs, which are recognized legally or tacitly in certain cases by settled custom, and may be created conventionally in certain other cases.

LEGAL OR TACIT HYPOTHECS[68]

Feudal superior's hypothec

A feudal superior of lands has a right of hypothec[69] over the fruits of the feu in security of his feu-duty, preferable to the landlord's hypothec. It extends also to *invecta et illata*.[70]

Landlord's hypothec

A landlord similarly has a right of hypothec over the tenant's *invecta et illata* in security of his claim for rent.[71] Landlord's hypothec has been abolished in respect of all subjects let for agriculture or pasture and exceeding two acres in extent,[72] and, in the case of lets regulated by the House Letting and Rating Act, 1911, there are excepted all bedding materials, all tools and implements of trade used or to be used by the occupier or any member of his family as a means of livelihood, which are in the house, and also such further furniture and plenishing as the occupier may select to the value of £10 according to the sheriff-officer's inventory.[73] In cases where it applies, such as houses, shops, market gardens, and mines and quarries, hypothec covers all the *invecta et illata*, including all goods obtained on hire or hire-purchase,[74] though not to goods held on hire in premises let furnished.[75]

Hypothec does not cover goods not belonging to the tenant, such as those of one of his family, or of a lodger,[76] or in the tenant's possession for a limited purpose, such as repair.[77] The goods of a subtenant, however, may be attached for the subrent and also for the principal tenant's rent.[78] Goods comprised in a hire-purchase or conditional sale

---

[67] Stair I, 13, 14; Ersk. III, 1, 34; Bell, *Comm.* II, 24; *Prin.* §1385.

[68] Bell, *Comm.* II, 26.

[69] Bell, *Comm.* II, 26.

[70] *Yuille* v. *Lawrie* (1823) 2 S. 155.

[71] Ersk. II, 6, 56; Bell, *Comm.* II, 27; *Prin.* §1234, 1275, 1887.

[72] Hypothec Abolition Act, 1880; as to effect see *McGavin* v. *Sturrock's Tr.* (1891) 18 R. 576.

[73] 1911 Act, S. 10.

[74] *Penson* v. *Robertson*, 6 June 1820, F.C.; *Nelmes* v. *Ewing* (1883) 11 R. 193; *McIntosh* v. *Potts* (1905) 7 F. 765; *Dundee Corpn.,* v. *Marr*, 1971 S.C. 96; *Scottish & Newcastle Breweries* v. *Edinburgh District Council*, 1979 S.L.T. (Notes) 11.

[75] *Edinburgh Albert Bldg. Co.* v. *General Guarantee Corpn.*, 1917 S.C. 239.

[76] *Bell* v. *Andrews* (1885) 12 R. 961.

[77] *Pulsometer Co.* v. *Gracie* (1887) 14 R. 316.

[78] *Stewart* v. *Stables* (1878) 5 R. 1024.

agreement and not yet vested in the debtor are not subject to landlord's hypothec between the service of a default notice by the creditor and expiry of or compliance with the notice, or, if the agreement is enforceable on order of the court only, between commencement and termination of an action by the creditor to enforce the agreement.[79]

The landlord may obtain interdict against removal of *invecta et illata* to preserve his security and, if they have been removed, may after intimation to the tenant, unless the judgment states an exceptional reason to the contrary,[80] obtain warrant to have them brought back. Such remedies are, however, exceptional and the landlord will be liable in damaged if interdict is obtained on unfounded statements,[81] or if there is a dispute as to the rent and such extreme steps are unnecessary.[82]

Enforcement

Enforcement of hypothec is by petitioning the Sheriff Court[83] for warrant to sequestrate the tenant's goods which are then inventoried and valued by a sheriff-officer and, failing payment, warrant is sought from the court to have them sold by auction to satisfy the landlord's claim for rent. Once inventoried the goods are deemed to be in the court's custody and any party intromitting with them must account for their value and, if he acts in bad faith, is liable for the rent.[84]

Hypothec secures only one year's rent, and falls if not enforced within three months of the last term of payment. Prior arrears can be recovered only by action.[85]

Solicitor's hypothec

A solicitor who has advanced money on outlays and expenses for a litigation has at common law a claim of hypothec over any expenses awarded to his client, which entitles him to move for decree for expenses in his own favour as agent-disburser, in which case he obtains a right thereto preferable to any ordinary creditor of the client. He may obtain decree therefor even after the client has been sequestrated.[86] His claim is preferable to a claim by the other party under a plea of compensation, unless cross awards of expenses are made in the same

---

[79] Consumer Credit Act, 1974, S. 104. This appears to apply only to hire-purchase or conditional sale regulated by that Act. See Ch. 5.34, *Infra.*

[80] *Johnston* v. *Young* (1890) 18 R. (J.) 6; *Jack* v. *Black*, 1911 S.C. 691.

[81] *Jack, supra; Shearer* v. *Nicoll*, 1935 S.L.T. 313.

[82] *Gray* v. *Weir* (1891) 19 R. 25.

[83] *Duncan* v. *Lodijensky* (1904) 6 F. 408.

[84] Bell, *Prin.* §1244.

[85] *Young* v. *Welsh* (1833) 12 S. 233.

[86] Bell, *Comm.* II, 34, *Prin.* §1388; *Hunter* v. *Pearson* (1835) 13 S. 495; *Cullen* v. *Smith* (1845) 8 D. 771; *Peddie* v. *Davidson* (1856) 18 D. 1306.

action or in two actions arising from the same matters, in which case the claim of compensation is preferable to the solicitor's claim under hypothec.[87] This qualification, it has been said, will not be extended[88] and does not apply where decree in one action has been extracted before the other action has been raised.[89]

The solicitor may even move that he be sisted as a party to the action to make his hypothec over expenses effectual; he is entitled to be sisted where decree for expenses has been actually pronounced, or where an interlocutor has been pronounced on which decree for expenses necessarily follows, or where the action has been settled in the knowledge that the client was insolvent, and with the intention of defeating the solicitor's right.[90]

If decree for expenses is granted in the client's favour, the solicitor's hypothec is unaffected and, if his claim is intimated to the party liable in expenses, is preferable to that of the trustee in his client's sequestration,[91] but it may be excluded by a prior arrestment of the expenses,[92] or by a duly intimated assignation,[93] and is liable to a plea of compensation by the party liable in expenses.[94]

Statutory charge over property recovered

By statute[95] the court may in any action declare the solicitor entitled to a charge on and a right to payment out of, property of any kind or tenure, which has been recovered or preserved on behalf of the client, for his expenses; if such a declaration be granted, the court may make an order for raising and payment of such expenses as may seem proper, and acts or deeds by the client thereafter, unless in favour of a bona fide purchaser or lender, are void as against the solicitor's right. Such a declaration is probably precluded by the client's sequestration,[96] but not by a prior arrestment,[97] or by the client company's liquidation.[98] It is competent though the fund sought to be charged is outwith Scotland.[98] The court has a general discretion to make or refuse a

---

[87] *Lochgelly Iron Co. v. Sinclair*, 1907 S.C. 442; *Fine v. Edinburgh Life Assce. Co.*, 1909 S.C. 636; *Byrne v. Baird*, 1929 S.C. 624.
[88] *Jack v. Laing*, 1929 S.C. 426.
[89] *Baird v. Campbell*, 1928 S.C. 487.
[90] *McLean v. Auchinvole* (1824) 3 S. 190; *Macgregor & Barclay v. Martin* (1867) 5 M. 583; *Cornwall v. Walker* (1871) 8 S.L.R. 442; *Crawford v. Smith* (1900) 8 S.L.T. 249; *Ammon v. Tod*, 1912 S.C. 306; *Peek v. P.*, 1926 S.C. 565.
[91] *McTavish v. Pedie* (1828) 6 S. 593.
[92] *Stephen v. Smith* (1830) 8 S. 847.
[93] *Fleeming v. Love* (1839) 1 D. 1097.
[94] *Fleeming, supra.*
[95] Solicitors (Sc.) Act, 1980, S. 62.
[96] *Tait v. Wallace* (1894) 2 S.L.T. 252.
[97] *Automobile Syndicate v. Caledonian Ry.*, 1909, 1 S.L.T. 499.
[98] *Philip v. Willson*, 1911 S.C. 1203.

declaration[99] and the Court of Session may grant one in favour of a country agent,[1] or of an agent for a litigant on the poor's roll,[2] but a charge cannot be granted to the prejudice of a counter-claim for expenses by the other party to the action.[3]

Maritime hypothec or liens

Maritime hypothecs (commonly called maritime liens) are rights in security over a ship without possession, recognized only in definite and known cases of necessity,[4] and preferable to the rights of mortgagees.[5]

The ship's master has a lien for his wages and for disbursements properly made by him on account of the ship.[6] Members of the crew similarly have a lien for their wages, which they cannot exclude by contract.[7] A third party who pays the seaman's wages is subrogated to their lien, without written assignation, unless he is shown to have paid in reliance on the owner's personal credit, when he ranks only as an ordinary creditor and postponed to a mortgagee.[8]

A salvor has a lien over the ship for his salvage rewards.[9]

Another vessel, damaged in collision, has a lien for its claim of damages against the vessel in fault.[10]

Persons who supply goods to, or execute repairs on, the vessel in a foreign port have no lien for their charges;[11] and there is no such right for goods supplied in a home port.[12]

The owners of goods shipped may have a lien for loss caused by improper interruption of the voyage, or damage done by improper stowage,[13] or for average loss.[14]

---

[99] *Carruthers' Tr.* v. *Finlay & Wilson* (1897) 24 R. 363; *Stenhouse* v. *S's Tr.* (1903) 10 S.L.T. 684; *Smart* v. *Stewart*, 1911, 2 S.L.T. 340.

[1] *Bannatyne, Kirkwood, France & Co.*, 1907 S.C. 705.

[2] *Cameron* v. *McDonald*, 1935 S.N. 25.

[3] *O'Keefe* v. *Grieve's Trs.*, 1917, 1 S.L.T. 305.

[4] Bell, *Prin.* §1397; see also *Clydesdale Bank* v. *Walker & Bain*, 1926 S.C. 72, 90.

[5] *Harmer* v. *Bell* (1851) 7 Moo. P.C. 267.

[6] Ersk. III, 2, 34; Bell, *Comm.* I, 562; *Prin.* §1400; *Seamen of the Golden Star* v. *Miln* (1682) Mor. 6259; *Sands* v. *Scott* (1708) Mor. 6261; M.S.A., 1894, S. 167(2); *Morgan* v. *Castlegate S.S. Co.* [1893] A.C. 38; *The Orienta* [1895] P. 49; *McConnachie*, 1914 S.C. 853.

[7] M.S.A., 1894, S. 156.

[8] *Clark* v. *Bowring*, 1908 S.C. 1168 (but doubted in *Clydesdale Bank, infra*).

[9] *Duncan* v. *Dundee, Perth & London Shipping Co.* (1878) 5 R. 742; *Hatton* v. *A/S Durban Hansen*, 1919 S.C. 154.

[10] *Currie* v. *McKnight* (1896) 24 R. (H.L.) 1; *Clan Line* v. *E. Douglas Steamship Co.*, 1913 S.C. 967; *Dorie S.S. Co.*, 1923 S.C. 593. Not so where damage is done not by the other vessel, but by its master or crew, without collision.

[11] *Constant* v. *Christensen*, 1912 S.C. 371.

[12] *Wood* v. *Hamilton* (1789) 3 Paton 148; *Northcote* v. *Henrich Bjorn (Owners)* (1886) 11 App. Cas. 270; *Clydesdale Bank* v. *Walker and Bain*, 1926 S.C. 72.

[13] Bell, *Comm.* II, 38; *Prin.* §1399.

[14] Bell, *Comm.* II, 39; *Prin.* §1401.

Enforcement of a maritime lien is by petition to the court to declare the lien and to order judicial sale of the ship in satisfaction thereof.[15]

CONVENTIONAL HYPOTHEC[16]

Bond of bottomry

The only conventional hypothecs recognized in Scots law are bonds of bottomry and of respondentia. A bond of bottomry is a bond granted by the owner, or master of a ship, creating security over the ship itself without possession or entry on the ship's register. A bond by an owner is now unknown. The master has implied power to grant a bottomry bond if his ship is in a foreign port, is unable to proceed on its voyage for lack of money, no money is procurable on the owner's personal credit, and communication with the owner is impracticable.[17] If communication were practicable, it must be made and authority obtained.

The essentials of the bond are that it specify the ship, the voyage, the risk, and the event on which it becomes exigible, failing which, if not authorized by the owner, it is unenforceable.[18]

The lender has no claim if communication with the owner were not made, if practicable, if the circumstances did not justify the master's action, or if the ship fail to arrive at her destination. Bottomry bonds are preferred in reverse order of dates, as it is presumed that the latest was that which secured the ship's completion of her voyage.[19]

If the bond is valid the lender may enforce it by arresting the ship and insisting on judicial sale.[20] His claim ranks before any mortgagee of the ship or any ordinary creditor, but is postponed to the maritime lien of the master and seamen.

Bond of respondentia

A respondentia bond may be granted by the owner or master, creating security over the ship's cargo, without possession thereof, or endorsation or delivery of a bill of lading. The ship's master has implied power to grant such a bond if there is no other means of raising money to enable him to prosecute his voyage.[22]

---

[15] *Clan Line, supra; McConnachie*, 1914 S.C. 853; *Clydesdale Bank, supra.*
[16] Bell, *Comm.* II, 24.
[17] Bell, *Comm.* I, 578; Bell, *Prin.* §452, 1386; *Kleinworth, Cohen & Co. v. Cassa Maritima* (1877) 2 App. Cas. 156.
[18] *Miller* v. *Potter, Wilson & Co.* (1875) 3 R. 105.
[19] Bell, *Prin.* §456.
[20] *Lucovitch, Petr.* (1885) 12 R. 1090.
[21] *The Daring* (1868) L.R. 2 Adm. & Ecc. 260.
[22] *Anderston Foundry Co.* v. *Law* (1869) 7 M. 836; *Dymond* v. *Scott* (1877) 5 R. 196.

If communication with the cargo owner is practicable, it must be made.

Even if the ship does not arrive at her destination, but the cargo does, the bond in enforceable.[23] Enforcement is by the holders of the bond attaching the cargo and, if not repaid, selling it by judicial authority.

The grant of such a bond renders the shipowners liable to indemnify the cargo owners if the cargo is attached or sold under the bond.[24]

Seller's security by reservation of right of disposal

By the Sale of Goods Act, 1979, S. 19, a seller of specific goods may by the contract reserve the right of disposal of the goods until certain conditions are fulfilled and in such a case, notwithstanding delivery, the property does not pass to the buyer until the conditions are satisfied. Hence the seller may reserve the right of disposal until he is paid in full and authorize the buyer to resell or deal with the goods as seller's agent only or require him to hold them in trust for the seller. This may give the seller as owner a right preferable to the buyer's other creditors over the goods sold or the money received for them.[25] Whether in Scotland, it entitles the sellers to trace the proceeds of sale into and recover from the buyer's general account is questionable. Such a right, if given by a company, may be a floating charge and invalid unless registered.[26]

STATUTORY HYPOTHECS

Agricultural credits

By the Agricultural Credits (Sc.) Act, 1929, a society registered under the Industrial and Provident Societies Acts, having for its principal object the provision and sale of agricultural requisites or the sale of agricultural produce may create by instrument in writing in favour of a bank an agricultural charge on all or any of the stocks of merchandise from time to time belonging to and in the possession of the society in pursuance of its objects, as security for sums advanced or to be advanced or paid on its behalf by the bank, and for interest and charges.[27] The security created thereby ranks after any right of hypothec competent to the landlord or the superior.[28] *Inter se* such charges have priority in accordance with the times of registration with

---

[23] Bell, *Comm.* I, 584; *Anderston Foundry Co., supra.*

[24] *Anderston Foundry Co., supra.*

[25] *Aluminium Industrie Vaassen* v. *Romalpa Aluminium Ltd.* [1976] 2 All E.R. 552; see also *Re Bond Worth* [1979] 3 All E.R. 919; *Borden* v. *Scottish Timber Products Ltd.* [1979] 3 All E.R. 961; *Clark Taylor* v. *Quality Site Development Ltd.*, 1981 S.L.T. 310.

[26] *Re Bond Worth, supra; Borden, supra.*

[27] 1929 Act, Ss. 5, 9.

[28] Ibid., S. 6(2).

the Assistant Register of Friendly Societies for Scotland.[29] The security
may be enforced by sequestration and sale in the same way as a landlord's
hypothec.[30]

Floating charge

At common law the competency of a floating charge, i.e. a charge or
security attaching without possession to whatever property and assets
belonged for the time being to the debtor, was not recognized by Scots
law, even in respect of assets situated in England where a floating
charge was competent.[31] By the Companies (Floating Charges and
Receivers) (Sc.) Act, 1972[32] it is competent for an incorporated company or an industrial and provident society, for the purpose of securing
any debt or other obligation incurred or to be incurred, to create a
floating charge over all or any of the property, heritable or moveable,
which may from time to time be comprised in its property and undertaking.[33] It may be created only by the execution under the seal of the
company of an instrument of charge or of a bond or written acknowledgement of debt or obligation which purports to create such a
charge. It may except certain property from its application.[34] On the
commencement of winding-up it attaches to the property then comprised in the company's property and undertaking, apart from any
excepted property, subject to the rights of any person who (a) has
effectually executed diligence on any of the property; (b) holds a fixed
security over any of the property ranking in priority to the floating
charge; or (c) holds over any of the property another floating charge so
ranking.[35] A floating charge affects heritable property though not
recorded in the Register of Sasines.[36]

Charges (including floating charges) created by companies registered in Scotland are void against the liquidator and any creditor of the
company unless the prescribed particulars and a copy of the instrument of charge are delivered to the registrar of companies for registration within twenty-one days.[37]

A fixed security arising by operation of law has priority over a
floating charge, and any other fixed security has priority unless the
contract creating the fixed security was made after the 1961 Act, and
the floating charge was registered before the fixed security was made a

---

[29] Ibid., Ss. 7, 8.
[30] Ibid., S. 6(1).
[31] *Carse* v. *Coppen*, 1951 S.C. 233.
[32] Replacing Act of 1961 which introduced the floating charge into Scots law.
[33] 1972 Act, S. 1(1).
[34] 1972 Act, S. 2.
[35] 1972 Act, S. 1(2). 'Fixed security' is defined by S. 8(1)(c).
[36] 1972 Act, S. 3.
[37] Companies Act, 1948, S. 106A, added by 1961 Act, Sched. II.

real right, and the instrument creating the floating charge prohibited the company from subsequently creating any fixed security having priority over, or ranking equally with, the floating charge. *Inter se* floating charges rank according to the times of their registration, unless provided to rank *pari passu*.[38]

The security right created by a floating charge is enforced by petition for the winding-up of the company,[39] or by appointing a receiver.[40]

The Industrial and Provident Societies Act, 1967, enables a society registered under the Industrial and Provident Societies Acts, 1965 to 1967, to create such a floating charge. The 1972 Act applies with modifications to such a charge.

Mortgages of ships

By the Merchant Shipping Act, 1894, S. 31, a ship or a share therein may be mortgaged in security by an instrument in the form of Sched. I, Form B, which must be recorded by the registrar of the ship's port of registry, in the order in which they are produced for registration.[41] On production of a mortgage with a receipt endorsed thereon, the registrar must record that the mortgage has been discharged (S. 32).[42] Mortgagees have priority *inter se* according to the dates when each mortgage is recorded in the register (S. 33).[43] A mortgagee is not deemed owner of the ship, save so far as necessary to make it available as a security for the mortgage debt (S. 34).[44] The mortgagor, so long as he retains possession, may use the ship for his own benefit so long as he does not impair the mortgagee's security and is probably bound to keep the ship in repair. A shipwright undertaking repairs may acquire a lien over the ship which is good against the mortgagee.[45] A mortgagee has a right to take possession of the ship[46] but if he takes possession he incurs liability for goods supplied to the ship.[47] He has power of sale (S. 35), and a mortgage is not affected by the mortgagor's bankruptcy and is preferred to any claim of the other creditors[48] or the trustee in bankruptcy (S. 36). But a bottomry bond and a maritime lien (hypothec) both take priority over a mortgage.[49]

[38] 1972 Act, S. 5.
[39] 1972 Act, Ss. 1(2) and 4.
[40] 1972 Act, ss. 11–28.
[41] The stipulations of the mortgage agreement may be in a separate deed: *The Benwell Tower* (1895) 8 Asp. M.L.C. 13.   [42] cf. *Duthie* v. *Aitken* (1893) 20 R. 214.
[43] *Black* v. *Williams* [1895] 1 Ch. 408.
[44] cf. *Laming* v. *Seater* (1889) 16 R. 828; *Tyne Dock Co.* v. *Royal Bank*, 1974 S.L.T. 57.
[45] *Tyne Dock Co., supra.*
[46] Bell, *Prin.* §1382A.
[47] *Havilland, Routh & Co.* v. *Thomson* (1864) 3 M. 313.
[48] *Clydesdale Bank* v. *Walker & Bain*, 1926 S.C. 72.
[49] *The Royal Arch* (1857) Swab. 269; *The Staffordshire* (1872) L.R. 4 P.C. 194; *The Arbonne* (1925) 33 Ll. L.R. 141.

A mortgage may be transferred by instrument (Sched. I, Form G) recorded by the registrar (S. 37) and on transmission by marriage, death or bankruptcy or other lawful means. The transmission has to be authenticated by a declaration of the transferee and recorded by the registrar (S. 38).

If a registered owner wishes to mortgage the ship outwith the country of the port of registry he may, subject to certain conditions, obtain from the registrar a certificate of mortgage (Ss. 39–42). The power of mortgage thereby conferred must be exercised in conformity with the directions in the certificate, and every mortgage made thereunder must be registered by endorsement of a record thereof on the certificate by a registrar or British consular officer. The discharge may be redelivered to the registrar and cancelled (S. 43). The owner may authorize the registrar to give notice that a certificate is revoked (S. 46).

A bill of sale, or other written conveyance of a ship, though not in statutory form nor registered is probably habile to effect a good security if completed by actual possession or by the receipt of the ship's earnings.[50]

Mortgages of aircraft

An aircraft may be mortgaged by an aircraft mortgage in statutory form,[51] which is effective without delivery of the aircraft, but must be registered in the Register of Aircraft Mortgages kept by the Civil Aviation Authority. A priority notice, stating intention to apply to enter a contemplated mortgage of an aircraft in the register may be entered therein. Mortgages may be assigned and discharged. Provision is made for priority of mortgages and the rights of parties on default in satisfying the debt secured by the mortgage. The Court of Session may grant warrant for possession and sale.

---

[50] *Watson* v. *Duncan* (1879) 6 R. 1247.
[51] Mortgaging of Aircraft Order, 1972 (S.I. 1972, No. 1268), Sch. 2.

DERIVATIVE ACQUISITION OF PROPERTY IN CORPOREAL MOVEABLE OBJECTS

Derivative acquisition of moveable property is the acquisition of a proprietary right to moveables which have hitherto been in the ownership of another. It implies the surrender of his proprietary right by the person hitherto the owner. A distinction falls to be drawn between the title for the transfer, *titulus transferendi dominii,* and the mode of effecting it, *modus transferendi dominii,* both of which are essential for an effectual transfer of ownership.[1]

Titulus transferendi dominii

The legal title for transfer of ownership is either a voluntary act of will, either unilateral, such as intention to gift, or bilateral, as by making a contract, or the involuntary operation of law, such as sale under statutory or other powers, decree of court, legal diligence, or succession on death.[2]

Particular grounds of voluntary transfer—donation inter vivos

In the case of donation or gift *inter vivos*[3] the intention is to transfer proprietary rights gratuitously. There is a presumption against donation and the possession of one's goods by another is deemed to be loan unless there is clear evidence of *animus donandi.*

Barter

In barter[3] the agreement to exchange perfects the contract but there is no passing of the property in either thing being exchanged until mutual delivery of both things has been made,[4] or at least the items to be exchanged have been identified and separated and delivery orders in respect thereof transmitted and intimated to the custodiers.[5]

---

[1] Voet, 41, 1, 35; Bell, *Prin.* §1299.
[2] For involuntary transfer see Ch. 5.35, *infra.*
[3] Ch. 5.32, *infra.*
[4] Stair I, 14, 1.
[5] cf. *Inglis* v. *Robertson & Baxter* (1898) 25 R. (H.L.) 70; *Widenmeyer* v. *Burn Stewart & Co.,* 1967 S.C. 85.

Sale

At common law, sale was a contract only and no right of property in the subject sold was transferred without, nor until, *traditio* was effected.[6] But by the Sale of Goods Act, 1979, Ss. 17–18,[6a] the right of property in goods sold passes when the parties intend it to pass, which is normally (S. 18, Rule 1) when the contract is made, even though payment or delivery or both be postponed. Where the right of disposal is reserved until certain conditions are fulfilled (S. 19) the right of property does not pass till then, notwithstanding the delivery of the goods to the buyer, or to a carrier or custodier for transmission to him. Accordingly under the 1979 Act a sale is a contract and may also be a conveyance of the right of property, independently of when *traditio* of the actual goods is effected.[7]

Credit sale

In credit sale agreement, which is a variety of sale, the property prima facie passes when the contract is made, whether or not possession is then transferred.[8]

Conditional sale

Under a conditional sale agreement the property in the goods remains in the seller, notwithstanding that the buyer is given possession of the goods, until the conditions as to payment by instalments or otherwise specified in the agreement are fullfilled.[9]

Hire-purchase

The completion of the contract normally transfers the right of property to the finance company as owner by sale, though delivery of possession by the seller to the hirer is necessary to complete the hiring relationship between him and the finance company which now owns the goods. The property in the goods hired does not pass to the hirer until he has completed the payments and has exercised the option to purchase.[10]

Other contracts

The only other contract implying intent to transfer ownership is *mutuum* or improper loan, whereby the borrower on delivery becomes

---

[6] Bell, *Prin.* (9th ed.) §86; For some of the consequences of this rule see *McEwan* v. *Smith* (1849) 6 Bell 340; *Melrose* v. *Hastie* (1851) 13 D. 880; *Mathison* v. *Alison* (1854) 17 D. 274; *Wyper* v. *Harvey* (1861) 23 D. 606.

[6a] Repleacing Sale of Goods Act, 1893, in similar terms.

[7] Ch. 5.33, *infra.*

[8] Sale of Goods Act, 1979, Ss. 16–19.   [9] Ibid.

[10] Common law, and under Hire-Purchase (Sc.) Act, 1965 and Consumer Credit Act, 1974.

proprietor of the thing lent, subject to an obligation to restore an equal quantity of the same kind and quality.[11]

Modus transferendi dominii

The leading principle on mode is that embodied in the maxim *traditionibus non nudis pactis dominia rerum transferuntur*.[12] In general ownership of moveables passes only when possession is transferred or delivered with the intention of transferring the right of property to the receiver, and neither intention nor agreement will pass any property in moveables without delivery.[13] Only exceptionally, under the Sale of Goods Act 1979, can ownership pass without delivery.[14] A right of property in moveables cannot be transferred by assignation or other deed without transfer of possession; such a deed at most confers a right to demand delivery.[15]

Delivery may be actual, constructive or symbolical.

Actual delivery

Actual delivery is effected by voluntarily transferring physical possession to the transferee, or an agent for him, together with the relinquishment on the transferor's side of any further *animus possidendi* and the acquisition on the transferee's side of *animus possidendi*.[16] It may be effected by handing over the key of the premises where the goods are stored,[17] but probably not by merely setting aside the goods within the transferor's premises.[18] But in the case of sale actual delivery to a carrier leaves the goods liable to stoppage *in transitu* if the buyer has become bankrupt or insolvent before the buyer or his agent has taken delivery from the carrier.[19]

Constructive delivery

Constructive delivery is effected by the transfer of some thing essential

[11] Ch. 5.27, *supra*.

[12] See Gordon, *Studies in the Transfer of Property by Traditio*, Ch. 12. cf. *Mathison* v. *Alison* (1854) 17 D. 274; *McArthur* v. *Brown* (1858) 20 D. 1232; *Moore* v. *Gledden* (1869) 7 M. 1016; *Orr's Tr.* v. *Tullis* (1870) 8 M. 936.

[13] Stair II, 1, 11; Ersk. II, 1, 19; Bell, *Prin.* §1300; Brown, *Sale*, 390; *Milne* v. *Grant's Exors.* (1884) 11 R. 887, 890; *Brownlee's Exrx.* v. *B.,* 1908 S.C. 232, 240.

[14] 1979 Act, Ss. 17–18.

[15] cf. *Clark* v. *West Calder Oil Co.* (1882) 9 R. 1017.

[16] Ersk. II, 1, 18; III, 3, 8; Bell, *Comm.* I, 183; *Prin.* §1302. cf. Sale of Goods Act, 1979, S. 62, wherein 'delivery' is defined as 'Voluntary transfer of possession from one person to another'. See also *Robertson and Aitken* (1801) Mor. Appx. Sale, 15; *Baxter* v. *Pearson* (1807) Hume 688; *Dunlop* v. *Lambert* (1839) MacL. & R. 663.

[17] Ersk. II, 1, 19; III, 3, 8; Bell, *Comm.* I, 186; *Prin.* §1302; *Maxwell & Co.* v. *Stevenson* (1831) 5 W. & S. 169; *W. Lothian Oil Co.* v. *Mair* (1892) 20 R. 64; cf. *Pattison's Trs.* v. *Liston* (1893) 20 R. 806.

[18] *Gibson* v. *Forbes* (1833) 11 S. 916; *Boak* v. *Megget* (1884) 6 D. 662. cf. *Anderson* v. *Buchanan* (1848) 11 D. 270.

[19] Sale of Goods Act, 1979, S. 45.

for the actual delivery of the goods, which transfer puts them beyond the control of the transferor and under the control of the transferee as effectively as actual transfer of them. It may be effected, where goods are in the store of an independent third party, and are adequately ascertained and distinguishable from others of the same kind in the store,[20] by giving the transferee a delivery order addressed to the storekeeper, or by endorsation and delivery of the storekeeper's warrant for the goods, and in either case, making intimation to the storekeeper,[21] who then holds the goods for the transferee, not the transferor.[22] In the case of sale of goods delivery is not effected until the custodier acknowledges to the buyer that he holds the goods on the buyer's behalf.[23]

Symbolical delivery

Symbolical delivery is effected by the transfer of a document of title recognized by mercantile custom as a symbol of, and equivalent to, the goods themselves. The main recognized case is the endorsation and transfer of a bill of lading received for goods shipped and in transit, which has the same effect as actual transfer of the goods themselves and enables a transferee to take delivery as owner or holder in security on their being unloaded.[24]

Apart from the bill of lading no kind of document has been held effective as symbolical delivery.[25]

WHO CAN TRANSFER TITLE OF OWNERSHIP OF GOODS

It is clear that any person who has an unqualified right of property in any corporeal moveable can confer a good title thereto on a donee or purchaser from him, and that a person not having such a right cannot, in general, confer any title.

The fundamental principle is that no one can transfer a better title to goods than he himself has: *nemo dat quod non habet*.[26] Hence a mere custodier or other non-owner in possession cannot transfer a title of

---

[20] It does not suffice to give an order to one's own storekeeper, even though other goods are also in that store: *Anderson* v. *McCall* (1866) 4 M. 765; *Pochin* v. *Robinow* (1869) 7 M. 622, 628.

[21] *Black* v. *Incorporation of Bakers* (1867) 6 M. 136; *Hayman* v. *McLintock,* 1907 S.C. 936; *Price & Pierce* v. *Bank of Scotland,* 1912 S.C. (H.L.) 19.

[22] *Inglis* v. *Robertson & Baxter* (1898) 25 R. (H.L.) 70.

[23] Sale of Goods Act, 1979, S. 29(3).

[24] Bell, *Prin.* §417, 1305; *Bogle* v. *Dunmore* (1787) Mor. 14216; *Young* v. *Stein's Crs.* (1789) Mor. 1448. *Lickbarrow* v. *Mason* (1793) 6 East 21.

[25] e.g. *Paul* v. *Cuthbertson* (1840) 2 D. 1286; *Stiven* v. *Cowan* (1878) 15 S.L.R. 422.

[26] *Whistler* v. *Forster* (1863) 14 C.B.N.S. 248; *Cole* v. *N.W. Bank* (1875) L.R. 10 C.P. 354; *Cundy* v. *Lindsay* (1878) 3 App. Cas. 459, 463; *Banque Belge* v. *Hambrouck* [1921] 1 K.B. 321.

ownership by transferring goods, or otherwise. This principle is embodied in the Sale of Goods Act, 1979, S. 21(1). A hirer or borrower cannot transfer to a third party to the effect of conferring any title of property on him. But to this principle various exceptions have, for reasons of commercial convenience, been accepted, both at common law and under statute, under which a person who has no title, or less than a full title of ownership, may give a transferee a full title of ownership, and under which a transferee who takes in good faith, for value and without notice of the transferor's defect in title, himself acquires a good title of ownership. These exceptions are (a) money and negotiable instruments; (b) sales by a non-owner; (c) sales under a voidable title; (d) sales by sellers or buyers having possession of the goods or of documents of title thereto; (e) dispositions by factors; (f) sales of motor vehicles by hire-purchasers; and (g) sales under statutory and other powers of sale.[27]

Hence under the general principle one who has no title at all, e.g., having obtained the goods by fraud which induced essential error, can pass no title at all to a purchaser from him;[28] but in the exceptional cases the transferor can pass a good title, so long as the transferee takes in good faith, for value, and without notice of the seller's defective title.

Theft

It follows also from the general principle of *nemo dat quod non habet* that a thief or embezzler, who has *ex hypothesi* no title of ownership to the goods in question at all[29] cannot pass any title to even an honest transferee who takes in good faith, for value and without knowledge of the theft, still less to a resetter. Stolen property, except money and negotiable instruments, is tainted by a *vitium reale* which is not purged by any transmissions.[30] The goods are recoverable from the thief if he still has possession or he is liable to compensate for their value.[31] They are recoverable from any party into whose hands they have come and he is liable for the value of any not recovered.[32] An intermediate party who has in good faith parted with stolen property is

[27] In English law a further exception is the sale in market overt (Sale of Goods Act, 1979, S. 22).
[28] cf. *Morrisson* v. *Robertson*, 1908 S.C. 332; *Ingram* v. *Little* [1961] 1 Q.B. 31. See also *Henderson* v. *Gibson*, 17 June 1806, F.C.; *Todd* v. *Armour* (1882) 9 R. 901. But if the fraud gave the taker a title, though a voidable one, he can pass a title to a purchaser from him so long as his own title has not been avoided: *Brown* v. *Marr, Barclay* (1880) 7 R. 472; *Macleod* v *Kerr*, 1965 S.C. 253.
[29] He may have a right of custody: *O'Brien* v. *Strathern*, 1922 J.C. 55.
[30] *Bp. of Caithness* v. *Fleshers of Edinburgh* (1629) Mor. 9112; *Ferguson* v. *Forrest* (1639) Mor. 9112; *Henderson* v. *Gibson* (1806) Mor. Moveables, Appx. 1; *Todd* v. *Armour* (1882) 9 R. 901.
[31] *Gorebridge Co-operative Socy.* v. *Turnbull*, 1952 S.L.T. (Sh. Ct.) 91.
[32] *Oliver and Boyd* v. *Marr Typefounding Co.* (1901) 9 S.L.T. 170; *Dalhanna Knitwear Co.* v. *Mohammed Ali*, 1967 S.L.T. (Sh. Ct.) 74.

not liable to the true owner for restitution or for reparation, but only to recompense the dispossessed ultimate possessor.[33] He is liable to the true owner only for any profit made by selling the goods[34] or for their value if he sold them in bad faith.[35]

EXCEPTIONS

(a) MONEY, AND NEGOTIABLE INSTRUMENTS

Money, both notes and coin, is incapable of being earmarked or identified with any former owner and its circulation and transfer in satisfaction of a pecuniary obligation destroys the title of the previous owner and vests a new title in the person receiving the money so long as he has taken it in good faith, for value and without notice of any defect in the transferor's title.[36] Thus stolen money is recoverable from a thief or a resetter,[37] but not from an honest transferee who has given the thief value for it, e.g., taking it in payment for goods. Money regarded not as currency but as goods, or curios, falls under the ordinary rule applicable to moveables, and not under this exception.[38]

Similarly a holder in due course of a negotiable instrument[39] acquires a good title thereto notwithstanding defect in the title of the transferor. The category of negotiable instruments includes bills of exchange, cheques and promissory notes (including bank-notes), Treasury bills, scrip certificates issued to bearer,[40] share warrants issued to bearer,[41] debentures payable to bearer,[42] dividend warrants, banker's drafts and circular notes, but not share certificates or transfers thereof,[43] postal orders,[44] or pension receipts.[45] Bills of lading, dock warrants and

---

[33] Sale of Goods Act, 1979, S. 12.

[34] Ersk. III, 1, 10; *Scot* v. *Low* (1704) Mor. 9123; *Walker* v. *Spence & Carfrae* (1765) Mor. 12802.

[35] *Si dolo desiit possidere, dolus pro possessione habetur*; cf. *Kinniburgh* v. *Dickson* (1830) 9 S. 153; *Lockhart* v. *Cunningham* (1870) 8 S.L.R. 151.

[36] Bell, *Prin.* §527–9; 1333; *Hotchkis* v. *Royal Bank* (1797) Mor. 2673; *Swinton* v. *Beveridge* (1799) Mor. 10105; *Crawfurd* v. *Royal Bank* (1749) Mor. 875; *Lambton* v. *Marshall* (1799) Mor. Bill, Appx. 8; *Scott* v. *Kilmarnock Bank*, 27 Feb. 1812, F.C.

[37] *Gorebridge Co-operative Socy.* v. *Turnbull*, 1952 S.L.T. (Sh. Ct.) 91.

[38] cf. *Moss* v. *Hancock* [1899] 2 Q.B. 111.

[39] As defined by Bills of Exchange Act, 1882, S. 29(1).

[40] *Rumball* v. *Metropolitan Bank* [1877] 2 Q.B.D. 194; *Edelstein* v. *Schuler* [1902] 2 K.B. 144.

[41] Companies Act, 1948, S. 83.

[42] *Bechuanaland Exploration Co.* v. *London Trading Bank, Ltd.* [1898] 2 Q.B. 658; see also Companies Act, 1948, S. 93.

[43] *Colonial Bank* v. *Cady and Williams* [1890] 15 App. Cas. 267; *Longman* v. *Bath Electric Tramways* [1905] 1 Ch. 646.

[44] *Fine Arts Socy.* v. *Union Bank of London* [1886] 17 Q.B.D. 705.

[45] *Jones* v. *Coventry* [1909] 2 K.B. 1029.

similar documents of title to goods, though transferable, are not negotiable instruments.

(b) SALES BY A NON-OWNER

The Sale of Goods Act, 1979, S. 21, provides that, subject to that Act, where goods are sold by a person who is not their owner, and who does not sell them under the authority of or with the consent of the owner, the buyer acquires no better title to the goods than the seller had, unless the owner of the goods is by his conduct precluded from denying the seller's authority to sell. But nothing in the 1979 Act affects the provisions of the Factors Acts,[46] or any enactment enabling the apparent owner of goods to dispose of them as if he were the true owner thereof,[47] or the validity of any contract of sale under any special common law or statutory power of sale or under the order of a court.[48] This section restates the general principle but excepts cases where the owner is precluded from denying the seller's authority. The owner will be so precluded if the seller had actual or ostensible authority to act as his agent,[49] or the owner's consent,[50] or if the true owner, in allowing the seller the opportunity to sell, had failed to take reasonable care to prevent the buyer being deceived.[51]

(c) SALE UNDER A VOIDABLE TITLE

Where the seller of goods has only a voidable title to those goods, as where he obtained the goods himself under a contract voidable as having been induced by misrepresentation, but his title has not been avoided at the time of the sale, the buyer from him acquires a good title to the goods, provided he buys them in good faith and without notice of the seller's defect of title.[52] If the seller has no title, such as a thief, of a title under a contract wholly void, he can pass no title, even though the buyer takes in good faith, for value and without notice.[53] It may be sufficient to avoid a contract voidable within the meaning of the Sale of Goods Act, 1979, S. 23, and so prevent property passing, if the seller

[46] On these see exception (e), *infra*.
[47] e.g. sale of motor vehicles by a hire-purchaser: exception (f), *infra*.
[48] See exception (g), *infra*.
[49] *Eastern Distributors Ltd.* v. *Goldring* [1957] 2 Q.B. 600; contrast *Mercantile Credit Co.* v. *Hamblin* [1964] 3 All E.R. 592.
[50] e.g. *Mount* v. *Jay* [1960] 1 Q.B. 159.
[51] *Mercantile Credit Co., supra.*
[52] Sale of Goods Act, 1979, S. 23; *Phillips* v. *Brooks* [1912] 2 K.B. 243; *Lake* v. *Simmons* [1927] A.C. 487; *Butterworth* v. *Kingsway Motors* [1954] 2 All E.R. 694; *Macleod* v. *Kerr*, 1965 S.C. 253.
[53] *Cundy* v. *Lindsay* (1878) 3 App. Cas. 459; *Morrisson* v. *Robertson*, 1908 S.C. 332; *Ingram* v. *Little* [1961] 1 Q.B. 31.

takes all possible steps to regain the goods even though he does not communicate to the seller his decision to rescind the contract of sale to him.[54]

(d) DISPOSITIONS BY SELLERS AND BUYERS IN POSSESSION

(i) *Seller in possession*

Where a person having sold goods continues or is in possession of the goods, or of the documents of title to the goods, the delivery or transfer by that person, or by a mercantile agent[55] acting for him, of the goods or documents of title under any sale, pledge or other disposition thereof, to any person receiving the same in good faith and without notice of the previous sale, has the same effect as if the person making the delivery or transfer were expressly authorized by the owner of the goods to make the sale.[56] Hence a purchaser or pledgee from such a person obtains a good title provided he takes delivery, receives the goods in good faith, and has no notice of the previous sale. The seller need not have continued in possession with the buyer's consent.[57] The possession which the seller had must be possession continuing despite the sale and not be possession otherwise re-acquired as, e.g., where a garage sells a car and has it left with them for repainting.[58] It may be possession by an agent.[59] It is not essential that the seller has continued in possession with the buyer's consent.

(ii) *Buyer in possession*

Where a person, having bought or agreed to buy goods,[60] obtains, with the consent of the seller, possession of the goods or the documents of title to the goods, the delivery or transfer by that person, or by a mercantile agent[61] acting for him, of the goods or documents of title,

---

[54] But see *Macleod, supra.*

[55] Defined, 1979 Act, S. 26.

[56] Sale of Goods Act, 1979, S. 24, reproducing almost exactly Factors Act, 1889, S. 8, applied to Scotland by Factors (Sc.) Act, 1890.

[57] *Worcester Works Finance* v. *Cooden Eng. Co.* [1971] 3 All E.R. 708.

[58] *Staffs Motor Guarantees, Ltd.* v. *British Wagon Co., Ltd.* [1934] 2 K.B. 305, distinguished in *Union Tpt. Finance* v. *Ballardie* [1937] 1 K.B. 570; *Olds Discount Co.* v. *Krett and Krett* [1940] 2 K.B. 117. See also *Pacific Motor Auctions Pty., Ltd.* v. *Motor Credits (Hire Finance), Ltd.* [1965] A.C. 867.

[59] *City Fur Mfg. Co.* v. *Fureenbond (Brokers), Ltd.* [1937] 1 All E.R..799.

[60] A person who obtains possession under a hire-purchase contract has not 'bought or agreed to buy': *Helby* v. *Mathews* [1895] A.C. 471; *Belsize Motor Supply Co.* v. *Cox* [1914] 1 K.B. 244; but at common law a person has, though his contract to buy is conditional, or for purchase with payment by instalments: *Lee* v. *Butler* [1893] 2 K.B. 318. By S. 25(2) the buyer under a conditional sale agreement as defined by the Consumer Credit Act, 1974, is to be taken not to be a person who has bought or agreed to buy goods.

[61] Defined, 1979 Act, S. 26.

under any sale, pledge or other disposition thereof, to any person receiving them in good faith and without notice of any lien or other right of the original seller in respect of goods, has the same effect as if the person making the delivery or transfer were a mercantile agent in possession of the good or documents of title with the consent of the owner.[62] This provision deals with the unauthorized sale by a buyer in possession with the seller's consent, before ownership has vested in him, as where he has not yet paid the price or the whole of it, or he has merely agreed to buy under a conditional contract.[63] The possession must have been obtained with the seller's consent, though that consent may be afterwards withdrawn.[64] A buyer is not in possession with the seller's consent if he stole the goods, but he is if he obtained them by fraudulent misrepresentation or false pretences,[65] unless it induced error so essential as to render the transaction of obtaining void[66] or on approval, or on sale or return.[67]

(e) TRANSFERS BY FACTORS IN POSSESSION

A factor in possession has power to sell or pledge his principal's property. Where a mercantile agent[68] is, with the consent of the owner, in possession of goods or of the documents of title to goods,[69] any sale, pledge[70] or other disposition of the goods, made by him when acting in the ordinary course of business of a mercantile agent, is, subject to the Factors Act, 1889 and 1890, as valid as if he were expressly authorized by the owner of the goods to make that disposition, provided that the person taking under the disposition acts in good faith and has not at the time of the disposition notice that the person making the disposition has not authority to make it.[71]

The provision applies only to mercantile agents, not, e.g., to servants

---

[62] Sale of Goods Act, 1979, S. 25(1) reproducing almost exactly Factors Act, 1889, S. 9, applied to Scotland by Factors Act, 1980; cf. *Browne* v. *Ainslie* (1893) 21 R. 173; *Inglis* v. *Robertson & Baxter* (1898) 25 R. (H.L.) 70; *Graham* v. *Glenrothes Development Corpn.*, 1967 S.C. 284.

[63] *Marten* v. *Whale* [1917] 2 K.B. 480; *Wilkes* v. *Livingstone*, 1955 S.L.T. (Notes) 20.

[64] *Cahn* v. *Pockett's Bristol Channel S.P. Co.* [1899] 1 Q.B. 643.

[65] *London Jewellers* v. *Attenborough* [1934] 2 K.B. 206; *Du Jardin* v. *Beadman Bros., Ltd.* [1952] 2 Q.B. 712.

[66] *Morrisson* v. *Robertson*, 1908 S.C. 332.

[67] Sale of Goods Act, 1979, S. 18, R.4. Making a sale, pledge or other disposition is an act adopting the transaction within Rule 4: *London Jewellers, supra.*

[68] Defined, Factors Act, 1889, S. 1(1). cf. *Oppenheimer* v. *Attenborough* [1907] 1 K.B. 510; [1908] 1 K.B. 221.

[69] Defined, S. 1(2)–(4); cf. *Vickers* v. *Hertz* (1871) 9 M. (H.L.) 65; *Staffs. Motor Guarantee Ltd.* v. *British Wagon, Ltd.* [1934] 2 K.B. 305. A vehicle log-book is not a document of title: *Joblin* v. *Watkins & Rosevere (Motors) Ltd.* [1949] 1 All E.R. 47.

[70] Defined, S. 1(5).

[71] Factors Act, 1889, S. 2, applied to Scotland by Factors (Sc.) Act, 1890.

or carriers or brokers,[72] nor to commercial travellers.[73] Whether a person is a mercantile agent is a question of fact.[74] He must, moreover, have been a mercantile agent when entrusted with the possession of the goods, and not merely have become one later.[75]

He must have been entrusted with possession of the goods or documents and not obtained them by theft, though he may have obtained possession by misrepresentation, so long as not inducing error so essential as to render the obtaining void.[76]

He must have obtained possession as factor, and not in any other capacity or for another purpose.[77]

The sale or other disposition must be in the ordinary course of business; thus a sale, pledge or other disposition is not valid unless made for valuable consideration;[78] it must be effected at a proper place of business, during business hours, and in other respects be such as is normal in that business.[79]

A disposition by a mercantile agent, which would have been valid if the owner's consent to his possession of the goods or documents had continued, is valid notwithstanding the determination of the consent, provided that the person taking under the disposition had not notice at the time that the consent had been determined.[80] Hence if authority terminates by revocation or lapse of time but possession continues the factor can give a good title to an innocent purchaser or pledgee.[81]

A mercantile agent's possession of documents of title, as being or having been, with the consent of the owner in possession of the goods, represented thereby or of any other documents of title thereto, is for the purposes of the Factors Act, deemed to be with the consent of the owner.[82] The owner's consent is to be presumed in the absence of evidence to the contrary.[83]

(f) SALES OF MOTOR VEHICLES SUBJECT TO HIRE-PURCHASE AGREEMENTS

Where a motor vehicle has been let under a hire-purchase agreement

[72] *Heyman* v. *Flewker* (1863) 13 C.B. (N.S.) 519.

[73] *International Sponge Importers* v. *Watt*, 1909, 2 S.L.T. 24.

[74] *Weiner* v. *Harris* [1910] 1 K.B. 285; *Lowther* v. *Harris* [1927] 1 K.B. 393.

[75] *Heap* v. *Motorists Advisory Agency, Ltd.* [1923] 1 K.B. 577.

[76] *Vickers* v. *Hertz* (1871) 9 M. (H.L.) 65; *Folkes* v. *King* [1923] 1 K.B. 282; *Pearson* v. *Rose and Young, Ltd.* [1951] K.B. 275 (where sale not 'in the ordinary course of business').

[77] *Brown & Co.* v. *Bedford Pantechnicon Co.* (1889) 5 T.L.R. 449; *Staffs Motor Guarantee, Ltd.* v. *British Wagon Co.* [1934] 2 K.B. 305.

[78] Factors (Sc.) Act, 1890, S. 1(2); as to consideration see 1889 Act, S. 5.

[79] See *Oppenheimer* v. *Attenborough* [1908] 1 K.B. 221; *Heap, supra; Pearson, supra.*

[80] Factors Act, 1889, S. 2(2), overruling *Fuentes* v. *Monti* (1868) L.R. 4 C.P. 93.

[81] *Moody* v. *Pall Mall Deposit Co.* (1917) 33 T.L.R. 306.

[82] 1889 Act, S. 2(3).   [83] 1889 Act, S. 2(4).

or been agreed to be sold under a conditional sale agreement, and, before the property in the vehicle has become vested in the hirer or buyer, he disposes of it[84] to another person, the disposition has effect as if the title of the owner or seller had been vested in the hirer or buyer immediately before the disposition, provided the disposition is to a private purchaser and he is a purchaser of the motor vehicle in good faith and without notice of the hire-purchase or conditional sale agreement.[85] Where a disposition is made to a trade or finance purchaser,[86] then if the first private purchaser after that disposition is a purchaser in good faith and without notice of the hire-purchase or conditional sale agreement, the disposition to the first private purchaser has effect as if the title of the owner or seller had been vested in the hirer or purchaser immediately before he disposed of it to the trade or finance purchaser.[87] Where the disposition to the first private purchaser in good faith and without notice is a letting under a hire-purchase agreement and the owner disposes of the vehicle by way of transferring to him the property in the vehicle in pursuance of a provision in the hire-purchase agreement in that behalf, the latter disposition (whether the person to whom it is made is then a purchaser in good faith and without a notice of the original agreement or not) shall, as well as the former disposition, have effect as mentioned in S. 27(3).[88]

These provisions have effect notwithstanding the Sale of Goods Act, 1979, S. 21, but without prejudice to the Factors Acts, 1889 and 1890, or of any other enactment enabling the apparent owner of goods to dispose of them as if he were the owner, and they do not exonerate the hirer or buyer from any liability to which he would otherwise be subject.[89]

Certain presumptions in relation to dealings with motor vehicles are also created.[90]

(g) COMMON LAW AND STATUTORY POWERS OF SALE

At common law non-owners have powers of sale to the effect of giving a good title to a purchaser in certain cases:

---

[84] 'Dispose of' is defined in S. 29(1).

[85] Hire-Purchase Act, 1964, S. 27(1)–(2). Ss. 27–9 are restated with verbal changes in Consumer Credit Act, 1974, Sch. 4, para. 22. These provisions apply to all hire-purchase transactions relating to vehicles, without limitation of value or restriction to transactions by private persons. S. 27 protects a private purchaser if he is assured and honestly believes that any hire-purchase contract relative to the vehicle has been paid off: *Barker* v. *Bell* [1971] 2 All E.R. 867.

[86] Defined S. 29(2).

[87] Ibid., S. 27(3); *N.W. Securities* v. *Barrhead Coachworks*, 1976 S.C. 68.

[88] Ibid., S. 27(4).

[89] Ibid., S. 27(5)–(6).

[90] Ibid., S. 28.

Common law powers

(i) *Negotiorum gestor:* a *negotiorum gestor* may sell or pledge moveables of which he has taken possession in the exercise of his *gestio* to the effect of conferring a good title on the purchaser. But if the sale were unjustifiable in the circumstances the gestor will be liable in damages to the owner.[91]

(ii) Agent of necessity: an agent of necessity, whose action is justified by necessity and who is unable to communicate with the owners, may validly sell or pledge the goods.[92] If there is no emergency, or the goods are not perishable, the sale is unjustifiable and wrongful.[93]

(iii) Pledgee of goods: a pledgee of goods or of the documents of title to goods may sell, if the time fixed for repayment has expired, but only if he has been given express power to sell, or obtains warrant from the sheriff to do so.[94]

(iv) Superior or landlord exercising hypothec: a superior or landlord who in the exercise of his right of hypothec (where it exists) has sequestrated *invecta et illata* for feu-duty or rent unpaid may sell the sequestrated goods under warrant from the sheriff.

(v) Creditor in exercise of diligence: a creditor holding a decree may have the debtor charged to pay and, failing payment, poind his goods and sell them under judicial warrant.

Statutory powers

(i) Pawnbrokers have power to sell by auction unredeemed pledges above £15 in value.[95]

(ii) Innkeepers have power, subject to formalities, to sell goods brought to the inn by a guest indebted for his entertainment.[96]

(iii) Property found and not claimed by the owner or finder may be sold by order of a magistrate, and property stolen and unclaimed may also be sold.[97]

(iv) An unpaid seller of goods has a right of resale notwithstanding that the property in the goods has passed to the buyer.

(v) Warehousemen may sell imported goods in respect of which they have incurred expense.[99]

---

[91] *Koblin* v. *United Shipping Co.*, 1931 S.C. (H.L.) 128, 138.

[92] *Sims* v. *Midland Ry.* [1913] 1 K.B. 103; cf. *Prager* v. *Blatspiel, Stamp and Heacock* [1924] 1 K.B. 566; *Jebara* v. *Ottoman Bank* [1927] 2 K.B. 254.

[93] *Springer* v. *G.W. Ry.* [1921] 1 K.B. 257. cf. *Sach* v. *Miklos* [1948] 2 K.B. 23; *Munro* v. *Willmott* [1949] 1 K.B. 295.

[94] Bell, *Prin.* §207; see also *Duncan* v. *Mitchell* (1893) 21 R. 37.

[95] Consumer Credit Act, 1974, S. 121.

[96] Innkeepers Act, 1878, S. 1.

[97] Burgh Police (Sc.) Act, 1892, Ss. 412, 415.

[98] Sale of Goods Act, 1979, Ss. 39, 48(2).

[99] Merchant Shipping Act, 1894, Ss. 497–8.

(vi) Trustees in bankruptcy may sell the bankrupt's property.[1]

(vii) Liquidators of companies can sell the company's property.[2]

(viii) Receivers appointed to a company's property can sell any of the company's property.[3]

Court authority

In many cases sale is competent on warrant obtained from the sheriff on summary application; such cases include sale following sequestration for rent, sale of rejected goods, sale of strayed cattle, sale of perishable goods, and it is thought that all such sales confer a good title on the purchaser.

---

[1] Bankruptcy (Sc.) Act, 1913, Ss. 78, 133; see also *Robertson* v. *Adam* (1857) 19 D. 502; *Stewart* v. *Crookston,* 1910 S.C. 609.

[2] Companies Act, 1948, Ss. 245, 303.

[3] Companies (Floating Charges and Receivers) (Sc.) Act, 1972, S. 15(1)(b).

CHAPTER 5.32

GIFT AND BARTER OF MOVEABLES

In gift and barter the intention is to transfer proprietary rights in a moveable object, in gift, wholly gratuitously, or, in barter, in exchange for another moveable object, but in neither case for money.

DONATION *INTER VIVOS*[1]

The intention to donate or transfer gratuitously, *animus donandi,* is frequently evidenced only by the fact of delivery or by the donor's manner or expressions uttered at the time of actual transfer.[2] It may be proved by parole evidence, which must be clear and convincing.[3] Proof is easier where there existed circumstances inferring a natural obligation to support or assist the donee.[4] If evidenced by the writ or admission on oath of the donor his announced intention or promise constitutes an enforceable unilateral gratuitous obligation.[5] A *pactum donationis,* however, confers on the donee merely a right to claim delivery, and no right in the thing itself passes without delivery. If the intention is not proveable in the ways prescribed the donee has not even a right to claim delivery.[6] If the donor has orally promised a thing to one and gives it to another the latter becomes the owner.[7]

The *animus donandi* must be effectuated by delivery of the thing gifted, to dispossess the donor and invest the donee with the property in the thing gifted.[8]

---

[1] For donation *mortis causa,* see Ch. 7.4 *infra.*

[2] cf. *Little* v. *L.* (1856) 18 D. 701.

[3] *Sharp* v. *Paton* (1883) 10 R. 1000.

[4] *Wilson* v. *Paterson* (1826) 4 S. 817; *Macalister's Trs.* v. *M.* (1827) 5 S. 219; *Farquhar's Trs.* v. *Stewart* (1841) 3 D. 658; *Nisbet's Trs.* v. *N.* (1868) 6 M. 567; *Forbes* v. *F.* (1869) 8 M. 85; *Malcolm* v. *Campbell* (1889) 17 R. 255; cf. *Fairgrieves* v. *Hendersons* (1885) 13 R. 98.

[5] Ersk. III, 3, 88. cf. *Balfour* v. *Simpson* (1837) 11 M. 604; *Shaw* v. *Muir's Exrx.* (1892) 19 R. 997; *Cambuslang West Church* v. *Bryce* (1897) 25 R. 322.

[6] Ersk. III, 3, 90.

[7] Ersk. III, 3, 90.

[8] *Crosbie's Trs.* v. *Wright* (1880) 7 R. 823; *Milne* v. *Scott* (1880) 8 R. 83; *Thompson* v. *Dunlop* (1884) 11 R. 453; *L.A.* v. *Galloway* (1884) 11 R. 541; *Milne* v. *Grant's Exors.* (1884) 11 R. 887; *McNicol* v. *McDougall* (1889) 17 R. 25; *Brownlee's Exor.* v. *B.,* 1908 S.C. 232; *Hubbard* v. *Dunlop's Trs.,* 1933 S.N. 62; cf. *Newton* v. *N.,* 1923 S.C. 15.

A gift can be declined, by non-acceptance or return of the thing sought to be gifted.[9]

A donation is not now revocable, whether on the ground of the donee's ingratitude[10] nor as being *inter virum et uxorem*.[11]

In dubio there is a presumption against donation, and actual transfer of goods is to be ascribed to another legal category such as loan, unless the evidence of *animus donandi* is clear.[12] Whether payments by way of aliment are donation or loan is a question of circumstances.[13] If A's property is in B's hands the onus is on B to prove donation, not on A to prove deposit or agency or other reason for the property being in B's possession.[14] As a consequence of this, *debitor non praesumitur donare*, so that where a debtor gives money or goods to his creditor, the natural presumption is that he intends to reduce or extinguish his debt. This presumption may be overcome by stronger contrary presumption or evidence.[15] One person may sue another who has actually received money as a gift on the ground that the gift was intended for the pursuer and that the defender is unjustifiably withholding it.[16]

PERMUTATION OR BARTER OF GOODS

Permutation, barter or exchange[17] is the contract whereby one or more items of moveable property are exchanged for other items of moveable property, not for money. The contract of exchanging goods for goods and money is probably sale rather than barter.[18] The contract may be constituted in any way and proved by parole evidence.[19] It is regulated by common law and analogies with the common law of sale may be invoked.[20]

---

[9] Stair I, 10, 4; III, 2, 4; Ersk. III, 3, 88.

[10] Bankt. I, 9, 4; Ersk. III, 3, 90; Bell, *Prin.* §64.

[11] Married Women's Property (Sc.) Act, 1920, S. 5, altering Stair I, 4, 16; Ersk. I, 6, 29.

[12] Stair I, 8, 2; IV, 45, 17(14); Ersk. III, 3, 92; *Garthland's Trs.* v. *McDowall*, 26 May 1820, F.C.; *Drummond* v. *Swayne* (1834) 12 S. 342; *Farquhar's Trs.* v. *Stewart* (1841) 3 D. 658; *Murray* v. *M.* (1834) 6 D. 176; *B.L. Co.* v. *Martin* (1849) 11 D. 1004; *Robertson* v. *R.* (1858) 20 D. 371; *Heron* v. *McGeoch* (1851) 14 D. 25; *Forbes* v. *F.* (1869) 8 M. 85; *Sharp* v. *Paton* (1883) 10 R. 1000; *Milne* v. *Grant's Exors.* (1884) 11 R. 887; *Dawson* v. *McKenzie* (1829) 19 R. 261; *Brownlee's Exrx.* v. *B.*, 1908 S.C. 232.

[13] *Turnbull* v. *O'Brien*, 1908 S.C. 313.

[14] *Sharp, supra; Dawson, supra; Brownlee's Exrx., supra; Malcolm* v. *Campbell* (1889) 17 R. 255; *Penman* v. *White*, 1957 S.C. 338; *McVea* v. *Reid*, 1958 S.L.T. (Sh. Ct.) 60.

[15] Ersk. III, 3, 93; *Edgar* v. *Hamilton's Trs.* (1828) 6 S. 963; *Black* v. *Booth* (1835) 14 S. 113; *Johnstone* v. *Haviland* (1896) 23 R. (H.L.) 6.

[16] *Costin* v. *Hume*, 1914 S.C. 134.

[17] Stair I, 10, 14; I, 14, 1; Bankt. I, 19, 1; Ersk. III, 3, 4 and 13; Bell, *Prin.* §92(3); cf. Sale of Goods Act, 1979, S. 2.

[18] e.g. trading in a car and money for a new car; cf. *Aldridge* v. *Johnson* (1857) 7 E. & B. 885; *Dawson* v. *Dutfield* [1936] 2 All E.R. 232.

[19] *McMurrich's Trs.* v. *McM's Trs.* (1903) 6 F. 121, 125.

[20] The Sale of Goods Act, 1979, does not apply.

The right of property does not pass until delivery,[21] but the risk passes at the time when the contract is completed and the acquirer has right to a specific thing.[22] If the goods have been identified and appropriated to the contract the property passes even though the transferee has not assented to or accepted that appropriation.[23]

The goods must conform to any description given and if, by reason of non-conformity thereto, are unsuitable for the contemplated purpose, the contract is voidable if they are rejected timeously.[24] If the goods are in breach of warranty the taker's only remedy is rejection; he cannot retain them and bring an *actio quanti minoris*.[25] If the contract is for the exchange of trading stamps for goods certain stipulations are implied.[26]

If either party fails to implement his part of the contract, the other's remedy is to sue for specific implement,[27] failing which for damages, measured by the value of the thing not delivered.[28]

---

[21] Stair I, 14, 1; Ersk. III, 3, 8.

[22] Bell, *Comm.* I, 473; Ersk. III, 3, 7; *Widenmeyer* v. *Burn Stewart & Co.*, 1967 S.C. 85.

[23] *Widenmeyer, supra.*

[24] *MacGregor* v. *Bannerman* (1948) 64 Sh. Ct. Rep. 14.

[25] *Urquhart* v. *Wylie*, 1953 S.L.T. (Sh. Ct.) 87.

[26] Trading Stamps Act, 1964, S. 4, as substituted by Supply of Goods (Implied Terms) Act, 1973, S. 16.

[27] cf. *Widenmeyer, supra.*

[28] cf. *Harrison* v. *Luke* (1845) 14 M. & W. 139, 141.

CHAPTER 5.33

SALE OF CORPOREAL MOVEABLES

At common law the Scots law on sale of goods followed closely the principles of the Roman law of sale.[1] The Sale of Goods Act, 1893, did not abrogate the common law, save in so far as inconsistent with its express provision,[2] but in large measure it provided a code of law substantially common throughout the United Kingdom based mainly on English common law and substantially altering Scots law on many matters.[3] In particular at common law in Scotland a concluded contract of sale of specific goods was a contract only and left ownership of the goods with the seller till delivery, the purchaser having a right to demand delivery; it was merely *titulus transferendi dominii* conferring on the buyer only *jus ad rem specificam,* and requiring a conveyance, by delivery, to pass the right of property. In English law the conclusion of the contract passed the property in the goods, independently of delivery; it was both a contract and a conveyance, not only *titulus* but *modus transferendi dominii,* passing a *jus in re.* Also, if the goods were not yet in existence, or not yet deliverable, in neither country did the agreement transfer ownership; in Scotland it required delivery, but in England ownership passed as soon as the goods were appropriated to the contract and ready for delivery.[4] The Mercantile Law Amendment (Sc.) Act, 1856, Ss. 1–5, assimilated the Scottish rules to those of England in many respects and the 1893 Act carried the process further by accepting English theory as well as principles.[5] However commercially convenient the result is legally confusing. The 1893 Act, as later amended, is restated in the Sale of Goods Act, 1979.[6]

[1] See generally: De Zulueta, *Roman Law of Sale;* Stair I, 14, 1; Ersk. III, 3, 2; Bell, *Comm.* I, 166, 434; Bell, *Prin.* (9th ed.) §85, 1229; M. P. Brown, *Sale.*   [2] 1893 Act, S. 61(2)

[3] See generally: Bell, *Prin.* (10 ed.) §85 et seq.; R. Brown. *Sale of Goods Act*; Benjamin; Chalmers; and Atiyah on *Sale.*

[4] See Bell, *Prin.* §86; *Seath* v. *Moore* (1886) 13 R. (H.L.) 57.

[5] The Acts of 1893 and 1979, as codifying Acts must be interpreted uninfluenced by considerations derived from the previous state of the law, except is so far as the common law is saved, or the Act is ambiguous or unclear: *Vagliano* v. *Bank of England* [1891] A.C. 107, 145; *Bristol Tramways* v. *Fiat Motors* [1910] 2 K.B. 831, 836; *Nicol's Trs.* v. *Sutherland,* 1951 S.C. (H.L.) 21.

[6] Most of the section (but not subsection) numbers of the 1979 Act correspond to those of the 1893 Act and cases decided on the 1893 Act are frequently still valuable guides to interpretation of the 1979 Act, though in some respects the wording has been changed significantly.

The Act contains no special provisions as to, and consequently the general common law principles of contract as to, capacity and power to contract, principal and agent, and the effect of error, misrepresentation, fraud, duress or coercion, mistake or other invalidating cause, continue to apply to sales of goods.[7] The rules of bankruptcy, landlord's hypothec and sequestration for rent are unaffected by the Act.[8]

Nature of sale

Sale of goods is a mutual consensual contract, absolute or conditional,[9] by which the seller transfers or agrees to transfer the property in goods to the buyer in exchange for a pecuniary price.[10] Goods' include[11] all corporeal moveables[12] except money,[13] industrial growing crops,[14] and things attached to or forming part of the land which are agreed to be severed before sale or under the contract of sale.[15] The 1979 Act does not apply to any transaction in the form of a sale intended to operate by way of pledge, charge or other security.[16] It is distinguishable from barter,[17] hiring,[18] and the contract for services and materials.[19]

Sale and agreement to sell

Where the right of property in the goods is transferred the contract is a sale, but where the transfer of the right of property is to take place at

---

[7] For all these see Chs. 4.3–4.5, supra.

[8] 1979 Act, S. 62.

[9] The condition may be suspensive: Brandt v. Dickson (1876) 3 R. 375; or resolutive: The conditions may include one empowering the seller to buy back in certain circumstances, the pactum de retrovendendo; see Allan & Co's Tr. v. Gunn (1883) 10 R. 997; Gavin's Tr. v. Fraser, 1920 S.C. 674.

[10] S. 2; cf. Bell, Prin. §85, 109–10; Murdoch v. Greig (1889) 16 R. 396. Hence for a members' club to supply goods to members is not sale: Crossgates Bristol Legion Club v. Davidson, 1954 J.C. 35. The price may be partly paid by 'trading in' goods: see e.g. Dawson v. Dutfield [1936] 2 All E.R. 232.

[11] S. 61.

[12] Including ships; McConnachie v. Geddes, 1918 S.C. 391; though special rules apply to the transfer of title; cf. Manchester Ship Canal Co v. Horlock [1914] 2 Ch. 199; Behnke v. Bede Shipping Co. [1927] 1 K.B. 649.

[13] A coin, as a curio, is goods and not money: Moss v. Hancock [1899] 2 Q.B. 111; R. v. Dickinson [1920] 3 K.B. 552.

[14] cf. Paton's Trs. v. Finlayson, 1923 S.C. 872.

[15] This covers trees and fruit: Morison v. Lockhart, 1912 S.C. 1017; Kursell v. Timber Operators [1927] 1 K.B. 298; Saunders v. Pilcher [1949] 2 All E.R. 1097; Munro v. Balnagown Estates, 1949 S.C. 49.

[16] S. 62(4); cf. Robertson v. Hall's Tr. (1896) 24 R. 120; Jones' Tr. v. Allan (1902) 4 F. 374; Rennet v. Mathieson (1903) 5 F. 591; Hepburn v. Law, 1914 S.C. 918; Gavin's Tr. v. Fraser, 1920 S.C. 674; Scottish Transit Trust v. Scottish Land Cultivators, 1955 S.C. 254; G. and C. Finance Corpn. v. Brown, 1961 S.L.T. 408.

[17] Ch. 5.32, supra.

[18] Ch. 5.29, supra.

[19] Ch. 4.16, supra.

a future time or subject to some condition thereafter to be fulfilled it is an agreement to sell.[20] An agreement to sell becomes a sale when the time elapses or the conditions, subject to which the property is to be transferred, are fulfilled.[20]

Capacity

The capacities of the parties to buy and to sell are regulated by the general law of contract. When necessaries[21] are sold and delivered to a minor a person incompetent to contract by mental incapacity or drunkenness he must pay a reasonable price therefor.[21]

Offer and acceptance: error and misrepresentation

Offer and acceptance are determined by principles of common law. In self-service stores they are made at the checkout.[22] When buying from a vending machine the machine make a continuing offer, and acceptance is made by inserting the requisite coin.[23] Questions of error and misrepresentation are also determined by common law principles.[24]

Formalities

The contract may, subject to any special statute,[25] be constituted in any form, and proved by any evidence.[26]

Obligations of the parties

The seller's obligations are to transfer, or permit or authorize transfer of, the property in the thing sold to the buyer,[27] and to comply with the terms and conditions, express and statutorily implied, of the contract.[28] The buyer's obligations are to pay the agreed price, and to take delivery of the goods, unless they do not comply with the contract.[29]

[20] 1979 Act, S. 2: a sale is accordingly a contract and also a conveyance or transfer of title; an agreement to sell is a contract only; a credit sale agreement is an agreement to sell under the Act: *Lee* v. *Butler* [1893] 2 Q.B. 318; cf. *Helby* v. *Matthews* [1895] A.C. 471; *Bryce* v. *Ehrmann* (1904) 7 F. 5. A contract to sell a ship is only an agreement to sell, the transfer of the property being effected by the bill of sale: *Aurdal* v. *Estrella*, 1916 S.C. 882. An order for goods to be manufactured and delivered is an agreement to sell: *Stark's Trs.* v. *S.*, 1948 S.C. 41.
[21] 1979 Act, S. 3. *Ryder* v. *Wombwell* (1868) L.R. 4 Ex. 32, 38; approved in *Keane* v. *Mount Vernon Colliery Co.*, 1933 S.C. (H.L.) 1, 13. This liability truly arises quasi-contractually; *Re Rhodes* (1890) 44 Ch. D. 94, 105. Necessaries are defined as goods suitable to the condition in life of such minor or other person and to his actual requirements at the time of the sale and delivery; cf. *Nash* v. *Inman* [1908] 2 K.B.1.
[22] *Pharmaceutical Socy.* v. *Boots* [1953] 1 Q.B. 401.
[23] *Thornton* v. *Shoe Lane Parking Ltd.* [1971] 2 Q.B. 163.
[24] e.g. *Morrisson* v. *Robertson*, 1908 S.C. 332.
[25] e.g. Merchant Shipping Act, 1894 Ss. 24, 65, as to sale of ships.
[26] S. 4. Bell, *Prin.* §89; *Ireland* v. *Rosewall Coal Co.* (1900) 7 S.L.T. 445; The sale of mixed lot of items, predominantly moveable, may be proved *prout de jure*: *Allan* v. *Millar*, 1932 S.C. 620.
[27] cf. S. 27.
[28] Bell, *Prin.* §112, 121.
[29] Bell, *Prin.* §127, 128.

Subject of contract

The subject of contract may be existing goods, or goods subsequently to be manufactured or acquired by the seller ('future goods'),[30] or goods the acquisition of which by the seller depends on an uncertain contingency.[31] If a seller purports to sell future goods, the contract operates as an agreement to sell them.[32] They may also be specific goods, identified and agreed upon when the contact is made,[33] or ascertained goods, which may be identified subsequently,[34] or unascertained goods, which may be generic[35] or an undivided part of a larger consignment.[36] If specific goods were sold but have perished, unknown to the seller, before the contract was made, it is void.[37] If after an agreement to sell specific goods they perish without any fault of either party before the risk passes to the buyer, the contract is avoided.[38] These sections are not exclusive of the common law principles of avoidance by frustration or supervening illegality.[39]

Price

The price may be fixed by the contract, or left to be fixed in manner thereby agreed,[40] or determined by the course of dealing between the parties.[41] *Certum est quod certum reddi potest.* Failing such determination the buyer must pay a reasonable price, which is a question of fact in the circumstances of each case.[42] Hence there can be a valid

---

[30] *Ajello* v. *Worsley* [1899] 1 Ch. 274; *Sainsbury* v. *Street* [1972] 3 All E.R. 1127.
[31] S. 5; *Hale* v. *Rawson* (1858) 4 C.B.N.S. 85; cf. *emptio spei.*
[32] S. 5(3).
[33] e.g. 'my Bentley car'.
[34] e.g. 'a BL Metro'.
[35] e.g. '1 cwt. of potatoes'.
[36] e.g. '500 tons of wheat from load of' a named ship: cf. *Re Wait* [1927] 1 Ch. 606.
[37] S. 6; cf. *Couturier* v. *Hastie* (1856) 5 H.L.C. 673. But in the case of generic goods the rule is *genus nunquam perit* and the sale is valid; sell also *Barrow Lane & Ballard* v. *Phillips* [1929] 1 K.B. 574. Perishing or destruction after the contract is not within this section, but within the rule of impossibility of performance.
[38] S. 7; *Elphick* v. *Barnes* (1880) 5 C.P.D. 321; *In re Wait* [1927] 1 Ch. 606. If part of the goods have perished the sale is void if it was a sale of an indivisible lot of goods for a single price: *Barrow, Lane and Ballard Ltd.* v. *Phillip Phillips & Co.* [1929] 1 K.B. 574. If not indivisible the contract in enforceable in part: *Sainsbury* v. *Street* [1972] 3 All E.R. 1127. Deteriorated goods have not 'perished': *Horn* v. *Minister of Food* [1948] 2 All E.R. 1036.
[39] cf. *McMaster* v. *Cox, McEuen & Co.,* 1921 S.C. (H.L.) 24.
[40] Bell, *Prin.* §92; The price may be fixed by one party: *Lavaggi* v. *Pirie* (1872) 10 M. 312. As to valuation see *Macdonald* v. *Clark,* 1927 S.N. 6.
[41] S. 8(1); e.g. *Arcos Ltd.* v. *Aronson* (1930) 36 Ll.L.R. 108. Where the contract provided for 'prices to be agreed on from time to time' the H.L. held there was no contract: *May and Butcher* v. *The King* [1934] 2 K.B. 17n.
[42] S. 8(2); *Valpy* v. *Gibson* (1847) 4 C.B. 837, 864. It is not necessarily the market price: *Acebal* v. *Levy* (1834) 10 Bing. 376; *Leslie* v. *Millers* (1714) Mor. 14197; *Glynwed* v. *Koronka,* 1977 S.C. 1; but must not be illusory, which makes it donation: Bell, *Prin.* §92. As to effect of price rises made by ultimate supplier, see *Stark's Trs.* v. *S.,* 1948 S.C. 41.

contract though there is no agreement on price.[43] Where there is an agreement to sell goods at a third party's valuation and he cannot or does not make it, the agreement is avoided, but the buyer must pay a reasonable price for any goods delivered to the buyer. If the valuation is prevented by either party, the other has an action of damages against the party in fault.[44] Stipulation for part-payment of the price, as for a deposit payable on contracting and liable to forfeiture in certain circumstances, is valid and a buyer cannot found on his own breach of contract to claim a return thereof.[45] Unless otherwise indicated, stipulations as to the time of payment are not deemed of the essence of the contract, but the materiality of other stipulations as to time depends on the terms of the contract.[46] Where after the making of a contract for the supply of goods there is a change in VAT then, unless the contract otherwise provides, the change must be given effect to in the price.[47]

Price fixed by supplier

In general the price may not be one fixed by a third party who has supplied goods to the seller on condition of his not reselling below a fixed resale price, though a supplier may notify sellers of prices recommended as appropriate for the resale of particular goods.[48]

Trading stamps

Where a retail trader selling goods operates a trading stamps scheme[49] he must keep posted a notice stating the cash value of the trading stamps issued under the scheme and a copy of any current catalogue issued by the promoters.[50] There are restrictions on the persons who may carry on business as promoters of a trading stamp scheme.[51] Each stamp must state its cash value,[52] and the promoter must redeem stamps for cash on request if their face value is 25 pence or more.[53] Where trading stamps are redeemed by the promoters for goods notwithstanding any terms to the contrary on which the redemption is made, there is (a) an implied warranty on the part of the promoter that he has a right to give the goods in exchange; (b) an implied stipulation that the goods are free from any charge or encumbrance not disclosed

---

[43] *Glynwed, supra.*
[44] S. 9; *Vickers* v. *V.* (1867) L.R. 4 Eq. 529.
[45] *Commercial Bank* v. *Beal* (1891) 18 R. 80; *Roberts & Cooper* v. *Salvesen*, 1918 S.C. 794
[46] S. 10; *Martindale* v. *Smith* (1841) 1 Q.B. 389; *Mersey Steel Co.* v. *Naylor* (1884) 9 App. Cas. 434; *Shaw, Macfarlane & Co.* v. *Waddell* (1900) 2 F. 1070; *Payzu* v. *Saunders* [1919] 2 K.B. 581; contrast *Ryan* v. *Ridley* (1902) 8 Com. Cas. 105.
[47] Finance Act, 1972, S. 42.
[48] Resale Prices Act, 1976, Ss. 1, 9.
[49] Defined, Trading Stamps Act, 1964, S. 10.
[50] S. 7; as to catalogues see also S. 5.
[51] S. 1.   [52] S. 2; see also S. 6.   [53] S. 3.

or known to the person obtaining the goods before, or at the time of, redemption and that that person will enjoy quiet possession of the goods except so far as it may be disturbed by the owner or other person entitled to the benefit of any charge or encumbrance so disclosed or known; (c) an implied stipulation that the goods are of merchantable quality,[54] except that there is no such stipulation (i) as regards defects specifically drawn to the attention of the person obtaining the goods before or at the time of redemption; or (ii) if that person examines the goods before or at the time of redemption, as regards defects which that examination ought to reveal.[55]

TERMS OF THE CONTRACT

Trade descriptions

The application of a false trade description, within the Trade Descriptions Act, 1968, to goods is a criminal offence of strict liability[56] but a contract for the supply of any goods is not void or unenforceable by reason only of a contravention of the Act.[57] But a description may be a misrepresentation or warranty at common law, in which case the buyer may be entitled on general principles of contract to rescind the contract or to claim damages for the loss sustained in consequence.

Stipulations about time

Unless a different intention appears from the terms of the contract stipulations as to time of payment are not of the essence of the contract. Whether any other stipulation as to time is or is not of the essence depends on the terms of the contract. In a contract of sale a month is prima facie a calendar month.[58]

Conditions and warranties

The conditions and warranties, or terms and stipulations of the contract relative to the goods, depend primarily on the express terms

---

[54] Goods are of merchantable quality if they are as fit for the purpose or purposes for which goods of that kind are commonly bought as it is reasonable to expect having regard to any description applied to them and all the other relevant circumstances: subs. (2).

[55] S. 4, as substituted by Supply of Goods (Implied Terms) Act, 1973, S. 16. Subs. (3) substitutes the word 'stipulation' for 'warranty' in the section as applied to Scotland. The section assimilates the warranties implied on redemption of trading stamps to those implied in a contract of sale of goods.

[56] *Macnab* v. *Alexanders of Greenock*, 1971 S.L.T. 121.

[57] 1968 Act, S. 35.

[58] 1979 Act, S. 10. Any stipulation as to time may be expressly made of the essence. The point is important in relation to entitlement or not to rescind the contract for delay: *McDougall* v. *Aeromarine* [1958] 3 All E.R. 431.

and stipulations of the parties' contract,[59] and secondly on the terms implied by Ss. 12–15 of the 1979 Act. The Act, using English terminology, distinguishes[60] between conditions, or fundamental stipulations the breach of which gives rise to a right to treat the contract as repudiated,[61] and warranties, or less material stipulations, collateral to the main purpose of the contract,[62] the breach of which gives rise to a claim for damages but not to a right to treat the contract as repudiated.[62] In Scotland this corresponds generally to the distinction between material and less material breaches of contract,[63] though in Scottish usage a warranty is a more important stipulation than a mere term or condition, connoting something guaranteed, for breach of which the contract may be rescinded.[64] It is provided[65] that in Scotland a breach of warranty shall be deemed to be a failure to perform a material part of the contract. Accordingly it matters little in Scotland whether a term, express or implied by any of Ss. 12–15, is called a stipulation, a condition, or a warranty; the question is whether failure to implement it is a fundamental or material breach or a less important or non-material breach.[66] In Scotland, failure by the seller to perform any material part of a contract of sale is a breach of contract, which entitles the buyer within a reasonable time after delivery to reject the goods and treat the contract as repudiated,[67] or to retain the goods and treat the failure to perform such material part as a breach which may give

---

[59] These are, moreover, independent of any advertising statements, opinions, or collateral representations, made at the time of the making of the contract, and of any representations which may have induced the making of the contract. See e.g. *Campbell* v. *Henderson* (1886) 23 S.L.R. 712; *Wilson* v. *Turnbull* (1896) 23 R. 714; *Malcolm* v. *Cross* (1898) 25 R. 1089; *Robey* v. *Stein* (1900) 3 F. 278; *Cranston* v. *Mallow & Lien* 1912 S.C. 112. What express warranties, if any, were given is a question of fact and evidence. The pursuer must prove the exact words of any alleged express warranty given when the contract was made: *Mackie* v. *Riddell* (1874) 2 R. 63; *Robeson* v. *Waugh* (1874) 2 R. 63; *Rose* v. *Johnston* (1878) 5 R. 600; *Dunn* v. *E. Newington Garage Co.*, 1946 S.N. 144. See also *Hyslop* v. *Shirlaw* (1905) 7 F. 875; *Kyle* v. *Sim*, 1925 S.C. 425; *Flynn* v. *Scott*, 1949 S.C. 442. By the Agriculture Act, 1970, S. 68, a person who sells material of a prescribed description for use as a fertilizer or feeding stuff must give the purchaser a statement in writing containing prescribed particulars.

[60] Ss. 11(3) (not applicable to Scotland, but the words reappear in Ss. 12–15 and 53), and 61, *sub voce* 'Warranty'. 'Condition' is not defined in S. 61.

[61] *Wallis* v. *Pratt & Haynes* [1910] 2 K.B. 1003, 1012; [1911] A.C. 394. Whether a stipulation is a condition or a warranty depends on the construction of the contract; the word used is not conclusive; S. 11 (3) (not Scotland).

[62] S. 61(1); *Wallis, supra.*

[63] *Wade* v. *Waldon*, 1909 S.C. 571; as in England, any stipulation may by agreement become a material term, but failing agreement it is a question of the construction of the contract.

[64] See e.g. *Cranston* v. *Mallow & Lien*, 1912 S.C. 112; cf. *Campbell* v. *Henderson* (1886) 23 S.L.R. 712; *Wilson* v. *Turnbull* (1896) 23 R. 714; *Malcolm* v. *Cross* (1898) 25 R. 1089; *Hyslop* v. *Shirlaw* (1905) 7 F. 875.

[65] S. 61(2).

[66] cf. *Birkett, Sperling & Co.* v. *Engholm* (1871) 10 M. 170; *Shaw, Macfarlane & Co.* v. *Waddell* (1900) 2 F. 1070.

[67] Where the goods perished and could not be rejected, the buyer was held entitled to refuse payment: *Kinnear* v. *Brodie* (1901) 3 F. 540; cf. *Rough* v. *Moir* (1875) 2 R. 529.

rise to a claim for compensation or damages.[68] The buyer is entitled to a reasonable time to try the object bought to ascertain if it matches up to the warranty.[69] Failure to perform any less material part of the contract justifies only a claim for damages.[70] Nothing in S. 11 affects the case of any condition or warranty, fulfilment of which is excused by law by reason of impossibility or otherwise.[71]

Where goods are delivered in several consignments, if each is to be deemed a separate contract,[72] one or more may be rejected and others accepted, but if it is a single contract performed in stages, it is a difficult question whether defective performance of one justifies rejection of all.[73] Where there is a breach of warranty by the seller the buyer may set it up against the seller in diminution or extinction of the price, or maintain an action against the seller for damages.[74] Where a buyer has elected to accept goods which he might have rejected he may, in a seller's action for the price, be required in the court's discretion, to consign or pay into court the price of the goods or part thereof, or give other reasonable security for payment thereof.[75]

Implied undertakings as to title

By S. 12[76] it is provided: (1) in every contract of sale, other than one to which subsection (3) applies, there is an implied condition on the part of the seller that in the case of a sale, he has a right to sell the goods, and in the case of an agreement to sell, he will have a right to sell the goods at the time when the property is to pass;[77] and (2) there is also an implied warranty that (a) the goods are free, and will remain

---

[68] S. 11(5). See *Couston* v. *Chapman* (1872) 10 M. (H.L.) 74; *Aird & Coghill* v. *Pullan* (1904) 7 F. 258; *Nelson* v. *Chalmers*, 1913 S.C. 441; *Pollock* v. *Macrae*, 1922 S.C. (H.L.) 192; *Mechans* v. *Highland Marine Charters*, 1964 S.C. 48; *Millars of Falkirk* v. *Turpie*, 1976 S.L.T. 66.

The second alternative introduced the *actio quanti minoris* into the Scots law, subject to S. 58, whereby the buyer may, in an action by the seller for the price, be required to consign the price in court or give other reasonable security for payment thereof.

[69] *Kinnear* v. *Brodie* (1901) 3 F. 540; *Crowther* v. *Shannon* [1975] 1 All E.R. 139.

[70] *Fewson* v. *Gemmell* (1904) 11 S.L.T. 153, 697.   [71] S. 11(6).

[72] E.g. *Rosenthal* v. *Ismail* [1965] 2 All E.R. 860.

[73] *Mersey Steel Co.* v. *Naylor Benzon* (1884) 9 App. Cas. 434; *Maple Flock Co.* v. *Universal Furniture Products Ltd.* [1934] 1 K.B. 148.   [74] S. 53.

[75] S. 58. In *Cohen* v. *Jamieson & Paterson*, 1963 S.C. 289, it was held that S. 58 probably did not apply to S. 53 cases but that at common law the court could order consignation where a buyer elected to set up the breach in diminution or extinction of the price.

[76] This was substituted for original S. 12 by Supply of Goods (Implied Terms) Act, 1973, S. 1.

[77] This repeats S. 12(1) as originally enacted: see *Anderson* v. *Croall* (1903) 6 F. 153; *Niblett* v. *Confectioners' Materials Co.* [1921] 3 K.B. 387; *McDonald* v. *Provan* (*of Scotland St.*), 1960 S.L.T. 231. Subsections (1) and (2) deal with all cases except where there is a limitation on the title to be transferred; subsections (3) to (5) deal with the case where it is known that the seller may have a limited title and the buyer is taking only that title. Hence under subs. (1) a person in possession under a void title has no title and is in breach of S. 12(1) if he purports to sell: *Morrisson* v. *Robertson*, 1908 S.C. 332; but a person in possession under a voidable title can sell: *Robin & Rambler Coaches Ltd.* v. *Turner* [1947] 2 All E.R. 284; *MacLeod* v.*Kerr*, 1965 S.C. 253.

free until the time when the property is to pass, from any charge or encumbrance not disclosed or known to the buyer before the contract is made, and (b) the buyer will enjoy quiet possession of the goods except so far as it may be disturbed by the owner or other person entitled to the benefit of any charge or encumbrance so disclosed or known.[78] (3) In a contract of sale, in the case of which there appears from the contract or is to be inferred from the circumstances of the contract an intention that the seller should transfer only such title as he or a third person may have, there is (4) an implied warranty that all charges or encumbrances known to the seller and not known to the buyer have been disclosed before the contract is made; and (5) an implied warranty that none of the following will disturb the buyer's quiet possession of the goods, namely (i) the seller; (ii) in a case where the parties to the contract intend that the seller should transfer only such title as a third party may have, that person; (iii) anyone claiming through or under the seller or that third person otherwise than under a charge or encumbrance disclosed or known to the buyer before the contract is made.[79] Any term of a contract which purports to exclude or restrict liability for breach of the oblgations arising from S. 12 is void.[80]

Implied terms—sale by description, or sample and description

In the case of a sale by description[81] there is an implied condition that the goods shall correspond with the description;[82] and if the sale be by

[78] This replaces with modifications S. 12(2) and (3) as originally enacted. As to quiet possession see *Mason v. Burningham* [1949] 2 K.B. 545; *Microbeads v. Vinhurst* [1975] 1 All E.R. 529.

[79] This was a new provision in 1973: for cases where a seller purported to sell only a limited title: see *Payne v. Elsden* (1900) 17 T.L.R. 161; *Niblett, supra; Rowland v. Divall* [1923] 2 K.B. 500.   [80] Unfair Contract Terms Act, 1977, S. 20(1).

[81] This includes flax yarn containing jute: *Jaffe v. Ritchie* (1861) 23 D. 242; kind or species of goods: *Rutherford v. Miln*, 1941 S.C. 125; the constituents of a mixture: *McCallum v. Mason*, 1956 S.C. 50; every item in a description which constitutes a substantial ingredient in the identity of the thing sold is a condition: *Couchman v. Hill* [1947] 1 K.B. 554. Sale by description applies to all cases where the purchaser has not seen the goods: *Varley v. Whipp* [1900] 1 Q.B. 513; it consequently applies to all cases of mail-order; and may apply where he has seen the goods if the difference between description and reality is not apparent: *Beale v. Taylor* [1967] 3 All E.R. 253. All contracts for purchase of unascertained goods will be sales by description. Description may include particulars of quantity, quality, and packaging: *Manbre Saccharine Co. v. Corn Products Co.* [1919] 1 K.B. 198; *Re Moore & Co. and Landauer & Co.* [1921] 2 K.B. 519. See also S. 30(3). There is no breach of description of engine capacity by the appearance of a defect: *Britain S.S. Co. v. Lithgows*, 1975 S.C. 110.

[82] S. 13(1); *Bowes v. Shand* (1877) 2 App. Cas. 455; *Roberts v. Yule* (1896) 23 R. 855; *Varley v. Whipp* [1900] 1 Q.B. 513; *Wallis v. Pratt* [1911] A.C. 394; *Re Moore & Co., supra; Paul v. Pim* [1922] 2 K.B. 360; *Andrews Bros. v. Singer* [1934] 1 K.B. 17; *Macpherson Train v. Ross* [1955] 2 All E.R. 445; *McCallum v. Mason*, 1956 S.C. 50; *Beale v. Taylor* [1967] 3 All E.R. 253. A defect in quality is not actionable under this head; cf. *Rowan v. Coats Iron Co.* (1885) 12 R. 395; *McCallum, supra.* In *West Stockton Iron Co. v. Nielson & Maxwell* (1880) 7 R. 1055 and *Johnson & Reay v. Nicoll* (1881) 8 R. 437, it was held to be no breach to supply goods of different origin but equally answering the description.

sample and description, the bulk must correspond with the sample and the goods with the description.[83] A sale of goods is not prevented from being a sale by description by reason only that, being exposed for sale or hire, they are selected by the buyer.[84] Statements of incidental qualities, not serving to identify the goods are not part of the description. Supply of goods of a totally different kind,[85] or goods so defective as not really to answer the description of the goods sold,[86] or goods so deteriorated as to have lost their identity,[87] are breaches of condition. A contract is not affected merely by the fact that a false trade description has been applied to the goods and an offence thereby committed.[88] Any term in a contract which purports to exclude or restrict liability for breach of obligations arising from S. 13 is, in the case of a consumer contract void against the consumer, and in any other case, ineffective if it was not fair and reasonable to incorporate the term in the contract.[89]

Implied undertakings as to quality or fitness

S.14 provides: (1) Except as provided by this section and S. 15 of the Act and subject to any other enactment,[90] there is no implied condition or warranty as to the quality or fitness for any particular purpose of goods supplied under a contract of sale.[91] (2) Where the seller sells goods in the course of a business,[92] there is an implied condition that

---

[83] S. 13(2); Bell, *Prin.* §94A; *Nichol* v. *Godts.* (1854) 10 Ex. 191. Goods may be different from what was contracted for in a commercially significant way without failing to answer the description: *Gill & Dufus S.A.* v. *Berger* [1981] 2 Lloyd's Rep. 233.

[84] S. 13(3); e.g. if the buyer asks for 'a loaf' and, being shown several, says 'that one'.

[85] cf. *Chanter* v. *Hopkins* (1838) 4 M. & W. 399, 404 (to supply beans when peas were ordered is beach of description).

[86] cf. *Karsales* v. *Wallis* [1956] 2 All E.R. 866 (car incapable of self-propulsion without extensive repairs).

[87] *Ashington Piggeries* v. *Hill* [1972] A.C. 441.

[88] Trade Descriptions Act, 1968, S. 35.

[89] Unfair Contract Terms Act, 1977, S. 20(2). 'Consumer contract' is defined by S. 25 thereof.

[90] e.g. Heating Appliances (Fireguards) Act, 1952; Food and Drugs (Sc.) Act, 1956; Road Traffic Act, 1972, S. 60; Anchors and Chain Cables Act, 1967, S. 1; Trade Descriptions Act, 1968; Agriculture Act, 1970, S. 68; *Dobell* v. *Barber & Garrett* [1931] 1 K.B. 219; *Badham* v. *Lambs* [1946] K.B. 45.

[91] The general rule is accordingly *caveat emptor;* the buyer should satisfy himself as to the quality or fitness for his contemplated purpose of what he intends to buy; cf. *Hamilton* v. *Robertson* (1878) 5 R. 839. By common law the seller warranted the quality of the goods if the buyer had not seen them, and in certain other cases: see Bell, *Prin.* §96. The Mercantile Law Amdt. (Sc.) Act, 1856, S. 5, sought to assimilate the Scottish and English rules by providing that if the seller were without knowledge that the goods were defective, he was not to be held to have warranted their quality or sufficiency, but goods sold with all faults were to be at the purchaser's risk, unless the seller gave an express warranty. The 1893 Act made and the 1979 Act now makes uniform provision for Scotland and England on the former English lines.

[92] This excludes non-business transactions, e.g. between friends. As to 'business' see 1979 Act, S. 61(1); *Buchanan-Jardine* v. *Hamilink*, 1981 S.L.T. (Notes) 60.

the goods supplied under the contract are of merchantable quality,[93] except that there is no such condition (a) as regards defects specifically drawn to the buyer's attention before the contract is made; or (b) if the buyer examines the goods before the contract is made, as regards defects which that examination ought to reveal.[94] (3) Where the seller sells goods in the course of a business[92] and the buyer, expressly or by implication, makes known (a) to the seller, or (b) where the purchase price or part of it is payable by instalments and the goods were previously sold by a credit-broker[95] to the seller, to that credit-broker, any particular purpose for which the goods are being bought,[96] there is an implied condition that the goods supplied under the contract are reasonably fit for that purpose, [97] whether or not that is a purpose for

[93] Merchantable quality, by S. 14(6) of the 1979 Act, means that goods are as fit for the purpose or purposes for which goods of that kind are commonly bought as it is reasonable to expect having regard to any description applied to them, the price (if relevant), and all the other relevant circumstances. For older cases on merchantable quality see *Wren* v. *Holt* [1903] 1 K.B. 610; *Bristol Tramways* v. *Fiat Motors, Ltd.* [1910] 2 K.B. 831; *Jackson* v. *Rotax Motor Co.* [1910] 2 K.B. 937; *Sumner, Permain & Co.* v. *Webb* [1922] 1 K.B. 55; *Morelli* v. *Fitch & Gibbons* [1928] 2 K.B. 636; *Cammell Laird* v. *Manganese Bronze Co.* [1934] 4 A.C. 402; *Grant* v. *A.K.M. Ltd.* [1936] A.C. 85; *Daniels & Daniels* v. *White* [1938] 4 All E.R. 258; *Bartlett* v. *Marcus* [1965] 2 All E.R. 753; *Kendall* v. *Lillico* [1969] 2 A.C. 31; *Cehave N.V.* v. *Bremer Handelgesellschaft* [1976] Q.B. 44; goods are merchantable if capable of use for various purposes, even though not fit for the purpose the buyer intended: *Brown* v. *Craiks*, 1970 S.C. (H.L.) 51. See also *Williamson* v. *Macpherson* (1904) 6 F. 863.

[94] This replaces subs. (2) of S. 14 as originally enacted but is wider.

[95] Defined: S. 61(1).

[96] Where the goods are normally usable for one purpose only the buyer's purpose is adequately disclosed to the seller by merely asking for those goods; e.g. bunker coal: *Gillespie* v. *Cheney* [1896] 2 Q.B. 59; *Crichton & Stevenson* v. *Love*, 1908 S.C. 818; *Manchester Liners Ltd.* v. *Rea* [1922] 2 A.C. 74; food: *Wallis* v. *Russell* [1902] 2 I.R. 585; hot-water bottle: *Priest* v. *Last* [1903] 2 K.B. 148; milk: *Frost* v. *Aylesbury Dairy Co.* [1905] 1 K.B. 608; bun: *Chaproniere* v. *Mason* (1905) 21 T.L.R. 633; condenser-tubes: *Williamson* v. *Macpherson* (1904) 6 F. 863; tinned food: *Jackson* v. *Watson* [1909] 2 K.B. 193; salt mutton: *Knutsen* v. *Mauritzen*, 1918, 1 S.L.T. 85; house-coal: *Duke* v. *Jackson*, 1921 S.C. 362, disapproved in *Wilson* v. *Rickett, Cockerell & Co.* [1954] 1 Q.B. 598; shoes: *Thomson* v. *Sears*, 1926 S.L.T. 221; a car: *Crowther* v. *Shannon* [1975] 1 All E.R. 139.

But in *Hardie* v. *Austin* (1870) 8 M. 798; *Hamilton* v. *Robertson* (1878) 5 R. 839; and *Dunlop* v. *Crawford* (1886) 13 R. 937 (all under the Mercantile Law Amdt. (Sc.) Act, 1856) it was held that the 'particular purpose' must be other than the usual one. Where the goods are capable of various uses, e.g. a van to carry goods: *Flynn* v. *Scott*, 1949 S.C. 442; the particular purpose contemplated needs to be brought home to the seller to bring the case within the exception, expecially if the particular purpose will or might involve special or unusual stresses, e.g. use in wet or hot climate, unusual pressure. See e.g. *Teheran Europe Co.* v. *Belton* [1968] 2 All E.R. 886. So, too, if the particular purpose contemplated is other than the obvious one for which that king of goods are normally bought, e.g. food for scientific experiments rather than for eating; cf. *Gwynne* v. *Walker* (1873) 11 S.L.R. 116. Disclosure of one purpose of use does not cover a similar use on another occasion: *McCallum* v. *Mason*, 1956 S.C. 50.

There is no breach of fitness of a ship for its purpose by failure of its engines: *Britain S.S. Co.* v. *Lithgows Ltd.*, 1975 S.C. 110.

[97] There is breach accordingly if the goods break in normal use, or are poisonous, injurious or otherwise unfit; see e.g. *Fleming* v. *Airdrie Iron Co.* (1882) 9 R. 473; *Campbell* v. *Henderson* (1886) 23 S.L.R. 712; *Jacobs* v. *Scott* (1899) 2 F. (H.L.) 70; *Priest* v. *Last* [1903] 2 K.B. 148; *Williamson* v. *Macpherson* (1904) 6 F. 863; *Frost*, *supra*: *Chaproniere*, *supra*; *Jackson*, *supra*;

which such goods are commonly supplied, except where the circumstances show that the buyer does not rely, or that it is unreasonable for him to rely, on the skill or judgment of the seller or credit-broker.[98] (4) An implied condition or warranty about quality or fitness for a particular purpose may be annexed to a contract of sale by usage. (5) These provisions apply to a sale by a person who in the course of a business is acting as an agent for another as they apply to a sale by a principal in the course of a business, except where that other is not selling in the course of a business and either the buyer knows that fact or reasonable steps are taken to bring it to the notice of the buyer before the contract is made. (6) Goods of any kind are of merchantable quality if they are as fit for the purpose or purposes for which goods of that kind are commonly bought as it is reasonable to expect having regard to any description applied to them, the price (if relevant) and all the other relevant circumstances.

Any term of a contract which purports to exclude or restrict liability for breach of the obligations arising from S. 14 is, in the case of a consumer contract, void against the consumer, and in any other case, ineffective if it was not fair and reasonable to incorporate the term in the contract.[99]

Implied terms—sale by sample

In a sale by sample,[1] which is when there is a term, express or implied, in the contract to that effect, there are implied conditions (a)

Crichton v. *Love*, 1908 S.C. 818; *Duke* v. *Jackson*, 1921 S.C. 362, criticized in *Wilson* v. *Rickett, Cockerell & Co.* [1954] 1 Q.B. 598; *Buchanan & Carswell* v. *Eugene*, 1936 S.C. 160; *McCallum* v. *Mason*, 1956 S.C. 50; *Crowther* v. *Shannon* [1975] 1 All E.R. 139; *Kendall* v. *Lillico* [1969] 2 A.C. 31; *Vacwell Engineering Co.* v. *B.D.H. Chemicals* [1971] 1 Q.B. 111; *Ashington Piggeries* v. *Hill* [1972] A.C. 441; *Lambert* v. *Lewis* [1980] 1 All E.R. 978. But if the goods are of a different description from those purchased, the claim lies under S. 13; *Jaffe* v. *Ritchie* (1861) 23 D. 242; *McCallum, supra.*

[98] This subs. replaced S. 14(1) as enacted. Normally purchase under a patent or trade name indicates non-reliance on the sellers' skill and judgment; *Paul* v. *Glasgow Corpn.* (1900) 3 F. 119; *McMillan* v. *Dick* (1903) 11 S.L.T. 210; but even though a thing is bought under its patent or trade name, e.g. 'one eight-cylinder Bugatti car', the buyer may still show that he relied on the seller's skill or judgment: *Baldry* v. *Marshall* [1925] 1 K.B. 260. See also *Pommer & Thomsen* v. *Mowat* (1906) S.L.T. 373; *Harrison & Jones* v. *Bunten and Lancaster* [1953] 1 Q.B. 646. 'Unreasonable ... to rely' probably covers cases where the seller disclaims knowledge of suitability of the goods, or the buyer wants goods for a wholly unforeseeable special purpose.

[99] Unfair Contract Terms Act, 1977, S. 20(2): 'Consumer contract' is defined by S.25 thereof: *McCrone* v. *Boots Farm Sales*, 1981 S.L.T. 103.

[1] S. 15; it is not enough that a sample was exhibited; it must be a term of the contract that the sale was by sample; *White* v. *Dougherty* (1891) 18 R. 972; *Glasgow Mags.* v. *Ireland* (1895) 22 R. 818; as to the function of a sample, see *Drummond* v. *Van Ingen* (1887) 12 App. Cas. 284, 297.

that the bulk will correspond with the sample in quality,[2] (b) that the buyer will have a reasonable opportunity of comparing the bulk with the sample,[3] and (c) that the goods shall be free from any defect rendering them unmerchantable[4] which would not be apparent on reasonable examination of the sample.[5] Any term of a contract which purports to exclude or restrict liability for breach of the obligations arising from S. 15 is, in the case of a consumer contract, void against the consumer, and in any other case, ineffective if it was not fair and reasonable to incorporate the term in the contract.[6]

Exclusion of implied terms

The conditions and warranties implied by the Act might originally be negatived or varied[7] by express agreement[8] or by the course of dealing between the parties[9] or by usage if the usage be such as to bind both parties to the contract.[10] Now S. 55 provides: (1) Where a right, duty or liability would arise under a contract of sale of goods by implication of law, it may (subject to the Unfair Contract Terms Act, 1977) be negatived by or varied by express agreement, or by the course of dealing between the parties, or by such usage as binds both parties to the contract. (2) An express condition or warranty does not negative a condition or warranty implied by the Act unless inconsistent therewith.[11]

It has been held that an exclusion of liability for breach of implied warranties did not exclude liability for breach of express warranties,[12]

---

[2] *Macfarlane* v. *Taylor* (1868) 6 M. (H.L.) 1; *Champanhac* v. *Waller* [1948] 2 All E.R. 724; *Ruben* v. *Faire* [1949] 1 K.B. 254.
[3] The right to reject is not lost merely by payment if there had been no chance to inspect: *Polenghi* v. *Dried Milk Co.* (1904) 92 L.T. 64. Where part of consignment is inferior to sample the buyer may reject the whole or keep the whole and claim damages: *Aitken* v. *Boullen,* 1908 S.C. 490; contrast *Jackson* v. *Rotax* [1910] 2 K.B. 937; see also Act, S. 30. Prima facie the place for inspection is the place of delivery: *Couston Thomson & Co.* v. *Chapman* (1872) 10 M. (H.L.) 74; *Perkins* v. *Bell* [1893] 1 Q.B. 193.
[4] i.e. not satisfying S. 14(6) above.
[5] *Heilbutt* v. *Hickson* (1872) L.R. 7 C.P. 438; *Drummond* v. *Van Ingen* (1887) 12 App. Cas. 284; *Godley* v. *Perry* [1960] 1 All E.R. 36. If part of the goods are defective the buyer cannot reject them unless they amount to goods of a different description under S. 30(3): *Aitken* v. *Boullen,* 1908 S.C. 490.
[6] Unfair Contract Terms Act, 1977, S. 20(2). 'Consumer contract' is defined by S. 25 thereof.
[7] 1893 Act, S. 55.
[8] *Ward* v. *Hobbs* (1878) 4 App. Cas. 13; *Smith* v. *Waite Nash & Co.* (1888) 15 R. 533; *Wallis* v. *Pratt and Haynes* [1911] A.C. 394; *Pinnock Bros.* v. *Lewis & Peat* [1923] 1 K.B. 690; *Baldry* v. *Marshall* [1925] 1 K.B. 260; *Van Til-Hartman* v. *Thomson,* 1931 S.N. 30; *Rutherford* v. *Miln,* 1941 S.C. 125. See also *Andrews* v. *Singer* [1934] 1 K.B. 17; *L'Estrange* v. *Graucob* [1934] 2 K.B. 394.
[9] *Re Marquis of Anglesey* [1910] 2 Ch. 548; *Pocahontas Fuel Co.* v. *Ambatielos* (1922) 27 Com. Cas. 148.
[10] *Produce Brokers Co.* v. *Olympia Oil and Cake Co.* [1916] 1 A.C. 314.
[11] This repeats S. 14(4) of the 1893 Act. See *Douglas* v. *Milne* (1895) 23 R. 163; *Baldry* v. *Marshall* [1925] 1 K.B. 260.   [12] *Andrews* v. *Singer* [1934] 1 K.B. 17.

that any purported exclusion of warranties has to be construed strictly and *contra proferentem*,[13] and a purported exclusion by written conditions of sale may be negatived by a subsequent express oral warranty.[14] An exclusion is also ineffective if the goods suffer from so many defects as to be wholly disconform to contract.[15]

The Unfair Contract Terms Act, 1977, provides that the purported exclusion of liability for breach of obligations arising from S. 12 is void, and for breach of obligations arising from any of Ss. 13, 14 or 15 is, in the case of a consumer contract, void against the consumer, and in any other case ineffective if it was not fair and reasonable to incorporate the term in the contract.[16]

Buyer's remedies for breach of warranty or condition

At common law the buyer in Scotland could only reject goods disconform to contract (*actio redhibitoria*) and not, save by special agreement, retain them, claiming an abatement from the price by way of damages (*actio quanti minoris*).[17] Under the Act, however,[18] in Scotland, failure by the seller to perform any material part of a contract of sale is a breach of contract which entitles the buyer either within a reasonable time after delivery to reject the goods and treat the contract as repudiated,[19] or to retain the goods and treat the failure to perform such material part as a breach which may give rise to a claim for compensation or damages.

Where there is a breach of warranty (in the English sense, i.e. breach of a non-fundamental term) by the seller, the buyer may not reject the goods but may (a) set up the breach in diminution or extinction of the price;[20] or (b) claim damages for breach of warranty,[21] measured by the estimated loss directly and naturally resulting in the ordinary course from the breach of warranty.[22] In the case of breach of warranty of

[13] *Andrews, supra; L'Estrange, supra.*

[14] *Couchman v. Hill* [1947] 1 K.B. 554; *Harling v. Eddy* [1951] 2 All E.R. 212.

[15] *Pollock v. Macrae,* 1912 S.C. (H.L.) 192; *Mechans v. Highland Marine Charters,* 1964 S.C. 48.

[16] 1977 Act, S. 20(2). 'Consumer contract' is defined by S. 25 thereof.

[17] Bell, *Prin.* §99A; *McCormick v. Rittmeyer* (1869) 7 M. 854; *Bryson v. B.,* 1916, 1 S.L.T. 361. For exceptional pre-1893 cases see *Spencer v. Dobbie* (1879) 7 R. 396; *Dick & Stevenson v. Woodside Steel Co.* (1888) 16 R. 242; *Hope v. Crookston Bros.* (1890) 17 R. 868.

[18] S. 11(5).   [19] *Nelson v. Chalmers,* 1913 S.C. 441.

[20] S. 53 (1)(a); *Kinnear v. Brodie* (1901) 3 F. 540; *British Motor Body Co. v. Shaw,* 1914 S.C. 922; see also: *Jones v. Just* (1868) L.R. 3 Q.B. 197; *Bostock v. Nicholson* [1904] 1 K.B. 725; *Jackson v. Watson* [1909] 2 K.B. 193; *Slater v. Hoyle & Smith* [1920] 2 K.B.11; *Bunting v. Tory* (1948) 64 T.L.R. 353; *Minster Trust v. Traps Tractors* [1954] 3 All E.R. 136. In a case within this subsection the court has at common law a discretion to order consignation of the price or part thereof: *Cohen v. Jamieson & Paterson,* 1963 S.C. 289.

[21] S. 53(1)(b).

[22] S. 53(2); cf. *Randall v. Newson* (1877) 2 Q.B.D. 102; *Hammond v. Bussey* (1887) 20 Q.B.D. 79; *Bennett v. Kreeger* (1925) 41 T.L.R. 609; *Mason v. Burningham* (1949) 2 K.B. 545; *Cullinan v. British Rema Mfg. Co.* [1954] 1 Q.B. 292.

quality such loss is prima facie the difference between the value of the goods at the time of delivery and their value if they had answered to the warranty.[23] The fact that the breach has been used in diminution or extinction of the price does not prevent the buyer claiming for the same breach of warranty if he has suffered further damage.[24] This section does not prejudice the buyer's right of rejection in Scotland declared by S. 11(2).[25] Furthermore S. 58 provides that where a buyer has elected to accept goods which he might have rejected and to treat a breach of contract as only giving rise to a claim for damages, he may, in an action by the seller for the price, be required in the discretion of the court, to consign the price of the goods or part thereof, or to give other reasonable security for the due payment thereof. S. 58 does not deal with cases under S. 53 but is intended to guard against the abuse of the remedy under S. 11(2).[26] Apart from S.58 the court has a common law power to order consignation in a case under S. 53.[26]

Buyer's right of examining goods

Where goods are delivered which the buyer has not previously examined, he is not deemed to have accepted them unless and until he has had a reasonable opportunity of examining them to ascertain whether they are in conformity with the contract.[27] Unless otherwise agreed,[28] when the seller tenders delivery, he is bound, on request, to afford the buyer a reasonable opportunity of examining the goods to ascertain whether they conform to the contract.[29] The buyer should accordingly examine goods on delivery and unless the defect is latent and only discoverable after use, the buyer may be barred from subsequently rejecting them.[30]

If the buyer on examination rejects the goods as not corresponding with the contract notice of definite rejection is desirable; the buyer may then sue for non-delivery or specific implement or claim repayment of the price paid.[31]

---

[23] S. 53(3).   [24] S. 53(4).

[25] S. 53(5). Accordingly is Scotland, even if the stipulation is called by the Act a warranty, if the breach is a material breach, the buyer may reject.

[26] *Cohen* v. *Jamieson & Paterson*, 1963 S.C. 289; see also *Findlay* v. *Donaldson* (1846) 5 Bell 105; *Porter Spiers (Leicester) Ltd.* v. *Cameron* [1950] C.L.Y. 5329.

[27] S. 34(1); *Chalmers* v. *Paterson* (1897) 24 R. 1020; *Pommer & Thomsen* v. *Mowat* (1906) 14 S.L.T. 373; if after reasonable inspection of samples of the consignment some lots are found defective the buyer may still reject them and claim damages: *McCaw, Stevenson & Orr* v. *McLaren* (1893) 20 R. 437.

[28] *E. Clemens Horst Co.* v. *Biddell* [1912] A.C. 18.

[29] S. 34(2). The buyer has been held not entitled to reject without further trial where the test applied was in the court's view not conclusive: *Wilson* v. *Turnbull* (1896) 23 R. 714. The seller's claim for the price was refused in *Kinnear* v. *Brodie* (1901) 3 F. 540, where a horse was sold, was disconform to warranty and was killed before it had been accepted.

[30] *Carter* v. *Campbell* (1885) 12 R. 1075; *Pini* v. *Smith* (1895) 22 R. 699; *Strachan* v. *Marshall*, 1910, 2 S.L.T. 108.   [31] Ss. 51, 52.

Acceptance

The buyer is deemed to have accepted the goods[32] when he intimates acceptance to the seller,[33] or (except where S. 34 otherwise provides)[34] when the goods have been delivered and he does any act in relation to them inconsistent with the ownership of the seller,[35] or when after the lapse of a reasonable time he retains the goods without intimating rejection to the seller.[36] It is not competent to accept goods and then seek to reject them on the appearance of latent defects.[37] Rejection is not precluded by delay if it is attributable to the seller's representations that the goods were satisfactory and his attempts to make them satisfy the specification.[38] The right to reject may be barred by the contract, expressly or by implication,[39] or by a compromise agreement.[40]

Buyer not bound to return rejected goods

Unless otherwise agreed where goods are delivered to the buyer and he has the right to and refuses to accept them, he is not bound to return them to the seller, but need only intimate to the seller that he refuses to accept them.[41]

Rejection, or retention and damages

If the buyer elects to reject the goods and rescind the contract he must to so timeously.[42] If the breach is patent he must intimate rejection

---

[32] S. 35.

[33] *Mechans Ltd.* v. *Highland Marine Charters*, 1964 S.C. 48.

[34] Words in brackets added by Misrepresentation Act, 1967, S. 4(2).

[35] e.g. consuming or using them: *Blenkhorn, Richardson & Co.* v. *Milnathort Spinning Co.* (1883) 20 S.L.R. 707; breaking the bulk of a cargo: *Wallace & Brown* v. *Robinson, Fleming & Co.* (1885) 22 S.L.R. 830; or offering them for resale: *Hunt* v. *Barry* (1905) 13 S.L.T. 34; fitting them into a subject under construction: *Mechan* v. *Bow, McLachlan & Co.*, 1910 S.C. 758; taking delivery and shipping abroad: *Pini* v. *Smith* (1895) 22 R. 699; *Strachan* v. *Marshall*, 1910, 2 S.L.T. 108; *Dick* v. *Cochrane & Fleming*, 1935 S.L.T. 432; baling hay: *Woodburn* v. *Motherwell*, 1917 S.C. 533; or resale and delivery to a third party: *Ruben* v. *Faire* [1949] 1 K.B. 254; but see *McCarter* v. *Stewart & Mackenzie* (1877) 4 R. 890; *Pommer & Thomsen* v. *Mowat* (1906) 14 S.L.T. 373; *Cunningham* v. *Munro* (1922) 28 Com. Cas. 42; *Hardy* v. *Hillerns and Fowler* [1923] 1 K.B. 658.

[36] Rejection must accordingly be made, if at all, within a reasonable time, which is a question of fact: S. 56; cf. *Carter* v. *Campbell* (1885) 12 R. 1075.

[37] *Mechans, Ltd., supra.*

[38] *Aird & Coghill* v. *Pullan & Adams* (1904) 7 F. 258; *Munro* v. *Bennett*, 1911 S.C. 337.

[39] *Leary* v. *Briggs* (1904) 6 F. 857; *Cowell* v. *Glasgow Motor Car Co.* (1904) 11 S.L.T. 758. It is not necessarily barred by a provision in the contract that the property would pass on a particular instalment of the price being paid: *McDougall* v. *Aeromarine Ltd.* [1958] 3 All E.R. 431.

[40] *Smith Bros.* v. *Scott* (1875) 2 R. 601; *Bradley* v. *Dollar* (1886) 13 R. 893.

[41] S. 36; *Couston, Thomson & Co.* v. *Chapman* (1872) 10 M. (H.L.) 74; *Grimoldby* v. *Wells* (1875) L.R. 10 C.P. 391; *Carter* v. *Campbell* (1885) 12 R. 1075.

[42] The length of time is not conclusive: regard must be had to the circumstances: *Burrell* v. *Harding's Exrx.*, 1931 S.L.T. 76. Timeous rejection: *McBey* v. *Gardiner* (1858) 20 D. 1151 (3 days); *McCarter* v. *Stewart* (1877) 4 R. 890 (5 days); *Fleming* v. *Airdrie Iron Co.* (1882) 9 R. 473.

at once, but if it is latent it is sufficient if rejection is intimated as soon as the defect is discovered, so long as the goods have not been expressly accepted.[43] The right to reject may by agreement be kept open for a time.[44] In any case, though the rejecting buyer is not obliged to restore the goods to the seller or place them in neutral custody,[45] he must keep them intact till removal,[46] and may be barred if he refuses to allow the sellers to remove them without replacing them,[47] or purports to reject on the ground that a defect remedied might recur,[48] or continues to use the goods.[49] In the case of machinery the need for a period of trial after delivery is recognized as necessary.[50] It is not essential to examine all of a consignment.[51] Conversely if the seller takes back the rejected goods and uses them he cannot seek to insist on the buyer accepting and paying the price.[52] The buyer's right to reject is barred by acceptance of the goods,[53] or by excessive delay in rejecting, even if the defect were latent.[54] If the buyer elects to keep the goods and claim damages no notice to the seller is necessary. If the buyer seeks to reject but is held to have accepted the goods or to have allowed more than a reasonable time to elapse, he is not thereby precluded from invoking the alternative

---

(6 weeks): *Caledonian Ry.* v. *Rankin* (1882) 10 R. 63 (6 weeks); *Wallace* v. *Ronbinson* (1885) 22 S.L.R. 830 (7 days); *Glasgow Mags.* v. *Ireland* (1895) 22 R. 818; *Roberts* v. *Yule* (1896) 23 R. 855; *Aird & Coghill* v. *Pullan & Adams* (1904) 7 F. 258; *Munro* v. *Bennett*, 1911 S.C. 337; *Cranston* v. *Mallow & Lien*, 1912 S.C. 112 (7 days). Rejection too late: *Jardine* v. *Pendreigh* (1869) 6 S.L.R. 272; *Couston, Thomson & Co.* v. *Chapman* (1872) 10 M. (H.L.) 74 (2 months); *Smith Bros.* v. *Scott* (1875) 2 R. 601 (2 weeks); *Carter* v. *Campbell* (1885) 12 R. 1075; *Chaplin* v. *Jardine* (1886) 23 S.L.R. 487 (2 months); *Sinclair* v. *McEwan* (1887) 25 S.L.R. 76 (6 months); *Wilson* v. *Carmichael* (1894) 21 R. 732 (8 months); *Pini* v. *Smith* (1895) 22 R. 699 (1 month); *Morrison & Mason* v. *Clarkson* (1898) 25 R. 427; *Malcolm* v. *Cross* (1898) 25 R. 1089 (6 weeks); *Hyslop* v. *Shirlaw* (1905) 7 F. 875 (20 months); *Hunt* v. *Barry* (1905) 13 S.L.T. 34 (10 days); *Burrell* v. *Harding's Exrx.*, 1931 S.L.T. 76 (2 years); *Dick* v. *Cochrane & Fleming*, 1935 S.L.T. 432; *Flynn* v. *Scott*, 1949 S.C. 442 (3 weeks).

[43] *Morrison & Mason* v. *Clarkson* (1898) 25 R. 427; *Mechans* v. *Highland Marine Charters*, 1964 S.C. 48.

[44] *Paton* v. *Payne* (1897) 35 S.L.R. 112.

[45] On this see *Caledonian Ry.* v. *Rankin* (1882) 10 R. 63; *Malcolm* v. *Cross* (1898) 25 R. 1089.

[46] *Couston, Thomson & Co.* v. *Chapman* (1872) 10 M. (H.L.) 74.

[47] *Jardine, supra*; cf. *Newlands* v. *Leggat* (1885) 12 R. 820.

[48] *Sinclair, supra.*

[49] *Electric Construction Co.* v. *Hurry & Young* (1897) 24 R. 312; *Croom & Arthur* v. *Stewart* (1905) 7 F. 563.

[50] *Pearce Bros.* v. *Irons* (1869) 7 M. 571; *Fleming* v. *Airdrie Iron Co.* (1882) 9 R. 473; *Aird & Coghill, supra*; cf. *Bradley* v. *Dollar* (1886) 13 R. 893.

[51] *McCaw, Stevenson & Orr* v. *Maclaren* (1893) 20 R. 437.

[52] *Croan* v. *Vallance* (1881) 8 R. 700.

[53] *Morrison & Mason* v. *Clarkson* (1898) 25 R. 427; *Mechans, Ltd.* v. *Highland Marine Charters, Ltd.*, 1964 S.C. 48.

[54] *Mechans, Ltd., supra*, disapproving dictum in *Mechan* v. *Bow, McLachlan & Co.*, 1910 S.C. 758, 763.

remedy of damages,[55] provided he states a case to this effect in his pleadings.[56] A buyer is not barred from rejecting by having resold part of the goods before the defect was discovered, but in this case he must pay to the seller the value, not the price, of the goods not returned.[57] Where the goods are perishable it is permissible to reject but to resell at once so as to minimize loss.[58]

Where a buyer has elected to accept goods which he might have rejected and to claim damages only, he may, in an action by the seller for the price, be required, in the discretion of the Court, to consign the price of the goods in court, or part thereof, or to give other reasonable security for the due payment thereof.[59] This is intended to prevent abuse of the remedy of rejection and probably does not apply to the *actio quanti minoris,* though in the latter case consignation may be ordered at common law.[60] The buyer who rejects the goods may not retain them against the seller in respect of his claim for damages or expenses[61] but may, after due notice, do so in security of repayment of the price.[62]

A claim of damages may also be brought where, by reason of defect in the goods supplied, the pursuer has been held liable to a third party for injuries caused by the defective goods.[63]

Buyer's liability for not taking delivery

When the seller is ready and willing to deliver the goods and requests the buyer to take delivery, and the buyer does not within a reasonable time after such request take delivery of the goods he is liable to the seller for any loss occasioned by his neglect or refusal to take delivery, and for a reasonable charge for the care and custody of the goods. This does not affect the rights of the seller where the neglect or refusal of the buyer to take delivery amounts to a repudiation of the contract.[64]

Other remedies

The remedies given by the Act are against the seller and the only ones on the basis of breach of contract. If, however, the goods have, by reason of defect, caused personal injuries or damage to property, the

[55] *Paton* v. *Payne* (1897) 35 S.L.R. 112, (H.L.) in effect overruling *Electric Construction Co.* v. *Hurry & Young* (1897) 24 R. 312, on this point; *Aitken Campbell & Co.* v. *Boullen & Gatenby,* 1908 S.C. 490; *Pollock* v. *Macrae,* 1922 S.C. (H.L.) 192.

[56] *Mechans, Ltd., supra.*

[57] *McCormick* v. *Rittmeyer* (1869) 7 M. 854.

[58] *Pommer & Thomsen* v. *Mowat* (1906) 14 S.L.T. 373. Contrast *Hunt* v. *Barry* (1905) 13 S.L.T. 34.

[59] S. 58; *Motor Plants, Ltd.* v. *Stewart* (1909) 1 S.L.T. 478.

[60] *Cohen* v. *Jamieson & Paterson,* 1963 S.C. 289.

[61] *McCormick, supra,* 858; *Padgett* v. *McNair* (1852) 15 D. 76; *Lupton* v. *Schulze* (1900) 2 F. 1118.   [62] *Melville* v. *Critchley* (1856) 18 D. 643; *Laing* v. *Westren* (1858) 20 D. 519.

[63] *Buchanan & Carswell* v. *Eugene,* 1936 S.C. 160.   [64] S. 37.

buyer has a remedy on the basis of delict against the maker, whether he be also the seller or not.[65]

Stipulations as to time

Unless a different intention appears from the terms of the contract stipulations as to time of payment are not deemed to be of the essence of a contract of sale,[66] but whether any other stipulation as to time is of the essence of the contract or not depends on the terms of the contract.[67]

Condition as to resale prices

A term in a contract for sale of goods is void in so far as it purports to establish or provide for the establishment of minimum prices to be charged on resale, and it is unlawful to include in a contract any such term, to require the inclusion of any such term as a condition of supplying goods, or the giving of any undertaking to the like effect, or to notify to dealers a price stated or calculated to be understood as the minimum resale price, though prices may be recommended as appropriate for resale.[68] Particular classes of goods may be exempted by the Restrictive Practices Court.[69]

EFFECTS OF THE CONTRACT

Transfer of right of property

Under the Act, altering Scottish common law, the right of property in the goods may pass independently of actual transfer or delivery of the goods.

Where there is a contract for the sale of unascertained[70] goods no property in the goods is transferred to the buyer unless and until the goods are ascertained.[71]

[65] *Duke* v. *Jackson* 1921 S.C. 362; *Donoghue* v. *Stevenson*, 1932 S.C. (H.L.) 31; *Daniels* v. *White* [1938] 4 All E.R. 258.

[66] *Martindale* v. *Smith* (1841) 1 Q.B. 389; *Mersey Steel & Iron Co.* v. *Naylor* (1884) 9 App. Cas. 434; *Ryan* v. *Ridley* (1902) 8 Com. Cas. 105; *Payzu* v. *Saunders* [1919] 2 K.B. 581.

[67] S. 10; *Grieve* v. *Konig* (1880) 7 R. 521; *Forbes* v. *Campbell* (1885) 12 R. 1065; *Paton* v. *Payne* (1897) 35 S.L.R. 112; *Shaw, Macfarlane & Co.* v. *Waddell* (1900) 2 F. 1070; *Hartley* v. *Hymans* [1920] 3 K.B. 475; *Rickards* v. *Oppenheim* [1950] 1 K.B. 616; *McDougall* v. *Aeromarine Ltd.* [1958] 3 All E.R. 431.

[68] Resale Price Act, 1976, S.9.   [69] 1976 Act, Ss. 14–21.

[70] Unascertained or generic goods are goods not identified but referred to by description only, e.g. ten cows. Future goods are unascertained goods. Specific goods are goods identified and agreed upon at the time the contract is made: S. 61. 'Ascertained' means identified after the contract is made: *Re Wait* [1927] 1 Ch. 606; e.g. by selecting and segregating the 10 cows sold from the herd.

[71] S. 16; *Pochin* v. *Robinow* (1869) 7 M. 628; *Hayman* v. *McLintock*, 1907 S.C. 936; *Laurie & Morewood* v. *Dudin* [1926] 1 K.B. 223; *Kursell* v. *Timber Operators, Ltd.* [1927] 1 K.B. 298; *In re Wait* [1927] 1 Ch. 606.

Where there is a contract for the sale of specific or ascertained goods[72] the property in them is transferred to the buyer at such times as the parties intend it to be transferred. For the purpose of ascertaining the intention of the parties regard is to be had to the terms of the contract, the conduct of the parties, and the circumstances of the case.[73] Unless a different intention appears[74] the following rules are provided[75] for ascertaining the intention of the parties as to the time at which the property in the goods is to pass to the buyer.

'Rule 1.—Where there is an unconditional contract for the sale of specific goods, in a deliverable state,[76] the property in the goods passes to the buyer when the contract is made, and it is immaterial whether the time of payment or the time of delivery, or both, be postponed.'[77]

'Rule 2.—Where there is a contract for the sale of specific goods and the seller is bound to do something to the goods, for the purpose of putting them in a deliverable state,[76] the property does not pass until such thing be done, and the buyer has notice that it has been done.'[78]

'Rule 3.—Where there is a contract for the sale of specific goods in a deliverable state,[79] but the seller is bound to weigh, measure, test or do some other act or thing with reference to the goods for the purpose of ascertaining the price, the property does not pass until such act or thing be done, and the buyer has notice that it has been done.'[80]

'Rule 4.—When goods are delivered to the buyer on approval[81] or

---

[72] See note 70, supra.

[73] S. 17; *Brandt* v. *Dickson* (1876) 3 R. 375; *McBain* v. *Wallace* (1881) 8 R. (H.L.) 106; *Clarke & Co.* v. *Miller & Son's Tr.* (1885) 12 R. 1035; *Henckell Du Buisson* v. *Swan* (1889) 17 R. 252; *Brewer* v. *Duncan* (1892) 20 R. 230; *Kennedy's Tr.* v. *Hamilton & Manson* (1897) 25 R. 252; *Peebles* v. *Kerr* (1902) 9 S.L.T. 372; *Reid* v. *Macbeth & Gray* (1904) 6 F. (H.L.) 25; *Pommer & Thomsen* v. *Mowat* (1906) 14 S.L.T. 372; *Badische Anilin Fabrik* v. *Hickson* [1906] A.C. 419; *Laing* v. *Barclay Curle*, 1908 S.C. (H.L.) 1; *Nelson* v. *Chalmers*, 1913 S.C. 441; *McLaren's Tr.* v. *Argylls, Ltd.*, 1915, 2 S.L.T. 241; *Penney* v. *Clyde Shipping Co.*, 1920 S.C. (H.L.) 68; *Munro* v. *Balnagown Estates Liqdr.*, 1949 S.C. 49. If the property has passed it remains with the buyer though the goods be returned for repair: *Beasley* v. *McEwan* (1884) 12 R. 384.

[74] *Young* v. *Matthews* (1886) L.R. 2 C.P. 127; *Anchor Line (Henderson Bros.) Ltd.* [1937] 1 Ch. 1; *McDougall* v. *Aeromarine Ltd.* [1958] 3 All E.R. 431.

[75] S. 18. These are prima facie presumptions only and yield to evidence (S. 17(2)) of contrary intention, but the contrary intention must be present at the time of the contract: *Dennant* v. *Skinner* [1948] 2 K.B. 164.   [76] S. 61(5).

[77] See contrast with common law drawn in *Seath* v. *Moore* (1886) 13 R. (H.L.) 57; see also *Brown Bros.* v. *Carron Co.* (1898) 6 S.L.T. 231; *Gowans* v. *Bowe*, 1910, 2 S.L.T. 17; *Morison* v. *Lockhart*, 1921 S.C. 1017; *Shankland* v. *Robinson*, 1920 S.C. (H.L.) 103; *Underwood Ltd.* v. *Burgh Castle* [1922] 1 K.B. 343; *Dennant* v. *Skinner* [1948] 2 K.B. 164.

[78] *Brown Bros.* v. *Carron Co.* (1898) 6 S.L.T. 231; *Cockburn's Tr.* v. *Bowe*, 1910, 2 S.L.T. 17; *Woodburn* v. *Motherwell*, 1917 S.C. 533; *Underwood* v. *Burgh Castle Cement Syndicate* [1922] 1 K.B. 343.   [79] See *Morrison* v. *Lockhart*, 1912 S.C. 1017.

[80] *Nanka Bruce* v. *Commonwealth Trust* [1926] A.C. 77. Note that it is the seller's act of weighing, etc., and giving notice that fixes the time of passing of the property.

[81] On difference between sale under warranty and sale on approval, see *Cranston* v. *Mallow & Lien*, 1912 S.C. 112.

"on sale or return"[82] or other similar terms the property in the goods passes to the buyer:

(a) when he signifies his approval or acceptance to the seller or does any other act adopting the transaction;[83]

(b) If he does not signify his approval or acceptance to the seller but retains the goods without giving notice of rejection, then, if a time has been fixed for the return of the goods, on the expiration of such time, and, if no time has been fixed, on the expiration of a reasonable time. What is a reasonable time is a question of fact.[84]

'Rule 5.—(1) Where there is a contract for the sale of unascertained or future goods by description, and goods of that description and in a deliverable state are unconditionally appropriated to the contract, either by the seller with the assent of the buyer, or by the buyer with the assent of the seller, the property in the goods then passes to the buyer; and the assent may be express or implied, and may be given either before or after the appropriation is made.[85]

(2) Where, in pursuance of the contract, the seller delivers the goods to the buyer or to a carrier or other custodier (whether named by the buyer or not) for the purpose of transmission to the buyer, and does not reserve the right of disposal, he is deemed to have unconditionally appropriated the goods to the contract.'[86]

Reservation of right of disposal

Where there is a contract for the sale of specific goods or where goods are subsequently appropriated to the contract, the seller may, by the terms of the contract or appropriation, reserve the right of disposal of the goods until certain conditions are fulfilled; and in such case, notwithstanding the delivery of the goods to the buyer, or to a carrier or other custodier for transmission to the buyer, the property in the goods does not pass to the buyer until the conditions imposed by the seller are fulfilled.[87] Hence a seller may stipulate that until the price has been paid in full the buyer may resell or otherwise deal with the goods only as agent for the seller and subject to accounting to the seller for moneys received.[88] Where goods are shipped, and by the bill of lading

[82] See distinction drawn in *Brown* v. *Marr, Barclay & Co.* (1880) 7 R. 427.

[83] *Kirkham* v. *Attenborough* [1897] 1 Q.B. 201; *Bryce* v. *Ehrmann* (1904) 7 F. 5; *London Jewellers* v. *Attenborough* [1934] 2 Q.B. 206; contrast *Weiner* v. *Gill* [1906] 2 K.B. 574; see also *Bell, Rannie & Co.* v. *Smith* (1885) 22 S.L.R. 597; *Macdonald* v. *Westren* (1888) 25 R. 988; *Ross & Co.* v. *Piano Mfg. Co.* (1903) 11 S.L.T. 7.

[84] *Elphick* v. *Barnes* (1880) 5 C.P.D. 321; *Poole* v. *Smith's Car Sales* [1962] 2 All E.R. 482.

[85] *Pignataro* v. *Gilroy* [1919] 1 K.B. 459; *Warder's Co.* v. *Norwood* [1968] 2 All E.R. 602.

[86] *Badische Anilin Fabrik* v. *Basle Chemical Works* [1898] A.C. 200; cf. *Delaurier* v. *Wyllie* (1889) 17 R. 167.

[87] S. 19(1); Bell, *Prin.* §102A; *Eastwood & Holt* v. *Studer* (1926) 31 Com. Cas. 251.

[88] *Aluminium Industrie Vaassen* v. *Romalpa Aluminium Co.* [1976] 2 All E.R. 552; *Re Bond Worth* [1979] 3 All E.R. 919; *Borden* v. *Scottish Timber Products Ltd.* [1979] 3 All E.R. 961.

are deliverable to the order of the seller or his agent, the seller is prima facie deemed to reserve the right of disposal.[89] Where the seller of goods draws on the buyer for the price, and transmits the bill of exchange and bill of lading to the buyer together to secure acceptance or payment of the bill of exchange, the buyer is bound to return the bill of lading if he does not honour the bill of exchange, and if he wrongfully retains the bill of lading, the property in the goods does not pass to him.[90]

Passing of the risk

The risk of loss, deterioration or destruction of the goods is on the owner, unless otherwise agreed, and they are consequently at the buyer's risk once the property passes, whether delivery has been made or not.[91] The general rule is *res perit domino*. But if delivery has been delayed by the fault[92] of either party the goods are at the risk of the party in fault as regards any loss which might not otherwise have occurred.[93] Nor does anything in the section affect the duties or liabilities of either party as custodier of the goods of the other party.[94]

TRANSFER OF TITLE

Sale by non-owner

A person who is owner of the goods can pass an indefeasible title to the goods to the buyer thereof. But, subject to the provisions of the Act,[95] where goods are sold by a person who is not the owner thereof, and who does not sell them under the authority or with the consent of the owner, the buyer acquires no better title to the goods than the seller had, unless the owner of the goods is by his conduct precluded from denying the seller's authority to sell.[96] It is provided, however,[97] that nothing in the Act affects the provisions of the Factors Acts,[98] or any enactment enabling the apparent owner of goods to dispose of them as if he were the true owner thereof,[99] nor the validity of any contract of

---

[89] S. 19(2): This applies where goods are shipped under a bill of lading: *Biddell Bros.* v. *E. Clemens Horst Co.* [1911] 1 K.B. 934.

[90] S. 19(3): This is likely under a c.i.f. contract, on which see *infra*: *The Prinz Adelbert* [1917] A.C. 586; *The Orteric* [1920] A.C. 724.

[91] S. 20; Bell, *Prin.* §87; *Bevington* v. *Dale* (1902) 7 Com. Cas. 112.

[92] Fault is 'wrongful act or default': S. 61 (1).

[93] S. 20; *Demby Hamilton & Co.* v. *Barden* [1949] 1 All E.R. 435.

[94] S. 30; *Wiehe* v. *Dennis Bros*, (1913) 29 T.L.R. 250; *Shaw* v. *Symmons* [1917] 1 K.B. 799; *Rutter* v. *Palmer* [1922] 2 K.B. 87.   [95] Ss. 21, 23, 25.

[96] S. 21(1); The basic rule is *nemo dat quod non habet*.   [97] S. 21(2).

[98] Factors Act, 1889; Factors (Sc.) Act, 1890.   [99] e.g. S. 25.

sale under any special common law[1] or statutory power of sale[2] or under the order of a court or competent jurisdiction. Hence a person possessing goods obtained by finding[3] or theft[4] or a void contract[5] can pass no title to a buyer from him. *Nemo plus juris in alium transferre potest quam ipse habet.* A *vitium reale* inheres in such property and affects the title of even a bona fide purchaser for value without notice of the defect, and accordingly the true owner can recover from the purchaser.[5]

The English rule that, if goods are sold in market overt, the buyer obtains a good title if he bought in good faith and without notice of any defect or want of title on the seller's part, is not law in Scotland[6] but a title to goods thereby acquired in England will be recognized in Scotland.[7] Hence in Scotland a person who has obtained goods by theft or fraud inducing essential error can never, even by sale to a bona fide buyer, confer a good title.[8]

But[9] when the seller of goods has a voidable[10] title thereto, but his title has not been avoided at the time of the sale, the buyer acquires a good title to the goods, provided he buys them in good faith and without notice of the seller's defect of title.

Disposition by buyer or seller in possession after sale

Where a buyer having sold goods continues or is in possession of the goods, or of the documents of title to the goods, the delivery or transfer by that person, or by a mercantile agent[11] acting for him, of the goods or documents of title under any sale, pledge, or other disposition thereof, to any person receiving them in good faith and without notice of the previous sale has the same effect as if the person making the deliver or transfer were expressly authorized by the owner of the goods

---

[1] e.g. an agent of necessity, or *negotiorum gestor.*

[2] e.g. S. 48(3); innkeepers (Innkeepers Act, 1878, S. 1); pawnbrokers (Pawnbrokers Act, 1872, S. 19).

[3] cf. *Hibbert* v. *McKiernan* [1948] 2 K.B. 142.

[4] cf. *McDonald* v. *Provan (of Scotland St.) Ltd.,* 1960 S.L.T. 231.

[5] e.g. *Cundy* v. *Lindsay* (1878) 3 App. Cas. 459; *Morrisson* v. *Robertson,* 1908 S.C. 332; *Ingram* v. *Little* [1961] 1 Q.B. 31.

[6] S. 22.

[7] *Todd* v. *Armour* (1882) 9 R. 901.

[8] cf. *Morrisson* v. *Robertson,* 1908 S.C. 332; *Oliver & Boyd* v. *Marr* (1901) 9 S.L.T. 170.

[9] S. 23.

[10] Voidable only, not void; e.g. goods obtained by misrepresentation, but not so essential as to render the contract void; cf. *Phillips* v. *Brooks* [1919] 2 K.B. 243, explained in *Lake* v. *Simmons* [1927] A.C. 487.

In such a case as *Morrisson* v. *Robertson,* 1908 S.C. 332, the seller to Robertson had not a voidable title, but no title, so could not pass any title to Robertson. Contrast *McLeod* v. *Kerr,* 1965 S.C. 253, where the seller's title was voidable only.

[11] To have the same meaning as in the Factors Acts; S. 26.

to make it.[12] Where a person having bought or agreed to buy[13] goods obtains, with the consent of the seller, possession of the goods or the documents of title to the goods, the delivery or transfer by that person, or by a mercantile agent acting for him, of the goods or documents of title, under any sale, pledge or other disposition thereof, to any person receiving them in good faith and without notice of any lien or other right of the original seller in respect of the goods, has the same effect as if the person making the delivery or transfer were a mercantile agent in possession of the goods or documents of title with the consent of the owner.[14] For the purposes of this section—(a) The buyer under a conditional sale agreement is to be taken not to be a person who has bought or agreed to buy goods, and (b) 'conditional sale agreement' means an agreement for the sale of goods which is a consumer credit agreement within the meaning of the Consumer Credit Act, 1974, under which the purchase price or part of it is payable by instalments, and the property in the goods is to remain in the seller (notwithstanding that the buyer is to be in possession of the goods) until such conditions as to the payment of instalments or otherwise as may be specified in the agreement are fulfilled.

In Sections 24 and 25 'mercantile agent' means a mercantile agent having in the customary course of his business as such agent authority either (a) to sell goods, or (b) to consign goods for the purpose of sale, or (c) to buy goods, or (d) to raise money on the security of goods.[15]

PERFORMANCE OF THE CONTRACT

Delivery

The seller must deliver the goods and the buyer must accept and pay for them in accordance with the contract.[16] Unless otherwise agreed payment and delivery are concurrent conditions.[17] By agreement either or both may be deferred, or be performed by instalments. It depends on

---

[12] S. 25(1), substantially re-enacting Factors Act, 1889, S. 8, applied to Scotland by Factors (Sc.) Act, 1980.
      City Fur Mfg. Co. v. *Fureenbond* [1937] 1 All E.R. 799 This section protects the purchaser from a seller in possession, not from a custodier or depositary.
[13] A person holding goods under a hire-purchase agreement has not 'bought or agreed to buy' them, but is a hirer with en evential option to purchase: *Belsize Motor Co.* v. *Cox* [1914] 1 K.B. 244. Contrast *Marten* v. *Whale* [1917] 2 K.B. 480.
[14] S. 25(2), substantially re-enacting Factors Act, 1889, S. 9, applied to Scotland by Factors (Sc.) Act, 1890; *Graham* v. *Glenrothes Development Corpn.*, 1967 S.C. 284.
[15] S. 26.
[16] S. 27; Bell, *Prin.* §114–19; cf. *West Limerigg Colliery Co.* v. *Robertson* (1873) 10 S.L.R. 467.
[17] S. 28; *Forbes* v. *Campbell* (1885) 12 R. 1065.

the contract whether it is for the buyer to take possession of the goods or for the seller to send them.[18] Apart from contract the place of delivery is the seller's place of business, if any, or his residence. But if the contract is for the sale of specific goods, known when the contract was made to be in some other place, that is the place of delivery. If the seller is bound to send and no time is fixed, he must do so within a reasonable time.[19] Where the goods are in the possession of a third party, there is no delivery unless and until he acknowledges to the buyer that he holds the goods on the buyer's behalf, but this does not affect the issue or transfer of any document of title to goods.[20] Demand or tender of delivery must be made at a reasonable hour, which is a question of fact. The expenses of and incidental to putting the goods into a deliverable state must be borne by the seller.[21] A seller is justified in rescinding the contract if the buyer is in breach in failing to take delivery timeously.[22]

Delivery of wrong quantity

Where the seller delivers a lesser quantity[23] than he contracted to sell, the buyer may reject them, but if he accepts he must pay for them at the contract rate.[24] Where the seller delivers a greater quantity than he contracted to sell the buyer may accept the contractual quantity and reject the rest, or reject the whole, or accept the whole, paying for them at the contract rate.[25] Where the seller delivers the goods he contracted to sell mixed with goods of a different description[26] not included in the contract, the buyer may accept the goods which are in accordance with the contract and reject the rest, or reject the whole.[27] These provisions

[18] S. 29(1): Delivery to a person apparently authorized to receive is good delivery: *Galbraith & Grant* v. *Block* [1922] 2 K.B. 155.

[19] S. 29(2) and (3): cf. *Taylors* v. *Maclellans* (1891) 19 R. 10; *British Motor Body Co.* v. *Shaw*, 1914 S.C. 922.

[20] S. 29(4). See Bills of Lading Act, 1855; cf. *Hayman* v. *McLintock*, 1907 S.C. 936.

[21] S. 29(5) and (6).

[22] *Merry & Cuninghame* v. *Stevenson* (1895) 2 S.L.T. 489; *Shaw, Macfarlane & Co.* v. *Waddell* (1900) 2 F. 1070.

[23] The quantity fixed by the contract is part of the 'description' of the goods under S. 13, so that tender of a wrong quantity is a breach of the condition implied by S. 13, entitling the buyer to the remedies of S. 11(2).

[24] S. 30(1); *Harland & Wolff* v. *Burstall* (1901) 84 L.T. 324; *Behrend* v. *Produce Brokers Co.* [1920] 3 K.B. 530; *Beck* v. *Szymanowski* [1924] A.C. 43; see also *Robertson* v. *Stewart*, 1928 S.N. 31.

[25] S. 30(2) and (3); *Cunliffe* v. *Harrison* (1851) 6 Ex. 903; *Shipton Anderson & Co.* v. *Weil* [1912] 1 K.B. 574.

[26] Including goods wrongly packed: *Re Moore & Co. & Landauer & Co.* [1921] 2 K.B. 519; or of the wrong size: *Barker Junior & Co.* v. *Agius* (1927) 32 Com. Cas. 220; but not goods inferior to sample: *Aitken, Campbell & Co.* v. *Boullen & Gatenby*, 1908 S.C. 490.

[27] S. 30(4); *Nicholson* v. *Bradfield Union* (1866) L.R. 1 Q.B. 620; *Paul* v. *Pim* [1922] 2 K.B. 360. This was held inapplicable where part of the goods were merely of inferior quality: *Aitken* v. *Boullen*, 1908 S.C. 490.

are subject to any usage of trade, special agreement, or course of dealing between the parties.[28] In questions of quantity a reasonable margin of error is permissible—*de minimis no curat lex*—and a seller may within limits protect himself by selling 'about' so may tons,[29] or so much 'more or less'.[30]

Instalment deliveries

Unless otherwise agreed, the buyer is not bound to accept delivery by instalments.[31] Where there is a contract for delivery by stated instalments which are to be separately paid for and the seller makes defective deliveries in one or more instalments or the buyer fails to take delivery of or pay for one or more instalments, it depends in each case on the terms of the contract and the circumstances of the case whether the breach is a repudiation of the whole contract or a severable breach giving rise to a claim for compensation but not to a right to treat the whole contract as repudiated.[32] It may be provided that each instalment is to be treated as a separate contract,[33] or that payment therefor is to be a condition precedent to future deliveries.[34]

Delivery to carrier

Where the seller is authorized or required to send the goods to the buyer, delivery to a carrier, named by the buyer or not, for transmission to the buyer is prima facie deemed to be a delivery to the buyer.[35] Unless otherwise authorized, the seller must make such contract with the carrier on behalf of the buyer as may be reasonable having regard to the nature of the goods and the other circumstances. If he omits to do so, and the goods are lost or damaged in transit, the buyer may decline to treat the delivery to the carrier as a delivery to

---

[28] S. 30(5).

[29] cf. *Re Harrison & Micks* [1917] 1 K.B. 755.

[30] cf. *Tancred Arrol & Co.* v. *Steel Co. of Scotland* (1890) 17 R. (H.L.) 31.

[31] S. 31(1); *Angus Bros.* v. *Scott,* 1916, 2 S.L.T. 181; Unless agreed, tender by instalments is tender of the wrong quantity under S. 30; *Behrend & Co.* v. *Produce Brokers Co. Ltd.* [1920] 3 K.B. 530. See also *Barr* v. *Waldie* (1893) 21 R. 224; *Veit* v. *Ireland* (1896) 4 S.L.T. 4 (H.L.).

[32] S. 31(2); *Turnbull* v. *McLean* (1874) 1 R. 730; *Mersey Steel & Iron Co.* v. *Naylor* (1884) 9 App. Cas. 434; *Barr* v. *Waldie* (1893) 21 R. 224; *Govan Rope Co.* v. *Weir* (1897) 24 R. 368; *Millars Karri Co.* v. *Weddell* (1908) 100 L.T. 128; *Dominion Coal Co.* v. *Dominion Iron Co.* [1909] A.C. 293; *Angus Bros.* v. *Scott,* 1916, 2 S.L.T. 181; *Claddagh S.S. Co.* v. *Steven,* 1919 S.C. (H.L.) 132; *Payzu* v. *Saunders* [1919] 2 K.B. 581; *Maple Flock Co.* v. *Universal Furniture Products* [1934] 1 K.B. 148.

[33] *Higgins* v. *Pumpherston Oil Co.* (1893) 20 R. 532; *Munro* v. *Meyer* [1930] 2 K.B. 312.

[34] *Ebbw Vale Steel Co.* v. *Blaina Iron Co.* (1901) 6 Com. Cas. 33.

[35] S. 32(1); *Calcutta Co.* v. *De Mattos* (1863) 32 L.J.Q.B. 322; *Wimble* v. *Rosenberg* [1913] 3 K.B. 743.

The carrier is deemed the buyer's agent for the purpose of transmitting the goods to him, but not for accepting them in implement of the contract.

himself or may hold the seller responsible in damages.[36] Unless otherwise agreed, where goods are sent by a route involving sea transit,
under circumstances where it is usual to insure, the seller must give
such notice to the buyer as may enable him to insure them during their
sea transit, and if he fails to do so, the goods are at his risk during the
sea transit.[37] If the goods are lost in transit prima facie it is for the seller
to sue the carrier. Delivery to a carrier does not make the carrier the
buyer's agent to accept the goods.

Risk where goods delivered at distant place

Where the seller agrees to deliver goods at his own risk at a place
other than that where they are when sold, the buyer must nevertheless,
unless otherwise agreed, take any risk of deterioration in the goods
necessarily incident to the course of transit.[38]

Buyer's right of examination

Where goods, not previously examined by him, are delivered to the
buyer, he is not deemed to have accepted them unless and until he has
had a reasonable opportunity of examining them to ascertain whether
they are in conformity with the contract.[39] Unless otherwise agreed,
when the seller tenders delivery he is bound, on request, to give the
buyer a reasonable opportunity of examining the goods to ascertain
whether they are in conformity with the contract.[40]

Acceptance by buyer

The buyer is deemed to have accepted the goods when he intimates
to the seller that he has accepted them, or when the goods have been
delivered to him and he does any act in relation to them which is
inconsistent with the ownership of the seller,[41] or when after the lapse
of a reasonable time he retains the goods without intimating to the
seller that he has rejected them.[42] Once goods have been accepted in
any of these ways the right to reject is lost, but the buyer may still claim
damages for breach in a non-material respect. Acceptance is not to be
inferred so long as goods are under trial. The buyer need not return
rejected goods; it suffices if he intimates to the seller that he refuses to

[36] S. 32(2); *Young* v. *Hobson* (1949) 54 T.L.R. 365.
[37] S. 32(3); this provision applies only where sea transit is involved; such transit is normally part of an f.o.b. or c.i.f. contract, on which see *infra*.
[38] S. 33; cf. *Bull* v. *Robison* (1854) 10 Ex. 342; *Healy* v. *Howlett* [1917] 1 K.B. 337; *Ollett* v. *Jordan* [1918] 2 K.B. 41; *Broome* v. *Pardess Coop. Soc.* [1940] 3 All E.R. 603.
[39] S. 34(1).
[40] S. 34(2); *Chalmers* v. *Paterson* (1897) 24 R. 1020.
[41] e.g. using the goods, altering them, fitting them in, reselling them to another: *Wallis* v. *Pratt* [1911] A.C. 394; *Ruben* v. *Faire* [1949] 1 K.B. 254.
[42] S. 35; *Mechan* v. *Bow McLachlan & Co.* 1910 S.C. 758; *Leaf* v. *International Galleries* [1950] 2 K.B. 86.

accept them.[43] A buyer who finds that the seller will not uplift rejected goods can claim damages for storage.[44]

Liability of buyer for neglecting or refusing delivery

When the seller is ready and willing to deliver and requests the buyer to take delivery, and the buyer does not within a reasonable time thereafter take delivery, he is liable to the seller for any loss occasioned by his neglect or refusal, and also for a reasonable charge for the care and custody of the goods. This provision does not affect the rights of the seller where the neglect or refusal amounts to a repudiation of the contract.[45]

UNPAID SELLER'S RIGHTS AGAINST GOODS

UNPAID SELLER'S RIGHTS—(a) LIEN OR RETENTION

An unpaid seller,[46] notwithstanding that the property in the goods may have passed to the buyer, has by legal implication, subject to the Act and to any other Act in that behalf,[47] various rights against the goods. Firstly he has a lien on the goods (or right of retention of them) for the price while he is in possession of them.[48] This arises[49] (a) where the goods have been sold without any stipulation as to credit; (b) where the goods have been sold on credit, but the term of credit has expired; (c) where the buyer becomes insolvent.[50] The seller may exercise his right of retention notwithstanding that he is in possession of the goods as agent or custodier for the buyer.[51] Where the seller has made part delivery of the goods, he may exercise his right of retention on the remainder, unless the partial delivery has been made in such circumstances as to show an agreement to waive the right.[52] The seller's right of lien or retention is founded on possession, actual or

---

[43] S. 36

[44] Kolfor v. Tilbury Plant (1977) 121 Sol. Jo. 390.

[45] S. 37; as to seller's liability for neglecting or refusing delivery, see S. 51. S. 37 applies where the property has passed but the buyer fails to take delivery of his goods.

[46] Defined, S. 38, as a seller (a) when the whole price has not been paid or tendered; (b) when a bill of exchange or other negotiable instrument has been received as conditional payment and the condition has not been fulfilled by its dishonour or otherwise: cf McDowall & Neilson's Tr. v. Snowball Co. (1904) 7 F. 35. 'Seller', by S. 38(2), includes any person in the position of a seller, such as an agent of the seller.

[47] Factors Act, 1889; Factors (Sc.) Act, 1890.

[48] S. 39(1)(a).

[49] S. 41(1).

[50] Ex parte Lambton (1875) 10 Ch. App. 405, 415; Gunn v. Bolckow Vaughan & Co. (1875) 10 Ch. App. 491; Paton's Tr. v. Finlayson, 1923 S.C. 872.

[51] S. 41(2).

[52] S. 42.

constructive.[53] It is a claim in security only, and for the price only and renders the seller liable to the buyer for damages for non-delivery if claimed for a wrong cause or amount.[54] The buyer can secure the release of the goods from the seller's lien by tendering the whole price. The exercise by the seller of his right of lien or retention does not automatically rescind the contract of sale.[55]

Loss of lien or retention

The unpaid seller loses his right of retention[56] (a) when he delivers the goods to a carrier or other custodier for transmission to the buyer[57] without reserving the right of disposal of the goods; (b) when the buyer or his agent lawfully obtains possession of the goods;[58] and (c) by waiver.[59] He does not lose it merely be taking decree for the price of the goods.[60]

UNPAID SELLER'S RIGHTS—(b) STOPPAGE *IN TRANSITU*

The unpaid seller[61] also has the right, though the property in the goods may have passed to the buyer, in the case of the buyer's insolvency,[62] of stopping the goods *in transitu* after he has parted with possession of them;[63] he may accordingly resume possession of the goods as long as they are in course of transit, and retain them until payment or tender of the price.[64] Goods are deemed to be in course of transit from the time when they are delivered to a carrier or other custodier for transmission to the buyer, until the buyer or his agent takes delivery of them from the carrier or custodier.[65] The transit is at an end if the buyer or his agent obtains delivery before their arrival at the appointed destination.[66] If after arrival at the destination the

---

[53] cf. *Paton's Tr., supra.*

[54] *G. E. Ry.* v. *Lord's Tr.* [1909] A.C. 109.

[55] S. 48(1).

[56] S. 43.

[57] *Bolton* v. *L. & Y. Ry.* (1866) L.R. 1 C.P. 431.

[58] *Cooper* v. *Bill* (1865) 3 H. & C. 722; *Paton's Tr.* v. *Finlayson*, 1923 S.C. 872.

[59] *Robertson & Baxter* v. *McPherson* (1893) 1 S.L.T. 159.

[60] S. 43(2).

[61] Defined, S. 38.

[62] Defined S. 61(4).

[63] S. 39(1)(b). This principle was introduced into Scots law by the H.L. in *Jeffrey* v. *Allan, Stewart & Co.* (1790) 3 Pat. 191, disapproving a doctrine that if a buyer took delivery within the three days before stopping payment, he was presumed to have taken them fraudulently, and his trustee in bankruptcy could not retain them in an issue with the seller.

[64] S. 44; *Schotsmans* v. *L. & Y. Ry.* (1867) L.R. 2 Ch. App. 332; *Kendall* v. *Marshall, Stevens & Co.* (1883) 11 Q.B.D. 356.

[65] S. 45(1) cf. *McLeod* v. *Harrison* (1880) 8 R. 227; *Bethell* v. *Clark* (1888) 20 Q.B.D. 615; *McDowall & Neilson's Tr.* v. *Snowball* (1904) 7 F. 35. See also *Booker* v. *Milne* (1870) 9 M. 314.

[66] S. 45(2).

carrier acknowledges to the buyer that he holds the goods on his behalf and continues in possession of them as custodier for the buyer, the transit is at an end, though a further destination for the goods may have been indicated by the buyer.[67] If the buyer rejects the goods, and the carrier or other custodier continues in possession of them, the transit is not deemed to be at an end, even if the seller has refused to take them back.[68] When goods are delivered to a ship chartered by the buyer it depends on the circumstances of the case whether they are in the possession of the master as a carrier, or as agent to the buyer.[69] Where the carrier or other custodier wrongfully refuses to deliver the goods to the buyer or his agent, the transit is deemed to be at an end.[70] Where part delivery of the goods has been made to the buyer or his agent, the remainder of the goods may be stopped *in transitu*, unless such part delivery has been made under such circumstances as to show an agreement to give up possession of the whole of the goods.[71]

Stoppage *in transitu* is effected by taking actual possession of the goods, or by giving notice of the seller's claim to the carrier or other custodier in whose possession the goods are, either to the person in actual possession or to his principal, in time to prevent delivery to the buyer; the carrier or other custodier must then redeliver the goods to, or to the directions of, the seller, and at his expense.[72] A seller who effectively exercises the right of stoppage *in transitu* recovers possession of the goods and his lien or right of retention over them for the price revives.[73] He does not thereby recover the right of property in the goods,[74] nor does the mere exercise of the right of lien or of stoppage *in transitu* rescind the contract of sale.[75] He may retain possession only till the buyer tenders the price; if the buyer does not do so, the seller may proceed to his statutory power of resale.[76]

A seller who wrongfully stops *in transitu* goods, the property in which has passed to the buyer, is liable in damages for detention of the goods; if the property has not passed, he is liable to the buyer for

[67] S, 45(3); *Kendall v. Marshall, Stevens & Co.* (1883) 11 Q.B.D. 356; *Muir v. Rankin* (1905) 13 S.L.T. 60.

[68] S. 45(4); *Bolton v. L. & Y. Ry.* (1866) L.R. 1 C.P. 431.

[69] S. 45(5); *Berndtson v. Strang* (1867) L.R. 4 Eq. 481; 3 Ch. App. 588; *Cowdenbeath Coal Co. v. Clydesdale Bank* (1895) 22 R. 682.

[70] S. 45(6); *Bird v. Brown* (1850) 4 Ex. 786.

[71] S. 45(7); *Bolton, supra; Kemp v. Falk* (1882) 7 App. Cas. 573; cf. *Mechan v. N. E. Ry.*, 1911 S.C. 1348.

[72] S. 46; *Whitehead v. Anderson* (1842) 9 M. & W. 518; *U.S. Steel Products Co. v. G. W. Ry.* [1916] 1 A.C. 189; *Booth S.S. Co. v. Cargo Fleet Iron Co.* [1916] 2 K.B. 570.

[73] S. 44.

[74] *U.S. Steel Products Co. v. G. W. Ry.* [1916] 1 A.C. 189; *Booth S.S. Co. v. Cargo Fleet Iron Co.* [1916] 2 K.B. 570.

[75] S. 48(1).

[76] S. 48(3).

non-delivery.[77] If the seller duly notifies the carrier and the latter makes delivery in face of the notice of stoppage, the carrier is liable to the sellers in damages for the loss caused thereby.[78]

Effect of sub-sale or pledge by buyer

Subject to the Act,[79] the unpaid seller's right of retention or stoppage *in transitu* is not affected by any sale or other disposition of the goods which the buyer may have made,[80] unless the seller has assented thereto.[81] But where a document of title to goods has been lawfully transferred to any person as buyer or owner of the goods and that person transfers the document to a person who takes it in good faith and for value, such transaction, if by way of sale, defeats the seller's right of retention or stoppage *in transitu*, and if a pledge or other diposition for value, the seller's rights can only be exercised subject to the right of the transferee.[82]

UNPAID SELLER'S RIGHTS—(c) RESALE

The unpaid seller[83] also has a right of resale.[84] The first sale is not rescinded by the mere exercise of the seller's right of retention or of stoppage,[85] but the unpaid seller who has exercised either right may resell and the second buyer acquires a good title as against the original buyer.[86] Where the goods are of a perishable nature, or where the unpaid seller intimates to the buyer his intention to resell, and the buyer does not within a reasonable time pay or tender the price, the unpaid seller may resell and recover damages from the original buyer for any loss occasioned by his breach.[87] Where the seller expressly reserves a right of resale in case of default and on default resells, the original contract is thereby rescinded without prejudice to the seller's claim for damages.[88] The first sale is rescinded by resale or notice of intention to resell under S. 48(3) and when the seller resells he does so as full owner,[89] and resale under S. 48(4) is a sale by a full owner in

[77] S. 51(1).
[78] *Mechan* v. *N. E. Ry.*, 1911 S.C. 1348.
[79] Ss. 21–6.
[80] S. 47(1); *Farmeloe* v. *Bain* (1876) 1 C.P.D. 445 (lien); *Kemp* v. *Falk* (1882) 7 App. Cas. 573 (stoppage).
[81] *Merchant Banking Co.* v. *Phoenix Bessemer Co.* (1877) 5 Ch. D. 205.
[82] S. 47(2); *Dobell, Beckett & Co.* v. *Neilson* (1904) 7 F. 281; *Mordaunt Bros.* v. *B.O.C.M.* [1910] 2 K.B. 502; *Jurgens* v. *Dreyfus* [1914] 3 K.B. 40.
[83] Defined, S. 38.
[84] S. 39(1)(c).
[85] S. 48(1).
[86] S. 48(2).
[87] S. 48(3); *Lord* v. *Price* (1874) L.R. 9 Exch. 54; *Ex parte Stapleton* (1879) 10 Ch. D. 586; *Ward* v. *Bignall* [1967] 1 Q.B. 534, overruling *Gallagher* v. *Shilcock* [1949] 2 K.B. 765.
[88] S. 48(4).   [89] *Ward, supra.*

whom the property has revested. If the seller resells under S. 48(3) at a profit he probably has to account to the first buyer for the profit, but not if he resells under S. 48(4). If he resells at a loss he may in either case recover from the first buyer damages for the loss caused by his failure to pay for the goods.

UNPAID SELLER'S RIGHTS—(d) WITHHOLDING DELIVERY

Where the property in goods has not passed to the buyer the unpaid seller[90] has, in addition to his other remedies, a right of withholding delivery similar to and co-extensive with his rights of retention and stoppage *in transitu* where the property has passed to the buyer.[91] It is essential that the seller should still have possession of the goods.

UNPAID SELLER'S RIGHTS—(e) ARRESTMENT OR POINDING

In Scotland a seller may also attach the goods while in his own hands or possession by arrestment or poinding to the same effect as if done by a third party.[92]

ACTIONS FOR BREACH OF THE CONTRACT

Unpaid seller's rights—action for price

Where the property in the goods has passed to the buyer, and the buyer wrongfully[93] neglects or refuses to pay for the goods according to the terms of the contract, the seller may bring an action against him for the price.[94] If the price is payable on a day certain irrespective of delivery,[95] and the buyer wrongfully neglects or refuses to pay it, the seller may sue for the price, though the property has not passed nor the goods been appropriated to the contract.[96] The seller in Scotland may claim interest on the price from the date of tender of the goods, or the due date of payment, as the case may be.[97] The claim for the price is the only remedy where the property has passed to the buyer and he has

---

[90] Defined, S. 38.

[91] S. 39(2). Being still owner, a seller in this case could not logically claim either a lien or a right to stop *in transitu*, both being appropriate only to goods the property of another.

[92] S. 40, superseding Mercantile Law Amdt. (Sc.) Act, 1856, S. 3.

[93] Payment may be postponed or depend on a contingency. Refusal to pay is justified if the goods are defective.

[94] S. 49(1); *British Motor Body Co. v. Shaw*, 1914 S.C. 922.

[95] *Stein Forbes & Co. v. County Tailoring Co.* (1916) 86 L.J.K.B. 448.

[96] S. 49(2).

[97] S. 49(3).

accepted the goods; if the property has passed but the buyer refuses to accept the goods, or the property has not passed but the purchase price is payable on a day certain, either an action for the price or for damages for non-acceptance[98] is competent. Action for the price is competent also only where the buyer wrongfully refuses to pay; if he is entitled to refuse payment, as for a breach of condition, this action is not competent. Where the seller is in breach of contract, as by late delivery, the buyer may retain the price.[99] It is no defence that the purchase had been made for resale and had been rejected by the sub-purchasers as disconform to contract; the validity of the third party's rejection is *res inter alios*.[1]

Unpaid seller's rights—damages for non-acceptance

Where the buyer wrongfully neglects or refuses to accept and pay for the goods, the seller may claim damages for non-acceptance,[2] measured by the estimated loss directly and naturally resulting in the ordinary course from the buyer's breach of contract,[3] and where there is an available market for the goods, prima facie to be ascertained by the difference between the contract price and the market or current price when the goods should have been accepted or if no time was fixed for acceptance when they were refused.[4] This is the only remedy where the property has not passed to the buyer, and he has not accepted the goods; if the property has passed but the buyer refuses to accept the goods, or the property has not passed but the price is payable on a day certain, either an action for the price[5] or for damages for non-acceptance is competent.[6] The defence that earlier deliveries under the contract had not been of the stipulated quality has been held relevant.[7] In special circumstances the prima facie measure of damages is inapplicable, particularly where sub-sales were foreseeable and the contract breaker should have known of something which made the ordinary measure of damages inadequate, in which case damages are the difference between contract price and sub-sale price, but also where there

---

[98] S. 50.

[99] *British Motor Body Co.* v. *Shaw*, 1914 S.C. 922.

[1] *Brush Elec. Eng. Co.* v. *Scott Stirling & Co.* (1907) 14 S.L.T. 751.

[2] S. 50(1).

[3] S. 50(2). This measure of damages is based on the principle of *Hadley* v. *Baxendale* (1854) 9 Ex. 341; see Ch. 4.9, *supra;* and *Rodocanachi* v. *Milburn* (1886) 18 Q.B.D. 67; *Williams* v. *Agius* [1914] A.C. 510. If the seller has resold to another at as good a price no damages are due: *Lazenby Garages* v. *Wright* [1976] 2 All E.R. 770.

[4] S. 50(3).

[5] S. 49.

[6] *Heskell* v. *Continental Express* [1950] 1 All E.R. 1033; see also *Hall* v. *Pim* (1928) 33 Com. Cas. 324; *Finlay* v. *Kwik Hoo Tong* [1929] 1 K.B. 400; *Biggin* v. *Permanite* [1951] 2 All E.R. 191.

[7] *Govan Rope Co.* v. *Weir* (1897) 24 R. 368.

is no available market for the goods, where damages will include the cost of the unsaleable article and loss of profit thereon.[8]

Buyer's remedies—damages for non-delivery

Where the seller wrongfully neglects or refuses to deliver, the buyer may claim damages for non-delivery,[9] measured by the estimated loss directly and naturally arising, in the ordinary course, from the seller's breach,[10] and where there is an available market for the goods[11] prima facie to be ascertained by the difference between the contract price and the market or current price when they should have been delivered or if no time was fixed when the seller refused to deliver.[12] This action lies also where the seller has delivered goods which the buyer is entitled to reject, unless he has accepted those goods. In the case of instalment deliveries, if each instalment is a separate contract, the buyer's remedy is exercisable in respect of non-delivery in any period.[13]

The Act does not deal expressly with damages for delay in delivery. If the date of delivery is part of the description of the goods, delay is a breach of warranty[14] and the buyer may exercise his rights under S. 11(5). Otherwise delay in delivery is a breach of contract at common law justifying damages for the loss caused thereby, measured prima facie by the difference between the contract price and the market price, or the difference between the contract price and the resale price.[15]

Buyer's remedies—specific performance

In an action for breach of contract to deliver specific or ascertained goods the court may direct that the contract shall be performed specifically, without giving the defender the option of retaining the goods on payment of damages. This decree may be unconditional or on such conditions as the court may deem just. This is supplementary to the general Scottish right to claim specific implement.[16] Specific

[8] Re Vic Mill Ltd. [1913] 1 Ch. 465; Swift v. B.O.T. [1925] A.C. 520.
[9] S. 51(1).
[10] S. 51(2); founded on the principle of Hadley v. Baxendale (1854) 9 Ex. 341; see Ch. 4.9, supra; Millett v. Van Heek [1921] 2 K.B. 369; Tai Hing Cotton Co. v. Kamsing Knitting Co. [1978] 1 All E.R. 515.
[11] cf. Marshall v. Nicoll, 1919 S.C. (H.L.) 129.
[12] S. 51(3); cf. Williams v. Agius [1914] A.C. 510. As to case where no 'available market' see Marshall, supra. The second limb of S. 51(3) does not apply in any case of anticipatory breach of contract: Tai Hing Co., supra.
[13] Higgins v. Pumpherston Oil Co. (1893) 20 R. 532. cf. West Limerigg Coal Co. v. Robertson (1873) 10 S.L.R. 467; Barr v. Waldie (1893) 21 R. 224; Ireland v. Merryton Coal Co. (1894) 21 R. 989.
[14] S. 13.
[15] Wertheim v. Chicoutimi Pulp Co. [1911] A.C. 30, expld. Williams v. Agius [1914] A.C. 510; British Motor Body Co. v. Shaw, 1914 S.C. 922.
[16] S. 52; cf. Aurdal v. Estrella, 1916 S.C. 882. On this common law right in Scotland see Stewart v. Kennedy (1890) 17 R. (H.L.) 1.

implement may be claimed whether the property has passed or is still vested in the seller.

Interest and special damages

Nothing in the Act affects the right of the buyer or seller[17] to recover interest[18] or special damages[19] where by law interest or special damages may be recoverable, or to recover money paid where the consideration for the payment of it has failed.[20]

Buyer's remedies—damages for wrongful detention

Where the property in the goods has passed to the buyer and the seller neglects or refuses to deliver the buyer may also, at common law, claim damages for wrongful detention or withholding of the buyer's goods, measured by the value of the goods. This is normally claimed alternatively to specific implement. This remedy is also competent, and indeed the only remedy competent, against a third party who has possession of the buyer's goods, unless such third party can rely on Ss. 21–6 or 47–8 or the Act.

Buyer's remedies—return of the price

If the buyer has already paid the price and neither the property has passed nor the goods been delivered to him, the buyer can at common law seek repetition of the price under the principle *condictio causa data causa non secuta.*[21]

SPECIAL KINDS OF SALE

Auction sales

In a sale by auction, where goods are put up for sale in lots, each lot is prima facie deemed to be the subject of a separate contract of sale.[22] A sale by auction is complete when the auctioneer announces its completion by the fall of the hammer, or in other customary manner.

---

[17] S. 54.

[18] On interest see Bell, *Comm.* I, 694.

[19] i.e. damages for loss foreseeable only if knowledge of special circumstances was communicated to the party in breach when the contract was made: *Victoria Laundry* v. *Newman* [1949] 2 K.B. 528.

[20] cf. *Cantiere San Rocco* v. *Clyde Shipbuilding* Co. 1923 S.C. (H.L.) 105; *Rowland* v. *Divall* [1923] 2 K.B. 500; *Mason* v. *Burningham* [1949] 2 K.B. 545; *Butterworth* v. *Kingsway,* [1954] 2 All E.R. 694.

[21] *Cantiere San Rocco* v. *Clyde Shipbuilding Co.,* 1923 S.C. (H.L.) 105.

[22] S. 57(1); Bell, *Prin.* §130; *Couston, Thomson & Co.* v. *Chapman* (1872) 10 M. (H.L.) 74.

Till then any bidder may retract his bid.[23] A sale by auction may be notified to be subject to a reserve or upset price,[24] and a right to bid may be reserved expressly by or on behalf of the seller, in which case only the seller or any one person on his behalf may bid.[25] Where a sale by auction is not notified to be subject to a right to bid on behalf of the seller, the seller may not bid himself, nor employ anyone to bid at the sale, nor may the auctioneer knowingly take any bid from the seller or any such person. A sale contravening this rule may be treated as fraudulent by the buyer.[26] The auctioneer, if acting for a disclosed seller and in accordance with his instructions, is not liable for implement or damages to a purchaser,[27] though he is if he has sold without authority and the purchaser loses the bargain.[28] He may sue the buyer for the price in his own name[29] and has a lien over the goods for his charges and commission.[30]

The Auctions (Bidding Agreements) Acts, 1927 and 1969, make it an offence for a dealer to give or receive consideration or reward for abstaining or having abstained from bidding; such agreements are illegal and on the offender's conviction may be treated as fraudulent by the seller.[31] The Mock Auctions Act, 1961, makes unlawful the auction of certain kinds of property if any lot is sold at a price below the highest bid, or the right to bid is restricted to persons who have bought one or more articles or any articles are given away or offered by way of gift.[32]

A sale by auction is excluded from the definition of 'consumer contract' in the Unfair Contract Terms Act, 1977, S. 25, so that the protections given to consumers by that Act do not apply in auction sales.

Sale on approval, or on 'sale or return' terms

A sale on such terms is a sale subject to suspensive or resolutive condition.[33] The property in the goods passes when the buyer signifies

---

[23] S. 57(2); *Shankland* v. *Robinson*, 1920 S.C. (H.L.) 103. Conversely the seller may withdraw the goods from the sale until the hammer falls: *Fenwick* v. *Macdonald Fraser & Co.* (1904) 6 F. 850.

[24] S. 57(3). cf. *McManus* v. *Fortescue* [1907] 2 K.B. 1, and principle of *Anderson* v. *Croall* (1904) 6 F. 153.

[25] S. 57(6); *Brodie* v. *Dowell* (1894) 2 S.L.T. 9.

[26] S. 57(4) and (5); *Morrice* v. *Craig* (1902) 9 S.L.T. 193; see also *Union Bank* v. *Munster* (1887) 37 Ch. D. 51.   [27] *Fenwick, supra.*

[28] *Anderson* v. *Croall* (1903) 6 F. 153.

[29] *Couston Thomson & Co.* v. *Chapman* (1872) 10 M. (H.L.) 74; *Mackenzie* v. *Cormack* 1950 S.C. 183.   [30] *Mackenzie, supra.*

[31] *Rawlings* v. *General Trading Co.* [1921] 1 K.B. 635; *Cohen* v. *Roche* [1927] 1 K.B. 169; *R.* v. *Barnett* [1951] 1 T.L.R. 899.

[32] *Clements* v. *Rydeheard* [1978] 1 All E.R. 658; *Allen* v. *Simmons* [1978] 3 All E.R. 662.

[33] cf. *Kirkham* v. *Attenborough* [1897] 1 Q.B. 201; *Weiner* v. *Gill* [1906] 2 K.B. 574; *Weiner* v. *Harris* [1910] 1 K.B. 285.

his approval or acceptance or does any other act adopting the transaction, or retains the goods without giving notice of rejection within
any time fixed for rejection, or within a reasonable time.[34] Such a sale
has been held not to be a transaction under which a person is in
possession of goods under an agreement to buy within S. 25,[35] nor does
it become a sale because the goods are damaged or perish while in the
potential buyer's possession though without his fault.[36]

Credit sale

A credit sale is a sale in which, by agreement, payment of the price is
deferred in whole or in part. It may be payable by instalments. It is a
'sale' within the meaning of the 1979 Act and governed by that Act.[37]
Accordingly prima facie the property passes when the contract is
made[38] and the seller has only a personal claim for the unpaid price and
no right in security over the goods sold.[39] The buyer can validly resell
notwithstanding that he has not paid the full price. But if the agreement provides for the price to be payable by instalments and it is not a
conditional sale agreement and is in other respects within the scope of
the Consumer Credit Act, 1974, Ss. 8–9, it is governed by that Act.[40]

Conditional sale

Conditional sale is a sale or an agreement for sale of goods, subject
to certain conditions, suspensive or resolutive, which may include
conditions as to payment[41] or performance[42] or as to the passing of the
property.[43] Such a transaction is a 'sale' or an 'agreement for sale'
within the meaning of the 1979 Act.[44] Payment of the price may be
suspended in whole or in part and it may be payable by instalments. If
there is no condition suspensive of the passing of the property prima
facie it passes when the contract is made,[45] in which case the seller no

[34] 1979 Act, S. 18, R. 4. cf. *R.* v. *Eaton* (1966) 50 Cr. App. R. 189.
[35] *Edwards* v. *Vaughan* (1910) 26 T.L.R. 545.
[36] *Elphick* v. *Barnes* (1880) 5 C.P.D. 321; see also *Poole* v. *Smith's Car Sales* [1962] 2 All E.R. 482.
[37] See 1979 Act, Ss. 28, 41(1)(a) and (b).
[38] 1979 Act, Ss. 17–18.
[39] cf. *Cropper* v. *Donaldson* (1880) 7 R. 1108.
[40] Ch. 5.34, *infra*.
[41] e.g. payment by bill: *Brandt* v. *Dickson* (1876) 3 R. 375 *Clarke* v. *Miller* (1885) 12 R. 1035; payment by instalments; *Murdoch* v. *Greig* (1889) 16 R. 396.
[42] e.g. subject to testing: *Mackay* v. *Dick & Stevenson* (1881) 8 R. (H.L.) 37; subject to period of trial: *Cranston* v. *Mallow & Lien*, 1912 S.C. 112; condition as to quality: *Jacobs* v. *Scott* (1899) 2 F. (H.L.) 70; condition as to delivery: *Higgins* v. *Pumpherston Oil Co.* (1893) 20 R. 532; ship not to be held as delivered until trials passed: *Barclay, Curle & Co.* v. *Laing*, 1908 S.C. 82.
[43] e.g. *Murdoch* v. *Greig* (1889) 16 R. 396.
[44] S. 2.
[45] cf. *Lee* v. *Butler* [1893] 2 Q.B. 318, where held purchaser could resell though he had not completed payments.

longer has any right over the goods, unless he is unpaid. If there is a condition suspensive of the passing of the property the buyer is still one who has agreed to buy, not merely one who has an option to buy, and he must therefore complete the purchase or be liable in damages. He has no option to return the goods. The implied terms and conditions of the Sale of Goods Act 1979 apply.

But if the agreement is one for the sale of goods under which the purchase price or part of it is payable by instalments, and the property in the goods is to remain in the seller (notwithstanding that the buyer is to be in possession of the goods) until such conditions as to the payment of instalments or otherwise as may be specified in the agreement are fulfilled, and it is in other respects within the scope of the Consumer Credit Act, 1974, Ss. 8–9, it is governed by that Act.[46]

Sale overseas

Certain specialities arise where the sale of goods is to a buyer abroad and mercantile custom has developed particular sets of contractual documents usual in import and export trading.

Sale C.I.F.

Under a sale c.i.f. (i.e. at a price including cost, insurance and freight)[47] the seller's duty is to make a contract of affreightment for the goods to be carried to their contractual destination and delivered there, to effect an insurance for the buyer, to deliver the goods on board ship,[48] or on transport to it, for loading, and to forward the bill of lading, as symbol of the goods described therein, the insurance policy, and invoice to the buyer.[49] The property passes on delivery of the documents against which the buyer's liability to pay the price arises.[50] Payment may be agreed to be made by bill of exchange against delivery of documents, in which case a bill is forwarded with the documents and the property does not pass unless the buyer accepts the bill of exchange.[51] If he does not, the property does not pass and he must return the bill of lading.[52] The risk passes on shipment and if the

---

[46] Ch. 5.34, *infra*.

[47] See generally Kennedy, *C.I.F. Contracts*; Schmitthoff, *The Export Trade*.

[48] cf. *McDowell & Neilson's Tr.* v. *Snowball Co.* (1904) 7 F. 35.

[49] *Biddell Bros.* v. *E. Clemens Horst Co.* [1911] 1 K.B. 214, 220; [1912] A.C. 18. Other documents may be necessary, e.g. export licence, consular invoice, certificate of origin. See also *Harrower, Welsh & Co.* v. *McWilliam*, 1928 S.C. 326; *Comptoir d'Achat* v. *Ridder* [1949] A.C. 293.

[50] *Biddell Bros.* v. *E. Clemens Horst Co.* [1911] 1 K.B. 214; *Harrower, supra*; *Smyth* v. *Bailey* [1940] 3 All E.R. 60, 68; *Chao* v. *British Traders* [1954] 2 Q.B. 459.

[51] Sale of Goods Act, 1979, S. 19(3); *The Prinz Adalbert* [1917] A.C. 586; *The Orteric* [1920] A.C. 724.

[52] Ibid.; *Shepherd* v. *Harrison* (1871) L.R. 5 H.L. 116.

goods are lost the buyer is covered by the insurance.[53] By accepting the documents the buyer does not lose his right to reject the goods on delivery if they are disconform to contract.[54] Prima facie the place of delivery is the proper place for their examination.[55]

Sale F.O.B.

Under an f.o.b. contract (free on board)[56] the seller's duty is at his own expense to deliver the goods on board ship at the agreed port for carriage to the buyer. He may make the contract of affreightment on the buyer's behalf, the buyer being liable for the freight.[57] The buyer will be liable for damages for non-acceptance if he fails to nominate an effective ship for the carriage.[58] The seller must give the buyer adequate notice to enable the buyer to insure the goods during transit;[59] if he fails to do so, the goods are deemed to be at seller's risk.[60] There is no duty to give further notice where the contract contained sufficient information to enable the buyer to insure.[61] The property passes, prima facie, on shipment,[62] as does the risk.[63] The price covers expenses up to and including delivery on board; further expenses, including freight, insurance, import duties, etc. fall on the buyer.[64] Payment is due on delivery to ship, but the contract may provide for payment by 'cash against documents', or by acceptance of a bill of exchange against tender of a bill of lading, or by a confirmed letter of credit. The effect of such terms may be that the property shall pass only on such an event as the buyer's acceptance fo the bill of exchange.

F.A.S. and F.O.R. contracts

Under as f.a.s. contract (free alongside) the seller is bound to deliver the goods at his own expense alongside the ship, ready for loading;[65] under an f.o.r. contract (free on rail) the seller undertakes to deliver the goods at his own expense at the station or into railway wagons. These

---

[53] *Groom v. Barber* [1915] 1 K.B. 316; it is immaterial that the seller knows when he tenders the documents that the goods have been lost: *Manbre Saccharine Co. v. Corn Products Co.* [1919] 1 K.B. 198.

[54] *Biddell Bros., supra.*

[55] *Heilbutt v. Hickson* (1872) L.R. 7 C.P. 438; *Perkins v. Bell* [1893] 1 Q.B. 193.

[56] See generally Schmitthoff, *The Export Trade.*

[57] *Inglis v. Stock* (1885) 10 App. Cas. 263.

[58] *Colley v. Overseas Exporters* [1921] 3 K.B. 302.

[59] *W.L.R. Trades (London) Ltd. v. British and Northern Shipping Agency Ltd.* [1955] 1 Lloyd's Rep. 554.

[60] 1979 Act, S. 32(3); Bell, *Prin.* §118.

[61] *Wimble v. Rosenberg* [1913] 3 K.B. 743.

[62] *Inglis, supra.*

[63] *Inglis, supra; Pyrene Co. v. Scindia S.N. Co.* [1954] 2 Q.B. 402.

[64] *Glengarnock Iron Co. v. Cooper* (1895) 22 R. 672.

[65] *Pini v. Smith* (1895) 22 R. 699; see also *Glengarnock Iron Co. v. Cooper* (1895) 22 R. 672.

contracts are variations of the ordinary contract of sale only in respect of the place and cost of delivery, and in fixing prima facie the time at which the property and risk pass and the price becomes payable.[66]

Ex-ship contract

Under an ex-ship contract the seller undertakes to have delivery made to the buyer from a ship which has arrived at the port of destination and a place therein usual for delivery of that kind of goods. The seller has to load, and pay insurance and freight, and to furnish the buyer with an effectual order on the ship to deliver.[67] The property and risk pass only when the goods are delivered over the ship's rail at the port of delivery, and only then is the price payable.[68]

International sales

The Uniform Laws on International Sales Act, 1967,[69] gives the force of law in the United Kingdom to rules adopted by international conventions dealing respectively with a Uniform Law on the International Sale of Goods (Sch. 1) and a Uniform Law on the Formation of Contracts for the International Sale of Goods (Sch. 2).

---

[66] cf. *Healy* v. *Howlett* [1917] 1 K.B. 337.
[67] Bell, *Prin.* §108; *Yangtze Ins. Assoc.* v. *Lukmanjee* [1918] A.C. 585, 589.
[68] *Yangtze Ins. Assoc., supra.*
[69] Not yet in force.

CHAPTER 5.34

HIRE-PURCHASE, CREDIT SALE OR CONDITIONAL SALE OF MOVEABLES

The desire of persons to acquire the immediate possession and use of goods for which they cannot pay outright, and the desires of manufacturers and dealers to satisfy their customers' wishes for deferred payment has led to the evolution of various modes of acquisition of goods on credit.[1] Three similar but distinct legal transactions having these desired results have developed, hire-purchase, credit sale and conditional sale. The legal relationships are somewhat confused because in economic reality the intending purchaser is advanced money to acquire the goods from the dealer, by a third party who in return acquires rights over the goods but without possession thereof in security of his loan. In some cases it may be uncertain whether a transaction is one of hire or of hire-purchase.[2] In modern practice where the buyer wishes to utilize one of the forms of purchase by deferred payments, the seller normally sells the goods in question outright to a finance or hire-purchase company and is paid by it; the buyer then contracts to hire and ultimately to buy those goods from the hire-purchase company, to pay the instalments to it, and, if he ultimately acquires the property, he does so from it.[3] The dealer commonly acts as agent for the hire-purchase company in making the contract and receiving the payments.[4] Or the buyer buys on credit or subject to conditions from the seller or a finance company.

These three kinds of contract each exist in two forms: at common law and regulated by statute.

---

[1] Early Scottish examples are *Marston* v. *Kerr's Tr.*(1879) 6 R. 898; *Murdoch* v. *Greig* (1889) 16 R. 396. The same result could be obtained by sale under suspensive condition: see *Cowan* v. *Spence* (1824) 3 S. 42; *Wright* v. *Forman* (1828) 7 S. 175.

[2] e.g. *Galbraith* v. *Mitchenall Estates, Ltd.* [1964] 2 All E.R. 653.

[3] The hirer obtains credit for all the unpaid instalments: *Maclean* v. *McCord*, 1965 S.L.T. (Sh. Ct.) 69 seems unsound.

[4] See the system described in *Re Finance Houses Association's Agreement* [1965] 3 All E.R. 509.

HIRE-PURCHASE AT COMMON LAW

At common law the contract of hire-purchase is a contract whereby an owner lets goods on hire to a hirer in return for periodical payments, and further grants him an option, in certain circumstances and subject to certain conditions, to purchase the goods outright. Under the option, the hirer is not bound to buy, but the owner is bound to sell if the hirer exercises the option and satisfies the conditions. The hirer may, on conditions, surrender the goods and terminate the hiring before the option is exercisable. The payments, nominally of hire, are calculated to amount to instalments of the price with an allowance for interest on the unpaid balance thereof, and the option is normally exercisable on payment of a final small payment.[5] A contract of hire-purchase is neither a sale, nor an agreement to sell, neither at common law nor under the Sale of Goods Act, 1979, nor is it simply a hiring, as the existence of the option gives the hirer from the outset a semi-proprietary interest in the goods.[6] Having merely an option to buy, the hirer is not owner nor in possession of the goods under an agreement to buy, and consequently cannot confer any title on a purchaser from him under the Factors Acts or the Sale of Goods Act, 1979, S. 25.[7] The property does not pass to him until the option is exercised and good payment made of all sums due in respect thereof.[8] Goods held by a tenant on hire-purchase fall under the landlord's hypothec[9] and may be poinded for local rates,[10] but do not pass to the trustee on the hirer's sequestration,[11] nor are they attached by a poinding of the hirer's goods.[12]

Formation of contract of hire-purchase at common law

At common law the general principles of contract apply to the agreement of parties.[13] Writing is not required to constitute or prove a common law hire-purchase agreement,[14] but writing is now in practice

---

[5] See explanations of hire-purchase contracts at common law in *Helby* v. *Matthews* [1895] A.C. 471; *Muirhead & Turnbull* v. *Dickson* (1905) 7 F. 686; *Taylor* v. *Wylie & Lochhead*, 1912 S.C. 978; *Darngavil Coal Co.* v. *I.R.*, 1913 S.C. 602. Contrast cases of sale with attempted security without possession till price paid: *Cropper* v. *Donaldson* (1880) 7 R. 1108.

[6] *Whiteley* v. *Hilt* [1918] 2 K.B. 808; *Karflex Ltd.* v. *Poole* [1933] 2 K.B. 251.

[7] *Helby* v. *Matthews* [1895] A.C. 471; but see *Brechin Auction Co.* v. *Reid* (1895) 22 R. 711.

[8] *McLaren's Tr.* v. *Argylls, Ltd.*, 1915, 2 S.L.T. 241.

[9] *Rudman* v. *Jay*, 1908 S.C. 552. cf. *Dundee Corpn.* v. *Marr*, 1977 S.C. 96 (hire).

[10] *Orchard Trust Ltd.* v. *Glasgow Corpn.* (1951) 67 Sh. Ct. Rep. 59.

[11] *Marston* v. *Kerr's Tr.* (1879) 6 R. 898; cf. *Duncanson* v. *Jefferis' Trs.* (1881) 8 R. 563; *Murdoch* v. *Greig* (1889) 16 R. 396.

[12] *Hopkinson* v. *Napier*, 1953 S.C. 139.

[13] *Bell Bros. (H.P.) Ltd.* v. *Aitken*, 1939 S.C. 577; *Bell Bros. (H.P.) Ltd.* v. *Reynolds*, 1945 S.C. 213

[14] *Muirhead & Turnbull* v. *Dickson* (1905) 7 F. 686; *Campbell Discount Co.* v. *Gall* [1961] 1 Q.B. 431.

invariable; it need not be probative.[15] In modern practice as to formation of the contract the prospective hirer completes both a proposal form that the finance company buy the goods from the dealer and let them on hire-purchase to him, and the hire-purchase agreement with the finance company as prospective owner of the goods to take the goods from it on hire-purchase terms. The contract is concluded if and when the finance company for its part executes these agreements, and this is notified to the hirer.[16] The contract normally binds the hirer to pay the instalments, keep the goods in repair, keep them insured, not to remove them from his premises, and not to resell or pledge them.

The contract may be induced by misrepresentations[17] and may include express warranties.[18] At common law the dealer is not necessarily an agent of the finance house, though in some cases he may have some *ad hoc* agency.[19]

The forms of the agreement so far as concerning payment may be challengeable as in extortionate credit bargain, regardless of the amount involved.[20]

Collateral guarantees

The finance company frequently requires the hirer's undertaking to be reinforced by the guarantee of a third party. Such a guarantee must conform to the normal requirements for such a contract.[21] Alternatively it may require the dealer or a third party to undertake to indemnify it against loss on the transaction with the hirer.[22] Such an undertaking is probably a guarantee within the Mercantile Law Amdt. (Sc.) Act, 1856, S. 6.

Cancellation at common law

At common law the hirer or buyer has no right to cancel his agreement unless the owner agrees, and such an attempt is a breach of contract.

---

[15] cf. *Pollok* v. *Whiteford*, 1936 S.C. 402, 412; *Terret* v. *Frew*, 1951 S.L.T. (Sh. Ct.) 29. As to signature in blank, see *British Wagon Co.* v. *Russell*, 1962 S.L.T. (Sh. Ct.) 55.

[16] The dealer is not the finance company's agent to accept the hirer's offer unless expressly authorized to do so. As to the hirer signing a blank form, leaving it to the dealer to complete it, see *U.D.T. Ltd.* v. *Western* [1976] Q.B. 513.

[17] e.g. *Oscar Chess, Ltd.* v. *Williams* [1957] 1 All E.R. 325.

[18] e.g. *Bentley* v. *Smith* [1965] 2 All E.R. 65.

[19] *Mercantile Credit Ltd.* v. *Hamblin* [1965] 2 Q.B. 242, 269; *Branwhite* v. *Worcester Works Finance Ltd.* [1969] 1 A.C. 552.

[20] Consumer Credit Act, 1974, Ss. 137–40 (applicable to unregulated agreements as well as to regulated).

[21] Ch. 4.21, *supra*. See e.g. *Unity Finance Ltd.* v. *Woodcock* [1963] 2 All E.R. 270. As to proceeding against guarantor see *Woodfield Finance Trust* v. *Burrow*, 1962 S.L.T. (Sh. Ct.) 6.

[22] See e.g. *Yeoman Credit, Ltd.* v. *Latter* [1961] 2 All E.R. 294; *Park Motors* v. *Blackmore*, 1964, S.L.T. (Sh. Ct.) 30.

Representations and stipulations in common law cases

In common law cases representations may be made[23] and warranties given, but the contract normally negatives all warranties. There were until 1973 probably no warranties or stipulations implied by law beyond those implied in any contract of simple hiring,[24] but the stipulations implied by the 1973 Act *(infra)* apply to all common law as well as statutory cases.

Duties of owner at common law

The owner's duty is to deliver possession of the thing hired on completion of the contractual documents and usually on payment of the initial payment. Undue delay to deliver is a breach of contract, and may be so material as to justify rescission of the contract. The hiring commences only when possession of the goods has been delivered to the hirer. He should not sign a delivery receipt until he has actually taken delivery.[25] If the goods let are totally unfit for the purpose of the hiring there is a material breach of contract entitling the hirer to rescind the contract and claim damages.[26] If, however, the hirer in such circumstances elects to affirm the contract he is entitled to damages but is otherwise still bound by the agreement.[27] A non-material breach by the owner does not entitle the hirer to rescind the contract but only to claim damages.[28] Independently of contract an owner may be liable *ex delicto* if the hirer is injured by reason of a defect causing him foreseeable injury.[29]

Duties of hirer at common law

The hirer must take delivery of the goods and take reasonable care of them, and will be liable in damages for non-acceptance,[30] for loss or damage attributable to fault or lack of reasonable care, the onus of disproof of which is on him,[31] or due to use in a dangerous or unusual way, but not for fair wear and tear or accidental destruction or theft.[32]

---

[23] cf. *Bell Bros. (H.P.) Ltd.* v. *Reynolds,* 1945 S.C. 213; *Andrews* v. *Hopkinson* [1957] 1 Q.B. 229.

[24] *Drury* v. *Buckland* [1941] 1 All E.R. 269; *Karsales* v. *Wallis* [1956] 2 All E.R. 866. In *Karflex* v. *Poole* [1933] 2 K.B. 251 there was held to be a warranty that the lessor, when he let on hire-purchase, was owner; in *Mercantile Union Ltd* v. *Wheatley* [1938] 1 K.B. 490; and *Warman* v. *Southern Counties Car Finance Corpn.* [1949] 2 K.B. 576 it was held that the lessor had to be entitled to dispose when he delivered the goods on hire-purchase.

[25] *Bell Bros. (H.P.) Ltd.* v. *Reynolds,* 1945 S.C. 213; *Karsales, supra.*

[26] *Karsales, supra; Charterhouse Credit Co.* v. *Tolly* [1963] 2 Q.B. 683.

[27] *Charterhouse Credit Co., supra.*

[28] cf. *Sc. Midland Guarantee Trust* v. *Gray,* 1951 S.L.T. (Sh. Ct.) 8.

[29] cf. *Andrews* v. *Hopkinson* [1957] 1 Q.B. 229.

[30] *Interoffice Telephones, Ltd.* v. *Freeman* [1958] 1 Q.B. 190.

[31] cf. *Pullars* v. *Walker* (1858) 20 D. 1238; *Wilson* v. *Orr* (1879) 7 R. 266.

[32] cf. *Bell, Prin.* §141; *Smith* v. *Melvin* (1845) 8 D. 264.

The hirer is usually taken bound to carry out normal repairs, maintenance and renewals.[33] He is frequently taken bound to insure the goods.[34] He must pay the rent by the due dates. He is not obliged to pay rent for any period during which the goods let are wholly unfit for the purpose of the hire from a cause not attributable to the hirer, nor to fair wear and tear.[35]

Hirer's rights of possession

The hirer has possession of the goods with the owner's consent and may recover them from any third party who has custody of them.[36] But until he has exercised the option to purchase neither he, nor an agent on his behalf, can validly, without the owner's consent, sell the goods.[37]

Hirer's breach of contract at common law

At common law the contract normally provides that if the hirer defaults in payment, does not perform all the obligations incumbent on him under the contract, purports to sell, pledge or otherwise dispose of the goods, has diligence done against him, or is sequestrated,[38] or in any other stated way acts in breach of his contract, the contract is automatically terminated, or that the owner may without notice terminate the agreement, the hirer remaining liable for all rent accrued down to the date of termination. The owner might, however, merely sue for any unpaid instalments. Failure to make punctual payment of an instalment does not necessarily evidence intention to repudiate the contract.[39] The agreement may provide for a minimum payment being due on termination on the hirer's default, as agreed depreciation on the goods, but such a provision may be open to challenge as a penalty.[40] Alternatively the owner may claim damages for his loss of profit on the transaction.[41]

---

[33] cf. Bell, *Prin.* §145; *Lamonby v. Foulds*, 1928 S.C. 89. See also *Brady v. St. Margaret's Trust* [1963] 2 Q.B. 494.
[34] There may be no duty to do so if it is not in the agreement.
[35] *McEwan's Utility House, Ltd. v. Currie*, 1953 S.L.T. (Sh. Ct.) 79.
[36] *McArthur v. O'Donnell*, 1969 S.L.T. (Sh. Ct.) 41.
[37] *F.C. Finance, Ltd. v. Brown*, 1969 S.L.T. (Sh. Ct.) 41.
[38] The goods being owned by the lessor do not pass to the trustee in bankruptcy: *McEntire v. Crossley Bros.* [1895] A.C. 457.
[39] *Financings, Ltd. v. Baldock* [1963] 2 Q.B. 104; *Brady, supra.*
[40] *Bell Bros. (H.P.) Ltd. v. Aitken*, 1939 S.C. 577; *Mercantile Credit Co. Ltd. v. Brown*, 1960 S.L.T. (Sh. Ct.) 41; *Union Tpt. Finance v. McQueen* (1961) S.L.T. (Sh. Ct.) 35; *Phonographic Equipment Ltd. v. Muslu* [1961] 3 All E.R. 626; *Lombank, Ltd. v. Excell* [1963] 3 All E.R. 486; *Anglo-Auto Finance Co. v. James* [1963] 3 All E.R. 566; *Bowmaker (Commercial) Ltd. v. McDonald*, 1965 S.L.T. (Sh. Ct.) 33.
[41] *Yeoman Credit Ltd. v. Waragowski* [1961] 3 All E.R. 145.

Right to terminate agreement at common law

At common law a hirer or buyer may terminate the agreement at any time, but usually only on making further payments up to an agreed minimum amount, frequently two-thirds of the total hire-purchase price, by way of compensation for the owner's loss on the transaction. Questions have arisen whether a minimum payment clause imposed a penalty or was a liquidate damages provision.[42] The owner is always entitled to terminate the agreement if the hirer or buyer commits a material breach of contract, and is usually entitled by the contract to do so on the happening of specified events, material or not. He may also recover any instalments of rental in arrears at the date of termination.[43]

Recovery of possession at common law

At common law the owner has no right to recover goods lawfully in the hirer's possession on his default save by action,[44] unless by the agreement the hirer has waived this right and empowered the owner summarily to retake possession from the hirer, in which case summary repossession is competent.[45] The owner must in either case be able to show that the hiring has been terminated; if it has not, repossession is wrongful. Unless the agreement gives liberty to enter on the hirer's premises to take the goods, it is a trespass to do so. By recovering possession the owner does not abandon his right to sue for arrears of rental.[46]

Assignation

An owner of goods let on hire-purchase may assign his interest in the agreement, or assign his interest in the goods themselves. The hirer can, unless it is contractually excluded, assign his interest in the agreement, but not his interest in the goods.

Discharge by performance

An agreement is discharged when the hirer has paid all sums due and

[42] U.D.T. (Commercial) Ltd. v. Bowden, 1958 S.L.T. (Sh. Ct.) 10; Union Tpt. Finance, Ltd. v. McQueen, 1961 S.L.T. (Sh. Ct.) 35; Mercantile Credit Ltd. v. McLachlan, 1962 S.L.T. (Sh. Ct.) 58; Bridge v. Campbell Discount Co. [1962] A.C. 600; Financings Ltd. v. Baldock [1963] 2 Q.B. 104; Bowmaker (Commercial) Ltd. v. McDonald, 1965 S.L.T. (Sh. Ct.) 33. See also Phonographic Equipment Ltd. v. Muslu [1961] 3 All E.R. 626; Lombank Ltd. v. Cook [1962] 3 All E.R. 491; Lombank Ltd. v. Excell [1963] 3 All E.R. 486; Anglo-Auto Finance Ltd. v. James [1963] 3 All E.R. 566; E.P. Finance Co. Ltd. v. Dooley [1964] 1 All E.R. 527.
[43] Overstone v. Shipway [1962] 1 All E.R. 52; Financings Ltd. v. Baldock [1963] 2 Q.B. 104.
[44] Ersk. II, 1, 20.
[45] e.g. Rudman v. Jay, 1908 S.C. 552; N. Central Wagon & Finance Co. v. Graham [1950] 2 K.B. 7; Moorgate Mercantile Co. v. Finch [1962] 1 Q.B. 701.
[46] Brooks v. Beirnstein [1909] 1 K.B. 98.

exercised the option to purchase. If a third party does so he is deemed to do so on behalf of the hirer and title vests in the hirer.[47]

Credit sale at common law

At common law a credit sale is a sale of goods, payment of the price being deferred in whole or in part and payable later. The buyer does not have merely an option to purchase, nor has he merely agreed to purchase, but he has purchased, though he has not paid in full. Credit sale is regulated by the common law of sale as modified by the Sale of Goods Act, 1979.[48] The implied terms are those of the 1979 Act.

Conditional sale at common law

At common law a conditional sale is an agreement to sell and buy goods, subject to some conditions thereafter to be fulfilled.[49] The buyer does not have merely an option to purchase, but has actually agreed to purchase, subject to the condition. Conditional sale is regulated by the common law of sale as modified by the Sale of Goods Act, 1979.[50] The implied terms are those of the 1979 Act.

REGULATED AGREEMENTS

Statutory protection

Widespread abuses of hire-purchase and similar transactions by dealers provoked statutory intervention for the protection of the purchasers.[51] The legislation does not provide a code of hire-purchase law, and cases not covered thereby[52] must be determined by common law.

Hire-purchase—regulated agreement

A hire-purchase agreement is an agreement, other than a conditional sale agreement, under which goods are hired in return for periodical payments and the property in the goods will pass if the terms of the agreement are complied with and there occurs the exercise of an option to purchase, or the doing of any other specified act by any party

---

[47] *Bennett* v. *Griffin Finance Ltd.* [1967] 2 Q.B. 46.

[48] See Ch. 5.33, *supra*. These rules alone apply to all credit sales not falling also within the Consumer Credit Act, 1974.

[49] cf. *Allan & Co.'s Tr.* v. *Gunn* (1883) 10 R. 997; *Murdoch* v. *Greig* (1889) 16 R. 396; Sale of Goods Act, 1979, S. 2(3). The conditions do not necessarily relate to payment: e.g. *Minster Trust* v. *Traps* [1954] 3 All E.R. 136 (condition that goods 'reconditioned').

[50] See Ch. 5.33, *supra*. These rules alone apply to all conditional sales not falling also within the Consumer Credit Act, 1974.

[51] Consumer Credit Act, 1974, replacing earlier Acts, particularly Hire-Purchase (Sc.) Act, 1965. Cases not regulated by the 1974 Act are controlled by common law, not the repealed 1965 Act.

[52] Cases where the price exceeds £5000 and certain other cases are excepted.

to the agreement, or the happening of any other specified event.[53] If the value for which credit is given does not exceed £5000 it is a regulated consumer credit agreement for restricted-use credit and a debtor–creditor–supplier agreement.[54] Such an agreement will normally be made by completing copies of dealer's and finance company's standard forms. It is subject to all the requirements of a regulated consumer credit agreement,[55] with respect to advertisements and canvassing,[56] entry into and withdrawal from agreements[57] and matters arising during the currency of the agreement.[58] In particular the creditor (finance house) is liable to the debtor (hirer) jointly and severally with the supplier for a misrepresentation or breach of contract by the supplier.[59]

Statutorily implied stipulations

The Supply of Goods (Implied Terms) Act, 1973, Ss. 8–13 and 15, as substituted by the 1974 Act, Sched. 4, implies certain stipulations into every hire-purchase agreement (not merely those otherwise subject to the 1974 Act) but not into credit sale or conditional sale agreements which are, for this purpose all regulated by the Sale of Goods Act, 1979. The 1973 Act as substituted provides:

(1) In every hire-purchase agreement[60] other than one to which subsection (2) below applies, there is (a) an implied condition[61] on the part of the creditor that he will have a right to sell the goods at the time when the property is to pass; and (b) an implied warranty

    (i) that the goods are free and will remain free until the time when the property is to pass, from any charge or encumbrance not disclosed or known to the person to whom the goods were hired before the agreement is made, and

    (ii) that the person will enjoy quiet possession of the goods except so far as it may be disturbed by any person entitled to the benefit of any charge or encumbrance so disclosed or known.

(2) In a hire-purchase agreement, where there appears from the agreement or is to be inferred from the circumstances of the agreement

---

[53] Consumer Credit Act, 1974, S. 189.

[54] Ss. 8, 9, 11–13.

[55] Ch. 4.12, *supra*.

[56] Ss. 43–54.

[57] Ss. 55–74. Under S. 56 'negotiations' for an agreement include representations, conditions, warranties and any other statement or undertaking, oral or in writing: S. 189. In certain cases a person conducting negotiations is deemed to do so as agent of the creditor as well as personally; thus a dealer is to be regarded as agent of the finance company.

[58] Ss. 75–86. See also *U.D.T.* v. *Taylor*, 1980 S.L.T. (Sh. Ct.) 28.

[59] S. 75. Common law determines whether something said or done is a misrepresentation. cf. *Andrews* v. *Hopkinson* [1957] 1 Q.B. 229.

[60] Defined: S. 15.

[61] Deemed by S. 15(1) to be material to the agreement.

an intention that the owner should transfer only such title as he or a third person may have, there is (a) an implied warranty that all charges or encumbrances known to the creditor and not known to the person to whom the goods are hired have been disclosed to that person before the agreement is made; and (b) an implied warranty that neither (i) the creditor; nor (ii) in a case where the parties to the agreement intend that any title which may be transferred shall be only such title as a third person may have; that person; nor (iii) anyone claiming through or under the creditor or that third person otherwise than under a charge, or encumbrance disclosed or known to the person to whom the goods are hired before the agreement is made; will disturb the quiet possession of the person to whom the goods are hired.[62]

Letting on hire-purchase by description

Where under a hire-purchase agreement goods are hired by description, there is an implied condition[63] that the goods will correspond with the description; and if under the agreement the goods are hired by reference to a sample as well as a description, it is not sufficient that the bulk of the goods corresponds with the sample if the goods do not also correspond with the description. Goods are not prevented from being hired by description by reason only that, being exposed for sale or hire, they are selected by the person to whom they are hired.[64]

Implied undertakings as to quality or fitness

(1) Except as provided by Ss. 10 and 11 of the 1973 Act and subject to the provisions of any other enactment, there is no implied condition or warranty as to the quality or fitness for any particular purpose of goods hired under a hire-purchase agreement. (2) Where the creditor hires goods under a hire-purchase agreement in the course of a business,[65] there is an implied condition[66] that the goods are of merchantable quality,[67] except that there is no such condition (a) as regards defects specifically drawn to the attention of the person to whom the goods are hired before the agreement is made; (b) if that person examines the goods before the agreement is made, as regards defects

---

[62] Supply of Goods (Implied Terms) Act, 1973, S. 8, as substituted by 1974 Act, Sched. 4, replacing 1965 Act, S. 17(1). By S. 15 'stipulation' is equivalent in Scotland to 'condition' or 'warranty' in the Act as applied in England. cf. Sale of Goods Act, 1979, S. 12.

[63] By S. 15(1) it is deemed material.

[64] 1973 Act, S. 9, as substituted. cf. Sale of Goods Act, 1979, S. 13.

[65] Defined, 1973 Act, S. 15.

[66] By S. 15(1) it is deemed material.

[67] Defined, 1973 Act, S. 15(3) as meaning as fit for the purpose or purposes for which goods of that kind are commonly bought as it is reasonable to expect having regard to any description applied to them, the price (if relevant) and all other relevant circumstances. cf. Sale of Goods Act, 1979, S. 14(6) As to second-hand goods see *Bartlett* v. *Marcus* [1965] 2 All E.R. 753; *Crowther* v. *Shannon Motor Co.* [1975] 1 All E.R. 139.

which that examination ought to reveal. (3) Where the creditor hires goods under a hire-purchase agreement in the course of a business[65] and the person to whom the goods are hired, expressly or by implication, makes known (a) to the creditor in the course of negotiations conducted by the creditor in relation to the making of the hire-purchase agreement or (b) to a credit-broker in the course of negotiations conducted by that broker in relation to goods sold by him to the creditor before forming the subject matter of the hire-purchase agreement, any particular purpose for which the goods are being hired, there is an implied condition that the goods supplied under the agreement are reasonably fit for that purpose, whether or not that is a purpose for which such goods are commonly supplied,[68] except where the circumstances show that the person to whom the goods are hired does not rely, or that it is unreasonable for him to rely,[69] on the skill or judgment of the creditor or credit-broker. (4) An implied condition or warranty as to quality or fitness for a particular purpose may be annexed to a hire-purchase agreement by usage. (5) These provisions apply to a hire-purchase agreement made by a person who in the course of a business is acting as agent for the creditor as they apply to an agreement made by the creditor in the course of a business, except where the creditor is not hiring in the course of a business and either the person to whom the goods are hired knows that fact or reasonable steps are taken to bring it to the notice of that person before the agreement is made.[70]

Letting on hire-purchase by sample

Where under a hire-purchase agreement goods are hired by reference to a sample, there is an implied condition[71] (a) that the bulk will correspond with the sample in quality; and (b) that the person to whom the goods are hired will have a reasonable opportunity of comparing the bulk with the sample; and (c) that the goods will be free from any defect rendering them unmerchantable, which would not be apparent on reasonable examination of the sample.[72]

Breach of implied terms

Breach entitles the debtor to rescind the contract and claim damages for loss resulting from the breach, or to claim damages alone.[73]

---

[68] cf. *Lowe* v. *Lombank Ltd.* [1960] 1 All E.R. 611.
[69] cf. *Yeoman Credit Co.* v. *Apps* [1962] 2 Q.B. 508; *Astley Industrial Trust* v. *Grimley* [1963] 2 All E.R. 33.
[70] 1973 Act, S. 10, as substituted by 1974 Act, Sched. 4. cf. Sale of Goods Act, 1979; S. 14.
[71] By S. 15(1) it is deemed material.
[72] 1973 Act, S. 11, as substituted by 1974 Act, Sched. 4. cf. Sale of Goods Act, 1979; S. 15.
[73] On measure of damages see *Yeoman Credit Co.* v. *Apps* [1962] 2 Q.B. 508; *Charterhouse Credit Co.* v. *Tolly* [1963] 2 Q.B. 683.

Exclusion of implied terms and conditions

S. 12 of the 1973 Act[74] provides: (1) An express condition or warranty does not negative a condition or warranty implied by the 1973 Act unless inconsistent therewith. The Unfair Contract Terms Act, 1977, provides (S. 20) that any term in a contract which purports to exclude or restrict liability for breach of the obligations arising from S. 8 of the 1973 Act is void, and that any term in a contract which purports to exclude or restrict liability for breach of the obligation arising from sections 9, 10 or 11 of the 1973 Act is, in the case of a consumer contract,[75] void against the consumer, and in any other case, ineffective if it was not fair and reasonable to incorporate the term in the contract.

Conflict of laws

Where the proper law of a hire-purchase agreement would, apart from a term that it sould be the law of some other country or to the effect, be the law of a part of the United Kingdom, or where any such agreement contains a term which purports to substitute, or has the effect of substituting, provision of the law of some other country for all or any of the provisions of Ss. 8–12 of the 1973 Act, these sections apply to the agreement notwithstanding that term.[76]

Default

In general remedies given to the creditor by the agreement against the possibility of default by the debtor are enforceable; these may include power to demand the whole outstanding balance due, power to terminate the agreement in specified circumstances, power to remedy breaches and charge the debtor with the cost, power of repossession and sale, and fixing in advance the damages payable for a breach.[77]

The creditor may not enforce a term of a regulated agreement by demanding earlier payment, recovering possession of goods, or treating any right under the agreement as terminated, restricted or deferred, save after giving seven days' notice of intention to do so.[78]

Before the creditor is entitled by reason of a breach by the debtor of a regulated agreement to terminate the agreement, recover possession of goods or otherwise act on default he must serve a default notice.[79] If

[74] As substituted by 1974 Act, Sched. 4, amended by Unfair Contract Terms Act, 1977, Sched. 4. cf. Sale of Goods Act, 1979, S. 55.
[75] Defined by S. 25.
[76] 1973 Act, S. 13.
[77] Such may be challengeable as being a penalty: *Bridge* v. *Campbell Discount Co.* [1962] A.C. 600; *Anglo-Auto Finance Co.* v. *James* [1963] All E.R. 566.
[78] Consumer Credit Act, 1974, S. 76.
[79] Consumer Credit Act, 1974, Ss. 87–9.

the debtor is in breach of a regulated hire-purchase agreement and has paid at least one-third of the total price, the goods are protected goods and the creditor is not entitled to recover possession except on an order of the court. If goods are recovered in contravention of this the regulated agreement terminates, the debtor is released from all liability thereunder and is entitled to recover all sums paid thereunder.[80] Save by order of the court, the creditor may not enter any premises to take possession of goods.[81] Interest is not to be increased on his default.[82]

Termination

The creditor may not terminate a regulated agreement save after giving at least seven days' notice.[83] The debtor is entitled to complete his payments ahead of time on giving notice and may be entitled to a rebate for early settlement.[84] At any time before the final payment is due the debtor may terminate the agreement by giving notice.[85] The debtor is liable, unless the agreement provides for a smaller, or no, payment, to pay the creditor the difference between half of the total price and the total of sums paid and sums due before the termination or such lesser sum as the court considers equal to the loss sustained by the creditor. A further sum may be allowed if the debtor has not taken reasonable care of the goods.[86]

Sureties

The creditor under a regulated hire-purchase agreement may require the debtor to find a surety. Any obligation undertaken by a surety provided by him, if not embodied in the agreement, must be expressed in writing and information must be given him and notice served on him also.[87] The provisions of the Consumer Credit Act are without prejudice to the common law principles concerning cautioners.[88]

Giving security

The primary security will normally be the goods let to the debtor under the hire-purchase agreement and recoverable by the creditor in certain circumstances of default. Any security provided in relation to a regulated agreement but not embodied in the agreement must be expressed in writing properly executed and copies given to the debtor and any surety.[89] If not expressed in writing, or the security instrument is improperly executed, the security is enforceable against the surety on an order of the court only; provision is made for ineffective securities.[90]

[80] Ss. 90-1.   [81] S. 92.   [82] S. 93.
[83] S. 98.   [84] Ss. 94-7.   [85] S. 99.
[86] Ss. 100-1.   [87] Ss. 105-12.   [88] S. 105.
[89] S. 105. 'Security is defined widely in S. 189, covering both personal security (guarantees, notes) and real security (pledge).   [90] Ss. 105-7.

A creditor or owner may not take a negotiable instrument, other than a banknote or cheque, in discharge of a sum payable by a debtor or hirer, or by a surety, nor negotiate a cheque except to a banker, nor take a negotiable instrument as security for discharge of such a sum, save under a non-commercial agreement.[91]

On default if the creditor wishes to recover possession of goods, he must serve a default notice,[92] and if the goods are protected goods he may recover them only by court order.[93] Regulations may provide for the sale or other realization of property over which a right has been given in security.[94] A land mortgage securing a regulated agreement is enforceable by order of the court only.[95]

On application to the court for an enforcement order or to enforce a security the court may make a time order, allowing payment by instalments or extension of time to pay.[96]

Resale and pledge of goods subject to agreements

At common law a hirer under hire-purchase has no title to resell the goods, but a buyer under a credit sale, being the owner, has, and a buyer under a conditional sale agreement, being in possession under an agreement to sell, may sell and confer a good title.[97] In cases within the 1974 Act, however, the buyer under a conditional sale agreement is deemed not to be a person who has bought or agreed to buy goods,[98] and he cannot therefore confer any title. A hire-purchase or conditional sale agreement normally makes a purported sale a breach of an express term of the agreement. If a hirer does sell the owner can recover as damages the outstanding instalments, less discount for early payment.[99]

But by statute[1] a hire-purchaser or conditional buyer may make a disposition[2] of a motor vehicle[3] to another person before the property therein has become vested in him; if the purchaser is a private purchaser in good faith and without notice of the hirer's or conditional buyer's agreement, the disposition has effect as if the title of the owner or seller had been vested in the hirer or conditional buyer immediately before the disposition. If the disponee is a trade or finance purchaser[4] and the first private purchaser of the vehicle takes in good faith and without notice of the original agreement, the disposition to the first private

---

[91] Ss. 123–4.   [92] Ss. 87–9.   [93] Ss. 90–2.
[94] S. 112.   [95] S. 126.   [96] Ss. 132–3.
[97] Sale of Goods Act, 1979, S. 25.
[98] 1974 Act, S. 189.
[99] *Wickham Holdings* v. *Brooke House Motors* [1967] 1 All E.R. 117.
[1] Hire-Purchase Act, 1964, S. 27(1) and (2) as substituted by 1974 Act, Sched. 4. These provisions apply even if the hirer is a body corporate or the price exceeds £2,000.
[2] Defined, 1964 Act, S. 29(1).
[3] Defined, 1964 Act, S. 29(2).
[4] Defined, 1964 Act, S. 29(2).

purchaser has effect as if the title of the owner or seller to the vehicle
has been vested in the hirer or buyer immediately before he disposed of
it to the trade or finance purchaser.[5] Where in such a case the disposition to the first private purchaser is itself a letting on hire-purchase,
and the disposition is by way of transferring to the purchaser the
property in the vehicle in pursuance of a provision in the agreement in
that behalf, both dispositions have effect as if the title of the owner or
seller had been vested in the hirer or buyer immediately before he
disposed of it to the original purchaser.[6] These provision are without
prejudice to civil or criminal liability which would otherwise have
arisen.[7] Presumptions as to good faith arise in certain cases.[8]

The hirer or conditional buyer may be contractually prohibited
from pledging or creating any lien over the goods for repairs done
thereto. Such may be held to destroy the hirer's implied authority to
pledge or create a lien,[9] but may be ineffective if unknown to the
repairer,[10] or if the repair is a necessary incident of the use of the goods
in the way contemplated.[11] Goods comprised in a hire-purchase or
conditional sale agreement are not to be treated as subject to landlord's
hypothec for rent during either of the stated periods.[12]

Assignation of rights under agreement

The right of a hirer or conditional buyer to assign the benefit of the
hire and of the ultimate option to buy is normally excluded by the
contract. The owner may assign the right to recover the hire or price,
his right of property in the goods, and his right to repossess them,
reserving always the hirer's rights under the agreement.

Extinction of agreement

A hire-purchase, credit sale or conditional sale agreement is extinguished by the hirer or buyer making all payments due in respect of
hire and option to buy, or of the instalments of the price, and thereby
becoming indefeasible owner of the goods. Only the hirer has any right
to pay off the owner and acquire title to the goods.[13] A hirer is not

---

[5] 1964 Act, S. 27(3); accordingly a trade or finance purchaser acquires no title from a hirer or
conditional buyer, but a good title can pass despite his intervention: *North West Securities Ltd.* v.
Barrhead Coachworks Ltd. 1976 S.C. 68.

[6] 1964 Act, S. 27(4).

[7] 1964 Act, S. 27(6).

[8] 1964 Act, S. 28.

[9] *Lamonby* v. *Foulds*, 1928 S.C. 89.

[10] *Albemarle Sy. Co.* v. *Hind* [1928] 1 K.B. 307.

[11] *Jowitt* v. *Union Cold Storage Co.* [1913] 3 K.B. 1; *Green* v. *All Motors Ltd.* [1917] 1 K.B.
625.

[12] Consumer Credit Act, 1974, S. 104.

[13] *Bennett* v. *Griffin Finance* [1967] 2 Q.B. 46.

entitled to insist on doing so, but is usually allowed to anticipate payments due and to complete the contract prematurely; he may be allowed discount therefor but may not himself deduct anything as discount.[14]

Failure of consideration

The consideration for a hire-purchase contract may wholly fail, as where the lessor fraudulently falsifies or alters the contract form. In this case the hirer is not bound and may recover any goods or money transferred on the faith of the contract being valid.[15]

Court's power to modify agreements

When the court is dealing with a regulated hire-purchase agreement it may modify the agreement as may be just, order the return of goods to the creditor, order transfer of the creditor's title to some goods and return of others to the creditor, and order enforcement of any security.[16] If the creditor brings an action or applies to recover possession of goods and proves that a demand for them was made, then the debtor's possession is deemed adverse to the creditor. This does not affect a claim for damages for delict.[17] The court may make a term in its order conditional, suspend its operation, or vary a provision, and include such provision as it considers just for amending any agreement or security in consequence of its order.[18]

Credit sale—regulated agreements

A credit sale is an agreement for the sale of goods under which the purchase price or part of it is payable by instalments but which is not a conditional sale agreement.[19] This accordingly covers cases where the property passes in accordance with the ordinary law of sale though the price has not been, or not all been, paid. If the price, or part of it, for which credit is given does not exceed £5000 the contract is a regulated consumer credit agreement for restricted-use credit and subject to all the regulations of the Consumer Credit Act applicable to money-lending.[20]

Conditional sale—regulated agreements

A conditional sale is an agreement for the sale of goods under which the price or part of it is payable by instalments and the property in the

---

[14] *Taylor* v. *Wylie & Lochhead*, 1912 S.C. 978.
[15] *Branwhite* v. *Worcester Works Finance* [1969] 1 A.C. 552.
[16] S. 133.
[17] S. 134.
[18] Ss. 135–6.
[19] Consumer Credit Act, 1974, S. 189.
[20] Ss. 8, 9, 11; Ch. 4.12, *supra*.

goods is to remain in the seller, although the buyer is to have possession of the goods, until the conditions as to payment of instalments or otherwise specified in the agreement are fulfilled.[21] If the price, or part of it, for which credit is given does not exceed £5000 it is a regulated consumer credit agreement for restricted-use credit and subject to all the regulations of the Consumer Credit Act applicable to money-lending.[22]

Linked transactions

Linked transactions[23] are transactions entered into by a debtor with another party, except one for provision of security, in stated circumstances, such as for insurance or maintenance of goods. Linked transactions are important in that charges due under a linked transaction are part of the total charge for credit, withdrawal from a prospective regulated agreement operates as a withdrawal from a linked transaction,[24] cancellation operates to cancel a linked transaction,[25] on cancellation of a linked transaction money becomes repayable or ceases to be due,[26] and discharge of a debtor may discharge him from liability under a linked transaction.[27]

Other similar transactions

Certain other kinds of transactions may be of similar effect to hire-purchase. A shop may sell goods to a customer who has opened a personal credit account with it, or an allied organization, under which the customer is granted credit to a specified amount in return for periodical payments.[28] Or a customer may purchase checks or tokens to a certain nominal value, outright or by instalments, and exchange them for goods at shops which accept such checks.[29] Or a person may obtain a personal loan or overdraft from a bank, or a loan from a friend or moneylender, wherewith to make a purchase.[30] Hire-purchase forms may not validly be used as part of a simulate transaction seeking to create a security over moveables without delivery.[31]

[21] Consumer Credit Act, 1974, S. 189. This definition is narrower that that of conditional sale at common law in that instalment payment is part of the definition.

[22] Ss. 8, 9, 11; Ch. 4.12, *supra*.

[23] Defined S. 19.

[24] Ss. 57, 69.

[25] S. 69.

[26] S. 70.

[27] S. 96.

[28] Such has been held·to be a credit sale agreement infringing a statutory control: *Napier* v. *Patterson*, 1959 J.C. 48; *Napier* v. *Corbett*, 1962 S.L.T. (Sh. Ct.) 90; but not to be moneylending: *MacDonald* v. *Napier*, 1960 J.C. 123.

[29] cf. *Premier Clothing Co.* v. *Hillcoat* [1969] C.L.Y. 2279a.

[30] On these see Ch. 5.27, *supra*.

[31] *Scottish Transit Trust, Ltd.* v. *Scottish Land Cultivators, Ltd.*, 1955 S.C. 254; *G. & C. Finance Corpn. Ltd.* v. *Brown*, 1961 S.L.T. 408.

CHAPTER 5.35

INVOLUNTARY TRANSFER OF RIGHTS IN CORPOREAL MOVEABLES

In a number of cases a person may have his proprietary title to moveables transferred from him to another without, or contrary to, his will.

Sale under common law or statutory powers

The valid exercise of a power of sale by a non-owner under a common law or statutory power of sale[1] divests the former owner and confers a good title on the buyer. If the power of sale were exercised invalidly, no property passes.[2]

Decree of court

The title to moveables may be decided and transferred by decree in various kinds of actions. Thus title may be determined by declarator, such as that certain testamentary writings made a valid bequest in the pursuers' favour,[3] or by decree in an action of multiplepoinding which determines which of two or more parties claiming right to one thing of fund is or are truly entitled thereto.[4] The right to demand a conveyance of property may be determined in a multiplepoinding.[5]

Statutes imposing criminal penalties may provide for the court ordering forfeiture of moveables.[6]

Diligence

Title to moveables may be transferred by various forms of diligence. Money or other valuables belonging to a debtor but in the hands of a third party may be attached there by arrestment and made available to the creditor by action of furthcoming or be sold.[7] Decree establishes in the purchaser a judicial title to the object.[8] Property in the debtor's

---

[1] For such powers see Ch. 5.31, *supra*.
[2] *Springer* v. *G.W. Ry.* [1921] 1 K.B. 257; *Prager* v. *Blatspiel* [1924] 1 K.B. 566.
[3] *Dundee Mags.* v. *Morris* (1856) 19 D. 168; cf. *Falconer Stewart* v. *Wilkie* (1892) 19 R. 630.
[4] e.g. *Macleod* v. *Kerr*, 1965 S.C. 253.
[5] *Campbell* v. *E. Craufurd* (1783) Mor. 3973.
[6] e.g. *Loch Lomond Sailings* v. *Hawthorn*, 1962 J.C. 8.
[7] Bell, *Prin.* §2272–83; Graham Stewart, 1; Ch. 9.1, *infra*.
[8] *Muirhead* v. *Corrie* (1735) Mor. 687; *Stevenson* v. *Paul* (1680) Mor. 5405; *Stevenson* v. *Grant* (1767) Mor. 2762.

own hands may be attached by poinding followed by sale of the poinded goods under warrant from the sheriff.[9] In the case of debts preferably secured over land, *debita fundi,* the creditor may by poinding of the ground attach moveables while on the lands for the debt and have them sold.[10] A vassal's moveables on the subjects feued to him may be attached by the process of superior's sequestration for feu-duty and sold.[11] A tenant's moveables on the subjects let to him may be attached by the process of landlord's sequestration and sold.[12]

Sequestration

The Act and Warrant issued to the trustee in bankruptcy *ipso jure* vests in the trustee, *inter alia,* the moveable estate of the bankrupt, wherever situated, so far as attachable for debt to the same effect as if actual delivery or possession had been obtained, subject always to such preferable securities as existed at the date of the sequestration and are not null or reducible.[13] He may sell moveables by public roup or by private bargain and, having by statute[13] an absolute title to the moveable property, can pass an absolute title by sale.

Succession on death

On the death of any person, testate or intestate, every part of his estate falling to be administered under the law of Scotland, by virtue of confirmation thereto, vests for the purpose of administration in the executor thereby confirmed.[14] The executor must deal with the estate as directed by the deceased's will or the rules of intestate succession.[15]

---

[9] Bell, *Prin.* §2286–8; Graham Stewart, 274; Law Reform (Diligence) (Sc.) Act, 1973.
[10] Bell, *Prin.* §2385; Graham Stewart, 491.
[11] Bell, *Prin.* §701; Graham Stewart, 489.
[12] Bell, *Prin.* §1233–47; Graham Stewart, 460.
[13] Bankruptcy (Sc.) Act, 1913, S. 97(1).
[14] Succession (Sc.) Act, 1964, S. 14(1).
[15] Chs. 7.1–7.6, *infra.*

CHAPTER 5.36

EXTINCTION OF RIGHTS IN CORPOREAL
MOVEABLE OBJECTS

Loss of possession

A person's right of possession is extinguished when he has lost or surrendered actual possession and also ceased to have *animus possidendi,* as when he gives up goods for lost, but not merely by cessation of either *factum* or *animus* of possession.

Extinction of ownership—consumption

Apart from cases where ownership is extinguished by being transferred, voluntarily or involuntarily, to another, it is extinguished when moveable objects are used up, consumed, destroyed or perish. If one's goods are used by another and made up into a new thing the claims arising from *specificatio* arise.[1]

Abandonment

Where property has been put out with the apparent intention of abandoning it the owner may be criminally liable for doing so.[2] If he is not known the property in the things abandoned may vest in the Crown under the principle *quod nullius est fit domini regis.*

Property may be put out however, with the intention that another take it away as rubbish, for salvage or destruction. Till collected it remains in the former owner's ownership and possession.[3] Possession and ownership pass constructively when the intended person removes the articles, and any third party who take the articles for his own purposes commits theft.[3]

Loss

Where an object has been lost the right of property probably continues so that the goods, if they can be identified and ownership

---

[1] Ch. 5.26, *supra.*

[2] See Litter Act, 1958; Refuse Disposal (Amenity) Act, 1978 (abandoned vehicles, etc.).

[3] cf. *Ellerman Wilson Line* v. *Webster* [1952] 1 Lloyd's Rep. 179; *Digby* v. *Heelan* [1952] C.L.Y. 790; *R.* v. *Samuel* (1956) 40 Cr. A.R. 8; *Williams* v. *Phillips* (1957) 41 Cr. A.R. 5. cf. Sewerage (Sc.) Act, 1968, S. 39 (sewage becomes property of local authority).

established, can be vindicated from a finder or other possessor.[4] It is questionable whether any lapse of time can exclude the right of a true owner to reclaim his own.[5] Valuable goods of the nature of treasure, to which no person can now prove ownership, fall to the Crown under the principle *quod nullius est fit domini regis.*[6]

[4] Ersk. II, 1, 12; III, 1, 10; Bell, *Prin.* §527, 1291; *Bp. of Caithness* v. *Edinburgh Fleshers* (1629) Mor. 9112; *Ferguson* v. *Forrest* (1639) Mor. 9112; *Ramsay* v. *Wilson* (1666) Mor. 9113; *Forsyth* v. *Kilpatrick* (1680) Mor. 9120; *Henderson* v. *Gibson,* 17 June 1806, F.C.; but see Stair I, 7, 3, who indicates that finders may keep found property: *sed quaere.*

[5] The Burgh Police (Sc.) Act, 1892, S. 412, provides for lost property being sold after six months. The Dogs Act, 1906, S. 3, provides for stray dogs held by the police being sold or destroyed after seven days. But if X borrows, or steals, a Raeburn from Y, can Y, on finding that X has it, reclaim it from him after 20 years? cf. *Ramsay, supra; Sands* v. *Bell and Balfour,* 22 May 1810, F.C.

[6] Stair II, 1, 5; III, 3, 27; Mack. II, 1; Bankt, I, 3, 16; I, 8, 4; Ersk. II, 1, 11; Bell, *Prin.* §1294; *Lord Advocate* v. *Aberdeen University,* 1963 S.C. 533.

PART 5

RIGHTS IN INCORPOREAL MOVEABLE OBJECTS OF PROPERTY

CHAPTER 5.37

RIGHTS IN INCORPOREAL MOVEABLE OBJECTS OF PROPERTY

Incorporeal moveable objects of property comprise certain kinds of immaterial or incorporeal abstractions, which exist only as rights or bodies of legal claims and rights and have no physical existence which can be actually possessed, and which, moreover, are deemed not connected with or like land and are accordingly moveable rather than heritable in succession.[1]

Kinds of incorporeal moveable property

Incorporeal moveable property includes a wide variety of particular rights or groups of rights; the main kinds are decrees of court, claims of debt, claims of damages, rights of relief, rights under contract, rights under negotiable instruments, bills of lading, other documents of title to goods, obligations of debt, book debts, some rights in security over property, reversionary rights, policies of insurance, salary and pension rights, *jura crediti* under wills and trusts, interests in partnerships and companies, business rights, rights to registered trade marks, to patents, of copyright, in registered designs, and in plant breeders' rights.

The objects of incorporeal moveable property sometimes consist of a single right, such as to payment of debt or damages, but sometimes of groups of various interrelated rights and interests, which can be dealt with separately, such as the various rights which collectively amount to the copyright of a book. Some of these groups of rights exist in relation to a corporeal object, but are distinct from rights in and to that corporeal object,[2] while others exist only in the contemplation of the

---

[1] Ersk. II, 2, 7; Bell, *Comm.* I, 100; *Prin.* §1338; 1476–1505; cf. Inst. II, 2.

[2] Thus the rights which comprise an author's copyright are quite distinct from his rights in and to the manuscript or book which contains the words which are the subject of his copyright. The copyright is incorporeal moveable property; the manuscript or book is corporeal moveable property.

law, unrelated to any corporeal subject, e.g. a claim to payment for work done.

Whether a right or group of rights can be described as an incorporeal moveable object of property depends on whether the right or groups of rights can be turned into money, is assignable *inter vivos,* transmits to executors on death and passes to the trustee in bankruptcy on the holder's sequestration. If it is not assignable or transmissible it is a purely personal right and not an object of property.[3]

Interests in incorporeal moveable property.

As objects of property of this class consist only in legal rights and claims, capable of legal enforcement and of being assigned and transmitted, the only interest which can subsist in any object of this class of property is ownership, in the sense of being the person entitled to enforce some or all of the legal rights amounting to such property. They are vested by the completion of the *jus exigendi.*[4] Objects of property of this class cannot be possessed separately from ownership. To own something within one of these categories means to have the legal rights and claims which attach by law to the person entitled to such a group of rights; what rights and claims do attach to each kind of incorporeal property are defined by common law or statute, and differ from one category to another. The ownership may, however, be burdened by a disposition in security of some or all of the rights, or it may in some cases be divided, some of the rights being vested in one person, others in another.

Incorporeal property may be held in liferent or in fee, and a liferenter is not a trustee but a full owner, but for life only.[5]

In respect of each kind of incorporeal moveable property the relevant questions are how such property is created, how it is evidenced, what rights and claims against other people are conferred by ownership of it, how the rights may be enforced or protected, whether and, if so, how they may be transferred in security or outright, and how they are extinguished or terminated.

Personal claims and privileges

Distinct from rights in incorporeal moveable property are mere personal claims and privileges, which an individual is allowed to exercise but which he does not have as a matter of law. Still less are such personal privileges assignable or transmissible to another.[6]

[3] *Trevalion* v. *Blanche,* 1919 S.C. 617; *Tawse's Trs.* v. *L.A.,* 1934 S.C. 124. Thus many kinds of licences are personal only, not proprietary nor assignable or transmissible.
[4] Bell, *Prin.* §1338.
[5] *Fogo's J.F.* v. *F's Tr.,* 1929 S.C. 546.
[6] cf. E. *Ancaster* v. *Doig,* 1960 S.C. 203; *Wallace* v. *Simmers,* 1960 S.C. 255.

CHAPTER 5.38

ACQUISITION OF RIGHTS IN INCORPOREAL MOVEABLE OBJECTS

Creation of incorporeal moveable property

The modes of creation and of a person's acquisition of rights in incorporeal moveable objects of property are various; in some cases they come into being *ipso jure*, sometimes by registration, by decree of court, by contract, by disposition or bequest of another.

DECREES AND RIGHTS OF ACTION

Decrees

A decree of court for payment or *ad factum praestandum*, pronounced in due course by a court of competent jurisdiction, imposes on the defender against whom it has passed an obligation to obtemper it and vests the party in right of the decree with a *jus exigendi* enforceable by diligence. Hence a decree for the payment of money can be assigned by the party in right[1] and passes on death to and is exigible by the entitled party's executor.[2] Where a third party relieves the debtor by paying his debt, he is entitled to an assignation of the decree from the creditor,[3] and where one joint wrongdoer satisfies a joint and several decree held by a pursuer he is entitled to an assignation of the decree to enable him to recover relief *pro tanto* from the other joint wrongdoers.[4]

Claims of debt

A claim of debt arises from the non-performance of the pecuniary obligation under a contract, as by non-payment at the due date of a liquidated sum due under the contract. Such a claim is an asset of the

---

[1] *Stewart* v. *Kidd* (1852) 14 D. 527; *Rose* v. *Stevenson* (1888) 15 R. 336; *Purnell* v. *Shannon* (1894) 22 R. 74; *Steven* v. *Broady Norman & Co.*, 1928 S.C. 351.
[2] *Morrison* v. *M's Exrx.*, 1912 S.C. 892; *Mackay* v. *M.*, 1914 S.C. 200.
[3] *Smith* v. *Gentle* (1844) 6 D. 1164.
[4] *Palmer* v. *Wick and Pulteneytown S.S. Co.* (1894) 21 R. (H.L.) 39; see also Law Reform (Misc. Prov.) (Sc.) Act, 1940, S. 3(2); *Central S.M.T. Co.* v. *Lanarkshire C.C.*, 1949 S.C. 450; *N.C.B.* v. *Thomson*, 1959 S.C. 353.

creditor's estate which may be assigned[5] or bequeathed and is exigible by his executor[6] or trustee in bankruptcy.[7] A provision that a debt is not to be assigned may bar a claim by a gratuitous assignee,[8] but is of doubtful validity against an onerous assignee.

Claims of damages

A right of action for damages arising from a breach of obligation, whether *ex contractu* or *ex delicto*, is an incorporeal right capable of vindication by action.[9] It arises *ex lege* on the occurrence of a breach of a valid and enforceable contract, or on the breach of a duty of care not to cause unjustifiable harm owed in the circumstances to the injured person.

A claim arising *ex contractu* transmits as moveable property on the claimant's death, is enforceable by his executor and assignable to a third party.[10]

A claim arising *ex delicto*, if of a personal character, as for injuries to the claimant's person, or character, is purely personal, and though assignable *inter vivos*,[11] if not pursued by him does not pass to his trustee in bankruptcy,[12] and lapses on his death.[13] If, however, action has been initiated during the claimant's lifetime, the claim passes to his executor and may be enforced by the executor for behoof of the estate,[14] and probably assigned by him.

If, on the other hand, the claim is of a proprietary character, for patrimonial loss, such as for loss of earnings or damage to property, the claim if not pursued by the injured person, is assignable *inter vivos*[15] and, on his death, transmits to his executor and is enforceable

---

[5] Stair III, 1, 3; Ersk. III, 5, 2; Bell, *Prin.* §1341, 1459; *Fraser* v. *Duguid* (1838) 16 S. 1130.

[6] *Walker* v. *Orr's Trs.*, 1958 S.L.T. 63; cf. *Morrison* v. *M's Exrx.*, 1912 S.C. 893.

[7] Bankruptcy (Sc.) Act, 1913, Ss. 70, 97; *Gallie* v. *Lockhart* (1840) 2 D. 445; *Hallowell* v. *Niven* (1843) 5 D. 655.

[8] *Boswall* v. *Arnott* (1759) Mor. 12578; see also *Strachan* v. *Barclay* (1683) Mor. 4310.

[9] Ersk. II, 2, 17; *Milne* v. *Gauld's Trs.* (1841) 3 D. 345, 350; *Caledonian Ry.* v. *Watt* (1875) 2 R. 917, 921.

[10] *Levett* v. *L.N.W. Ry.* (1866) 2 S.L.R. 207; *Constant* v. *Kincaid* (1902) 4 F. 901; *Riley* v. *Ellis*, 1910 S.C. 934.

[11] *Traill* v. *Dalbeattie* (1904) 6 F. 798; *Cole-Hamilton* v. *Boyd*, 1963 S.C. (H.L.) 1; *Bentley* v. *Macfarlane*, 1963 S.C. 279; 1964 S.C. 76.

[12] *Muir's Tr.* v. *Braidwood*, 1958 S.C. 169.

[13] *Bern's Exor.* v. *Montrose Asylum* (1893) 20 R. 859; *Stewart* v. *L.M.S. Ry.*, 1943 S.C. (H.L.) 19; *Smith* v. *Stewart*, 1960 S.C. 329; Damages (Sc.) Act, 1976 S. 2.

[14] Bell, *Prin.* §546; *Milne* v. *Gauld's Trs.* (1841) 3 D. 345; *Neilson* v. *Rodger* (1853) 16 D. 325; *Darling* v. *Gray* (1892) 19 R. (H.L.) 31; *Borthwick* v. *B.* (1896) 24 R. 211; *Reid* v. *Lanarkshire Traction Co.*, 1934 S.C. 79; *Stewart, supra; Smith, supra.*

[15] *Symington* v. *Campbell* (1894) 21 R. 434; *Cole-Hamilton* v. *Boyd*, 1963 S.C. (H.L.) 1; *Bentley* v. *Macfarlane*, 1964 S.C. 76 (claim for both injuries and property damage); cf. *Liqdr. of Larkhall Collieries* v. *Hamilton* (1906) 14 S.L.T. 202; *Corvi* v. *Ellis*, 1969 S.C. 312.

for the benefit of the estate.[16] It passes on his bankruptcy to the trustee.[17] A claim by a company against a director for breach of trust is proprietary.[18] Even a claim for damages for loss of or injury to heritable property is incorporeal moveable property.[19]

The claim competent to certain close relatives of a person killed by the fault of another, formerly for solatium and now for loss of society award,[20] and for damages for the patrimonial loss caused to the claimant by the death,[21] if initiated by the claimant, transmitted at common law to the claimant's executor,[22] and was probably assignable *inter vivos*. It does not now transmit.[23] If action is not initiated by the entitled claimant, the right to do so lapses on his death.

A right of action which has been assigned can be retrocessed.[24]

Rights of relief

The right of relief possessed by a party who has satisfied a claim of damages for which another party is allegedly truly liable[25] is also a proprietary right.[26] It may exist by contract,[27] or *ex lege*,[28] but arises under statute in the case of joint delinquents[29] and where one of possible joint delinquents has been sued and had the claim of damages judicially constituted against him, though not where he has compromised the claim against him.[30]

---

[16] *Mein* v. *Call* (1844) 6 D. 1112; *Davidson* v. *Tulloch* (1863) 3 Macq. 783; *Garden* v. *Davidson* (1864) 2 M. 758; *Auld* v. *Shairp* (1875) 2 R. 191; *Fraser* v. *Livermore Bros.* (1900) 7 S.L.T. 450; *Riley* v. *Ellis*, 1910 S.C. 934; *Smith* v. *Stewart*, 1961 S.C. 91; *McGhie* v. *B.T.C.*, 1964 S.L.T. 25. cf. *Hendry* v. *United Collieries*, 1908 S.C. 1215.

[17] *Muir's Tr.*, *supra*.

[18] *Larkhall Collieries Liqdr.* v. *Hamilton* (1906) 14 S.L.T. 202.

[19] *Heron* v. *Espie* (1856) 18 D. 917, 951; *Caledonian Ry.* v. *Watt* (1875) 2 R. 917; *Kelvinside Estate Co.* v. *Donaldson's Trs.* (1879) 6 R. 995.

[20] Damages (Sc.) Act, 1976, S. 1.

[21] Under the principle of *Eisten* v. *N.B. Ry.* (1870) 8 M. 980.

[22] *Kelly* v. *Glasgow Corpn.*, 1951 S.C. (H.L.) 15; cf. *Hendry* v. *United Collieries*, 1909 S.C. (H.L.) 19, but see *Fraser* v. *Livermore* (1900) 7 S.L.T. 450.

[23] Damages (Sc.) Act, 1976, S. 3.

[24] *Bentley* v. *Macfarlane*, 1964 S.C. 76.

[25] *Caledonian Ry.* v. *Colt* (1860) 3 Macq. 833; *Ovington* v. *McVicar* (1864) 2 M. 1066; *McIntyre* v. *Gallacher* (1883) 11 R. 64; *Duncan's Trs.* v. *Steven* (1897) 24 R. 880; *Glasgow Corpn.* v. *Turnbull*, 1932 S.L.T. 457; *Buchanan and Carswell* v. *Eugene*, 1930 S.C. 160.

[26] cf. *Harvey* v. *O'Dell* [1958] 2 Q.B. 78.

[27] *Binnie* v. *Parlane* (1825) 4 S. 122; *Hamilton* v. *Anderson*, 1953 S.C. 129.

[28] e.g. right of person held vicariously liable to relief from person actually in fault: *Semtex* v. *Gladstone* [1954] 2 All E.R. 206; *Lister* v. *Romford Ice Co.* [1957] A.C. 555; or agent's relief from principal: *Eastern Shipping Co.* v. *Quah Beng Kee* [1924] A.C. 177.

[29] Law Reform (Misc. Prov.) (Sc.) Act, 1940, S. 3(1); e.g. *Drew* v. *Western S.M.T. Co.*, 1947 S.C. 222.

[30] Law Reform (Misc. Prov.) (Sc.) Act, 1940, S. 3(2); *N.C.B.* v. *Thomson*, 1959 S.C. 353; see also *Wimpey* v. *B.O.A.C.* [1955] A.C. 169; *Central S.M.T. Co.* v. *Lanarkshire C.C.*, 1949 S.C. 450.

JURA CREDITI UNDER CONTRACTS

A right under contract to performance of an obligation is personal and not proprietary if the contract involves an element of *delectus personae creditoris*[31] but if it does not, so that it is a matter of indifference to the debtor to or for whom he must tender performance, the creditor's right is proprietary in nature, assignable,[32] and the *jus exigendi* passes to the creditor's executors on his death.

Similarly a contractual right is personal and non-proprietary if the party bound is bound personally only and the obligation does not transmit against his executors,[33] or others who come to stand in his right.[34]

A right constituted by contract restrictive of the liberty of one party to carry on a business or profession may be assignable by the party in right thereof along with the business protected thereby.[35]

The right to enforce a restrictive condition relative to heritable property, such as contained in a condition relative to construction or use of buildings, or a servitude transmits with the superiority or dominant tenement to a new creditor in the obligation.[36]

A restrictive condition relative to moveable property does not, in general, transmit with those moveables so as to bind a party subsequently acquiring those goods.[37] An exception exists in the case of goods sold by a supplier subject to a condition as to the price at which they may be resold.[38]

Price of land

The sale of land, whether voluntary or compulsory, operates conversion and the price thereof is moveable, falling to the seller's ex-

---

[31] *Hoey* v. *McEwan & Auld* (1867) 5 M. 814; *Grierson, Oldham & Co.* v. *Forbes, Maxwell & Co.* (1895) 22 R. 812; *International Fibre Syndicate* v. *Dawson* (1901) 3 F. (H.L.) 32; *Berlitz School* v. *Duchene* (1903) 6 F. 181; *Asphaltic Co.* v. *Glasgow Corpn.*, 1907 S.C. 463; *Cole* v. *Handasyde*, 1910 S.C. 68.

[32] Stair III, 1, 2; Ersk. III, 5, 2; Bell, *Prin.* §1459; *Aurdal* v. *Estrella*, 1916 S.C. 882; *Westville Shipping Co.* v. *Abram Steamship Co.*, 1923 S.C. (H.L.) 68.

[33] *Gilmour* v. *Nunn's Trs.* (1899) 7 S.L.T. 292.

[34] *Melrose* v. *Aitken Melrose & Co.*, 1918, 1 S.L.T. 109.

[35] *Fraser* v. *Renwick* (1906) 14 S.L.T. 443; *Methven Simpson, Ltd.* v. *Jones*, 1910 2 S.L.T. 14; contrast *Berlitz School* v. *Duchene* (1903) 6 F. 181; *Rodger* v. *Herbertson*, 1909 S.C. 256, where held personal.

[36] e.g. *E. Zetland* v. *Hislop* (1882) 9 R. (H.L.) 40; *Royal Exchange Buildings, Glasgow* v. *Cotton*, 1912 S.C. 1151.

[37] *Morton* v. *Muir Bros.*, 1907 S.C. 1211, is an exceptional, and rather doubtful, case.

[38] Resale Prices Act, 1976, S. 26, *County Laboratories* v. *Mindel* [1957] Ch. 295; *Goodyear Tyre Co.* v. *Lancashire Batteries, Ltd.* [1958] 3 All E.R. 7.

ecutor,[39] unless it has been constructively reconverted by a direction to lay it out on the purchase of other heritage.

Arrears of feu-duties and interest on heritable bonds

Though the superior's right to recover feu-duties is heritable and the creditor's right in heritable bonds sometimes heritable, arrears of payments due are deemed moveable, though secured over land.[40]

Arrears of rent

Accruing payments of rent become moveable once they have vested.[41]

Options in relation to land

An option in relation to land, to buy, extend a lease or otherwise,[42] is normally personal, non-assignable and accordingly not proprietary.

NEGOTIABLE INSTRUMENTS

Negotiable instruments are a special class of incorporeal moveable rights. Negotiability is the quality which attaches by law, following mercantile usage, to certain kinds of documents evidencing indebtedness and conferring a right to obtain payment of money. This quality cannot be conferred by private agreement to the effect of affecting the rights of third parties to the agreement, though such a stipulation may be good as between the parties to it.[43]

The quality of negotiability imports that (a) the document is transferable by delivery alone, if payable to bearer, or by endorsement and delivery if payable to order, and needs no assignation or intimation thereof; and (b) it confers a good title, notwithstanding lack of, or defect in, the title of the transferor, on a transferee who takes in good faith, for value, and without notice of any defect in the title of the transferor. Both characteristics must attach to any document before it can be regarded as a negotiable instrument.[44]

Negotiability attaches to bills of exchange, promissory notes (in-

---

[39] Bell, *Prin.* §1479; *Heron* v. *Espie* (1856) 18 D. 917.

[40] Ersk. II, 9, 64; Bell, *Prin.* §1479, 1505; *Martin* v. *Agnew* (1755) Mor. 5457; 5 B.S. 830; *Spalding* v. *S.* (1792) Mor. 5257; *Johnston* v. *Cochran* (1829) 7 S. 226; *Hughes' Trs.* v. *Corsane* (1890) 18 R. 299; *Logan's Trs.* v. *L.* (1896) 23 R. 848; *Watson's Trs.* v. *Brown*, 1923 S.C. 228.

[41] Bell, *Prin.* §1496–504.

[42] e.g. *Commercial Union Assce. Co.* v. *Watt & Cumine*, 1964 S.C. 84.

[43] *Bovill* v. *Dixon* (1856) 3 Macq. 1; *Crouch* v. *Credit Foncier* (1873) L.R. 8 Q.B. 374.

[44] *London Joint Stock Bank* v. *Simmons* [1891] 1 Ch. 270, 294; [1892] A.C. 201; *Walker* v. *Watson & Sturrock* (1897) 35 S.L.R. 26.

cluding banknotes[45]) and cheques, Treasury bills, share warrants issued to bearer,[46] scrip certificates issued to bearer,[47] debentures payable to bearer,[48] bankers' drafts and circular notes, and dividend warrants. It does not attach to postal orders,[49] share certificates and transfers,[50] pension receipts,[51] letters of credit,[52] nor to deposit receipts.[53]

The recognized categories of negotiable instruments are not finally closed, and if the Court finds that a category of documents have, by the general usage and custom of business and trade, been treated as negotiable, it will recognize such a category as entitled to the privileges of negotiability.[54]

The protection of the taker of a negotiable instrument extends only to one who takes in good faith, for value and without knowledge of any defect in the title of the transferor. A transferee may take in good faith notwithstanding negligence or folly in not suspecting from the circumstances that there is defect in the transferor's title, but not if the circumstances raise actual suspicion or doubt and the instrument is accepted without further inquiry.[55]

In the hands of a bona fide holder for value and without notice of any defect in the title of the transferor to him, a negotiable instrument is property, transferable *inter vivos* by delivery, or endorsement and delivery, which passes on death to his executor, and confers a right to payment from the drawee.

A bill of exchange accepted payable at a banker's[56] and a cheque drawn for value[57] operate an assignation of the funds of the acceptor or drawer in the banker's hands.[58]

A bill of lading is not a negotiable instrument as the transferee

[45] cf. Bell, *Prin.* §1340.
[46] Companies Act, 1948, S. 83.
[47] *Rumball* v. *Metropolitan Bank* (1877) 2 Q.B.D. 194; *Edelstein* v. *Schuler* [1902] 2 K.B. 144.
[48] *Bechuanaland Exploration Co.* v. *London Trading Bank* [1898] 2 Q.B. 658.
[49] *Fine Arts Socy.* v. *Union Bank of London* (1886) 17 Q.B.D. 705.
[50] *Colonial Bank* v. *Cady & Williams* (1890) 15 App. Cas. 267; *Longman* v. *Bath Electric Tramways, Ltd.* [1905] 1 Ch. 646.
[51] *Jones* v. *Coventry* [1909] 2 K.B. 1029.
[52] *Morgan* v. *Larivière* (1875) L.R. 7 H.L. 423, 432.
[53] *Barstow* v. *Inglis* (1857) 20 D. 230; *Wood* v. *Clydesdale Bank*, 1914 S.C. 397; cf. *Dickson* v. *National Bank*, 1917 S.C. (H.L.) 50.
[54] *Goodwin* v. *Robarts* (1875) L.R. 11 Ex. 337; (1876) 1 App. Cas. 476; *Bechuanaland Exploration Co.* v. *London Trading Bank* [1898] 2 Q.B. 658.
[55] *Jones* v. *Gordon* (1877) 2 App. Cas. 616; *London Joint Stock Bank* v. *Simmons* [1892] A.C. 201.
[56] *B.L. Co.* v. *Rainey's Tr.* (1885) 12 R. 825.
[57] *Sutherland* v. *Commercial Bank* (1882) 20 S.L.R. 139; *B.L. Co.* v. *Carruthers* (1883) 10 R. 923.
[58] Bills of Exchange Act, 1882, S. 53(2).

acquires no better title than the transferor,[59] nor are documents of title under the Factors Acts.

BILLS OF LADING

A bill of lading for goods is not only a receipt for goods shipped and evidence of the contract of carriage, but it is also by mercantile custom deemed a symbol of the goods. Possession of it is equivalent to possession of the goods and it is capable of transfer outright or in security by endorsement and delivery in the same way as the goods themselves.[60] The goods need not be specifically ascertained or identified.[61] It is not, however, a negotiable instrument as the transferee never acquires any better title to the goods than the transferor himself had.[62]

Bills of lading are usually drawn in sets of three and if more than one is endorsed to different endorsees the goods belong to the one who first takes an endorsed bill.[63] The shipowner may, however, in the absence of notice of a prior claim, deliver the goods to the person who first presents one of a set of bills.[64] If he has notice of conflicting claims he should warehouse the goods and have the claims determined in a multiplepoinding.

On transfer of the bill, the property in the goods represented thereby passes, and the right of the original consignor to stop the goods *in transitu* is wholly defeated (in the case of transfer outright) or becomes subject to the security (in the case of transfer in security).[65]

If the holders of a bill in security nevertheless allow actual delivery to be made to an onerous third party, such as purchase from the party who delivered the bill in security, the holders lose their security.[66]

Other documents of title to goods

Dock warrants, delivery orders, warehouse keepers' certificates and similar documents granted by the custodiers of goods and used as proof of the possession or control of goods,[67] do not, like a bill of

[59] *Lickbarrow* v. *Mason* (1794) 5 T.R. 683; *Gunn* v. *Bolckow, Vaughan & Co.* (1875) 10 Ch. D. 491.

[60] Bell, *Prin.* §417; *Sewell* v. *Burdick* (1884) 10 App. Cas. 74; *Sanders* v. *Maclean* (1883) 11 Q.B.D. 327; *Hayman* v. *McLintock*, 1907 S.C. 936.

[61] *Hayman, supra.*

[62] *Lickbarrow* v. *Mason* (1794) 5 Term Rep. 683.

[63] *Barber* v. *Meyerstein* (1870) L.R. 4 H.L. 317; *Sanders, supra.*

[64] *Glynn* v. *E. & W. India Docks Co.* (1882) 7 App. Cas. 591.

[65] *Lickbarrow, supra; Leask* v. *Scott* (1877) 2 Q.B.D. 376; *Kemp* v. *Falk* (1882) 7 App. Cas. 573.

[66] *Tod* v. *Merchant Banking Co. of London* (1883) 10 R. 1009.

[67] cf. Factors Act, 1889, S. 1(4) applied by Factors (Sc.) Act, 1890, S. 1, and Sale of Goods Act, 1979, S. 61(1).

lading, represent the goods themselves but, if endorsed and delivered, authorize the possessor to receive the goods referred to in the documents.[68] Endorsation and delivery of such a document and intimation thereof to the custodier accordingly entitles the endorsee to take possession of the goods from the custodier and is accordingly the mode in which the goods may be constructively delivered on sale or in security.[69]

For the transfer of the documents to be effective as constructive delivery of the goods themselves, the custodier must be an independent third party and neither a servant of the granter[70] nor a party having control but with no claim to custody, such as an exciseman.[71] The goods must be sufficiently identified and appropriated to the holder of the documents of title.[72]

The holder of a delivery order obtained in good faith and for value, has a preferable title to that of the original seller of goods as against the purchaser who granted the delivery orders so long as the goods concerned have been sufficiently identified and appropriated to the transferees of the order.[73]

OBLIGATIONS OF DEBT

Claims of aliment

A claim for aliment arises *ex lege* in certain relationships.[74] In other cases it may be furnished *ex pietate*, though not due *ex lege*.

I.O.U.

An I.O.U. is an acknowledgement of debt and imports an obligation to repay, but is not a promissory note or other form of negotiable instrument. It may doubtless be assigned, but only by assignation, not by mere delivery or endorsement and delivery, and will pass to the creditor's executor on his death.[75]

---

[68] *Farina* v. *Home* (1846) 16 M. & W. 119; *McEwan* v. *Smith* (1849) 2 H.L. Cas. 309; *Gunn* v. *Bolckow, Vaughan & Co.* (1875) 10 Ch. App. 491.

[69] *Hamilton* v. *Western Bank* (1856) 19 D. 152; *Fleming* v. *Smith* (1881) 8 R. 548; *Inglis* v. *Robertson & Baxter* (1898) 25 R. (H.L.) 70.

[70] *Dobell, Beckett & Co.* v. *Neilson* (1904) 7 F. 281; cf. *Roy's Tr.* v. *Colville & Drysdale* (1908) 5 F. 769.

[71] *Rhind's Tr.* v. *Robertson & Baxter* (1891) 18 R. 623; cf. *Distillers Co.* v. *Russell's Tr.* (1889) 16 R. 479; *Browne* v. *Ainslie* (1893) 21 R. 173. See also *Pochin* v. *Robinow & Marjoribanks* (1869) 7 M. 622.

[72] *Price & Pierce, infra.*

[73] *Price & Pierce* v. *Bank of Scotland*, 1912 S.C. (H.L.) 19; cf. *Connal & Co.* v. *Loder* (1868) 6 M. 1095.

[74] See Chs. 3.3–3.4, *supra.*

[75] *Thiem's Trs.* v. *Collie* (1899) 1 F. 764.

Personal bonds

A personal bond confers on the holder a right to payment from the granter in accordance with the terms of the bond. Such a bond is assignable[76] and transmits to the creditor's executor.[77] If once extinguished by payment it cannot be assigned to a new creditor in security of another debt of the same debtor.[78]

Debentures

A debenture is an instrument of debt granted by a company providing for repayment, with interest so long as the principal is unpaid, and usually creating a security by way of floating charge over the company's property. It is commonly issued as a series of debentures ranking *pari passu*. Debentures may be issued payable to bearer,[79] in which case they are negotiable instruments. A debenture may equally be created in favour of a trustee for debenture holders to whom debenture stock is issued evidencing title to a fractional share of the debenture. In all cases the interest of the debenture-holder is moveable and he may transfer it in the same way as a personal bond or as stock in the company.[80]

British Government stock

The interest of a stockholder in any stock issued by the Government is moveable,[81] and is transferable by instrument in writing, as provided by Treasury regulations.[82]

Local authority securities

Local authorities may create mortgages or stock[83] as securities for money lent them. Mortgages are in statutory form, and may be renewed, transferred or discharged by endorsement thereon,[84] and their issue, transfer, renewal or discharge is recorded in a register of mortgages maintained by the authority.[85] Redeemable stock may be created in accordance with regulations made by the Secretary of State, which provide for stock certificates, and the transfer of stock.[86]

---

[76] Bell, *Prin.* §1459.
[77] cf. *Reid's Exrx.* v. *R.* 1943 S.C. 362 (bond of annuity).
[78] *Jackson* v. *Nicoll* (1870) 8 M. 408.
[79] Companies Act, 1948, S. 93.
[80] Companies Act, 1948, Ss. 73–82, 86–94.
[81] National Debt Act, 1870, S. 23; *Hog* v. *Hog* (1791) Mor. 5479; 3 Pat. 247.
[82] Finance Act, 1942, S. 47.
[83] Local Govt. (Sc.) Act, 1947, S. 260(1).
[84] 1947 Act, S. 267 and Sched. 7; see also Stock Transfer Act, 1963, S. 1.
[85] 1947 Act, S. 268.
[86] 1947 Act, S. 271; S.I. 1975, No. 236. By S. 270 certain other statutory authorities have similar powers. See e.g. *Downie* v. *D's Trs.* (1866) 4 M. 1067.

RIGHTS IN SECURITY OVER PROPERTY

A right in security over heritage constituted by bond and disposition in security is now[87] moveable in the creditor's succession. The bond, however, remains heritable, as at common law, for the purposes of the Crown right to escheat and as regards legal rights of children. A bond made moveable by the statute is assignable[88] and passes on the creditor's death to his executors and next-of-kin.[89]

A right in security over corporeal moveables constituted by pledge and delivery of possession, or by lien over goods possessed, is assignable[90] and passes to the creditor's executor on his death.

A right in security over incorporeal moveable rights constituted by assignation in security is itself in incorporeal right capable of assignation, and transmits to the assignee's executor.

REVERSIONARY RIGHTS

Where a person conveys a fund or other property to trustees for administrative purposes he retains a reversionary right which can be carried by his will;[91] it would be otherwise if he irrevocably divested himself in favour of trustees or anyone else.

Where a person conveys heritable or moveable property to another in security in the appropriate way he retains a right of reversion therein, which can be exercised by paying off the sum due with interest and claiming a reconveyance of the security. This reversionary right, though not exercised, is, so long as it may be exercised, a right capable of assignation outright or in security.[92] Where subjects were disponed *ex facie* absolutely to a bank, but truly in security, the back-letter not being recorded, and the true owner subsequently assigned the right of reversion to another bank, which assignation was intimated to the first bank, after which both banks made further advances, it was held that

---

[87] Titles to Land Consolidation (Sc.) Act, 1868, S. 117 amd. Succession (Sc.) Act, 1964, Sched. 3; cf. *Hughes' Trs.* v. *Corsane* (1890) 18 R.299.

[88] *McCutcheon* v. *McWilliam* (1876) 3 R. 565; *Bruce* v. *Sc. Amicable Life Assce. Soc.*, 1907 S.C. 637.

[89] 1868 Act, S. 117, as amd. 1964 Act.

[90] *Moore* v. *Gledden* (1869) 7 M. 1016.

[91] *Byres's Trs.* v. *Gemmell* (1896) 23 R. 332; *Bulkeley-Gavin's Trs.* v. *B.G.'s Trs.*, 1971 S.C. 209.

[92] *Forbes* v. *Welsh & Forbes* (1894) 21 R. 630; cf. *McCallum's Trs.* v. *McNab* (1877) 4 R. 520. Where a heritable proprietor grants security by bond and disposition in security he retains the radical right subject to the encumbrance, and can sell his property, subject to the bond. See also *Campbell's J.F.* v. *National Bank*, 1944 S.C. 495. As to shares, see *Nelson* v. *National Bank*, 1936 S.C. 570.

the first bank's security was limited to advances made prior to the intimation of the assignation of the reversionary right.[93] The appointment of a judicial factor has the same effect as an intimated assignation.[94]

The reversionary right gives the true owner of land a title to sue for the protection of the land against the encroachment of a stranger[95] or for damages for injury to the property by a third party.[96]

In the case of security over moveables the reversionary right of the debtor is not generally assignable in security, as a right in security without possession generally avails nought, and pledged subjects cannot be sold outright and the right to recover possession assigned outright to the buyer, possession being exigible when the first security-holder surrenders possession.[97]

Similarly, a fiar, during the subsistence of a liferent, has a reversionary right capable of assignation, transmissible and subject to diligence.[98]

POLICIES OF LIFE ASSURANCE

A policy of life assurance has an increasing value as time passes towards its maturity and its surrender value increases. A policy by a husband on his wife's life is part of his moveable estate on his death, survived by her, and legitim is due from it.[99] The sums in policies on the husband's life fall under *jus relictae*.[1] A policy is assignable outright or in security[2] but bare custody without assignation confers no security right on the custodier,[3] nor does payment of premiums by a third party confer any right on the payer.[4]

A life policy passes on bankruptcy to the trustee; even if its existence is not disclosed to him and it is kept up by the bankrupt till his death, the trustee is entitled to it.[5] Similarly if an undischarged bankrupt

[93] *Union Bank* v. *National Bank* (1886) 14 R. (H.L.) 1.
[94] *Campbell's J.F.* v. *National Bank*, 1944 S.C. 495.
[95] *Vincent* v. *Wood* (1899) 6 S.L.T. 297.
[96] *McBride* v. *Caledonian Ry.* (1894) 21 R. 620.
[97] Such a transaction being a sale 'intended to operate by way of security' the Sale of Goods Act, 1979, particularly Ss. 17–18, whereby the subjects could be sold without delivery of possession, does not apply, by S. 62(4) thereof, but the common law applies and requires delivery.
[98] *Brower's Exor.* v. *Ramsay's Trs.*, 1912 S.C. 1374.
[99] *Pringle's Trs.* v. *Hamilton* (1872) 10 M. 621.
[1] *Muirhead* v. *M's J.F.* (1867) 6 M. 95.
[2] Policies of Assurance Act, 1867; *Crossley* v. *City of Glasgow Life Assce. Co.* (1876) 4 Ch. D. 421.
[3] *United Kingdom Life Assce. Co.* v. *Dixon* (1838) 16 S. 1277.
[4] *Wylie's Exrx.* v. *McJannet* (1901) 4 F. 195.
[5] *Tapster* v. *Ward* (1900) 101 L.T. 503.

effects a life policy and pays premiums after he has obtained his
discharge, it still vests in the trustee who can recover the proceeds for
the benefit of the creditors.[6] Discharge in bankruptcy does not revest in
the bankrupt a life policy owned by him or acquired before discharge,
even though it then has little or no surrender value, but a retrocession
of the policy is necessary.

If the policy is void or voidable as against the assured, it is equally so
against even an onerous assignee.[7]

SALARY AND PENSION RIGHTS

Entitlement to a salary is a personal claim, which is probably assignable, but is not transmissible on death.

The entitlement to a pension, whether under a contract of employment or under statute, is personal rather than proprietary and the right
is assignable unless statutorily declared inalienable, but not transmissible. It may be declared alimentary, in which case it is not attachable
by creditors.[8]

JURA CREDITI ON INTESTACY OR UNDER WILLS OR TRUSTS

Spouses' prior rights on intestacy

A surviving spouse's prior rights on intestacy to a dwelling-house or
the value thereof,[9] furniture and plenishing[10] and financial provision
from the estate[11] are *jura crediti* exigible from the estate, rather than
rights of property in, or of succession to, portions of the deceased's
estate, but postponed to the claims of creditors. Once vested the rights
are probably proprietary, assignable, and transmit to executors.

Legal rights

Legal rights are *jura crediti* for payment of a certain portion of a
deceased's estate at the date of death.[12] They are similarly proprietary,

---

[6] *Re Bennett, ex p. Official Receiver* [1907] 1 K.B. 149; *Re Phillips* [1914] 2 K.B. 689; *Re Stokes, ex p. Mellish* [1919] 2 K.B. 256.
[7] *Scottish Widows' Fund* v. *Buist* (1876) 3 R. 1078.
[8] *Union Bank Superannuation Fund Trs.* v. *Cooper*, 1976 S.L.T. (Sh. Ct.) 2. cf. *Sinton* v. *S.* 1976 S.L.T. (Sh. Ct.) 95.
[9] Succession (Sc.) Act, 1964, S. 8(1), (2) and (4).
[10] Ibid., S. 8(3).
[11] Ibid., S. 9.
[12] *Wright* v. *Brown* (1849) 11 D. 459; *Muirhead* v. *M's J.F.* (1867) 6 M. 95; *Inglis* v. *I.* (1869) 7 M. 435; *Cameron's Trs.* v. *Maclean*, 1917 S.C. 416 (*jus relictae*); *Fisher* v. *Dixon* (1843) 2 Bell 63; *McMurray* v. *McM's Trs.* (1852) 14 D. 1048; *Dalhousie* v. *Crokat* (1868) 6 M. 659; *Ross* v. *R.* (1896) 23 R. 802; *Gams* v. *Russell's Trs.* (1899) 7 S.L.T. 289 (*legitim*).

once they have vested. The right to elect between legal rights and testamentary provisions is not carried to trustees by a conveyance of acquirenda, but remains an independent right.[13]

Rights on intestacy

The rights of persons entitled, on a deceased's intestacy, to shares in the free estate,[14] once vested in them by relationship and survivance, are proprietary rights, assignable[15] and transmissible.

Liferent

A right of improper liferent is an incorporeal claim to the whole or part of the income of an estate in trust for the period of one's life, or a shorter determinate period. Unless declared alimentary, the right is assignable outright or in security, but only for the duration of its continuance.[16]

Alimentary provisions

A provision enjoyed by a person, as under a liferent, which is declared alimentary or for his alimentary use allenarly is prima facie not a proprietary right capable of assignation, outright or in security,[17] nor attachable by creditors. In so far, however, as the provision exceeds what the cover considers a reasonable provision, it is attachable by creditors,[18] and assignable to them[19] or to third parties.[20] Each term's payment, when paid, is at the beneficiary's absolute disposal, and the protection as alimentary may be ended by the beneficiary in certain circumstances.[21] A wife's alimentary liferent for the duration of her marriage ceases to be alimentary on her husband's death;[22] if for her life or for the children, and the marriage is dissolved, it remains alimentary even though part of the capital is paid to the children.[23] A

[13] *Mackenzie's Trs.* v. *Beveridge's Trs.*, 1908 S.C. 1185.

[14] 1964 Act, S.2.

[15] *Secus, Stevenson's Trs.* v. *Macnaughton*, 1932 S.C. 46, *sed quaere*.

[16] *Bailey's Trs.* v. *B.*, 1954 S.L.T. 282; cf. *Fraser* v. *Carruthers* (1875) 2 R. 595. There is no right to a conveyance of the trust estate in liferent: *Ker's Trs.* v. *Justice* (1868) 6 M. 627.

[17] Ersk. III, 5, 2; *Mackenzie* v. *Morison* (1791) Mor. 10413; *McDonnell* v. *Clark*, 25 Mar. 1819, F.C.; *Rennie* v. *Ritchie* (1845) 4 Bell, 221; *Hewats* v. *Robertson* (1881) 9 R. 175.

[18] *Lewis* v. *Anstruther* (1852) 15 D. 260; *Livingstone* v. *L.* (1886) 14 R. 43; *Haydon* v. *Forrest's Trs.* (1895) 3 S.L.T. 182; *L. Ruthven* v. *Pulford*, 1909 S.C. 951. cf. *Hardie* v. *Macfarlane's J.F.*, 1912 S.C. 502.

[19] *E. Buchan* v. *His Creditors* (1835) 13 S. 1112; *Harvey* v. *Calder* (1840) 2 D. 1095; *Lewis* v. *Anstruther* (1852) 14 D. 875; 15 D. 260.

[20] *Claremont's Trs.* v. *C.* (1896) 4 S.L.T. 144; *Craig* v. *Pearson's Trs.*, 1915, 2 S.L.T. 183. See also *Cuthbert* v. *C's Trs.*, 1908 S.C. 967.

[21] *Dempster's Trs.* v. *D.*, 1949 S.C. 92; *Sturgis's Tr.* v. *S.*, 1951 S.C. 637; contrast *Kennedy* v. *K's Trs.*, 1953 S.C. 60; cf. *Hewats* v. *Roberton* (1881) 9 R. 175.

[22] *Martin* v. *Bannatyne* (1861) 23 D. 705; *Strange*, 1966 S.L.T. 59; *Pearson*, 1968 S.C. 8.

[23] *Sturgis's Tr.* v. *S.*, 1951 S.C. 637, 648; *Sutherland*, 1968 S.C. 200.

person cannot create an alimentary liferent in favour of himself,[24] save that a women in her ante-nuptial marriage-contract may do so.[25]

The court has, however, declined to sanction the assignation of part of an alimentary provision in order to raise a capital sum, as such a sanction would not be *res judicta* in any future question between the beneficiary and possible alimentary creditors.[20]

Rights of beneficiary

A designated beneficiary, having a vested right under a will or trust settlement, has a *jus crediti* against the executor or trustee for delivery or payment of the property or rights destined to him under the will or trust. This right is heritable or moveable according to the nature of the subject held for his behalf, and may be affected by the testator's or trustee's directions for constructive conversion of parts of the estate. In so far as the estate on which the beneficiary has a claim is, or is constructively deemed to be, moveable or is general or uncertain his *jus crediti* is moveable.[26]

Such a right may, before it is reduced to possession, be assigned *inter vivos*,[27] attached by creditors,[28] and passes to executors under the beneficiary's will or intestacy.

An option conferred by a will may, depending on the language used, be a personal privilege exercisable by the donee only, or be a proprietary right transmissible to the donee's representatives.[29]

Jura crediti *under marriage-contract trusts*

To be a *jus crediti* a provision under a marriage-contract trust must confer a present right on the claimant, availing in competition with outside creditors, though not giving a preference. Under an ante-nuptial marriage-contract provisions in favour of the wife are of this class.[30] Under a post-nuptial contract a provision for the wife confers a

[24] *L. Ruthven* v. *Drummond*, 1908 S.C. 1154; *Douglas Gardiner & Mill* v. *Mackintosh's Trs.* 1916 S.C. 125; *Dempster's Trs., supra.*

[25] *Pearson*, 1968 S.C. 8; *Sutherland*, 1968 S.C. 200. She cannot do so by post-nuptial marriage-contract: *Cargill*, 1965 S.C. 122.

[26] *Buchanan* v. *Angus* (1862) 4 Macq. 374; *Wardlaw's Trs.* v. *W.* (1880) 7 R. 1070.

[27] *Ker's Trs.* v. *Justice* (1868) 6 M. 627; *Rothwell* v. *Stuart's Trs.* (1898) 1 F. 81; *Train* v. *Buchanan's Trs.*, 1908 S.C. (H.L.) 26; *Macpherson's J.F.* v. *Mackay*, 1915 S.C. 1011; *Murdoch's Trs.* v. *Stock*, 1923 S.C. 906. See also *Macknight* (1875) 2 R. 667; *Brigg's Trs.* v. *B.*, 1923 S.L.T. 755; *Robinson* v. *R's Trs.*, 1934 S.L.T. 183; as to intimation of assignation see *Jameson* v. *Sharp* (1887) 14 R. 643; *Browne's Tr.* v. *Anderson* (1901) 4 F 305.

[28] *Brower's Exor.* v. *Ramsay's Trs.*, 1912 S.C. 1374.

[29] *Adam's Trs.* v. *Russell*, 1955 S.C. 232.

[30] Ersk. III, 9, 22; III, 8, 36; *Wilson's Trs.* v. *W.* (1856) 18 D. 1096; *Carphin* v. *Clapperton* (1867) 5 M. 797.

jus crediti only so far as reasonable and provided that the husband was solvent at the time of making the provision.[31]

The right conferred on children under a marriage-contract may be a *jus crediti*,[32] but the presumption is against conferment of any such right, and such a right will normally be a *spes successionis* only.[31] Children have a *jus crediti* secured against other creditors only if it secured against the father himself.[33] Provisions for children in post-nuptial contracts are accounted gratuitous and are reducible in a competition with creditors if the granter were not solvent at the time of granting.

A *jus crediti* renders the party entitled a creditor of the trust, having a right which is assignable and transmissible.[34]

Spes successionis

A *spes successionis* is a contingent or defeasible right in succession, either on intestacy or under a testamentary deed.[35] *Spes successionis* may mean that A hopes to benefit by the will of B who is still alive, or that A has a right under the said will of B, who is dead, subject to a certain contingency.[36] Among such are a legal right of legitim, so long as the parent is alive,[37] or the right of children under a destination of heritage to a husband or wife in liferent and the children of the marriage in fee,[38] or the right of children under a destination in a marriage-contract to the children of the marriage, the father having in such a case full power of administration, subject to the obligation to leave the estate to the children at his death,[39] or the right of a beneficiary, subject to a liferent and with a gift-over if the beneficiary should predecease the liferentrix,[40] or the right of any substitute under a destination, whose right may be defeated by the institute.

It differs from a *jus crediti* in that in the latter case the right has vested and is indefeasible though it may not be yet exigible. A person may have a *jus crediti* as against certain claimants and only a *spes successionis* against others.[41]

---

[31] *Craig v. Galloway* (1861) 4 Macq. 267; *Walkinshaw's Trs. v. W.* (1872) 10 M. 763.

[32] *Goddard v. Stewart's Children* (1844) 6 D. 1018; *Cruikshank's Trs. v. C.* (1853) 16 D. 7.

[33] *Fotheringham v. F.* (1734) Mor. 12941; *Gordon v. Sutherland* (1748) Mor. 12915; *Herries, Farquhar & Co. v. Brown* (1838) 16 S. 948; *Mackinnon's Trs. v. Dunlop*, 1913 S.C. 232.

[34] *Harvey v. Ligertwood* (1872) 10 M. (H.L.) 33.

[35] *Reid v. Morrison* (1893) 20 R. 510; *Scott v. S.*, 1930 S.C. 903.

[36] *Salaman v. Tod*, 1911 S.C. 1214, 1223; *Wright v. Bryson*, 1934 S.C. 557.

[37] *Coats v. Bannochie's Trs.*, 1912 S.C. 329.

[38] *E. Wemyss v. E. Haddington* (1818) 6 Pat. 390; *Macdonald v. Hall* (1893) 20 R. (H.L.) 88.

[39] *Arthur & Seymour v. Lamb* (1870) 8 M. 928.

[40] *Rothwell v. Stuart's Tr.* (1898) 1 F. 81.

[41] *Goddard v. Stewart's Children* (1844) 6 D. 1018; *Murray v. Macfarlane's Trs.* (1895) 22 R. 927.

A *spes successionis* has a present value, depending on the likelihood of its realization and the value of the hoped-for benefit.[42] It is assignable, absolutely or in security, to the effect of giving the assignee a good title against the assignor to the succession, though the assignation can become effective only if and when the right vests.[43] It will not be assigned by a general conveyance by a person of his property.[44]

It is now[45] carried to the trustee in sequestration on the entitled party's sequestration,[46] but is not attachable by diligence.[47]

An assignee of a contingent interest in a trust has been held entitled to inspect the trust accounts.[48]

Radical right under trusts

A truster retains a radical or reversionary right in assets put in trust by him and is entitled to them in the event of failure of all the trust purposes.[49]

INTERESTS IN PARTNERSHIPS AND COMPANIES

Interest in partnership

The interest of a partner in a partnership is a proprietary right, and moveable, even though the partnership assets or business are mainly heritable.[50]

The right to claim an accounting and payment of the partner's entitlement passes to his executor.[51]

Though a partner's interest is assignable, the assignee is not entitled to participate in the management of the partnership business or otherwise to act as a partner, but only to receive the share of profits which the assignee would otherwise have been entitled to receive, as agreed by the partners.[52]

---

[42] *Bradshaw* v. *Kirkwood* (1904) 7 F. 249.

[43] *Wood* v. *Begbie* (1850) 12 D. 963; *Trappes* v. *Meredith* (1871) 10 M. 38; *Rothwell* v. *Stuart's Tr.* (1898) 1 F. 81; see also *Reid* v. *Morrison* (1893) 20 R. 510; *Browne's Tr.* v. *Anderson* (1901) 4 F. 305; *Salaman* v. *Tod*, 1911 S.C. 1214; *Coats* v. *Bannochie's Trs.*, 1912 S.C. 329; *Wright* v. *Bryson*, 1935 S.C. (H.L.) 49.

[44] *McEwan's Trs.* v. *Macdonald*, 1909 S.C. 57.

[45] For former law, see *Beaton and McAndrew* v. *McDonald* (1821) 1 S. 49; *Kirkland* v. *K's Trs.* (1886) 13 R. 798; *Trappes, supra; Reid, supra.* See also *Obers* v. *Paton's Trs.* (1897) 24 R. 719.

[46] Bankruptcy (Sc.) Act, 1913, S. 97.

[47] *Reid* v. *Morrison* (1893) 20 R. 510.

[48] *Salamon* v. *Morrison's Trs.*, 1912 2 S.L.T. 499.

[49] *Coat's Trs.* v. *L.A.*, 1964 S.C. 249.

[50] Partnership Act, 1890, S. 22; *Murray* v. *M.* (1805) Mor. Heritable and Moveable Appx. 4; *Minto* v. *Kirkpatrick* (1833) 11 S. 632; *L.A.* v. *Macfarlane's Trs.* (1893) 31 S.L.R. 357; see also *Irvine* v. *I.* (1851) 13 D. 1367.

[51] *Morrison* v. *M's Exrx.*, 1912 S.C. 892.

[52] Partnership Act, 1890, S. 31.

Shares in companies

A share in a company limited by shares is a right to a fractional part of the ownership of the company, comprising rights to participate in and vote at meetings, and to receive a proportional part of the dividends declared and of the assets on a winding-up, subject to the liability to pay the full nominal value of the share.[53] The precise rights attaching to classes of shares are determined by the Memorandum and Articles of Association of the particular company. The shares or other interest of a member of a company are moveable property, even if the company's sole objects relate to land or all its property is land.[54]

Shares in a public company are prima facie freely transferable, but those of a private company must be,[55] and shares in a public company may be,[56] subject to restriction on transfer imposed by the company's Articles of Association. Subject thereto shares may be transferred outright or in security, attached by creditors, and pass under the owner's will or on intestacy.[57]

Dividends

A dividend, once declared by a company, is a debt owed by the company to each shareholder entitled by virtue of the ownership of shares at the date of closure of the company's transfer books.[58]

Uncalled share capital of companies

A company the share capital of which is partly uncalled and which consequently has a claim against its shareholders may assign the uncalled capital but this must be intimated to all the debtors, i.e. the shareholders.[59]

[53] *Colonial Bank* v. *Whinney* (1886) 11 App. Cas. 426; *Re Paulin* [1935] 1 K.B. 26, 57.
[54] Companies Act, 1948, S. 73; *Hog* v. *H.* (1791) Mor. 5457.
[55] Companies Act, 1948 S. 28(1)(a).
[56] e.g. *I.R.C.* v. *Crossman* [1937] A.C. 26.
[57] For sale of whole share capital see *Spencer* v. *Macmillan's Trs.*, 1958 S.C. 300.
[58] *Wallace, Hamilton & Co.* v. *Campbell* (1824) 2 Shaw's App. 467; *Re Irving, ex p. Brett* (1877) 7 Ch. D. 419; *Re Severn and Wye and Severn Bridge Rail Co.* [1896] 1 Ch. 559; *Bond* v. *Barrow Haematite Co.* [1902] 1 Ch. 353. As to payment, see *Thailwall* v. *G.N. Ry.* [1910] 2 K.B. 509.
[59] *Union Club Liqdr.* v. *Edinburgh Life Assce. Co.* (1906) 8 F. 1143; *Ballachulish Slate Quarries* v. *Malcolm* (1908) 15 S.L.T. 963; *Same* v. *Menzies* (1908) 16 S.L.T. 48.

ACQUISITION OF RIGHTS IN INTELLECTUAL PROPERTY

Intellectual property is a convenient general name for a group of kinds of incorporeal moveable objects of property most of which are regulated by statute and all of which are principally concerned with the protection of exclusive business rights against trade competitors or misuse by others.[1]

GOODWILL

Goodwill is the identity attaching to a professional, industrial or commercial undertaking rendering it probable that it will continue to do substantial business, to a greater extent than a new, though otherwise similar, undertaking. It is the value attaching to the likelihood that customers will again do business where they have done it before.[2] Goodwill may arise from the personal capacities and qualities of the person conducting the business,[3] or may be associated with the site and premises in which the undertaking is carried on,[4] or from the name, reputation and business connections of the undertaking,[5] or may arise from more than one of these elements. There may be a business goodwill though there are neither premises nor staff.[6] In some circumstances goodwill may be of no value.[7] Whether a particular business has a goodwill or not is a question of fact.[8]

Goodwill is distinguishable as an asset from both the premises in

---

[1] Generally Bell, *Comm.* I, 103; *Prin.* §1349 *et seq.*

[2] Bell, *Prin.* §1361 c (2). cf. *Cruttwell* v. *Lye* (1810) 17 Ves. 335; *Churton* v. *Douglas* (1859) John. 174; *Trego* v. *Hunt* [1896] A.C. 7.

[3] cf. *Bain* v. *Munro* (1878) 5 R. 416; *Drummond* v. *Leith Assessor* (1886) 13 R. 540; *Thatcher* v. *T.* (1904) 11 S.L.T. 605; *Rodger* v. *Herbertson*, 1909 S.C. 256; *Corbin* v. *Stewart* (1911) 28 T.L.R. 99.

[4] cf. *Bain* v. *Munro* (1878) 5 R. 416; *Bell's Tr.* v. *B.* (1884) 12 R. 85; *Philp's Exor.* v. *P's Exor.* (1894) 21 R. 482; *Brown* v. *Robertson* (1896) 4 S.L.T. 17.

[5] *Morrison* v. *M.* (1900) 2 F. 382; see also *Hughes* v. *Stirling Assessor* (1892) 19 R. 840.

[6] *Donald* v. *Hodgart's Trs.* (1893) 21 R. 246.

[7] *Bell's Tr.* v. *B.* (1884) 12 R. 85; *Graham* v. *G's Trs.* (1904) 6 F. 1015; *Mackenzie* v. *Macfarlane*, 1934 S.N. 16.

[8] *Reid* v. *R.*, 1938 S.L.T. 415.

which an existing business is conducted and from its business name,[9] its trade marks, trade names and stock-in-trade.[10] It may be sold,[11] attached for debt, bequeathed, or pass on intestacy.[12] It may be heritable,[13] moveable,[14] or partly both;[15] which it is is a question of fact in each case.[16] It may be protected by an action for passing off.[17]

A transfer of a practice or business carries the exclusive right to carry on the old business and represent the new as a continuation of the old business,[18] and includes rights to the sole use of the trade name,[19] to the exclusive use of trade marks,[20] to the delivery of business books and records,[21] and to the benefit of any existing contracts in restraint of trade.[22] But, unless there is an express restriction, it does not prevent the transferor commencing a new business of the same kind and even in adjacent premises.[23] A voluntary transferor may not solicit the business of former customers,[24] though he may deal with them if they come voluntarily to him,[25] and an involuntary transferor is not thus restricted.[26]

In other cases the transfer of a business identified with certain premises is hardly separable from the premises; the person acquiring the premises acquires the goodwill of the business,[27] and a person acquiring the goodwill acquires the transferor's interest to obtain a renewal of the lease.[28]

---

[9] *Barr* v. *Lions, Ltd.*, 1956 S.C. 59.

[10] *Guest's Exor.* v. *I.R.C.*, 1921 S.C. 440.

[11] cf. *Donald* v. *Hodgart's Trs.* (1893) 21 R. 246.

[12] *Brown* v. *Robertson* (1896) 4 S.L.T. 17; *Morrison's Tr.* v. *M.*, 1915 2 S.L.T. 296; contrast *Philp's Exor.*, *supra*.

[13] *Ross* v. *Ross's Trs.* (1901) 9 S.L.T. 340; *Town and Country Bank* v. *McBain* (1902) 9 S.L.T. 485; *Muirhead's Tr.* v. *M.* (1905) 7 F. 496.

[14] cf. *Bain* v. *Munro* (1878) 5 R. 416.

[15] *Murray's Tr.* v. *McIntyre* (1904) 6 F. 588.

[16] *Leishman* v. *Glen & Henderson* (1899) 6 S.L.T. 328.

[17] *Haig* v. *Forth Blending Co.*, 1954 S.C. 35.

[18] *Churton*, *supra*; *Walker* v. *Mottram* (1882) 19 Ch. D. 355.

[19] *Churton*, *supra*; *Bradbury* v. *Dickens* (1859) 27 Beav. 53; *Levy* v. *Walker* (1879) 10 Ch. D. 436; *Smith* v. *McBride* (1888) 16 R. 36.

[20] Trade Marks Act, 1938; cf. *Cotton* v. *Gillwood* (1875) 44 L.J. Ch. 90; *Ex p. Lawrence* (1881) 44 L.T. (N.S.) 98.

[21] *Morrison* v. *M.* (1900) 2 F. 382.

[22] *Townsend* v. *Jarman* [1900] 2 Ch. 698; *Automobile Carriage Builders* v. *Sayers* (1909) 101 L.T. 419.

[23] *Cruttwell*, *supra*; *Churton*, *supra*; *Trego*, *supra*.

[24] *Trego*, *supra*; *Dumbarton Steamboat Co.* v. *MacFarlane* (1899) 1 F. 993.

[25] *Curl Bros.* v. *Webster* [1904] 1 Ch. 685.

[26] *Ginesi* v. *Cooper* (1880) 14 Ch. D. 596; *Walker* v. *Mottram* (1882) 19 Ch. D. 355; *Dawson* v. *Benson* (1822) 22 Ch. D. 504.

[27] *Bain* v. *Munro* (1878) 5 R. 416; *Bell's Tr.* v. *B.* (1884) 12 R. 85; *Brown* v. *Robertson* (1896) 33 S.L.R. 570; *Leishman* v. *Glen & Henderson* (1899) 6 S.L.T. 328; *Thomson* v. *T.* (1899) 1 F. 1134.

[28] *Brown*, *supra*.

Goodwill, unless purely personal, passes on sequestration to the trustee in bankruptcy.[29]

It is a question of fact and degree at what point a discontinued business loses its goodwill.[30]

TRADE NAMES

A person has a prima facie right to trade under his own name and the court is reluctant to prevent him doing so.[31] But he may be prevented from doing so if the consequence is the probability of deceiving the public into thinking that his business or goods are those of another.[32] Intent to deceive need not be proved.[33] A person may not carry on business or trade under a name likely to mislead the public into thinking that it is the business of another.[34] An individual or firm carrying on business under a name other than his own name or the true names of all partners must disclose it in prescribed ways.[35]

A trade name passes with the goodwill of the business and, in view of the greater risk of confusion, the court is more ready to limit the seller's liberty to carry on business thereafter under the same, or a deceptively similar, name.[36]

The court will readily restrict the use as a trade name of a fancy name if it has become associated with the pursuer's goods and there is material risk of confusion,[37] but will less readily restrict the use of a descriptive name.[38]

[29] Bankruptcy (Sc.) Act, 1913, S. 97; *Coupland's Tr.* v. C. (1886) 23 S.L.R. 456; *Stewart's Tr.* v. *Stewart's Exrx.* (1896) 23 R. 739; *Melrose-Drover, Ltd.* v. *Heddle* (1902) 4 F. 1120.

[30] *Ad-Lib Club* v. *Granville* [1971] 2 All E.R. 300.

[31] *Turton* v. *T.* (1889) 42 Ch. D. 128; *Wright, Layman and Umney, Ltd.* v. *Wright* (1949) 66 R.P.C. 149.

[32] *Smith* v. *McBride and Smith* (1888) 16 R. 36; *Bayer* v. *Baird* (1898) 25 R. 1142; *Cooper & McLeod* v. *McLachlan* (1901) 9 S.L.T. 41; *Williamson, infra; Rodgers, infra; Marengo* v. *Daily Sketch* (1948) 65 R.P.C. 242; *Baume* v. *Moore* [1958] Ch. 907; *John Haig & Co.* v. *John D. D. Haig, Ltd.,* 1957 S.L.T. (Notes) 36; cf. *Boswell* v. *Mathie* (1884) 11 R. 1072.

[33] *Singer Mfg. Co.* v. *Kimball & Morton* (1873) 11 M. 267; *G.N.S. Ry.* v. *Mann* (1892) 19 R. 1035; *Rolls Razor, Ltd.* v. *Rolls Lighter, Ltd.* (1949) 66 R.P.C. 299; *Baume, supra.*

[34] *Cowan* v. *Millar* (1895) 22 R. 833; *Resartus Co.* v. *Sartor Resartus Co.* (1908) 16 S.L.T. 210; *Williamson* v. *Meikle,* 1909 S.C. 1272; *Rodgers* v. *Rodgers* (1924) 41 R.P.C. 227; *Office Cleaning Services, Ltd.* v. *Westminster Window and General Cleaners, Ltd.* (1946) 63 R.P.C. 39; cf. *Baird & Tatlock (London), Ltd.* v. *Baird & Tatlock, Ltd.,* 1917 1 S.L.T. 46.

[35] Companies Act, 1981, Ss. 28–30.

[36] *Melrose-Drover* v. *Heddle* (1901) 4 F. 1120; *Townsend* v. *Jarman* [1900] 2 Ch. 698; cf. *Barr* v. *Lions, Ltd.,* 1956 S.C. 59.

[37] *Premier Cycle Co.* v. *Premier Tube Co.* (1896) 12 T.L.R. 481; *Crystalate Gramophone Record Mfg. Co.* v. *British Crystalite Co., Ltd.* (1934) 51 R.P.C. 315; *Exxon Corpn.* v. *Exxon Insurance Consultants Ltd.* [1981] 2 All E.R. 495.

[38] *General Radio Co.* v. *General Radio Co. (Westminster), Ltd.* [1957] R.P.C. 471; cf. *Bile Bean Mfg. Co.* v. *Davidson* (1906) 8 F. 1181; *Scottish Union and National Ins. Co.* v. *Sc. National Ins. Co.,* 1909 S.C. 318.

The court may restrain the use as a trade name of a place of business if likely to confuse,[39] or of a local name.[40]

Similarly a person or body may not adopt a professional designation, or abbreviation thereof, liable to lead the public to believe that he or they belong to an existing, recognized, body using that designation or abbreviation.[41]

Trade name of goods

Independently of registered trade marks, no trader has any right of property in a trade name or mark, but he may by interdict prevent another trader representing his goods to be those of the complainer,[42] or of a different quality or class,[43] and this right is a proprietary one.[44] No fraudulent representation need be proved,[45] but only the likelihood of deception of a substantial section of the trade or of the public.[46] There is no right or interest in the 'Scottishness' of a product save where that is part of a trade description.[47]

The pursuer must prove that the name, mark or other feature in question has by exclusive use by him for some time become regarded as indicative of his goods,[48] and that its use by the defender was calculated or likely to deceive and to cause confusion and damage to the goodwill of his business.[49]

The wrong of passing off is wider than misuse of a party's trade name or trade mark of goods and may include use of slogans or visual

---

[39] G.N.S. Ry. v. Mann (1892) 19 R. 1035; Cowan v. Millar (1895) 22 R. 833; Cooper & McLeod v. Maclachlan (1901) 18 R.P.C. 380; Boussod, Valadon & Co. v. Marchant (1907) 25 R.P.C. 42; cf. Charleson v. Campbell (1876) 4 R. 149; Crawford's trs. v. Lennox (1896) 23 R. 747.

[40] Montgomerie v. Donald (1884) 11 R. 506; Rugby Portland Cement Co. v. Rugby and Newbold Portland Cement Co., Ltd. (1891) 9 R.P.C. 46; Grand Hotel Co. of Caledonia Springs, Ltd. v. Wilson [1904] A.C. 103; cf. Lochgelly Iron Co. v. Lumphinnans Iron Co. (1879) 6 R. 482; Dunnachie v. Young (1883) 10 R. 874.

[41] Socy. of Accountants in Edinburgh v. Corporation of Accountants (1893) 20 R. 750; Corporation of Accountants v. Society of Accountants in Edinburgh (1903) 11 S.L.T. 424.

[42] Reddaway v. Banham [1896] A.C. 199; Birmingham Brewery Co. v. Powell [1897] A.C. 710; Bass, Ratcliff & Gretton v. Laidlaw (1908) 16 S.L.T. 660; Oertli v. Bowman [1959] R.P.C. 1.

[43] Spalding v. Gamage (1915) 32 R.P.C. 273; Britains v. Morris [1961] R.P.C. 217.

[44] Reddaway, supra; Spalding, supra; Bollinger v. Costa Brava Wine Co. [1960] Ch. 262.

[45] Spalding, supra; Baume v. Moore [1958] Ch. 907.

[46] Cellular Clothing Co. v. Maxton & Murray (1899) 1 F. (H.L.) 29; Office Cleaning Services, supra; Haig v. Forth Blending Co., 1954 S.C. 35.

[47] Lang Bros v. Goldwell, 1977 S.C. 74.

[48] Singer Mfg. Co. v. Kimball & Morton (1873) 11 M. 267; Birmingham Brewery Co. v. Powell [1897] A.C. 710; Bayer v. Baird (1898) 25 R. 1142; Cellular Clothing Co. v. Maxton & Murray (1899) 1 F. (H.L.) 29; Kinnell v. Ballantyne, 1910 S.C. 246. See also John Dewar v. Dewar (1900) 7 S.L.T. 462; Woolley v. Morrison (1904) 6 F. 451; Dunlop Tyre Co. v. Dunlop Motor Co., 1907 S.C. (H.L.) 15.

[49] Haig v. J. D. D. Haig Ltd., 1957 S.L.T. (Notes) 36; Erven Warnink Besloten Vernootschap v. Townsend [1979] 2 All E.R. 927.

images associated by advertising with the pursuer's product, if that material has become so associated with the pursuer's product that he has acquired a proprietary right in it.[50]

TRADE SECRETS

Trade secrets are bodies of knowledge, whether relating to customers, markets, sources of supply or methods of manufacture or otherwise, which a person in business or trade regards as and seeks to preserve as peculiarly his own. No exclusive or proprietary right is, however, legally recognized in trade secrets as such, except in so far as they are the subject of trade marks, patents, registered designs, copyright, or plant breeders' rights, and there is no appropriation of property by discovering or annexing or publishing another's trade secrets.[51]

The disclosure of trade secrets may be restricted by restrictive conditions in the contracts of employment of certain employees, in which case they are enforceable if reasonable,[52] and may be actionable as in breach of confidentiality.[53] Apart from these cases an employer cannot prevent or restrain an employee from using, after the employment has ended, any knowledge or skill gained during the employment.[54]

Trade secrets may be sold or shared but no form of assignation is required.

TRADE MARKS

A trade mark means a mark used in relation to goods for the purpose of indicating or so as to indicate a connection in the course of trade between the goods and some person having the right either as proprietor or as registered user to use the mark, whether with or

---

[50] *Cadbury Schweppes Ltd.* v. *Pub Squash Co. Ltd.* [1981] 1 All E.R. 213.

[51] cf. *Massam* v. *Thorley's Cattle Food Co.* (1877) 6 Ch. D. 574; *United Indigo Co.* v. *Robinson* (1932) 49 R.P.C. 178.

[52] It probably may be reasonable even if unlimited in space or time; see *Leather Cloth Co.* v. *Lorsont* (1869) L.R. 9 Eq. 345; *Davies* v. *D.* (1887) 36 Ch. D. 359; *Forster* v. *Suggett* (1918) 35 T.L.R. 87; *Vandervell Products* v. *McLeod* [1957] R.P.C. 185.

[53] *Neuman* v. *Kennedy* (1905) 12 S.L.T. 763; *Mustad* v. *Allcock* (1928) in [1963] 3 All E.R. 416; *Saltman Eng. Co.* v. *Campbell Eng. Co.* (1948) 65 R.P.C. 203; *Peter Pan Mfg. Corpn.* v. *Corsets Silhouette, Ltd.* [1963] 3 All E.R. 402; *Levin* v. *Caledonian Produce (Holdings)*, 1975 S.L.T. (Notes) 69. cf. *Brown's Trs.* v. *Hay* (1898) 25 R. 1112; *Schering Chemicals* v. *Falkman* [1981] 2 All E.R. 321.

[54] *Morris* v. *Saxelby* [1916] 1 A.C. 688; *Attwood* v. *Lamont* [1920] 3 K.B. 571.

without any indication of the identity of that person.[55] A mark includes a device, brand, heading, label, ticket, name, signature, word, letter, numeral, or any combination thereof.[55]

At common law a trader who attached a distinctive name or mark to his goods could prevent others copying it in a way misleading to the public on proof that the name had become so associated with his goods as to connote in the market that they were his manufacture or supply.[56]

Since 1875 trade marks may be registered whereby the proprietor obtains a statutory title and need not prove long association to establish his title to the mark.[57] No person may institute any proceeding to prevent or recover damages for the infringement of an unregistered trade mark, without prejudice to the right of action for passing-off goods as those of another.[58]

Registration

There is maintained at the Patent Office, a register of trade marks, divided into Part A and Part B, wherein are entered all registered trade marks with the names, addresses and descriptions of their proprietors, notifications of assignations and transmissions, the names, addresses and descriptions of all registered users, disclaimers, conditions, limitations and such other matters as may be prescribed.[59] A trade mark must be registered in respect of particular goods or classes of goods.[60]

The register may be rectified,[61] or a registration varied or expunged for breach of a condition,[62] or it may be corrected,[63] or the trade mark altered in any manner not substantially affecting its identity.[64]

The registrar may give preliminary advice as to distinctiveness to a person proposing to apply for the registration of a trade mark.[65]

REGISTRABILITY—PART A

To be registrable in Part A a trade mark must contain or consist of at least one of the essentials: (a) the name of a company, individual, or firm, represented in a special or particular manner; (b) the signature of the applicant for registration or some predecessor in his business; (c)

---

[55] Trade Marks Act, 1938, S. 68(1). The mark may cover the whole of the visible surface of the goods to which it is applied: *Smith-Kline* v. *Sterling-Winthrop* [1975] 2 All E.R. 578.

[56] *Singer Mfg. Co.* v. *Loog* (1880) 18 Ch. D. 395; *Reddaway* v. *Banham* [1896] A.C. 199; *Kinnell* v. *Ballantine*, 1910 S.C. 246.

[57] *Boord* v. *Thom & Cameron*, 1907 S.C. 1326, 1342; *Champagne Heidsieck* v. *Buxton* [1930] 1 Ch. 330.

[58] 1938 Act, S. 2.

[59] 1938 Act, S. 1; Trade Marks Rules, 1938; Marks may also be registered at Sheffield in respect of cutlery, and at Manchester for textiles: Ss. 38–9.

[60] 1938 Act, S. 3.   [61] 1938 Act, S. 32.   [62] 1938 Act, S. 33.
[63] 1938 Act, S. 34.   [64] 1938 Act, S. 35.   [65] 1938 Act, S. 42.

an invented word or words; (d) a word or words having no direct reference to the character or quality of the goods, and not being according to its ordinary signification a geographical name or surname, (e) any other distinctive mark, but a name or a surname, signature or word or words, other than under the foregoing heads, is not registrable except upon evidence of its distinctiveness.[66]

In all legal proceedings relating to registration the original registration in Part A is to be taken, after seven years, as valid in all respects, unless it were obtained by fraud, or the trade mark is likely to deceive or cause confusion, or is contrary to law or morality, or scandalous.[67]

The mark must always be distinctive;[68] it need satisfy only one of the five essentials.[69]

(a) Name

If a name is used, it must be that of a real, not an imaginary person,[70] unless used in the possessive case,[71] or a surname used alone,[72] or a name printed in the ordinary manner.[73]

(c) Invented word

An invented word must have been substantially new when first used by the applicant or at the date of registration, but need not have required great ingenuity to invent.[74] The use of an old word in a new sense is not invention, and the addition of an affix to a known word may not make it an invented word.[75] The combination of ordinary words,[76] a variant spelling,[77] a common descriptive foreign word,[78] a foreign place name[79] and an American slang term[79] will not normally be accepted as invented words.

(d) No direct reference to character or quality

A word 'having no direct reference to the character or quality of the

[66] 1938 Act, S. 9(2); 'distinctive' is defined: S. 9(2).
[67] 1938 Act, S. 13.
[68] Re Fanfold, Ltd.'s Appln. (1928) 45 R.P.C. 325; Smith-Kline v. Sterling-Winthrop [1975] 2 All E.R. 578.
[69] Re Diamond T. Motor Co. [1921] 2 Ch. 583.
[70] Re Holt & Co.'s T.M. [1896] 1 Ch. 711.
[71] Pirie's T.M. [1892] 1 Ch. 35.
[72] Re Teofani & Co.'s T.M. (1913) 30 R.P.C. 446.
[73] Re Fanfold, Ltd.'s Appln., supra; Staines v. La Rosa (1953) 70 R.P.C. 62.
[74] Re Eastman Co., Ltd.'s Appln. [1898] A.C. 571; Re Kodak, Ltd.'s T.M. (1903) 20 R.P.C. 337.
[75] Re Eastman Co., supra; Re T. M. Haematogen (1904) 20 T.L.R. 585.
[76] Re Eastman Co., supra; Re Minnesota Co.'s Appln. (1924) 41 R.P.C. 237.
[77] Re Eastman Co., supra; cf. Stuart & Co. v. Scottish Val de Travers Co. (1885) 13 R. 1.
[78] Re Boots Drug Co.'s T.M. [1938] Ch. 54.
[79] Re La Marquise Footwear's Appln. (1946) 64 R.P.C. 27.

goods' permits the registration of words though they may suggest some object or quality of such goods.[80]

A word 'not being . . . a geographical name' excludes well known place names, but not necessarily every name attaching to some place in the world.[81]

(e) *Any other distinctive mark*

A surname is not registrable under the fourth head, but may be under the fifth, if distinctiveness is established.[82] In determining distinctiveness the court may consider the inherent qualities of the mark and how far other circumstances have rendered it adapted to distinguish.[83]

REGISTRABILITY—PART B

To be registrable in Part B a trade mark must be capable, in relation to the goods in respect of which it is registered or proposed to be registered, of distinguishing goods with which the proprietor of the trade mark is or may be connected in trade from goods in the case of which no such connection subsists either generally, or, where the trade mark is registered or proposed to be registered subject to limitations, in relation to use within the extent of the registration.[84] A trade mark may be registered in Part B notwithstanding any registration in Part A in the name of the same proprietor of the same trade mark. A Part B mark does not acquire any presumed validity after seven years.

Registrations prohibited

It is not lawful to register as a trade mark or part thereof any matter the use of which would, by reason of its being likely to deceive or cause confusion or otherwise, be disentitled to protection in as court of justice, or contrary to law or morality, or any scandalous design.[85] The registration of identical and resembling trade marks, save exceptionally, is prohibited.[86]

Registration may be allowed only subject to disclaimer by the proprietor of any right to the exclusive use of the mark.[87]

---

[80] e.g. *Re Compagnie Industrielle des Petroles' Appln.* [1907] 2 Ch. 435; *Re J. & P. Coats, Ltd.'s Appln.* [1936] 2 All E.R. 975.

[81] *Boots Pure Drug Co.* [1938] Ch. 540.

[82] *Re Teofani & Co.'s T.M.* [1913] 2 Ch. 545; *Re Barford & Co., Ltd.'s Appln.* [1919] 2 Ch. 28.

[83] *Yorkshire Copper Works. Ltd. v. T.M. Registrar* [1954] 1 All E.R. 570.

[84] 1938 Act, S. 10; see *H. Quennell, Ltd.'s Appln.* (1955) 72 R.P.C. 36; *Goodyear Tyre and Rubber Co.'s Appln.* [1957] R.P.C. 173.

[85] 1938 Act, S. 11; *G.E. Co. of U.S.A. v. G.E. Co.* [1972] 2 All E.R. 507.

[86] 1938 Act, S. 12; cf. *Electrolux, Ltd. v. Electrix, Ltd.* (1954) 71 R.P.C. 23; *Kidax (Shirts), Ltd.'s Appln.* [1960] R.P.C. 117. [87] 1938 Act, S. 14.

The use of the Royal Arms without authority may be restrained.[88]
The use of the Red Cross and associated emblems is also restricted.[89]

A registration does not become invalid by reason of the use, subsequent to the registration, of words in the trade mark as the name or description of an article or substance.[90]

Application for registration

Registration is obtained by application in writing to the registrar by a person claiming to be the proprietor of a trade mark used or proposed to be used by him. The person who first designed or used a trade mark is entitled to claim to be proprietor.[91] For the purposes of registration goods are classified in thirty-four classes.[92] The registrar may, instead of refusing it, treat an application for Part A as one for Part B. The Registrar's decision may be appealed to the Department of Trade or to the Court of Session.[93]

Once accepted an application must be advertised and any person may give notice of opposition to the registration, whereupon the registrar must decide whether and subject to what conditions, if any, the registration is to be permitted. His decision may be appealed to the Court.[94] Thereafter the Registrar registers the trade mark as of the date of the application, and issues the applicant a certificate in the prescribed form.[95] Notice of a trust will not be entered in the register.[96]

In all legal proceedings registration is prima facie evidence of the validity of the original registration and of all subsequent assignations and transmissions.[97] If the validity of registration is challenged in any case and decided in favour of the proprietor the court may give a certificate of validity.[98]

Duration of Registration

Registration endures for seven years and may be renewed for fourteen years at a time.[99] If renewal be not requested at the due time the registrar may remove the mark from the register, but may later, if satisfied that it is just to do so, restore it.[99]

[88] 1938 Act, S. 61; see *Royal Warrant Holder's Assoc.* v. *Deane & Beal* [1912] 1 Ch. 10; *Re Imperial Tobacco Co.'s Appln.* [1915] 2 Ch. 27; *Royal Warrant Holder's Assocn.* v. *Robb*, 1935 S.N. 32.
[89] Geneva Conventions Act, 1957, S. 6.
[90] 1938 Act, S. 15.
[91] *Gynomin T.M.* [1961] R.P.C. 408.
[92] Trade Mark Rules, 1938, Sched. IV.
[93] 1938 Act, S. 17.
[94] 1938 Act, S. 18.
[95] 1938 Act, S. 19.
[96] 1938 Act, S. 64.
[97] 1938 Act, S. 46.
[98] 1938 Act, S. 47.
[99] 1938 Act, S. 20.

False representation of registration

It is an offence falsely to represent that a mark is a registered trade mark and in various other respects.[1]

Rights on registration: infringement

Registration in Part A as proprietor of a trade mark, if valid, gives that person the exclusive right to the use of the trade mark in relation to those goods, and that right is infringed by any person who, not being the proprietor or a registered user using by way of the permitted use, uses a mark identical with it or so nearly resembling it as to be likely to deceive or cause confusion, in the course of trade, in relation to any goods in respect of which it is registered, and in such manner as to render the use of the mark likely to be taken either as being used as a trade mark, or as importing a reference to some person having the right either as proprietor or as registered user to use the trade mark or to goods with which such a person as aforesaid is connected in the course of trade. The right to the use of a trade mark is subject to any conditions or limitations entered on the register.[2]

Registration in Part B as proprietor of a trade mark in respect of any goods, if valid, gives that person the same rights as if the registration had been in Part A. In an action for infringement of the right to the use of a trade mark given by registration in Part B, otherwise than by infringements under S. 6, no interdict or other remedy shall be granted to the pursuer if the defender satisfies the court that the use of which the pursuer complains is not likely to deceive or cause confusion or to be taken as indicating a connection in the course of trade between the goods and some person having the right as proprietor or as registered user to use the trade mark.[3]

The use complained of as infringing must be in the course of trade,[4] and the likelihood of deception must be considered in relation to the place of sale of the goods.[5] Use in an advertisement is infringement.[6] Use of the essential features of a trade mark, though added to or modified, is infringement.[7]

---

[1] 1938 Act, S. 60.

[2] 1938 Act, S. 4; *Aristoc v. Rysta* [1945] A.C. 68; *Coca- Cola Co. v. Struthers*, 1968 S.C. 214. The right to use is not deemed infringed by certain uses, specified in S. 4(3) and (4).

[3] 1938 Act, S. 5.

[4] *Aristoc, Ltd. v. Rysta, Ltd.* [1945] A.C. 68; *Ravok v. National Trade Press, Ltd.* [1955] 1 Q.B. 554.

[5] *Ballantine v. Ballantyne Stewart & Co.* [1959] R.P.C. 273; cf. *Cowie Bros. v. Herbert* (1897) 24 R. 353.

[6] *Hindhaugh v. Inch*, 1923 S.L.T. 667; *Reuter v. Mulhens* [1954] Ch. 50.

[7] *Saville Perfumery Co. v. Perfect* (1941) 58 R.P.C. 147; cf. *Board v. Thom & Cameron*, 1907 S.C. 1326.

Exceptions

Exclusive right to the use of a registered trade mark is not, however, infringed if the goods are to be sold or traded in a place to which the registration does not extend, or where the proprietor has applied the mark or impliedly consented to its use for the goods, or the use of the mark is reasonably necessary to describe parts for articles which bear or might bear the mark,[8] or the use is by a person who can prove continuous use by himself or his predecessors prior to the registration and use by the proprietor or his predecessors,[9] or there is bona fide use by a person of the name, or the name of the place of business, of himself or any of his predecessors in business,[10] or use by any person of a bona fide description of the character or quality of his goods, provided that this does not import a prohibited reference,[11] or by reason of concurrent use the defender is entitled to be registered for the mark used.[12]

Assignation and transmission

A registered trade mark is assignable and transmissible in connection with the goodwill of a business or separately, in respect of some or all of the goods in respect of which it is registered, except where the result would be that more than one person would enjoy exclusive rights to use identical or similar trade marks the use of which is likely to deceive. The Registrar may certify to a proprietor proposing to assign whether his proposed assignment would be invalid.[13]

Associated trade marks, registered by the same proprietor in respect of the same description of goods or nearly resembling each other, are assignable and transmissible as a whole only, unless the registrar dissolves the association.[14]

The registered proprietor may assign and give receipts for any consideration.[15] Assignees or beneficiaries by transmission must apply to the Registrar for registration as proprietors of the trade mark.[16]

Registered users

A person other than the proprietor of a trade mark may be registered as a registered user in respect of any or all of the goods in respect of which it is registered. A registered user may call on the proprietor to

---

[8] 1938 Act, S. 4(2) and (3).
[9] 1938 Act, S. 7.
[10] 1938 Act, S. 8(a): *Baume* v. *Moore* [1958] Ch. 907.
[11] 1938 Act, S. 8(b).
[12] 1938 Act, S. 12(2).
[13] 1938 Act, S. 22.
[14] 1938 Act, S. 23.
[15] 1938 Act, S. 24.
[16] 1938 Act, S. 25.

take proceedings to prevent infringement and, if the latter fails to do so, may do so himself. He may not assign or transmit the right to the use of the trade mark.[17]

Removal from register

A registered trade mark may be removed from the register, on the application of a person aggrieved, on the ground of non-use.[18]

Defensive registration

If a trade mark consisting of an invented word or words has become so well known in respect of certain goods that its use in relation to other goods would be likely to be taken as indicating a connection between them and the proprietor of the trade mark, he may register it in respect of the other goods as a defensive trade mark.[19]

PATENTS

A patent is a Crown grant, formerly under letters patent sealed with the Great Seal, now in a form authorized by statutory rules and sealed with the seal of the Patent Office but having the same effect,[20] of monopoly rights in respect of an invention. The issue of patents is regulated on behalf of the Crown by the Comptroller General of Patents, Designs and Trade Marks, subject to the supervision of the Department of Trade,[21] and appeal from most decisions of the comptroller lies to an Outer House judge of the Court of Session, with further appeal to the Inner House in certain circumstances or on the ground that the decision of the Outer House judge is wrong in law.[22] Nothing in the 1949 Act abridges or prejudices the Crown prerogative in relation to letters patent.[23]

There is maintained at the Patent Office a register of patents in which are entered particulars of patents in force, assignations and transmissions of patents and notice of all matters required by the Acts to be entered in the register and of all other matters affecting the validity or proprietorship of patents as the comptroller thinks fit. It is open to the public. No notice of any trust is entered therein and the comptroller is not affected by notice thereof.[24] The court may order

---

[17] 1938 Act, S. 28.
[18] 1938 Act, S. 26; cf. *John Dewar & Sons* v. *Dewar* (1900) 7 S.L.T. 461.
[19] 1938 Act, S. 27.
[20] Patents Act, 1949, S. 21(1). For form see Patents Rules, 1958, Sched. III.
[21] The Patents Act, 1949, as amended, regulates patents granted under it. New applications are made under the Patents Act, 1977, and the Patents Rules, 1978 (S.I. 216, 1978).
[22] 1977 Act, Ss. 97–8. See also Ss. 99–108.
[23] 1949 Act, S. 102.   [24] 1977 Act, S. 32.

rectification of the register[25] and the comptroller may correct errors in a patent, application or relative document.[26]

The comptroller must on request furnish information as to any patent or application for a patent.[27]

The false representation that any article sold is a patented article is an offence;[28] so also is the false representation that a patent has been applied for.[29]

The monopoly right prevents any other person from making or using the patented article or process; it does not confer on the patentee any right to manufacture the invention, for that he was without any patent.[30]

There are now three kinds of patents, patents under the 1977 Act, patents (U.K.), and Community patents. The rules applicable to patents under the Act are closely modelled on the European system and differ in many respects from those under earlier U.K. legislation.

PATENTS UNDER DOMESTIC LAW

Domestic law—what is patentable

A patent may be granted for an invention only if it is new,[31] involves an inventive step,[32] is capable of industrial application[33] and is not declared excluded as not being an invention. Among things declared not to be inventions are (a) a discovery, scientific theory or mathematical method,[34] (b) a literary, dramatic, musical or artistic work or any other aesthetic creation whatsoever,[35] (c) a scheme, rule or method for performing a mental act, playing a game or doing business, or a program for a computer, (d) the preservation of information. A patent cannot be granted for an invention the publication or exploitation of which would be generally expected to encourage offensive, immoral or anti-social behaviour, or for any variety of animal or plant or any essentially biological process, for the production of animals or plants, not being a micro-biological process or the product of such a process.

---

[25] Ibid., S. 34.
[26] Ibid., S. 117.
[27] Ibid., S. 118.
[28] Ibid., S. 110.
[29] Ibid., S. 111.
[30] *Steers* v. *Rodger* (1893) 10 R.P.C. 245.
[31] 1977 Act, S. 2, *infra*.
[32] Ibid., S. 3, *infra*.
[33] Ibid., S. 4, *infra*.
[34] cf. *Neilson* v. *Househill Coal Co.* (1842) 4 D. 1187, 1201; (sequel 5 D. 86, 180); *Reynolds* v. *Smith* (1903) 20 R.P.C. 123; *B.T.H.* v. *Charlesworth Peebles & Co.* (1925) 42 R.P.C. 180.
[35] These are covered by copyright and industrial designs.

The Secretary of State has power to vary the list of things not inventions.[36]

Novelty

An invention is taken to be new if it does not form part of the state of the art, which comprises all matter (whether a product, process, information about either, or anything else) which has at any time before the priority date of that invention been made available to the public in the U.K. or elsewhere by written or oral description, by use or otherwise, and, in the case of an invention to which an application for, or a patent, relates, comprises also matter contained in an application for another patent published on or after the priority date of that invention, subject to certain conditions. Certain recent disclosures of matter are to be disregarded.[37]

Inventive step

An invention is taken to involve an inventive step if it is not obvious to a person skilled in the art, having regard to any matter which forms part of the state of the art by virtue only of S. 2(2).[38]

Industrial application

An invention is capable of industrial application if it can be made or used in any kind of industry, including agriculture; this excludes a method of treatment of the human or animal body by surgery, therapy or diagnosis but not necessarily a product consisting of a substance or composition invented for use in any such method.[39]

Priority date

The priority date of an invention to which an application for a patent relates or for which a patent has been granted is the date of filling the application for a patent. In certain circumstances it may be up to twelve months earlier.[40]

Right to apply for and obtain a patent

A person may apply alone or jointly with another and a patent may be granted to the inventor, i.e. actual deviser of the invention, or joint inventors, or, in preference to them, to a person who was entitled to

---

[36] Ibid., S. 1. On extent of invention see also S. 125.
[37] Ibid., S. 2. cf. *Molins v. Industrial Machinery Co.* [1937] 4 All E.R. 295; *Allmanna Svenska Elektriska A/B v. Burntisland Shipping Co.* (1952) 69 R.P.C. 63; *Lyle & Scott Ltd. v. Wolsey*, 1955 S.L.T. 322.
[38] Ibid., S. 3.
[39] Ibid., S. 4.
[40] Ibid., Ss. 5–6.

the whole of the property in the invention when it was made, or the successors in title of any of these persons.[41] Before a patent has been granted a person may refer to the comptroller whether he is entitled to a grant.[42] Questions about entitlement to foreign and convention patents may similarly be referred.[43] An inventor is entitled to be mentioned in any patent granted and an applicant must identify the inventor.[44]

Application

Application for a patent is made in the prescribed form to the Patent Office and contains (a) a request for the grant of a patent and (b) a specification containing a description of the invention disclosing the invention in a manner clear and complete enough for the invention to be performed by a person skilled in the art, a claim or claims and any drawing referred to in the description or any claim, and (c) an abstract. The claim or claims must define the matter for which the applicant seeks protection, be clear and concise, be supported by the description, and relate to one invention or to a group of inventions which are so linked as to form a single inventive concept.[45] The purpose of the abstract is to give technical information, and the comptroller may reference it to ensure that it does so adequately. An application may be withdrawn and the withdrawal is not revocable.[46]

The date of filing an application is the earliest date on which the documents filed disclose the necessary information.[47] The comptroller then publishes the application as filed and advertises the fact in the journal, containing particulars of applications and grants.[48]

Preliminary examination and search

On request being made within the prescribed period the comptroller refers the application to an examiner for preliminary examination, to determine whether it complies with the Act and other formal requirements, and for search, or such investigation as is reasonably practicable and necessary to identify the documents which the examiner thinks will be needed to decide on substantive examination under S. 18 whether the invention is new and involves an inventive step. If search would not serve a useful purpose, the examiner reports this to the comptroller.[49]

---

[41] Ibid., S. 7.
[42] Ibid., S. 8. Appeal lies to the Outer House and then to the Inner House.
[43] Ibid., S. 12.
[44] Ibid., S. 13.
[45] cf. *Mullard Radio Valve Ltd.* v. *Philco Radio Corpn.* (1936) 53 R.P.C. 323.
[46] Ibid., S. 14.   [47] Ibid., S. 15.
[48] Ibid., S. 16.   [49] Ibid., S. 17.

Substantive examination and grant or refusal of patent

On request made after preliminary examination and search the comptroller refers the application to an examiner for substantive examination. The examiner investigates whether the application complies with the Act and rules; the application may be amended. If it complies with the requirements the comptroller grants a patent.[50] Third parties may make observations to the comptroller on whether the invention is patentable or not.[51] Information in an application prejudicial to the defence of the realm or the public safety may be withheld from publication.[52] United Kingdom residents may not apply for a patent outside the U.K. unless they have done so in the U.K.[53]

Patents after grant—duration

When a patent has been granted the comptroller publishes in the journal a notice of this fact, and publishes the specification, the names of the proprietor and inventor, and other matters which he thinks should be published.[54] A patent is deemed granted and takes effect on the date on which notice of the grant is published in the journal and continues in force for twenty years from the date of filing the application. It may be renewed within six months of expiry on payment of fees.[55] A patent is not to be impugned for lack of unity.[56]

The comptroller may allow the specification to be amended retrospectively after grant.[57]

A patent which has expired and not been renewed may be restored within one year under certain conditions.[58] It may be surrendered on certain conditions.[59]

A patent or application for one and any right in or under either is, in Scotland, incorporeal moveable property, and may be assigned or security granted over it, by writing probative or holograph of the parties. A licence may be granted for working the invention, a sub-licence granted, and either may be assigned or security granted over it. An assignation or an exclusive licence may confer on the assignee or licensee the right to bring proceedings under Ss. 58, 61 or 69.[60]

Register of patents

There is kept at the Patent Office a register of patents which records grants, published applications, transactions, instruments or events affecting rights in or under patents and applications, and certain other information. No notice of any trust may be entered in the register.[61]

---

[50] Ibid., Ss. 18–20.   [51] Ibid., S. 21.   [52] Ibid., S. 22.
[53] Ibid., S. 23.   [54] Ibid., S. 24.   [55] Ibid., S. 25.
[56] Ibid., S. 26.   [57] Ibid., S. 27.   [58] Ibid., S. 28.
[59] Ibid., S. 29.   [60] Ibid., S. 31.   [61] Ibid., S. 32.

Property acquired in a patent or application by a registered assignation, grant in security, licence or sub-licence, death of a proprietor or
order of a court transferring a patent or application has priority over
any unregistered transaction, instrument or event of these kinds.[62] The
register may be rectified and it and certificates of entry in it are
admissible and sufficient evidence of anything required or authorized
to be registered.[63]

Co-ownership

Where a patent is granted to two or more persons each is entitled to
an equal individed share therein and each may do independently
anything which would otherwise be an infringement.[64]

After a patent has been granted any person may refer to the comptroller the question of entitlement to ownership of the patent and an
order transferring ownership may be made.[65]

Employees' inventions

An employee's inventions belong to his employer if made in the
course of his duties, with entitlement to compensation.[66] A term in a
contract relating to an employee's inventions which diminishes his
rights in inventions is unenforceable against him to the extent that it
diminishes his rights in an invention or in or under a patent therefor.[67]

Contracts as to patented products

Any condition or term of a contract for the supply of a patented
product or a licence to work a patented invention, or of a contract
relating to any such supply or licence is, subject to certain exceptions,
void in so far as it purports to impose certain restrictive conditions.[68]
Such a contract may, after the patents have ceased to be in force, be
determined to the extent that the contract or licence relates to the
product or invention by either party on three months' notice, without
prejudice to the rules of frustration or other rights to determine a
contract or licence.[69]

Licences

A patentee has power to grant licences; a licence may be granted
orally,[70] by deed, or by implication from conduct.[71] A licence permits
the doing of what would otherwise be an infringement. A licence,
unless it states to the contrary, is personal and not assignable.[72]

---

[62] Ibid., S. 33.   [63] Ibid., Ss. 34–5.   [64] Ibid., S. 36.
[65] Ibid., Ss. 37–8.   [66] Ibid., Ss. 39–41.   [67] Ibid., Ss. 42–3.
[68] Ibid., S. 44.   [69] Ibid., S. 45.
[70] *Crossley* v. *Dixon* (1863) 10 H.L. Cas. 293.
[71] *Tweedale* v. *Howard and Bullough Ltd.* (1896) 13 R.P.C. 522.
[72] *National Carbonising Co.* v. *British Coal Distilleries Co. Ltd.* (1936) 54 R.P.C. 41.

Licences of right and compulsory licences

After a patent is granted the proprietor may apply to the comptroller for an entry in the register that licences are to be available as of right. In that event any peron is entitled as of right to a licence under the patent on terms settled by agreement or by the comptroller. The licensee under a licence of right may request the proprietor to take proceedings against infringement; if he does not the licensee may do so in his own name. Such entry in the register may be cancelled.[73]

After three years from the grant of a patent any person may apply to the comptroller on stated grounds for a compulsory licence, or an entry in the register that licences are available as of right, or, where the applicant is a government department, the grant to a specified person of a licence.[74] In a case of monopoly or merger a Minister may apply for relief in respect of the patent, by cancellation or modification of conditions in the licence or order that licences are available as of right.[75]

Use of patented inventions for services of the Crown

Any government department and authorized person may, for the service of the Crown, without the consent of the proprietor of the patent, make use, import or keep the product, use the process, sell or offer to sell the invented drug or medicine, supply or offer to supply any of the means for putting the invention into effect, or dispose or offer to dispose of anything made, used, imported or kept in the exercise of these statutory powers, in some cases free of royalty, in other cases on terms to be agreed. Wider powers of use are permissible in a period of emergency.[76]

Infringement

A person infringes a patent only if, while the patent is in force, without the proprietor's consent, he makes, disposes of, offers to dispose of, uses or imports a patented product or keeps it for disposal or otherwise, uses a process or offers it for use in the U.K. when he knows, or it is obvious, that its use there without the proprietor's consent would be an infringement, or disposes of, offers to dispose of, uses or imports any product obtained directly by means of the patented process or keeps any such product for disposal or otherwise, or supplies or offers to supply a person other than the licensee with any of the means for putting the invention into effect when he knows, or it is

[73] Ibid., Ss. 46–7.
[74] Ibid., Ss. 48–50.
[75] Ibid., Ss. 51–3.
[76] Ibid., Ss. 55–9.

obvious, that those means are suitable for putting and intended to put the invention into effect in the U.K. An act prima facie an infringement is not one if (a) it is done privately and for non-commercial purposes, (b) it is done for experimental purposes, (c) it is done as the preparation in a pharmacy of a medicine in accordance with a prescription, (d) it consists in the use of a product or process in a foreign ship where it is temporarily or necessarily in the internal or territorial waters of the U.K., (e) it consists in the use of a product or process in the operation of a foreign aircraft, which has temporarily or accidentally entered or is crossing the U.K., or (f) it consists in the use of an aircraft exempted from seizure which has lawfully entered or is lawfully crossing the U.K.[77]

The proprietor of the patent may sue in respect of any act alleged to infringe the patent and claim (a) interdict,[78] (b) an order to deliver up or destroy any patented product in relation to which the patent is infringed or any article in which it is comprised, (c) damages,[79] (d) an account of profits derived from the infringement, and (e) declarator that the patent is valid and has been infringed. Damages and an account of profits may not both be given. The question of infringement may be referred to the comptroller, but he may decline to deal with it.[80] In infringement proceedings damages are not to be awarded nor an order made for an account of profits against a defender who proves he was not aware and had no reasonable grounds for supposing that the patent existed, and the mere word 'patented' without its number does not prove knowledge. The court may decline to award damages or order an account in respect of infringement during any period after expiry and before the renewal fee is paid, and no damages are to be awarded for infringement committed before the decision to allow an amendment of the specification unless the specification as published was framed in good faith and with reasonable skill and knowledge.[81] Relief may be granted for infringement of a partially valid patent.[82] A person who before the priority date does in good faith what would otherwise be infringement may continue to do so in certain cases.[83] The court or comptroller may certify that the validity of the patent was

[77] Ibid., S. 60.
[78] cf. *Plasticisers Ltd.* v. *Stewart*, 1972 S.C. 268.
[79] As to measure of damages see *United Horse Shoe Co.* v. *Stewart* (1888) 15 R. (H.L.) 45; *Watson Laidlaw Co.* v. *Pott, Cassels & Williamson*, 1914 S.C. (H.L.) 18; *B.T.H. Co.* v. *Charlesworth Peebles & Co.*, 1923 S.C. 599.
[80] Ibid., S. 61. As to proceedings by co-owners see S. 66, and by exclusive licensees see S. 67. Non-registration affects infringement proceedings: S. 68.
[81] Ibid., S. 62.
[82] Ibid., S. 63.
[83] Ibid., S. 64.

contested in proceedings before it or him and it was found wholly or partially valid.[84]

Once an application for a patent has been published the applicant has from publication until the grant of the patent the same rights to bring proceedings for damages as if the patent had been granted, with certain qualifications.[85]

Remedy for groundless threats of proceedings

Where a person threatens another with proceedings for infringement,[86] a person aggrieved by the threats may take proceedings and, unless the defender proves that the acts constitute or would constitute an infringement, and the patent is not shown by the pursuer to be invalid in a relevant respect, is entitled to declarator that the threats are unjustifiable, interdict against continuance of the threats, and damages in respect of loss by the threats. Mere notification of the existence of a patent is not a threat of proceedings.[87] A mere warning to take proceedings if anyone infringes is not actionable.[88] In the case of malicious threats an action for slander of title might lie.[89] It is no defence that the threat was made in good faith.[90] The mode is immaterial,[91] and a threat may be made by implication.[92] It need not be made directly to the person against whom proceedings would be taken.[93]

Declarator of non-infringement

In certain circumstances the court may grant declarator that an act does not, or would not, constitute infringement.[94]

Revocation

The court or comptroller may revoke a patent only on any of the grounds that (a) the invention was not a patentable invention, (b) it was granted to a person who was not the only person entitled, (c) the specification does not disclose the invention clearly enough and com-

---

[84] Ibid., S. 65; *V.D. Ltd.* v. *Boston Deep Sea Fishing Co.* (1934) 52 R.P.C. 1; *Martin* v. *C.B. Protection (Eng.) Ltd.* (1948) 65 R.P.C. 361; *Plasticisers Ltd.* v. *Stewart*, 1972 S.C. 268.
[85] Ibid., S. 69.
[86] *C. & P. Developments Co. (London) Ltd.* v. *Sisabro Novelty Co.* (1953) 70 R.P.C. 277; *Rosedale Assoc. Mfrs.* v. *Airfix Products Ltd.* [1956] R.P.C. 360.
[87] Ibid., S. 70. cf. *Speedcranes Ltd.* v. *Thomson*, 1972 S.C. 324.
[88] *Speedcranes Ltd., supra.*
[89] *Montgomerie* v. *Paterson* (1894) 11 R.P.C. 633; cf. *Cars* v. *Bland Light Syndicate* (1911) 28 R.P.C. 33.
[90] *Skinner* v. *Perry* (1893) 10 R.P.C. 1.
[91] *Kurtz* v. *Spence* (1888) 5 R.P.C. 161; *Ellis* v. *Pogson* (1923) 40 R.P.C. 62; *Luna Advertising Co.* v. *Burnham* (1928) 45 R.P.C. 258.
[92] *Luna, supra.*
[93] *Summers* v. *Cold Metal Process Co.* (1948) 65 R.P.C. 75.
[94] Ibid., S. 71.

pletely enough for it to be performed by a person skilled in the art, (d) the matter disclosed in the specification extends beyond that disclosed in the application as filed, or earlier application, or (e) the protection has been extended by an amendment which should not have been allowed. Revocation may be unconditional or conditional on amendment to the comptroller's satisfaction.[95] The comptroller may revoke patents on his own initiative.[96]

Putting validity in issue

The validity of a patent may be put in issue (a) by defence in proceedings for infringement under S. 61 or under S. 69; (b) under S. 70; (c) under S. 71; (d) under S. 72; (e) under S. 58; but not in other proceedings, and the only grounds on which it may be put in issue are those on which it may be revoked under the section. There are further restrictions in certain cases.[97]

Amendment of patents and applications

In cases where the validity of a patent is put in issue the court or the comptroller may in certain circumstances allow amendment of a specification.[98] Amendments are not to include added matter.[99]

PATENTS UNDER INTERNATIONAL CONVENTIONS

European patents (U.K.)

A European patent (U.K.), i.e. a patent granted under the European Patent Convention, 1973, designating the U.K., is from the publication of the mention of its grant in the European Patent Bulletin treated for the purposes of Parts I and II (Ss. 1–76, 96–132) of the Act as if it were a patent under the 1977 Act; accordingly the proprietor as regards the U.K. has the same rights and remedies as the proprietor of a patent under the Act.[1] An application for a European Patent (U.K.) having a date of filing under the European Patent Convention is treated as an application for a patent under the Act having that date as its date of filing, subject to certain modifications.[2] An application for a European Patent (U.K.) may be treated as an application for a patent under the Act in certain cases.[3] The court and the comptroller have jurisdiction to determine questions as to right to a patent in certain cases[4] and

[95] Ibid., S. 72.   [96] Ibid., S. 73.
[97] Ibid., S. 74.   [98] Ibid., S. 75.   [99] Ibid., S. 76.
[1] Ibid., S. 77. Under the European Patent Convention a single application is made to the European Patent Office and, when granted, the applicant receives a separate patent for each designated country.
[2] Ibid., Ss. 78–80.   [3] Ibid., S. 81.   [4] Ibid., S. 82.

determinations of competent authorities of other states are to be recognized in the U.K. in certain cases.[5]

Community patents

All rights, powers, liabilities, obligations and restrictions created or arising by or under the Community Patent Convention, 1975, and all remedies and procedures provided by or under it have legal effect in the U.K. and are to be used there, recognized and available in law and enforced, allowed and followed accordingly. Certain sections of the Act do not apply to any application which is treated as an application for a Community patent.[6] Decisions on the Community Patent Convention, 1975, are to be questions of law in the U.K.[7] Provision is made as to jurisdiction in connection with the Community Patent Convention.[8]

International applications for patents

An international application for a patent (U.K.) for which a date of filing has been accorded by the Patent Office or any other body under the Patent Co-operation Treaty, 1970, is to be treated for the purposes of Parts I and III of the 1977 Act as if it were an application under the Act.[9]

REGISTERED DESIGNS

A design means[10] features of shape, configuration, pattern or ornament[11] applied to an article by any industrial process or means, being features which in the finished article appeal to and are judged solely by the eye, but does not include a method or principle of construction or features of shape or configuration which are dictated solely by the function which the article to be made in that shape or configuration has to perform.

---

[5] Ibid., S. 83.

[6] Ibid., S. 86. Community patents are granted by the European Patent Office in Munich and have application throughout the E.E.C.

[7] Ibid., S. 87.

[8] Ibid., S. 88.

[9] Ibid., S. 89. Under the Patent Co-operation Treaty when a date of filing has been given to an application in a foreign country and it is designated U.K. it will be treated as an application for a U.K. patent. The U.K. Patent Office can then dispense with examination and search as the comptroller thinks fit.

[10] Registered Designs Act, 1949, S. 1(3); cf. *Harvey* v. *Secure Fittings, Ltd.*, 1966 S.L.T. 121.

[11] It has been said that shape and configuration apply to three dimensions and pattern or ornament to two: *Re Kestos, Ltd., regd. design* (1935) 53 R.P.C. 139, 152; see also *Hunter, Walker & Co.* v. *Falkirk Iron Co.* (1887) 14 R. 1072; *Hecla Foundry Co.* v. *Walker, Hunter & Co.* (1889) 16 R. (H.L.) 27.

Registration

Under the Registered Designs Acts, 1949 to 1961, there is maintained at the Patent Office[13] a register of designs, in which are recorded the names and addresses of the proprietors of registered designs, notices of assignations and transmissions of designs and such other matters as may be prescribed or as the registrar may think fit. The register is in general open to the public and certified copies of any entry in the register must be given to anyone requiring them.[13] The register is prima facie evidence of any matters required or authorized to be entered therein, but no notice of any trust may be entered therein.[13] The court may order rectification of the register[14] and the registrar may correct any error in an application or the representation of a design or any error in the register.[15]

On application by the person claiming to be the proprietor, a design may be registered in respect of any article or set of articles specified in the application. A design shall not be registered unless it is new or original, and shall not be registered if it is the same as a design previously registered or differs only in immaterial details or in features which are variants commonly used in the trade.[16] The registrar grants a certificate of registration.[17] Thereafter the representation or specimen of the design registered is generally open to inspection at the Patent Office.[18] On request the registrar will inform an inquirer whether a design is registered, in respect of what articles, whether any extension has been granted, the date of registration and the name and address of the proprietor.[19]

Registrar's powers and duties

The Acts do not authorize or require the registrar to register a design the use of which would, in his opinion, be contrary to law or morality.[20] On the request of a proprietor, the registrar may cancel the registration of a design, and any person interested may apply for its cancellation on the ground that it was not new or original, or on any other ground on which the registrar could have refused to register the design.[21]

The registrar must give an applicant for registration an opportunity

---

[12] Another register of limited scope is maintained at Manchester: Design Rules, 1949, R. 72.
[13] 1949 Act, S. 17.
[14] 1949 Act, S. 20.
[15] 1949 Act, S. 21.
[16] 1949 Act, S. 1(1) and (2). As to proceedings for registration, see S. 3.
[17] 1949 Act, S. 18.
[18] 1949 Act, S. 22. The Department of Trade may delay the inspection of certain designs for time.
[19] 1949 Act, S. 23.   [20] 1949 Act, S. 43.   [21] 1949 Act, S. 11.

to be heard before exercising adversely to him any discretion he has under the Act.[22]

Appeals

Appeals from the registrar lie to the Court of Session.[23]

The design

A design may be registered in respect of any article or set of articles of manufacture, including any part made and sold separately, but it must perform some function other than merely carry the design.[24] Articles primarily literary or artistic in character are excluded from registration.[25]

The eye is the sole standard of judgment and a design must show some new effect distinguishable by the eye from previous designs.[26] But it need not possess artistic merit.[27] If the difference in design does not have artistic merit the court requires a more marked difference discernible by the eye.[28]

A design is not registrable for a method or principle of construction by itself, though it may do so incidentally,[29] nor in respect of features of shape and configuration dictated solely by the intended function of the article so shaped.[30]

The design must be new or original,[31] whether the purpose of this be beauty or utility or both, but a registration may be valid in respect of the application of an old pattern to a new kind of article.[32] It may be new or original though composed of constituents which are old[33] provided the whole is in some way an improvement on the parts alone.[34] Applications for registration must be accompanied by a statement saying for what features novelty is claimed.[35]

A design registered in respect of one article may be registered in

---

[22] 1949 Act, S. 29. As to expenses, evidence and representation, see Ss. 30–2.
[23] 1949 Act, Ss. 28, 45.
[24] 1949 Act, Ss. 1, 44; *Re Littlewoods Pools, Ltd.'s Appln.* (1949) 66 R.P.C. 309; *Sifam* v. *Sangamo Weston Ltd.* [1971] 2 All E.R. 1074. A fixed building is not, a portable building is, registrable: *Portable Concrete Buildings, Ltd.* v. *Bathcrete* [1962] R.P.C. 49.
[25] 1949 Act, S. 1(4); Design Rules, 1949, R. 26. Many such articles would come within the Copyright Act, 1956.
[26] *Re Smith's Regd. Design* (1889) 6 R.P.C. 200.
[27] *Hecla Foundry Co.* v. *Walker, Hunter & Co.* (1889) 16 R. (H.L.) 27.
[28] *Re Smith's Regd. Design, supra.*
[29] *Re Bayer's Design* (1907) 25 R.P.C. 56.
[30] 1949 Act, S. 1(3); *Stenor, Ltd.* v. *Whitesides* [1948] A.C. 107.
[31] 1949 Act, S. 1(2).
[32] *Saunders* v. *Wiel* [1893] 1 Q.B. 470.
[33] *Heath* v. *Rollason* [1898] A.C. 499.
[34] *Phillips* v. *Harbro Rubber Co.* (1919) 36 R.P.C. 79.
[35] Designs Rules, 1949, R. 14(2); cf. *Hunter, Walker & Co.* v. *Falkirk Iron Co.* (1887) 14 R. 1072.

respect of another or other articles later and is not invalidated by the prior registration.[36]

Effect of registration

Registration gives the registered proprietor the copyright in the registered design, i.e. the exclusive right in the U.K. and Isle of Man to make or import for sale or for use for the purposes of any trade or business, or to sell, hire or offer for sale or hire, any article in respect of which the design is registered, being an article to which the registered design has been applied, and to make anything for enabling any such article to be made as aforesaid in the U.K. or elsewhere.[37] It is an offence falsely to represent that a design applied to an article sold is registered in respect of that article.[38]

Duration of copyright

Subject to the Act, copyright in a registered design subsists for five years from the date of registration. On application before the expiry the registrar extends the copyright for a second and a third period of five years.[39]

Proprietorship of design

The author of a design is the proprietor, unles it is executed for another person for payment, in which case that other is the proprietor.[40]

Assignation and transmission

The right of property in a design is assignable and transmits as moveable property on intestacy or under a will[41] or to a trustee in bankruptcy. On assignation or transmission the assignee or beneficiary becomes proprietor.[42] A person who becomes entitled to a design or a share therein by assignation, transmission, or operation of law or as mortgagee of an interest in a design, must apply to the registrar for registration of his title or of notice of his interest.

Licences

The registered proprietor of a design may grant a licence to do any of the acts restricted to him by the copyright in the design. A person

[36] 1949 Act, S. 4(1).
[37] 1949 Act, S. 7; cf. *Haddon* v. *Bannerman* [1912] 2 Ch. 602; *Dorling* v. *Honnor Marine* [1965] Ch. 1.
[38] 1949 Act, S. 35.
[39] 1949 Act, S. 8.
[40] 1949 Act, S. 2.
[41] 1949 Act, S. 19(4).
[42] 1949 Act, S. 2.

becoming entitled as licensee to an interest in a registered design must have his interest noted in the register of designs.[43] No special form is provided but it must be clear that permission is being granted to apply the design.

Compulsory licences

After a design has been registered any person interested may apply to the registrar for the grant of a compulsory licence on the ground that the design is being applied in the U.K. by any industrial process to such an extent as is reasonable in the circumstances.[44] The registrar may allow a reasonable time to begin manufacture in the U.K. If made, an order for compulsory licence has the same effect as a grant of a licence by the proprietor.[44]

Infringement of design

Infringement consists in doing any act the exclusive right to do which is vested in the proprietor by the registration of his design. The question is frequently whether one design differs sufficiently from a registered design to be distinct from it; this must be determined by the eye alone[45] and depends only on shape or configuration, not on identity of function.[46] There is no infringement if the eye would not confuse the two designs under normal conditions.[47]

Defences other than non-infringement are that the registration is invalid or has expired, or the licence of the registered proprietor. The defender may claim that the registration should be cancelled.

Infringement claims may be brought only by the registered proprietor[48] and justify damages, interdict, an order for delivery of infringing goods,[49] or a count, reckoning and payment of profits.

Damages will not be awarded against a defender who proves that at that date of infringement he was not aware and had no reasonable grounds for supposing that the design was registered.[50]

Where the validity of the design is upheld, a certificate of contested validity may be given.[51]

---

[43] 1949 Act, S. 19.
[44] 1949 Act, S. 10.
[45] *Holdsworth* v. *McCrea* (1867) L.R. 2 H.L. 380; *Hecla Foundry Co.* v. *Walker, Hunter & Co.* (1889) 16 R. (H.L.) 27; *Re Kestos, Ltd., Regd. Design* (1935) 53 R.P.C. 139.
[46] *Hecla Foundry Co., supra.*
[47] *Hutchison Main & Co.* v. *St. Mungo Mfg. Co.* (1907) 24 R.P.C. 265.
[48] 1949 Act, S. 7(1).
[49] cf. *Knowles* v. *Bennett* (1895) 12 R.P.C. 137.
[50] 1949 Act, S. 9(1). *John Khalil Khawam* v. *Chellaram* [1964] 1 All E.R. 945. The marking 'Registered' without the number does not affect him with knowledge.
[51] 1949 Act, S. 25(1); *Harvey* v. *Secure Fittings, Ltd.*, 1966 S.L.T. 121.

Action for threats

Where any person by circulars, advertisements or otherwise threatens[52] any other person with proceedings for infringement of a registered design, any person aggrieved thereby may claim declarator that the threats are unjustified, interdict against the continuance of the threats, and damages sustained by reason of the threats. A mere notification that a design is registered is not a threat of proceedings.[53] A claim for threats may be adduced as a counterclaim in an action for infringement.[54] A malicious statement that another's products infringe a registered design may ground an action for injurious falsehood.

Unregistered designs

A design never registered, or one the registration of which has expired, confers no proprietary rights on the user and he has no ground for objection if another uses the same or a similar design, though he may have a right of action if the circumstances amount to passing off.

COPYRIGHT

Copyright is the exclusive right to exercise, and to authorize other persons to exercise, certain rights in literary, dramatic, musical or artistic material. The right is distinct from the property in the manuscript or book or other thing embodying the words or work created.[55] It subsists not in the ideas or theme but in the execution, presentation and order of words.[56] Copyright existed at common law[57] but now exists only under the Copyright Act, 1956.[58] Work no longer copyright is the common property of all, and anyone may republish at his will.

Copyright subsists, subject to the Act, in every original literary, dramatic or musical work which is unpublished and of which the author was a qualified person when the work was made.[59]

Copyright also subsists in an original literary, dramatic, or musical work which has been published if the first publication took place in the

[52] cf. *Paul Trading Co., Ltd.* v. *Marksmith* (1952) 69 R.P.C. 301; *Rosedale Assoc. Mfrs.* v. *Airfix Products, Ltd.* [1956] R.P.C. 360.
[53] 1949 Act, S. 26.
[54] e.g. *Kleeman* v. *Rosedale Assoc. Mfrs.* (1953) 71 R.P.C. 78.
[55] *Re Dickens* [1935] Ch. 267.
[56] *Donoghue* v. *Allied Newspapers Ltd.* [1938] Ch. 106; see generally Bell, *Comm.* I, 110–15; Copinger and Skone James on *Copyright*; Laddie on *Copyright*. Copyright legislation dates from 1709; the 1956 Act takes account of the International Copyright Convention of Berne, 1885, later revised, and the Universal Copyright Convention of Geneva, 1952.
[57] cf. *Tennyson* v. *Forrester* (1871) 43 S. Jur. 278.
[58] 1956 Act, S. 46(5).
[59] 1956 Act, S. 2(1). 'Qualified person' is defined: S. 1(5).

United Kingdom or in another country to which the section extends, or the author was a qualified person when the work was first published, or the author had died before that time, but was a qualified person immediately before his death.[60]

Originality

Originality relates not to idea or substance but to words, to independent skill or labour employed in collection, preparation or execution, not necessarily to originality of idea.[61] Hence collections,[62] compilations and formulae are protected. Skill and labour may be exercised by change of medium,[63] compiling works of information,[64] making selections,[65] adaptations,[66] or abridgements,[67] new arrangements of music.[68] A new edition may be so materially different from a former edition to be entitled to independent copyright.[69]

The title of a work can rarely be the subject of copyright, on the ground of lack of originality,[70] but the identity or similarity of one title to another may give rise to an action for passing-off.[71] An author may also be able to protect his pen name by a passing-off action.[72]

Publication

A work is published when reproductions have been issued to the public,[73] not by exhibiting a manuscript, allowing persons to read it, sending the text as a letter to a correspondent, delivering the text as

---

[60] 1956 Act, S. 2(2).

[61] *Harpers* v. *Barry, Henry & Co.* (1892) 20 R. 133.

[62] *Bailey & Taylor* (1830) 1 Russ. & My. 73 (mathematical tables); *Alexander* v. *Mackenzie* (1846) 9 D. 748 (collection of conveyancing styles); *Univ. of London Press* v. *Univ. Tutorial Press* [1916] 2 Ch. 601 (examination questions).

[63] e.g. translating: *Byrne* v. *Statist Co.* [1914] 1 K.B. 622; reporting: *Walter* v. *Lane* [1900] A.C. 539.

[64] *Exchange Telegraph Co.* v. *Gregory* [1896] 1 Q.B. 147; *B.B.C.* v. *Wireless League Gazette Pub. Co.* [1926] Ch. 433; *Football League, Ltd.* v. *Littlewoods Pools, Ltd.* [1959] Ch. 637; contrast *Cramp* v. *Smythson* [1944] A.C. 329.

[65] *Macmillan* v. *Suresh Chunder Deb.* (1890) 17 Ind. L.R. (Calcutta) 951.

[66] *Hatton* v. *Keane* (1859) 7 C.B. 268.

[67] *Macmillan* v. *Cooper* (1923) 40 T.L.R. 186; cf. *Sweet* v. *Benning* (1855) 16 C.B. 459.

[68] *Wood* v. *Boosey* (1867) L.R. 3 Q.B. 223; *Boosey* v. *Fairlie* (1877) 7 Ch. D. 301.

[69] cf. *Black* v. *Murray* (1870) 9 M. 341; *Blacklock* v. *Pearson* [1915] 2 Ch. 376.

[70] *Dicks* v. *Yates* (1881) 18 Ch. D. 76; *Ladbroke* v. *William Hill (Football), Ltd.* [1964] 1 All E.R. 465; cf. *Broemel* v. *Meyer* (1912) 29 T.L.R. 148; *Francis Day & Hunter* v. *Twentieth Century Fox Corpn.* [1940] A.C. 112.

[71] e.g. *Primrose Press Agency Co.* v. *Knowles* (1885) 2 T.L.R. 404; contrast *Outram* v. *London Evening Newspaper Co.* (1910) 27 T.L.R. 231; *Ridgway Co.* v. *Hutchinson* (1923) 40 R.P.C. 335; *Cooper* v. *Richmond Hill Press, Ltd.* [1957] R.P.C. 363; *Kark* v. *Odhams Press, Ltd.* [1962] 1 All E.R. 636; cf. *Constable* v. *Brewster* (1824) 3 S. 215; *Edinburgh Correspondent* (1822) 1 S. 407 n; *Exxon Corpn.* v. *Exxon Insurance Consultants Ltd.* [1981] 2 All E.R. 495.

[72] *Hines* v. *Winnick* [1947] Ch. 708; *Forbes* v. *Kemsley Newspapers, Ltd.* [1951] 2 T.L.R. 656.

[73] 1956 Act, S. 49(2); cf. Ss. 12(9), 13(10).

lectures,[74] performing a musical or dramatic work in public, exhibiting an artistic work, or constructing an architectural work of art. Public performance of a dramatic or musical work is not publication.[75] Presentation of copies to friends is not 'issue to the public'.[76]

Unauthorized publication does not amount to publication for copyright purposes.[77]

Publication which is merely colourable and not intended to satisfy the reasonable requirements of the public has to be disregarded.[78]

Letters remain unpublished though sent,[79] but letters to the editor of a newspaper imply a licence to the latter to publish and even to abbreviate or alter.[80]

Acquisition of statutory rights of copyright

Under the Copyright Act, 1842, no action could be brought for infringement of copyright in a book, unless it was duly registered at Stationers' Hall.[81] Since the 1911 Act, and under the 1956 Act, no registration or other procedure is necessary to acquire copyright. Copyright in an unpublished work attaches *ipso jure* when it is created, and in a published work when it is published.

Where public policy precludes acquisition of copyright

On grounds of public policy a claim to copyright in an immoral, obscene, libellous or scandalous work will not be enforced.[82] Nor can copyright be recognized in works purporting to be what they are not.[83]

Subjects of copyright—literary work

Literary work includes any written table or compilation;[84] i.e. expressed in any form of symbols or characters. It need not be

---

[74] *Caird* v. *Sime* (1887) 14 R. (H.L.) 37.

[75] 1956 Act, S. 49(2).

[76] *Prince Albert* v. *Strange* (1849) 1 M. & G. 25.

[77] 1956 Act, S. 49(3); cf. *Webb* v. *Rose* (1732) in (1766) 4 Burr. 2330; *Macklin* v. *Richardson* (1770) 2 Amb. 694.

[78] 1956 Act, S. 49(2)(b); *Francis, Day & Hunter* v. *Feldman* [1914] 2 Ch. 728.

[79] The recipient acquires the property in the letter as an object, but not the copyright; cf. *Philip* v. *Pennell* [1907] 2 Ch. 577.

[80] *Walter* v. *Lane* [1900] A.C. 539; *Springfield* v. *Thame* (1903) 89 L.T. 242, but see *Davis* v. *Miller* (1855) 17 D. 1166.

[81] 1842 Act, S. 24; cf. *Black* v. *Murray* (1870) 9 M. 341; *Thomas* v. *Turner* (1886) 33 Ch. D. 292.

[82] *Clementi* v. *Golding* (1809) 2 Camp. 25; *Hine* v. *Dale* (1809) 2 Camp. 27n.; *Lawrence* v. *Smith* (1822) Jac. 471; *Murray* v. *Benbow* (1822) Jac. 474n.; *Stockdale* v. *Onwhyn* (1826) 5 B. & C. 173; *Baschet* v. *London Illustrated Standard Co.* [1900] 1 Ch. 73; *Glynn* v. *Western Feature Film Co.* [1916] 1 Ch. 261; *Pasickniak* v. *Dojacek* (1928) 42 T.L.R. 545.

[83] *Wright* v. *Tallis* (1845) 1 C.B. 893; *Slingsby* v. *Bradford Patent Truck Co.* [1906] W.N. 51.

[84] 1956 Act, S. 48(1); cf. *Leslie* v. *Young* (1893) 21 R. (H.L.) 57 (timetables); *McNeil* v. *Rolled Steel Forge Co.*, 1930 S.N. 145 (catalogue). Maps and plans are 'drawings' and protected under S. 3(1).

'literature',[85] nor have any quality of style, nor need the written words be meaningful.[86] There must, however, be skill and labour in the arrangement of words: hence there is generally no copyright in the title of a book or article, nor in advertisement slogans or laudatory statements.[87] For a single word to be copyright, even though invented and original, it must have meaning.[88]

Literary work does not cover a cardboard sleeve pattern,[89] a photograph album,[90] a cricket scoring sheet,[91] or a single invented word used as a corporate name.[88]

Subjects of copyright—dramatic and musical works

In dramatic[92] and musical works[93] there may be copyright in the text or score, and separate rights to prevent public performance without consent, and to prevent broadcasting or reproduction on records or film without consent.

Duration of copyright

Copyright subsists till fifty years from the end of the calendar year in which the author died, and then expires.[94]

If before the death of the author the work had neither been published, nor performed in public, nor records thereof offered for sale to the public, nor been broadcast, copyright subsists till fifty years from the end of the calendar year in which one of these acts was first done.[94]

Acts restricted by copyright

The acts restricted by the copyright in a literary, dramatic or musical work are[95] (a) reproducing[96] the work in any material form; (b)

---

[85] *Maple* v. *Junior Army and Navy Stores* (1882) 21 Ch. D. 369; *Harpes* v. *Barry, Henry & Co.* (1892) 20 R. 133; *Univ. of London Press* v. *Univ. Tutorial Press* [1916] 2 Ch. 601, 608; *Purefoy Eng. Co.* v. *Sykes, Boxwell & Co.* (1955) 72 R.P.C. 89.

[86] *Anderson* v. *Lieber Code Co.* [1917] 2 K.B. 469 (telegraph code); *Pitman* v. *Hine* (1884) 1 T.L.R. 39 (shorthand); *Ladbroke* v. *William Hill (Football) Ltd.* [1964] 1 All E.R. 465.

[87] *Sinanide* v. *La Maison Kosmes* (1928) 139 L.T. 365.

[88] *Exxon Corpn.* v. *Exxon Ins. Consultants Ltd.* [1981] 2 All E.R. 495.

[89] *Hollinrake* v. *Truswell* [1894] 3 Ch. 420.

[90] *Schove* v. *Schminske* (1886) 33 Ch. D. 546.

[91] *Page* v. *Wisden* (1869) 20 L.T. 435.

[92] Defined, 1956, S. 48(1); see also *Tate* v. *Fullbrook* [1908] 1 K.B. 821.

[93] Not defined by 1956 Act, but see definition in (repealed) Musical (Summary Proceedings) Copyright Act, 1902, S. 3.

[94] 1956 Act, S. 2(3), 3(4).

[95] 1956 Act, S. 2(5).

[96] 1956 Act, S. 48(1). This includes unauthorized printing or photocopying: *Moorhouse and Angus & Robertson* v. *University of N.S.W.* [1975] R.P.C. 454.

publishing[97] the work; (c) performing[98] the work in public; (d) broadcasting the work; (e) causing the work to be transmitted to subscribers to a diffusion service; (f) making any adaptations[99] of the work; (g) doing, in relation to an adaptation of the work, any of acts (a) to (e). A record lending library does not authorize infringement by taping the sound made by the record merely because it knows that borrowers do this.[1]

Publication of unpublished manuscripts

Copyright is not infringed by the reproduction or publication of a copyright unpublished work, the manuscript or a copy of which is kept in a library or museum, if the author has been dead for fifty years and a hundred years have elapsed since the work was made.[2]

Publication in breach of confidence

Apart from infringement of copyright unauthorized reproduction or publication, as of letters received, may be actionable as a breach of confidence or of trust.[3] Action for breach of confidence may also protect where copyright does not, e.g. against the publication of ideas or information communicated in confidence.[4]

Copyright in published editions of works

Subject to the Act, copyright subsists in every published edition of any one or more literary, dramatic or musical works if the first publication took place in the U.K., or in another country to which the section extends, or the publisher of the edition was a qualified person. Such copyright vests in the publisher and subsists for twenty-five years; it restricts the making of a reproduction of the typographical arrangement of the edition, with an exception for libraries of particular classes.[5]

---

[97] 1956 Act, S. 49; *Warwick Film Productions Ltd.* v. *Eisinger* [1967] 3 All E.R. 367.
[98] 1956 Act, S. 48; *Jennings* v. *Stephens* [1936] Ch. 469; *P.R.S.* v. *Camelo* [1936] 3 All E.R. 557; *Turner* v. *P.R.S.* [1943] 1 All E.R. 413; *P.R.S.* v. *Rangers F.C. Supporters Club*, 1974 S.L.T. 151.
[99] 1956 Act, S. 2(6).
[1] *C.B.S. Inc.* v. *Ames Records Ltd.* [1981] 2 All E.R. 812.
[2] 1956 Act, S. 7(6) and (7).
[3] 1956 Act, S. 46(4); *Pope* v. *Curl* (1741) 2 Atk. 341; *Gee* v. *Pritchard* (1818) 2 Swans. 402; *Prince Albert* v. *Strange* (1849) 1 M. & G. 25; See also *White* v. *Dickson* (1881) 8 R. 896; *McCosh* v. *Crow* (1903) 5 F. 670.
[4] cf. *Exchange Telegraph* v. *Gregory* [1896] 1 Q.B. 147; see also *Chilton* v. *Progress Printing Co.* [1895] 2 Ch. 29; *Exchange Telegraph* v. *Howard* (1906) 22 T.L.R. 375; *Philip* v. *Pennell* [1907] 2 Ch. 577.
[5] 1956 Act, S. 15; see also S. 16. This protects reprints of works out of copyright. Thus the Stair Society acquired copyright in its photo-reprint (1962–4) of Balfour's *Practicks* (pub. 1754), the copyright of which had expired; cf. *Black* v. *Murray* (1870) 9 M. 341.

Copyright in artistic works

Copyright subsists in artistic work[6] which is unpublished[7] and of which the author was a qualified person when he made it or for a substantial part of the period of making. If original artistic work has been published[7] copyright subsists in it only if the first publication took place in the U.K. or in another country to which the section extends, or the author was a qualified person at the time when the work was first published, or the author had died before that time but was a qualified person immediately before his death.[8] As in literary, dramatic and musical works the expression, not the idea, is protected.[9]

Copyright under S. 3 subsists till the end of fifty years from the end of the calendar year in which the author died, and then expires, but in the case of an engraving, unpublished at the author's death, it subsists for fifty years from the year in which it is first published, and the copyright in a photograph subsists till fifty years from the end of the calendar year in which it is first published, and then expires.[10]

The acts restricted by copyright in an artistic work are (a) reproducing the work in any material form; (b) publishing the work; (c) including the work in a television broadcast; (d) causing a television programme which includes the work to be transmitted to subscribers to a diffusion service.

Copyright in sound recordings

Copyright subsists in every sound recording[11] of which the maker was a qualified person when it was made, if published[7] and if the first publication of the recording took place in the United Kingdom or another country to which the section extends. It subsists till fifty years from the end of the year in which the recording is first published and then expires; it vests in the maker of the sound recording, or, in the absence of contrary agreement, in the person who commissions the making of a sound recording and pays or agrees to pay for it, if the recording is made in pursuance of that copyright.[12]

[6] Defined (S. 3(1)) as paintings, sculptures, drawings, engravings and photographs, buildings or models for buildings, and works of artistic craftsmanship: artistic quality is irrelevant. See *Burke* v. *Spicer's Dress Designs* [1936] 1 All E.R. 99; *Dorling* v. *Honnor Marine* [1964] 1 All E.R. 241; *Hensher* v. *Restawile Upholstery Ltd.* [1974] 2 All E.R. 420; *Merchant Adventurers Ltd.* v. *Gress* [1971] 2 All E.R. 657; *Infabrics Ltd.* v. *Jaytex Ltd.* [1981] 1 All E.R. 1057. By S. 48(1) sculpture includes any cast or model made for the purpose of sculpture, drawings include any diagram, map, chart or plan, and engravings any etching, lithograph, wood-cut, print or similar work, not being a photograph.
[7] S. 49(2).
[8] 1956 Act, S. 3(2) and (3).
[9] *Kenrick* v. *Lawrence* (1890) 25 Q.B.D. 99.
[10] 1956 Act, S. 3(4).
[11] Defined, 1956 Act, S. 12(9).
[12] 1956 Act, S. 12(1)–(4).

The acts restricted by the copyright in a sound recording are (a) making the record embodying the recording; (b) causing the recording to be heard in public; and (c) broadcasting the recording; but certain acts are deemed not to be infringements.[13]

Copyright in cinematograph films

Subject to the Act copyright subsists in cinematograph films of which the maker was a qualified person, and in every such film which has been published, if the first publication took place in the U.K. or another country to which the section extends. Such copyright lasts for fifty years, vests in the maker of the film, and, with certain qualifications, restricts the rights to make a copy of the film, cause the film to be seen or heard in public, broadcast the film, or cause it to be transmitted to subscribers to a diffusion service.[14]

Copyright in television broadcasts and sound broadcasts

Subject to the Act, copyright subsists in every television broadcast made by the B.B.C. or I.B.A. from a place in the U.K. or another country to which the section extends, and in every sound broadcast made by either authority from such a place. It vests in the B.B.C. or I.B.A., subsists for fifty years, and restricts the making, otherwise than for private purposes, of a film or copy of a film of a television broadcast, the making, otherwise than for private purposes, of a sound recording or a record embodying such a recording of a sound broadcast or the sounds of a television broadcast, the causing of a broadcast to be seen or heard in public by a paying audience, or re-broadcasting a sound or television broadcast.[15]

Ownership of copyright

Copyright in a literary, dramatic, musical or artistic work attaches to the author thereof.[16] Subject to any contrary agreement, where a literary or dramatic or artistic work is made by an author in the course of his employment by a newspaper or periodical under a contract of service of apprenticeship and made for publication in a newspaper or

---

[13] 1956 Act, S. 12(5)–(8); see also S. 16, and *Harms v. Martans Club, Ltd.* [1927] 1 Ch. 526; *P.R.S. v. Hawthorn Hotel, Ltd.* [1933] Ch. 855; *Jennings v. Stephens* [1936] Ch. 469; *Phonographic Performance Ltd. v. Pontin's Ltd.* [1967] 3 All E.R. 736; *P.R.S. v. Harlequin Record Shops* [1979] 1 W.L.R. 851.

[14] 1956 Act, S. 13; See also S. 16; cf. *Milligan v. Broadway Cinema Productions*, 1923 S.L.T. 35. On infringement by video recording see *Rank Film v. Video Information Centre* [1981] 2 All E.R. 76.

[15] 1956 Act, S. 14; see also S. 16.

[16] 1956 Act, S. 4(1). 'Author' is not defined: as to who is author see *Tate v. Thomas* [1921] 1 Ch. 503; *Donoghue v. Allied Newspapers* [1938] Ch. 106. On presumption of ownership see *Warwick Films v. Eisinger* [1967] 3 All E.R. 367. In relation to a photograph the 'author' is the owner of the material on which it is taken: S. 48(1).

periodical, the copyright is in the newspaper proprietor in so far as it relates to publication in a newspaper or periodical, but no further, and where a person commissions a photograph, portrait or engraving and pays or agrees to pay for it, the person commissioning is entitled to any copyright therein,[17] and where in any other case a work is made in the course of the author's employment by another under a contract of service or apprenticeship, the employer is entitled to the copyright.[18] Copyright in sound records and films vests in the makers[19] and copyright in T.V. or sound broadcasts in the B.B.C. or I.B.A.[20] Provision is made for ownership of works published anonymously or pseudonymously, and works of joint authorship.[21]

Prospective ownership of copyright

Copyright which will or may come into existence in respect of future work may be assigned by the prospective owner, and it then vests in the assignee on coming into being.[22]

Transfer and transmission

Copyright is transferable by assignation or by will, or transmissible by operation of law, as moveable property.[23] It is a distinct object of property from the material objects which embody the expressions which are the subject of copyright, such as a manuscript, score or painting.[24] The copyright is deemed, failing contrary indication in the will, conveyed by a bequest of the manuscript of an unpublished literary, dramatic or musical work, or of an unpublished artistic work, in so far as the testator was owner of the copyright immediately before his death.[25]

An assignation of copyright may be total or limited as to classes of acts vested in the owner, or as to the countries in relation to which the owner has exclusive right, or as to the period for which it is to subsist, or in more than one of these ways.[26]

---

[17] cf. *Crooke* v. *Scots Pictorial Publishing Co.* (1906) 14 S.L.T. 127.

[18] 1956 Act, S. 4(2)–(5). As to works published anonymously or pseudonymously, see 1956 Act, S. 11 and Sched. II. As to works of joint authorship, see 1956 Act, S. 11 and Sched. III.

[19] Ss. 12(4), 13(4).

[20] S. 14(2).

[21] S. 11.

[22] 1956 Act, S. 37; cf. *Ward Lock & Co.* v. *Long* [1906] 2 Ch. 550; *Macdonald* v. *Eyles* [1921] 1 Ch. 631; *Chaplin* v. *Frewin* [1965] 3 All E.R. 764.

[23] 1956 Act, S. 36(1); cf. *Mackay* v. *M.*, 1914 S.C. 200; *Re Grant Richards* [1907] 2 K.B. 33 (bankruptcy). It is not clear what diligence, if any, is appropriate for attaching copyright, though royalties can be arrested.

[24] cf. *Cooper* v. *Stephens* [1895] 1 Ch. 567; but see *Caddell & Davies* v. *Stewart* (1804) Mor., Literary Property, Appx. 4; *Clark* v. *Adam* (1832) 6 W. & S. 141; *London Ptg. Alliance* v. *Cox* [1891] 3 Ch. 291.

[25] 1956 Act, S. 38.

[26] 1956 Act, S. 36(2); *Jonathan Cape Ltd.* v. *Consolidated Press Ltd.* [1954] 3 All E.R. 253.

An assignation must be in writing signed by or on behalf of the assignor.[27]

Once it has been assigned the author may not claim to exercise any of the rights protected by copyright.[28]

Licences in respect of copyright

A licence or permission may be granted in respect of any element of copyright, thereby legalizing something which would otherwise have been unlawful.[29] Any such licence granted by the owner of the relevant copyright binds every successor in title to his interest in the copyright except a purchaser in good faith for value without notice of the licence or a person deriving title from such a purchaser.[30] A licence may be oral, or implied by conduct,[31] but an exclusive licence must be in writing. It authorizes the licensee, to the exclusion of all others, to exercise a right which would otherwise be exercisable solely by the owner of the copyright.[32] A licence is probably assignable, unless there is *delectus personae.*[33]

Infringement

Infringement is constituted by the doing or authorizing of the doing, without licence from the owner,[34] of any act the exclusive right to do which[35] is vested in the owner of the copyright. Infringement is also constituted by certain importations, sales and other dealings with infringing articles.[36]

Certain dealings with literary, dramatic and musical works[37] and with artistic works[38] are however not deemed infringements.

[27] 1956 Act, S. 36(3). No particular form is necessary, and a receipt for money may be held to imply an assignation: *Jeffreys* v. *Kyle* (1855) 18 D. 906; *Levy* v. *Rutley* (1871) L.R. 6 C.P. 523; *London Ptg. Alliance* v. *Cox* [1891] 3 Ch. 291; *Savory* v. *World of Golf, Ltd.* [1914] 2 Ch. 566; *Ornamin (U.K.)* v. *Bacsa* [1964] R.P.C. 293.

[28] *Educ. Co. of Ireland* v. *Fallon Bros.* [1919] 1 I.R. 62.

[29] cf. 1956 Act, Ss. 1(2), 5(2). The commonest case is an author's agreement with a publisher to print and publish a book, the author retaining the copyright. cf. *Cunningham* v. *Maclachlan & Stewart's Tr.* (1891) 18 R. 460.

[30] 1956 Act, S. 36(4).

[31] *Blair* v. *Tomkins* [1971] 1 All E.R. 468; *Stovin-Bradford* v. *Volpoint* [1971] 3 All E.R. 570.

[32] 1956 Act, S. 19; on the licensee's right to make alterations see *Frisby* v. *B.B.C.* [1967] 2 All E.R. 106.

[33] cf. *Griffith* v. *Tower Publishing Co.* [1897] 1 Ch. 21; *Re Jude's Musical Compositions, Ltd.* [1907] 1 Ch. 651.

[34] S. 1(2).

[35] i.e. the acts listed in Ss. 2(5) and 3(5). See e.g. *Macfarlane* v. *Oak Foundry Co.* (1883) 10 R. 801.

[36] S. 5.

[37] Ss. 6–8; *Hubbard* v. *Vosper* [1972] 2 W.L.R. 389; *Beloff* v. *Pressdram Ltd.* [1973] 1 All E.R. 241; *Moorhouse and Angus & Robertson* v. *University of N.S.W.* [1976] R.P.C. 151.

[38] Ss. 9–10. See also Design Copyright Act, 1968; *Sifam Electrical Co.* v. *Sangamo Weston* [1971] 2 All E.R. 1074.

Infringement by reproduction involves making a substantial use of the form of expression, not the idea, plot or principle, of the copyright work,[39] taken from that work. It is frequently a question of degree whether the amount reproduced is so substantial as to amount to infringement.[40] Not only the quantity, but the value and importance of the matter reproduced matters.[41] The words or other mode of expression need not be copied exactly. There is no infringement merely by reason of identity of subject or similarity of statement, particularly where both works in question necessarily draw on the same sources.[42]

Infringement in other ways includes unauthorized reprinting, performing the work in public, broadcasting the work, adapting or translating it.

There are excepted from infringement any fair dealing with a literary, dramatic or musical work for purposes of research, private study, criticism or review and certain other purposes, in some cases subject to conditions, the making or supply of a copy of a periodical article, subject to conditions, the making of a record of a a musical work, subject to conditions, and fair dealing with an artistic work, subject to conditions.[43] Copyright is not infringed by certain uses for education.[44]

Indirect infringement is effected by anyone who without the licence of the copyright owner makes for sale or hire, sells or lets or exposes for sale an infringing work, exhibits it or imports it, unless for private or domestic use.[45]

Infringement is actionable at the instance of the copyright owner by way of claims for damages, interdict, count, reckoning and payment of profits, or otherwise. In certain circumstances particular remedies are excluded.[46] The copyright owner has also rights in respect of the intromission by a person with an infringing copy.[47] Provision is also made for cases where an exclusive licence has been granted in respect of the copyright,[48] for the proof of certain facts in copyright actions,

[39] *Lennie* v. *Pillans* (1843) 5 D. 416; *Alexander* v. *Mackenzie* (1847) 9 D. 748; *Hollinrake* v. *Truswell* [1894] 3 Ch. 420.

[40] *White* v. *Briggs* (1890) 18 R. 223.

[41] *Bramwell* v. *Helcomb* (1836) 3 M. & Cr. 737; *Saunders* v. *Smith* (1838) 3 M. & Cr. 711; *Neale* v. *Harmer* (1897) 13 T.L.R. 209; *Ladbroke* v. *William Hill (Football), Ltd.* [1964] 1 All E.R. 465.

[42] cf. *Kelly* v. *Morris* (1866) L.R. 1 Eq. 697; *Scott* v. *Stanford* (1867) L.R. 3 Eq. 718; *Cox* v. *Land and Water Journal Co.* (1869) L.R. 9 Eq. 324; *Pike* v. *Nicholas* (1870) L.R. 5 Ch. 251.

[43] Ss. 6–9.

[44] S. 41.

[45] S. 21.

[46] S. 17. As to measure of damages see *Sutherland Publishing Co.* v. *Caxton Publishing Co.* [1936] Ch. 323; *Beloff* v. *Pressdram Ltd.* [1973] 1 All E.R. 241; as to injunction see *Borthwick* v. *Evening Post* (1888) 37 Ch. D. 449.

[47] S. 18. Damages under S. 18 are cumulative with those under S. 17; *Caxton Pub. Co.* v. *Sutherland Pub. Co.* [1939] A.C. 178; *Infabrics Ltd.* v. *Jaytex Ltd.* [1981] 1 All E.R. 1057. As to measure of damages see also *Birn* v. *Keene* [1918] 2 Ch. 281. [48] S. 19.

and for penalties and summary proceedings in respect of dealings which infringe copyright.[49]

False attribution of authorship

The 1956 Act,[50] without prejudice to other civil or criminal remedies, imposes restrictions, the contravention of which is actionable as a breach of statutory duty, on falsely attributing literary, dramatic, musical or artistic work to a person not the author thereof, without the latter's permission, during his life or within twenty years of his death.

Use of copyright in education

Copyright is not infringed by reason only of the reproduction, or adaptation, of the work for educational purposes.[51]

Crown copyright

The Crown is entitled to copyright in literary, dramatic, musical or artistic work made by or under the direction or control of Her Majesty or a government department, and in work first published in the U.K. if by or under the direction or control of Her Majesty or a government department. Such copyrights subsist so long as the work is unpublished, or till fifty years after publication.[52] Special provisions are made as to the public records.[53] In Scotland the right of printing Bibles belongs to the Crown and is exercised by publishers under licence.[54]

Performing rights: the Performing Right Tribunal

The owner of copyright in a literary, dramatic or musical work, sound recording or television broadcast, may grant to another a licence to perform his work or to do another act restricted by copyright. Societies exist with the main object of negotiating the granting of such licences, as owner or as agent for the owner of the copyright, to persons wishing to perform the work in question[55] and pursuing parties performing without licence.[56] Such societies may

---

[49] Ss. 20–1.

[50] S. 43; see also *Carlton Illustrators* v. *Coleman* [1911] 1 K.B. 771; *Preston* v. *Raphael Tuck Ltd.* [1926] Ch. 667; *Moore* v. *News of the World* [1972] 1 All E.R. 915.

[51] 1956 Act, S. 41.   [52] 1956 Act, S. 39.   [53] 1956 Act, S. 42.

[54] *King'sPrinters* v. *Manners & Miller* (1828) 3 W. & S. 268. As to England see *Oxford and Cambridge Universities* v. *Eyre and Spottiswoode* [1963] 3 All E.R. 289.

[55] These include the Performing Right Society concerned with plays and music, Phonographic Performance Ltd., and British Phonographic Industry, Ltd. concerned with records and tapes, and Mechanical Copyright Protection Society Ltd. concerned with tapes. See *P.R.S.* v. *Edinburgh Mags.*, 1922 S.C. 165.

[56] *P.R.S.* v. *Rangers Supporters Club*, 1974 S.L.T. 151; *C.B.S. Inc.* v. *Ames Records* [1981] 2 All E.R. 812; *E.M.I. Records Ltd.* v. *Riley* [1981] 2 All E.R. 838.

make licence schemes setting out the classes of cases in which they are willing to grant licences, and on what terms and conditions.[57]

The Act establishes a Performing Right Tribunal to determine disputes between licensing bodies and persons requiring licences.[58] Licence schemes may be referred to the tribunal,[59] and persons claiming to have been refused a licence may apply to it for a licence.[60]

Performers' Protection Acts

The Performers' Protection Acts, 1958 and 1963, penalize the making of records, films on broadcasts without the consent of the performers, save in special cases.

PUBLIC LENDING RIGHT

Authors have a right known as public lending right,[61] to receive, in accordance with a scheme made by the Secretary of State,[62] from time to time payments from a central fund in respect of such of their books as are lent out to the public by local library authorities in the U.K. The scheme is administered by the Registrar of Public Lending Right who maintains registers of the books in respect of which the right subsists and the persons entitled to the right.[63] The duration of the right is from publication or the time at which application is made for registration until fifty years from the end of the year in which the author died, i.e. until it goes out of copyright.[64] The right is established by registration, transmissible by assignation, testamentary disposition or operation of law as moveable property and may be claimed by or on behalf of the person for the time being entitled and renounced in whole or in part, temporarily or for all time, on notice to the Registrar to that effect.

PLANT BREEDERS' RIGHTS

The Controller of the Plant Varieties Rights Office may on application grant plant breeders' rights to a person who has bred or discovered a variety of plant, or his successor in title.[65] Provision is made

[57] 1956 Act, S. 24.
[58] 1956 Act, S. 23; see also Ss. 29–30.
[59] 1956 Act, Ss. 25–6.
[60] 1956 Act, S. 27; Copyright (Amdt.) Act, 1971, S. 1.
[61] Public Lending Right Act, 1979, S. 1.
[62] Ibid., S. 3.
[63] Ibid., S. 4.
[64] Ibid., S. 1(6).
[65] Plant Varieties and Seeds Acts, 1964, Ss. 1–2, and Sched. 2.

for the protection of an applicant pending the decision of his application.[66] An appeal lies from the Controller to the Plant Variety Rights Tribunal.[67]

Rights are exercisable for a period prescribed by a scheme under the Act, but for not less that fifteen or eighteen and not exceeding twenty-five years, with possible extension by the Controller. Rights may be surrendered or terminated.[68]

The holder of plant breeders' rights in a plant variety has the exclusive right himself, and to authorize others, to sell the reproductive material of the plant variety, to produce the reproductive material in Great Britain for sale, and to exercise certain other rights.[69] Infringement is actionable for damages, interdict, count and reckoning for profits, as in the cases of other proprietary rights.[69] There is no right to damages for an innocent infringement.[70] A holder must be able to maintain reproductive material capable of producing the variety to which the rights relate.[71]

The Controller may grant an applicant, by way of compulsory licence, any rights as respects a plant variety which the holder might have granted.[72]

Plant breeders' rights may be assigned outright or in security,[73] attached by diligence and pass on intestacy or under a will like other proprietary rights.

---

[66] 1964 Act, S. 1(3) and Sched. I.
[67] 1964 Act, S. 1(4) and 10.
[68] 1964 Act, S. 3.
[69] 1964 Act, S. 4 and Sched. 3.
[70] 1964 Act, S. 4(3).
[71] 1964 Act, S. 6.
[72] 1964 Act, S. 7.
[73] cf. 1964 Act, S. 8.

TRANSFER IN SECURITY OF RIGHTS IN INCORPOREAL MOVEABLE OBJECTS

Any right in any incorporeal moveable object capable of being assigned outright may equally be conveyed in security of the payment of money or the performance of some similar obligation by assignation.[1] It proceeds on the basis of an undertaking or contract to transfer in security and no security right exists until the contract has been effected by assignation.[2] Assignation of incorporeal moveable rights may be conjoined with a personal obligation to repay contained in a bond and assignation in security. Assignation in security is effected by the same means as outright assignation,[3] but is subject to an obligation expressed in the assignation, or (where the assignation is *ex facie* absolute) contained in a separate back-bond or agreement,[4] to retrocess or reassign to the cedent or assignor the rights assigned, on repayment or due performance of the obligations secured by the assignation. It is completed by intimation to the debtor in the right assigned, preference being regulated by priority of intimation.[5] The equitable assignment recognized in English law, created by the deposit of the title deeds of property, or share certificates, or insurance policies, is ineffective in Scotland.[6]

In the case of mortgaging company shares the delivery to the assignee of an executed instrument of transfer with the relative share certificate enables the transferee to have himself registered as owner with the company,[7] without disclosure of his obligation to reconvey on being

---

[1] Transmission of Moveable Property (Sc.) Act, 1862; Policies of Assurance Act, 1867.

[2] *Bank of Scotland* v. *Hutchison, Main & Co. Liqdrs.*, 1914 S.C. (H.L.) 1.

[3] An understanding that an assignation is in security only can be proved by writ or oath only: *Purnell* v. *Shannon* (1894) 22 R. 74. See also *Walker* v. *Buchanan, Kennedy & Co.* (1857) 20 D. 259.

[4] *Caledonian Ins. Co.* v. *Beattie* (1898) 5 S.L.T. 349; Ch. 5.41, *infra*.

[5] *Allan* v. *Urquhart* (1887) 15 R. 56; *Union Club Liqdr.* v. *Edinburgh Life Assce. Co.* (1906) 8 F. 1143; cf. *Tod's Trs.* v. *Wilson* (1869) 7 M. 1100; *Campbell's Trs.* v. *Whyte* (1884) 11 R. 1078. Notarial intimation is still competent.

[6] *Christie* v. *Ruxton* (1862) 24 D. 1182 (title deeds); *Gourlay* v. *Mackie* (1887) 14 R. 403 (share cetificates); *Strachan* v. *McDougle* (1835) 13 S. 954; *Wylie's Exrx.* v. *McJannet* (1901) 4 F. 195; *Robertson's Tr.* v. *Riddell*, 1911 S.C. 14 (insurance policies); contrast *Sc. Provident Inst.* v. *Cohen* (1888) 16 R. 112, where deposit of insurance policy in England held valid.

[7] *Guild* v. *Young* (1884) 22 S.L.R. 520; *Morrison* v. *Harrison* (1876) 3 R. 406.

repaid, but such a security is defeasible by a subsequent transfer by the debtor registered earlier[8] or by arrestments by another creditor. To deposit the share certificates with the creditor together with transfers executed by the owner as transferor but blank as to the transferee is valid in England[9] but questionable in Scotland since the Blank Bonds and Trusts Act, 1696 (c. 25) declares void instruments delivered blank as to the creditor's name.[10] The only complete right in security is by transferring the shares *ex facie* absolutely to the creditor, subject to a back-bond or agreement requiring reconveyance on the debt being repaid, registration in the company's books securing preference over other claims.[11] If the shares are not fully paid up, the security-holder becomes liable for any calls made, and cannot require the mortgaging debtor to indemnify him unless he comes to redeem the shares.

Policies of life assurance are assignable in security by the person in whose favour the company has undertaken the beneficial obligation.[12] The assignee in security may keep up the policy by paying the premiums, but should take the cedent bound to pay them, or to reimburse him if he has to do so, and take power on the cedent's default to surrender or sell the policy.[13]

Exceptionally negotiable instruments may be transferred in security by negotiation, i.e. by delivery or endorsement and delivery, without assignation. The creditor obtains an indefeasible and unburdened title if he takes it in good faith, for value and without notice of any defect in the title of the debtor to it. He may probably retain the instrument in security only of the debt for which it was pledged.[14] It is doubtful whether the holder can realize the instrument without judicial authority while it is pledged. If the date of payment arrives while an instrument is held in security the creditor is bound to take steps to collect the sum due.[15]

Security-holder's rights

An assignee in security takes the assigned right *tantum et tale* as vested in the cedent, and subject to all defects and objections thereto.[16]

---

[8] *Rainford* v. *Keith* [1905] 1 Ch. 296.

[9] *Colonial Bank* v. *Cody* (1890) 15 App. Cas. 267.

[10] cf. *Shaw* v. *Caledonian Ry.* (1890) 17 R. 466, 478.

[11] *Morrison, supra.*

[12] *Thomson's Trs.* v. *T.* (1879) 6 R. 1227. Certain kinds of policies, e.g. under the Friendly Societies Acts, are not assignable. A husband cannot assign in security a policy effected under the Married Women's Policies of Assurance (Sc.) Act, 1880.

[13] cf. *Wood* v. *Anstruther* (1842) 4 D. 1363; *Bankhardt's Trs.* v. *Scottish Amicable Socy.* (1871) 9 M. 443.

[14] *Hamilton* v. *Western Bank* (1856) 19 D. 152; *Alston's Tr.* v. *Royal Bank* (1893) 20 R. 887. See also *Robertson's Tr.* v. *Royal Bank* (1890) 18 R. 12.

[15] cf. *Robertson's Tr., supra.*

[16] cf. *National Bank* v. *Dickie's Tr.* (1895) 22 R. 740, 754.

If the right was defeasible or terminable in the hands of the cedent it remains so in the hands of the assignee.[17] But he takes it free from latent trusts and claims prestable against the cedent, provided that he took the assignation in good faith, for value, and without notice of the trust or claim in question.[18]

The cedent may in the assignation expressly grant warrandice, normally from fact and deed, and this, if not expressed, is implied.[19] If a debt is assigned warrandice *debitum subesse* is implied,[20] and that the obligation is a continuing one,[21] but not that the debtor is solvent.[22]

If the object transferred in security is one such as company shares, yielding periodical profits, the creditor draws them under an obligation to account therefor to the debtor.[23]

Extent of security

Where rights, such as a policy of insurance, are assigned expressly in security, the presumption is that the security covers only the debt due at the time of assignation.[24] But it is competent to provide that the security is to extend to future advances also, and the same result follows where a security is granted to cover a particular debt and further advances are made expressly in reliance on that security.[25]

Where rights, such as company shares, are assigned in security by *ex facie* absolute transfer, the assignee is entitled to hold them as security both for advances made at the date of the transfer and for subsequent advances,[26] but if the transfer bears to be in security of a specific advance[27] or a limitation of the assignee's title appears in a collateral agreement a further assignation must be executed if it is desired to make the subjects available as security for further advances.[28]

[17] *Johnstone-Beattie* v. *Dalziel* (1868) 6 M. 333; *Buist* v. *Scottish Equitable Life Assce. Socy.* (1878) 5 R. (H.L.) 64; *Chambers's Trs.* v. *Smiths* (1878) 5 R. (H.L.) 151; *Train* v. *Clapperton*, 1907 S.C. 517.
[18] *Somervails* v. *Redfearn* (1813) 1 Dow 50; cf. *Burns* v. *Lawrie's Trs.* (1840) 2 D. 1348; contrast *Heritable Reversionary Co.* v. *Millar* (1892) 19 R. (H.L.) 43.
[19] Ersk. II, 3, 25–7.
[20] *Russell's Trs.* v. *Mudie* (1857) 20 D. 125.
[21] *Reid* v. *Barclay* (1879) 6 R. 1007.
[22] *Barclay* v. *Liddel* (1671) Mor. 16591. See also Bell, *Prin.* §1469.
[23] *Queensberry's Trs.* v. *Scottish Union Ins. Co.* (1842) 1 Bell 183. cf. *Dougall* v. *National Bank* (1892) 20 R. 8.
[24] *National Bank* v. *Forbes* (1858) 21 D. 79.
[25] *Clyne* v. *Dunnet* (1839) MacL. & R. 28.
[26] *Hamilton* v. *Western Bank* (1856) 19 D. 152; *Union Bank* v. *National Bank* (1886) 14 R. (H.L.) 1; *National Bank* v. *Dickie's Tr.* (1895) 22 R. 740; *Robertson's Tr.* v. *Riddell*, 1911 S.C. 14.
[27] *Anderson's Tr.* v. *Somerville* (1899) 36 S.L.R. 833.
[28] *National Bank, supra*, 753.

True owner's reversionary right

Despite the assignation the true owner retains a reversionary right in the rights assigned entitling him on implementing his obligation to the assignee to call for a retrocession.[29] The reversionary right may itself be of sufficient value to be assignable in security.[30] If it is so assigned and the assignation intimated to the assignee in security of the right itself, the assignee of the right has no security for advances made subsequently to the intimation that the reversionary right was no longer vested in the true owner.[31]

An assignee in security must, so long as he holds the rights in security, have regard to the true owner's reversionary right,[32] and must not, e.g., realize assets held in security any further than necessary,[33] nor ignore a rights issue of shares made to existing shareholders; he should communicate such an offer to the true owners, and is liable in damages if they lose by his failure to do so.[34]

Retrocession

On due performance of the obligation secured the assignee may be called on and, if need be, ordained by the court, to execute a retrocession of the assigned rights to the cedent, or to account to the borrower for his transactions with the assigned rights. In the case of the transfer of numbered company shares in security, the assignee is probably bound, failing express or implied authority to act otherwise, to retain and account for and reconvey the specific shares transferred, since the title to these shares is known to be good, whereas the title to other shares might depend on a forged transfer.[35]

Retention or realization of objects assigned

If the cedent fails to implement his obligation or repay the money in security of which the right were assigned, the creditor may not, if the rights were assigned expressly in security, retain the right as his own, the reversionary right remaining in the cedent, nor may he realize the rights unless power to do so on default was expressly conferred on him or he obtains power of sale from the court and exercises it.[36] But if the security were constituted *ex facie* absolute assignation qualified by

---

[29] cf. *Paul's Tr.* v. *Justice*, 1912 S.C. 103.
[30] e.g. *Nelson* v. *National Bank,* 1936 S.C. 570.
[31] *Union Bank* v. *National Bank* (1886) 14 R. (H.L.) 1.
[32] *Nelson, supra.*
[33] *Baillie* v. *Drew* (1884) 12 R. 199; *Nelson, supra.*
[34] *Waddell* v. *Hutton,* 1911 S.C. 575.
[35] *Crerar* v. *Bank of Scotland,* 1921 S.C. 736; affd. 1922 S.C. (H.L.) 137 (where owner had acquiesced in receiving back other shares of the same denomination).
[36] cf. Bell, *Prin.* §207; *Murray* v. *Smith* (1899) 6 S.L.T. 357.

back-bond the creditor may retain the objects and, if he disposes of the objects to a third party the latter, if he takes in good faith, for value and without notice of the cedent's rights, will obtain a title free from the latent claim enforceable against the creditor.[37] But if the third party knew that the object bought by him was truly held in security only, he will acquire no better right than the creditor had.

---

[37] *Somervail* v. *Redfearn* (1813) 5 Pat. 707; *Attwood* v. *Kinnear* (1882) 10 S. 817; *Burns* v. *Lawrie's Trs.* (1840) 2 D. 1348.

VOLUNTARY TRANSFER OF RIGHTS IN INCORPOREAL MOVEABLE OBJECTS

Incorporeal moveable objects of property, unless personal and non-assignable, may freely be transferred outright to another party, thereby substituting him in the granter's place to the same force and effect as if he had been the original owner of that property.

Rights assignable and non-assignable

Rights in incorporeals are in general assignable. Those non-assignable comprise rights strictly personal, into which an element of *delectus personae* enters, such as some rights under contract, rights under partnership, some personal privileges,[1] and goodwill depending on personal qualities,[2] and rights which are alimentary, from their nature or by express or implied provision. Rights alimentary by nature include, at common law, wages, salaries and allowances, at least so far as not exceeding what is necessary for aliment.[3] Rights alimentary by provision include rights of income,[4] as by annuity or liferent, provided by one for the aliment of another,[5] declared to be so, and protected against the beneficiary's own actings and the assaults of his creditors by the interposition of a trust.[6] In this case also the provision is protected only to the extent that it is reasonable; beyond this it may be assigned in security or outright.[7] Each termly payment when received is, however, at the unfettered disposal of the recipient,[8] and arrears may be assigned.[9] By statutes social security benefits are non-assignable.[10]

---

[1] *Arbroath Mags. v. Strachan's Trs.* (1842) 4 D. 538; *Leith Dock Commrs. v. Colonial Life Assce. Co.* (1861) 24 D. 64; *McCallum's Trs. v. McNab* (1877) 4 R. 520; *Orr-Ewing v. E. Cawdor* (1885) 12 R. (H.L.) 12.

[2] *Bain v. Munro* (1878) 5 R. 416 cf. *Rodger v. Herbertson,* 1909 S.C. 256.

[3] *Learmonth v. Paterson* (1858) 20 D. 418.

[4] *Ker v. Justice* (1866) 5 M. 4.

[5] Bell, *Comm.* I, 124; *Wink v. Speirs* (1867) 6 M. 77; *White's Trs. v. Whyte* (1877) 4 R. 786.

[6] *White's Trs., supra.*

[7] Stair III, 1, 37; Ersk. III, 6, 7; Bell, *Comm.* I, 126; *Lewis v. Anstruther* (1852) 14 D. 857; *Scott's Tr. v. S.* (1885) 12 R. 540; *Livingston v. L.* (1886) 14 R. 43.

[8] *Hewats v. Robertson* (1881) 9 R. 175.

[9] *Drew v. D.* (1870) 9 M. 163.

[10] Social Security Act, 1975, S. 87; Family Allowances Act, 1965, S. 10; Supplementary Benefits Act, 1976, S. 16.

Claims of debt and of damages are assignable *inter vivos,* but claims of damages for purely personal wrongs do not transmit on death.

Titulus et modus transferendi dominii

For valid transfer of an assignable right the transferor must have a right to transfer,[11] and there must be both *titulus et modus transferendi dominii.* The *tituli* in question in outright transfer are the intention to gift[12] and the contracts of barter and sale. The *modus* is in general assignation completed by intimation.

Gift

The intention to make a donation, whether *inter vivos* or *mortis causa,* of a right must be clearly evidenced. *In dubio* there is a presumption against gift, and intention to donate must be clearly proved;[13] if not proved, loan or other redeemable transfer will be inferred. To be effectual a unilateral deed of gift must generally be delivered.[14] Parole proof of intention to donate is competent only where there has been delivery to the donee or someone on his behalf of the document evidencing the right alleged to be donated.[15]

Donation inter vivos

A donation *inter vivos* requires evidence of the requisite *animus donandi*[16] and execution and delivery of the assignation or transfer requisite to transfer title to the right donated from donor to donee if registered or intimated by the donee. Delivery of a writ evidencing the right, such as a share certificate, will not suffice by itself. A negotiable instrument can be donated by delivery, or endorsement and delivery,[17] and the goods represented by a document of title by delivery, or endorsement and delivery thereof. Money in the form of notes or coin can be donated by bare delivery *animo donandi.*[18] Paying a debt due by another

---

[11] cf. *Mackay* v. *M.,* 1914 S.C. 200; *Bentley* v. *Macfarlane,* 1964 S.C. 76.

[12] cf. *Macfarlane's Exor.* v. *Miller* (1898) 25 R. 1201; *Scott's Trs.* v. *Macmillan* (1905) 8 F. 214; *Carmichael* v. *C's Exor.,* 1920 S.C. (H.L.) 195, 203; *Macpherson's Exor.* v. *Mackay,* 1932 S.C. 565 (donations *mortis causa*); *Brownlee* v. *Robb,* 1907 S.C. 1302; *I.R.* v. *Wilson* 1928 S.C. (H.L.) 42 (donation *inter vivos*).

[13] *Ross* v. *Mellis* (1871) 10 M. 197; *Jamieson* v. *McLeod* (1880) 7 R. 1131; *Thomson's Exor.* v. *T* (1882) 9 R. 911; *Sharp* v. *Paton* (1883) 10 R. 1000, 1056; *Milne* v. *Grant's Exors.* (1884) 11 R. 887; *Connell's Trs.* v. *C's Trs.* (1886) 13 R. 1175; *Dawson* v. *McKenzie* (1892) 19 R. 261, 271; *Penman's Trs.* v. *P.* (1896) 4 S.L.T. 66; *Brownlee* v. *Robb,* 1907 S.C. 1302; *Brownlee's Exrx.* v. *B.,* 1908 S.C. 232, 242; *Grant's Trs.* v. *Macdonald,* 1939 S.C. 448; *Penman* v. *White,* 1957 S.C. 338.

[14] *Jarvie's Tr.* v. *J's Trs.* (1887) 14 R. 411; *Connell's Trs.* v. *C's Tr.* 1955 S.L.T. 125. cf. *Tennent* v. *T's Trs.* (1869) 7 M. 936; *Cameron's Trs.* v. *C.,* 1907 S.C. 407.

[15] *Anderson's Trs.* v. *Webster* (1883) 11 R. 35; *Drummond* v. *Mathieson,* 1912, 1 S.L.T. 455.

[16] *Grants' Trs., supra.*

[17] cf. *Swan's Exors.* v. *McDougall* (1868) 5 S.L.R. 675.

[18] *Malcolm* v. *Campbell* (1889) 17 R. 255; cf. opening accound in donee's name: *Boucher's Trs.* v. *B's Trs.* (1907) 15 S.L.T. 157.

may be a donation to the real debtor.[19] It is essential that the transaction takes immediate effect; an intention to gift is unenforceable,[20] though a promise to give may be enforceable.

The gift may be conditional, but any condition may be invalid on the ground of illegality or contrariety to public policy.[21] Gifts to charitable funds may be conditional so that if the charitable purpose fails the gift is returnable,[22] or they may be held absolute in which case, if the charitable purpose fails, the moneys will fall to be applied *cy près*.[23]

A gift or bequest made by will may be declined, even one of an alimentary liferent.[24]

Donation mortis causa

An incorporeal moveable right may be donated *mortis causa,* in contemplation of though not necessarily in immediate apprehension of death. Such a donation is revocable if the donor recovers,[25] but becomes a perfected gift if he dies. It must be effected by such act or deed as is required to complete a transfer of title to the kind of property in question and, at least normally, completed by delivery to, or on behalf of, the donee.[26] The normal cases are of claims to money, particularly deposit receipts.[27]

Contract of barter or of sale

A contract of barter or of sale of rights in incorporeal moveables is regulated entirely by common law. The essentials are agreement on the parties, the subject-matter of contract, precisely which rights are to be transferred, and the thing to be taken in exchange or the price.[28] The contract is challengeable on the usual grounds.[29] Other matters may be specifically dealt with. There are no general requirements as to formalities of contract.[30] A person having notice of vice affecting his title to rights cannot validly assign them.[31]

---

[19] *Douglas's Trs. v. D.* (1868) 6 M. 223.
[20] *Allison v. Anderson* (1907) 15 S.L.T. 529.
[21] cf. *Parkinson v. College of Ambulance* [1925] 2 K.B. 1.
[22] cf. *Re Gillingham Bus Disaster Fund* [1959] Ch. 62.
[23] cf. *Re North Devon Relief Fund Trust* [1953] 2 All E.R. 1032; *Re Hillier* [1954] 2 All E.R. 59.
[24] *Ford v. F's Trs.,* 1961 S.C. 122.
[25] *Macfarquhar v. McKay* (1869) 7 M. 766.
[26] *Morris v. Riddick* (1867) 5 M. 1036.
[27] See *infra,* Ch. 7.4.
[28] *Lindsay v. Craig,* 1919 S.C. 139.
[29] e.g. *Young v. Healy,* 1909 S.C. 687.
[30] But see Banking Companies (Shares) Act, 1867, S. 1 (repealed, Statute Law Revision Act, 1966); see *Mitchell v. City of Glasgow Bank* (1878) 6 R. 420; 6 R. (H.L.) 66; *Neilson v. James* (1882) 9 Q.B.D. 546.
[31] *Moff v. Smith's Trs.,* 1930 S.N. 162.

Completion of contract

A completely constituted contract of sale of incorporeal rights, however, vests only an equitable claim in the buyer and requires to be complete by conveyance of the right, normally by assignation in writing, normally followed by intimation of the assignation to the debtor in the obligation or registration of the new owner in a public register.[32]

Mode of transfer of rights

The former mode of effecting the transfer of a right was by making the third party the creditor's mandatory for the exaction and discharge of the debt, but without imposing any obligation to account to the mandant.[33] While this is still competent, the modern practice is to transfer the claim by assignation. No particular form or words are in general essential and any words clearly indicating transference will operate an assignation.[34] Prior to 1862 two forms of assignation were in use; in one the cedent directly assigned the debt as well as the bond itself; in the other the cedent constituted the assignee the assignee to both sum and deed and surrogated the assignee in place of the cedent. The Transmission of Moveable Property (Scotland) Act, 1862, applicable primarily to personal bonds or conveyances[35] of moveable estate,[35] provides forms appropriate generally to moveable rights, which may be written on the deed assigned, or form a separate deed. They contain only a narrative clause, clause of assignation, and require to be attested in the usual way, or, presumably, be holograph or adopted as holograph. In an assignation of a bond warrandice is implied; if the transfer is gratuitous simple warrandice is implied; if onerous there are implied warrandice from fact and deed and *debitum subesse,* i.e. that the debt is subsisting and due by the debtor to the cedent.[36] He does not warrant that the debtor is solvent.[37] The assignation impliedly covers all writs relating exclusively to the debt assigned.[38] The 1862 Act, S. 1, declares an assignation registrable in the books of any court in terms of any clause of registration contained in the bond or conveyance assigned.

---

[32] *McMurrich's Trs.* v. *McM* (1904) 6 F. 121, 126.

[33] cf. *Ritchie* v. *McLachlan* (1870) 8 M. 815.

[34] *Carter* v. *McIntosh* (1862) 24 D. 925; *Caledonian Ins. Co.* v. *Beattie* (1898) 5 S.L.T. 349; *Brownlee* v. *Robb*, 1907 S.C. 1302; cf. *McCutcheon* v. *McWilliam* (1876) 3 R. 565.

[35] Defined in S. 4.

[36] *Ferrier* v. *Graham's Trs.* (1828) 6 S. 818; *Sinclair* v. *Wilson and Maclellan* (1829) 7 S. 401; *Reid* v. *Barclay* (1879) 6 R. 1007.

[37] Ersk. II, 3, 25; *Barclay* v. *Liddel* (1671) Mor. 16591.

[38] *Finlaw* v. *E. Northesk* (1670) Mor. 6544; *Lyell* v. *Christie* (1823) 2 S. 288; *Webster* v. *Reid's Trs.* (1859) 20 D. 83.

Interpretation

An assignation is open to interpretation to determine such questions as whether it is an assignation outright or in security,[39] and precisely what rights the assignation was intended to cover.[40]

Implications of assignation

A cedent impliedly confers on the assignee all powers necessary to make the assignation effectual, by intimation or otherwise.[41]

Intimation

While a delivered assignation is effective as between the cedent and the assignee[42] intimation of the assignation to the debtor or holder of the fund is necessary to acquaint him with the transfer, to interpel him from paying to the original creditor or any other assignee,[43] to divest the cedent,[44] and to complete the assignee's right and make if effectual against all parties.[45] It also renders it incompetent to prove any exception against the debt unless the subject had been rendered litigious before intimation or the assignee admits on oath that the assignation was gratuitous or in trust for the cedent.[46] The assignation is effective from the date of intimation in a question with other assignees or third parties.[47] It may be made after the death of the cedent.[48]

The debtors' actual knowledge of an assignation is sufficient to interpel him from paying the cedent,[49] but does not effect a transfer to the assignee in a competition with creditors.[50] An assignation delivered but not intimated to the debtor is good against the cedent and his executors but defeasible by a later assignation intimated first,[51] by payment by debtor to cedent,[52] by diligence by the cedent's creditors,

---

[39] *Eaglesham* v. *Grant* (1875) 2 R. 960; *Purnell* v. *Shannon* (1894) 22 R. 74.

[40] *Robertson* v. *Wright* (1873) 1 R. 237; *McCutcheon* v. *McWilliam* (1876) 3 R. 565; *Greenock Harbour Trs.* (1888) 15 R. 343; *Liqdr. of Larkhall Collieries* v. *Hamilton* (1906) 14 S.L.T. 202.

[41] *Miller* v. *Muirhead* (1894) 21 R. 658.

[42] Stair III, 1, 15; *Thome* v. *T.* (1683) 2 B. S. 49; *Grant* v. *Gray* (1828) 6 S. 489; *Brownlee* v. *Robb*, 1907 S.C. 1302.

[43] *McGill* v. *Laurestoun* (1558) Mor. 843; *McDowal* v. *Fullerton* (1714) Mor. 840; *Allan* v. *Urquhart* (1887) 15 R. 56.

[44] *Drummond* v. *Muschet* (1492) Mor. 843; *L. Rollo* v. *Niddrie* (1665) 1 B.S. 510.

[45] Stair III, 1, 6; Ersk. III, 5, 3; Bell, *Comm.* II, 16; *Liquidator of Union Club* v. *Edinburgh Life Assce. Co.* (1906) 8 F. 1143.

[46] *Lang* v. *Hislop* (1854) 16 D. 908.

[47] *Wallace* v. *Edgar* (1663) Mor. 837; *Shiells* v. *Ferguson, Davidson & Co.* (1876) 4 R. 250; *Chambers' J.F.* v. *Vertue* (1893) 20 R. 257; *Macpherson's J.F.* v. *Mackay*, 1915 S.C. 1011.

[48] *Brownlee* v. *Robb*, 1907 S.C. 1302.

[49] *Leith* v. *Garden* (1703) Mor. 865.

[50] *L. Rollo, supra*; *Dickson* v. *Trotter* (1776) Mor. 873.

[51] *L. Rollo, supra*; *Newlands* v. *Miller* (1882) 9 R. 1104; *Campbell's Trs.* v. *Whyte* (1884) 11 R. 1078.

[52] *Drummond, supra.*

confirmation of an executor-creditor to his estate,[53] or confirmation of a trustee on his sequestrated estates. An unintimated assignation does not prevent the subject assigned from passing to the trustee in the event of the assignor's sequestration.[54]

Mode of intimation

At common law the regular mode of intimation was for a procurator for the assignee to deliver to the debtor, in the presence of a notary and two witnesses, a copy of the assignation and a schedule of intimation, and to have the notary expede an instrument of intimation signed by the notary and the witnesses. Alternatively the assignee might produce the assignation to the debtor, deliver a copy of it, and obtain an attested or holograph acknowledgment of intimation.[55] These modes are still competent. Under the Transmission of Moveable Property (Scotland) Act, 1862, S. 2, intimation may be validly made by a notary public delivering a certified copy of the assignation to the debtor, and certifying intimation in the form set out in the Act, Sched. C, or by the assignee or his agent transmitting a certified copy of the assignation by post and obtaining the debtor's written acknowledgement of receipt by him of the copy. The copy need contain only such part of the deed containing the assignation as concerns the subject matter of the assignation. Where an interest in a testamentary trust has been assigned intimation to the solicitors of the trust is probably sufficient intimation to the trustees.[56] Though intimation should be made to each of joint and several debtors,[57] intimation to one trustee has been held sufficient.[58] An assignation of the uncalled capital of a company must be intimated to all the shareholders.[59] Intimation to an absent person may be made in the statutory modes, or by edictal citation, to a firm by intimation to all the partners,[60] and to a company at its registered office.

Equivalents of intimation

Various kinds of conduct are deemed equivalent to intimation of the assignation to the debtor. These include the assignee's taking possession of the right by entering into enjoyment of the rents or interest, which

[53] *Sinclair* v. *S.* (1726) Mor. 2793.
[54] *Moncrieff's Trs.* v. *Balfour,* 1928 S.N. 64, 139.
[55] Bell, *Convg.* I, 312.
[56] *Browne's Tr.* v. *Anderson* (1901) 4 F. 305.
[57] Ersk. III, 5, 5.
[58] *Jameson* v. *Sharp* (1887) 14 R. 643.
[59] *Liqdr. of Union Club* v. *Edinburgh Life Assce. Co.* (1906) 8 F. 1143; *Ballachulish Slate Quarries* v. *Malcolm* (1908) 15 S.L.T. 963; *Ballachulish Slate Quarries* v. *Menzies* (1908) 16 S.L.T. 48.
[60] *Hill* v. *Lindsay* (1846) 8 D. 472.

implies the debtor's knowledge of and compliance with the assignation;[61] action or diligence against the debtor, at the instance of the
assignee and founded on the assignation;[62] actual payment by the
debtor to the assignee of part of the principal, or of interest;[63] a written
promise by the debtor to pay the assignee;[64] participation by the debtor
as a party to the assignation,[65] but not merely as witness;[66] production
of the assignation by the assignee in an action to which the debtor is a
party;[67] intimation by the assignee by letter to the debtor and the
latter's answers thereto;[68] attendance and voting by an assignee of a
share in a firm at a meeting of the partners;[69] and intimation to the
debtor's factor and entry by him in the debtor's books.[70]

The registration of assignations of bonds or contracts in the Books
of Council and Session or Sheriff Court books for preservation, or for
preservation and execution, does not effect publication and is not
equivalent to intimation,[71] but registration of the deed in the Register
of Sasines is.[72] The debtor's actual knowledge is not equivalent to
intimation[73] particularly in a case of competition between an unintimated assignation and other claims.[74]

Where intimation unnecessary

If the assignation is granted by one who is the debtor himself,[75] or to
the person to whom intimation would otherwise have to be made, such
as the trustee of the debtor fund,[76] intimation is unnecessary. It is also
unnecessary in the case of the statutory assignation effected by the Act
and Warrant of a trustee on a sequestrated estate.[77] A bill of exchange

[61] Ersk. III, 5, 3.
[62] Ersk. III, 5, 4; *Whyte* v. *Neish* (1622) Mor. 854; *Dougall* v. *Gordon* (1795) Mor. 851.
[63] *Livingston* v. *Lindsay* (1626) Mor. 860.
[64] *Home* v. *Murray* (1674) Mor. 863.
[65] *L. Ballenden's Crs.* (1707) Mor. 865; *Turnbull* v. *Stewart* (1751) Mor. 868.
[66] *Murray* v. *Durham* (1622) Mor. 855.
[67] *Dougal* v. *Gordan* (1795) Mor. 851; cf. *Faculty of Advocates* v. *Dickson* (1718) Mor. 866.
[68] *Gray* v. *D. Hamilton* (1708) Rob. App. 1; *Wallace* v. *Davies* (1853) 15 D. 688.
[69] *Hill* v. *Lindsay* (1857) 10 D. 78.
[70] *E. Aberdeen* v. *E. March* (1730) 1 Pat. 44; but see Bell, *Convg.* I, 318.
[71] *Tod's Trs.* v. *Wilson* (1869) 7 M. 1100; *Cameron's Trs.* v. *C.*, 1907 S.C. 407.
[72] *Paul* v. *Boyd's Trs.* (1835) 13 S. 818; *Edmond* v. *Aberdeen Mags.* (1858) 3 Macq. 116;
Rodger v. *Crawfords* (1867) 6 M. 24.
[73] Stair II, 1, 24; More, *Notes*, cclxxi; Ersk. III, 5, 5; Bell, *Comm.* II, 18; *Adamson* v.
McMitchell (1624) Mor. 859; *L. Westraw* v. *Williamson & Carmichael* (1626) Mor. 859;
Dickson v. *Trotter* (1776) Mor. 873; *Fac. of Advocates* v. *Dickson* (1718) Mor. 866; cf. *Leith* v.
Garden (1703) Mor. 865.   [74] *L. Rollo* v. *Laird of Niddrie* (1665) 1 B.S. 510.
[75] *Browne's Tr.* v. *Anderson* (1901) 4 F. 305.
[76] *E. Argyle* v. *Macdonald* (1676) Mor. 842; *Russell* v. *Breadalbane* (1831) 5 W. & S. 256;
Miller v. *Learmonth* (1870) 42 S. Jur. 418; *Mounsey* (1896) 4 S.L.T. 46; *Ayton* v. *Romanes*
(1893) 3 S.L.T. 203.
[77] Bankruptcy (Sc.) Act, 1913, S. 97(1); *Tod's Tr.* v. *Wilson* (1869) 7 M. 1100; *Watson* v.
Duncan (1879) 6 R. 1247; *Kirkland* v. *K's Tr.* (1886) 13 R. 798; *Greenock Harbour Trs.* (1888)
15 R. 343.

accepted payable at a banker's operates on presentment as an intimated assignation of the acceptor's funds in the banker's hands.[78]

Effect of assignation

The effect of an intimated assignation is to divest the cedent completely and to put the assignee in his place, entitled to sue for the
enforcement of the assigned right, and do diligence thereon,[79] to
receive payment and grant a good discharge therefor: *Assignatus
utitur jure auctoris.*

Quality of assignee's right

By virtue of the maxim *nemo plus juris ad alium transferre potest
quam ipse habet* the assignee obtains no better right than the cedent
himself possessed. If the right was terminable or defeasible against the
cedent, it remains so against the assignee.[80] The debtor may utilize
against the assignee all pleas, rights of action, and defences which
would have been competent against the cedent, even though the assignee
took in good faith and for value.[81] But pleas emerging subsequently to
the assignation cannot competently be pleaded against the assignee.[82]
The debtor may, however, expressly undertake that pleas competent
between the original parties shall not be pleadable in a question with
an assignee,[83] or may bar himself by his conduct from challenging the
assignee's rights.[84]

Where cedent's right subject to latent trusts or claims

But an assignee who takes in good faith, for value, and without
notice of any latent trusts or claims affecting the cedent's right,[85]
obtains the assigned right free of any such claim, and accordingly
obtains a better title than his cedent had. Thus where a shareholder
assigned his share, which *ex facie* he held absolutely, to a creditor in

---

[78] *B.L. Co.* v. *Rainey's Tr.* (1885) 12 R. 825; *Sutherland* v. *Commercial Bank* (1882) 20 S.L.R.
139.

[79] *Grier* v. *Maxwell* (1621) Mor. 828.

[80] *Johnstone-Beattie* v. *Dalziel* (1868) 6 M. 333; *Chambers' Trs.* v. *Smiths* (1878) 5 R. (H.L.)
151; *Train* v. *Clapperton*, 1908 S.C. (H.L.) 26.

[81] Stair I, 10, 16; III, 1, 20; IV, 40, 21; Ersk. III, 5, 10; Bell, *Prin.* §1468; *McDowells* v. *Bell &
Rannie* (1772) Mor. 4974; *Shiells* v. *Ferguson, Davidson & Co.* (1876) 4 R. 250; *Scottish
Widows' Fund* v. *Buist* (1878) 5 R. (H.L.) 64; *Arnott's Trs.* v. *Forbes* (1881) 9 R. 89; cf. *Duncan*
v. *Brooks* (1894) 21 R. 760.

[82] *Shiells, supra; Macpherson's J.F.* v. *Mackay*, 1915 S.C. 1011.

[83] *Bovill* v. *Dixon* (1854) 16 D. 619; 3 Macq. 1.

[84] *Bovill, supra; Scottish Equitable Life Assce. Socy.* v. *Buist* (1877) 4 R. 1076.

[85] It is noteworthy that in many cases where ownership of a right is registered the register may
not notice any trust or similar equitable claim; see e.g. register of shares if company registered in
England (Companies Act, 1948, s. 117); register of trademarks (Trade Marks Act, 1938, S. 64);
register of patents (Patents Act, 1977, S. 32); register of designs (Registered Designs Act, 1949,
S. 17).

security of a private loan, the assignee was held entitled to it in preference to and free of the claim to the share by a partnership for which the cedent had held the share as trustee.[86]

This principle does not apply if the assignee did not take in complete good faith and in the belief that the cedent was entitled to assign absolutely, nor if the assignation were gratuitous, nor if the assignee had knowledge of the claim qualifying the cedent's right. Nor does it apply to the general assignation effected by sequestration to the trustee for the body of creditors in a sequestration, for they take the bankrupt's rights *tantum et tale* as vested in him, and are affected by even latent trusts and claims affecting his rights, having given no value for the assignation effected by the sequestration.[87]

Special cases

In various cases a formal assignation followed by intimation is unnecessary. A negotiable instrument is transferred by delivery, or by endorsement and delivery;[88] bills of lading by delivery or endorsement and delivery;[89] policies of marine insurance by endorsement thereon so long as the assured still has an interest in the subject-matter insured or had, before or at the time of losing his interest, expressly or impliedly agreed to assign the policy;[90] bottomry and respondentia bonds probably by assignation in common form;[91] and share warrants to bearer by delivery of the warrant.[92]

Special forms of assignation

In other cases a special form of assignation is utilized: life insurance policies are assigned either in one of the forms authorized by the Transmission of Moveable Property (Sc.) Act, 1862, or in the form authorized by the Policies of Assurance Act, 1867; interests in Government stock may be transferred in the same mode as shares or stock in limited companies;[93] local authority mortgages by transfer endorsed thereon in the form in the Local Government (Scotland) Act, 1947, Sched. 7, and attested, without prejudice to other mode of assignation, the transfer being registered in the register of mortgages maintained by the authority;[94] shares or stock or debentures of com-

[86] *Somervails* v. *Redfearn* (1813) 1 Dow 50; cf. *Burns* v. *Laurie's Trs.* (1840) 2 D. 1348.

[87] *Gordon* v. *Cheyne* (1824) 2 S. 675; *Heritable Reversionary Co.* v. *Millar* (1892) 19 R. (H.L.) 43; *Bank of Scotland* v. *Liquidators of Hutchison Main & Co.*, 1914 S.C. (H.L.) 1.

[88] Bills of Exchange Act, 1882.

[89] Bills of Lading Act, 1855, S. 1.

[90] Marine Insurance Act, 1906, Ss. 50–1.

[91] But see *The Petone* [1917] P. 198.

[92] Companies Act, 1948, S. 83.

[93] cf. National Debt Act, 1870, S. 23; Finance Act, 1942, S. 47 and Sched. II; Government Stock Regulations, 1943 (S.R & O. 1943, No. 1.) See also now Stock Transfer Act, 1963.

[94] Local Government (Sc.) Act, 1947, Ss. 267–8.

panies incorporated under the Companies Acts in the manner provided by the Articles of the company, which is normally a common form instrument of transfer signed by both transferor and transferee, each before one witness, and sent to the company's office for registration;[95] fully paid securities (including shares, stock, debenture stock, etc.) issued by any company within the Companies Act, 1948, except a company limited by guarantee or an unlimited company, or by any body incorporated in Great Britain by or under any enactment or by Royal Charter except a building society or a society registered under the Industrial and Provident Societies Act, 1893, or by the Government of the United Kingdom (with certain exceptions), or by any local authority, and units of an approved unit trust scheme may be transferred by an instrument in the form set out in the Stock Transfer Act, 1963, Sched. 1, executed by the transferor only without need for any witness,[96] and specifying the consideration, the description of the securities, the transferor's and transferee's names and addresses. The consideration may be inserted in the transfer or supplied by separate brokers' transfers in the form set out in Sched. 2.[97]

Trade Marks: Patents: Designs: Copyright: Public Lending Right: Plant Breeder's rights

A registered trade mark is assignable, in connection with the goodwill of a business or separately, and in respect of some or all of the goods in respect of which it is registered, the assignee being bound to apply to the Register of Trade Marks to register his title thereto.[98]

A patent may be assigned and notice of the assignation must be recorded in the Register of Patents.[99]

An assignee of a registered design or to a share therein must apply to the Register of Designs for the registration of his title as proprietor thereof.[1]

An assignation of copyrights, total or partial, is effective only if in writing signed by or on behalf of the assignor.[2]

An assignation of an author's public lending right must be in writing and registered in the Register of Public Lending Right.[3]

---

[95] Companies Act, 1948, Ss. 73–82; Stock Transfer Act, 1963; Stock Exchange (Completion of Bargains) Act, 1976. The right of property is transferred only when the new owner is registered by the company. *Tennant's Trs.* v. *T.* 1946 S.C. 420.

[96] Except, by Stock Transfer Act, 1963, S. 2(4), a transfer executed under the Conveyancing (Sc.) Act, 1924, S. 18, on behalf of a person who is blind or unable to write.

[97] Stock Transfer Act, 1963.

[98] Trade Marks Act, 1938, Ss. 22–5.

[99] Patents Act, 1977, Ss. 31–2.

[1] Registered Designs Act, 1949, S. 19.

[2] Copyright Act, 1956, S. 36.

[3] Public Lending Right Act, 1979, Ss. 1, 4.

Plant breeder's rights are assignable like other kinds of proprietary rights.[4]

Assignation of funds by bill or cheque

A bill of exchange accepted payable at a banker operates on presentment as an intimated assignation of the acceptor's funds in the banker's hands,[5] and a cheque drawn for value also operates assignation of the drawer's funds.[6]

PARTICULAR KINDS OF INCORPOREAL OBJECTS

Decrees of court, claims of debt or of damages

The sale of such a right is frequently part of a compromise whereby a defender settles the pursuer's claim and acquires his right, to aid him in working out relief against another defender,[7] but it may be to an independent third party,[8] or may be as part of a transaction whereby the corporeal subject, in respect of which the claim arises, was sold.[9]

Rights of relief

A person subject to a legal liability who has a right of relief against another person in respect of that liability may assign his right of relief.[10] The assignee may sue the party liable in relief only if the debtor has admitted liability or been found liable for the debt.[11]

Rights under contract

Rights under contract to payment are generally assignable; rights to performance are assignable only in cases where there is no *delectus personae creditoris* so that it does not matter to or for whom the debtor must perform his obligation,[12] and no *delectus personae debitoris* so that it does not matter which person performs the obligation.[13]

---

[4] Plant Varieties and Seeds Act, 1964, S. 4(4).

[5] *B.L. Co.* v. *Rainey's Tr.* (1885) 12 R. 825.

[6] *Sutherland* v. *Commercial Bank* (1882) 20 S.L.R. 139.

[7] e.g. *Gardiner* v. *Main* (1895) 22 R. 100; *Constant* v. *Kincaid* (1902) 4 F. 901; *Traill* v. *A/S. Dalbeattie* (1904) 6 F. 798; *Cole-Hamilton* v. *Boyd*, 1963 S.C. (H.L.) 1.

[8] *Bentley* v. *Macfarlane*, 1963 S.C. 279.

[9] *Symington* v. *Campbell* (1894) 21 R. 434.

[10] *Rollo* v. *Perth Mags.* (1902) 10 S.L.T. 25.

[11] *Duncan's Trs.* v. *Steven* (1897) 24 R. 880; *N.C.B.* v. *Thomson*, 1959 S.C. 353.

[12] Bell, *Prin.* §1459; *Aurdal* v. *Estrella*, 1916 S.C. 882; *Westville Shipping Co.* v. *Abram*, 1923 S.C. (H.L.) 68.

[13] *Asphaltic Limestone Co.* v. *Glasgow Corpn.*, 1907 S.C. 463; *Cole* v. *Handasyde*, 1910 S.C. 68.

Negotiable instruments

A bill of exchange or other negotiable instrument may be transferred by negotiation pursuant to an agreement to transfer the claim therein. But it may also be agreed to be sold[14] or assigned,[15] particularly as part of a sale of economic assets, and be transferred in pursuance thereof by assignation in the same way as other incorporeal rights. But until or unless the bill is actually transferred under the contract by assignation, the holder may negotiate it to any innocent third party who, if he gives value, acquires a good title by negotiation, leaving the disappointed buyer or assignee to a claim of damages for breach of contract.

Bills of lading

As a symbol of the goods described therein as shipped, a bill of lading may be agreed to be sold, unless its terms preclude transfer.[16] The contract must be completed by delivery or endorsement and delivery of the bill.[17] The whole property in the goods passes if the transfer of the bill was intended to have that effect. But a transfer passes no property in the goods where the transfer has been made without consideration,[18] where the transferor himself had no property in the goods and no authority to deal with the property in them, as where he had already sold the goods apart from the bill of lading,[19] or where the transfer is made to a transferee who does not take *in bona fide*, being aware of facts which make the transfer inoperative, such as the buyer's insolvency.[20]

Documents of title to goods

A warrant granted by a storekeeper or warehousekeeper acknowledging holding certain goods to the order of a named person is a species of property which may be sold or assigned in security. To complete the contract the warrants must be endorsed and transmitted to the purchaser, and intimation made to the storekeeper.[21]

Claims of aliment

A claim for aliment is personal to the individual entitled thereto and cannot be assigned.

[14] *Embiricos* v. *Anglo-Austrian Bank* [1905] 1 K.B. 677.
[15] *Dawson* v. *Isle* [1906] 1 Ch. 633.
[16] *Henderson* v. *Comptoir d'Escompte de Paris* (1873) L.R. 5 P.C. 253.
[17] *Sewell* v. *Burdick* (1884) 10 App. Cas. 74.
[18] *Sewell, supra*, 80.
[19] *Gurney* v. *Behrend* (1854) 3 E. & B. 622; *London Joint Stock Bank* v. *British Amsterdam Maritime Agency* (1910) 11 Asp. M.L.C. 571.
[20] *Cuming* v. *Brown* (1808) 9 East 506; *Pease* v. *Gloahec* (1866) L.R. 1 P.C. 219.
[21] *Connal* v. *Loder* (1868) 6 M. 1095; *Inglis* v. *Robertson & Baxter* (1898) 25 R. (H.L.) 70.

Obligations of debt

An I.O.U. or similar acknowledgment of debt is not a promissory note or bill, and cannot be negotiated but may be assigned.

Personal bonds

A personal bond is assignable and, if onerous, the assignation implies warrandice from fact and deed and *debitum subesse*, i.e. that the debt subsists and is due by the debtor to the assigning creditor.[22]

Debentures

Debentures are transferable by assignation.

Rights in security over corporeal objects

Some rights in security over corporeal moveables are saleable and assignable, namely, where documents of title have been pledged in security.[23] The assignee's right is completed not by assignation but by endorsement and delivery of the documents of title, and intimation to the actual holder of the goods.[24]

Reversionary rights

A reversionary right in an object transferred in security, by pledge, may be sold outright and transferred by assignation.[25]

Policies of life assurance

The right under a policy of life assurance to receive an agreed sum on the happening of an agreed event is a right of property[26] which may be sold outright before that event happens. It may be assigned though when the assured effected the policy he had the intention to assign it.[27] The contract to sell or assign may be constituted in any form.[28] The contract is void if the life assured has died before the contract was made.[29] A policy effected under the Married Women's Policies of Assurance (Sc.) Act, 1880, S. 2, cannot be validly assigned by husband

---

[22] *Ferrier* v. *Graham's Trs.* (1828) 6 S. 818; *Sinclair* v. *Wilson and Maclellan* (1829) 7 S. 401; *Reid* v. *Barclay* (1879) 6 R. 1007.
[23] cf. *Inglis* v. *Robertson & Baxter* (1898) 25 R. (H.L.) 70; *Price & Pierce* v. *Bank of Scotland*, 1912 S.C. (H.L.) 19.
[24] *Inglis, supra.*
[25] cf. *Mears* v. *L.S.W. Ry.* (1862) 11 C.B. (N.S.) 850 (owner can claim for damage done by third party to moveables lent to, hired by or pledged with another).
[26] *Re Moore* (1878) 8 Ch. D. 519; *Hadden* v. *Bryden* (1899) 1 F. 710.
[27] *McFarlane* v. *Royal London Friendly Socy.* (1886) 2 T.L.R. 755.
[28] For a special case see *Ballantyne's Trs.* v. *Scottish Amicable Life Assce. Socy.*, 1921, 2 S.L.T. 75.
[29] *Scott* v. *Coulson* [1903] 2 Ch. 249.

and wife to the former's creditors,[30] but may be surrendered by the trustee with the wife's concurrence.[31] A policy may be assigned by husband to wife as a provision for her if she survives, in which case, if she does not, it never vests in her.[32]

The contract must be completed by a deed of assignation[33] intimated by the assignee to the insurers, and to entitle the buyer to receive the sum due under the policy he must continue to pay the premiums and prove the death of the life assured.[34]

Salary and pension rights

Salaries and earnings from employment are generally assignable.[35]

The assignation of salaries paid to persons in the public service is forbidden by public policy. This principle covers all persons paid out of national funds, from judges[36] to telephone attendants.[37] It may apply to M.P.'s.[38]

A pension paid to a person for past services is assignable[39] unless assignation is forbidden by statute.[40] Social security benefits are declared non-assignable.[41]

Liferent

A liferent, whether proper or improper, may be assigned unless declared not assignable,[42] or, if improper, unless declared alimentary[43] and then only so far as excessive. If assignable, the right assigned subsists only for the duration of the cedent's, and not of the assignee's, life.[44]

[30] *Scottish Life Assce. Co. v. Donald* (1901) 9 S.L.T. 200; *Edinburgh Life Assce. Co. v. Balderston,* 1909, 2 S.L.T. 323.

[31] *Schumann v. Scottish Widows' Fund Socy.* (1886) 13 R. 678.

[32] *Galloway v. Craig* (1861) 4 Macq. 267; *Pirie v. P.,* 1921 S.C. 781.

[33] Statutory form in Policies of Assurance Act, 1867, Sched. But a deed of assignation in common form suffices, as does any equivalent deed: *Caledonian Ins. Co. v. Beattie* (1898) 5 S.L.T. 349; *Brownlee v. Robb,* 1907 S.C. 1302.

[34] The Presumption of Death (Sc.) Act, 1977, may not apply. See also *N.B. and Mercantile Ins. Co. v. Stewart* (1871) 9 M. 534.

[35] cf. *O'Driscoll v. Manchester Insurance Cttee.* [1915] 3 K.B. 499. As to merchant seamen see Merchant Shipping Act, 1970, Ss. 11, 13, 14.

[36] *Arbuthnot v. Norton* (1846) 5 Moo. P.C. 219.

[37] *Mulvenna v. The Admiralty,* 1926 S.C. 842.

[38] *Hollinshead v. Hazleton* [1916] 1 A.C. 428.

[39] See e.g. *Willcock v. Terrell* (1878) 3 Ex. D. 323; *Sansom v. S.* (1879) 4 P.D. 69.

[40] See Naval and Marine Pay and Pensions Act, 1865, S. 4; Army Act, 1955, S. 203; Air Force Act, 1955; S. 203; Police Pensions Act, 1948, S. 7; Fire Services Act, 1947, S. 26; 1951, S. 1; Superannuation Act, 1972, S. 5.

[41] Social Security Act, 1975, S. 87; Family Allowance Act, 1965, S. 10; Supplementary Benefits Act, 1976, S. 16.

[42] *Chaplin's Trs. v. Hoile* (1890) 18 R. 27; *Scottish Union and National Ins. Co. v. Smeaton* (1904) 7 F. 174.

[43] *Claremont's Trs. v. C.* (1896) 4 S.L.T. 144; *Craig v. Pearson's Trs.,* 1915, 2 S.L.R. 183. See also *Cuthbert v. C's Trs.,* 1908 S.C. 967.   [44] Ersk. II, 9, 41.

Beneficial interests in succession

A *spes successionis,* or non-vested contingent right of succession, is assignable, unless such a transaction with the right is prohibited by the deed under which the *spes* arises,[45] to the effect of giving the buyer a good title in a question with the seller to the right, estate or succession when it comes to be vested in the seller.[46] If the contingency whereby the right transmits to the seller never happens, *contractus perit emptori.* A legacy given, subject to postponed vesting, has been held to confer an assignable prospective interest between the testator's death and the date of vesting.[47]

A provision such as an annuity, made in succession, unless declared alimentary or non-assignable, is assignable onerously or gratuitously.[48]

Beneficial interests under trusts

Excepting interests declared alimentary,[49] and even then only so far as not excessive,[50] a beneficial interest under a trust may be assigned by contract followed by assignation, intimated to the trustees.[51] In such a case the assignees are not affected by the actings of their cedent subsequent to the intimation of the assignation.

Rights under marriage-contracts

A right under a marriage-contract, if vested, may be sold and assigned, but probably not if not yet vested.[52]

Interests in partnerships

The interest of one partner in a partnership may be assigned[53] but only to the effect of entitling the assignee to receive the share of profits to which the assignor would otherwise be entitled, and not to the effect of making the assignee a partner or entitling him to interfere in the management or administration of the firm,[54] to require any accounts of the partnership transactions or to inspect the partnership books.[55] On dissolution the assignee becomes entitled to the assigning partner's

---

[45] cf. *Kirkland* v. *K's Tr.* (1886) 13 R. 798; *Brown's Tr.* v. *Anderson* (1901) 4 F. 305.

[46] *Trappes* v. *Meredith* (1871) 10 M. 38; see also *Reid* v. *Morison* (1893) 20 R. 510; *Salaman* v. *Todd,* 1911 S.C. 1214; *Coats* v. *Bannochie's Trs.,* 1912 S.C. 329.

[47] *Rothwell* v. *Stuart's Trs.* (1898) 1 F. 81.

[48] *White's Trs.* v. *Whyte* (1877) 4 R. 786.

[49] *Rothwell* v. *Stuart's Trs.* (1898) 1 F. 81.

[50] *Claremont's Trs.* v. *C.* (1896) 4 S.L.T. 144; *Cuthbert* v. *C's Trs.,* 1908 S.C. 967.

[51] *Thow's Trs.* v. *Young,* 1910 S.C. 588; *Macpherson's J.F.* v. *Mackay,* 1915 S.C. 1011.

[52] *McDonald* v. *McGrigor* (1874) 1 R. 817. See also *Christie's Factor* v. *Hardie* (1899) 1 F. 703.

[53] On the contract to assign see *Dodson* v. *Downey* [1901] 2 Ch. 620.

[54] cf. *Re Garwood's Trusts* [1903] 1 Ch. 236.

[55] Partnership Act, 1890, S. 31(1).

share of the assets and, for the purpose of ascertaining that, to an account from the date of the dissolution.[56]

Sale of shares in company

Shares in companies are transferable by gift or sale.

A sale of shares or marketable securities may be concluded direct with the purchaser[57] or through the agency of brokers on the Stock Exchange. A contract for the sale of shares or securities may be made orally and proved by parole evidence.[58] It is challengeable on the ground of fraud.[59] Any person who buys or sells any stock or marketable security of the value of £5 or upwards as a broker or agent must forthwith make, execute and transmit a stamped contract note to his principal, or his vendor or purchaser.[60]

The purchaser may repudiate the contract if the seller delivers share warrants rather than registered shares,[61] but not if lots of the shares bought are tendered from several different sellers.[62]

The seller is under a duty to deliver the share or stock certificate and to execute an instrument of transfer,[63] and must do nothing to prevent the purchaser having himself registered as proprietor of the shares.[64] It is the duty of the buyer to prepare and tender a transfer,[65] but in stock exchange transactions the tranferor frequently tenders the transfer. The buyer may refuse payment for a transfer unaccompanied by the share certificate unless it is certified that the certificate is at the company's office. The seller does not guarantee the purchaser's registration.[66]

Time is of the essence of the contract.[67]

In the event of breach the injured party may claim specific implement, damages, or an indemnity, depending on the circumstances. Specific implement will not normally be granted of a contract to transfer government stock,[68] nor of a contract to sell shares readily

---

[56] S. 31(2); *Bergmann* v. *Macmillan* (1881) 17 Ch. D. 423; see also *Watts* v. *Driscoll* [1901] 1 Ch. 294; *Bonnin* v. *Neame* [1910] 1 Ch. 732.
[57] e.g. *Spence* v. *Crawford*, 1939 S.C. (H.L.) 52.
[58] *Devlin* v. *McKelvie*, 1915 S.C. 180.
[59] *Gibbs* v. *B.L. Co.* (1877) 4 R. 630; *Spence, supra.*
[60] Finance (1909–10) Act, 1910, S. 78.
[61] *Iredell* v. *General Securities Corpn., Ltd.* (1916) 33 T.L.R. 67.
[62] *Benjamin* v. *Barnett* (1903) 8 Com. Cas. 244; cf. *Lamont, Macquisten* v. *Inglis* (1903) 11 S.L.T. 10.
[63] *Neilson* v. *James* (1882) 9 Q.B.D. 546; *London Founders Assocn* v. *Clarke* (1888) 20 Q.B.D. 576.
[64] *London Founders Assocn., supra; Hooper* v. *Herts* [1906] 1 Ch. 549.
[65] *Lyle and Scott, Ltd.* v. *Scott's Trs.*, 1959 S.C. (H.L.) 64.
[66] *Marr* v. *Buchanan Younger & Co.* (1852) 14 D. 467.
[67] *Rothschild* v. *Hennings* (1829) 9 B. & C. 470; *Black* v. *Cullen* (1853) 15 D. 646.
[68] *Nutbrown* v. *Thornton* (1804) 10 Ves. 159.

available in the market, though it may if the market in the shares is restricted.[69] A purchase may be ordained to execute a transfer.[70]

In other cases damages are recoverable, as where a purchaser declines to accept stock or to pay therefor.[71]

The seller is entitled to an indemnity from the buyer in respect of a call, though made after the contract but before the date of completion,[72] and in respect of any liability as a contributory if the company has commenced winding-up.[73]

The gift or sale is completed by execution of a transfer under the Stock Transfer Act, 1963, or as provided by the articles of the company, and registration by the company.[74]

Transfer of goodwill

The goodwill of a business may in some cases be deemed so connected in whole or in part with the premises in which it has been carried on[75] as to require a contract for its sale to be constituted in writing, but in other cases the goodwill is quite separate from sale of the premises and business name,[76] and accordingly, in general, writing, though common,[77] is unnecessary. The sale of a going business implies sale of its goodwill.

Goodwill partakes of so many elements that it is desirable to specify what rights are contracted to be sold: *prima facie* a sale will pass the right to carry on the old business and use the old trade name,[78] and to the business books.[79] It will be a breach of contract for the seller subsequently to take advantage of the connection formed by him in the old business,[80] but, unless there is a restrictive clause in the sale, he may set up a new business in competition.

Assignation of trademarks, patents, registered designs, copyright, public lending right and plant breeders' rights

Each of these statutory forms of incorporeal property may be

---

[69] *Cheale* v. *Kenward* (1858) 3 De G. & J. 27.
[70] *Shaw* v. *Fisher* (1848) 2 De G. & Sm. 11.
[71] *Dorriens* v. *Hutchinson* (1804) 1 Smith 420;
[72] *Hawkins* v. *Maltby* (1867) L.R. 3 Ch. App. 188; 4 Ch. App. 200.
[73] *Rudge* v. *Bowman* (1868) L.R. 3 Q.B. 689; *Neilson* v. *James* (1882) 9 Q.B.D. 546.
[74] Companies Act, 1948, S. 73.
[75] cf. *Hughes* v. *Stirling Assessor* (1892) 19 R. 840; *Murray's Tr.* v. *McIntyre* (1904) 6 F. 588; *Graham* v. *G.s Trs.* (1904) 6 F. 1015; *Muirhead's Trs.* v. *M.* (1905) 7 F. 496; *Edinburgh Assessor* v. *Caira and Crolla*, 1928 S.C. 398.
[76] cf. *Barr* v. *Lions, Ltd.*, 1956 S.C. 59.
[77] cf. *Smith* v. *McBride & Smith* (1888) 16 R. 36; *Smart* v. *Wilkinson*, 1928 S.C. 383.
[78] *Churton* v. *Douglas* (1858) John. 174; *Walker* v. *Mottram* (1881) 19 Ch. D. 355; *Smith*, supra.
[79] *Morrison* v. *M.* (1900) 2 F. 382.
[80] *Trego* v. *Hunt* [1896] A.C. 7.

assigned, outright or in security, in accordance with the conditions in the relevant statute. The contract to assign need not be constituted in writing, but must be given effect to by assignation in writing.[81]

---

[81] e.g. *Mackay* v. *M.*, 1914 S.C. 200.

CHAPTER 5.42

INVOLUNTARY TRANSFER OF RIGHTS IN INCORPOREAL MOVEABLE OBJECTS

Rights in incorporeal moveable objects may be taken from the person having right to them, in certain cases by compulsory powers, in some cases by diligence in execution of decree, and in some cases by sequestration in bankruptcy.

Compulsory acquisition

In certain cases rights in incorporeals may be taken compulsorily, such as shares in and patents of companies which are nationalized.[1]

Diligence in execution

The diligence appropriate to most forms of incorporeal moveable objects is arrestment.[2] By it a creditor secures a prohibition on a third party, the arrestee, who is debtor to the principal or common debtor, paying the common debtor until the latter pays the arresting creditor. It may be used in security, to meet a debt not yet due, or in execution, where the arrester holds a decree of court or a decree by registration of a bill or bond.[3] Incorporeal objects arrestable include money due by a bank, the share of profits or stock in a partnership or joint adventure,[4] arrears of or current rents,[5] arrears of or current interest due on heritable bonds,[6] capital and interest of moveable bonds,[7] shares of ships,[8] the sum in a policy of insurance,[9] shares in a company[10] (though stock of the Bank of Scotland and The Royal Bank can be attached only by adjudication[11]), annuities,[12] moveable interests in trusts for family and testamen-

---

[1] See e.g. Coal Industry Nationalization Act, 1946, Ss. 5–7.
[2] Generally, Graham Stewart on *Diligence,* 24 *et seq.*
[3] Arrestment may alse be used in certain cases to found jurisdiction.
[4] Bell, *Comm.,* II, 3; *Rae* v. *Neilson* (1742) Mor. 716; *Neilson & Murdoch* v. *Colquhoun & Rae* (1745) Mor. 723.
[5] Bell, *Comm.* II, 72; *Prin.* §2276.
[6] Ibid.
[7] Arrestments (Sc.) 1661; *Stewart* v. *Dundas's Crs.* (1706) Mor. 705.
[8] *Clark* v. *Loos* (1853) 15 D. 750; *Lucovich* (1885) 12 R. 1090.
[9] *Strachan* v. *McDougle* (1835) 13 S. 954.
[10] *Lindsay* v. *L.N.W. Ry.* (1860) 22 D. 571; *Sinclair* v. *Staples* (1860) 22 D. 600.
[11] Bell, *Comm.* I, 102; *Royal Bank* v. *Fairholm* (1770) Mor. Appx. Adjudication, No. 3.
[12] Ersk. III, 6, 9; Bell, *Comm.* II, 8; *Prin.* §2276.

tary purposes,[13] but not trusts for behoof of creditors, the insured's interest in a life insurance policy payable on his death,[14] the sum contained in a deposit receipt,[15] articles lodged by the debtor with auctioneers for sale, they being liable to account to him,[16] sums due to the debtor from a trust estate,[17] money due to an executor by the solicitor administering the executry,[18] an obligation to account for a possible balance due to the debtor,[19] the sum due to the debtor under a third-party liability insurance policy,[20] instalments of the price about to become due under a contract,[21] legal rights on death,[22] and other similar claims.

Sums payable as salary or wages are arrestable, subject to the limitations imposed by the Wages Arrestment Limitation Acts, 1870 and 1960,[23] and some sums due in government employment.[24] A claim of damages has been held arrestable though the arrestments were used before the claim had been made.[25] Conversely a sum of damages awarded has been held non-arrestable when a new trial was allowed and the claim subsequently settled.[26]

Rights not arrestable include bills and promissory notes,[27] sums appropriated by the granter for special purposes,[28] alimentary rights for the maintenance of the grantee, except in so far as they exceed a reasonable maintenance,[29] *spes successionis*,[30] contingent and future claims,[31] wages of seamen and apprentices,[32] an obligation *ad factum praestandum*,[33] wages of labourers and manufacturers, so far as necessary for subsistence,[34] and various pension rights.

---

[13] *Learmonts* v. *Shearer* (1866) 4 M. 540.
[14] *Strachan* v. *McDougle, supra; Bankhardt's Trs.* v. *Scottish Amicable Socy.* (1871) 9 M. 443.
[15] *Allan's Exor.* v. *Union Bank*, 1909 S.C. 206.
[16] *Mackenzie* v. *Finlay* (1868) 7 M. 27.
[17] *Gracie* v. *G.*, 1910 S.C. 899.
[18] *Gibb* v. *Lee* (1908) 16 S.L.T. 260.
[19] *Baines & Tait* v. *Compagnie Générale des Mines* (1879) 6 R. 846.
[20] *Boland* v. *White Cross Ins. Co.*, 1926 S.C. 1066; contrast *Kerr* v. *R. & W. Ferguson*, 1931 S.C. 736.
[21] *Park Dobson & Co.* v. *Taylor*, 1929 S.C. 571.
[22] *Waddell* v. *W's Trs.*, 1932 S.L.T. 201.
[23] *McMurchy* v. *Emslie & Guthrie* (1888) 15 R. 375.
[24] *Mulvenna* v. *The Admiralty*, 1926 S.C. 842; Crown Proceedings Act, 1947, S. 46; Law Reform (Misc. Prov.) (Sc.) Act, 1966, S. 2.
[25] *Riley* v. *Ellis*, 1910 S.C. 934.
[26] *Mather* v. *Wilson* (1908) 15 S.L.T. 946.
[27] Ersk. III, 6, 7; Bell, *Prin.* §2276; but see Graham Stewart, 78.
[28] *Wright's Trs.* v. *Allan* (1840) 3 D. 243; *Dundee Mags.* v. *Taylor & Grant* (1863) 1 M. 701.
[29] *Livingstone* v. *L.* (1886) 14 R. 43.
[30] *Trappes* v. *Meredith* (1871) 10 M. 38.
[31] Stair, III, 1, 31; Bankt. III, 1, 35; Ersk. III, 6, 8; Bell, *Comm.* II, 72.
[32] M.S.A., 1894, S. 163.
[33] *Ross* v. *Renton* (1712) Mor. 690.
[34] Small Debt (Sc.) Act, 1837, S. 7 (repealed, but probably common law.)

It is uncertain what form of diligence is appropriate to copyright,[35] patents, trade marks, designs and plant breeders' rights, though royalties and licence fees due in respect of the exercise of such rights are arrestable.

Arrestments laid on may be loosed by the court,[36] or recalled or restricted with or without caution.[37]

When validly exercised arrestment attaches the creditor's right *tantum et tale* as it stands in the hands of the debtor and if the right is defeasible, e.g. by the trustee's (debtor's) exercise of a power, it may be defeated and be valueless.[38] The validity of arrestments may be tried in a petition for recall of arrestments but preferably in an action of furthcoming.[39]

Effect of arrestment

Arrestment interpels the arrestee from paying to his creditor (the common debtor). It affects the object arrested notwithstanding the death of the arrestee. If the arrestee parts with the object arrested he is liable to a claim for the value of the fund but the arrester is not entitled to claim from a third party who has acquired it bona fide and in ignorance, and the arrestee's conduct may also be treated as contempt of court.[40]

Preference among arrestments

Preference is determined by priority in time.[41] But preference gained thereby may be lost by delay in proceeding with furthcoming.

Prescription of arrestments

Arrestments for sums not exceeding £20 prescribe in three months unless renewed,[42] and all other arrestments in three years.[43]

Furthcoming

Arrestment is only an inchoate diligence. Claims attached by arrestment may be secured by the creditor by action of furthcoming, in which the arrestee may plead against the arrester every defence which

---

[35] In English law, none: *Edwards* v. *Picard* (1909) 78 L.J.K.B. 1108.
[36] Arrestments (Sc.) Act, 1617.
[37] Debtors (Sc.) Act, 1838, Ss. 20–1.
[38] *Chambers's Trs.* v. *Smiths* (1878) 5 R. (H.L.) 151; cf. *Baird* v. *B.*, 1910, 1 S.L.T.95.
[39] *Vincent* v. *Chalmers & Co's Tr.* (1877) 5 R. 43; *Brand* v. *Kent* (1892) 20 R. 29; see also *Barclay Curle* v. *Laing*, 1908 S.C. 82; *L. Ruthven* v. *Drummond*, 1908 S.C. 1154.
[40] *Inglis & Bow* v. *Smith & Aikman* (1867) 5 M. 320.
[41] *Hertz* v. *Itzig* (1865) 3 M. 813.
[42] Sheriff Courts (Sc.) Act, 1907, S. 45.
[43] Debtors (Sc.) Act, 1838, S. 22; *Jameson* v. *Sharp* (1887) 14 R. 643.

he could have pled against the debtor. Decree completes the arrester's right and is a judicial assignation of the object arrested to the arrester.[44]

Sequestration in bankruptcy

The Act and Warrant of confirmation of a trustee in sequestration transfers to and vests in him for behoof of the creditors, *inter alia,* the moveable estate of the bankrupt so far as attachable for debt or capable of voluntary alienation to the same effect as if intimation had been made at that date, but subject to such preferential securities as existed at the date of sequestration and are not null or reducible,[45] and any non-vested contingent right of succession or interest in property conceived in favour of the bankrupt under the will or settlement of any person deceased, or under marriage contract, or under any other deed, instrument, or writing of an irrevocable nature to the same effect as if an assignation of such right or interest had been executed by the bankrupt and intimation thereof made at the date of the sequestration, subject always to such preferable securities as existed at that date and are not null or reducible.[46]

---

[44] Ersk. III, 6, 17; *Muirhead* v. *Corrie* (1735) Mor. 687.
[45] Bankruptcy (Sc.) Act, 1913, S. 97(1).
[46] Ibid., S. 97(4); see also *Kirkland* v. *K's Trs.* (1886) 13 R. 798; *Reid* v. *Morison* (1893) 20 R. 510.

EXTINCTION OF RIGHTS IN
INCORPOREAL MOVEABLE OBJECTS

Rights in incorporeal moveable objects are extinguished in various ways, many being peculiar to particular kinds of rights.

They may all be lost completely, though the rights are not thereby extinguished, by outright assignation in pursuance of intention to gift, or of contract of barter or of sale, or by assignation in security and retention or realization by the creditor (assignee) on the cedent's failure to implement his obligation.

Decrees of court are extinguished by satisfaction of the decree.

Claims of debt, or kindred pecuniary claims, are extinguished by full payment, evidenced by a receipt,[1] or by a discharge,[2] or by facts and circumstances[3] or by cancellation and return to the debtor of any bill of exchange or bond which had evidenced the debt.[4]

Claims of damages are extinguished by full payment or by discharge proceeding on a compromise or settlement.[5] A right of action for damages for personal injuries must be brought within three years,[6] unless circumstances exist justifying an extension of that time,[7] failing which it is probably rendered merely unenforceable.

Policies of insurance are extinguished by payment in terms thereof.

Shares in companies are extinguished only by liquidation of the company, or by a reduction of capital which involves paying out the shareholders of that class.[8]

Claims to legal rights, to legacies, to shares in trust estates or intestate estates are extinguished by payment or transfer and discharge.

---

[1] *McLaren* v. *Howie* (1869) 8 M. 106.

[2] *Kippen* v. *K's Trs.* (1874) 1 R. 1171 (claim under marriage contract): *Neish's Trs.* v. *N.* (1897) 24 R. 306 (rights under marriage contract); *Obers* v. *Paton's Trs.* (1897) 24 R. 719 (legitim).

[3] *Chrystal* v. *C.* (1900) 2 F. 373.

[4] *Niven* v. *Burgh of Ayr* (1899) 1 F. 400.

[5] *McLean* v. *Hassard* (1903) 10 S.L.T. 593 (seduction); *McDonagh* v. *MacLellan* (1886) 13 R. 1000; *N.B. Ry.* v. *Wood* (1891) 18 R. (H.L.) 27 (personal injuries).

[6] Prescription and Limitation (Sc.) Act, 1973, S. 17.

[7] Ibid., Ss. 18–19A.

[8] e.g. *Wilsons and Clyde Coal Co.* v. *Scottish Ins. Corpn.*, 1949 S.C. (H.L.) 90.

Indefinite continuance

Such rights as copyright in unpublished literary work, or a trade name acquired by long use, may continue indefinitely.

Lapse of time

The rights conferred by registration of a trade mark, grant of a patent, registration of a design, creation and publication of a work the subject of copyright, registration of public lending right and the grant of plant breeder's rights, all lapse automatically after the expiry of the time for which the law grants the respective rights, except in so far as the right may be, and is, extended.[9]

Short prescription

Under the Prescription and Limitation (Sc.) Act, 1973,[10] rights to exact periodical payments by way of interest, annuity, feu-duty, ground annual, rent, periodical payment for the occupancy or use of land, periodical payment under a land obligation, claims based on unjust enrichment, *negotiorum gestio*, liability to make reparation, obligations under a bill or promissory note, obligations of accounting (other than for trust funds) and obligations arising from, or by breach of, contract or promise, but not[11] obligations under decrees of court, arising from a bank note, one constituted or evidenced by a probative writ (with exceptions), obligations under a contract of partnership or agency, obligations to satisfy a claim to legal rights or prior rights in succession, or obligations to make reparation for personal injuries or the death of any person from injuries, nor any imprescriptible obligation,[12] are extinguished after five years unless relevantly claimed[13] or relevantly acknowledged[14] within that time. Thus the running of the prescriptive period cuts off such claims as a claim of debt,[15] or to a *condictio indebiti*,[16] a claim of damages,[17] arrears of an annuity,[18] a balance allegedly due on current account with a bank,[19] and the right to levy harbour-dues.[20]

[9] Ch. 5.39, *supra*.
[10] S. 6 and Sch. 1, para. 1.
[11] S. 6 and Sch. 1, para. 2.
[12] Sch. 3.
[13] S. 9.
[14] S. 10.
[15] *Dundas* v. *D.* (1827) 5 S. 790; *Buchanan* v. *Bogle* (1847) 9 D. 686; *Murray* v. *Mackenzie* (1897) 4 S.L.T. 231.
[16] *Edinburgh Mags.* v. *Heriot's Trust* (1900) 7 S.L.T. 371.
[17] *Cooke* v. *Falconer's Reps.* (1850) 13 D. 157.
[18] *Henderson* v. *Burt* (1858) 20 D. 402.
[19] *Macdonald* v. *N. of S. Bank*, 1942 S.C. 369.
[20] *Renfrew Mags.* v. *Hoby* (1845) 16 D. 348; cf. *Dundee Harbour Trs.* v. *Dougall* (1852) 24 S. Jur. 385.

Long prescription

Incorporeal moveable rights other than imprescriptible rights not affected by the short prescription may be completely extinguished[21] by the long negative prescription, formerly of forty, now of twenty, years,[22] if within that period there has been no relevant claim and the subsistence of the obligation has not been relevantly acknowledged.[23] Thus the running of the long negative prescription extinguishes such claims as a claim of legitim,[24] or of *jus relictae*,[25] or to a legacy[26] or under a trust deed,[27] but does not extinguish the liability of a trustee to account for his intromissions.[28] Any right relating to property, heritable or moveable, not being a right specified as imprescriptible or falling within sections 6 or 7 of the 1973 Act as being a right correlative to an obligation to which either of those sections applies, if it has subsisted for twenty years continuously unexercised or unenforced and without any relevant claim in relation to it having been made, is extinguished from the expiration of that period.[29]

The prescriptive period runs from day to day commencing with the day when the property right vested and could first have been claimed by action and was not claimed, or when it was last claimed.[30]

Non valens agere

At common law the prescriptive period did not run so long as the creditor was *non valens agere,* i.e. not in a legal position to make his claim effectual. Under the old prescription Acts years of minority were excluded from deduction, but under the 1924 Act[31] no deduction is made for any period of minority or legal disability. A fiar is *valens* though the liferenter take no action to enforce his claim.[32] This plea has probably disappeared under the 1973 Act.

---

[21] Ersk. III, 7, 8; *Kermack* v. *K.* (1874) 2 R. 156.
[22] Prescription Acts, 1469, 1474 and 1617; Conveyancing Act, 1924, S. 17; *Sutherland C.C.* v. *Macdonald,* 1935 S.C. 915; *Marr's Exrx.* v. *Marr's Trs.,* 1936 S.C. 64; Prescription and Limitation (Sc.) Act, 1973, Ss 7 and 8.
[23] 1973 Act, S. 7.
[24] *Sanderson* v. *Lockhart-Mure,* 1946 S.C. 298.
[25] *Campbell's Trs.* v. *C's Trs.,* 1950 S.C. 48.
[26] *Briggs* v. *Swan's Exors.* (1854) 16 D. 385; *Jamieson* v. *Clark* (1872) 10 M. 399; *Pettigrew* v. *Harton,* 1956 S.C. 67.
[27] *Pollock* v. *Porterfield* (1779) 2 Pat. 495.
[28] *Bertram Gardner & Co.'s Tr.* v. *King's Remembrancer,* 1920 S.C. 555; *Hastie's J.F.* v. *Morham's Exors.,* 1951 S.C. 668; 1973 Act, Sch. 3.
[29] Prescription and Limitation (Sc.) Act, 1973, S. 8.
[30] *Campbell's Trs.* v. *C's Trs.,* 1950 S.C. 48.
[31] *Campbells Trs., supra;* see also *Harvie* v. *Robertson* (1903) 5 F. 338.
[32] *Pettigrew* v. *Harton,* 1956 S.C. 67.

Interruption

A period of prescription which has run is cancelled by interruption and it must start to run afresh. Interruption may take place down to the last moment of the period[33] but the longer the period has run the clearer must be the interruption.

Interruption may take place by making a 'relevant claim' to the right, i.e. making a claim for implement or part-implement of the obligation in certain kinds of legal proceedings or by doing diligence for enforcement of the obligation,[34] or by having the right 'relevantly acknowledged', i.e. by such performance by or on behalf of the debtor towards implement of the obligation as clearly indicates that the obligation still subsists, or by unequivocal written admission by or on behalf of the debtor to the creditor or his agent, clearly acknowledging that the obligation still subsists.[35]

---

[33] *Sinpson* v. *Marshall* (1900) 2 F. 447.

[34] 1973 Act, S. 9. cf. *E. Hopertoun* v. *York Bldgs. Co.* (1784) Mor. 11285.

[35] 1973 Act, S. 10. cf. *Aitken* v. *Malcolm* (1776) Hailes 148; *Vans* v. *Murray* 14 June 1816, F.C.; *Briggs* v. *Swan's Exor.* (1854) 16 D. 385; *Kermack* v. *K.* (1874) 2 R. 156; *Simpson* v. *Marshall* (1900) 2 F. 447.

INDEX